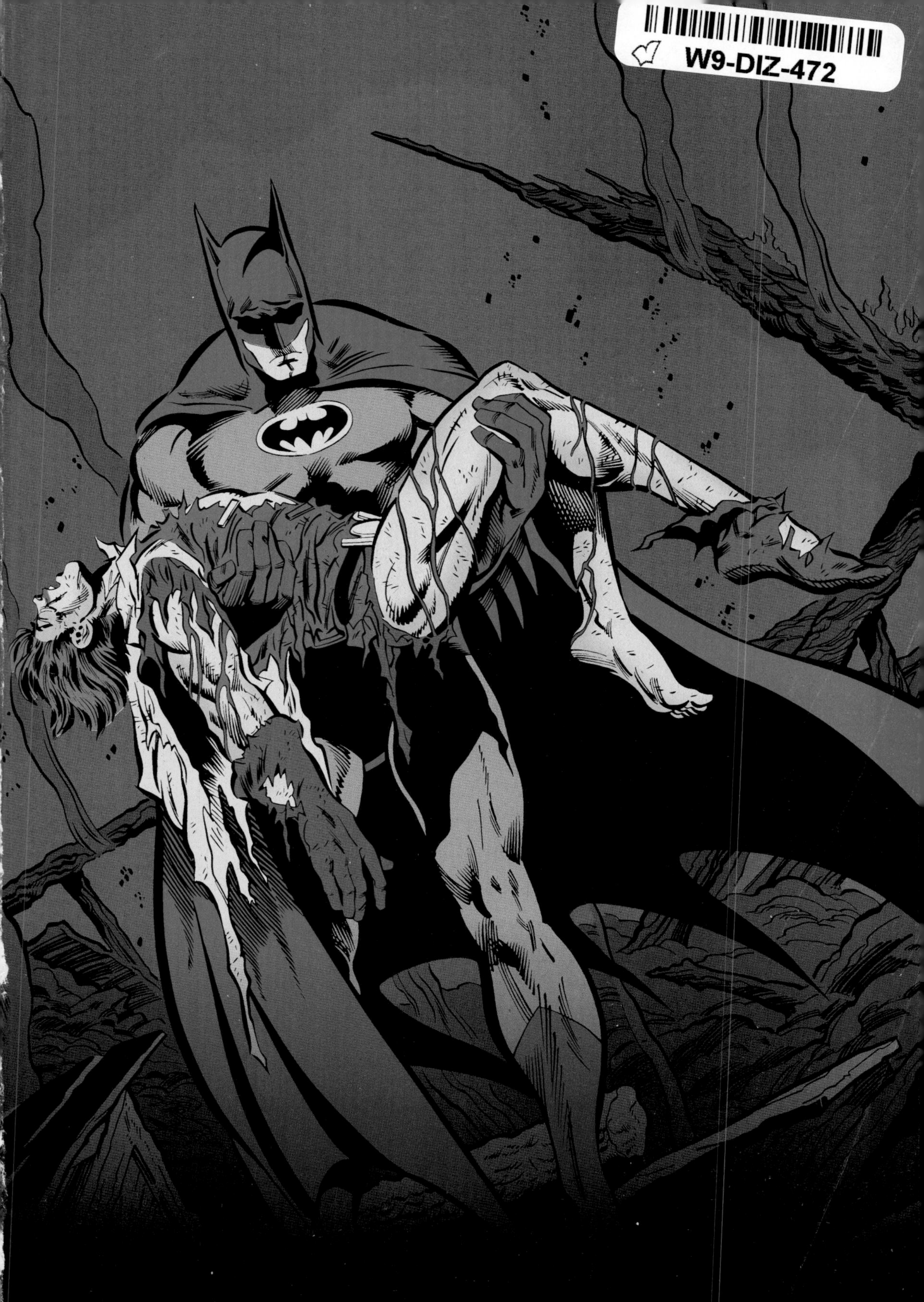

BATMAN: A DEATH IN THE FAMILY

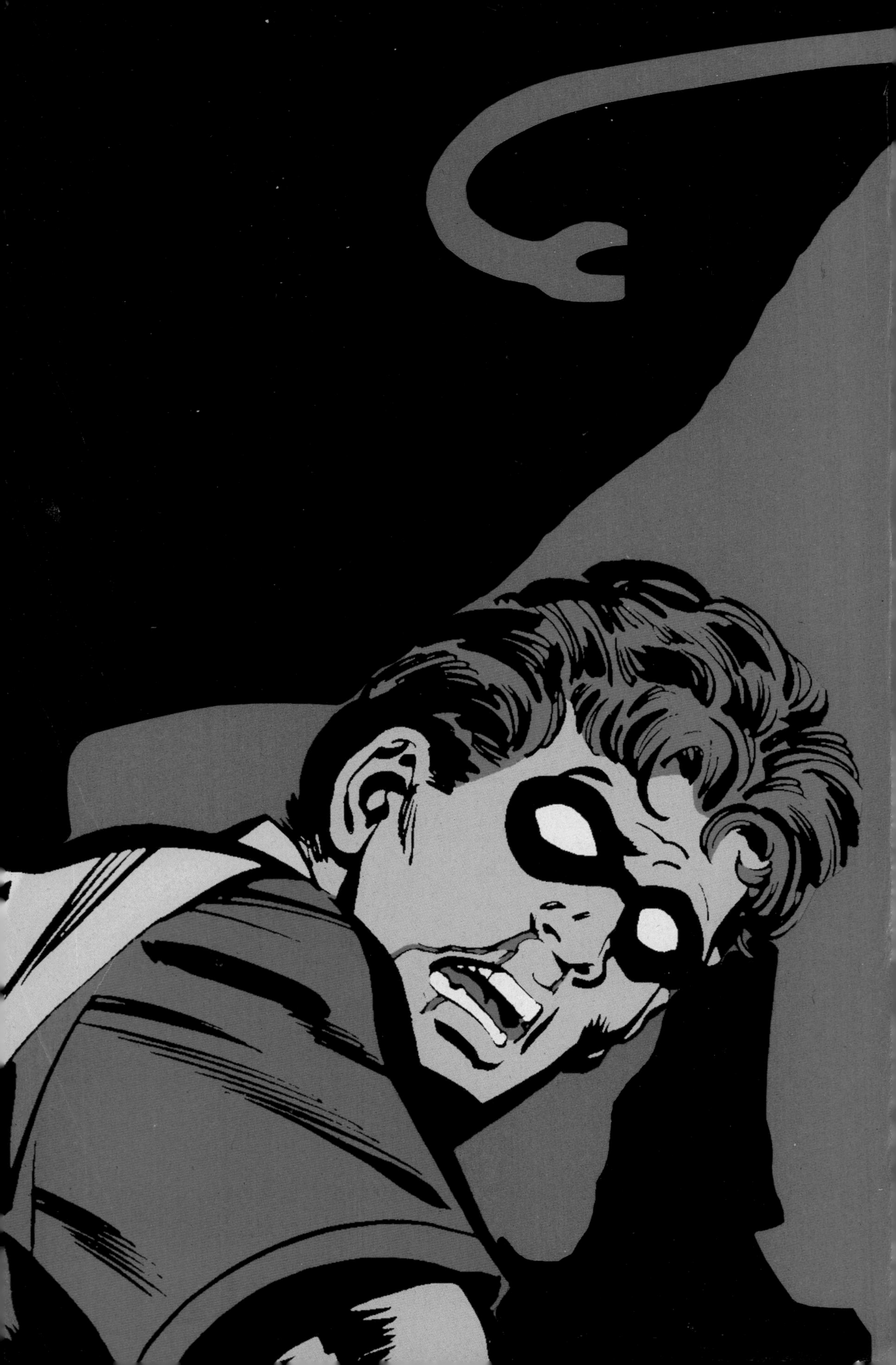

BATMAN:
A DEATH IN THE FAMILY

Writers
Jim Starlin — A DEATH IN THE FAMILY
Marv Wolfman — A LONELY PLACE OF DYING

Layouts and Co-Plotter
George Pérez — A LONELY PLACE OF DYING

Pencillers
Jim Aparo — A DEATH IN THE FAMILY
Tom Grummett — A LONELY PLACE OF DYING

Inkers
Mike DeCarlo — A DEATH IN THE FAMILY
Bob McLeod — A LONELY PLACE OF DYING

Letterer
John Costanza

Colorist
Adrienne Roy

Original Series Covers
Mike Mignola — A DEATH IN THE FAMILY
George Pérez — A LONELY PLACE OF DYING

BATMAN created by Bob Kane with Bill Finger

Mike Carlin
Dennis O'Neil Editors – Original Series
Jeb Woodard Group Editor – Collected Editions
Steve Cook Design Director – Books
Curtis King Jr. Publication Design

Bob Harras Senior VP – Editor-in-Chief, DC Comics

Diane Nelson President
Dan DiDio Publisher
Jim Lee Publisher
Geoff Johns President & Chief Creative Officer
Amit Desai Executive VP – Business & Marketing Strategy, Direct to
Consumer & Global Franchise Management
Sam Ades Senior VP – Direct to Consumer
Bobbie Chase VP – Talent Development
Mark Chiarello Senior VP – Art, Design & Collected Editions
John Cunningham Senior VP – Sales & Trade Marketing
Anne DePies Senior VP – Business Strategy, Finance &
Administration
Don Falletti VP – Manufacturing Operations
Lawrence Ganem VP – Editorial Administration & Talent Relations
Alison Gill Senior VP – Manufacturing & Operations
Hank Kanalz Senior VP – Editorial Strategy & Administration
Jay Kogan VP – Legal Affairs
Thomas Loftus VP – Business Affairs
Jack Mahan VP – Business Affairs
Nick J. Napolitano VP – Manufacturing Administration
Eddie Scannell VP – Consumer Marketing
Courtney Simmons Senior VP – Publicity & Communications
Jim (Ski) Sokolowski Senior VP – Publicity & Communications
Nancy Spears VP – Mass, Book, Digital Sales & Trade Marketing

Cover art by Jim Aparo.
Cover color by Allen Passalaqua.
Color reconstruction by Digikore.

BATMAN: A DEATH IN THE FAMILY

Published by DC Comics. Cover and compilation
Copyright © 2011 DC Comics. All Rights Reserved.

Originally published in single magazine form in
BATMAN 426-429, 440-442, THE NEW TITANS 60-61
and BATMAN ANNUAL 25. Copyright © 1988, 1989, 2006
DC Comics. All Rights Reserved. All characters, their
distinctive likenesses and related elements featured in
this publication are trademarks of DC Comics. The stories, characters
and incidents featured in this publication are entirely fictional.
DC Comics does not read or accept unsolicited submissions
of ideas, stories or artwork.

DC Comics, 2900 W. Alameda Avenue,
Burbank, CA 91505
Printed by Transcontinental Interglobe Beauceville,
Canada. 11/4/16.
Ninth Printing. ISBN: 978-1-4012-3274-0

Library of Congress Cataloging-in-Publication Data

Starlin, Jim.
  Batman : a death in the family / Jim Starlin, Marv
Wolfman, Jim Aparo, George Pérez.
    p. cm.
  "Originally published as Batman 426-429,
440-442, Batman Annual 25
and the New Teen Titans 60-61."
  ISBN 978-1-4012-3274-0
  1. Graphic novels. I. Wolfman, Marv. II. Aparo, Jim.
III. Pérez, George, 1954- IV. Title. V. Title: Death in
the family.
  PN6728.B36S7 2012
  741.5'973–dc23
                    2012032130

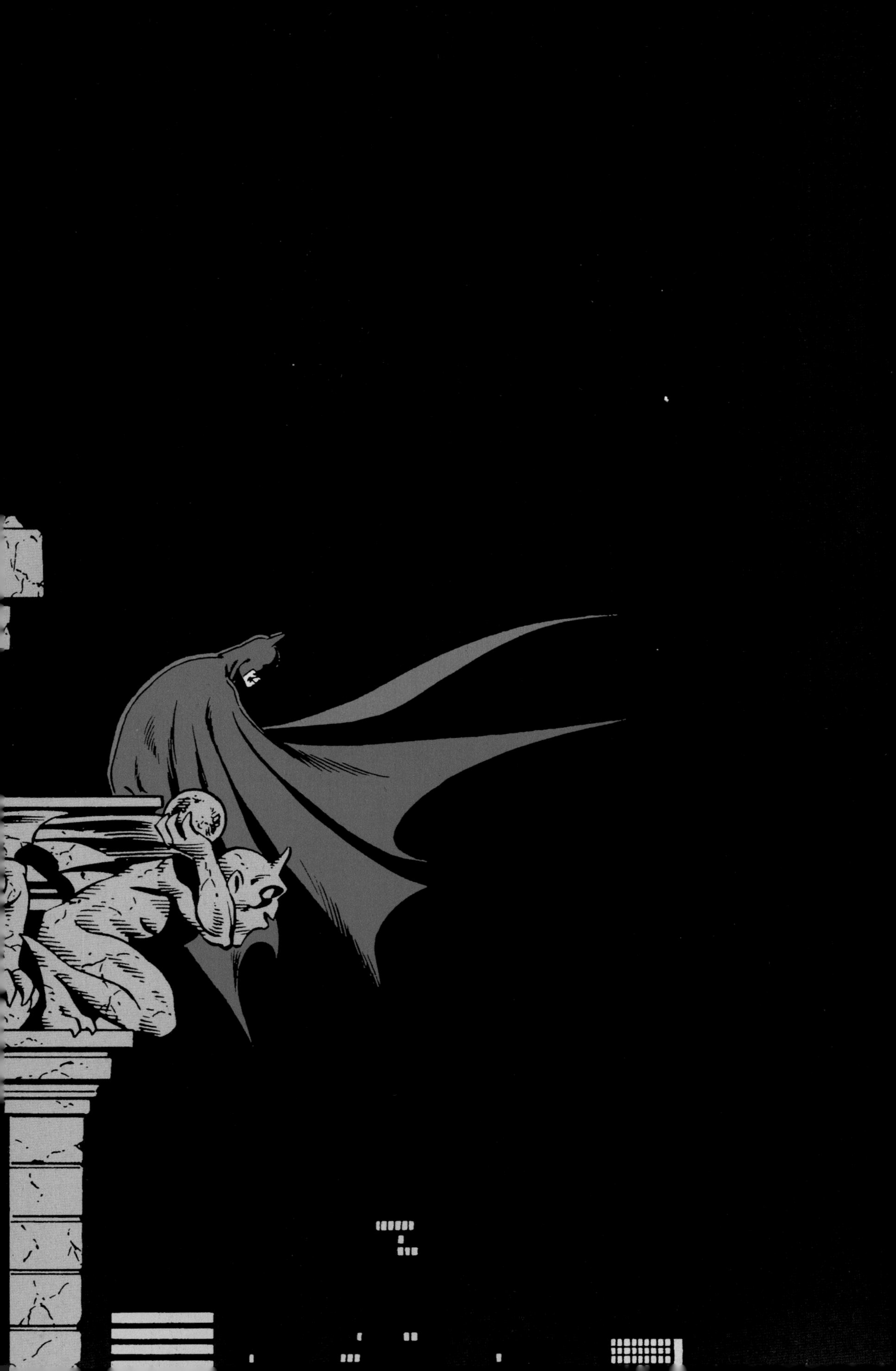

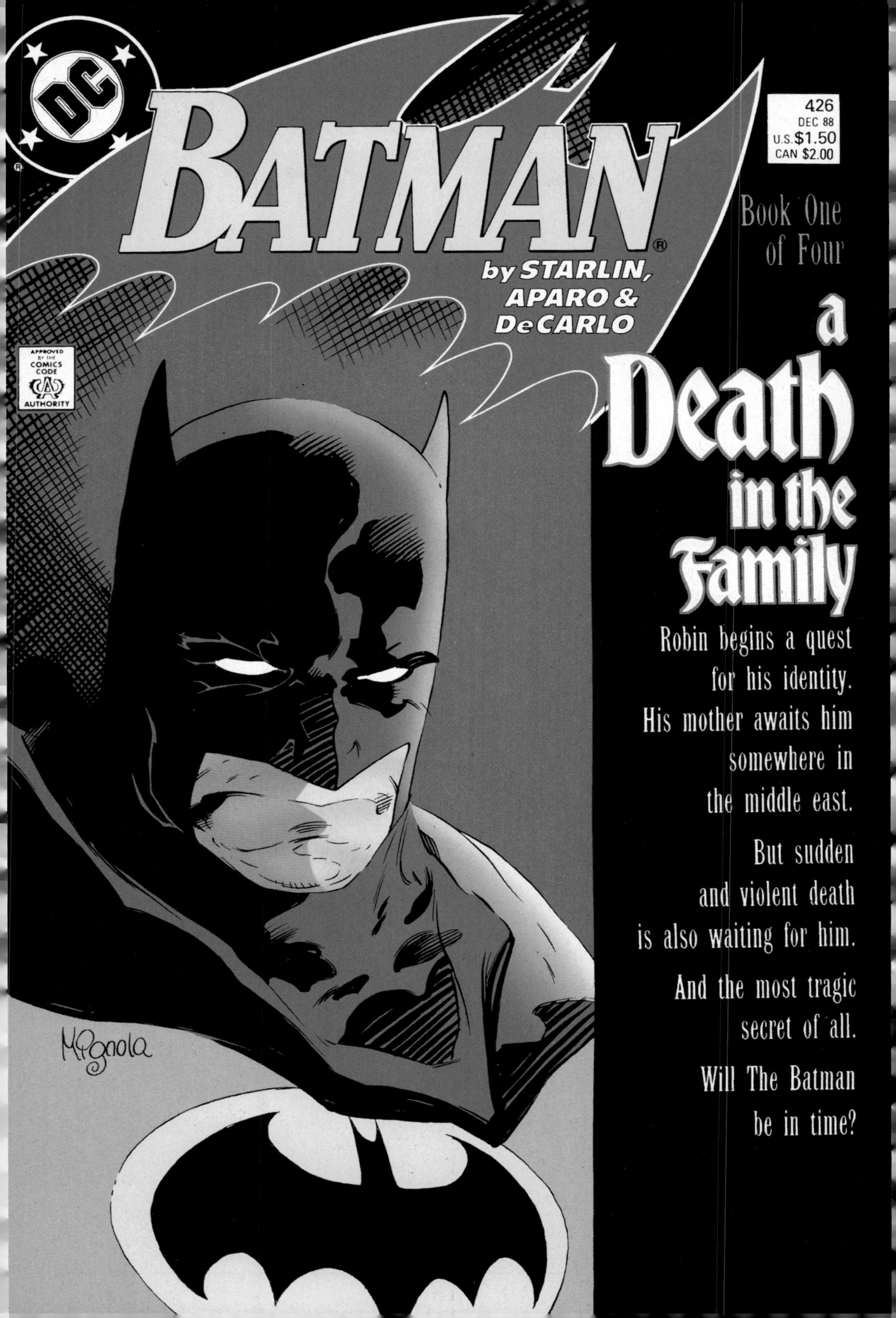
DC
BATMAN®
426
DEC 88
U.S. $1.50
CAN $2.00
Book One
of Four
by STARLIN,
APARO &
DeCARLO
APPROVED BY THE COMICS CODE AUTHORITY
a
Death
in the
Family
Robin begins a quest
for his identity.
His mother awaits him
somewhere in
the middle east.
But sudden
and violent death
is also waiting for him.
And the most tragic
secret of all.
Will The Batman
be in time?
MIGNOLA

A DEATH in the FAMILY

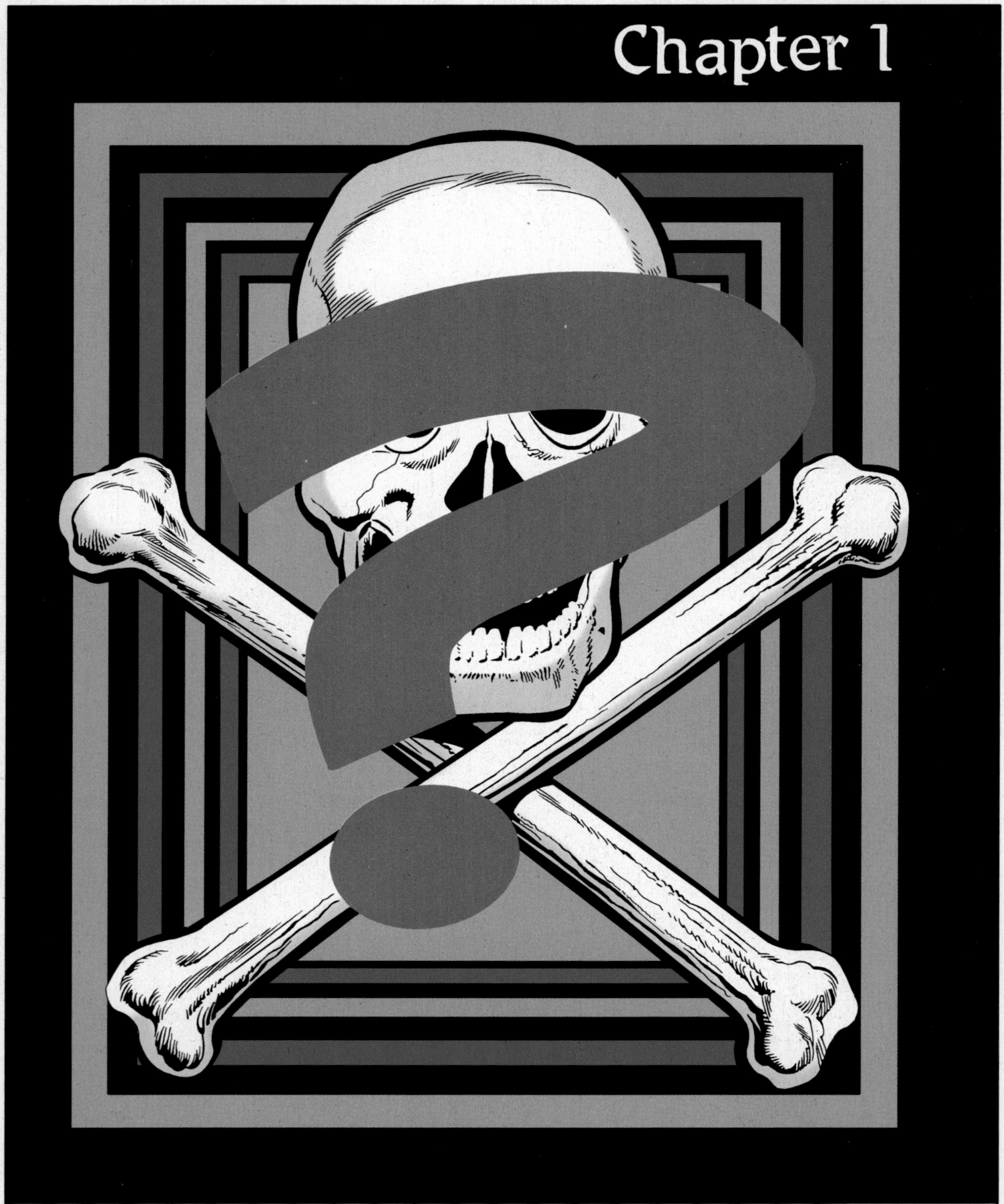
Chapter 1

JIM STARLIN . JIM APARO . MIKE DeCARLO . JOHN COSTANZA . ADRIENNE ROY
WRITER PENCILLER INKER LETTERER COLORIST
DAN RASPLER . DENNIS O'NEIL . BOB KANE
ASST. EDITOR EDITOR CREATOR

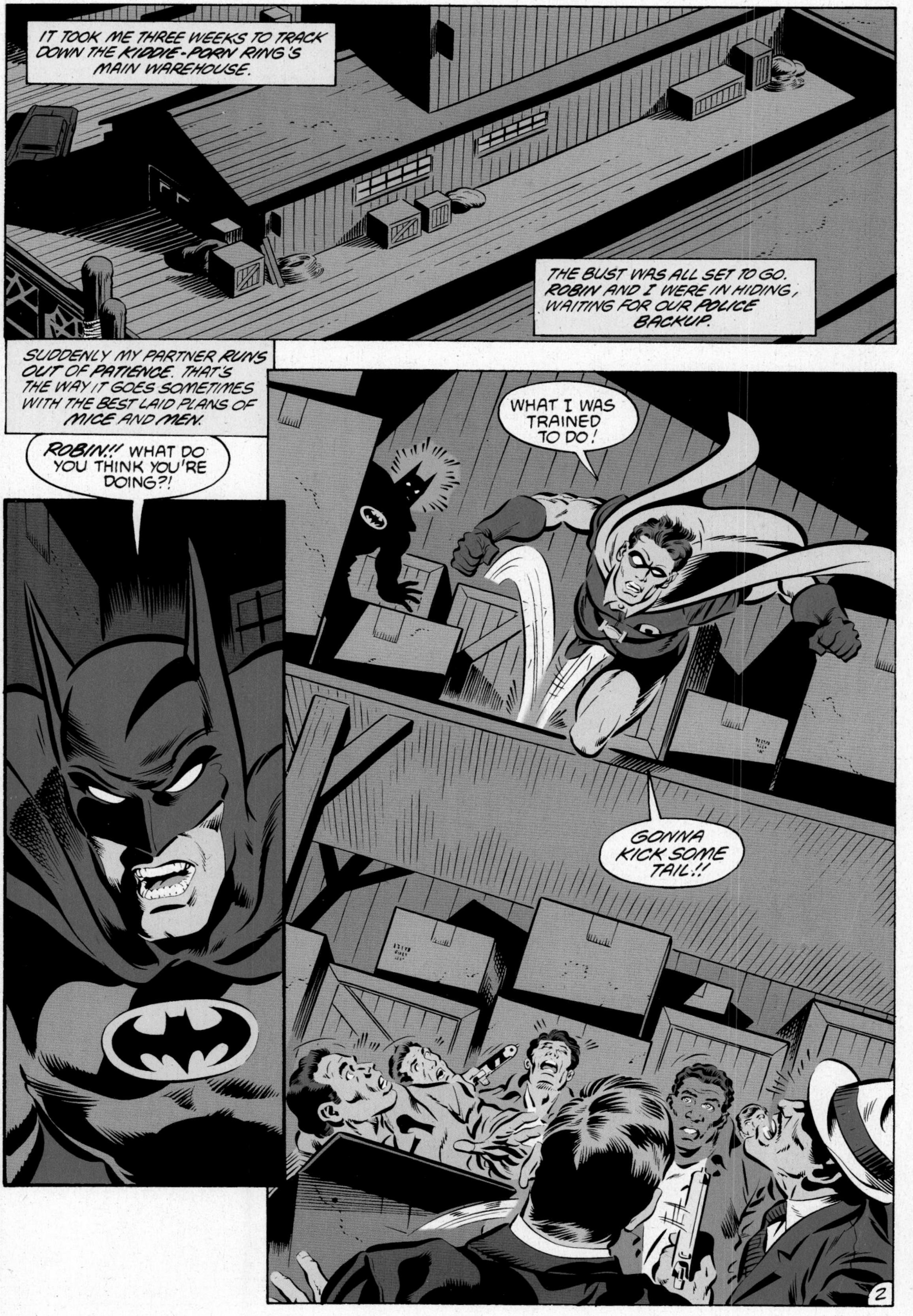
IT TOOK ME THREE WEEKS TO TRACK DOWN THE KIDDIE-PORN RING'S MAIN WAREHOUSE.
THE BUST WAS ALL SET TO GO. ROBIN AND I WERE IN HIDING, WAITING FOR OUR POLICE BACKUP.
SUDDENLY MY PARTNER RUNS OUT OF PATIENCE. THAT'S THE WAY IT GOES SOMETIMES WITH THE BEST LAID PLANS OF MICE AND MEN.
ROBIN!! WHAT DO YOU THINK YOU'RE DOING?!
WHAT I WAS TRAINED TO DO!
GONNA KICK SOME TAIL!!
2

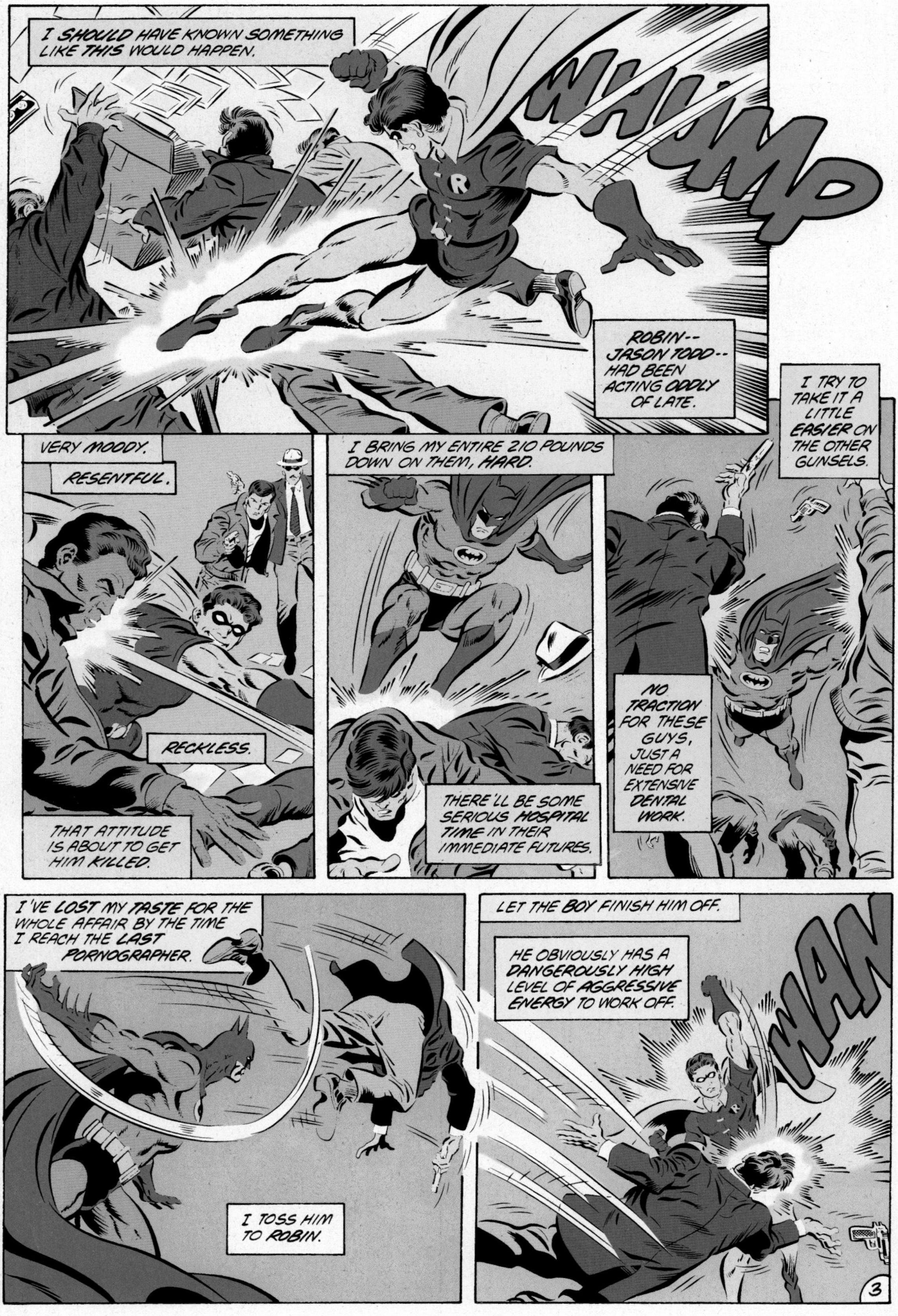
I SHOULD HAVE KNOWN SOMETHING LIKE THIS WOULD HAPPEN.
WHUMP
ROBIN-- JASON TODD-- HAD BEEN ACTING ODDLY OF LATE.
VERY MOODY.
RESENTFUL.
RECKLESS.
THAT ATTITUDE IS ABOUT TO GET HIM KILLED.
I BRING MY ENTIRE 210 POUNDS DOWN ON THEM, HARD.
THERE'LL BE SOME SERIOUS HOSPITAL TIME IN THEIR IMMEDIATE FUTURES.
I TRY TO TAKE IT A LITTLE EASIER ON THE OTHER GUNSELS.
NO TRACTION FOR THESE GUYS, JUST A NEED FOR EXTENSIVE DENTAL WORK.
I'VE LOST MY TASTE FOR THE WHOLE AFFAIR BY THE TIME I REACH THE LAST PORNOGRAPHER.
I TOSS HIM TO ROBIN.
LET THE BOY FINISH HIM OFF.
HE OBVIOUSLY HAS A DANGEROUSLY HIGH LEVEL OF AGGRESSIVE ENERGY TO WORK OFF.
WHA
3

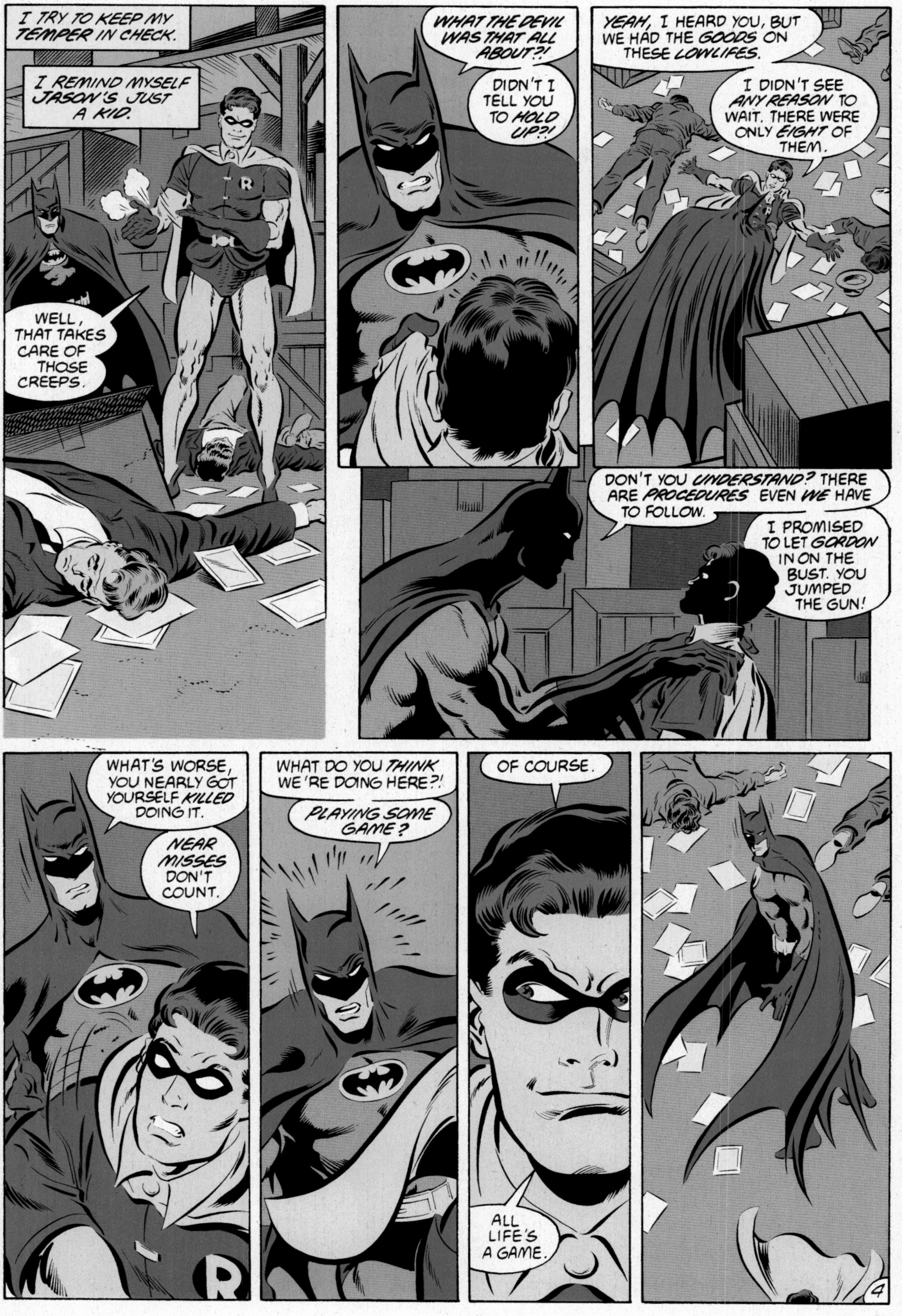
I TRY TO KEEP MY TEMPER IN CHECK.
I REMIND MYSELF JASON'S JUST A KID.
WELL, THAT TAKES CARE OF THOSE CREEPS.
WHAT THE DEVIL WAS THAT ALL ABOUT?!
DIDN'T I TELL YOU TO HOLD UP?!
YEAH, I HEARD YOU, BUT WE HAD THE GOODS ON THESE LOWLIFES.
I DIDN'T SEE ANY REASON TO WAIT. THERE WERE ONLY EIGHT OF THEM.
DON'T YOU UNDERSTAND? THERE ARE PROCEDURES EVEN WE HAVE TO FOLLOW.
I PROMISED TO LET GORDON IN ON THE BUST. YOU JUMPED THE GUN!
WHAT'S WORSE, YOU NEARLY GOT YOURSELF KILLED DOING IT.
NEAR MISSES DON'T COUNT.
WHAT DO YOU THINK WE'RE DOING HERE?!
PLAYING SOME GAME?
OF COURSE.
ALL LIFE'S A GAME.
4

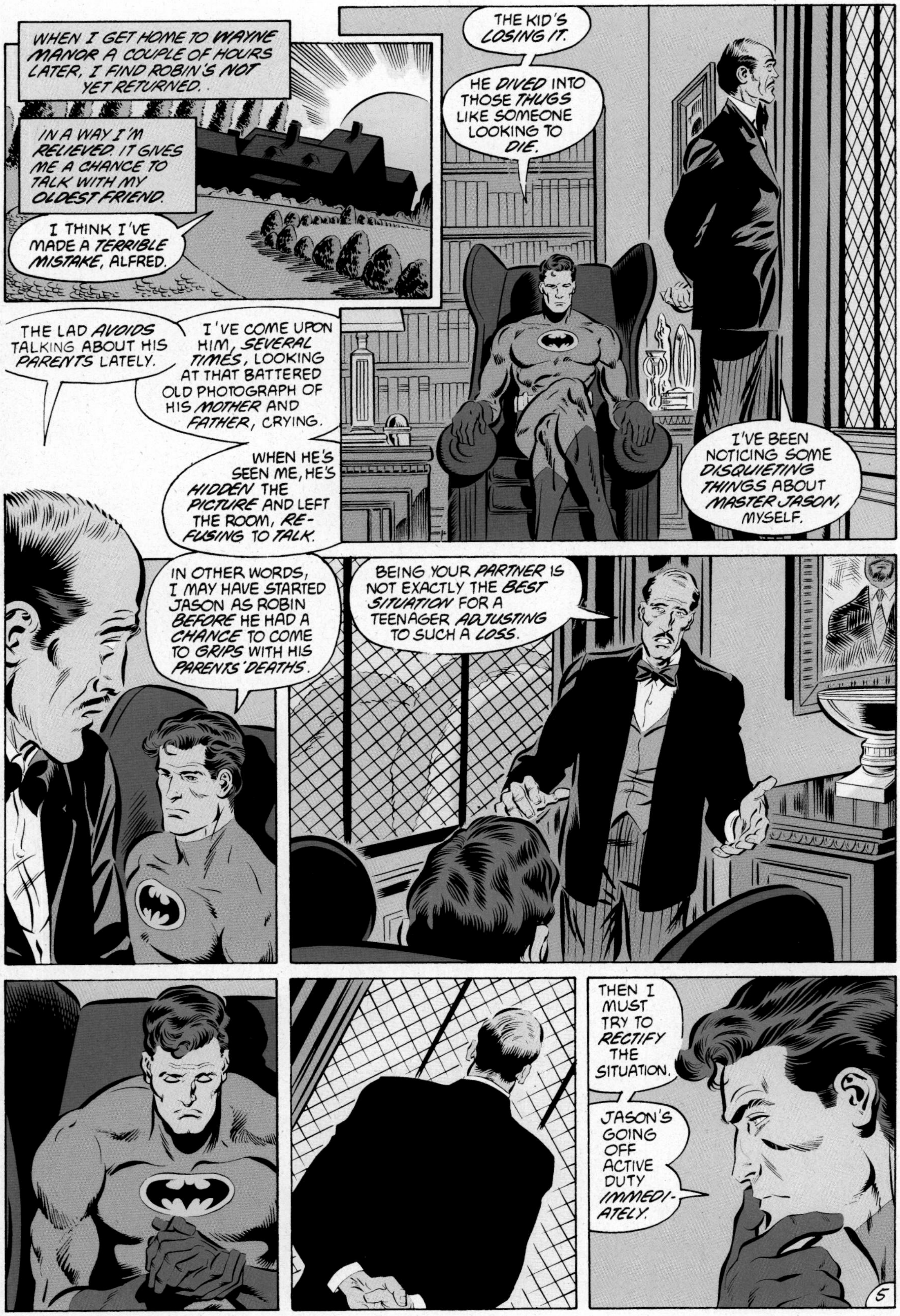
WHEN I GET HOME TO WAYNE MANOR A COUPLE OF HOURS LATER, I FIND ROBIN'S NOT YET RETURNED.
IN A WAY I'M RELIEVED. IT GIVES ME A CHANCE TO TALK WITH MY OLDEST FRIEND.
I THINK I'VE MADE A TERRIBLE MISTAKE, ALFRED.
THE KID'S LOSING IT.
HE DIVED INTO THOSE THUGS LIKE SOMEONE LOOKING TO DIE.
I'VE BEEN NOTICING SOME DISQUIETING THINGS ABOUT MASTER JASON, MYSELF.
THE LAD AVOIDS TALKING ABOUT HIS PARENTS LATELY.
I'VE COME UPON HIM, SEVERAL TIMES, LOOKING AT THAT BATTERED OLD PHOTOGRAPH OF HIS MOTHER AND FATHER, CRYING.
WHEN HE'S SEEN ME, HE'S HIDDEN THE PICTURE AND LEFT THE ROOM, RE-FUSING TO TALK.
IN OTHER WORDS, I MAY HAVE STARTED JASON AS ROBIN BEFORE HE HAD A CHANCE TO COME TO GRIPS WITH HIS PARENTS' DEATHS.
BEING YOUR PARTNER IS NOT EXACTLY THE BEST SITUATION FOR A TEENAGER ADJUSTING TO SUCH A LOSS.
THEN I MUST TRY TO RECTIFY THE SITUATION.
JASON'S GOING OFF ACTIVE DUTY IMMEDI-ATELY.
5

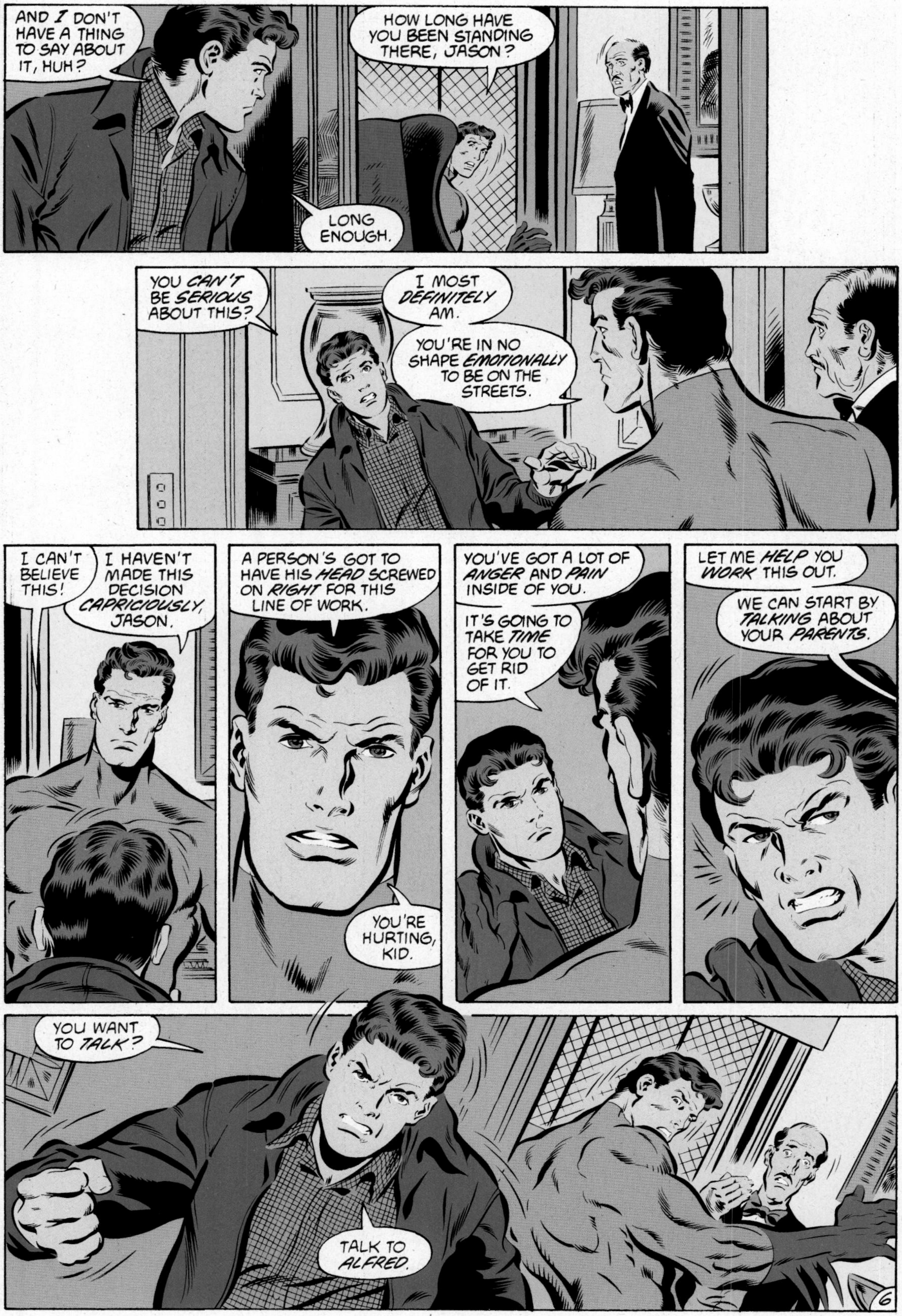
AND I DON'T HAVE A THING TO SAY ABOUT IT, HUH?
HOW LONG HAVE YOU BEEN STANDING THERE, JASON?
LONG ENOUGH.
YOU CAN'T BE SERIOUS ABOUT THIS?
I MOST DEFINITELY AM.
YOU'RE IN NO SHAPE EMOTIONALLY TO BE ON THE STREETS.
I CAN'T BELIEVE THIS!
I HAVEN'T MADE THIS DECISION CAPRICIOUSLY, JASON.
A PERSON'S GOT TO HAVE HIS HEAD SCREWED ON RIGHT FOR THIS LINE OF WORK.
YOU'RE HURTING, KID.
YOU'VE GOT A LOT OF ANGER AND PAIN INSIDE OF YOU.
IT'S GOING TO TAKE TIME FOR YOU TO GET RID OF IT.
LET ME HELP YOU WORK THIS OUT.
WE CAN START BY TALKING ABOUT YOUR PARENTS.
YOU WANT TO TALK?
TALK TO ALFRED.
6

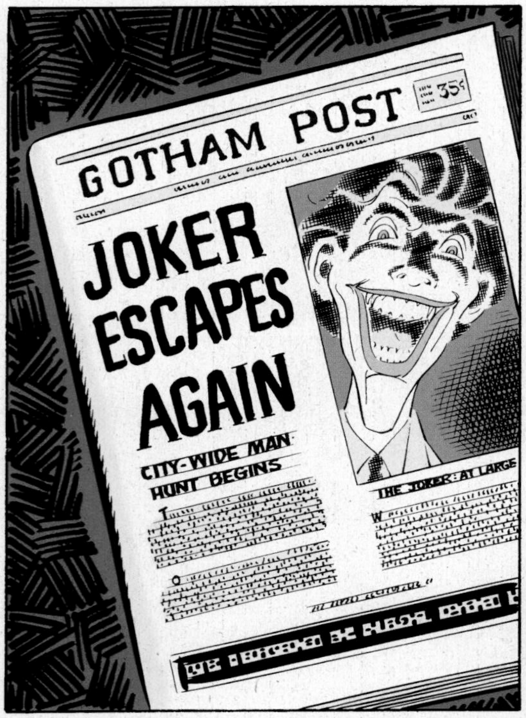
GOTHAM POST
35¢
JOKER ESCAPES AGAIN
CITY-WIDE MAN HUNT BEGINS
THE JOKER: AT LARGE

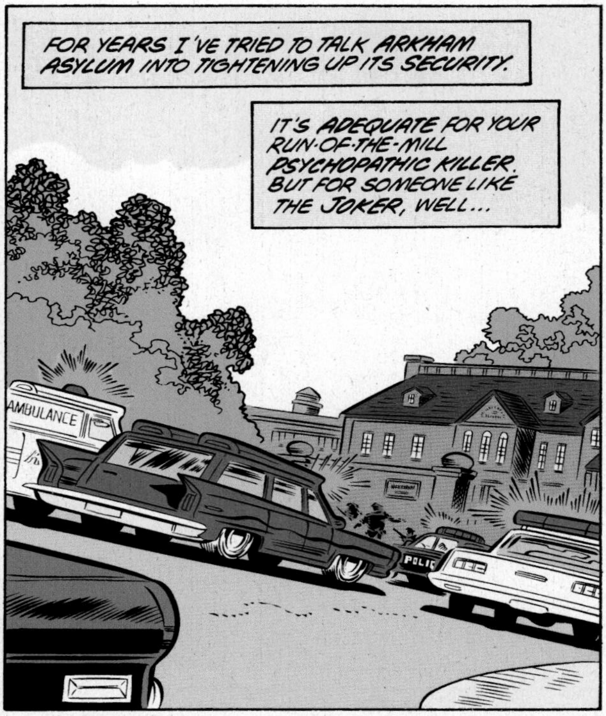
FOR YEARS I'VE TRIED TO TALK ARKHAM ASYLUM INTO TIGHTENING UP ITS SECURITY.
IT'S ADEQUATE FOR YOUR RUN-OF-THE-MILL PSYCHOPATHIC KILLER. BUT FOR SOMEONE LIKE THE JOKER, WELL...
AMBULANCE
POLICE

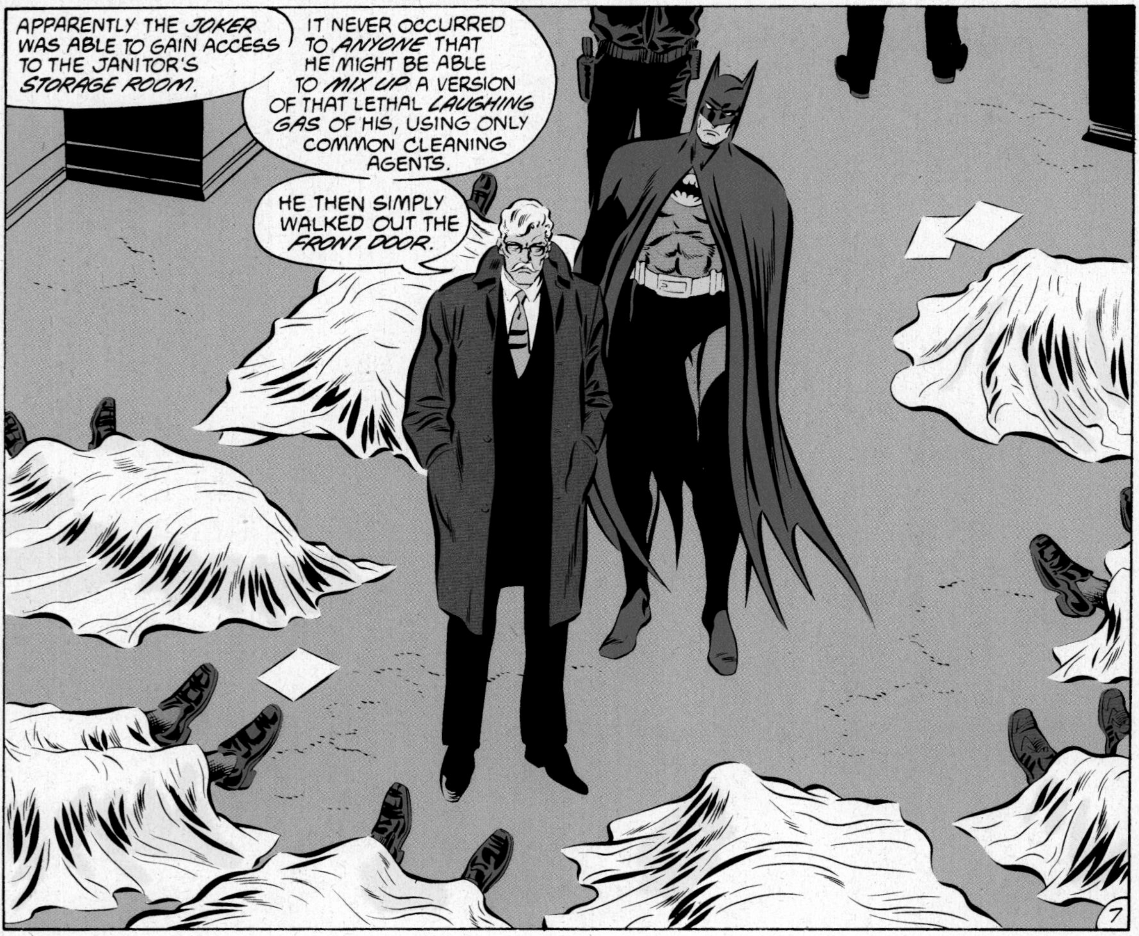
APPARENTLY THE JOKER WAS ABLE TO GAIN ACCESS TO THE JANITOR'S STORAGE ROOM.
IT NEVER OCCURRED TO ANYONE THAT HE MIGHT BE ABLE TO MIX UP A VERSION OF THAT LETHAL LAUGHING GAS OF HIS, USING ONLY COMMON CLEANING AGENTS.
HE THEN SIMPLY WALKED OUT THE FRONT DOOR.
7

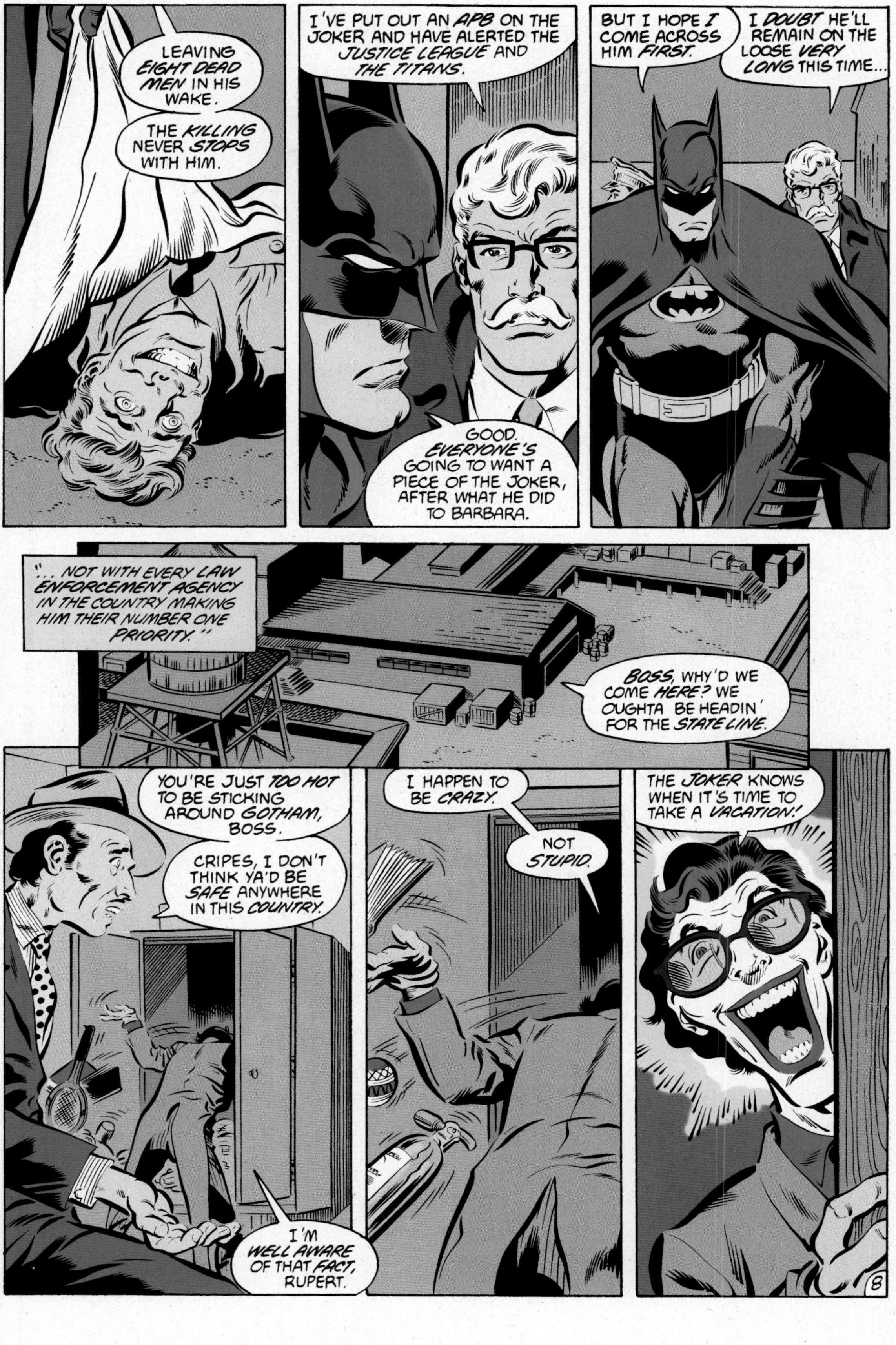
LEAVING EIGHT DEAD MEN IN HIS WAKE.
THE KILLING NEVER STOPS WITH HIM.
I'VE PUT OUT AN APB ON THE JOKER AND HAVE ALERTED THE JUSTICE LEAGUE AND THE TITANS.
GOOD. EVERYONE'S GOING TO WANT A PIECE OF THE JOKER, AFTER WHAT HE DID TO BARBARA.
BUT I HOPE I COME ACROSS HIM FIRST.
I DOUBT HE'LL REMAIN ON THE LOOSE VERY LONG THIS TIME...
"... NOT WITH EVERY LAW ENFORCEMENT AGENCY IN THE COUNTRY MAKING HIM THEIR NUMBER ONE PRIORITY."
BOSS, WHY'D WE COME HERE? WE OUGHTA BE HEADIN' FOR THE STATE LINE.
YOU'RE JUST TOO HOT TO BE STICKING AROUND GOTHAM, BOSS.
CRIPES, I DON'T THINK YA'D BE SAFE ANYWHERE IN THIS COUNTRY.
I'M WELL AWARE OF THAT FACT, RUPERT.
I HAPPEN TO BE CRAZY.
NOT STUPID.
THE JOKER KNOWS WHEN IT'S TIME TO TAKE A VACATION!
8

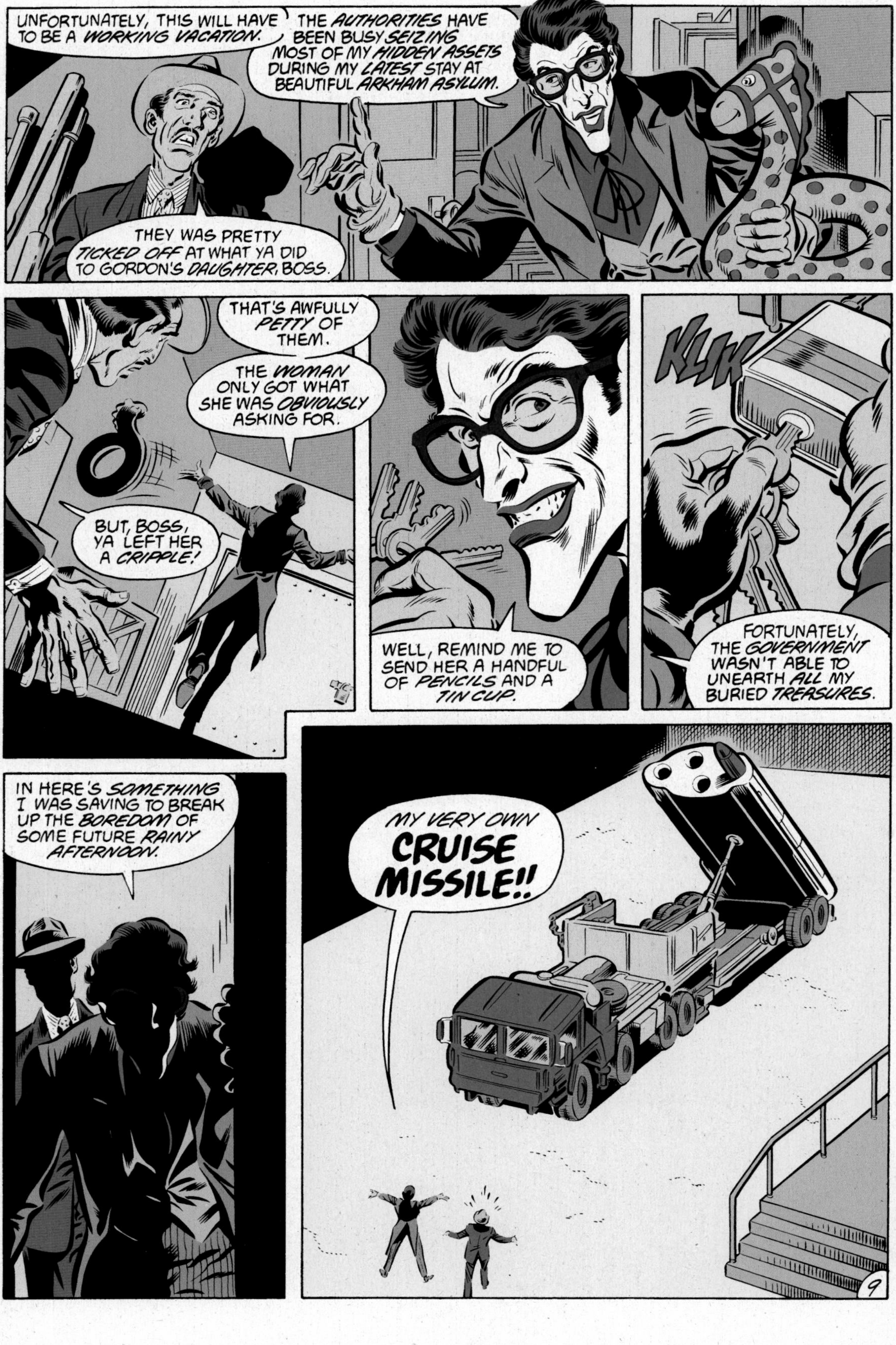

UNFORTUNATELY, THIS WILL HAVE TO BE A *WORKING VACATION*.
THE *AUTHORITIES* HAVE BEEN BUSY *SEIZING* MOST OF MY *HIDDEN ASSETS* DURING MY *LATEST* STAY AT BEAUTIFUL *ARKHAM ASYLUM*.
THEY WAS PRETTY *TICKED OFF* AT WHAT YA DID TO GORDON'S *DAUGHTER*, BOSS.
THAT'S AWFULLY *PETTY* OF THEM.
THE *WOMAN* ONLY GOT WHAT SHE WAS *OBVIOUSLY* ASKING FOR.
BUT, BOSS, YA LEFT HER A *CRIPPLE*!
WELL, REMIND ME TO SEND HER A HANDFUL OF *PENCILS* AND A *TIN CUP*.
KLIK
FORTUNATELY, THE *GOVERNMENT* WASN'T ABLE TO UNEARTH *ALL* MY BURIED *TREASURES*.
IN HERE'S *SOMETHING* I WAS SAVING TO BREAK UP THE *BOREDOM* OF SOME FUTURE *RAINY AFTERNOON*.
MY VERY OWN **CRUISE MISSILE!!**
9

HOW IN BLAZES DID YOU COME BY *THIS*, BOSS?

THROUGH A *FRIEND* OF MINE IN THE *MILITARY* WHO OWED ME A *BIG FAVOR*.

I PLANNED TO FIRE IT AT *CITY HALL* SOMEDAY.

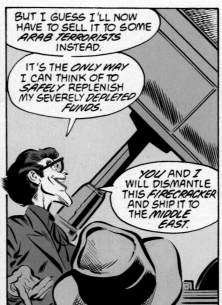

BUT I GUESS I'LL NOW HAVE TO SELL IT TO SOME *ARAB TERRORISTS* INSTEAD.

IT'S THE *ONLY WAY* I CAN THINK OF TO *SAFELY* REPLENISH MY SEVERELY *DEPLETED* FUNDS.

YOU AND *I* WILL DISMANTLE THIS *FIRECRACKER* AND SHIP IT TO THE *MIDDLE EAST*.

WE'LL *NEVER* GET IT OUTTA THE *COUNTRY*, BOSS! THAT *ROCKET'S* GOTTA BE *HOTTER* THAN EVEN YOU ARE!

NOT TO WORRY, RUPERT, MY LAD.

ON PAPER, THIS CRUISE MISSILE *DOESN'T* EVEN *EXIST*. NO ONE KNOWS IT'S MISSING.

IT'S *ANOTHER FAVOR* MY MILITARY FRIEND DID FOR ME BEFORE HIS *UNTIMELY DEMISE*.

YOU KNOW, RUPERT, IN A WAY I THINK THINGS HAVE *WORKED OUT* FOR THE *BEST*.

THE *TIME* HAS COME FOR ME TO MAKE A *FEW CHANGES* IN MY LIFE.

CRIME HASN'T BEEN ALL THAT *GOOD* TO ME OF LATE.

I'VE BEEN SPENDING MORE TIME *IN* ARKHAM ASYLUM THAN *OUT*.

I'VE BEEN SERIOUSLY THINKING OF GETTING INTO A *NEW LINE* OF WORK...

... SOME ENDEAVOR WHERE MY *SPECIAL TALENTS* WILL BE PROPERLY *APPRECIATED*.

SOMETHING LIKE *INTERNATIONAL POLITICS!*

⑩

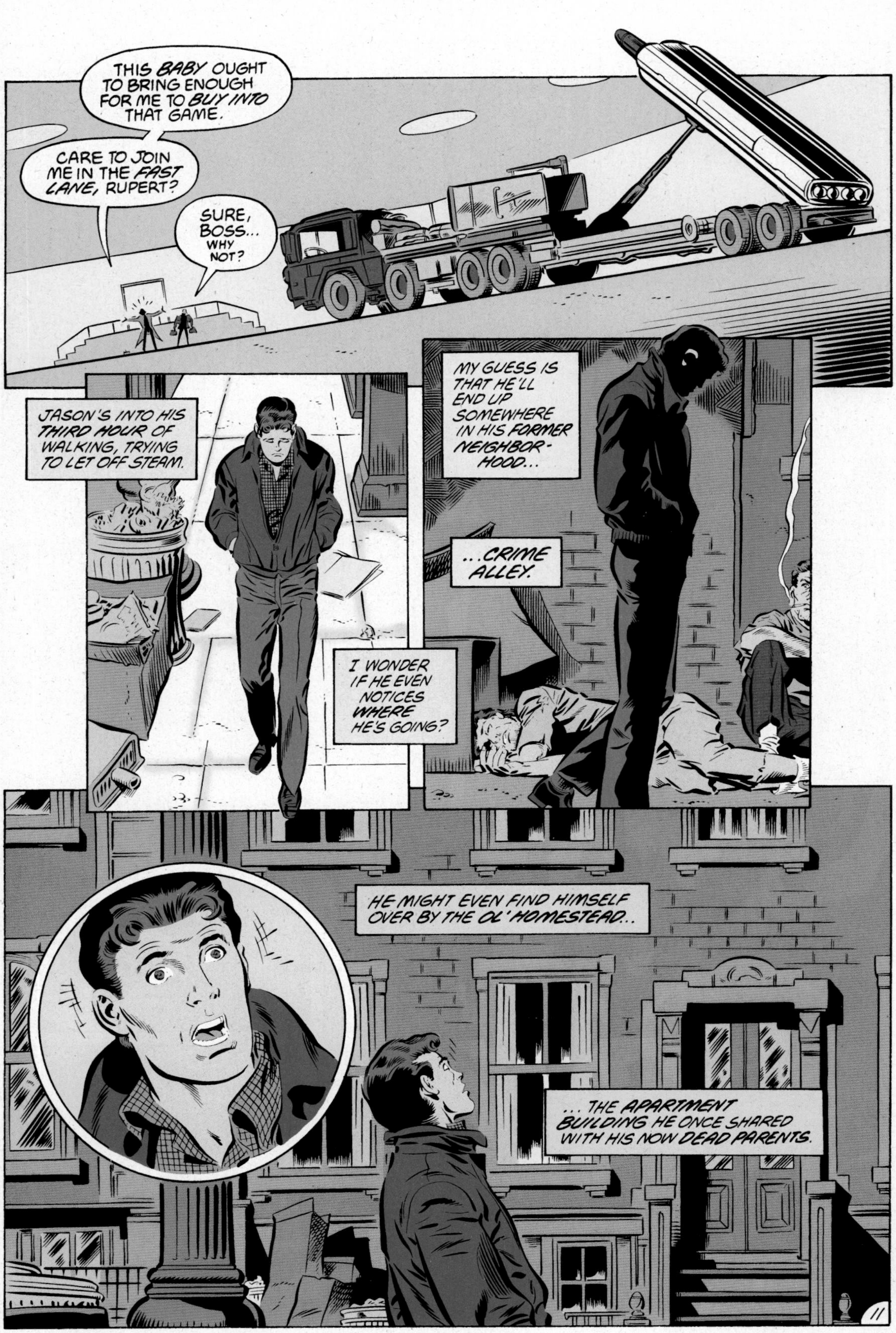
THIS BABY OUGHT TO BRING ENOUGH FOR ME TO BUY INTO THAT GAME.
CARE TO JOIN ME IN THE FAST LANE, RUPERT?
SURE, BOSS... WHY NOT?
JASON'S INTO HIS THIRD HOUR OF WALKING, TRYING TO LET OFF STEAM.
I WONDER IF HE EVEN NOTICES WHERE HE'S GOING?
MY GUESS IS THAT HE'LL END UP SOMEWHERE IN HIS FORMER NEIGHBOR-HOOD...
...CRIME ALLEY.
HE MIGHT EVEN FIND HIMSELF OVER BY THE OL' HOMESTEAD...
... THE APARTMENT BUILDING HE ONCE SHARED WITH HIS NOW DEAD PARENTS.
11

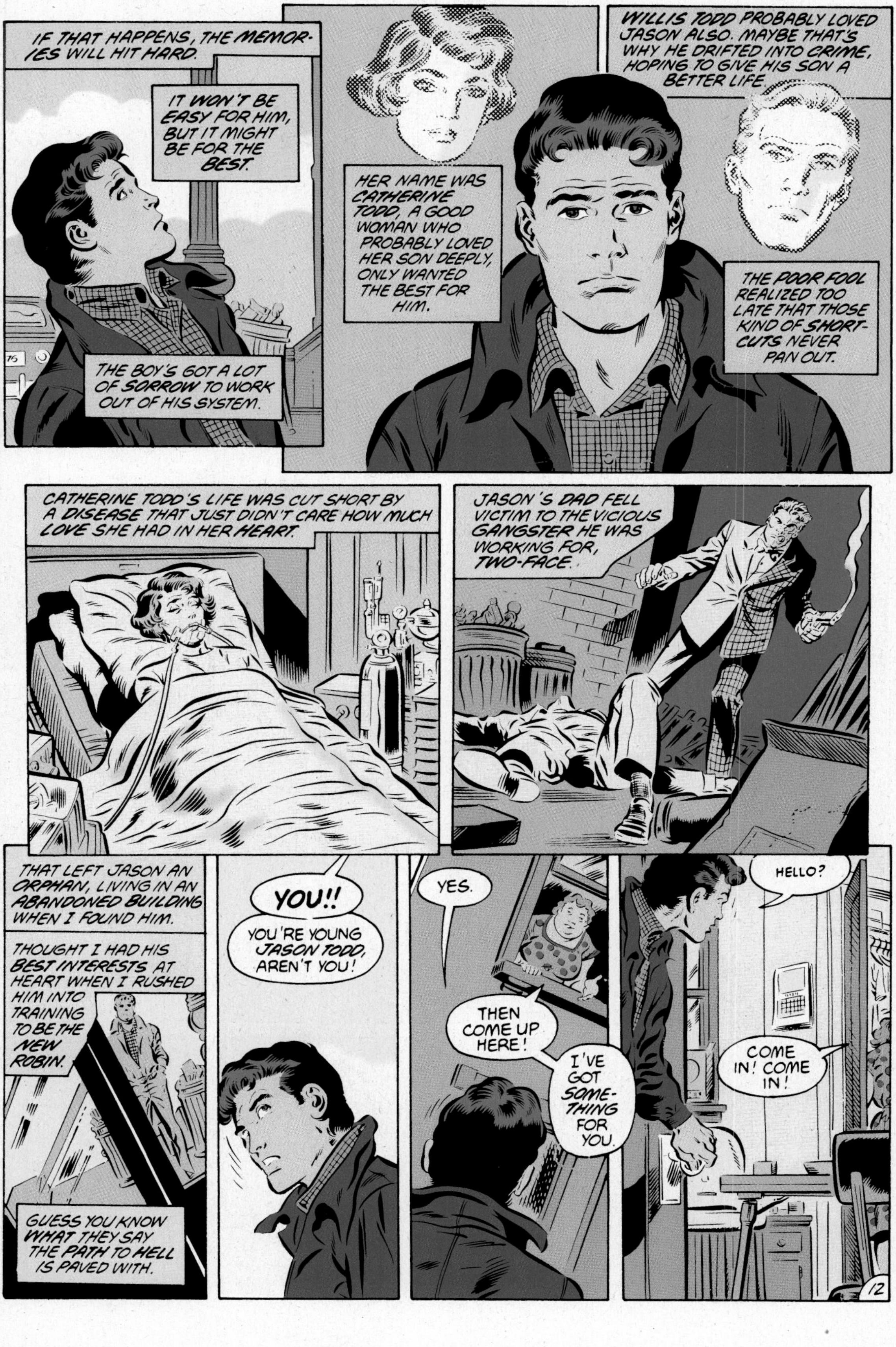
IF THAT HAPPENS, THE MEMORIES WILL HIT HARD.
IT WON'T BE EASY FOR HIM, BUT IT MIGHT BE FOR THE BEST.
THE BOY'S GOT A LOT OF SORROW TO WORK OUT OF HIS SYSTEM.
HER NAME WAS CATHERINE TODD, A GOOD WOMAN WHO PROBABLY LOVED HER SON DEEPLY, ONLY WANTED THE BEST FOR HIM.
WILLIS TODD PROBABLY LOVED JASON ALSO. MAYBE THAT'S WHY HE DRIFTED INTO CRIME, HOPING TO GIVE HIS SON A BETTER LIFE.
THE POOR FOOL REALIZED TOO LATE THAT THOSE KIND OF SHORT-CUTS NEVER PAN OUT.
CATHERINE TODD'S LIFE WAS CUT SHORT BY A DISEASE THAT JUST DIDN'T CARE HOW MUCH LOVE SHE HAD IN HER HEART.
JASON'S DAD FELL VICTIM TO THE VICIOUS GANGSTER HE WAS WORKING FOR, TWO-FACE.
THAT LEFT JASON AN ORPHAN, LIVING IN AN ABANDONED BUILDING WHEN I FOUND HIM.
THOUGHT I HAD HIS BEST INTERESTS AT HEART WHEN I RUSHED HIM INTO TRAINING TO BE THE NEW ROBIN.
GUESS YOU KNOW WHAT THEY SAY THE PATH TO HELL IS PAVED WITH.
YOU!!
YOU'RE YOUNG JASON TODD, AREN'T YOU!
YES.
THEN COME UP HERE!
I'VE GOT SOMETHING FOR YOU.
HELLO?
COME IN! COME IN!
12

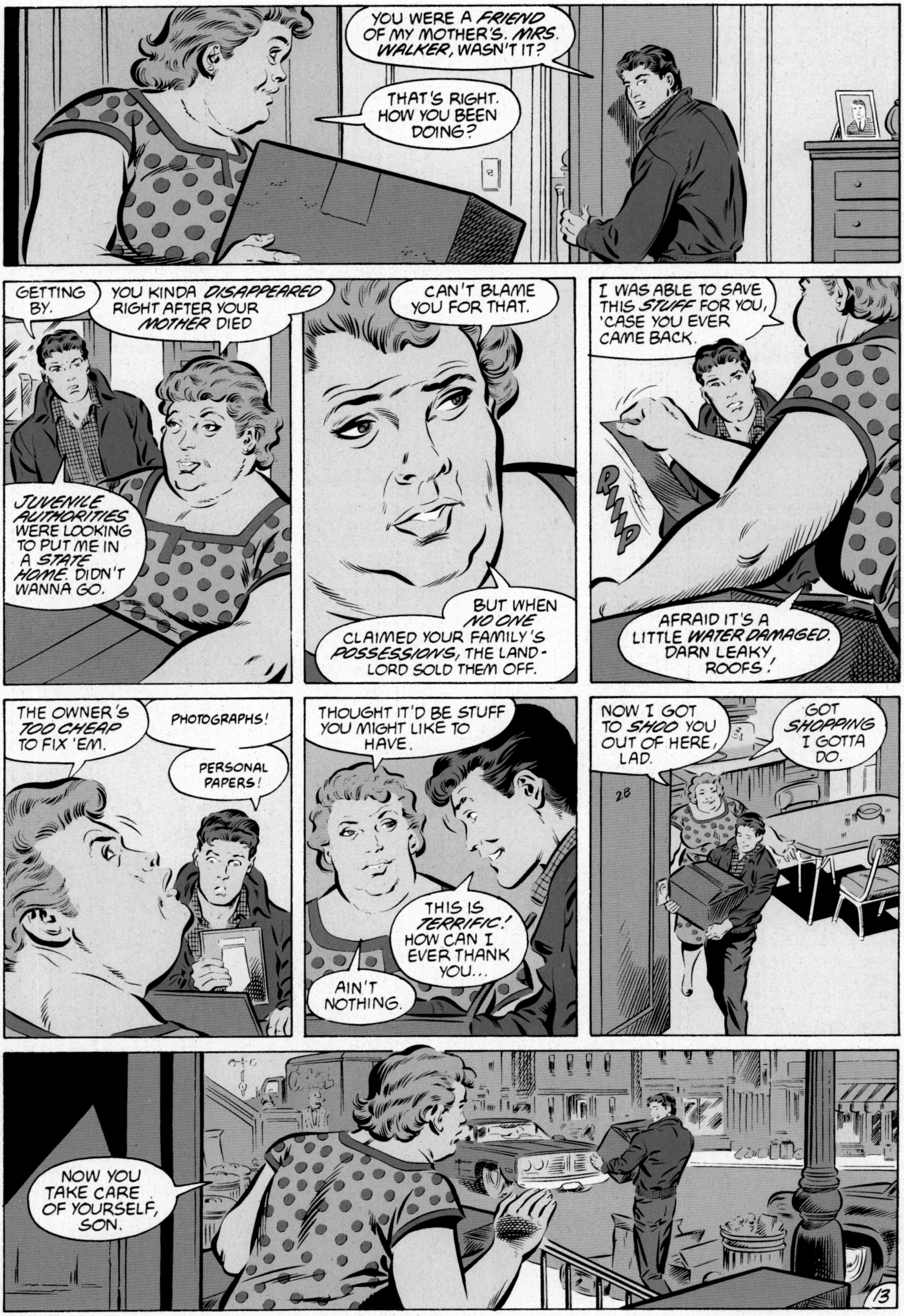
YOU WERE A *FRIEND* OF MY MOTHER'S. *MRS. WALKER*, WASN'T IT?
THAT'S RIGHT. HOW YOU BEEN DOING?
GETTING BY.
YOU KINDA *DISAPPEARED* RIGHT AFTER YOUR *MOTHER* DIED
JUVENILE AUTHORITIES WERE LOOKING TO PUT ME IN A *STATE HOME*. DIDN'T WANNA GO.
CAN'T BLAME YOU FOR THAT.
BUT WHEN *NO ONE* CLAIMED YOUR FAMILY'S *POSSESSIONS*, THE LAND-LORD SOLD THEM OFF.
I WAS ABLE TO SAVE THIS *STUFF* FOR YOU, 'CASE YOU EVER CAME BACK.
RIIP
AFRAID IT'S A LITTLE *WATER DAMAGED*. DARN LEAKY ROOFS!
THE OWNER'S *TOO CHEAP* TO FIX 'EM.
PHOTOGRAPHS!
PERSONAL PAPERS!
THOUGHT IT'D BE STUFF YOU MIGHT LIKE TO HAVE.
THIS IS *TERRIFIC!* HOW CAN I EVER THANK YOU...
AIN'T NOTHING.
NOW I GOT TO *SHOO* YOU OUT OF HERE, LAD.
GOT *SHOPPING* I GOTTA DO.
2B
NOW YOU TAKE CARE OF YOURSELF, SON.
13

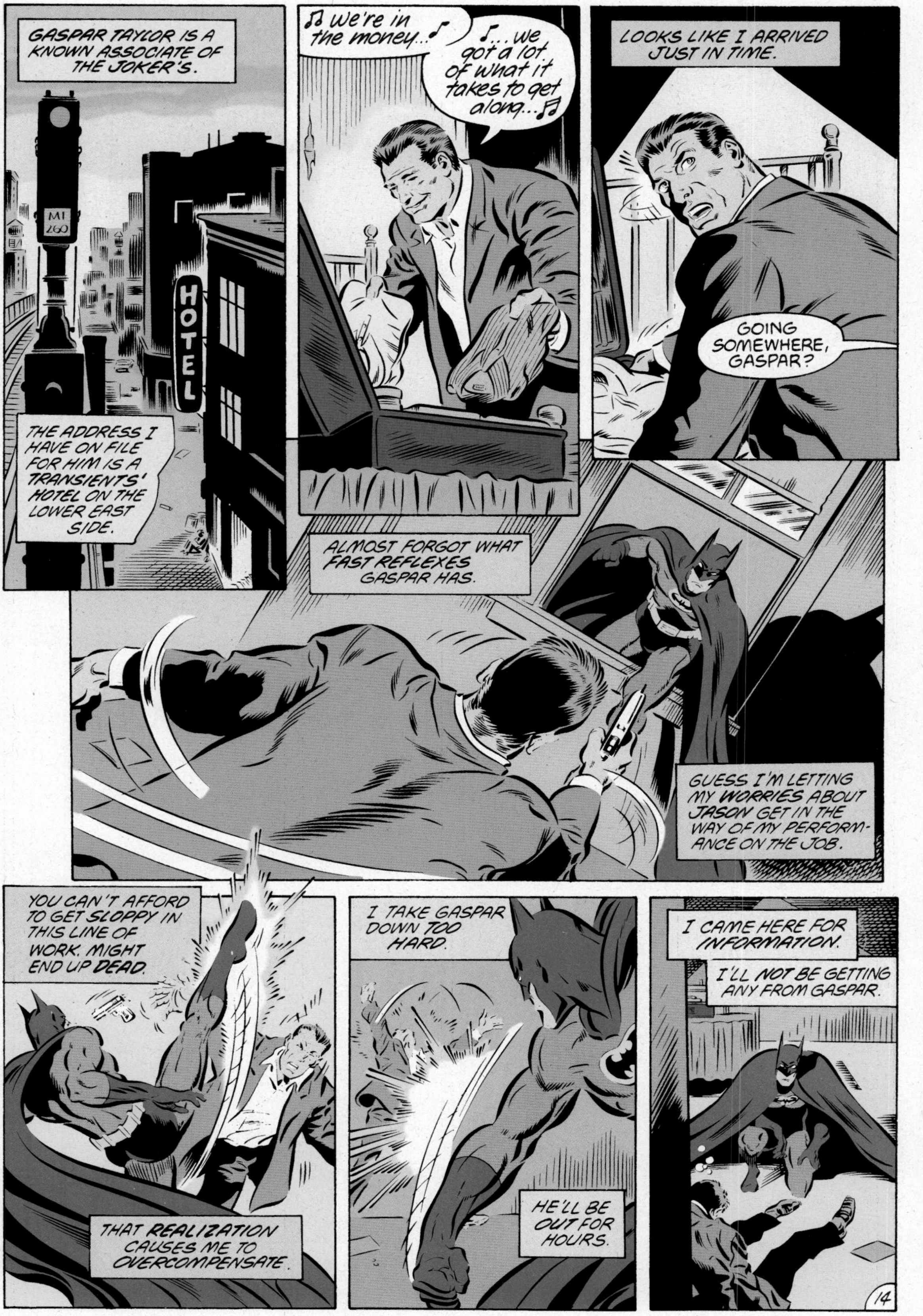
GASPAR TAYLOR IS A KNOWN ASSOCIATE OF THE JOKER'S.
MI 260
HOTEL
THE ADDRESS I HAVE ON FILE FOR HIM IS A TRANSIENTS' HOTEL ON THE LOWER EAST SIDE.
♫ We're in the money... ♪
♪... we got a lot of what it takes to get along... ♫
LOOKS LIKE I ARRIVED JUST IN TIME.
GOING SOMEWHERE, GASPAR?
ALMOST FORGOT WHAT FAST REFLEXES GASPAR HAS.
GUESS I'M LETTING MY WORRIES ABOUT JASON GET IN THE WAY OF MY PERFORMANCE ON THE JOB.
YOU CAN'T AFFORD TO GET SLOPPY IN THIS LINE OF WORK. MIGHT END UP DEAD.
THAT REALIZATION CAUSES ME TO OVERCOMPENSATE.
I TAKE GASPAR DOWN TOO HARD.
HE'LL BE OUT FOR HOURS.
I CAME HERE FOR INFORMATION.
I'LL NOT BE GETTING ANY FROM GASPAR.
14

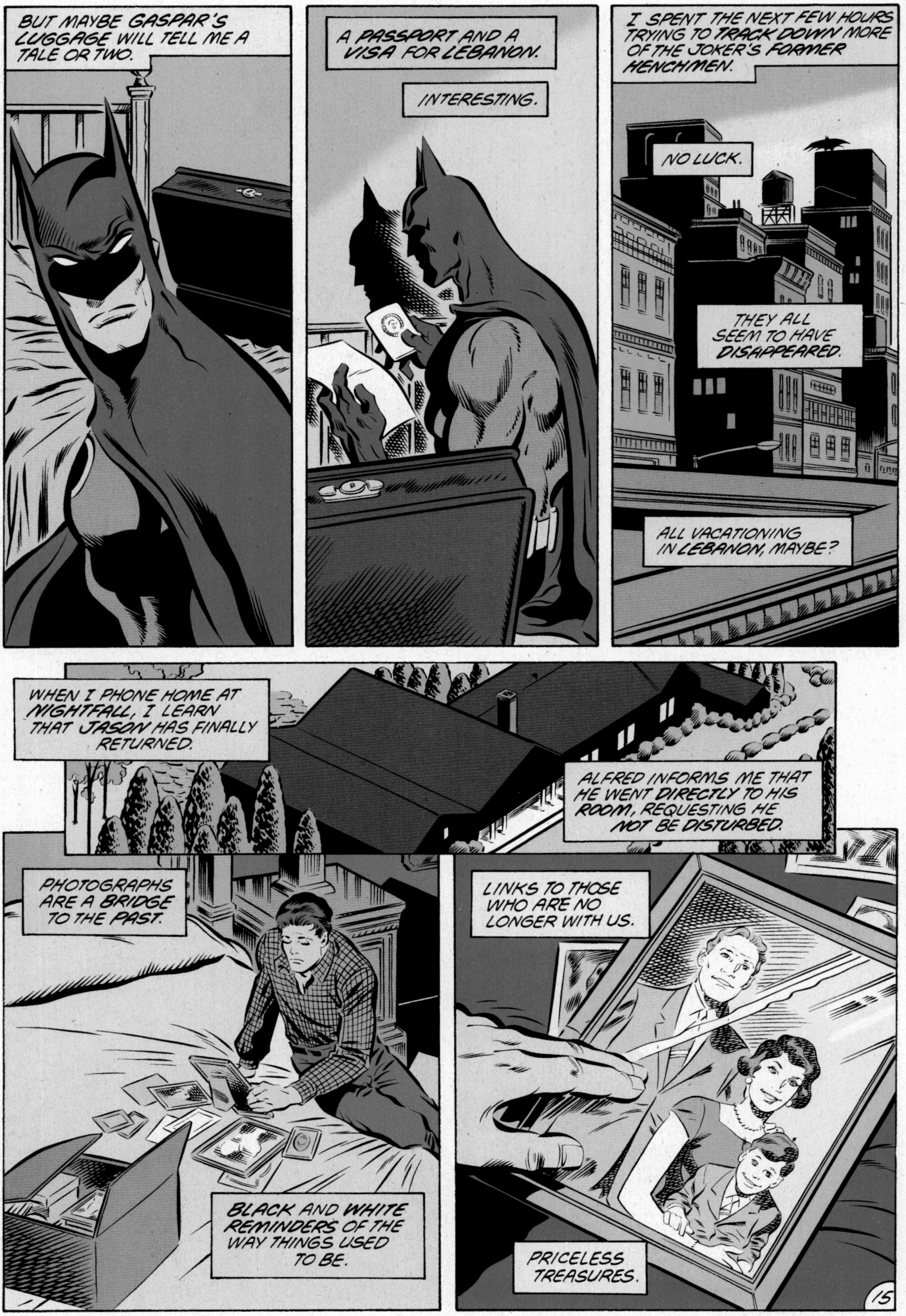

BUT MAYBE GASPAR'S LUGGAGE WILL TELL ME A TALE OR TWO.
A PASSPORT AND A VISA FOR LEBANON.
INTERESTING.
I SPENT THE NEXT FEW HOURS TRYING TO TRACK DOWN MORE OF THE JOKER'S FORMER HENCHMEN.
NO LUCK.
THEY ALL SEEM TO HAVE DISAPPEARED.
ALL VACATIONING IN LEBANON, MAYBE?
WHEN I PHONE HOME AT NIGHTFALL, I LEARN THAT JASON HAS FINALLY RETURNED.
ALFRED INFORMS ME THAT HE WENT DIRECTLY TO HIS ROOM, REQUESTING HE NOT BE DISTURBED.
PHOTOGRAPHS ARE A BRIDGE TO THE PAST.
BLACK AND WHITE REMINDERS OF THE WAY THINGS USED TO BE.
LINKS TO THOSE WHO ARE NO LONGER WITH US.
PRICELESS TREASURES.
15

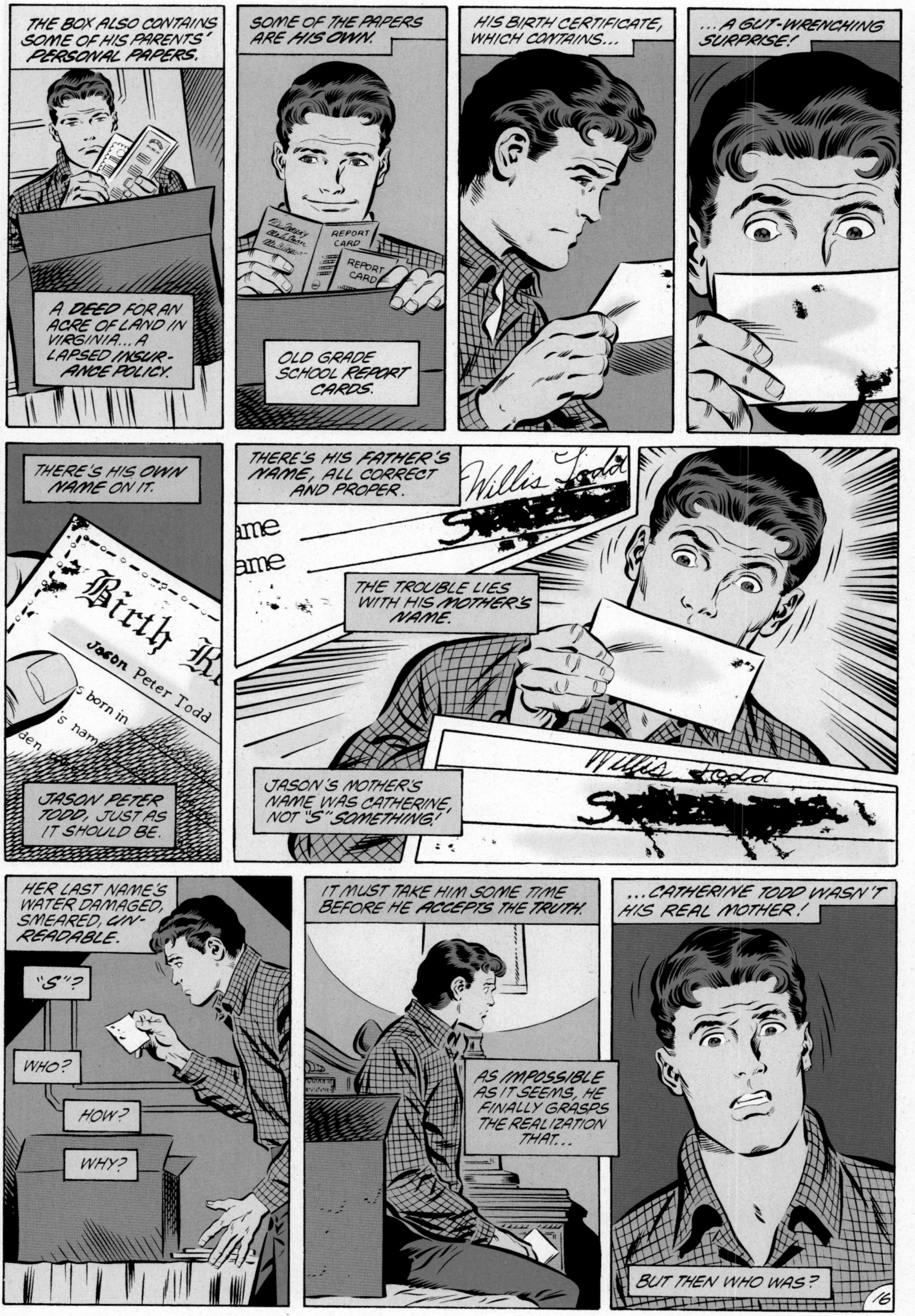
THE BOX ALSO CONTAINS SOME OF HIS PARENTS' PERSONAL PAPERS.
A DEED FOR AN ACRE OF LAND IN VIRGINIA... A LAPSED INSURANCE POLICY.
SOME OF THE PAPERS ARE HIS OWN.
REPORT CARD
REPORT CARD
OLD GRADE SCHOOL REPORT CARDS.
HIS BIRTH CERTIFICATE, WHICH CONTAINS...
...A GUT-WRENCHING SURPRISE!
THERE'S HIS OWN NAME ON IT.
Jason Peter Todd
s born in
JASON PETER TODD, JUST AS IT SHOULD BE.
THERE'S HIS FATHER'S NAME, ALL CORRECT AND PROPER.
Willis Todd
THE TROUBLE LIES WITH HIS MOTHER'S NAME.
JASON'S MOTHER'S NAME WAS CATHERINE, NOT "S" SOMETHING!
HER LAST NAME'S WATER DAMAGED, SMEARED, UNREADABLE.
"S"?
WHO?
HOW?
WHY?
IT MUST TAKE HIM SOME TIME BEFORE HE ACCEPTS THE TRUTH.
AS IMPOSSIBLE AS IT SEEMS, HE FINALLY GRASPS THE REALIZATION THAT...
...CATHERINE TODD WASN'T HIS REAL MOTHER!
BUT THEN WHO WAS?
16

HOW TO FIND OUT THE TRUTH?

HIS *MOTHER* AND *FATHER* ARE DEAD.

CAN'T ASK THEM.

MOTHER?

STEP-MOTHER--A BITTER REALIZATION.

HIS *REAL* MOTHER IS SOMEONE HE'S *NEVER* MET...

...SOMEONE WHO *MAY STILL BE ALIVE!*

THERE HAS TO BE A WAY TO FIND OUT!

I TAUGHT THE BOY HOW TO BE A *DETECTIVE.*

HE USES *THAT* SKILL.

AN *ADDRESS BOOK!!*

MY FATHER'S ADDRESS BOOK.

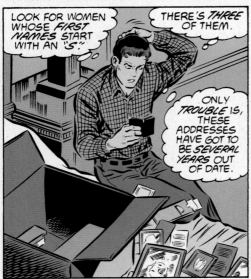

LOOK FOR WOMEN WHOSE *FIRST NAMES* START WITH AN *"S".*

THERE'S *THREE* OF THEM.

ONLY *TROUBLE* IS, THESE ADDRESSES HAVE GOT TO BE *SEVERAL YEARS* OUT OF DATE.

HOW DO I *LOCATE* THEM AFTER ALL THIS TIME?

OF COURSE! THE *COMPUTER* IN THE *BATCAVE.*

17

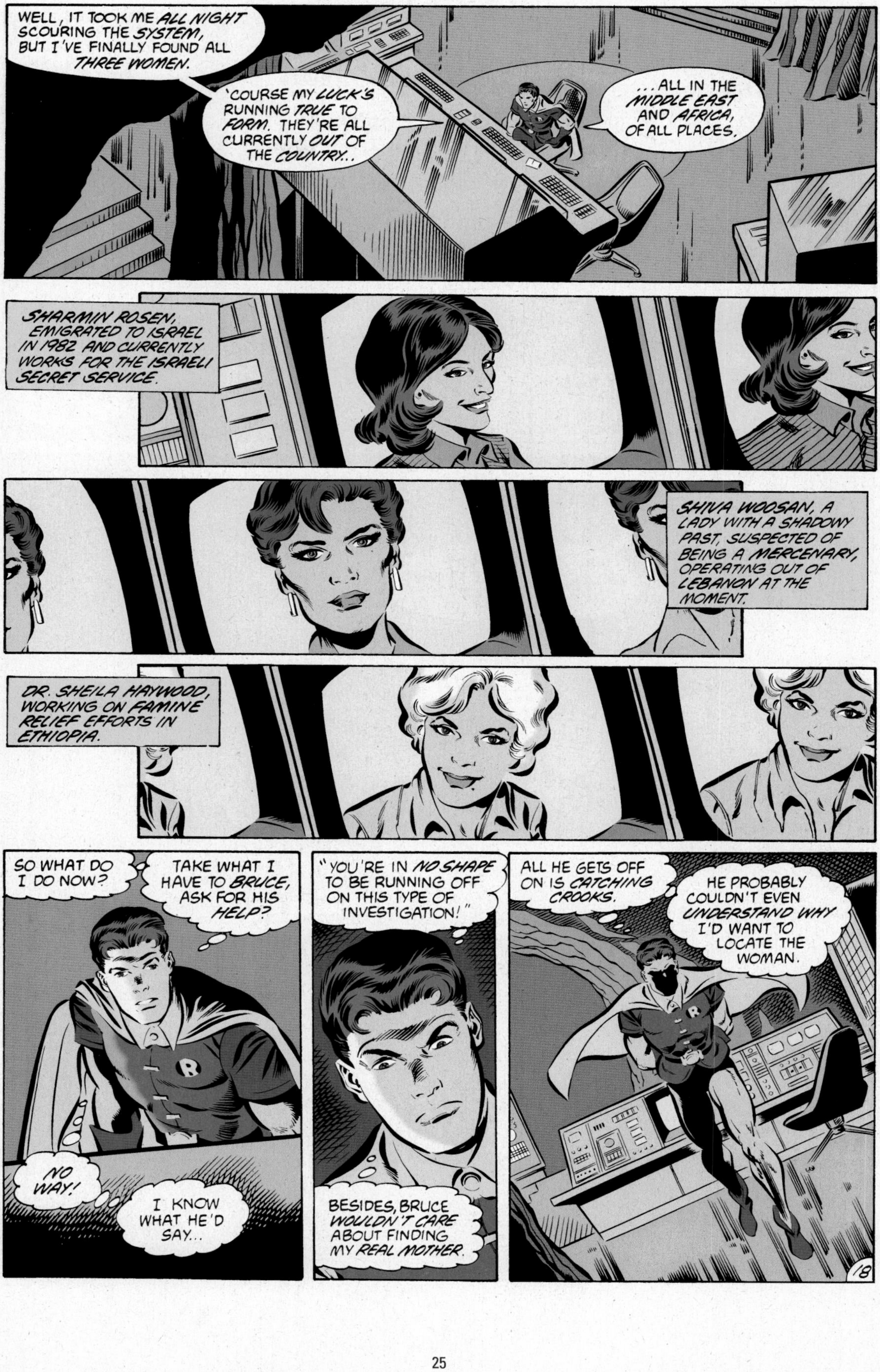
WELL, IT TOOK ME ALL NIGHT SCOURING THE SYSTEM, BUT I'VE FINALLY FOUND ALL THREE WOMEN.
'COURSE MY LUCK'S RUNNING TRUE TO FORM. THEY'RE ALL CURRENTLY OUT OF THE COUNTRY...
...ALL IN THE MIDDLE EAST AND AFRICA, OF ALL PLACES.
SHARMIN ROSEN, EMIGRATED TO ISRAEL IN 1982 AND CURRENTLY WORKS FOR THE ISRAELI SECRET SERVICE.
SHIVA WOOSAN, A LADY WITH A SHADOWY PAST, SUSPECTED OF BEING A MERCENARY, OPERATING OUT OF LEBANON AT THE MOMENT.
DR. SHEILA HAYWOOD, WORKING ON FAMINE RELIEF EFFORTS IN ETHIOPIA.
SO WHAT DO I DO NOW?
TAKE WHAT I HAVE TO BRUCE, ASK FOR HIS HELP?
NO WAY!
I KNOW WHAT HE'D SAY...
"YOU'RE IN NO SHAPE TO BE RUNNING OFF ON THIS TYPE OF INVESTIGATION!"
BESIDES, BRUCE WOULDN'T CARE ABOUT FINDING MY REAL MOTHER.
ALL HE GETS OFF ON IS CATCHING CROOKS.
HE PROBABLY COULDN'T EVEN UNDERSTAND WHY I'D WANT TO LOCATE THE WOMAN.
18

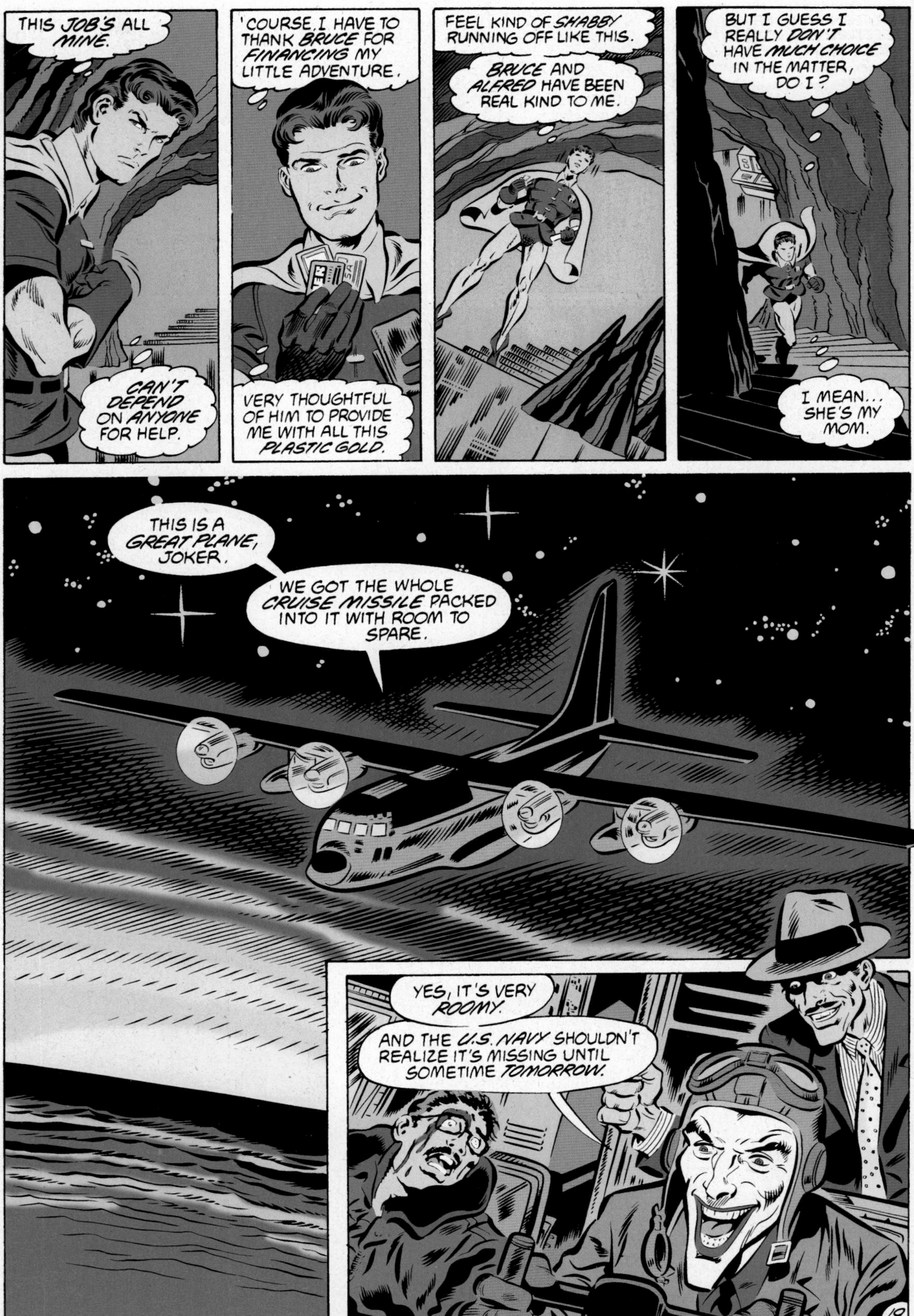
THIS JOB'S ALL MINE.
CAN'T DEPEND ON ANYONE FOR HELP.
'COURSE, I HAVE TO THANK BRUCE FOR FINANCING MY LITTLE ADVENTURE.
VERY THOUGHTFUL OF HIM TO PROVIDE ME WITH ALL THIS PLASTIC GOLD.
FEEL KIND OF SHABBY RUNNING OFF LIKE THIS.
BRUCE AND ALFRED HAVE BEEN REAL KIND TO ME.
BUT I GUESS I REALLY DON'T HAVE MUCH CHOICE IN THE MATTER, DO I?
I MEAN... SHE'S MY MOM.
THIS IS A GREAT PLANE, JOKER.
WE GOT THE WHOLE CRUISE MISSILE PACKED INTO IT WITH ROOM TO SPARE.
YES, IT'S VERY ROOMY.
AND THE U.S. NAVY SHOULDN'T REALIZE IT'S MISSING UNTIL SOMETIME TOMORROW.
19

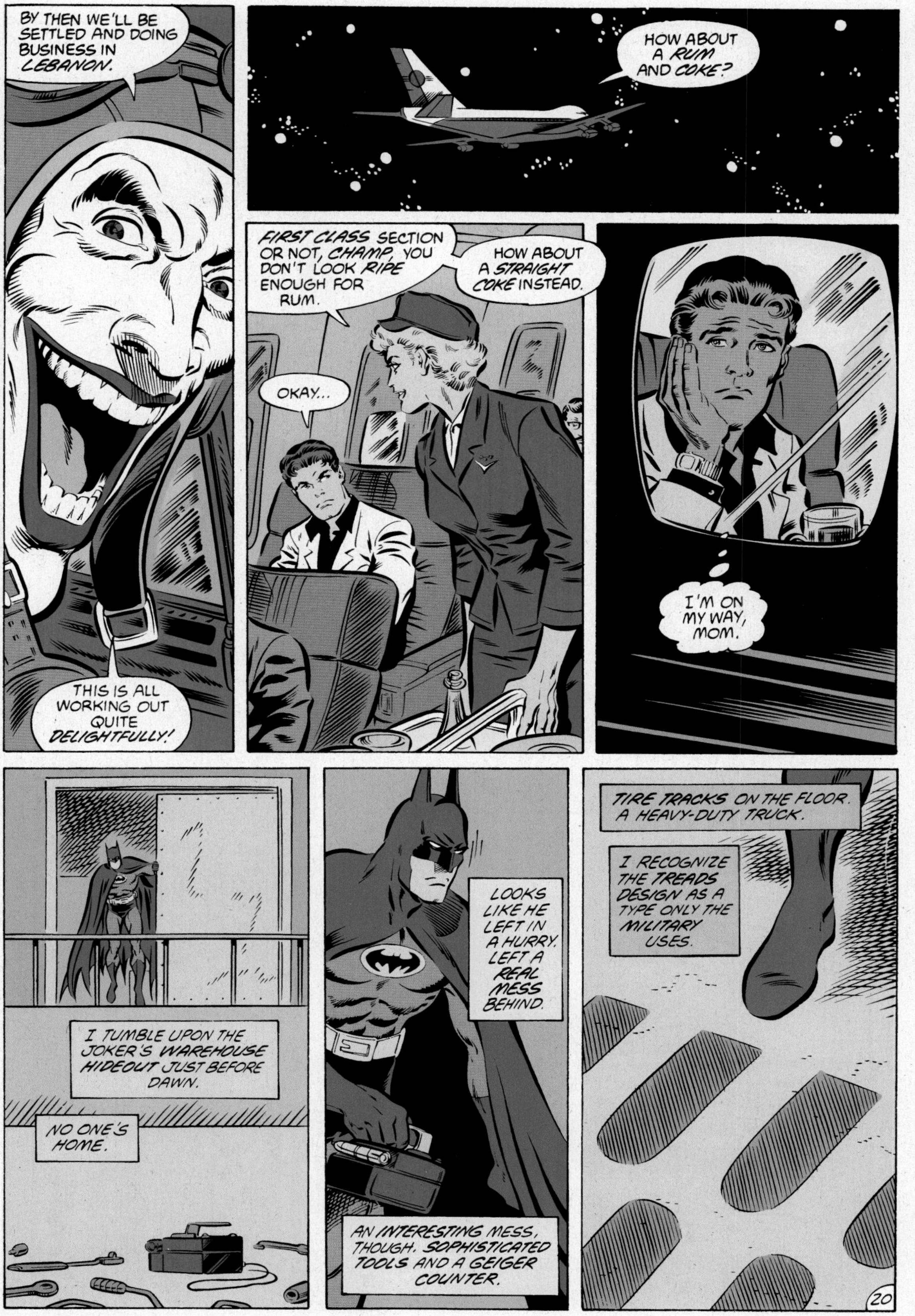
BY THEN WE'LL BE SETTLED AND DOING BUSINESS IN LEBANON.
THIS IS ALL WORKING OUT QUITE DELIGHTFULLY!
HOW ABOUT A RUM AND COKE?
FIRST CLASS SECTION OR NOT, CHAMP, YOU DON'T LOOK RIPE ENOUGH FOR RUM.
HOW ABOUT A STRAIGHT COKE INSTEAD.
OKAY...
I'M ON MY WAY, MOM.
I TUMBLE UPON THE JOKER'S WAREHOUSE HIDEOUT JUST BEFORE DAWN.
NO ONE'S HOME.
LOOKS LIKE HE LEFT IN A HURRY. LEFT A REAL MESS BEHIND.
AN INTERESTING MESS, THOUGH. SOPHISTICATED TOOLS AND A GEIGER COUNTER.
TIRE TRACKS ON THE FLOOR. A HEAVY-DUTY TRUCK.
I RECOGNIZE THE TREADS DESIGN AS A TYPE ONLY THE MILITARY USES.
20

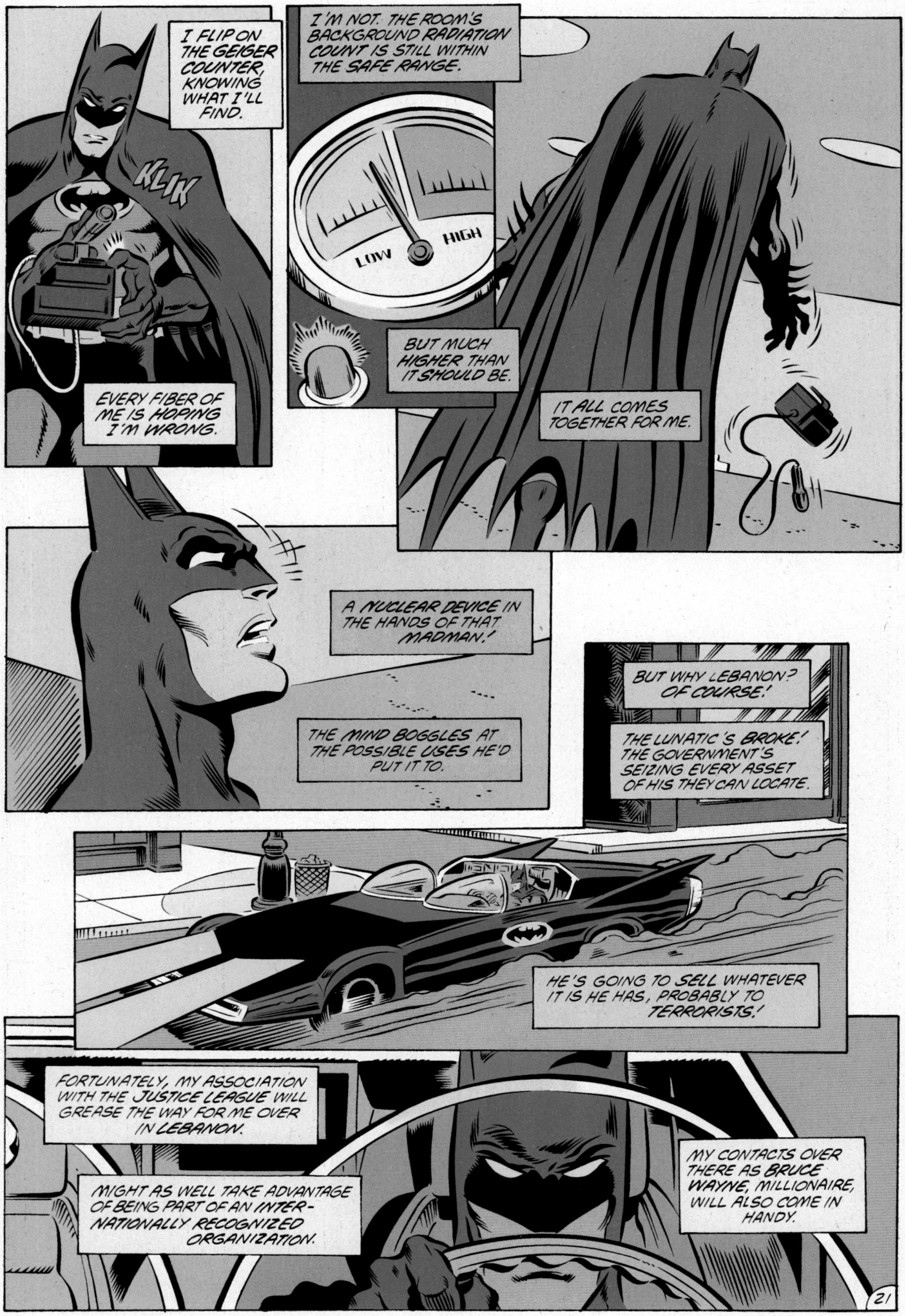
I FLIP ON THE GEIGER COUNTER, KNOWING WHAT I'LL FIND.
KLIK
EVERY FIBER OF ME IS HOPING I'M WRONG.
I'M NOT. THE ROOM'S BACKGROUND RADIATION COUNT IS STILL WITHIN THE SAFE RANGE.
LOW
HIGH
BUT MUCH HIGHER THAN IT SHOULD BE.
IT ALL COMES TOGETHER FOR ME.
A NUCLEAR DEVICE IN THE HANDS OF THAT MADMAN!
THE MIND BOGGLES AT THE POSSIBLE USES HE'D PUT IT TO.
BUT WHY LEBANON? OF COURSE!
THE LUNATIC'S BROKE! THE GOVERNMENT'S SEIZING EVERY ASSET OF HIS THEY CAN LOCATE.
HE'S GOING TO SELL WHATEVER IT IS HE HAS, PROBABLY TO TERRORISTS!
FORTUNATELY, MY ASSOCIATION WITH THE JUSTICE LEAGUE WILL GREASE THE WAY FOR ME OVER IN LEBANON.
MIGHT AS WELL TAKE ADVANTAGE OF BEING PART OF AN INTER-NATIONALLY RECOGNIZED ORGANIZATION.
MY CONTACTS OVER THERE AS BRUCE WAYNE, MILLIONAIRE, WILL ALSO COME IN HANDY.
21

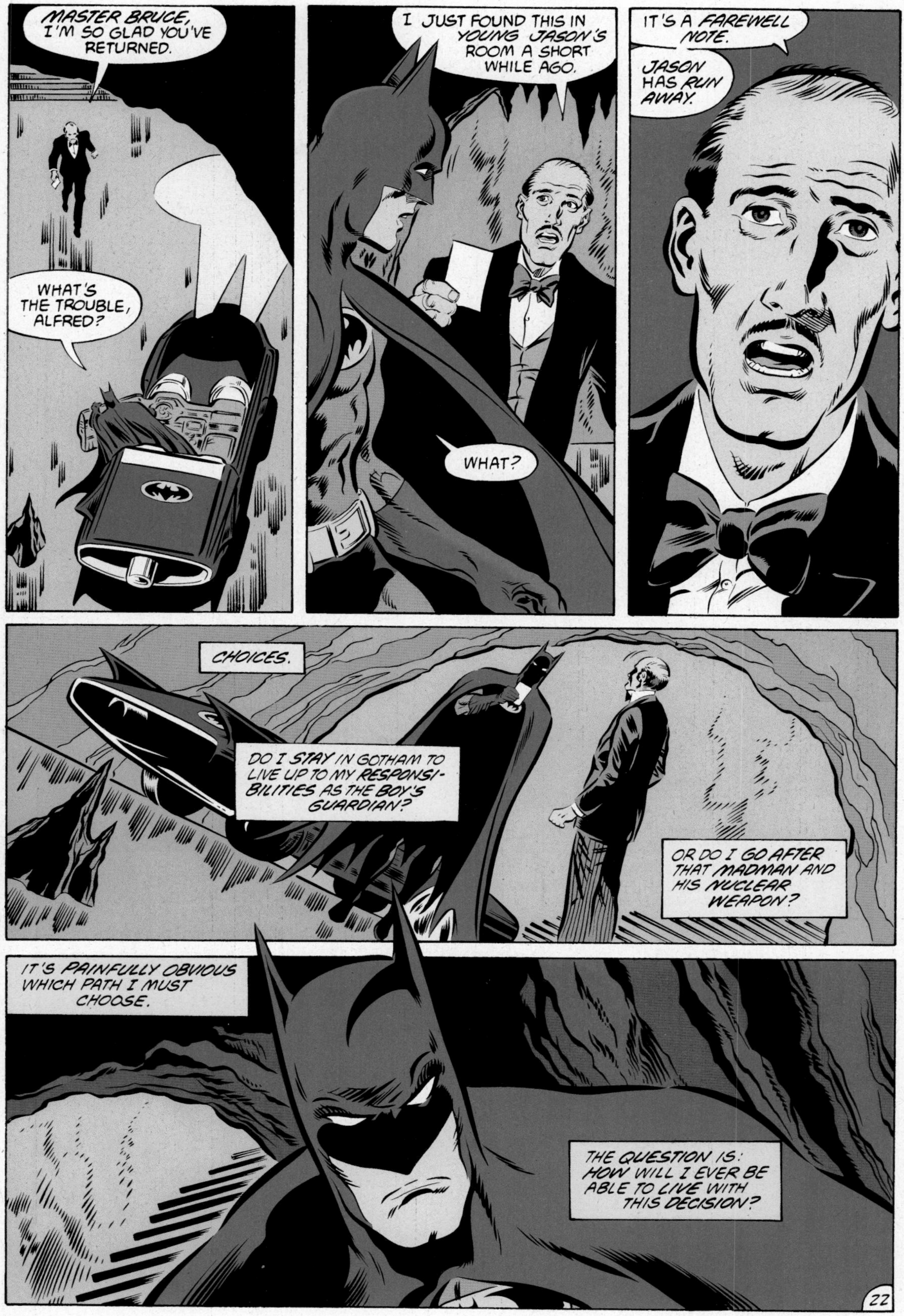
MASTER BRUCE, I'M SO GLAD YOU'VE RETURNED.
WHAT'S THE TROUBLE, ALFRED?
I JUST FOUND THIS IN YOUNG JASON'S ROOM A SHORT WHILE AGO.
WHAT?
IT'S A FAREWELL NOTE.
JASON HAS RUN AWAY.
CHOICES.
DO I STAY IN GOTHAM TO LIVE UP TO MY RESPONSIBILITIES AS THE BOY'S GUARDIAN?
OR DO I GO AFTER THAT MADMAN AND HIS NUCLEAR WEAPON?
IT'S PAINFULLY OBVIOUS WHICH PATH I MUST CHOOSE.
THE QUESTION IS: HOW WILL I EVER BE ABLE TO LIVE WITH THIS DECISION?
22

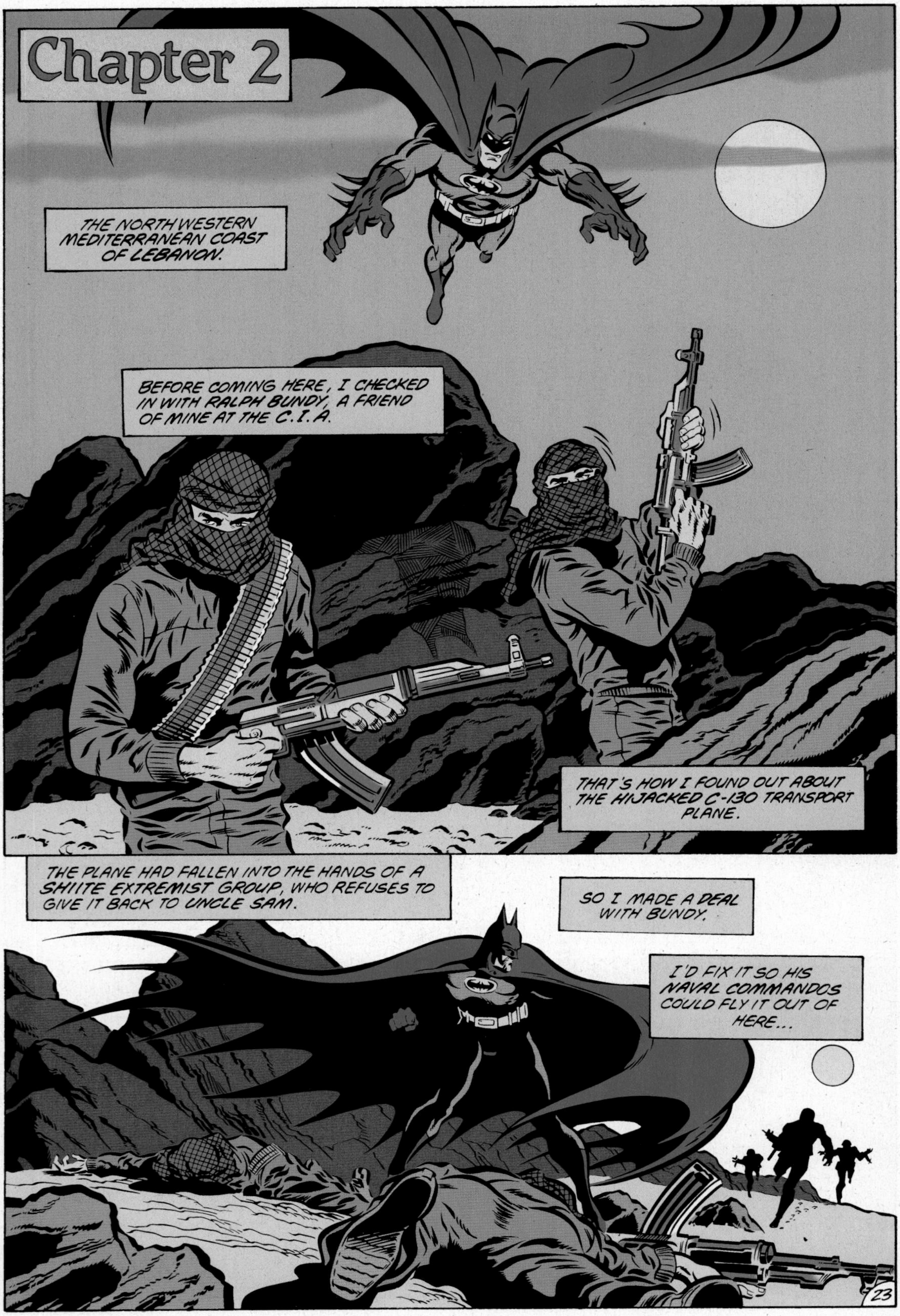
Chapter 2
THE NORTHWESTERN MEDITERRANEAN COAST OF LEBANON.
BEFORE COMING HERE, I CHECKED IN WITH RALPH BUNDY, A FRIEND OF MINE AT THE C.I.A.
THAT'S HOW I FOUND OUT ABOUT THE HIJACKED C-130 TRANSPORT PLANE.
THE PLANE HAD FALLEN INTO THE HANDS OF A SHIITE EXTREMIST GROUP, WHO REFUSES TO GIVE IT BACK TO UNCLE SAM.
SO I MADE A DEAL WITH BUNDY.
I'D FIX IT SO HIS NAVAL COMMANDOS COULD FLY IT OUT OF HERE...
23

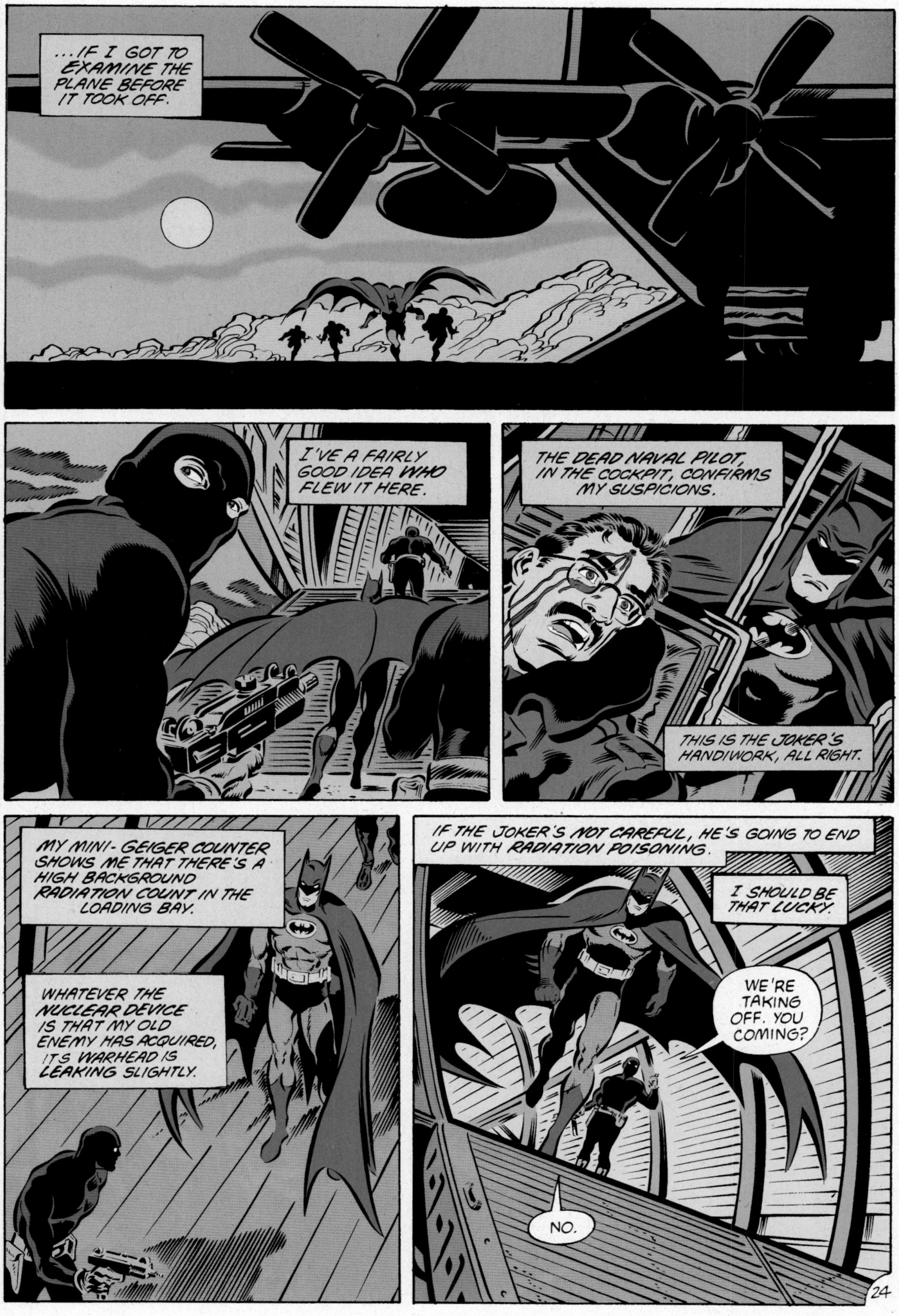

...IF I GOT TO EXAMINE THE PLANE BEFORE IT TOOK OFF.
I'VE A FAIRLY GOOD IDEA WHO FLEW IT HERE.
THE DEAD NAVAL PILOT, IN THE COCKPIT, CONFIRMS MY SUSPICIONS.
THIS IS THE JOKER'S HANDIWORK, ALL RIGHT.
MY MINI-GEIGER COUNTER SHOWS ME THAT THERE'S A HIGH BACKGROUND RADIATION COUNT IN THE LOADING BAY.
WHATEVER THE NUCLEAR DEVICE IS THAT MY OLD ENEMY HAS ACQUIRED, ITS WARHEAD IS LEAKING SLIGHTLY.
IF THE JOKER'S NOT CAREFUL, HE'S GOING TO END UP WITH RADIATION POISONING.
I SHOULD BE THAT LUCKY.
WE'RE TAKING OFF. YOU COMING?
NO.
24

THE JOKER'S GOTTEN THIS FAR--

--WHICH MEANS WHOEVER HE'S SELLING THE WEAPON TO IS IN *LEBANON.*

PROBABLY *TERRORISTS.*

HARD TO CONCENTRATE-- I KEEP WONDERING WHERE *JASON* IS.

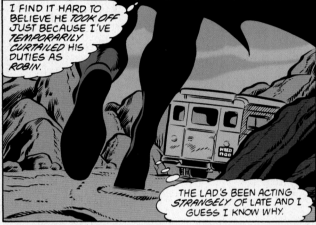

I FIND IT HARD TO BELIEVE HE *TOOK OFF* JUST BECAUSE I'VE *TEMPORARILY CURTAILED* HIS DUTIES AS *ROBIN.*

THE LAD'S BEEN ACTING *STRANGELY* OF LATE AND I GUESS I KNOW WHY.

SINCE HE'S NOT YET *ADJUSTED* TO THE *DEATH* OF HIS *PARENTS...*

...HE NEEDS *TIME* TO WORK OUT HIS *GRIEF,* TIME HE *WON'T FIND* FIGHTING CRIME BY MY SIDE.

WISH I COULD *TRACK DOWN* THE BOY AND BRING HIM HOME *MYSELF.*

BUT THIS *JOKER BUSINESS* TAKES PRIORITY. *LIVES ARE AT STAKE.*

BUT FORTUNATELY *ALFRED'S* BACK HOME, ON THE JOB.

IN FACT, IT'S TIME I CONTACT HIM VIA *SCRAMBLED SATELLITE RELAY.*

HOMEBASE, THIS IS *EL ZOOL.* ANY WORD ON THE *LOST BIRD* YET?

YES.

25

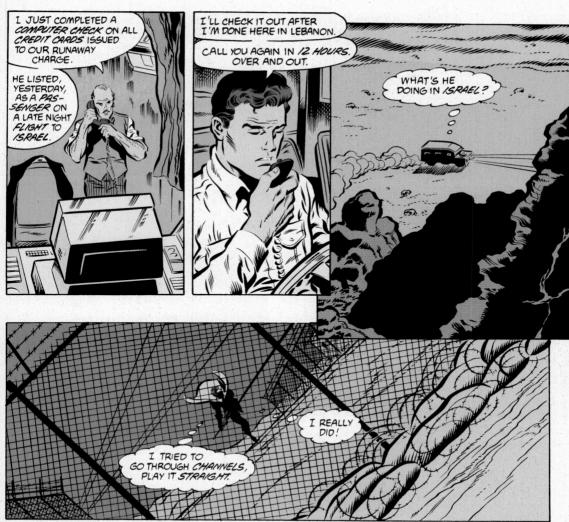

I JUST COMPLETED A *COMPUTER CHECK* ON ALL *CREDIT CARDS* ISSUED TO OUR RUNAWAY CHARGE.

HE LISTED, YESTERDAY, AS A *PAS-SENGER* ON A LATE NIGHT *FLIGHT* TO *ISRAEL*.

I'LL CHECK IT OUT AFTER I'M DONE HERE IN LEBANON.

CALL YOU AGAIN IN *12 HOURS.* OVER AND OUT.

WHAT'S HE DOING IN *ISRAEL?*

I TRIED TO GO THROUGH *CHANNELS,* PLAY IT *STRAIGHT.*

I REALLY DID!

BUT THEY JUST PLAIN *REFUSED* TO TELL ME WHERE *SHARMIN ROSEN* IS.

GUESS I CAN UNDERSTAND WHY.

GOVERNMENTS DON'T WILLINGLY GIVE OUT THE *LOCATIONS* OF THEIR *SECRET AGENTS.* STANDARD PROCEDURE.

BUT *NATIONAL SECURITY SECRETS* DON'T CUT A LOT OF ICE WITH ME.

I JUST GOTTA KNOW WHERE *MS. ROSEN* IS.

26

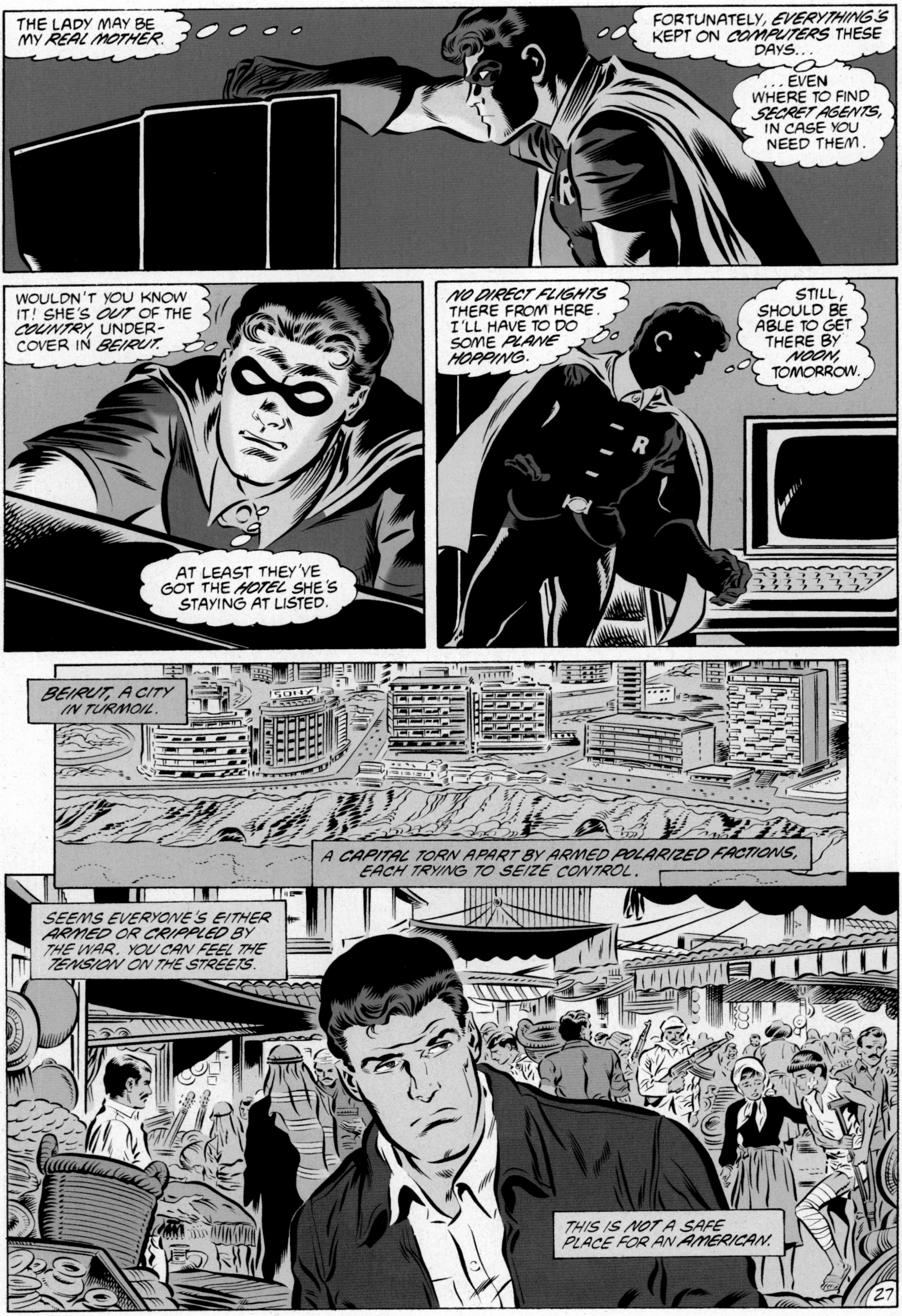

THE LADY MAY BE MY REAL MOTHER.
FORTUNATELY, EVERYTHING'S KEPT ON COMPUTERS THESE DAYS...
...EVEN WHERE TO FIND SECRET AGENTS, IN CASE YOU NEED THEM.
WOULDN'T YOU KNOW IT! SHE'S OUT OF THE COUNTRY, UNDER-COVER IN BEIRUT.
AT LEAST THEY'VE GOT THE HOTEL SHE'S STAYING AT LISTED.
NO DIRECT FLIGHTS THERE FROM HERE. I'LL HAVE TO DO SOME PLANE HOPPING.
STILL, SHOULD BE ABLE TO GET THERE BY NOON, TOMORROW.
BEIRUT, A CITY IN TURMOIL.
SONY
A CAPITAL TORN APART BY ARMED POLARIZED FACTIONS, EACH TRYING TO SEIZE CONTROL.
SEEMS EVERYONE'S EITHER ARMED OR CRIPPLED BY THE WAR. YOU CAN FEEL THE TENSION ON THE STREETS.
THIS IS NOT A SAFE PLACE FOR AN AMERICAN.
27

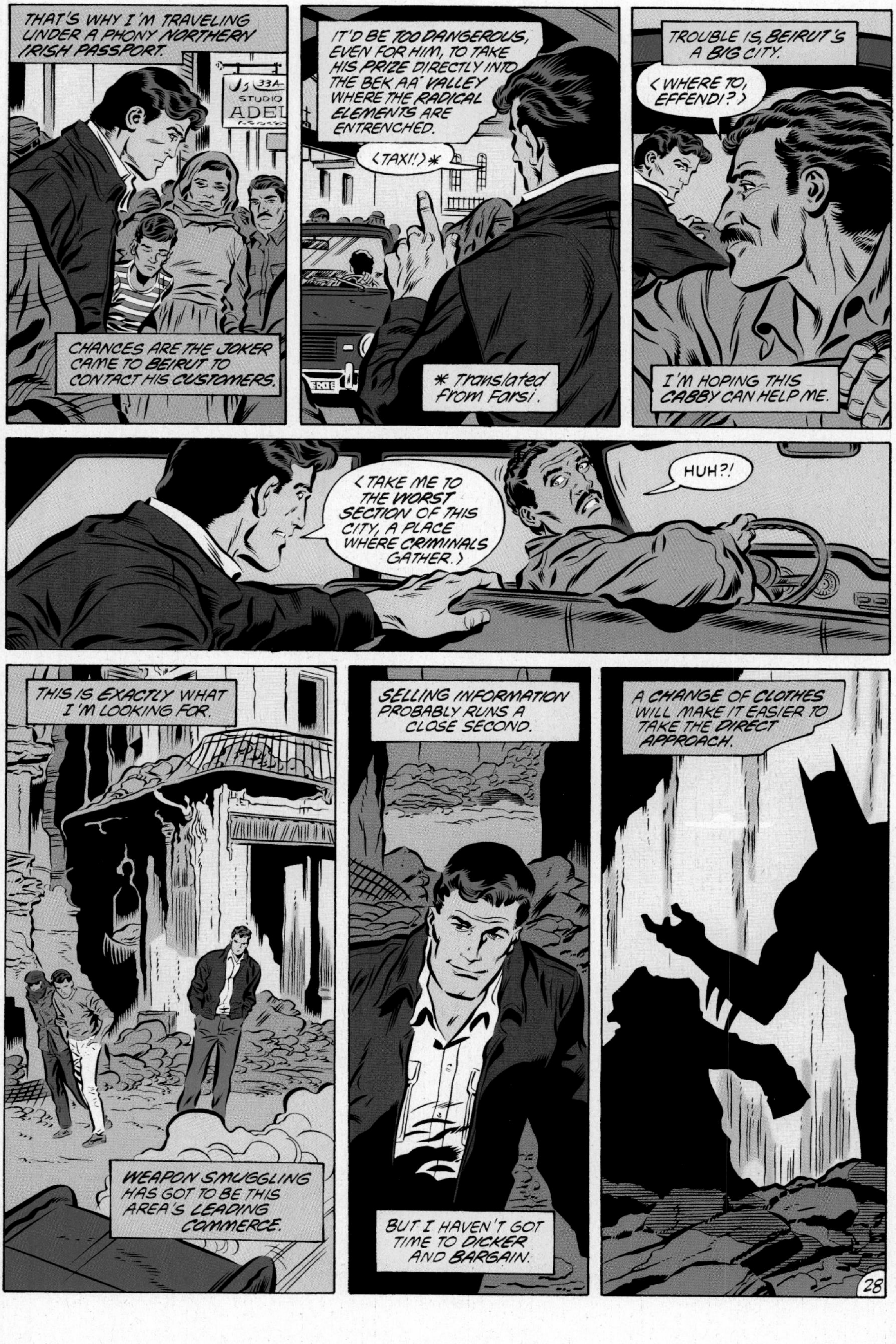
THAT'S WHY I'M TRAVELING UNDER A PHONY NORTHERN IRISH PASSPORT.
33A STUDIO ADEL
CHANCES ARE THE JOKER CAME TO BEIRUT TO CONTACT HIS CUSTOMERS.
IT'D BE TOO DANGEROUS, EVEN FOR HIM, TO TAKE HIS PRIZE DIRECTLY INTO THE BEK AA' VALLEY WHERE THE RADICAL ELEMENTS ARE ENTRENCHED.
<TAXI!>*
* Translated from Farsi.
TROUBLE IS, BEIRUT'S A BIG CITY.
<WHERE TO, EFFENDI?>
I'M HOPING THIS CABBY CAN HELP ME.
<TAKE ME TO THE WORST SECTION OF THIS CITY, A PLACE WHERE CRIMINALS GATHER.>
HUH?!
THIS IS EXACTLY WHAT I'M LOOKING FOR.
WEAPON SMUGGLING HAS GOT TO BE THIS AREA'S LEADING COMMERCE.
SELLING INFORMATION PROBABLY RUNS A CLOSE SECOND.
BUT I HAVEN'T GOT TIME TO DICKER AND BARGAIN.
A CHANGE OF CLOTHES WILL MAKE IT EASIER TO TAKE THE DIRECT APPROACH.
28

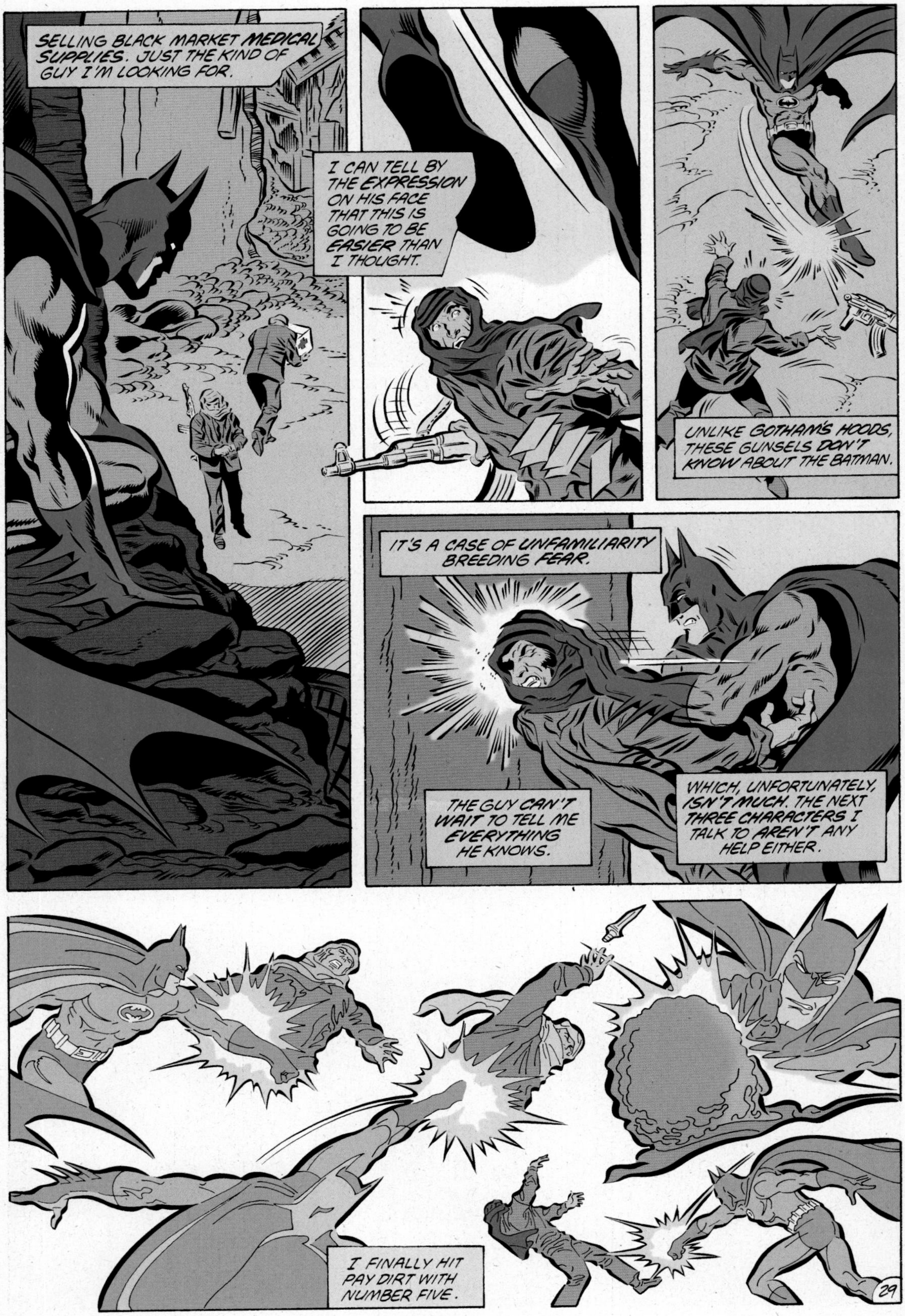
SELLING BLACK MARKET MEDICAL SUPPLIES. JUST THE KIND OF GUY I'M LOOKING FOR.
I CAN TELL BY THE EXPRESSION ON HIS FACE THAT THIS IS GOING TO BE EASIER THAN I THOUGHT.
UNLIKE GOTHAM'S HOODS, THESE GUNSELS DON'T KNOW ABOUT THE BATMAN.
IT'S A CASE OF UNFAMILIARITY BREEDING FEAR.
THE GUY CAN'T WAIT TO TELL ME EVERYTHING HE KNOWS.
WHICH, UNFORTUNATELY, ISN'T MUCH. THE NEXT THREE CHARACTERS I TALK TO AREN'T ANY HELP EITHER.
I FINALLY HIT PAY DIRT WITH NUMBER FIVE.
29

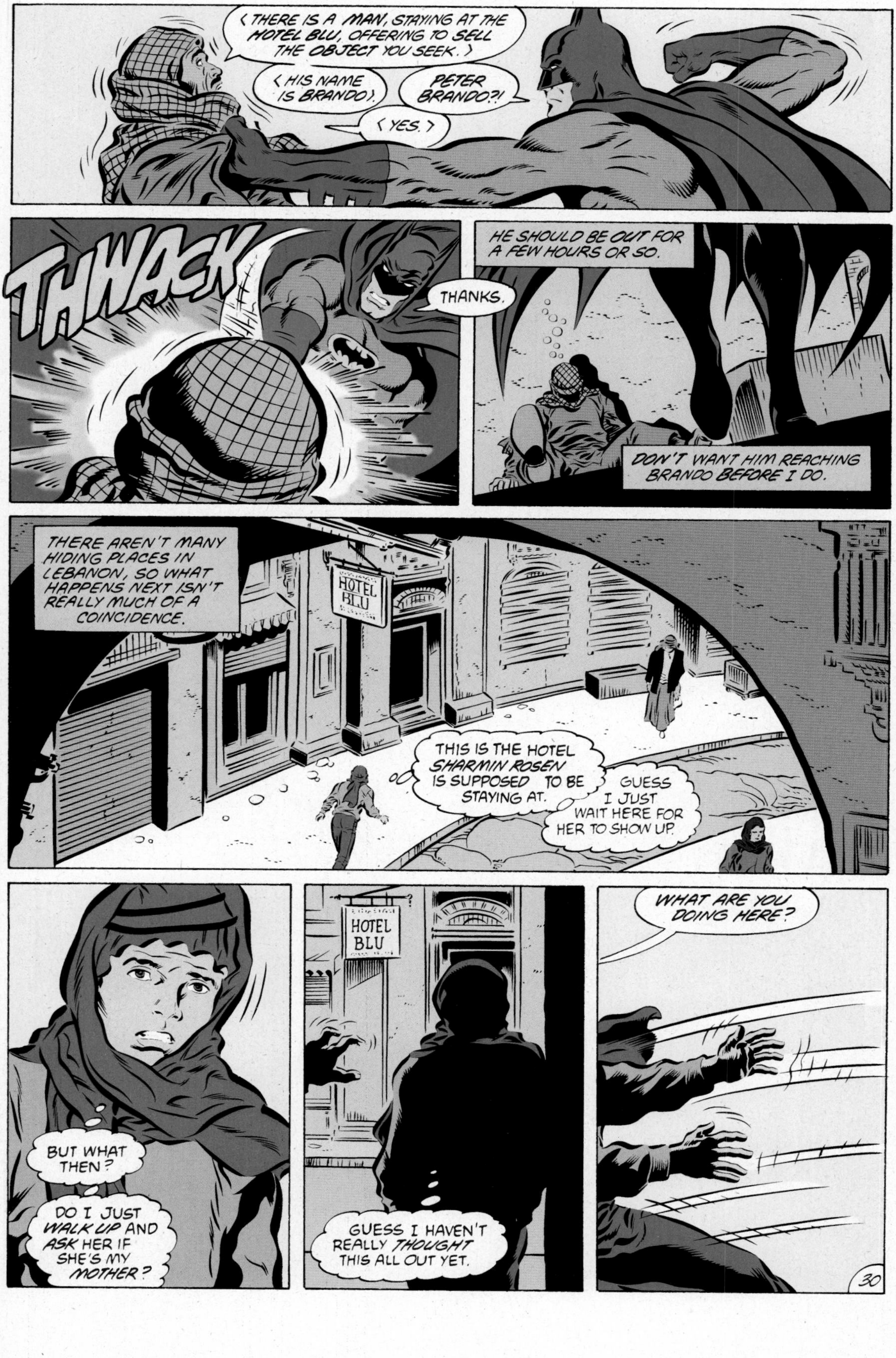
‹ THERE IS A MAN, STAYING AT THE HOTEL BLU, OFFERING TO SELL THE OBJECT YOU SEEK. ›
‹ HIS NAME IS BRANDO ›.
PETER BRANDO?!
‹ YES. ›
THWACK
THANKS.
HE SHOULD BE OUT FOR A FEW HOURS OR SO.
DON'T WANT HIM REACHING BRANDO BEFORE I DO.
THERE AREN'T MANY HIDING PLACES IN LEBANON, SO WHAT HAPPENS NEXT ISN'T REALLY MUCH OF A COINCIDENCE.
HOTEL BLU
THIS IS THE HOTEL SHARMIN ROSEN IS SUPPOSED TO BE STAYING AT.
GUESS I JUST WAIT HERE FOR HER TO SHOW UP.
BUT WHAT THEN?
DO I JUST WALK UP AND ASK HER IF SHE'S MY MOTHER?
HOTEL BLU
GUESS I HAVEN'T REALLY THOUGHT THIS ALL OUT YET.
WHAT ARE YOU DOING HERE?
30

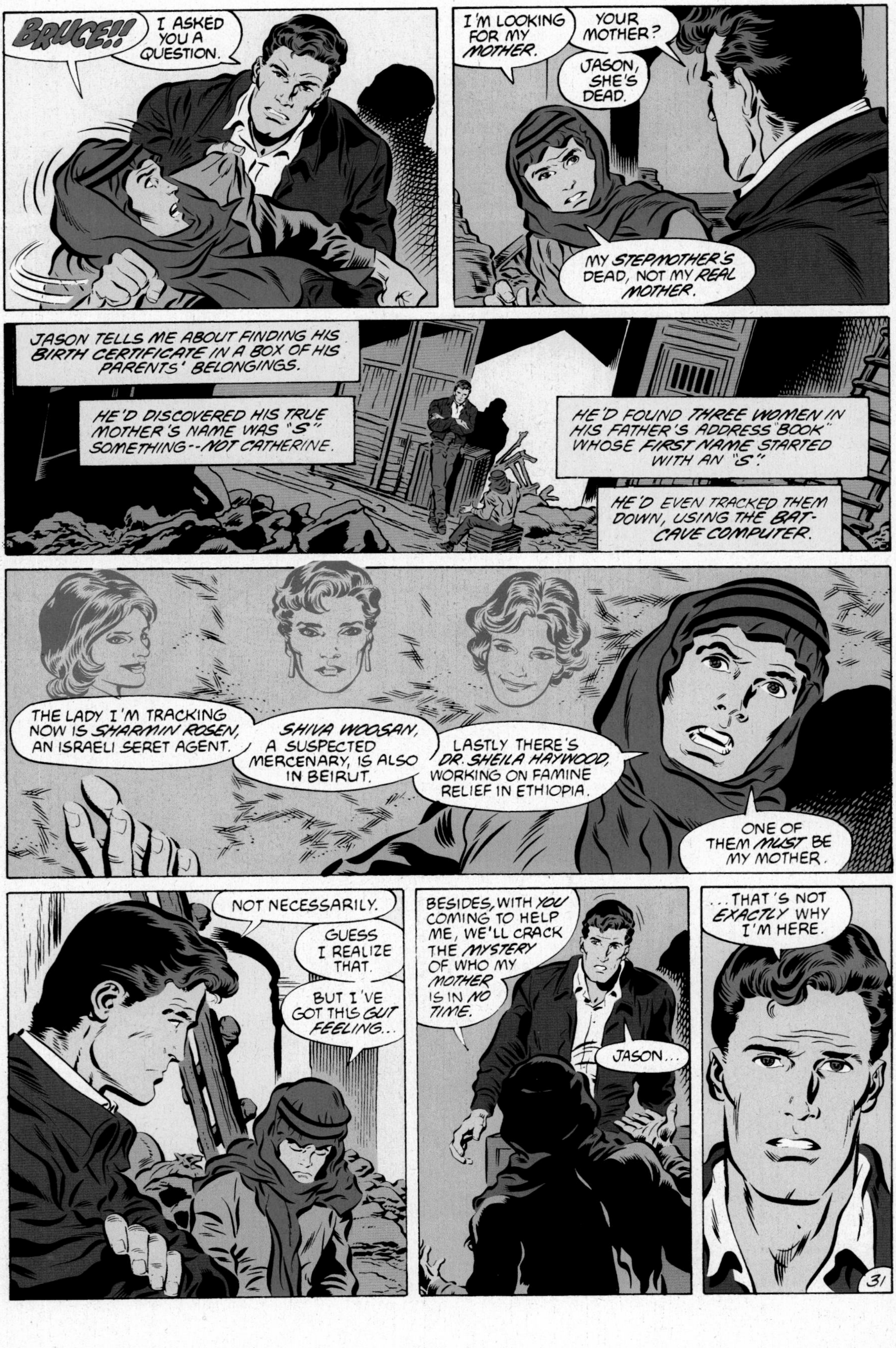

BRUCE!!
I ASKED YOU A QUESTION.
I'M LOOKING FOR MY MOTHER.
YOUR MOTHER?
JASON, SHE'S DEAD.
MY STEPMOTHER'S DEAD, NOT MY REAL MOTHER.
JASON TELLS ME ABOUT FINDING HIS BIRTH CERTIFICATE IN A BOX OF HIS PARENTS' BELONGINGS.
HE'D DISCOVERED HIS TRUE MOTHER'S NAME WAS "S" SOMETHING--NOT CATHERINE.
HE'D FOUND THREE WOMEN IN HIS FATHER'S ADDRESS "BOOK" WHOSE FIRST NAME STARTED WITH AN "S".
HE'D EVEN TRACKED THEM DOWN, USING THE BAT-CAVE COMPUTER.
THE LADY I'M TRACKING NOW IS SHARMIN ROSEN, AN ISRAELI SERET AGENT.
SHIVA WOOSAN, A SUSPECTED MERCENARY, IS ALSO IN BEIRUT.
LASTLY THERE'S DR. SHEILA HAYWOOD, WORKING ON FAMINE RELIEF IN ETHIOPIA.
ONE OF THEM MUST BE MY MOTHER.
NOT NECESSARILY.
GUESS I REALIZE THAT.
BUT I'VE GOT THIS GUT FEELING...
BESIDES, WITH YOU COMING TO HELP ME, WE'LL CRACK THE MYSTERY OF WHO MY MOTHER IS IN NO TIME.
JASON...
...THAT'S NOT EXACTLY WHY I'M HERE.
31

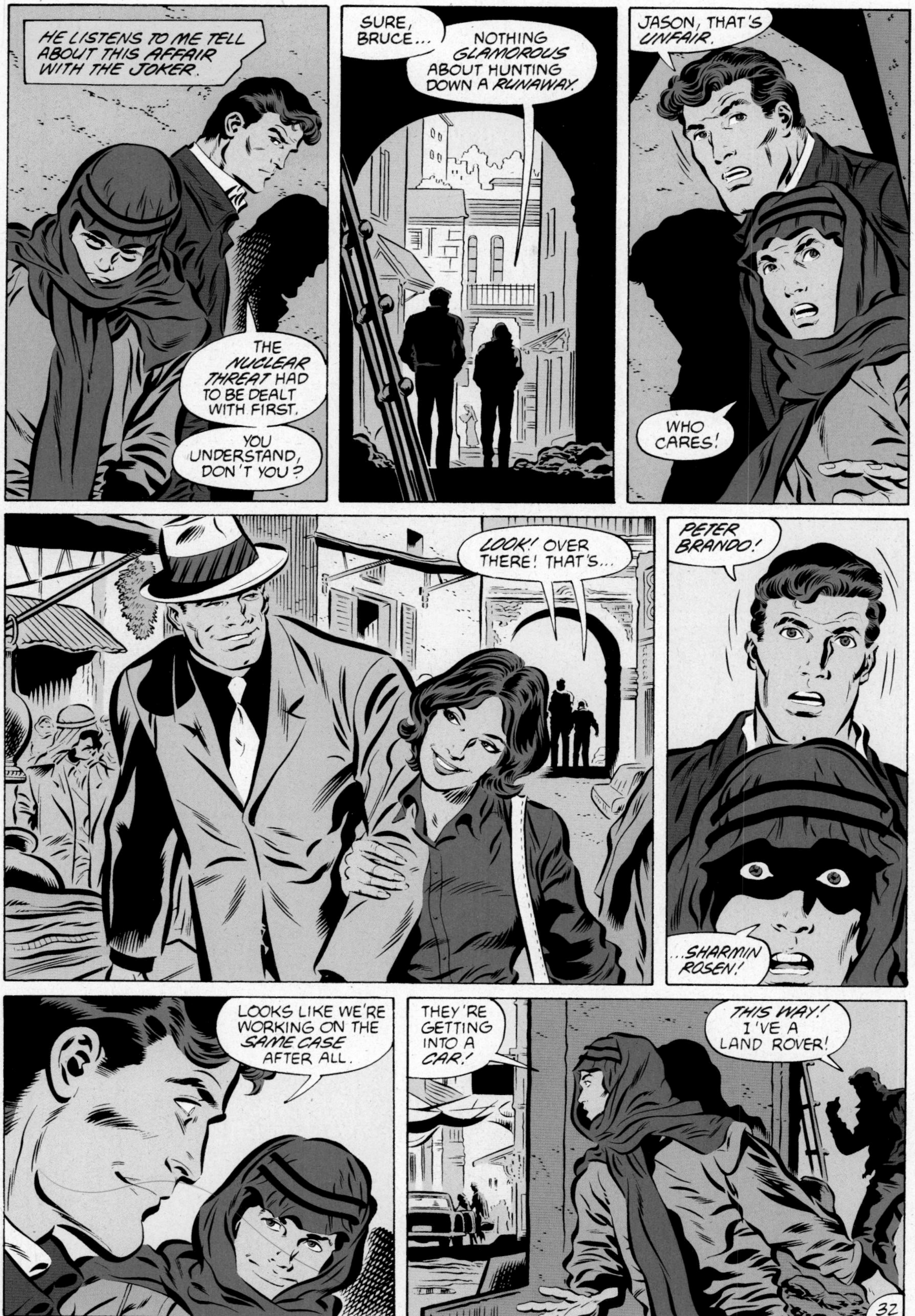
HE LISTENS TO ME TELL ABOUT THIS AFFAIR WITH THE JOKER.
THE NUCLEAR THREAT HAD TO BE DEALT WITH FIRST.
YOU UNDERSTAND, DON'T YOU?
SURE, BRUCE...
NOTHING GLAMOROUS ABOUT HUNTING DOWN A RUNAWAY.
JASON, THAT'S UNFAIR.
WHO CARES!
LOOK! OVER THERE! THAT'S...
PETER BRANDO!
...SHARMIN ROSEN!
LOOKS LIKE WE'RE WORKING ON THE SAME CASE AFTER ALL.
THEY'RE GETTING INTO A CAR!
THIS WAY! I'VE A LAND ROVER!
32

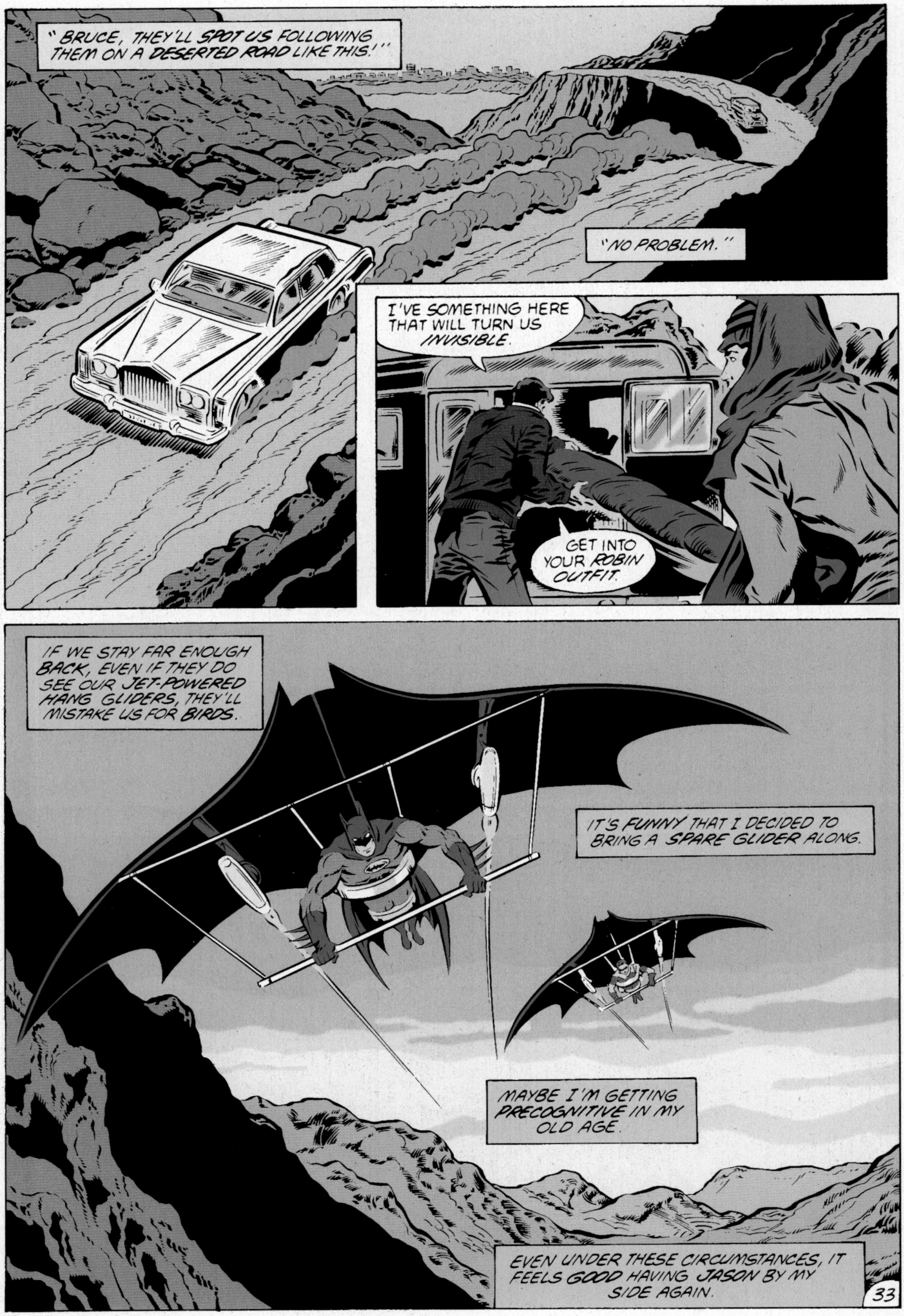
"BRUCE, THEY'LL SPOT US FOLLOWING THEM ON A DESERTED ROAD LIKE THIS!"
"NO PROBLEM."
I'VE SOMETHING HERE THAT WILL TURN US INVISIBLE.
GET INTO YOUR ROBIN OUTFIT.
IF WE STAY FAR ENOUGH BACK, EVEN IF THEY DO SEE OUR JET-POWERED HANG GLIDERS, THEY'LL MISTAKE US FOR BIRDS.
IT'S FUNNY THAT I DECIDED TO BRING A SPARE GLIDER ALONG.
MAYBE I'M GETTING PRECOGNITIVE IN MY OLD AGE.
EVEN UNDER THESE CIRCUMSTANCES, IT FEELS GOOD HAVING JASON BY MY SIDE AGAIN.
33

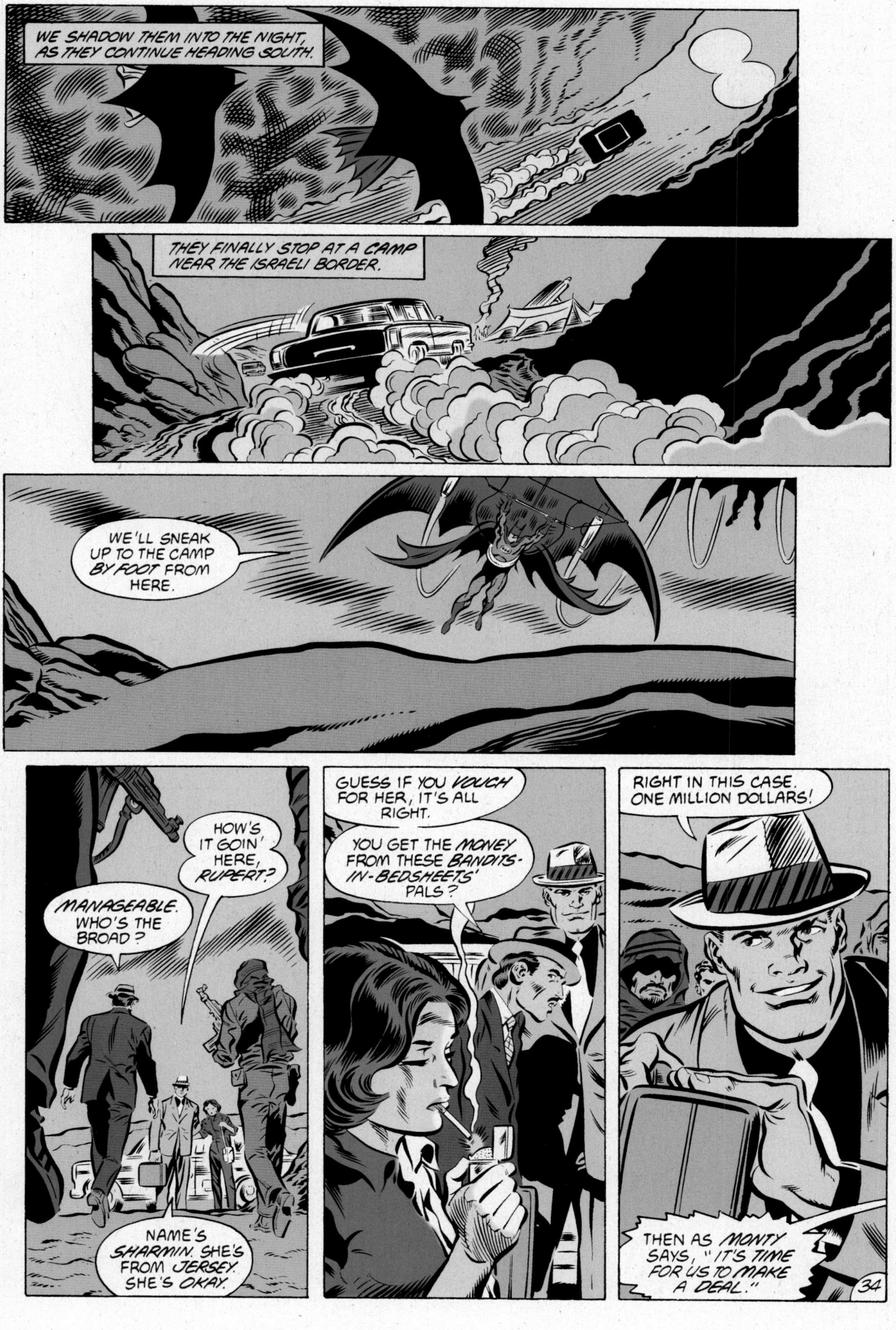
WE SHADOW THEM INTO THE NIGHT, AS THEY CONTINUE HEADING SOUTH.
THEY FINALLY STOP AT A CAMP NEAR THE ISRAELI BORDER.
WE'LL SNEAK UP TO THE CAMP BY FOOT FROM HERE.
HOW'S IT GOIN' HERE, RUPERT?
MANAGEABLE. WHO'S THE BROAD?
NAME'S SHARMIN. SHE'S FROM JERSEY. SHE'S OKAY.
GUESS IF YOU VOUCH FOR HER, IT'S ALL RIGHT.
YOU GET THE MONEY FROM THESE BANDITS-IN-BEDSHEETS' PALS?
RIGHT IN THIS CASE. ONE MILLION DOLLARS!
THEN AS MONTY SAYS, "IT'S TIME FOR US TO MAKE A DEAL."
34

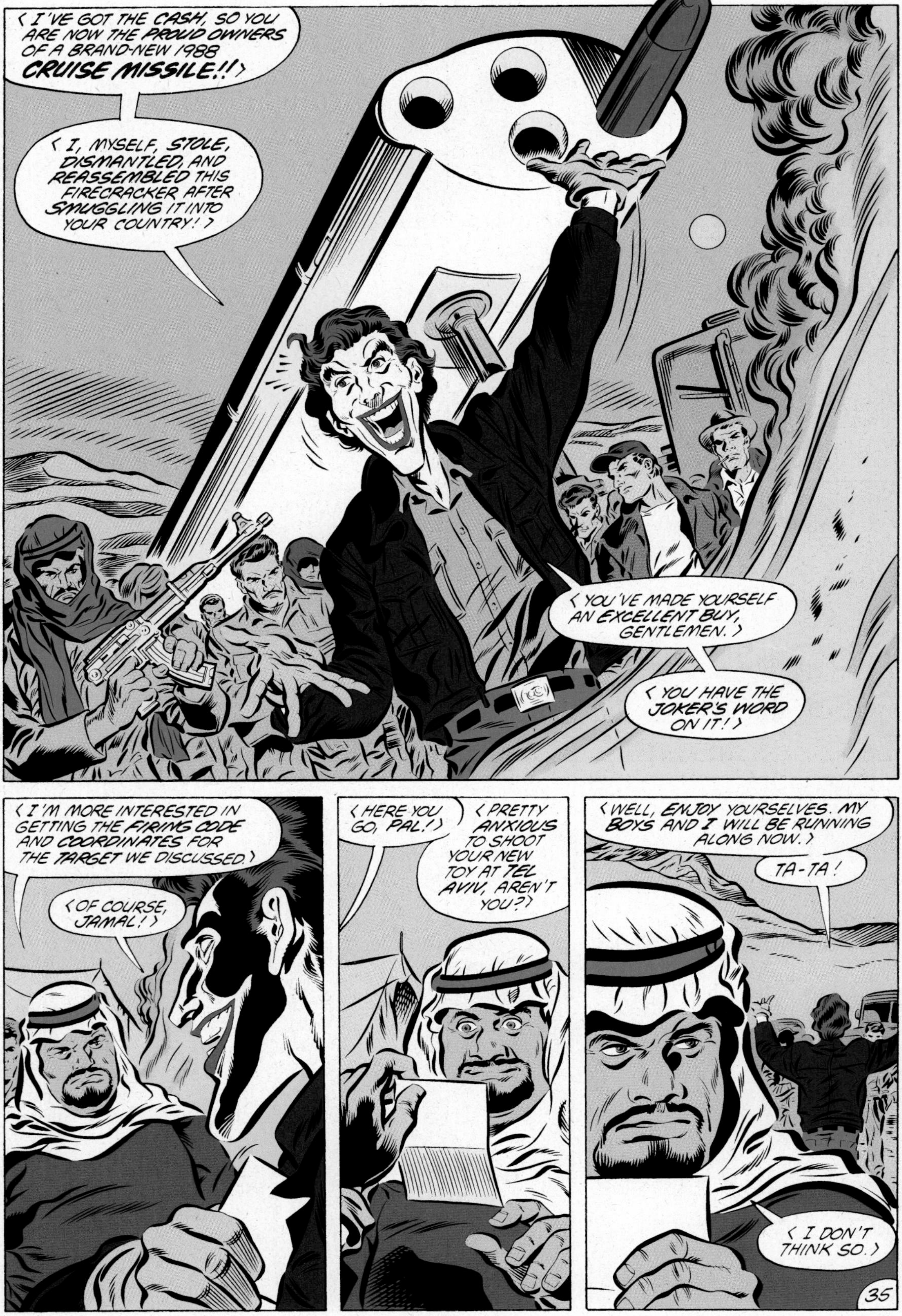
‹ I'VE GOT THE CASH, SO YOU ARE NOW THE PROUD OWNERS OF A BRAND-NEW 1988 CRUISE MISSILE!! ›
‹ I, MYSELF, STOLE, DISMANTLED, AND REASSEMBLED THIS FIRECRACKER AFTER SMUGGLING IT INTO YOUR COUNTRY! ›
‹ YOU'VE MADE YOURSELF AN EXCELLENT BUY, GENTLEMEN. ›
‹ YOU HAVE THE JOKER'S WORD ON IT! ›
‹ I'M MORE INTERESTED IN GETTING THE FIRING CODE AND COORDINATES FOR THE TARGET WE DISCUSSED. ›
‹ OF COURSE, JAMAL! ›
‹ HERE YOU GO, PAL! ›
‹ PRETTY ANXIOUS TO SHOOT YOUR NEW TOY AT TEL AVIV, AREN'T YOU? ›
‹ WELL, ENJOY YOURSELVES. MY BOYS AND I WILL BE RUNNING ALONG NOW. ›
TA-TA!
‹ I DON'T THINK SO. ›
35

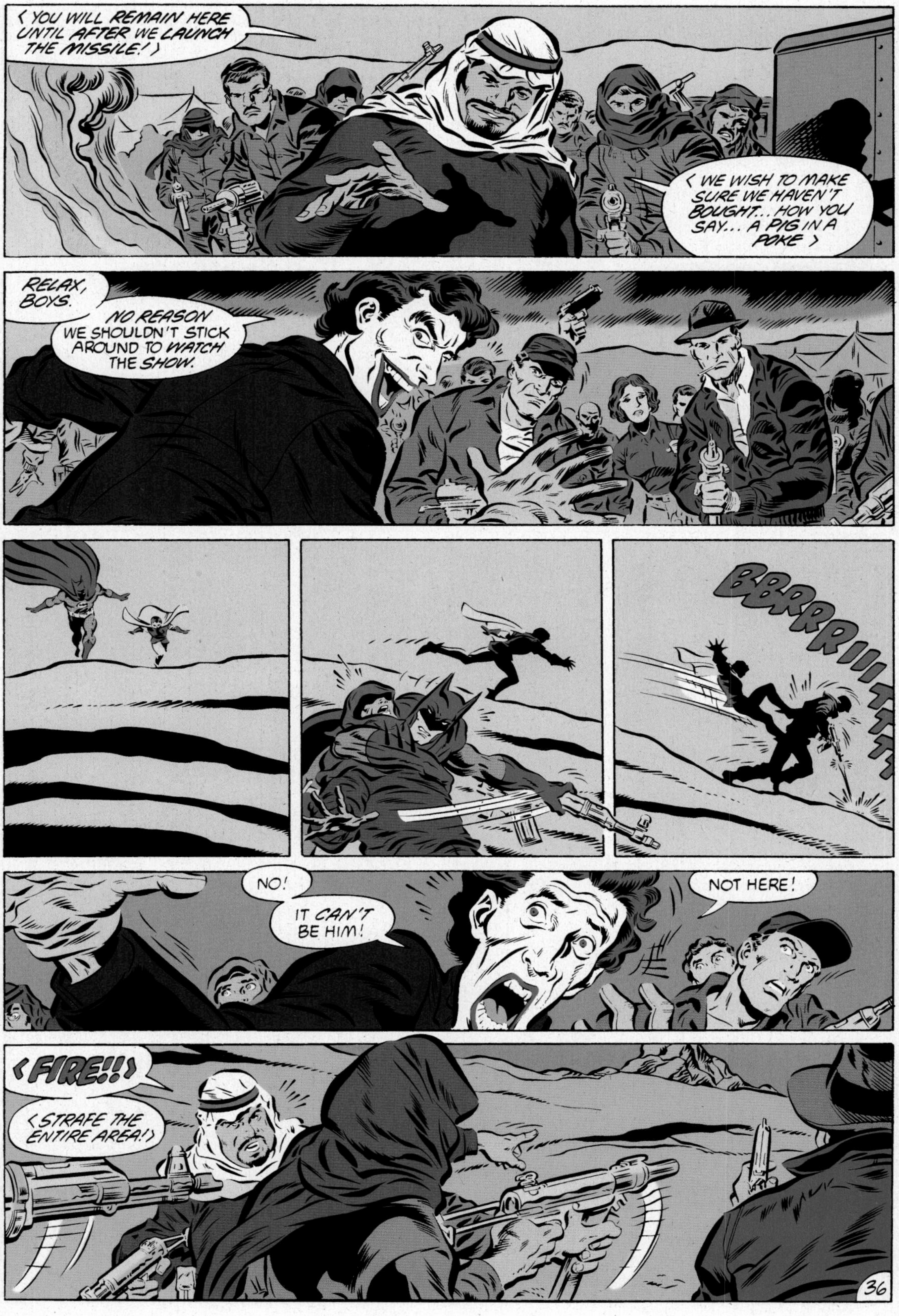
‹ YOU WILL REMAIN HERE UNTIL AFTER WE LAUNCH THE MISSILE! ›
‹ WE WISH TO MAKE SURE WE HAVEN'T BOUGHT... HOW YOU SAY... A PIG IN A POKE ›
RELAX, BOYS.
NO REASON WE SHOULDN'T STICK AROUND TO WATCH THE SHOW.
BBRRRRIIITTTT
NO!
IT CAN'T BE HIM!
NOT HERE!
‹ FIRE!! ›
‹ STRAFE THE ENTIRE AREA! ›
36

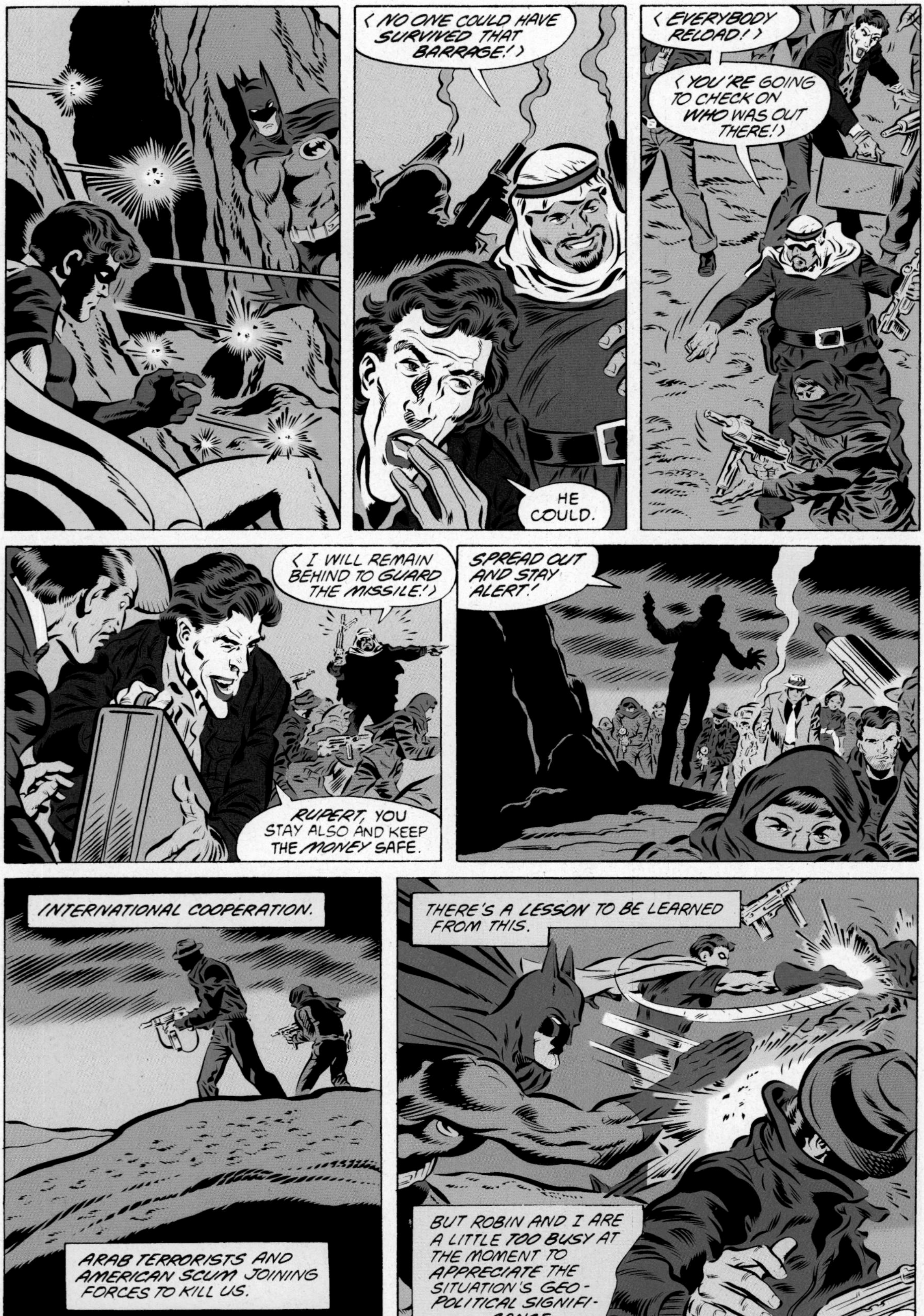
⟨ NO ONE COULD HAVE SURVIVED THAT BARRAGE! ⟩
HE COULD.
⟨ EVERYBODY RELOAD! ⟩
⟨ YOU'RE GOING TO CHECK ON WHO WAS OUT THERE! ⟩
⟨ I WILL REMAIN BEHIND TO GUARD THE MISSILE! ⟩
RUPERT, YOU STAY ALSO AND KEEP THE MONEY SAFE.
SPREAD OUT AND STAY ALERT!
INTERNATIONAL COOPERATION.
ARAB TERRORISTS AND AMERICAN SCUM JOINING FORCES TO KILL US.
THERE'S A LESSON TO BE LEARNED FROM THIS.
BUT ROBIN AND I ARE A LITTLE TOO BUSY AT THE MOMENT TO APPRECIATE THE SITUATION'S GEO-POLITICAL SIGNIFI-CANCE.
37

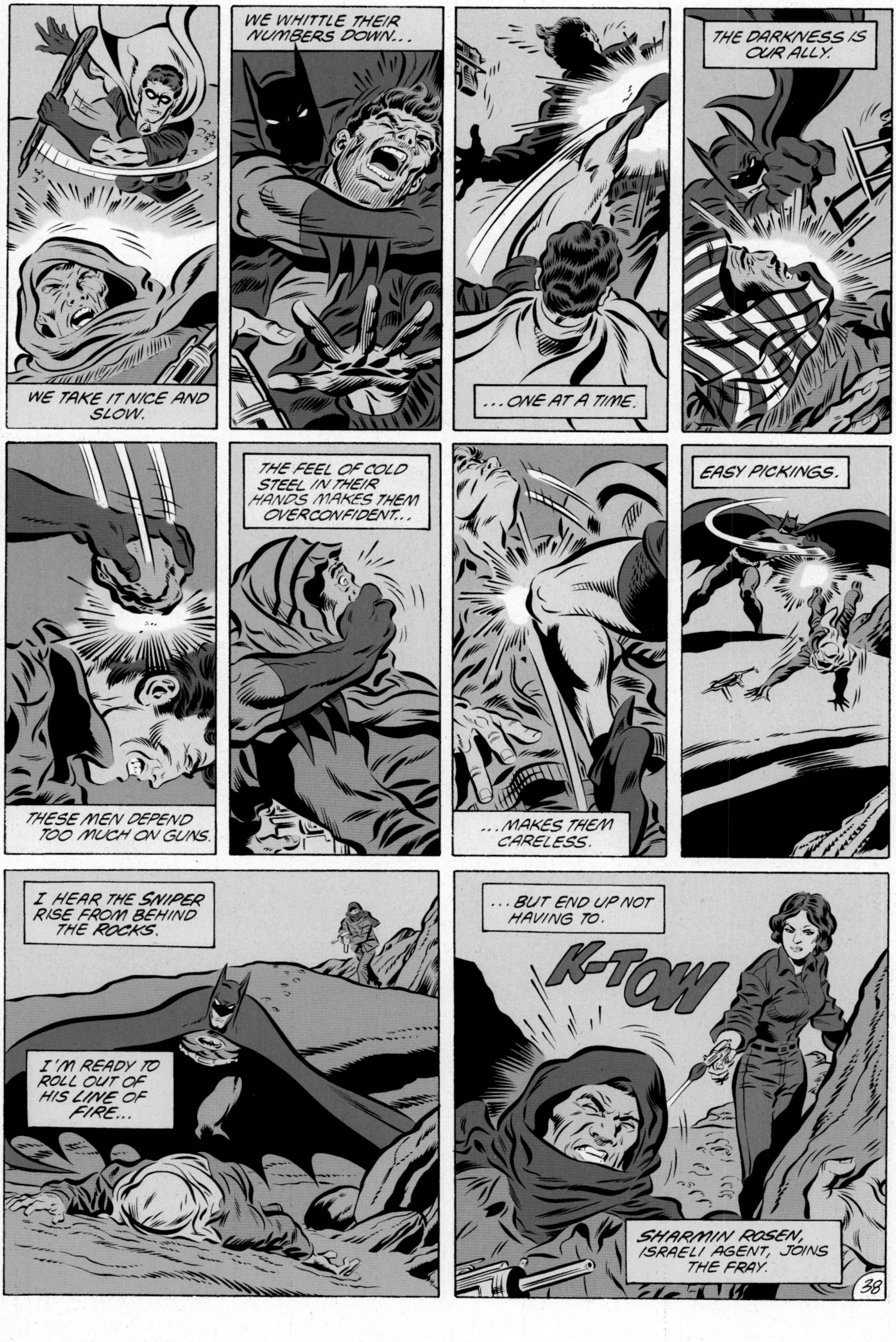
WE TAKE IT NICE AND SLOW.
WE WHITTLE THEIR NUMBERS DOWN...
...ONE AT A TIME.
THE DARKNESS IS OUR ALLY.
THESE MEN DEPEND TOO MUCH ON GUNS.
THE FEEL OF COLD STEEL IN THEIR HANDS MAKES THEM OVERCONFIDENT...
...MAKES THEM CARELESS.
EASY PICKINGS.
I HEAR THE SNIPER RISE FROM BEHIND THE ROCKS.
I'M READY TO ROLL OUT OF HIS LINE OF FIRE...
...BUT END UP NOT HAVING TO.
K-TOW
SHARMIN ROSEN, ISRAELI AGENT, JOINS THE FRAY.
38

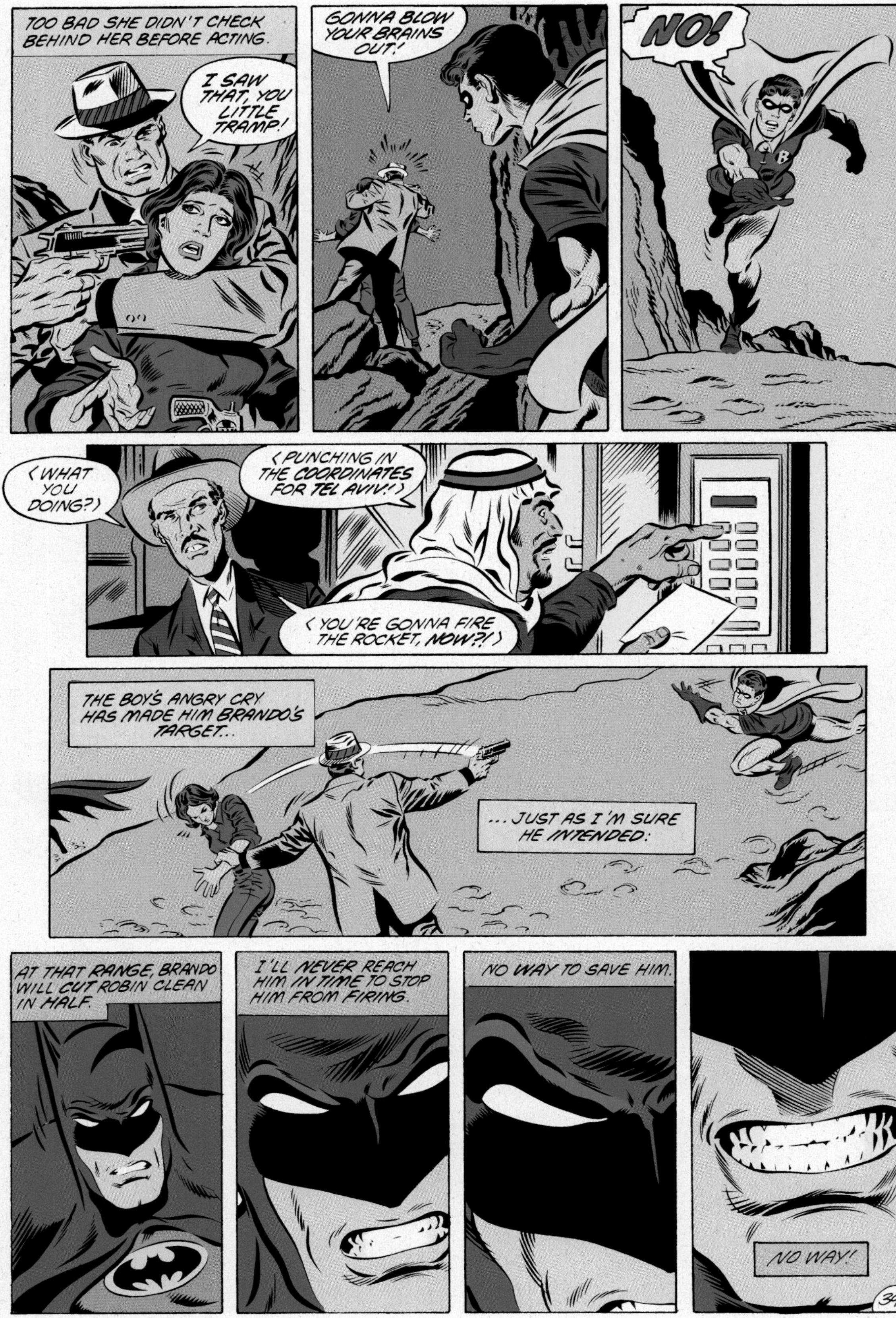
TOO BAD SHE DIDN'T CHECK BEHIND HER BEFORE ACTING.
I SAW THAT, YOU LITTLE TRAMP!
GONNA BLOW YOUR BRAINS OUT!
NO!
‹WHAT YOU DOING?›
‹PUNCHING IN THE COORDINATES FOR TEL AVIV!›
‹YOU'RE GONNA FIRE THE ROCKET, NOW?!›
THE BOY'S ANGRY CRY HAS MADE HIM BRANDO'S TARGET...
...JUST AS I'M SURE HE INTENDED:
AT THAT RANGE, BRANDO WILL CUT ROBIN CLEAN IN HALF.
I'LL NEVER REACH HIM IN TIME TO STOP HIM FROM FIRING.
NO WAY TO SAVE HIM.
NO WAY!
39

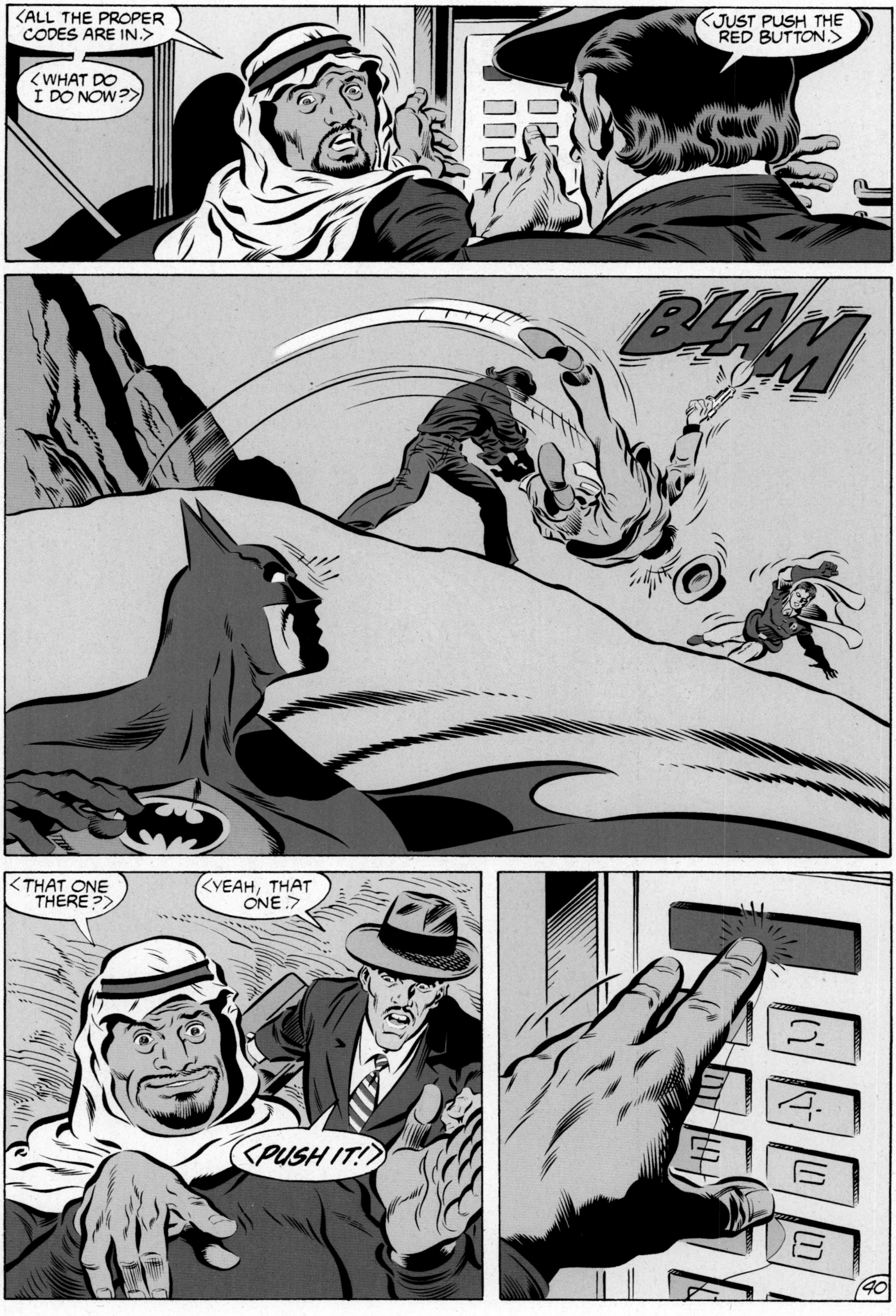
<ALL THE PROPER CODES ARE IN.>
<WHAT DO I DO NOW?>
<JUST PUSH THE RED BUTTON.>
BLAM
<THAT ONE THERE?>
<YEAH, THAT ONE.>
<PUSH IT!>
40

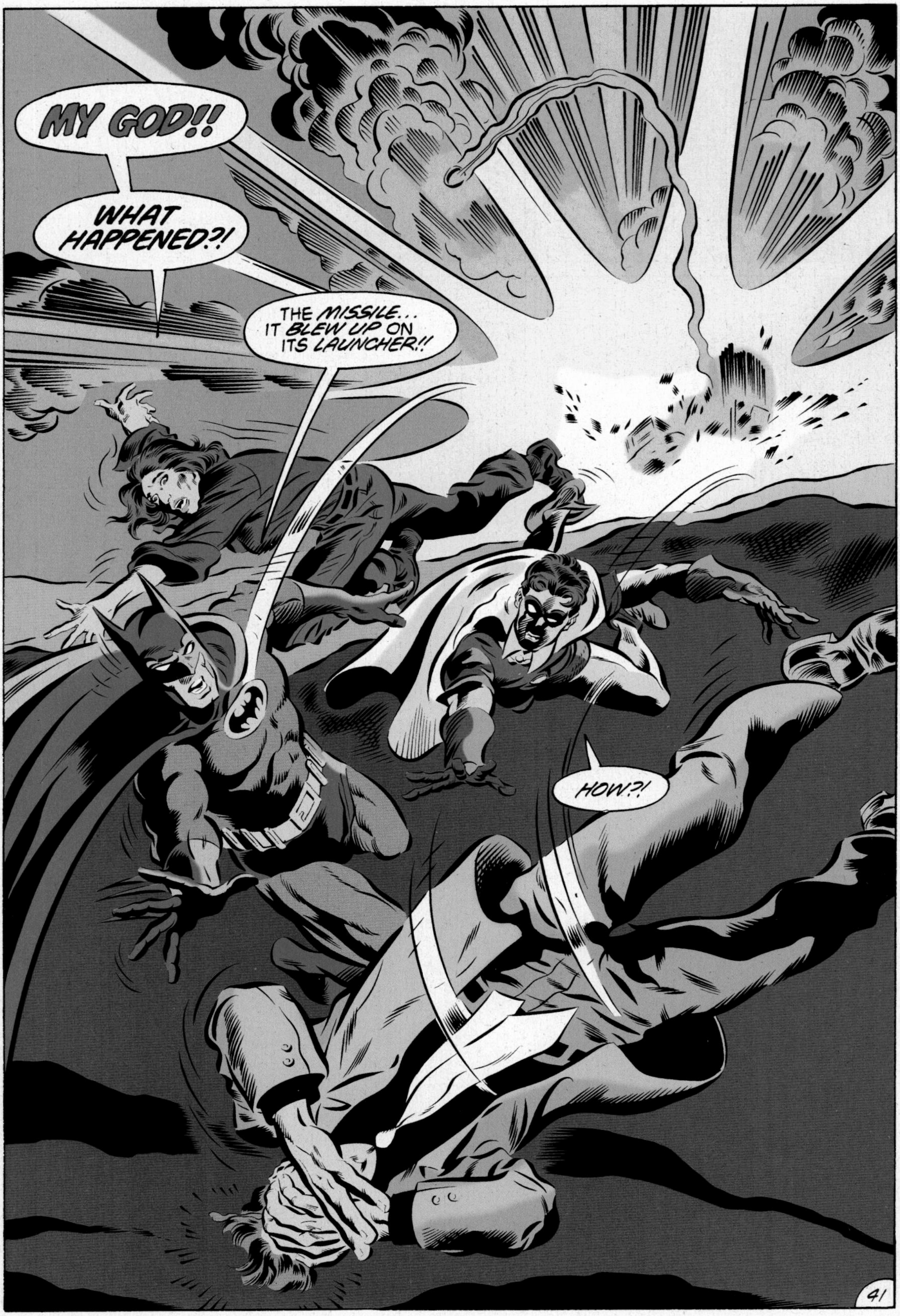
MY GOD!!
WHAT HAPPENED?!
THE MISSILE... IT BLEW UP ON ITS LAUNCHER!!
HOW?!
41

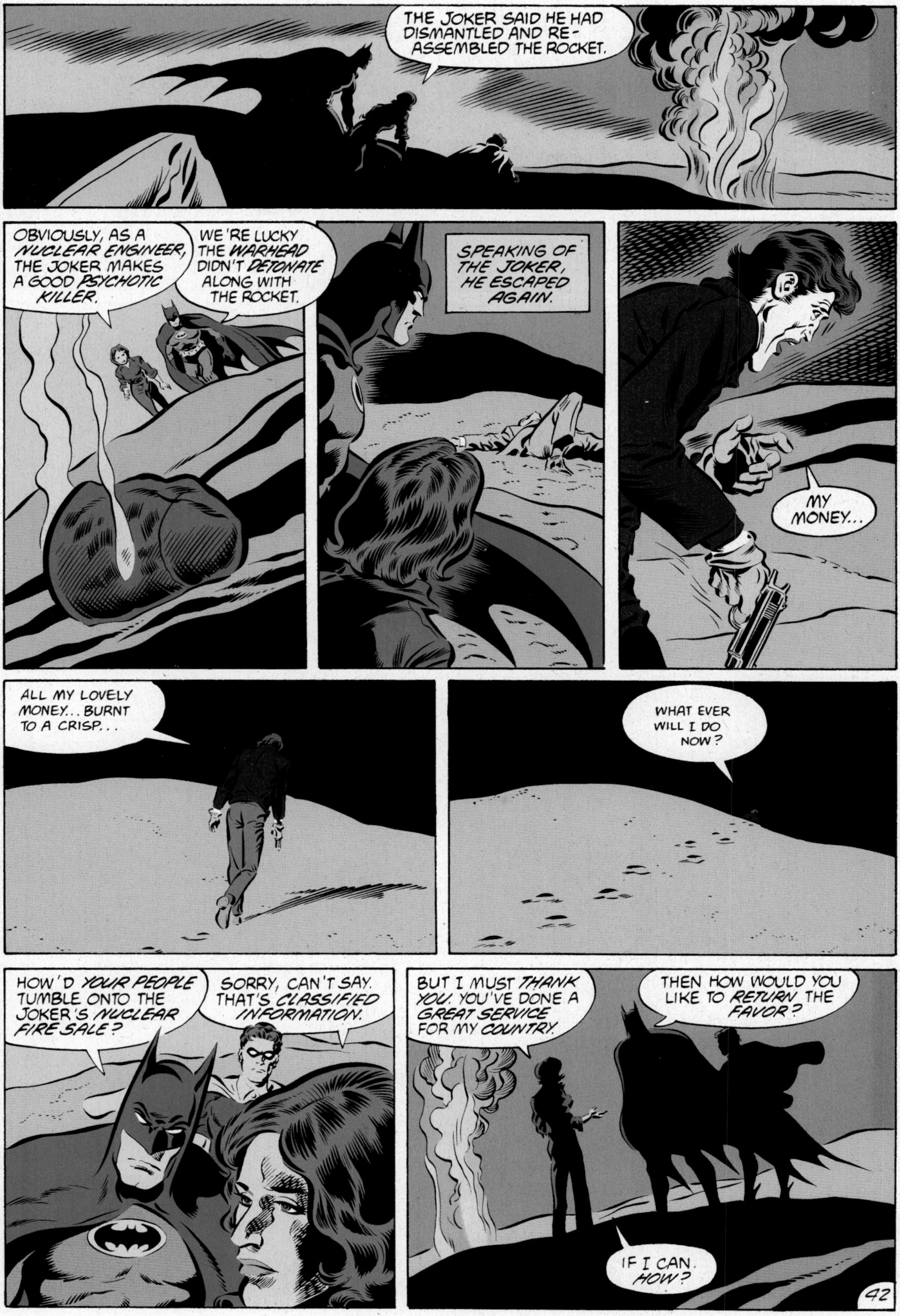
THE JOKER SAID HE HAD DISMANTLED AND RE-ASSEMBLED THE ROCKET.
OBVIOUSLY, AS A NUCLEAR ENGINEER, THE JOKER MAKES A GOOD PSYCHOTIC KILLER.
WE'RE LUCKY THE WARHEAD DIDN'T DETONATE ALONG WITH THE ROCKET.
SPEAKING OF THE JOKER, HE ESCAPED AGAIN.
MY MONEY...
ALL MY LOVELY MONEY... BURNT TO A CRISP...
WHAT EVER WILL I DO NOW?
HOW'D YOUR PEOPLE TUMBLE ONTO THE JOKER'S NUCLEAR FIRE SALE?
SORRY, CAN'T SAY. THAT'S CLASSIFIED INFORMATION.
BUT I MUST THANK YOU. YOU'VE DONE A GREAT SERVICE FOR MY COUNTRY.
THEN HOW WOULD YOU LIKE TO RETURN THE FAVOR?
IF I CAN. HOW?
42

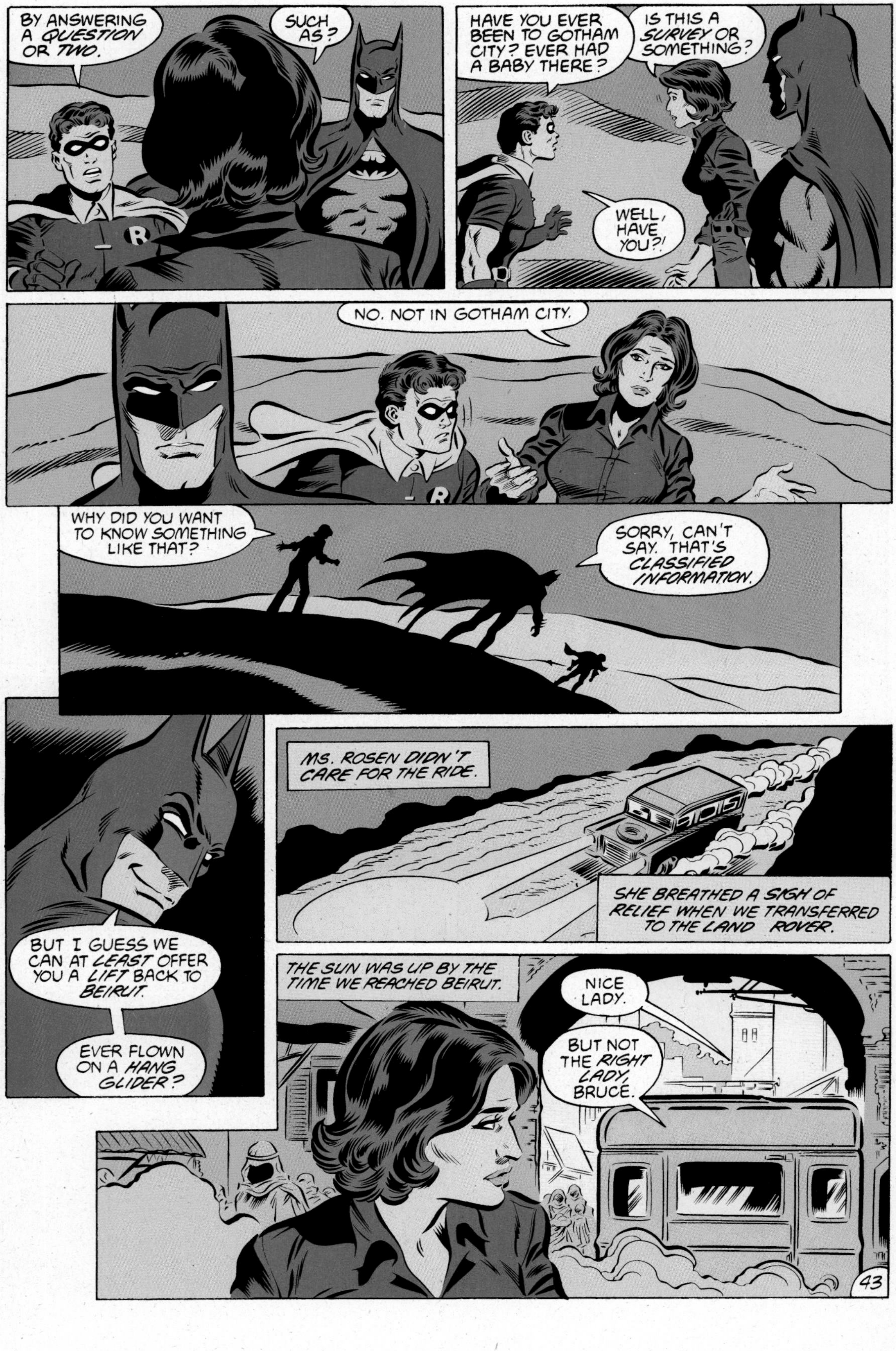

BY ANSWERING A QUESTION OR TWO.
SUCH AS?
HAVE YOU EVER BEEN TO GOTHAM CITY? EVER HAD A BABY THERE?
IS THIS A SURVEY OR SOMETHING?
WELL, HAVE YOU?!
NO. NOT IN GOTHAM CITY.
WHY DID YOU WANT TO KNOW SOMETHING LIKE THAT?
SORRY, CAN'T SAY. THAT'S CLASSIFIED INFORMATION.
BUT I GUESS WE CAN AT LEAST OFFER YOU A LIFT BACK TO BEIRUT.
EVER FLOWN ON A HANG GLIDER?
MS. ROSEN DIDN'T CARE FOR THE RIDE.
SHE BREATHED A SIGH OF RELIEF WHEN WE TRANSFERRED TO THE LAND ROVER.
THE SUN WAS UP BY THE TIME WE REACHED BEIRUT.
NICE LADY.
BUT NOT THE RIGHT LADY, BRUCE.
43

WHAT NOW?

I'M *NOT* GOING BACK TO THE *STATES.*

I'VE *TWO* MORE *WOMEN* TO CHECK OUT.

SHIVA WOOSAN IS SOMEWHERE IN *BEIRUT.*

DON'T TRY TO *STOP* ME FROM *FINDING* HER!

WOULDN'T THINK OF IT.

BUT WHAT IF SHE'S *NOT* YOUR MOTHER?

THEN I TRY *SHEILA HAYWOOD* IN ETHIOPIA.

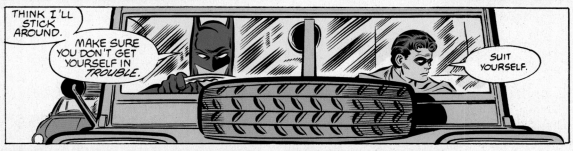

THINK I'LL STICK AROUND.

MAKE SURE YOU DON'T GET YOURSELF IN *TROUBLE.*

SUIT YOURSELF.

ONE TICKET TO *ADDIS ABABA, ETHIOPIA,* PLEASE.

‹ YES, SIR. HOW CAN I HELP YOU? ›

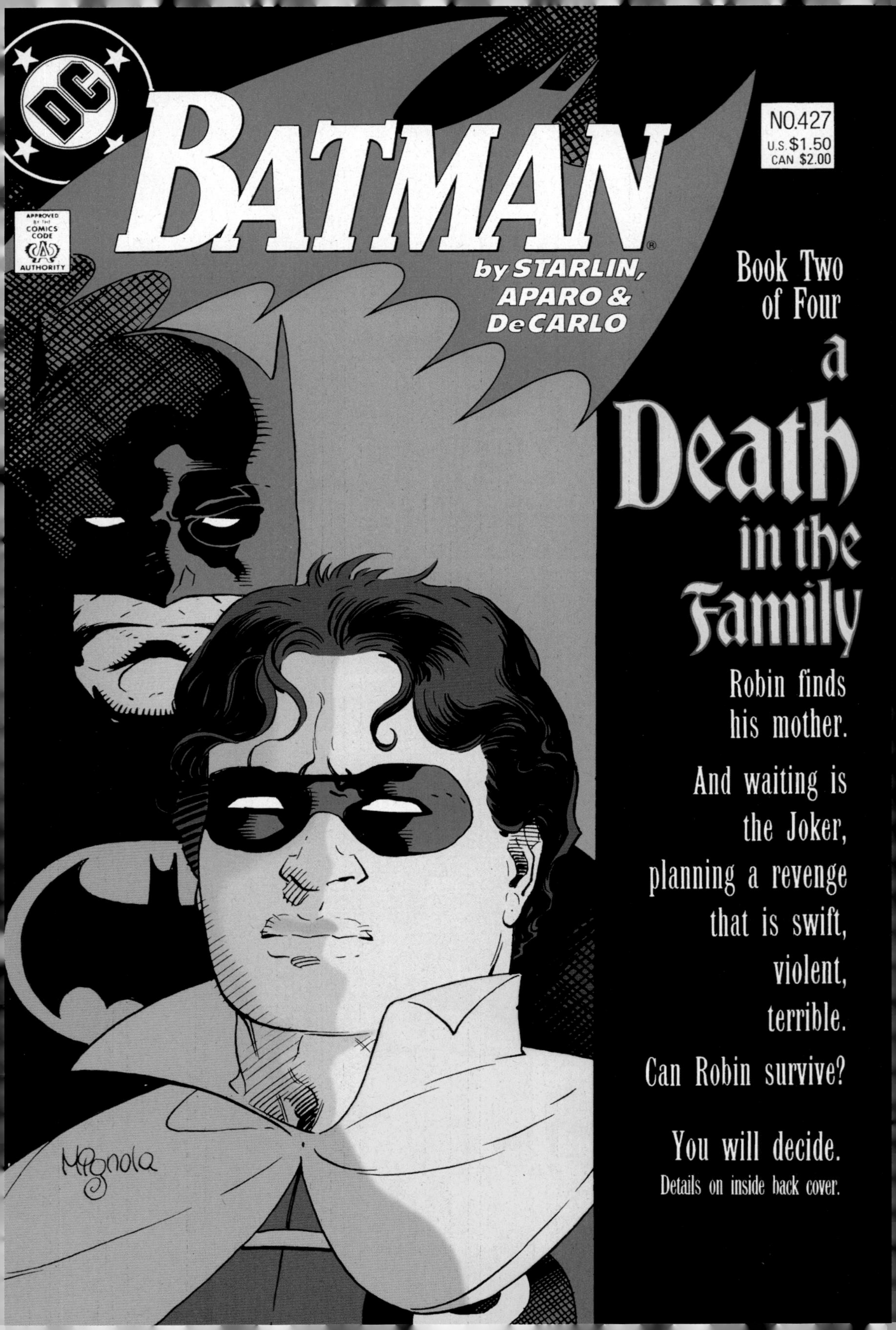
DC
BATMAN
NO.427
U.S. $1.50
CAN $2.00
APPROVED BY THE COMICS CODE AUTHORITY
by STARLIN, APARO & DeCARLO
Book Two of Four
a Death in the Family
Robin finds his mother.
And waiting is the Joker, planning a revenge that is swift, violent, terrible.
Can Robin survive?
You will decide.
Details on inside back cover.
Mignola

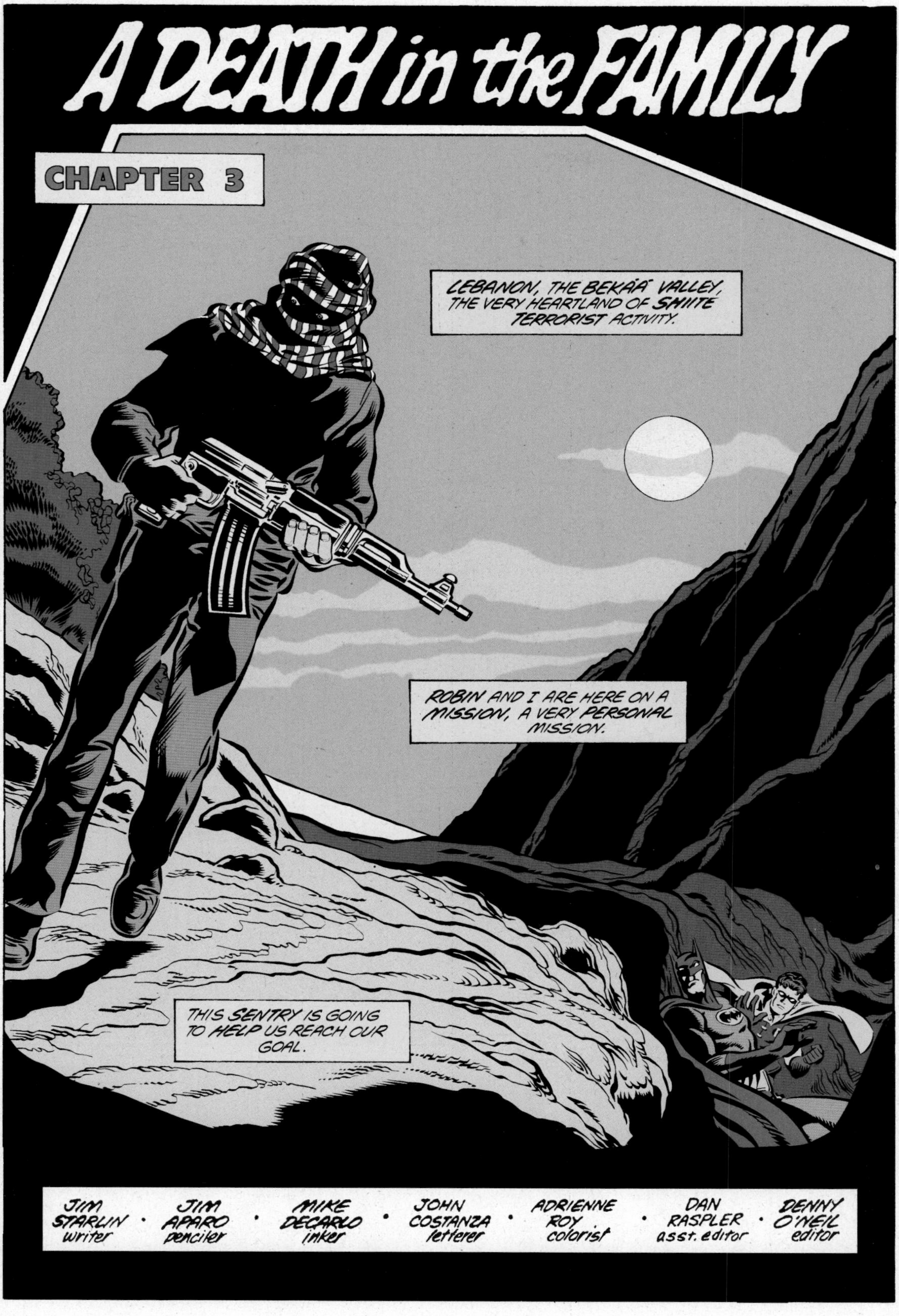
A DEATH in the FAMILY
CHAPTER 3
LEBANON, THE BEKÄÄ VALLEY, THE VERY HEARTLAND OF SHIITE TERRORIST ACTIVITY.
ROBIN AND I ARE HERE ON A MISSION, A VERY PERSONAL MISSION.
THIS SENTRY IS GOING TO HELP US REACH OUR GOAL.
JIM STARLIN · writer
JIM APARO · penciler
MIKE DECARLO · inker
JOHN COSTANZA · letterer
ADRIENNE ROY · colorist
DAN RASPLER · asst. editor
DENNY O'NEIL · editor

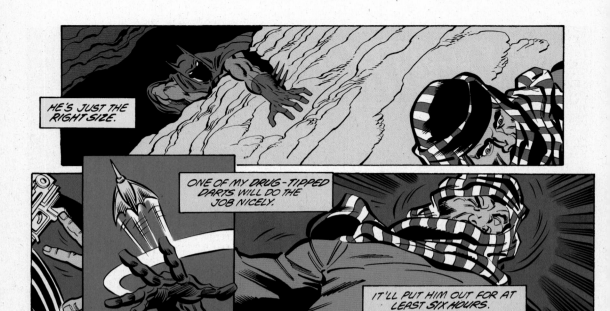

HE'S JUST THE RIGHT SIZE.

ONE OF MY DRUG-TIPPED DARTS WILL DO THE JOB NICELY.

IT'LL PUT HIM OUT FOR AT LEAST SIX HOURS.

THIS IS A TRICKY BUSINESS WE'RE INVOLVED IN, DEALING WITH COLD-BLOODED TERRORISTS.

EACH MOVE MUST BE CAREFULLY PLANNED AND EXECUTED. DEATH IS ONLY A MOMENT'S CARELESSNESS AWAY.

QUICKLY, GET HIM UNDRESSED.

WISH I COULD HAVE HANDLED THIS JOB WITHOUT JASON TAGGING ALONG.

BUT HE'S THE REASON WE'RE HERE.

MY HOPE IS THAT THIS MISSION WILL QUIET THE ANGRY FIRES THAT BURN WITHIN HIM.

HE STARTED GETTING OUT OF LINE BACK IN GOTHAM, TAKING RECKLESS CHANCES.

I QUICKLY REALIZED THE PROBLEM WAS THAT HE'D NOT YET ADJUSTED TO THE DEATH OF HIS PARENTS.

THAT'S WHY I DECIDED TO PUT JASON ON INACTIVE DUTY, TEMPORARILY.

I WANTED TO GIVE THE BOY TIME TO COME TO GRIPS WITH HIS GRIEF. OF COURSE, JASON DIDN'T SEE IT THAT WAY.

2

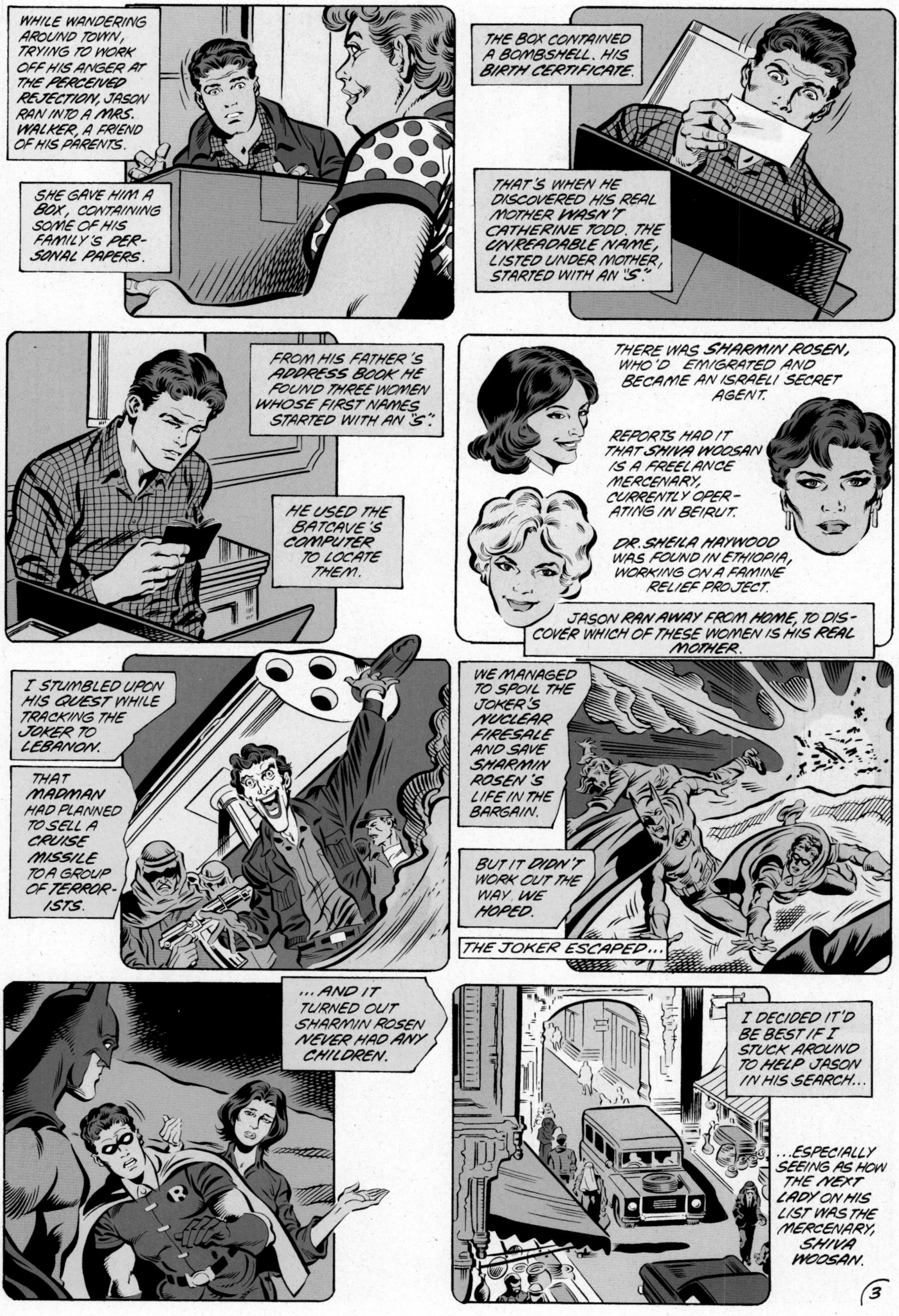
WHILE WANDERING AROUND TOWN, TRYING TO WORK OFF HIS ANGER AT THE PERCEIVED REJECTION, JASON RAN INTO A MRS. WALKER, A FRIEND OF HIS PARENTS.
SHE GAVE HIM A BOX, CONTAINING SOME OF HIS FAMILY'S PERSONAL PAPERS.
THE BOX CONTAINED A BOMBSHELL. HIS BIRTH CERTIFICATE.
THAT'S WHEN HE DISCOVERED HIS REAL MOTHER WASN'T CATHERINE TODD. THE UNREADABLE NAME, LISTED UNDER MOTHER, STARTED WITH AN "S."
FROM HIS FATHER'S ADDRESS BOOK HE FOUND THREE WOMEN WHOSE FIRST NAMES STARTED WITH AN "S".
HE USED THE BATCAVE'S COMPUTER TO LOCATE THEM.
THERE WAS SHARMIN ROSEN, WHO'D EMIGRATED AND BECAME AN ISRAELI SECRET AGENT.
REPORTS HAD IT THAT SHIVA WOOSAN IS A FREELANCE MERCENARY, CURRENTLY OPERATING IN BEIRUT.
DR. SHEILA HAYWOOD WAS FOUND IN ETHIOPIA, WORKING ON A FAMINE RELIEF PROJECT.
JASON RAN AWAY FROM HOME, TO DISCOVER WHICH OF THESE WOMEN IS HIS REAL MOTHER.
I STUMBLED UPON HIS QUEST WHILE TRACKING THE JOKER TO LEBANON.
THAT MADMAN HAD PLANNED TO SELL A CRUISE MISSILE TO A GROUP OF TERRORISTS.
WE MANAGED TO SPOIL THE JOKER'S NUCLEAR FIRESALE AND SAVE SHARMIN ROSEN'S LIFE IN THE BARGAIN.
BUT IT DIDN'T WORK OUT THE WAY WE HOPED.
THE JOKER ESCAPED...
...AND IT TURNED OUT SHARMIN ROSEN NEVER HAD ANY CHILDREN.
I DECIDED IT'D BE BEST IF I STUCK AROUND TO HELP JASON IN HIS SEARCH...
...ESPECIALLY SEEING AS HOW THE NEXT LADY ON HIS LIST WAS THE MERCENARY, SHIVA WOOSAN.
3

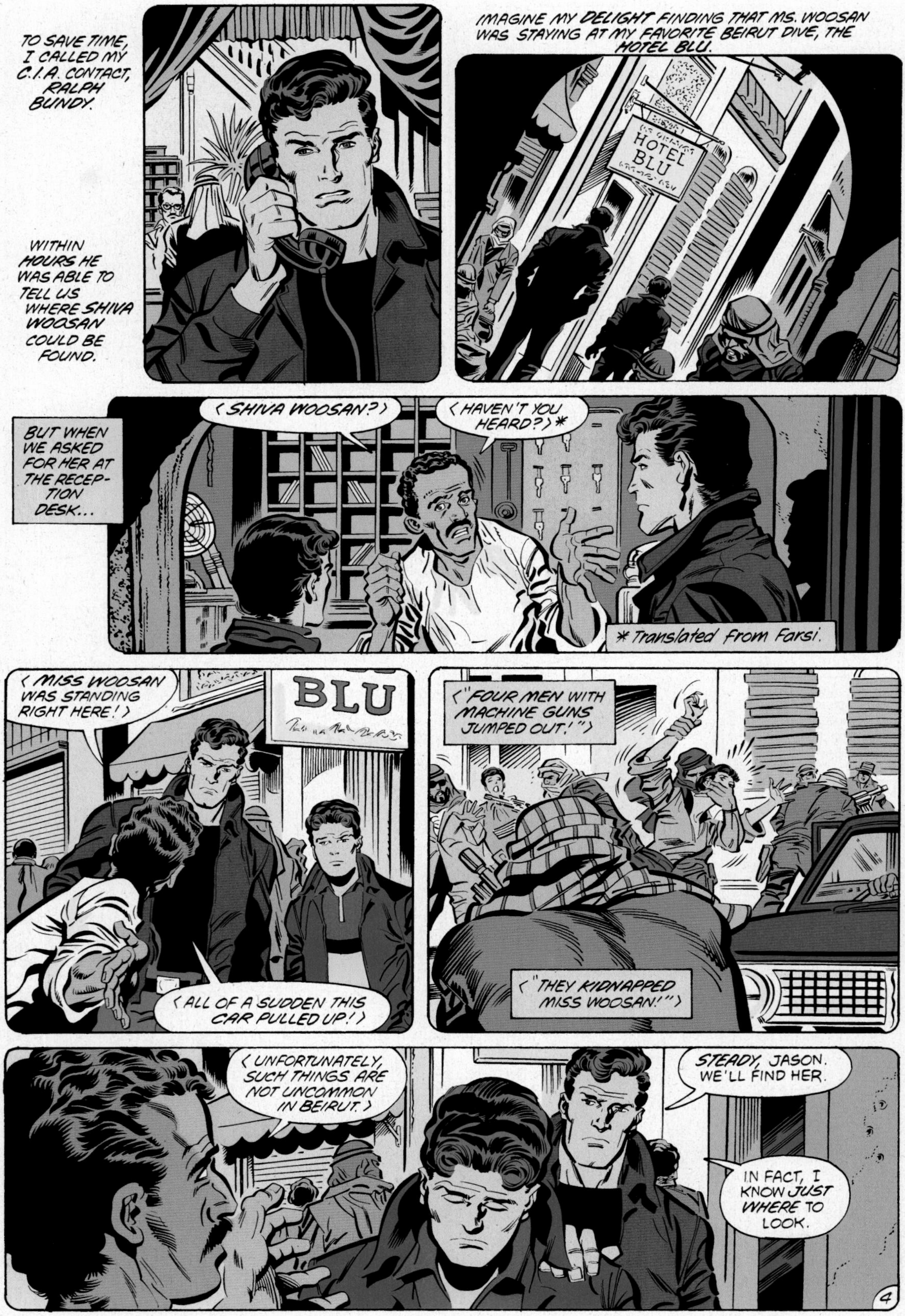
TO SAVE TIME, I CALLED MY C.I.A. CONTACT, RALPH BUNDY.
WITHIN HOURS HE WAS ABLE TO TELL US WHERE SHIVA WOOSAN COULD BE FOUND.
IMAGINE MY DELIGHT FINDING THAT MS. WOOSAN WAS STAYING AT MY FAVORITE BEIRUT DIVE, THE HOTEL BLU.
HOTEL BLU
BUT WHEN WE ASKED FOR HER AT THE RECEPTION DESK...
< SHIVA WOOSAN? >
< HAVEN'T YOU HEARD? >*
*Translated from Farsi.
BLU
< MISS WOOSAN WAS STANDING RIGHT HERE! >
< ALL OF A SUDDEN THIS CAR PULLED UP! >
< "FOUR MEN WITH MACHINE GUNS JUMPED OUT!" >
< "THEY KIDNAPPED MISS WOOSAN!" >
< UNFORTUNATELY, SUCH THINGS ARE NOT UNCOMMON IN BEIRUT. >
STEADY, JASON. WE'LL FIND HER.
IN FACT, I KNOW JUST WHERE TO LOOK.
4

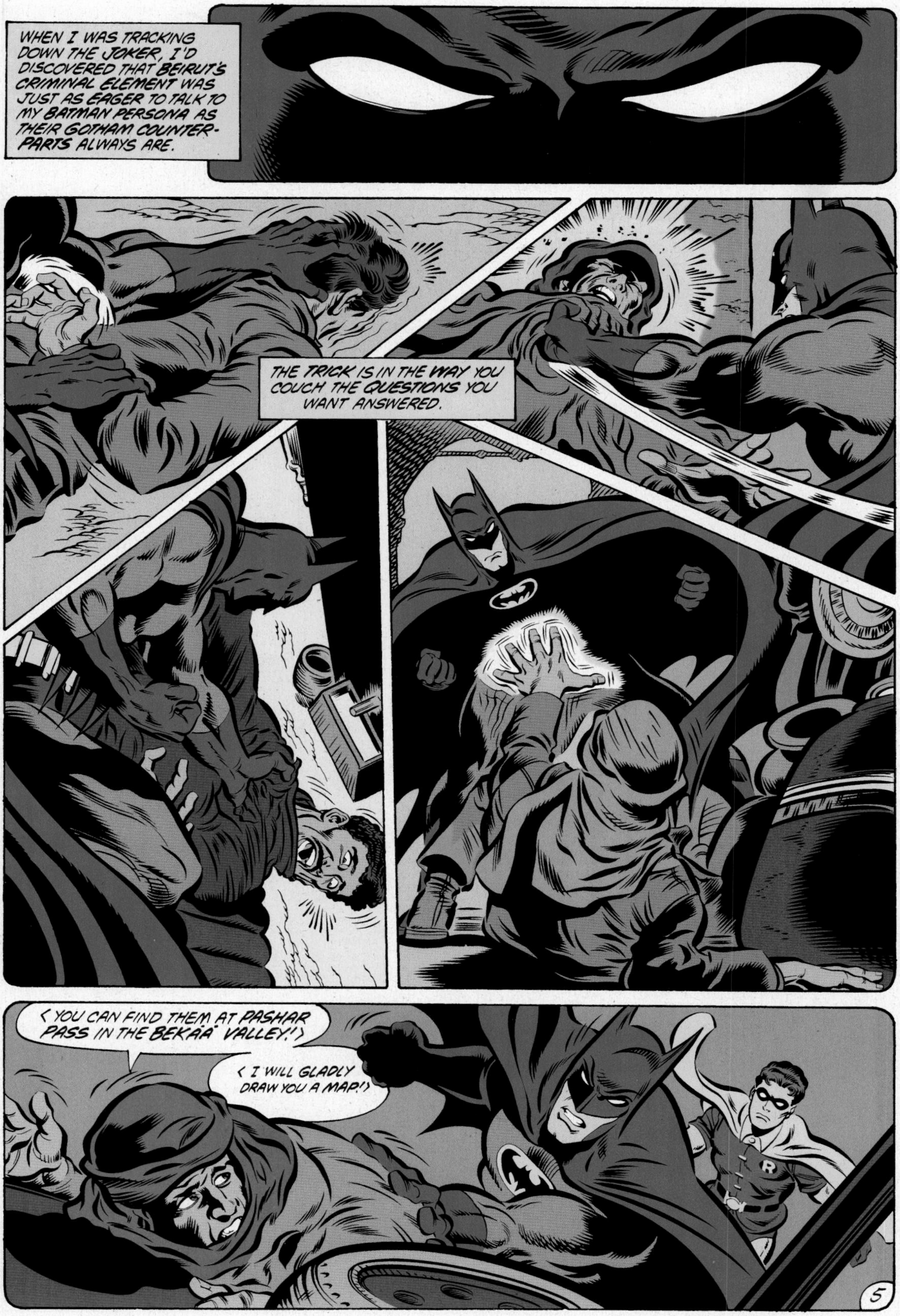
WHEN I WAS TRACKING DOWN THE JOKER, I'D DISCOVERED THAT BEIRUT'S CRIMINAL ELEMENT WAS JUST AS EAGER TO TALK TO MY BATMAN PERSONA AS THEIR GOTHAM COUNTER-PARTS ALWAYS ARE.
THE TRICK IS IN THE WAY YOU COUCH THE QUESTIONS YOU WANT ANSWERED.
< YOU CAN FIND THEM AT PASHAR PASS IN THE BEKAA VALLEY! >
< I WILL GLADLY DRAW YOU A MAP! >
5

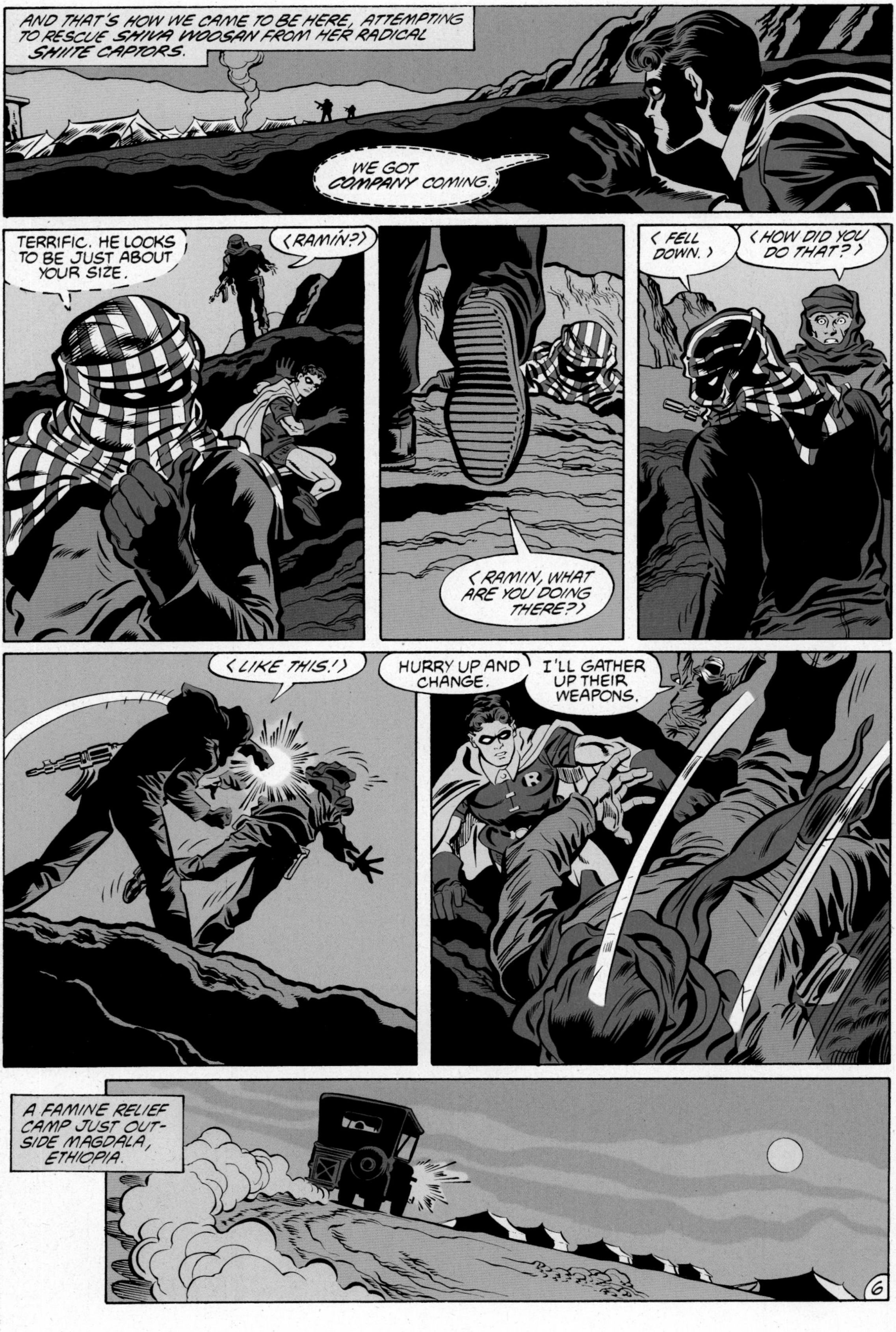
AND THAT'S HOW WE CAME TO BE HERE, ATTEMPTING TO RESCUE SHIVA WOOSAN FROM HER RADICAL SHIITE CAPTORS.
WE GOT COMPANY COMING.
TERRIFIC. HE LOOKS TO BE JUST ABOUT YOUR SIZE.
‹RAMIN?›
‹RAMIN, WHAT ARE YOU DOING THERE?›
‹FELL DOWN.›
‹HOW DID YOU DO THAT?›
‹LIKE THIS.!›
HURRY UP AND CHANGE.
I'LL GATHER UP THEIR WEAPONS.
A FAMINE RELIEF CAMP JUST OUTSIDE MAGDALA, ETHIOPIA.
6

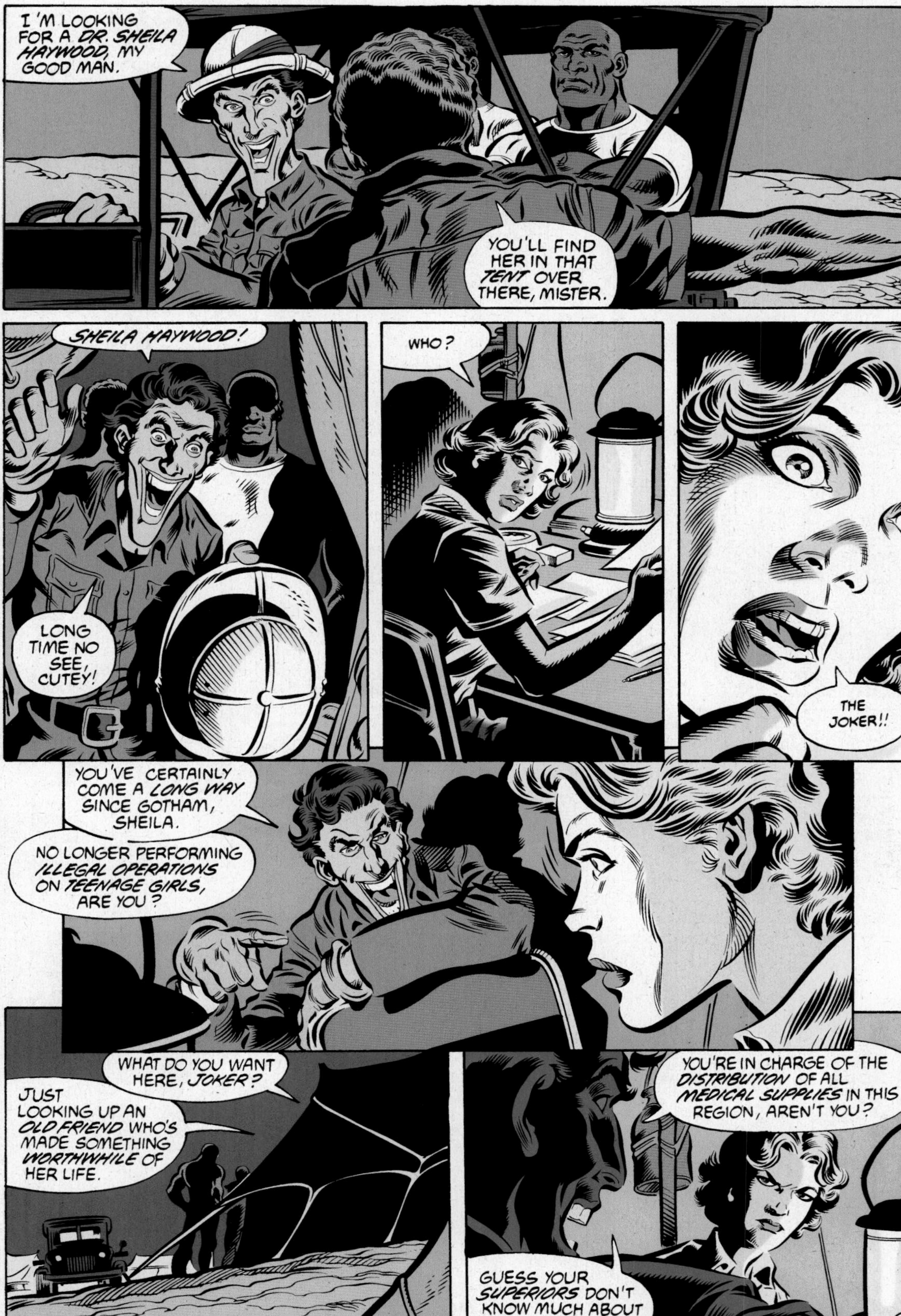

I'M LOOKING FOR A DR. SHEILA HAYWOOD, MY GOOD MAN.
YOU'LL FIND HER IN THAT TENT OVER THERE, MISTER.
SHEILA HAYWOOD!
LONG TIME NO SEE, CUTEY!
WHO?
THE JOKER!!
YOU'VE CERTAINLY COME A LONG WAY SINCE GOTHAM, SHEILA.
NO LONGER PERFORMING ILLEGAL OPERATIONS ON TEENAGE GIRLS, ARE YOU?
WHAT DO YOU WANT HERE, JOKER?
JUST LOOKING UP AN OLD FRIEND WHO'S MADE SOMETHING WORTHWHILE OF HER LIFE.
YOU'RE IN CHARGE OF THE DISTRIBUTION OF ALL MEDICAL SUPPLIES IN THIS REGION, AREN'T YOU?
GUESS YOUR SUPERIORS DON'T KNOW MUCH ABOUT YOUR PAST.
7

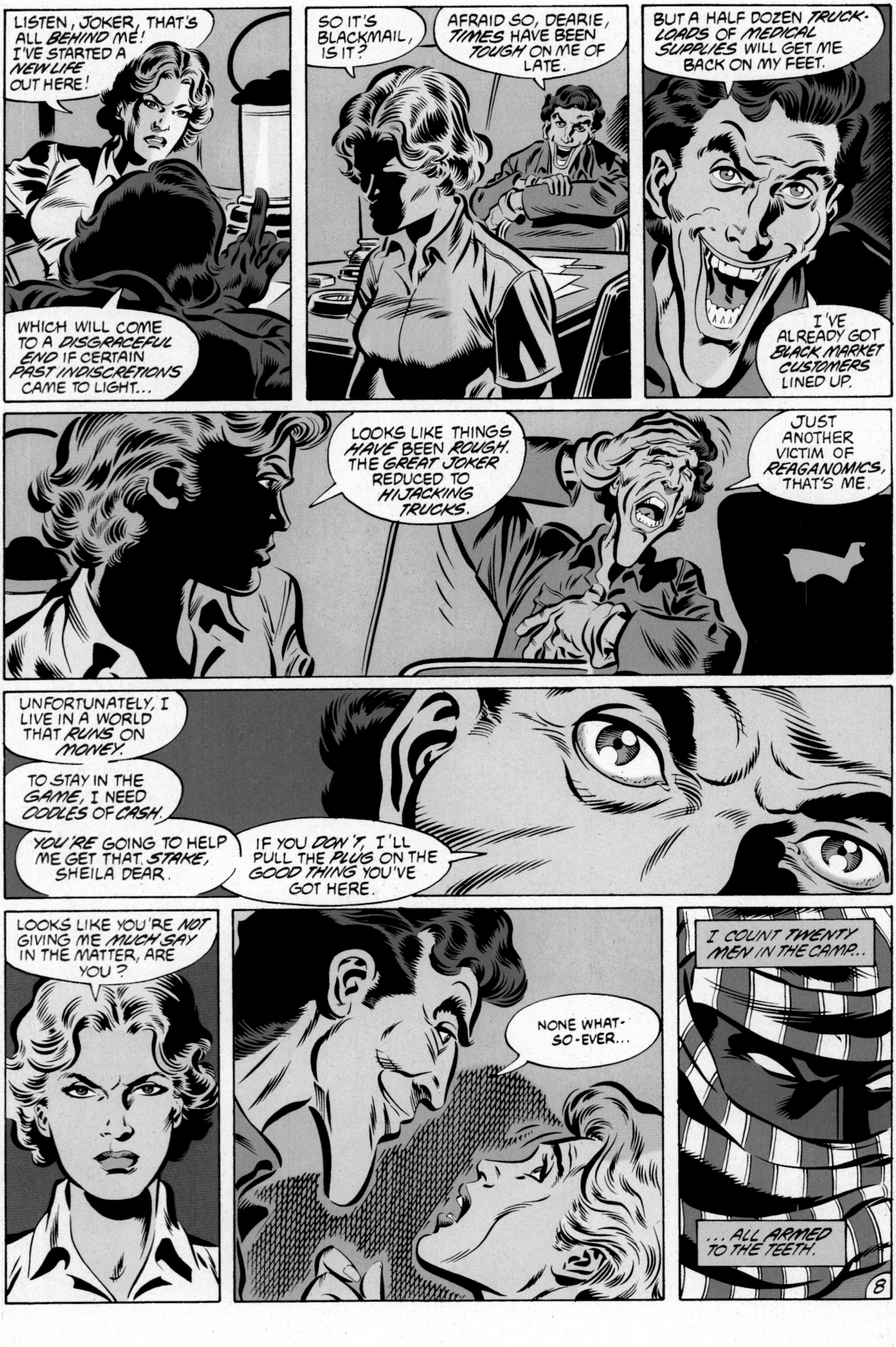
LISTEN, JOKER, THAT'S ALL BEHIND ME! I'VE STARTED A NEW LIFE OUT HERE!
WHICH WILL COME TO A DISGRACEFUL END IF CERTAIN PAST INDISCRETIONS CAME TO LIGHT...
SO IT'S BLACKMAIL, IS IT?
AFRAID SO, DEARIE, TIMES HAVE BEEN TOUGH ON ME OF LATE.
BUT A HALF DOZEN TRUCK-LOADS OF MEDICAL SUPPLIES WILL GET ME BACK ON MY FEET.
I'VE ALREADY GOT BLACK MARKET CUSTOMERS LINED UP.
LOOKS LIKE THINGS HAVE BEEN ROUGH. THE GREAT JOKER REDUCED TO HIJACKING TRUCKS.
JUST ANOTHER VICTIM OF REAGANOMICS, THAT'S ME.
UNFORTUNATELY, I LIVE IN A WORLD THAT RUNS ON MONEY.
TO STAY IN THE GAME, I NEED OODLES OF CASH.
YOU'RE GOING TO HELP ME GET THAT STAKE, SHEILA DEAR.
IF YOU DON'T, I'LL PULL THE PLUG ON THE GOOD THING YOU'VE GOT HERE.
LOOKS LIKE YOU'RE NOT GIVING ME MUCH SAY IN THE MATTER, ARE YOU?
NONE WHAT-SO-EVER...
I COUNT TWENTY MEN IN THE CAMP...
...ALL ARMED TO THE TEETH.
8

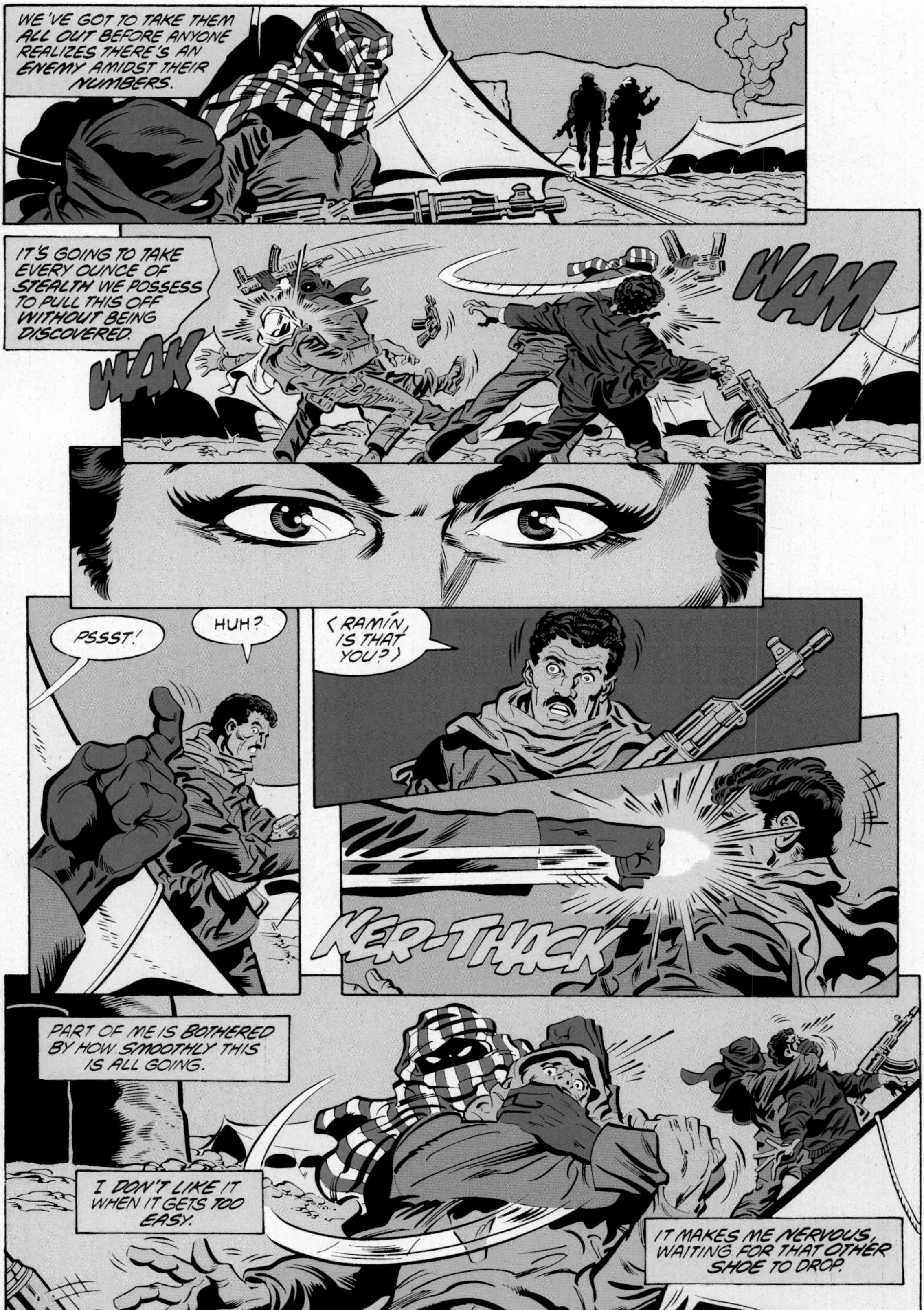
WE'VE GOT TO TAKE THEM ALL OUT BEFORE ANYONE REALIZES THERE'S AN ENEMY AMIDST THEIR NUMBERS.
IT'S GOING TO TAKE EVERY OUNCE OF STEALTH WE POSSESS TO PULL THIS OFF WITHOUT BEING DISCOVERED.
WAM
WAK
PSSST!
HUH?
<RAMIN, IS THAT YOU?>
KER-THACK
PART OF ME IS BOTHERED BY HOW SMOOTHLY THIS IS ALL GOING.
I DON'T LIKE IT WHEN IT GETS TOO EASY.
IT MAKES ME NERVOUS, WAITING FOR THAT OTHER SHOE TO DROP.
9

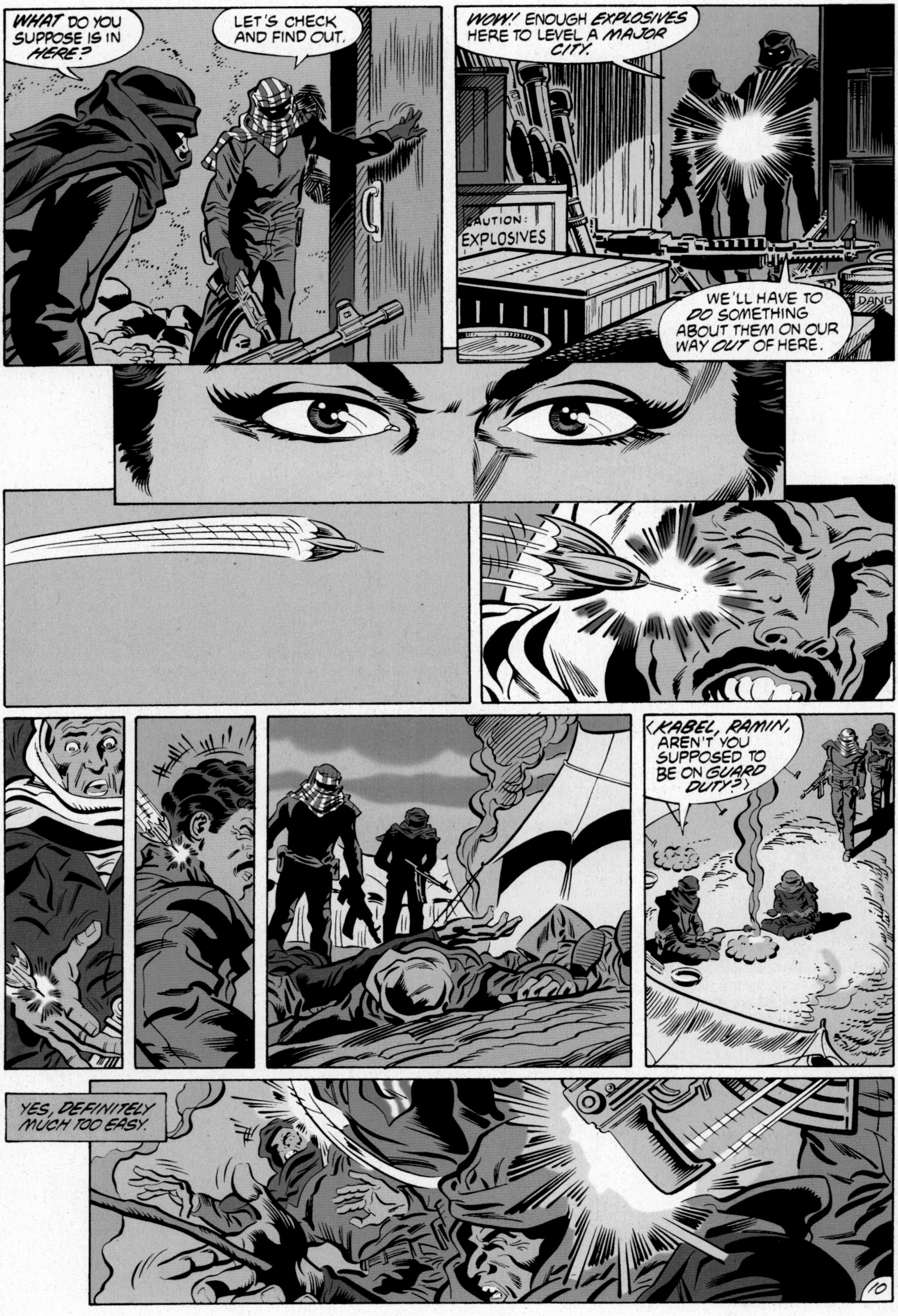
WHAT DO YOU SUPPOSE IS IN HERE?
LET'S CHECK AND FIND OUT.
WOW! ENOUGH EXPLOSIVES HERE TO LEVEL A MAJOR CITY.
CAUTION: EXPLOSIVES
WE'LL HAVE TO DO SOMETHING ABOUT THEM ON OUR WAY OUT OF HERE.
DANG
‹KABEL, RAMIN, AREN'T YOU SUPPOSED TO BE ON GUARD DUTY?›
YES, DEFINITELY MUCH TOO EASY.
10

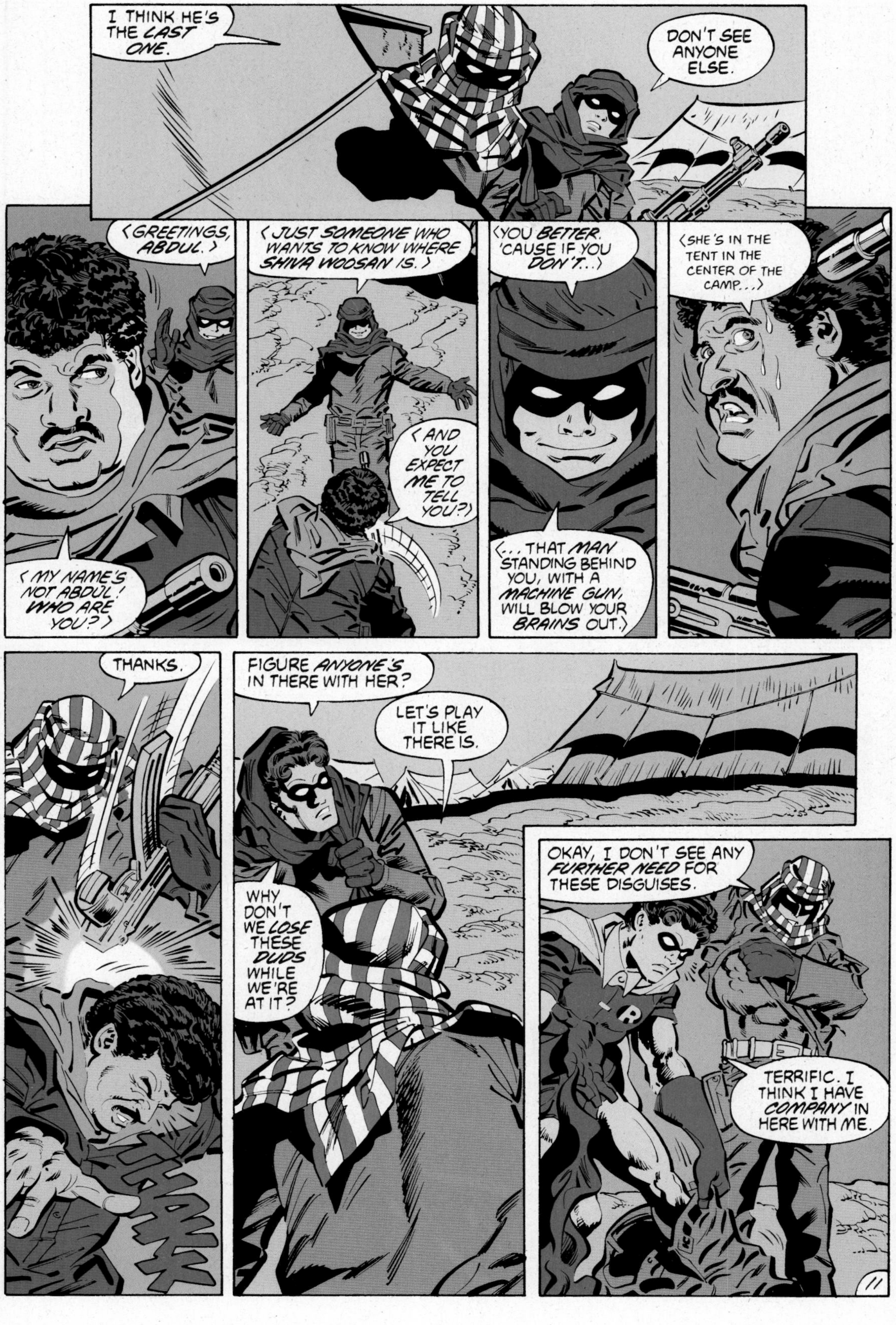

I THINK HE'S THE LAST ONE.
DON'T SEE ANYONE ELSE.
‹GREETINGS, ABDUL.›
‹MY NAME'S NOT ABDUL! WHO ARE YOU?›
‹JUST SOMEONE WHO WANTS TO KNOW WHERE SHIVA WOOSAN IS.›
‹AND YOU EXPECT ME TO TELL YOU?›
‹YOU BETTER. 'CAUSE IF YOU DON'T...›
‹...THAT MAN STANDING BEHIND YOU, WITH A MACHINE GUN, WILL BLOW YOUR BRAINS OUT.›
‹SHE'S IN THE TENT IN THE CENTER OF THE CAMP...›
THANKS.
THAK
FIGURE ANYONE'S IN THERE WITH HER?
LET'S PLAY IT LIKE THERE IS.
WHY DON'T WE LOSE THESE DUDS WHILE WE'RE AT IT?
OKAY, I DON'T SEE ANY FURTHER NEED FOR THESE DISGUISES.
TERRIFIC. I THINK I HAVE COMPANY IN HERE WITH ME.
11

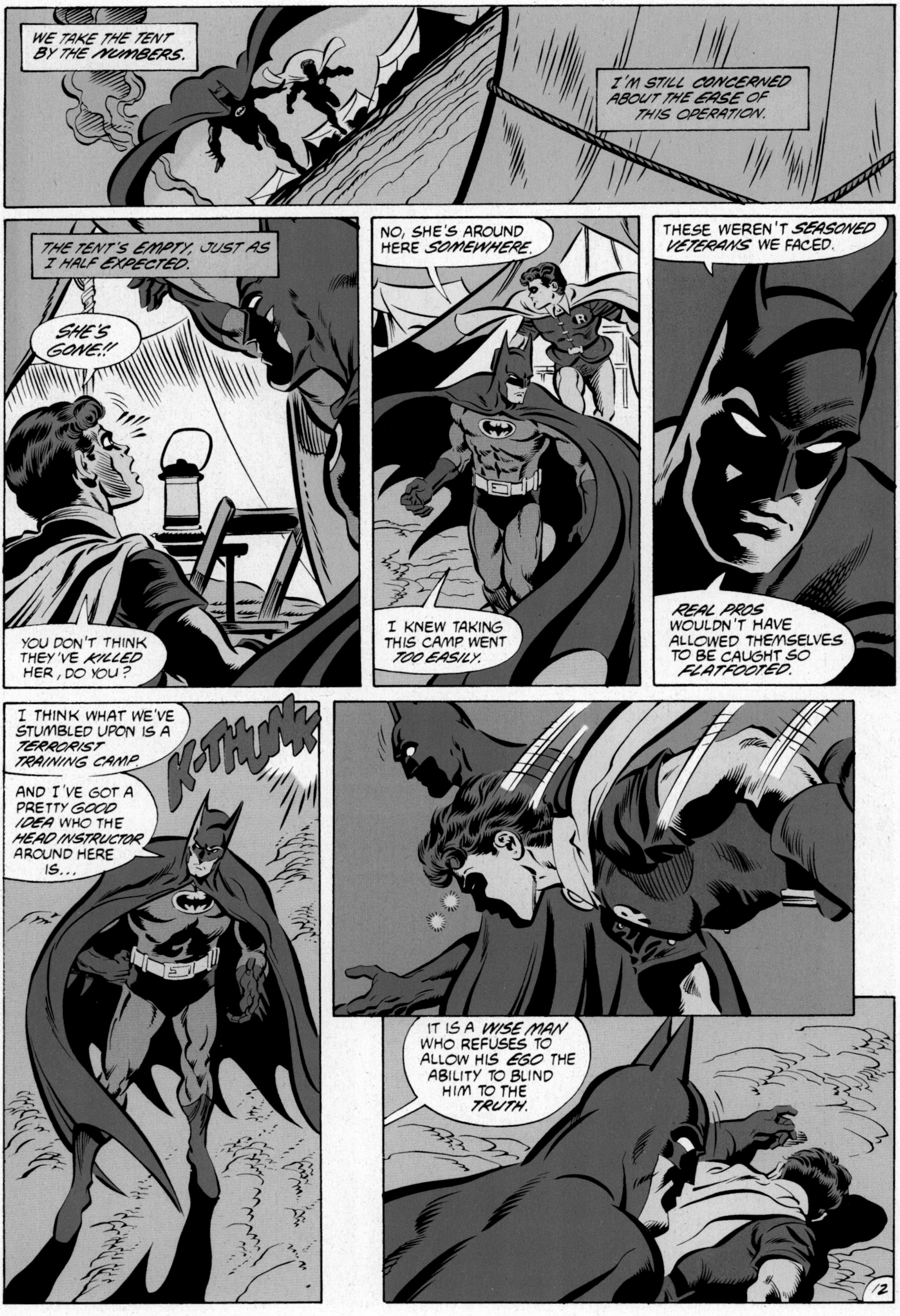
WE TAKE THE TENT BY THE NUMBERS.
I'M STILL CONCERNED ABOUT THE EASE OF THIS OPERATION.
THE TENT'S EMPTY, JUST AS I HALF EXPECTED.
SHE'S GONE!!
YOU DON'T THINK THEY'VE KILLED HER, DO YOU?
NO, SHE'S AROUND HERE SOMEWHERE.
I KNEW TAKING THIS CAMP WENT TOO EASILY.
THESE WEREN'T SEASONED VETERANS WE FACED.
REAL PROS WOULDN'T HAVE ALLOWED THEMSELVES TO BE CAUGHT SO FLATFOOTED.
I THINK WHAT WE'VE STUMBLED UPON IS A TERRORIST TRAINING CAMP.
AND I'VE GOT A PRETTY GOOD IDEA WHO THE HEAD INSTRUCTOR AROUND HERE IS...
K-THUNK
IT IS A WISE MAN WHO REFUSES TO ALLOW HIS EGO THE ABILITY TO BLIND HIM TO THE TRUTH.
12

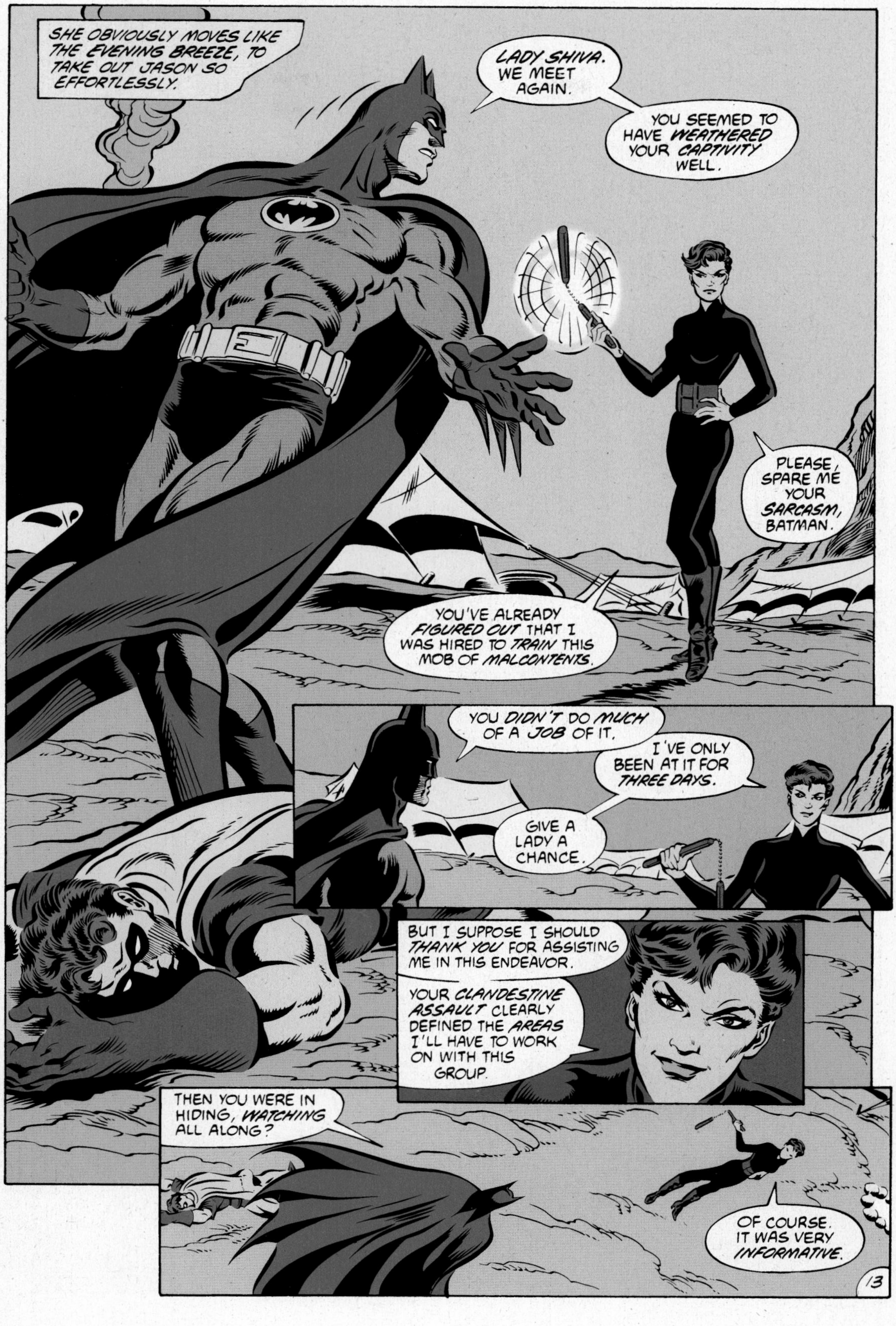
SHE OBVIOUSLY MOVES LIKE THE EVENING BREEZE, TO TAKE OUT JASON SO EFFORTLESSLY.
LADY SHIVA. WE MEET AGAIN.
YOU SEEMED TO HAVE WEATHERED YOUR CAPTIVITY WELL.
PLEASE, SPARE ME YOUR SARCASM, BATMAN.
YOU'VE ALREADY FIGURED OUT THAT I WAS HIRED TO TRAIN THIS MOB OF MALCONTENTS.
YOU DIDN'T DO MUCH OF A JOB OF IT.
I'VE ONLY BEEN AT IT FOR THREE DAYS.
GIVE A LADY A CHANCE.
BUT I SUPPOSE I SHOULD THANK YOU FOR ASSISTING ME IN THIS ENDEAVOR.
YOUR CLANDESTINE ASSAULT CLEARLY DEFINED THE AREAS I'LL HAVE TO WORK ON WITH THIS GROUP.
THEN YOU WERE IN HIDING, WATCHING ALL ALONG?
OF COURSE. IT WAS VERY INFORMATIVE.
13

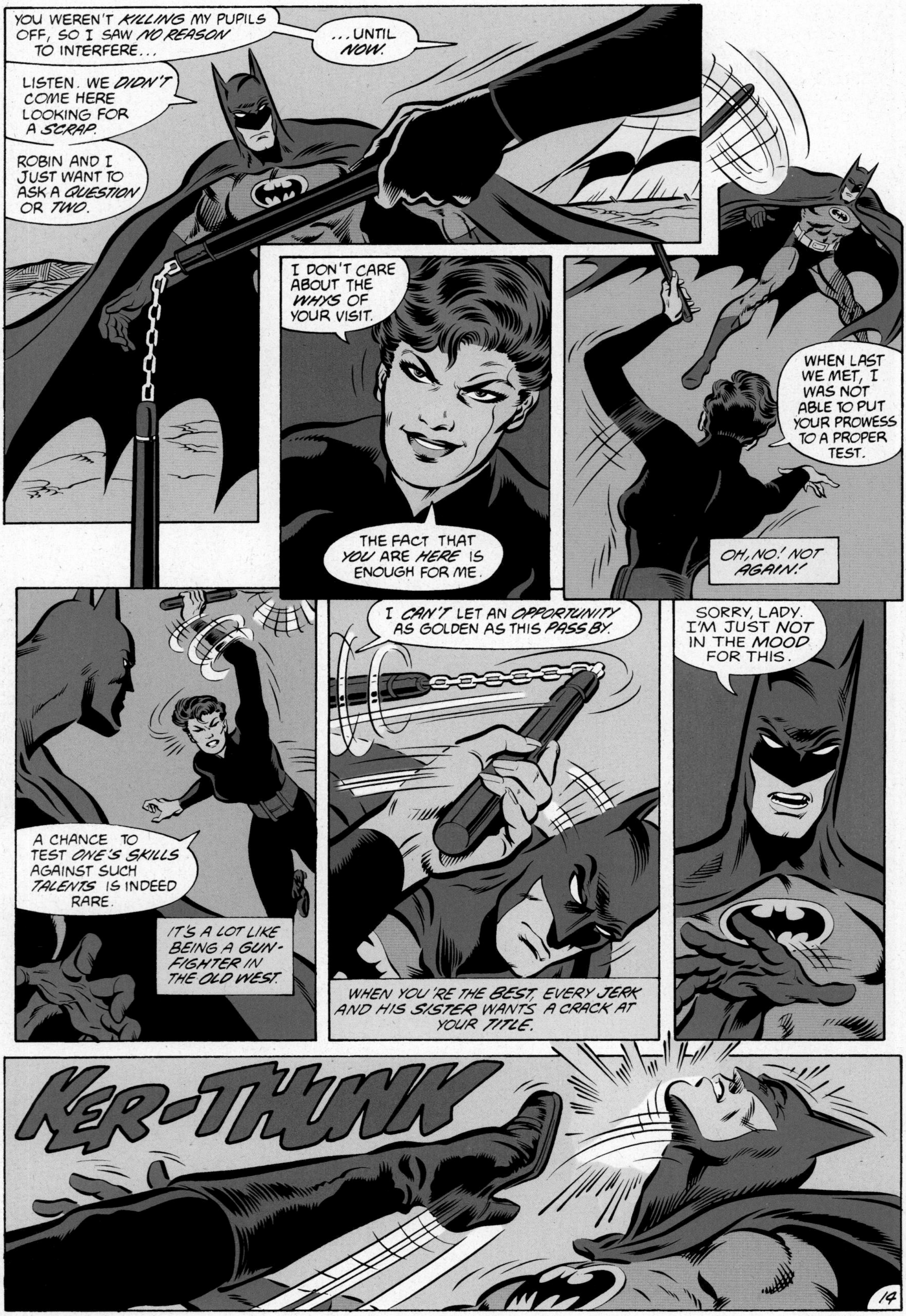
YOU WEREN'T KILLING MY PUPILS OFF, SO I SAW NO REASON TO INTERFERE...
...UNTIL NOW.
LISTEN. WE DIDN'T COME HERE LOOKING FOR A SCRAP.
ROBIN AND I JUST WANT TO ASK A QUESTION OR TWO.
I DON'T CARE ABOUT THE WHYS OF YOUR VISIT.
THE FACT THAT YOU ARE HERE IS ENOUGH FOR ME.
WHEN LAST WE MET, I WAS NOT ABLE TO PUT YOUR PROWESS TO A PROPER TEST.
OH, NO! NOT AGAIN!
A CHANCE TO TEST ONE'S SKILLS AGAINST SUCH TALENTS IS INDEED RARE.
IT'S A LOT LIKE BEING A GUN-FIGHTER IN THE OLD WEST.
I CAN'T LET AN OPPORTUNITY AS GOLDEN AS THIS PASS BY.
WHEN YOU'RE THE BEST, EVERY JERK AND HIS SISTER WANTS A CRACK AT YOUR TITLE.
SORRY, LADY. I'M JUST NOT IN THE MOOD FOR THIS.
KER-THUNK
14

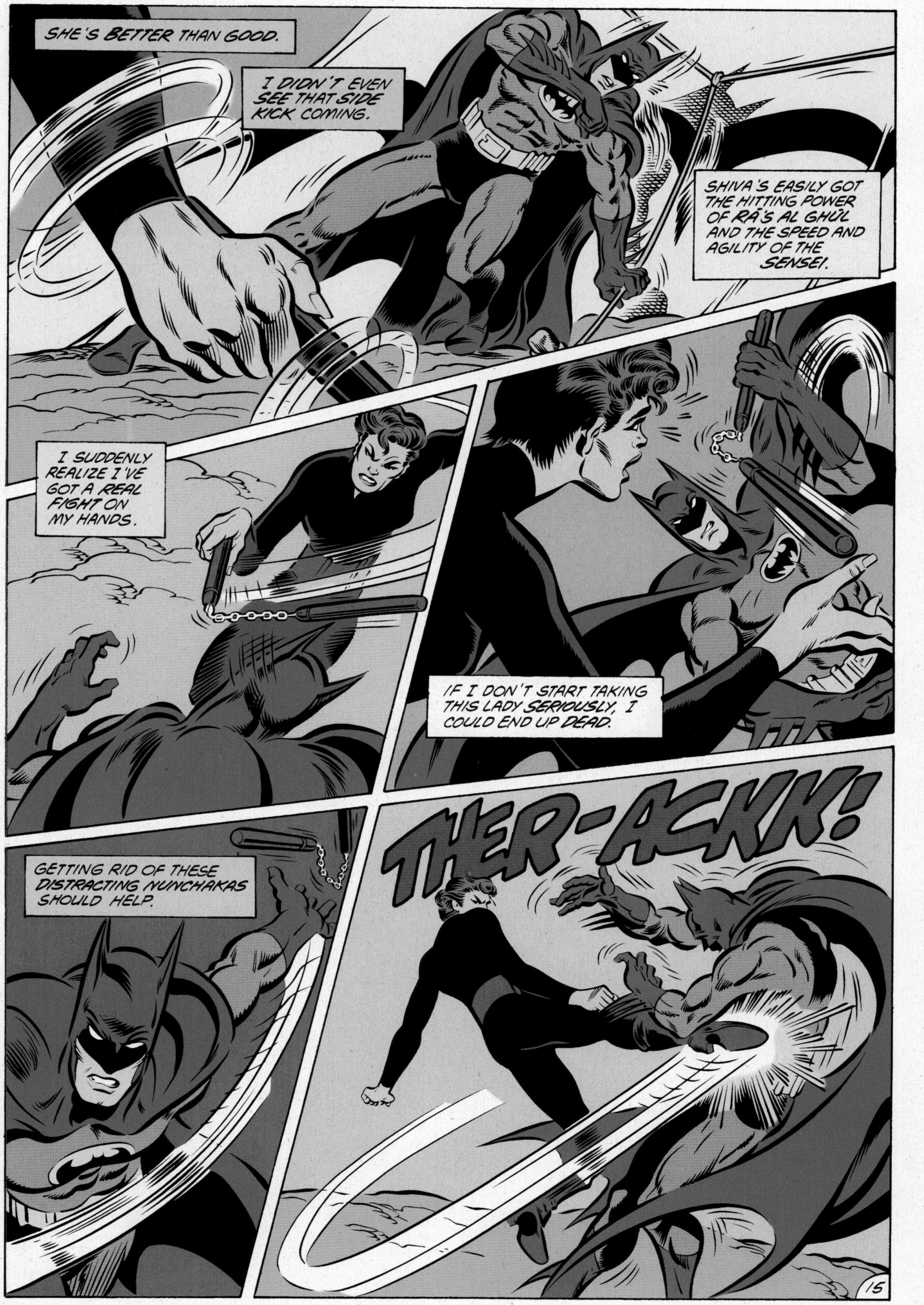
SHE'S BETTER THAN GOOD.
I DIDN'T EVEN SEE THAT SIDE KICK COMING.
SHIVA'S EASILY GOT THE HITTING POWER OF RÂ'S AL GHÛL AND THE SPEED AND AGILITY OF THE SENSEI.
I SUDDENLY REALIZE I'VE GOT A REAL FIGHT ON MY HANDS.
IF I DON'T START TAKING THIS LADY SERIOUSLY, I COULD END UP DEAD.
GETTING RID OF THESE DISTRACTING NUNCHAKAS SHOULD HELP.
THER-ACKK!
15

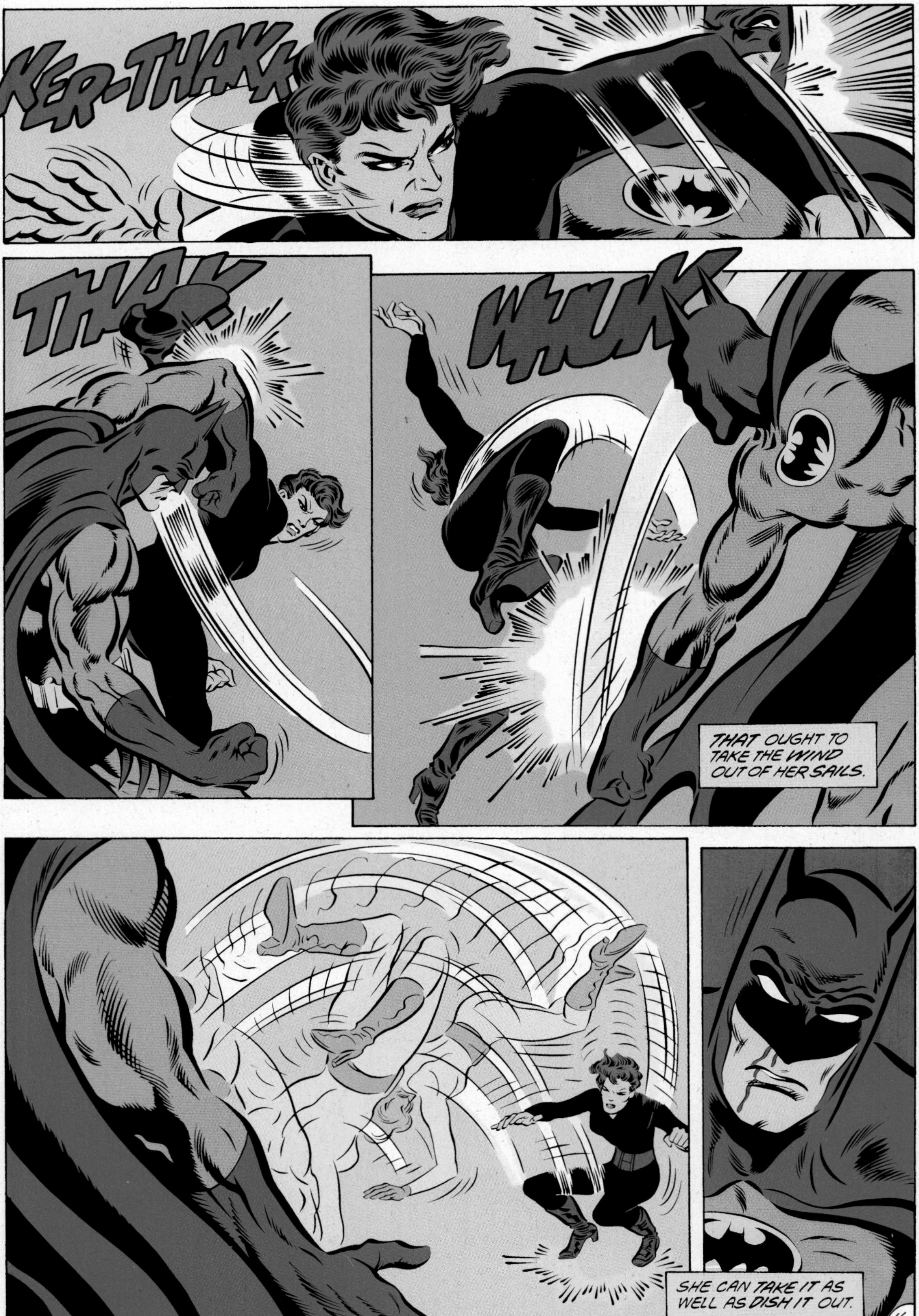
KER-THAKK
THAK
WHUK
THAT OUGHT TO TAKE THE WIND OUT OF HER SAILS.
SHE CAN TAKE IT AS WELL AS DISH IT OUT.
16

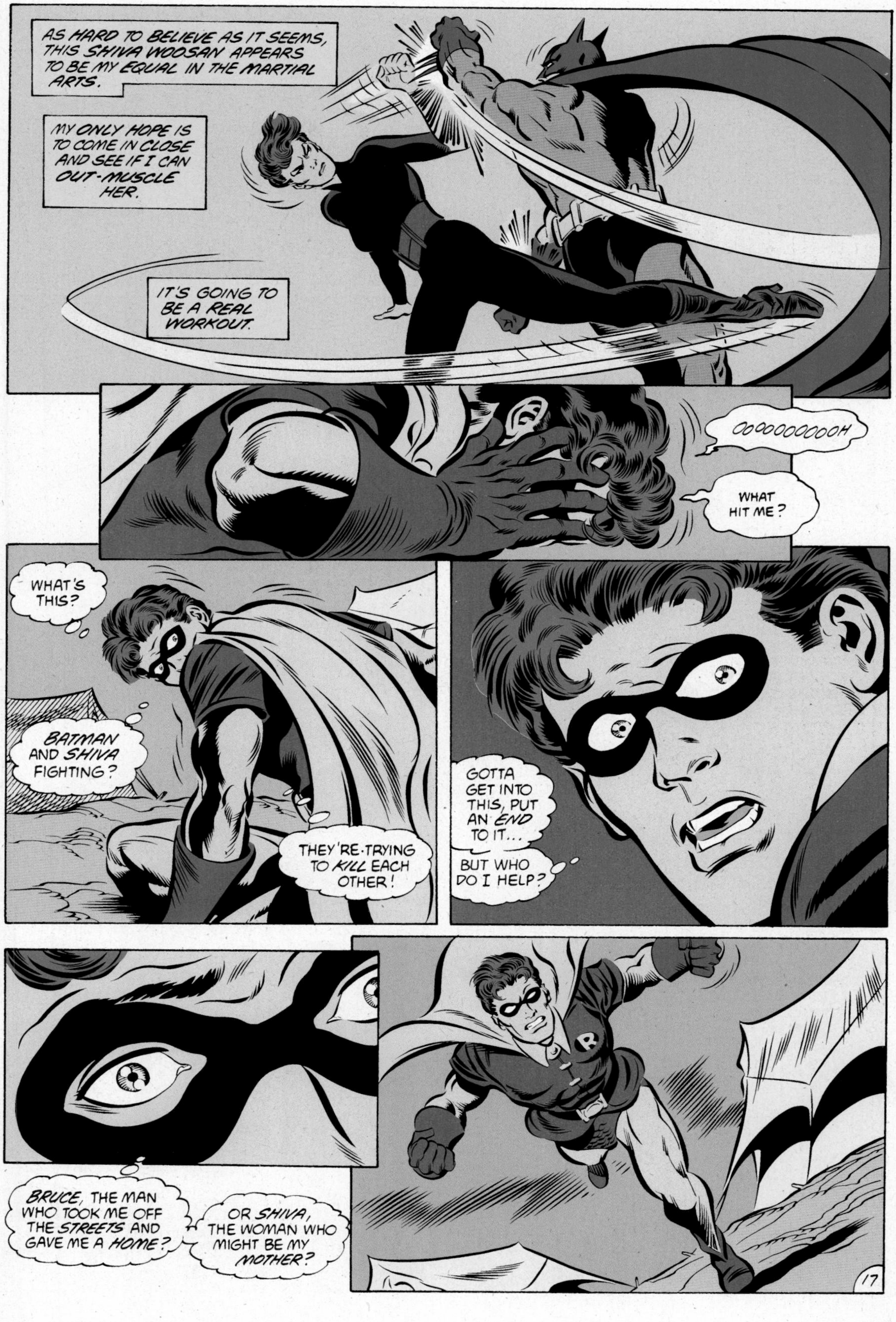

AS HARD TO BELIEVE AS IT SEEMS, THIS SHIVA WOOSAN APPEARS TO BE MY EQUAL IN THE MARTIAL ARTS.
MY ONLY HOPE IS TO COME IN CLOSE AND SEE IF I CAN OUT-MUSCLE HER.
IT'S GOING TO BE A REAL WORKOUT.
OOOOOOOOOOH
WHAT HIT ME?
WHAT'S THIS?
BATMAN AND SHIVA FIGHTING?
THEY'RE TRYING TO KILL EACH OTHER!
GOTTA GET INTO THIS, PUT AN END TO IT...
BUT WHO DO I HELP?
BRUCE, THE MAN WHO TOOK ME OFF THE STREETS AND GAVE ME A HOME?
OR SHIVA, THE WOMAN WHO MIGHT BE MY MOTHER?
17

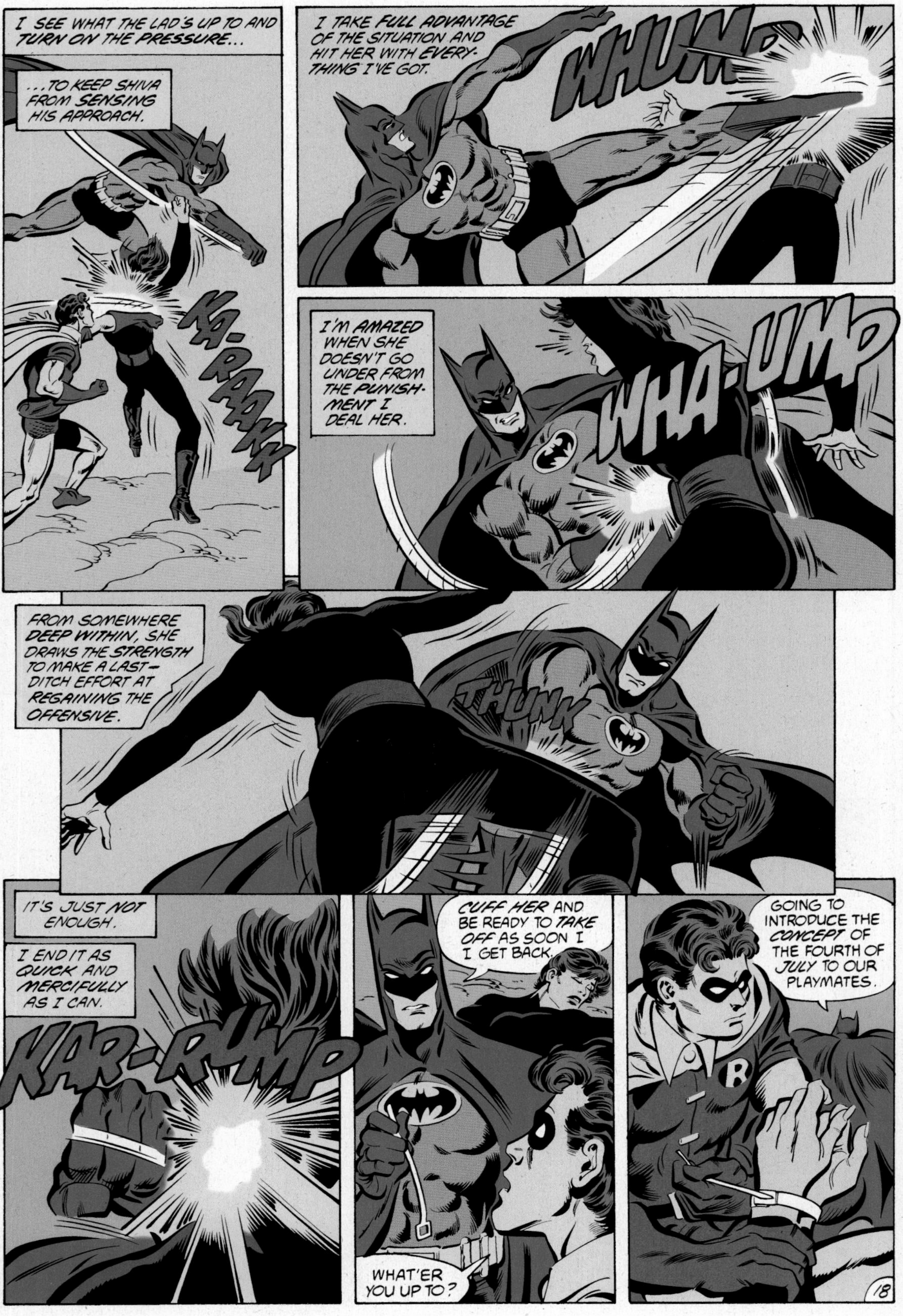
I SEE WHAT THE LAD'S UP TO AND TURN ON THE PRESSURE...
...TO KEEP SHIVA FROM SENSING HIS APPROACH.
KA-RAAAKK
I TAKE FULL ADVANTAGE OF THE SITUATION AND HIT HER WITH EVERY-THING I'VE GOT.
WHUMP
I'M AMAZED WHEN SHE DOESN'T GO UNDER FROM THE PUNISH-MENT I DEAL HER.
WHA-UMP
FROM SOMEWHERE DEEP WITHIN, SHE DRAWS THE STRENGTH TO MAKE A LAST-DITCH EFFORT AT REGAINING THE OFFENSIVE.
THUNK
IT'S JUST NOT ENOUGH.
I END IT AS QUICK AND MERCIFULLY AS I CAN.
KAR-RUMP
CUFF HER AND BE READY TO TAKE OFF AS SOON I I GET BACK.
WHAT'ER YOU UP TO?
GOING TO INTRODUCE THE CONCEPT OF THE FOURTH OF JULY TO OUR PLAYMATES.
18

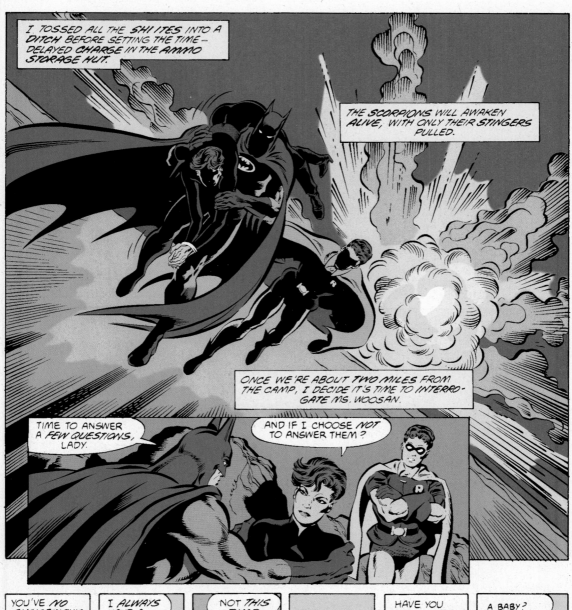

I TOSSED ALL THE *SHIITES* INTO A *DITCH* BEFORE SETTING THE TIME-DELAYED *CHARGE* IN THE *AMMO STORAGE HUT.*

THE *SCORPIONS* WILL AWAKEN *ALIVE,* WITH ONLY THEIR *STINGERS* PULLED.

ONCE WE'RE ABOUT *TWO MILES* FROM THE CAMP, I DECIDE IT'S TIME TO INTERRO-GATE MS. WOOSAN.

TIME TO ANSWER A *FEW QUESTIONS,* LADY.

AND IF I CHOOSE *NOT* TO ANSWER THEM?

YOU'VE *NO CHOICE* IN THIS MATTER, SHIVA.

I *ALWAYS* HAVE A CHOICE.

NOT *THIS TIME.*

HAVE YOU EVER HAD A *BABY?*

A BABY?

19

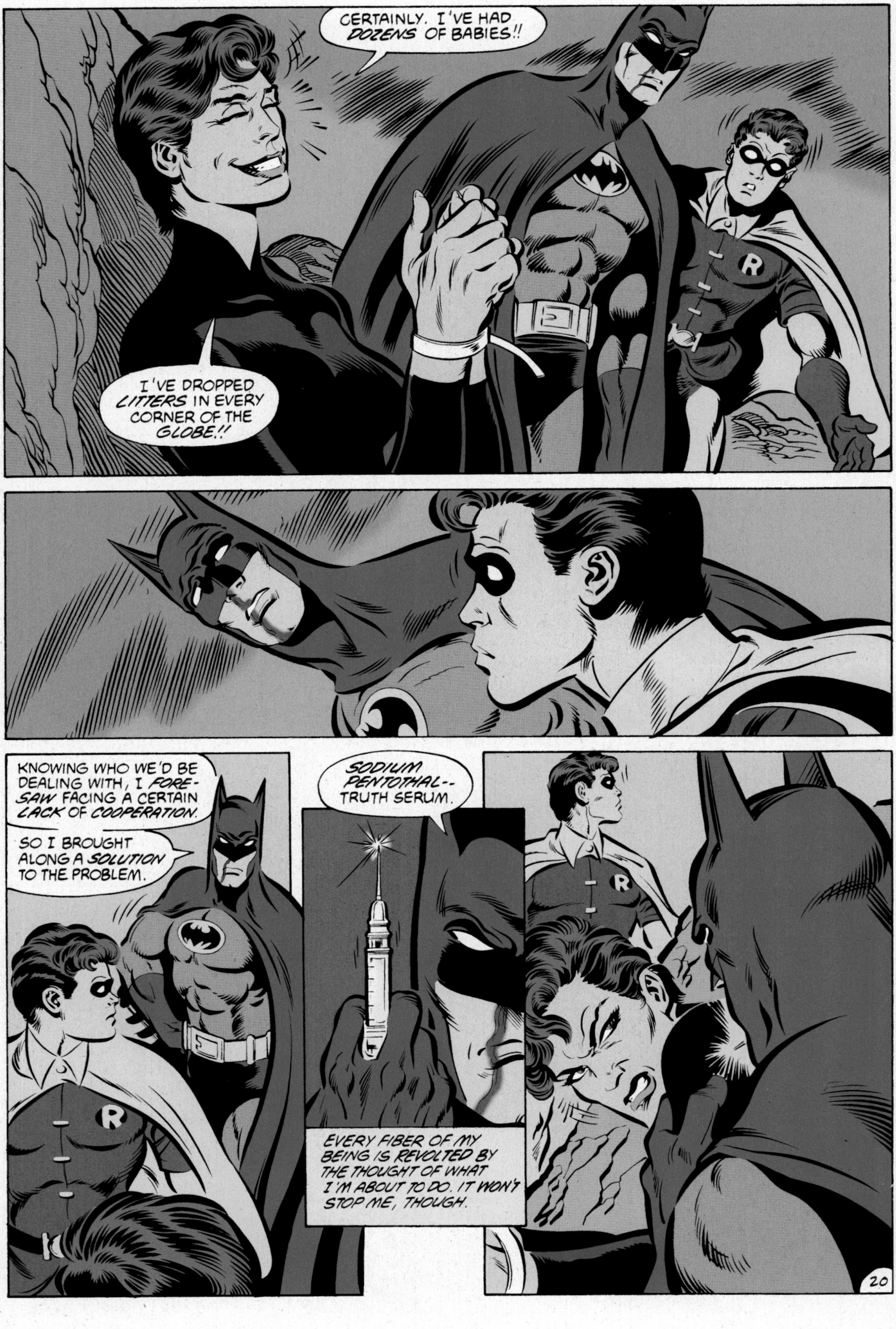
CERTAINLY. I'VE HAD DOZENS OF BABIES!!
I'VE DROPPED LITTERS IN EVERY CORNER OF THE GLOBE!!
KNOWING WHO WE'D BE DEALING WITH, I FORESAW FACING A CERTAIN LACK OF COOPERATION.
SO I BROUGHT ALONG A SOLUTION TO THE PROBLEM.
SODIUM PENTOTHAL-- TRUTH SERUM.
EVERY FIBER OF MY BEING IS REVOLTED BY THE THOUGHT OF WHAT I'M ABOUT TO DO. IT WON'T STOP ME, THOUGH.
20

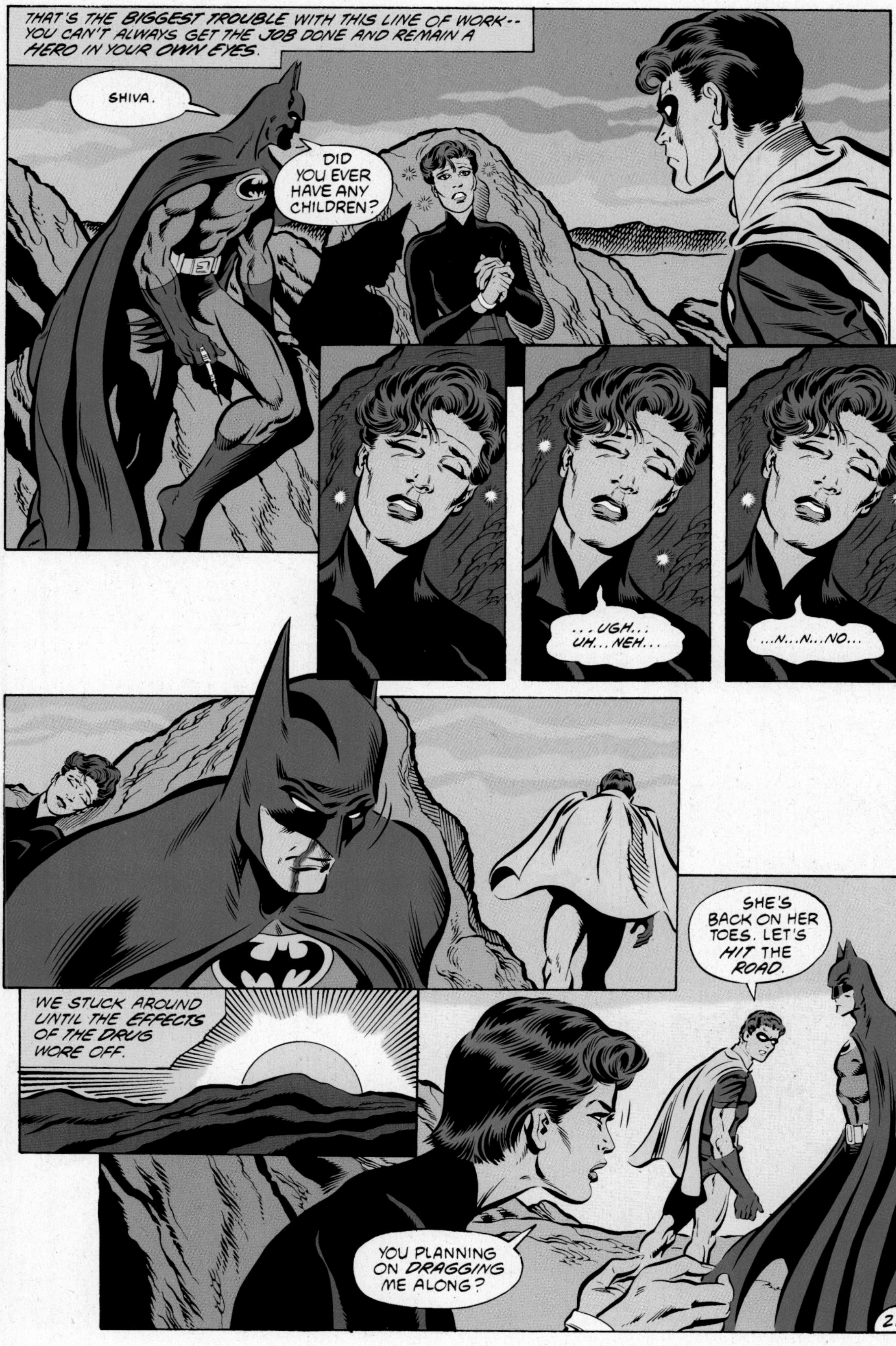

THAT'S THE BIGGEST TROUBLE WITH THIS LINE OF WORK-- YOU CAN'T ALWAYS GET THE JOB DONE AND REMAIN A HERO IN YOUR OWN EYES.
SHIVA.
DID YOU EVER HAVE ANY CHILDREN?
...UGH... UH...NEH...
...N...N...NO...
SHE'S BACK ON HER TOES. LET'S HIT THE ROAD.
WE STUCK AROUND UNTIL THE EFFECTS OF THE DRUG WORE OFF.
YOU PLANNING ON DRAGGING ME ALONG?
21

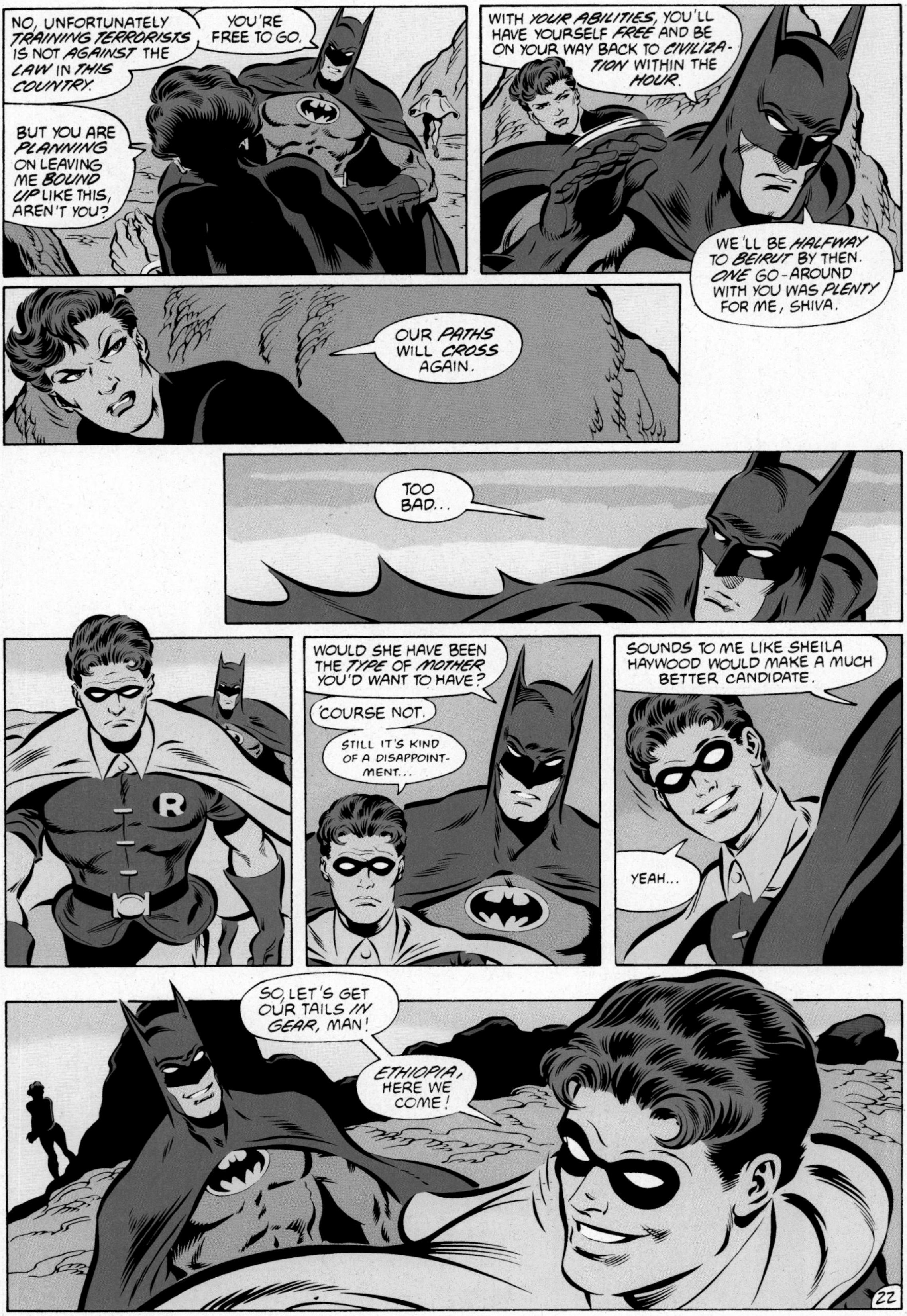
NO, UNFORTUNATELY TRAINING TERRORISTS IS NOT AGAINST THE LAW IN THIS COUNTRY.
YOU'RE FREE TO GO.
BUT YOU ARE PLANNING ON LEAVING ME BOUND UP LIKE THIS, AREN'T YOU?
WITH YOUR ABILITIES, YOU'LL HAVE YOURSELF FREE AND BE ON YOUR WAY BACK TO CIVILIZATION WITHIN THE HOUR.
WE'LL BE HALFWAY TO BEIRUT BY THEN. ONE GO-AROUND WITH YOU WAS PLENTY FOR ME, SHIVA.
OUR PATHS WILL CROSS AGAIN.
TOO BAD...
WOULD SHE HAVE BEEN THE TYPE OF MOTHER YOU'D WANT TO HAVE?
'COURSE NOT.
STILL IT'S KIND OF A DISAPPOINTMENT...
SOUNDS TO ME LIKE SHEILA HAYWOOD WOULD MAKE A MUCH BETTER CANDIDATE.
YEAH...
SO, LET'S GET OUR TAILS IN GEAR, MAN!
ETHIOPIA, HERE WE COME!
22

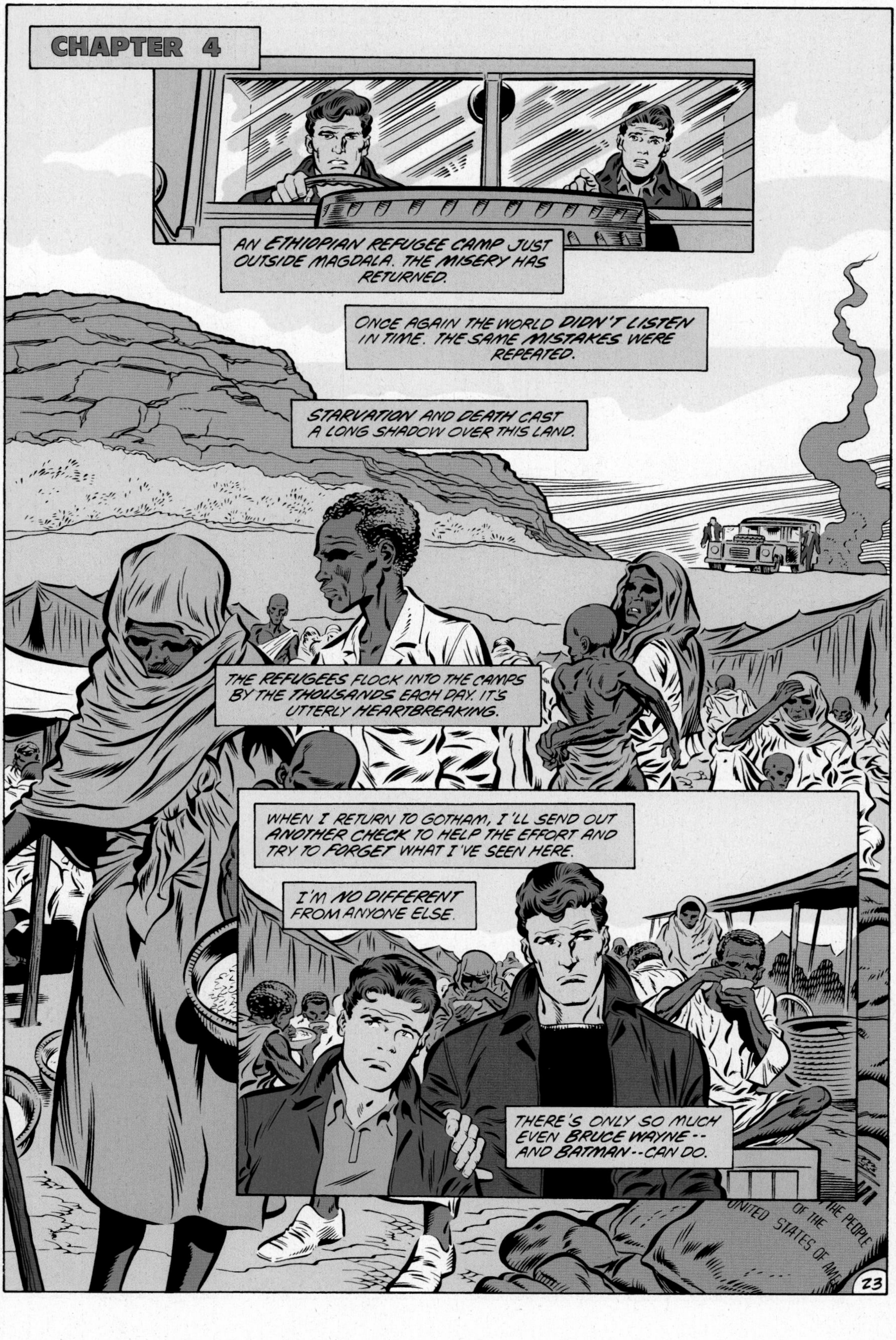
CHAPTER 4
AN ETHIOPIAN REFUGEE CAMP JUST OUTSIDE MAGDALA. THE MISERY HAS RETURNED.
ONCE AGAIN THE WORLD DIDN'T LISTEN IN TIME. THE SAME MISTAKES WERE REPEATED.
STARVATION AND DEATH CAST A LONG SHADOW OVER THIS LAND.
THE REFUGEES FLOCK INTO THE CAMPS BY THE THOUSANDS EACH DAY. IT'S UTTERLY HEARTBREAKING.
WHEN I RETURN TO GOTHAM, I'LL SEND OUT ANOTHER CHECK TO HELP THE EFFORT AND TRY TO FORGET WHAT I'VE SEEN HERE.
I'M NO DIFFERENT FROM ANYONE ELSE.
THERE'S ONLY SO MUCH EVEN BRUCE WAYNE -- AND BATMAN -- CAN DO.
23

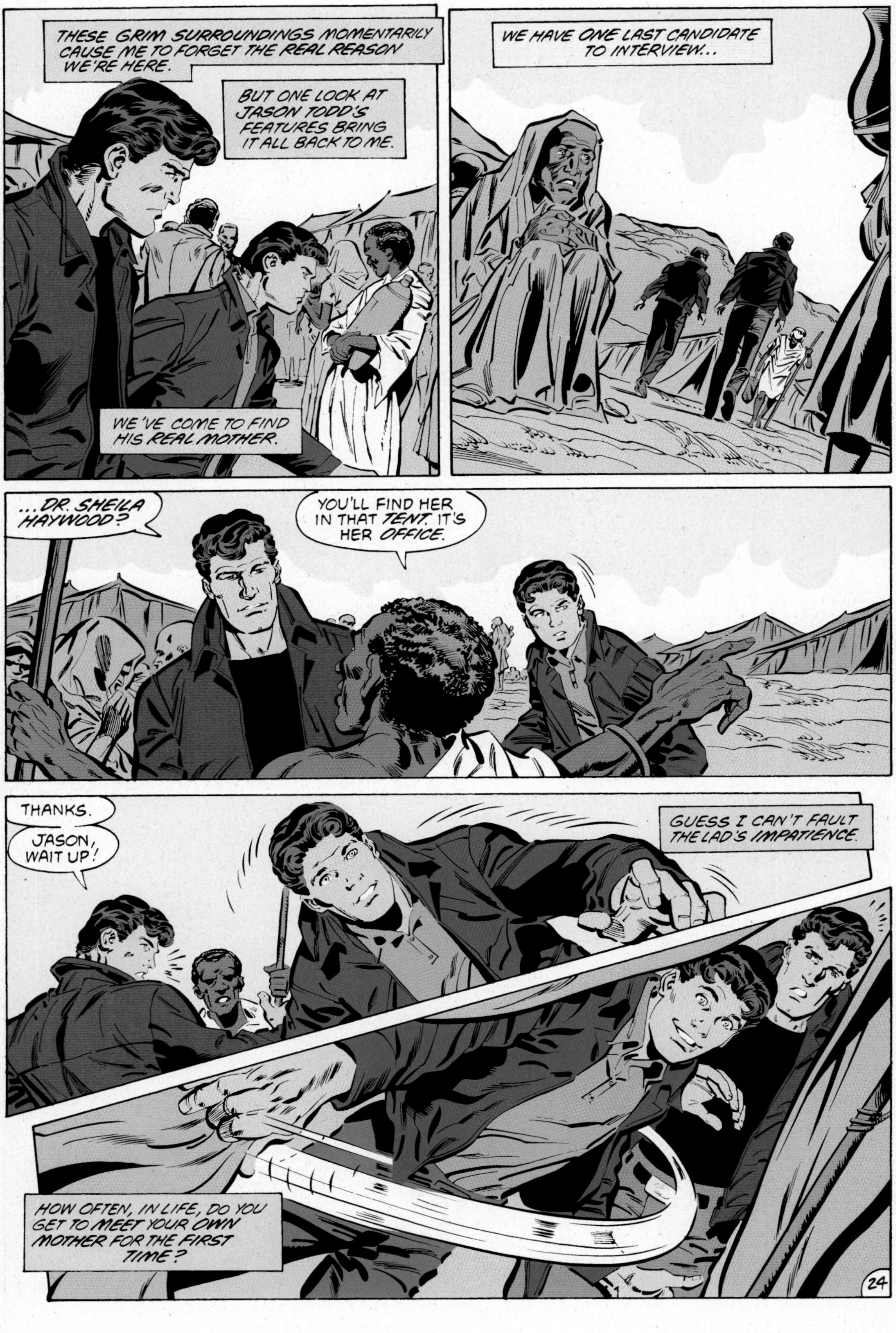
THESE GRIM SURROUNDINGS MOMENTARILY CAUSE ME TO FORGET THE REAL REASON WE'RE HERE.
BUT ONE LOOK AT JASON TODD'S FEATURES BRING IT ALL BACK TO ME.
WE'VE COME TO FIND HIS REAL MOTHER.
WE HAVE ONE LAST CANDIDATE TO INTERVIEW...
...DR. SHEILA HAYWOOD?
YOU'LL FIND HER IN THAT TENT. IT'S HER OFFICE.
THANKS.
JASON, WAIT UP!
GUESS I CAN'T FAULT THE LAD'S IMPATIENCE.
HOW OFTEN, IN LIFE, DO YOU GET TO MEET YOUR OWN MOTHER FOR THE FIRST TIME?
24

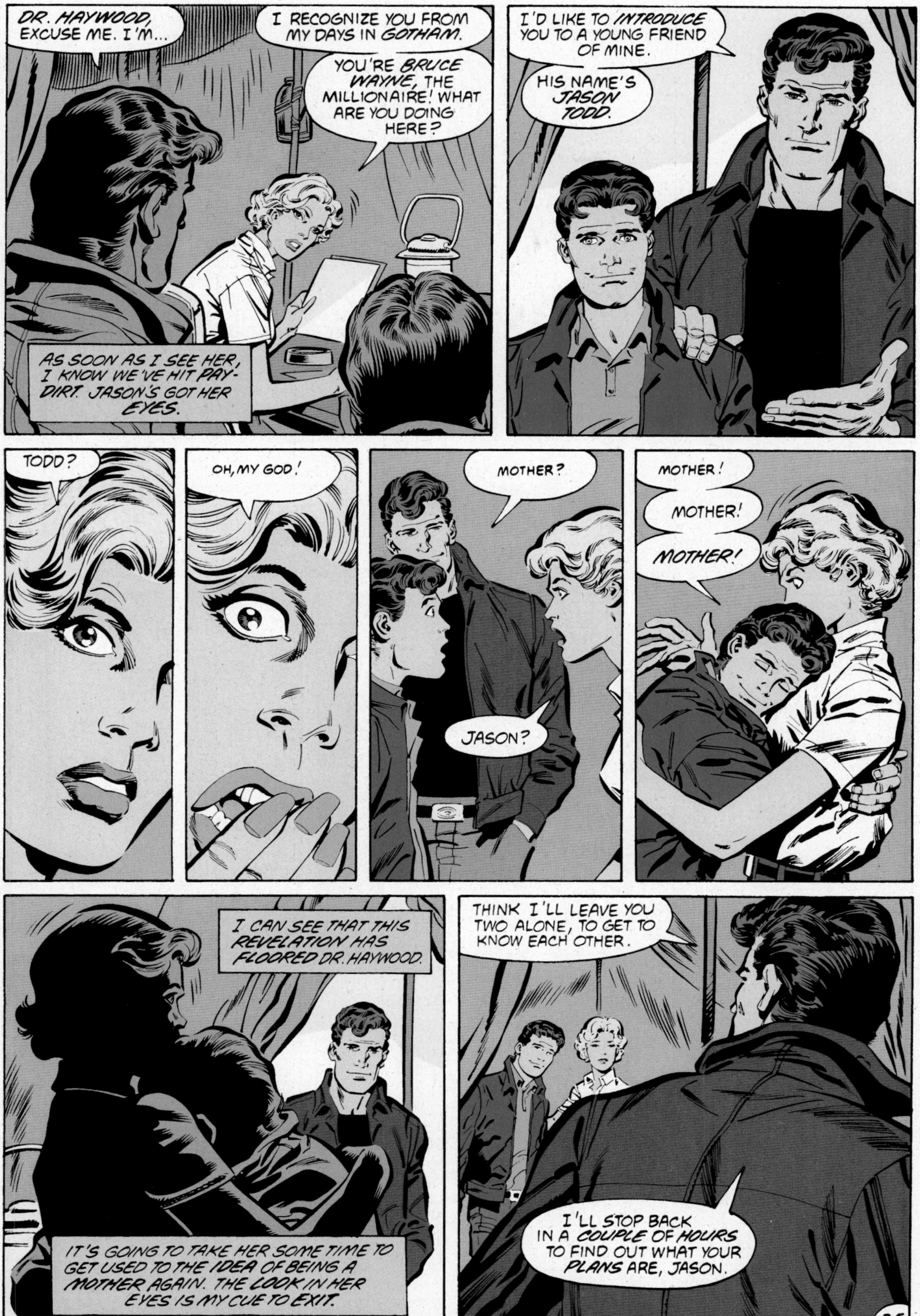
DR. HAYWOOD, EXCUSE ME. I'M...
I RECOGNIZE YOU FROM MY DAYS IN GOTHAM.
YOU'RE BRUCE WAYNE, THE MILLIONAIRE! WHAT ARE YOU DOING HERE?
AS SOON AS I SEE HER, I KNOW WE'VE HIT PAY-DIRT. JASON'S GOT HER EYES.
I'D LIKE TO INTRODUCE YOU TO A YOUNG FRIEND OF MINE.
HIS NAME'S JASON TODD.
TODD?
OH, MY GOD!
MOTHER?
JASON?
MOTHER!
MOTHER!
MOTHER!
I CAN SEE THAT THIS REVELATION HAS FLOORED DR. HAYWOOD.
IT'S GOING TO TAKE HER SOME TIME TO GET USED TO THE IDEA OF BEING A MOTHER AGAIN. THE LOOK IN HER EYES IS MY CUE TO EXIT.
THINK I'LL LEAVE YOU TWO ALONE, TO GET TO KNOW EACH OTHER.
I'LL STOP BACK IN A COUPLE OF HOURS TO FIND OUT WHAT YOUR PLANS ARE, JASON.
25

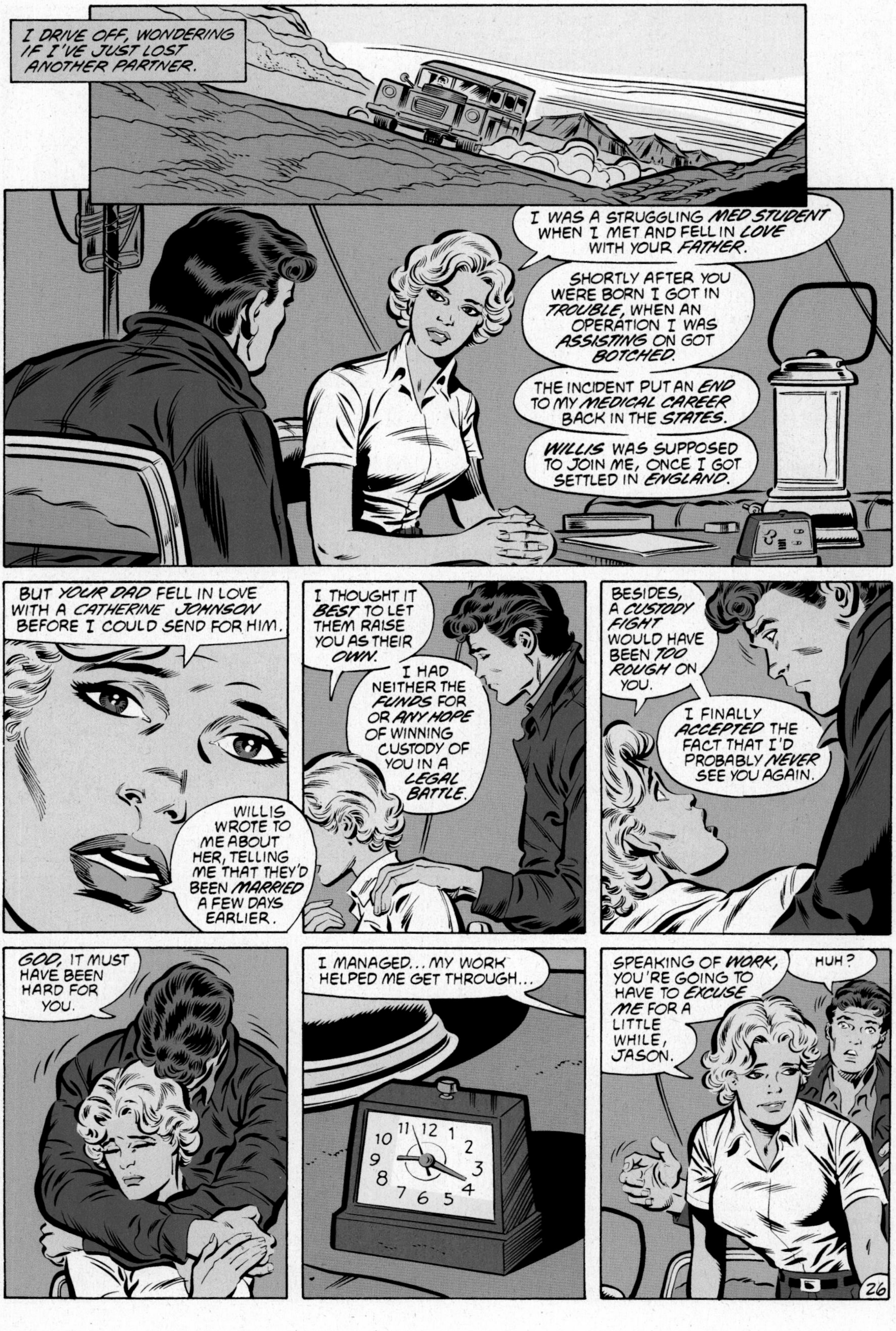
I DRIVE OFF, WONDERING IF I'VE JUST LOST ANOTHER PARTNER.
I WAS A STRUGGLING MED STUDENT WHEN I MET AND FELL IN LOVE WITH YOUR FATHER.
SHORTLY AFTER YOU WERE BORN I GOT IN TROUBLE, WHEN AN OPERATION I WAS ASSISTING ON GOT BOTCHED.
THE INCIDENT PUT AN END TO MY MEDICAL CAREER BACK IN THE STATES.
WILLIS WAS SUPPOSED TO JOIN ME, ONCE I GOT SETTLED IN ENGLAND.
BUT YOUR DAD FELL IN LOVE WITH A CATHERINE JOHNSON BEFORE I COULD SEND FOR HIM.
WILLIS WROTE TO ME ABOUT HER, TELLING ME THAT THEY'D BEEN MARRIED A FEW DAYS EARLIER.
I THOUGHT IT BEST TO LET THEM RAISE YOU AS THEIR OWN.
I HAD NEITHER THE FUNDS FOR OR ANY HOPE OF WINNING CUSTODY OF YOU IN A LEGAL BATTLE.
BESIDES, A CUSTODY FIGHT WOULD HAVE BEEN TOO ROUGH ON YOU.
I FINALLY ACCEPTED THE FACT THAT I'D PROBABLY NEVER SEE YOU AGAIN.
GOD, IT MUST HAVE BEEN HARD FOR YOU.
I MANAGED... MY WORK HELPED ME GET THROUGH...
SPEAKING OF WORK, YOU'RE GOING TO HAVE TO EXCUSE ME FOR A LITTLE WHILE, JASON.
HUH?
26

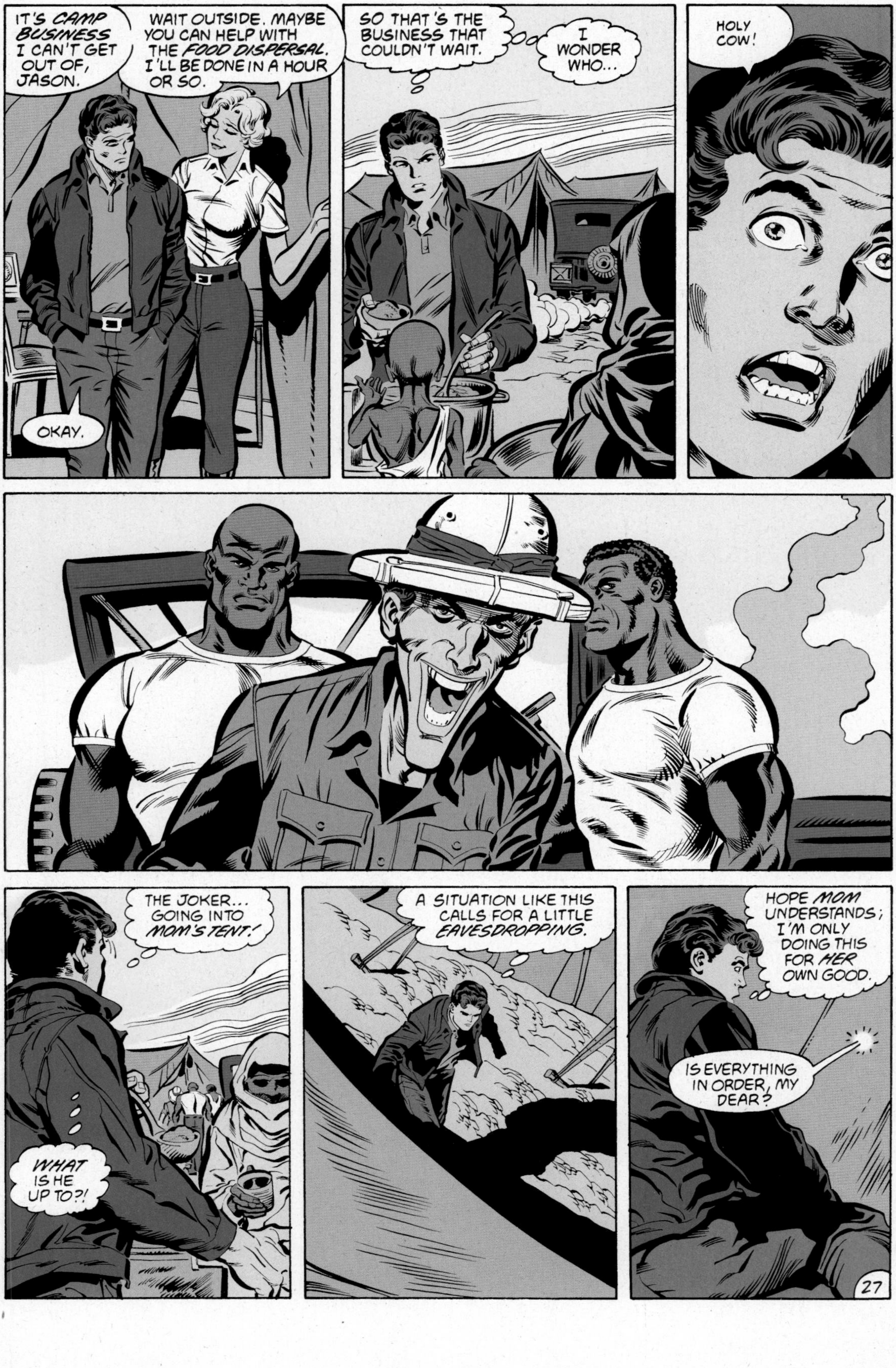

IT'S CAMP BUSINESS I CAN'T GET OUT OF, JASON.
WAIT OUTSIDE. MAYBE YOU CAN HELP WITH THE FOOD DISPERSAL. I'LL BE DONE IN A HOUR OR SO.
OKAY.
SO THAT'S THE BUSINESS THAT COULDN'T WAIT.
I WONDER WHO...
HOLY COW!
THE JOKER... GOING INTO MOM'S TENT!
WHAT IS HE UP TO?!
A SITUATION LIKE THIS CALLS FOR A LITTLE EAVESDROPPING.
HOPE MOM UNDERSTANDS; I'M ONLY DOING THIS FOR HER OWN GOOD.
IS EVERYTHING IN ORDER, MY DEAR?
27

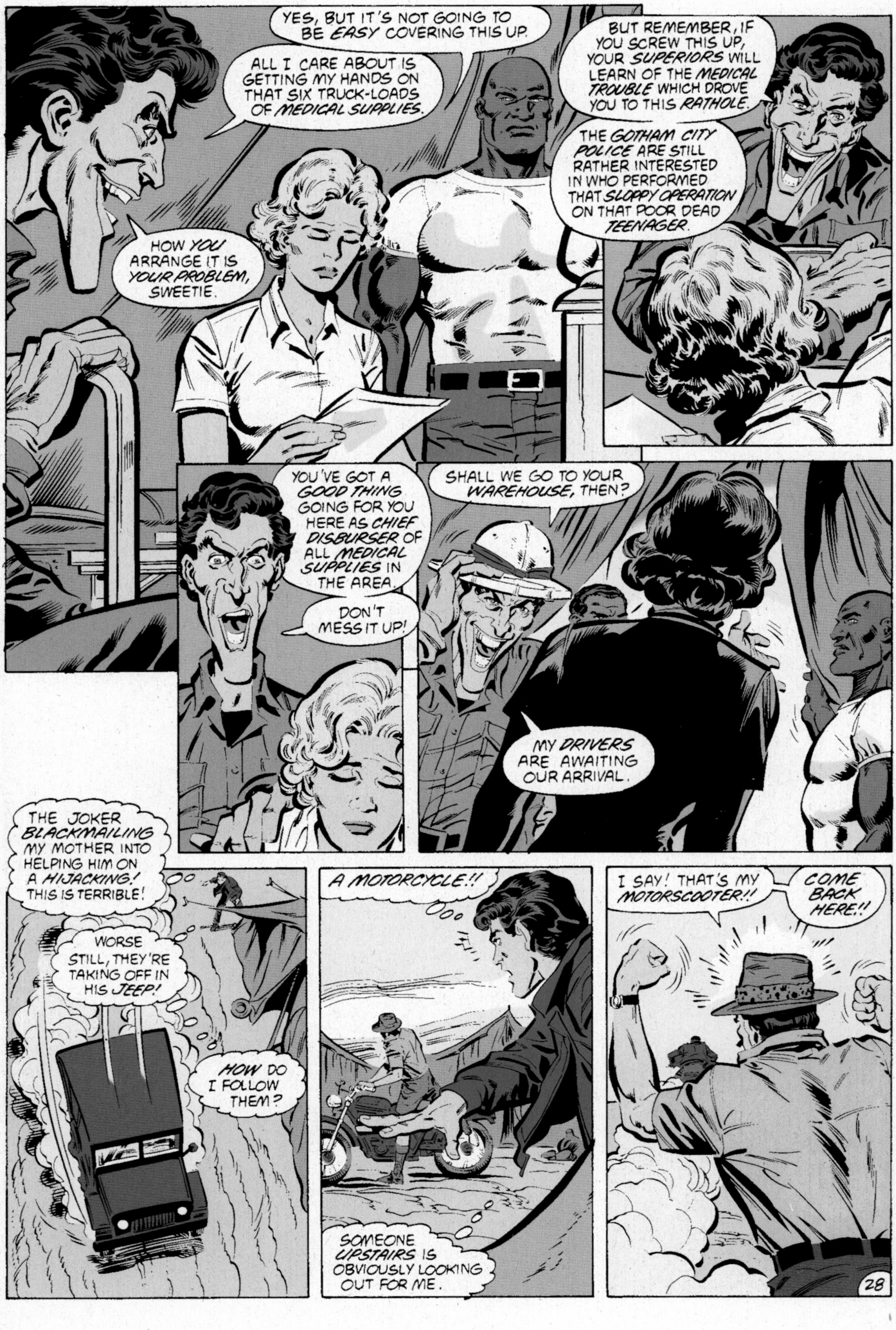
YES, BUT IT'S NOT GOING TO BE EASY COVERING THIS UP.
ALL I CARE ABOUT IS GETTING MY HANDS ON THAT SIX TRUCK-LOADS OF MEDICAL SUPPLIES.
HOW YOU ARRANGE IT IS YOUR PROBLEM, SWEETIE.
BUT REMEMBER, IF YOU SCREW THIS UP, YOUR SUPERIORS WILL LEARN OF THE MEDICAL TROUBLE WHICH DROVE YOU TO THIS RATHOLE.
THE GOTHAM CITY POLICE ARE STILL RATHER INTERESTED IN WHO PERFORMED THAT SLOPPY OPERATION ON THAT POOR DEAD TEENAGER.
YOU'VE GOT A GOOD THING GOING FOR YOU HERE AS CHIEF DISBURSER OF ALL MEDICAL SUPPLIES IN THE AREA.
DON'T MESS IT UP!
SHALL WE GO TO YOUR WAREHOUSE, THEN?
MY DRIVERS ARE AWAITING OUR ARRIVAL.
THE JOKER BLACKMAILING MY MOTHER INTO HELPING HIM ON A HIJACKING! THIS IS TERRIBLE!
WORSE STILL, THEY'RE TAKING OFF IN HIS JEEP!
HOW DO I FOLLOW THEM?
A MOTORCYCLE!!
SOMEONE UPSTAIRS IS OBVIOUSLY LOOKING OUT FOR ME.
I SAY! THAT'S MY MOTORSCOOTER!!
COME BACK HERE!!
28

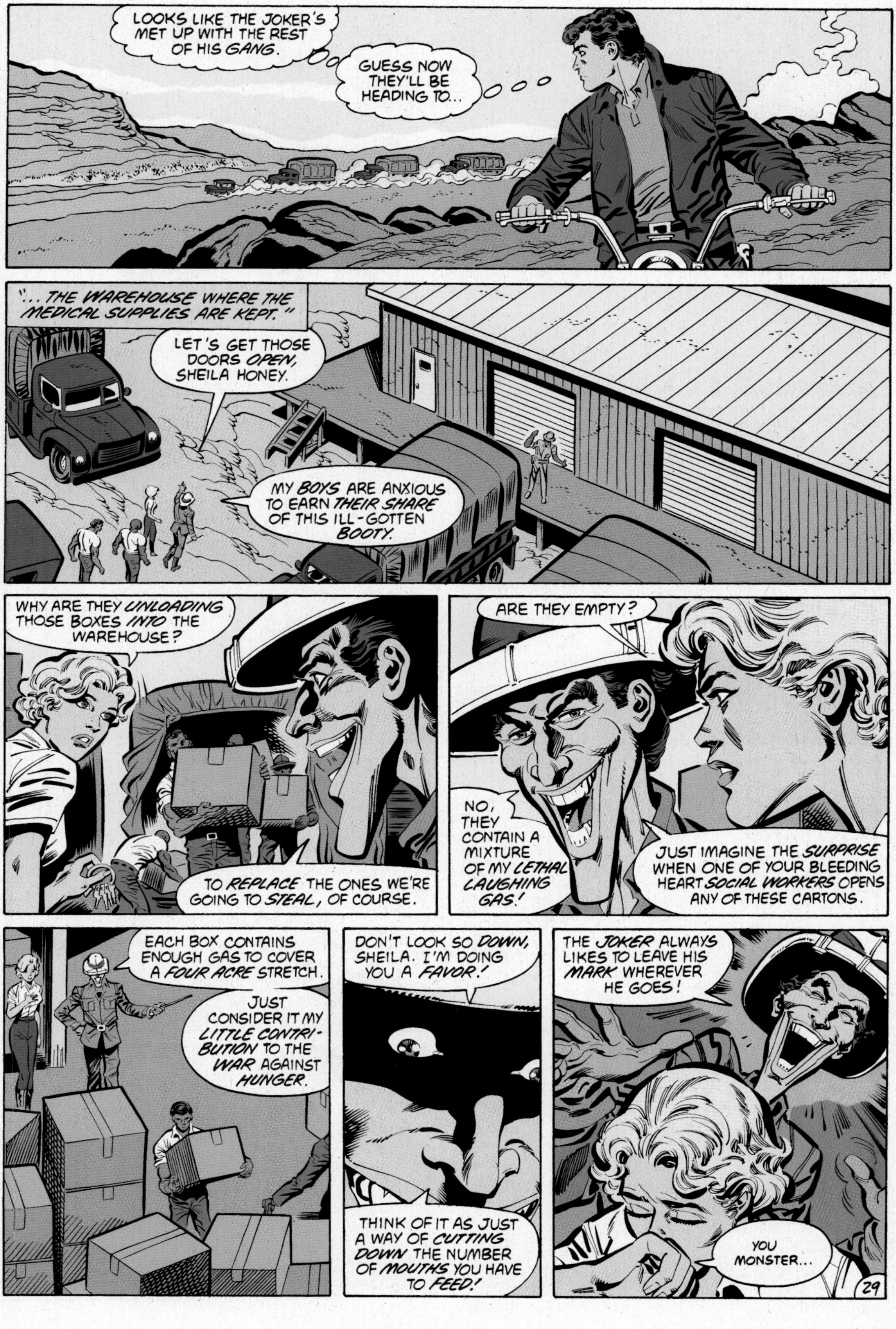
LOOKS LIKE THE JOKER'S MET UP WITH THE REST OF HIS GANG.
GUESS NOW THEY'LL BE HEADING TO...
"...THE WAREHOUSE WHERE THE MEDICAL SUPPLIES ARE KEPT."
LET'S GET THOSE DOORS OPEN, SHEILA HONEY.
MY BOYS ARE ANXIOUS TO EARN THEIR SHARE OF THIS ILL-GOTTEN BOOTY.
WHY ARE THEY UNLOADING THOSE BOXES INTO THE WAREHOUSE?
TO REPLACE THE ONES WE'RE GOING TO STEAL, OF COURSE.
ARE THEY EMPTY?
NO, THEY CONTAIN A MIXTURE OF MY LETHAL LAUGHING GAS!
JUST IMAGINE THE SURPRISE WHEN ONE OF YOUR BLEEDING HEART SOCIAL WORKERS OPENS ANY OF THESE CARTONS.
EACH BOX CONTAINS ENOUGH GAS TO COVER A FOUR ACRE STRETCH.
JUST CONSIDER IT MY LITTLE CONTRIBUTION TO THE WAR AGAINST HUNGER.
DON'T LOOK SO DOWN, SHEILA. I'M DOING YOU A FAVOR!
THINK OF IT AS JUST A WAY OF CUTTING DOWN THE NUMBER OF MOUTHS YOU HAVE TO FEED!
THE JOKER ALWAYS LIKES TO LEAVE HIS MARK WHEREVER HE GOES!
YOU MONSTER...
29

YOU SAID IT, MA. BUT DON'T WORRY, *I'LL GET YOU OUT OF THIS MESS.*

UNFORTUNATELY, THERE'S MORE TROUBLE HERE THAN I CAN HANDLE ON MY *OWN.*

THIS LOOKS LIKE A JOB FOR *BATMAN* AND *ROBIN.*

BRUCE! BOY, AM I *GLAD* TO SEE YOU!

WHAT'S GOING ON, JASON?!

WE'VE GOT *JOKER TROUBLE!*

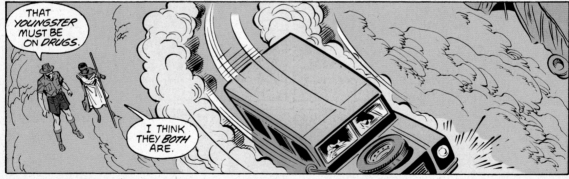

THAT *YOUNGSTER* MUST BE ON *DRUGS.*

I THINK THEY *BOTH* ARE.

LOOKS LIKE WE MADE IT BACK JUST IN TIME! THERE GOES THE *JOKER'S* CONVOY NOW!

NO!

30

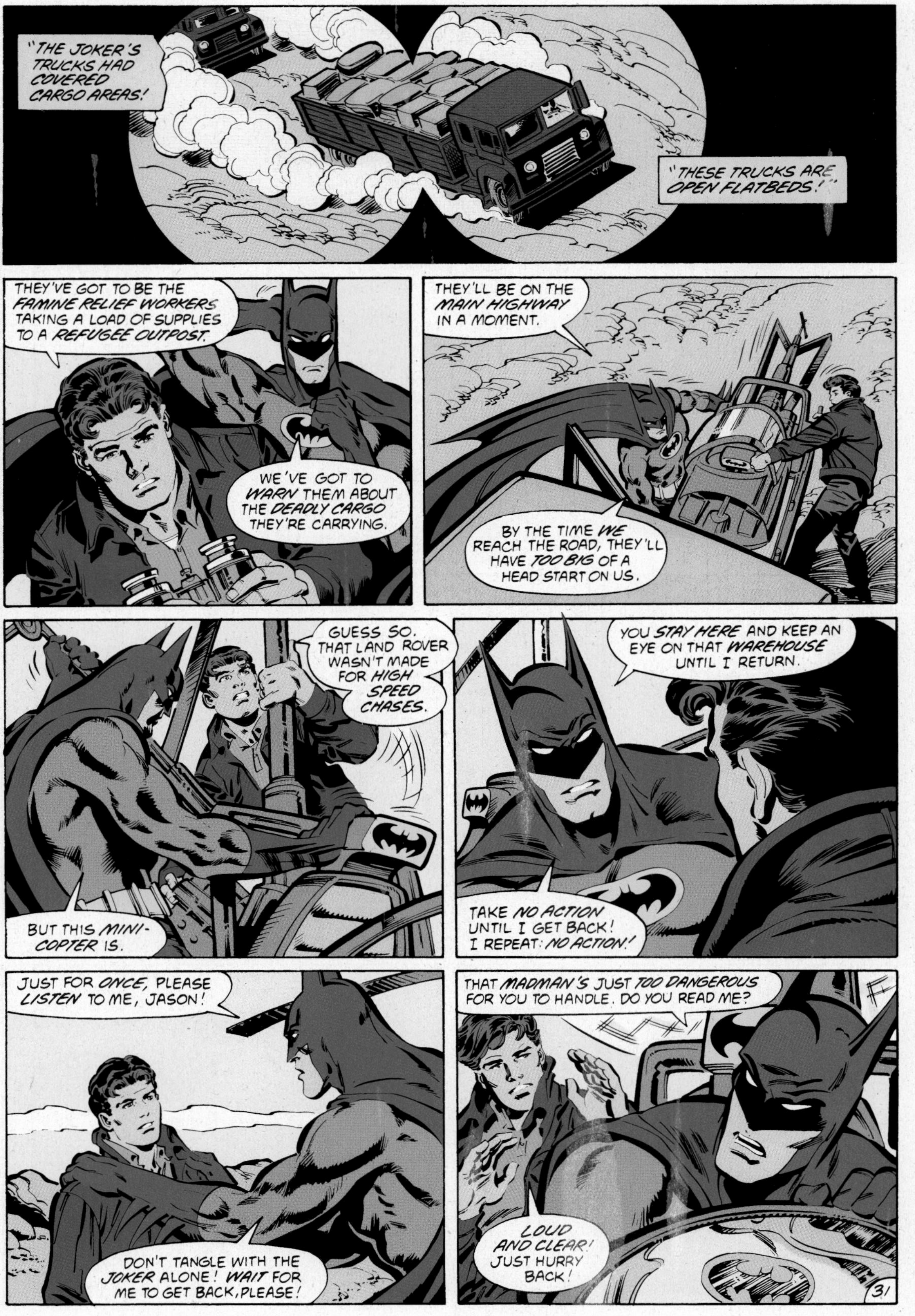

"THE JOKER'S TRUCKS HAD COVERED CARGO AREAS!
"THESE TRUCKS ARE OPEN FLATBEDS!"
THEY'VE GOT TO BE THE FAMINE RELIEF WORKERS TAKING A LOAD OF SUPPLIES TO A REFUGEE OUTPOST.
WE'VE GOT TO WARN THEM ABOUT THE DEADLY CARGO THEY'RE CARRYING.
THEY'LL BE ON THE MAIN HIGHWAY IN A MOMENT.
BY THE TIME WE REACH THE ROAD, THEY'LL HAVE TOO BIG OF A HEAD START ON US.
GUESS SO. THAT LAND ROVER WASN'T MADE FOR HIGH SPEED CHASES.
BUT THIS MINI-COPTER IS.
YOU STAY HERE AND KEEP AN EYE ON THAT WAREHOUSE UNTIL I RETURN.
TAKE NO ACTION UNTIL I GET BACK! I REPEAT: NO ACTION!
JUST FOR ONCE, PLEASE LISTEN TO ME, JASON!
DON'T TANGLE WITH THE JOKER ALONE! WAIT FOR ME TO GET BACK, PLEASE!
THAT MADMAN'S JUST TOO DANGEROUS FOR YOU TO HANDLE. DO YOU READ ME?
LOUD AND CLEAR! JUST HURRY BACK!
31

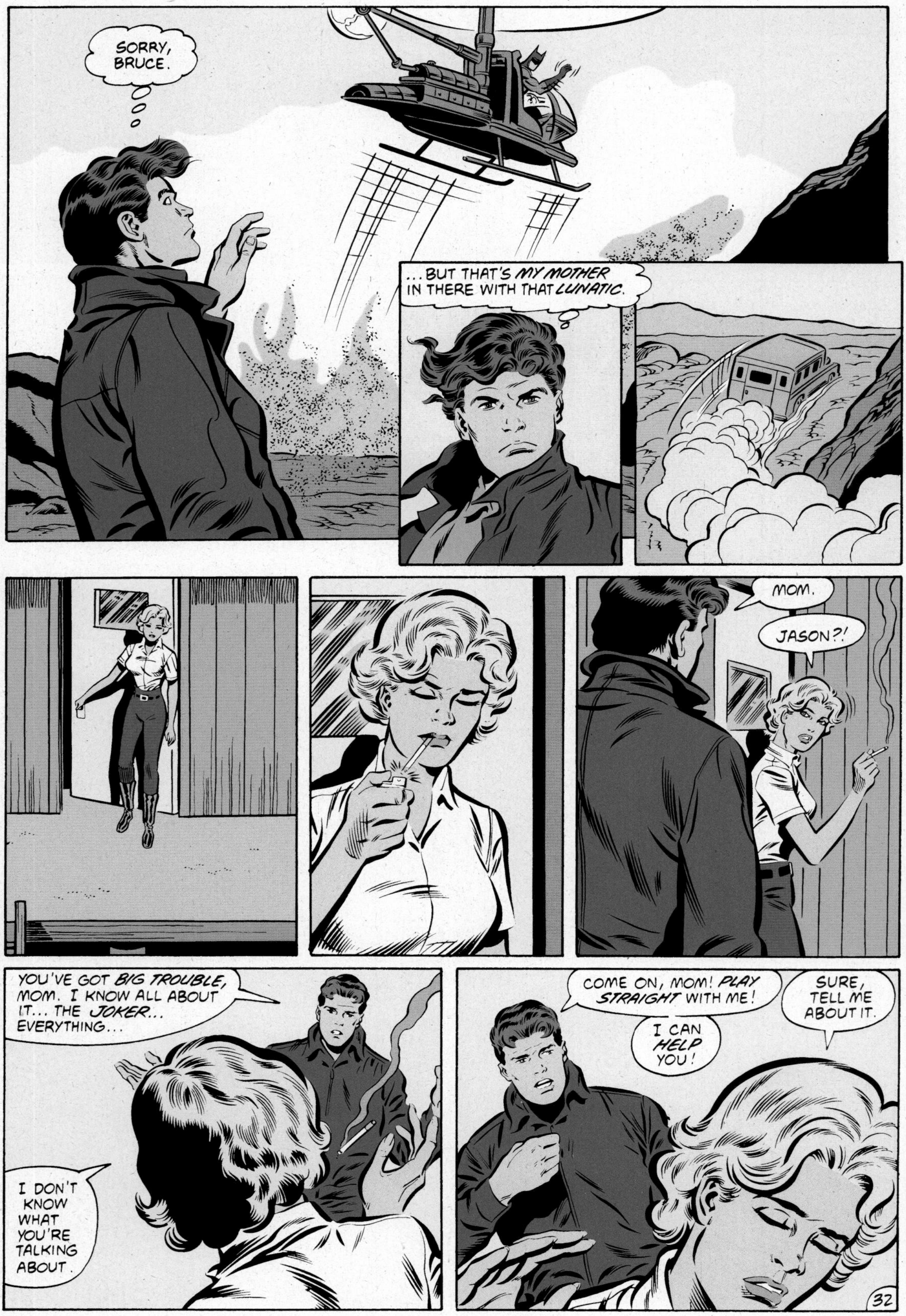
SORRY, BRUCE.
...BUT THAT'S MY MOTHER IN THERE WITH THAT LUNATIC.
MOM.
JASON?!
YOU'VE GOT BIG TROUBLE, MOM. I KNOW ALL ABOUT IT... THE JOKER... EVERYTHING...
I DON'T KNOW WHAT YOU'RE TALKING ABOUT.
COME ON, MOM! PLAY STRAIGHT WITH ME!
I CAN HELP YOU!
SURE, TELL ME ABOUT IT.
32

MOTHER, THERE'S A *LOT* ABOUT ME YOU *DON'T KNOW.*

HUH?

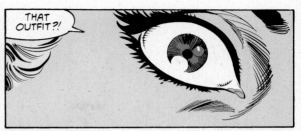

THAT OUTFIT?!

YOU'RE...

COME WITH ME.

WAIT! THE JOKER...

...IS LONG *GONE.* THERE'S *NOTHING* TO WORRY ABOUT. BUT I'VE *SOMETHING* YOU SHOULD SEE.

WHAT? WHAT'S GOING ON HERE?

JUST STEP OVER HERE AND YOU'LL *UNDER-STAND* EVERY-THING... *ROBIN.*

WHAT?!

BUT YOU SAID...

33

I LIED.

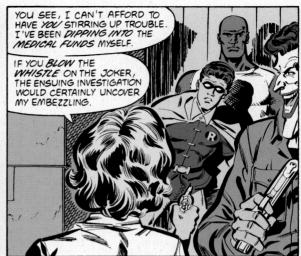

YOU SEE, I CAN'T AFFORD TO HAVE *YOU* STIRRING UP TROUBLE. I'VE BEEN *DIPPING INTO* THE *MEDICAL FUNDS* MYSELF.

IF YOU *BLOW* THE *WHISTLE* ON THE JOKER, THE ENSUING INVESTIGATION WOULD CERTAINLY UNCOVER MY EMBEZZLING.

SORRY ABOUT THAT, KID. LOOKS LIKE YOU CHOSE THE *WRONG PERSON* TO TRUST, THIS TIME.

WHAT SHOULD WE DO WITH HIM?

SOMETHING I'VE WANTED TO DO FOR *YEARS*...

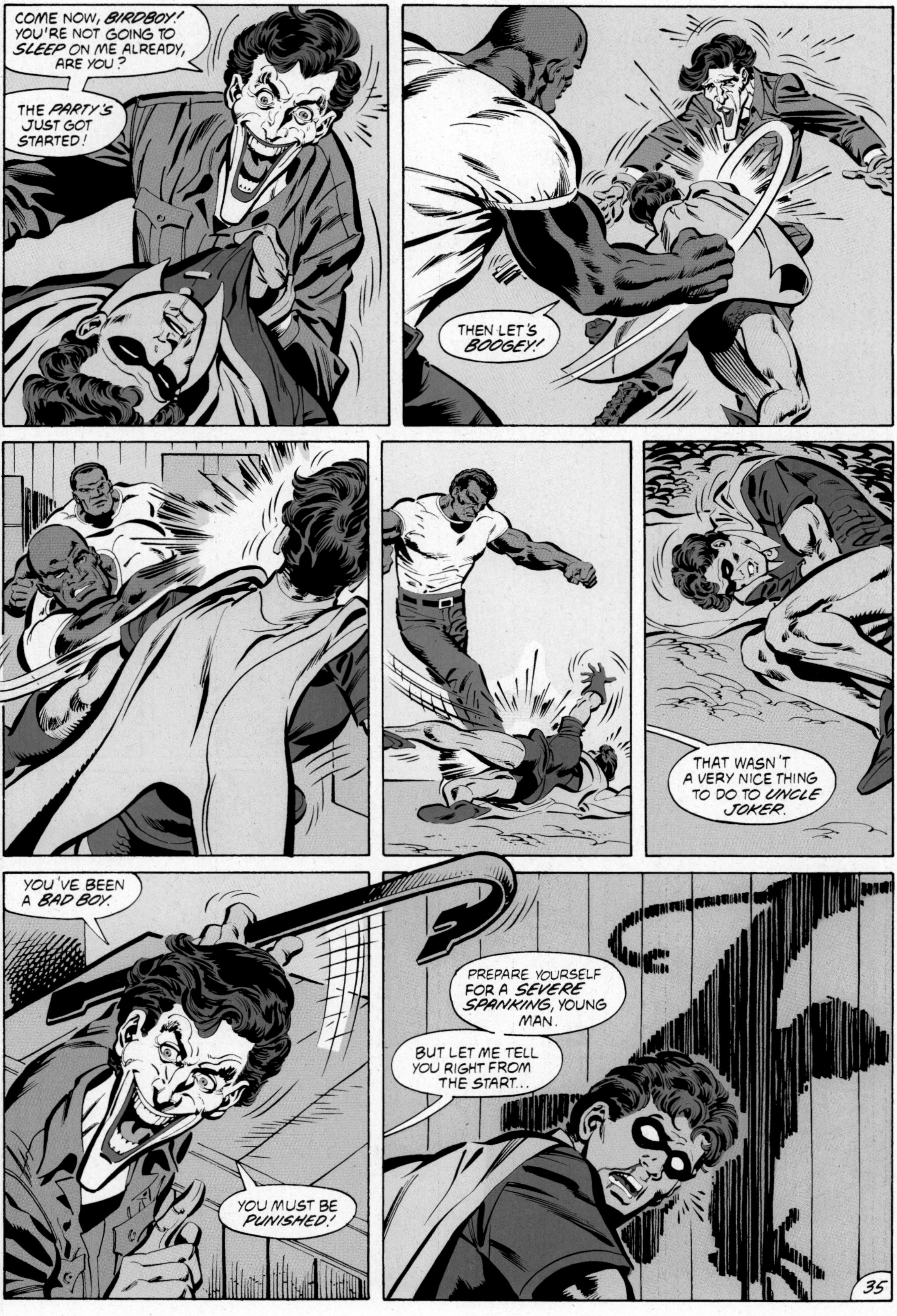
COME NOW, BIRDBOY! YOU'RE NOT GOING TO SLEEP ON ME ALREADY, ARE YOU?
THE PARTY'S JUST GOT STARTED!
THEN LET'S BOOGEY!
THAT WASN'T A VERY NICE THING TO DO TO UNCLE JOKER.
YOU'VE BEEN A BAD BOY.
YOU MUST BE PUNISHED!
PREPARE YOURSELF FOR A SEVERE SPANKING, YOUNG MAN.
BUT LET ME TELL YOU RIGHT FROM THE START...
35

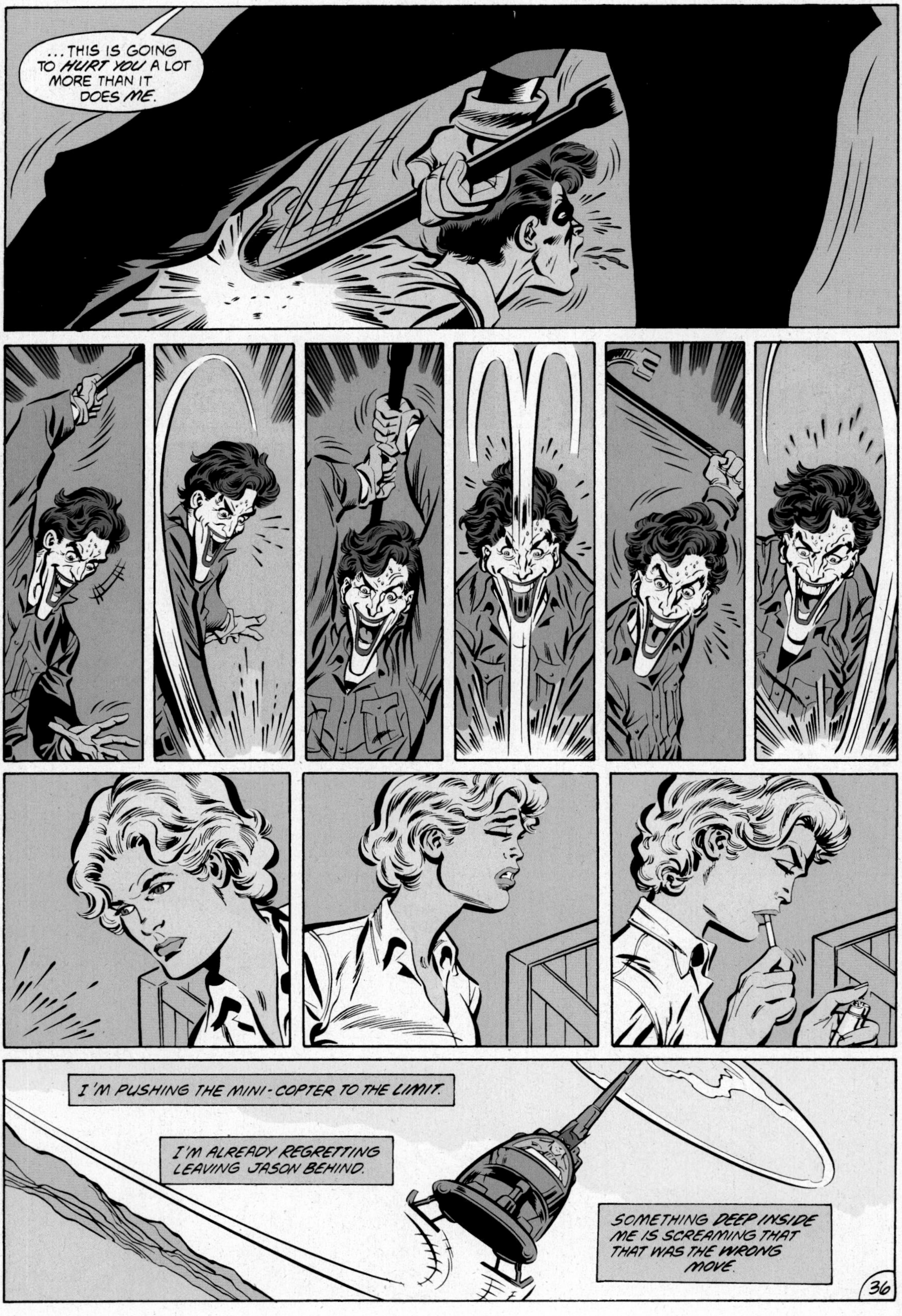

...THIS IS GOING TO HURT YOU A LOT MORE THAN IT DOES ME.
I'M PUSHING THE MINI-COPTER TO THE LIMIT.
I'M ALREADY REGRETTING LEAVING JASON BEHIND.
SOMETHING DEEP INSIDE ME IS SCREAMING THAT THAT WAS THE WRONG MOVE.
36

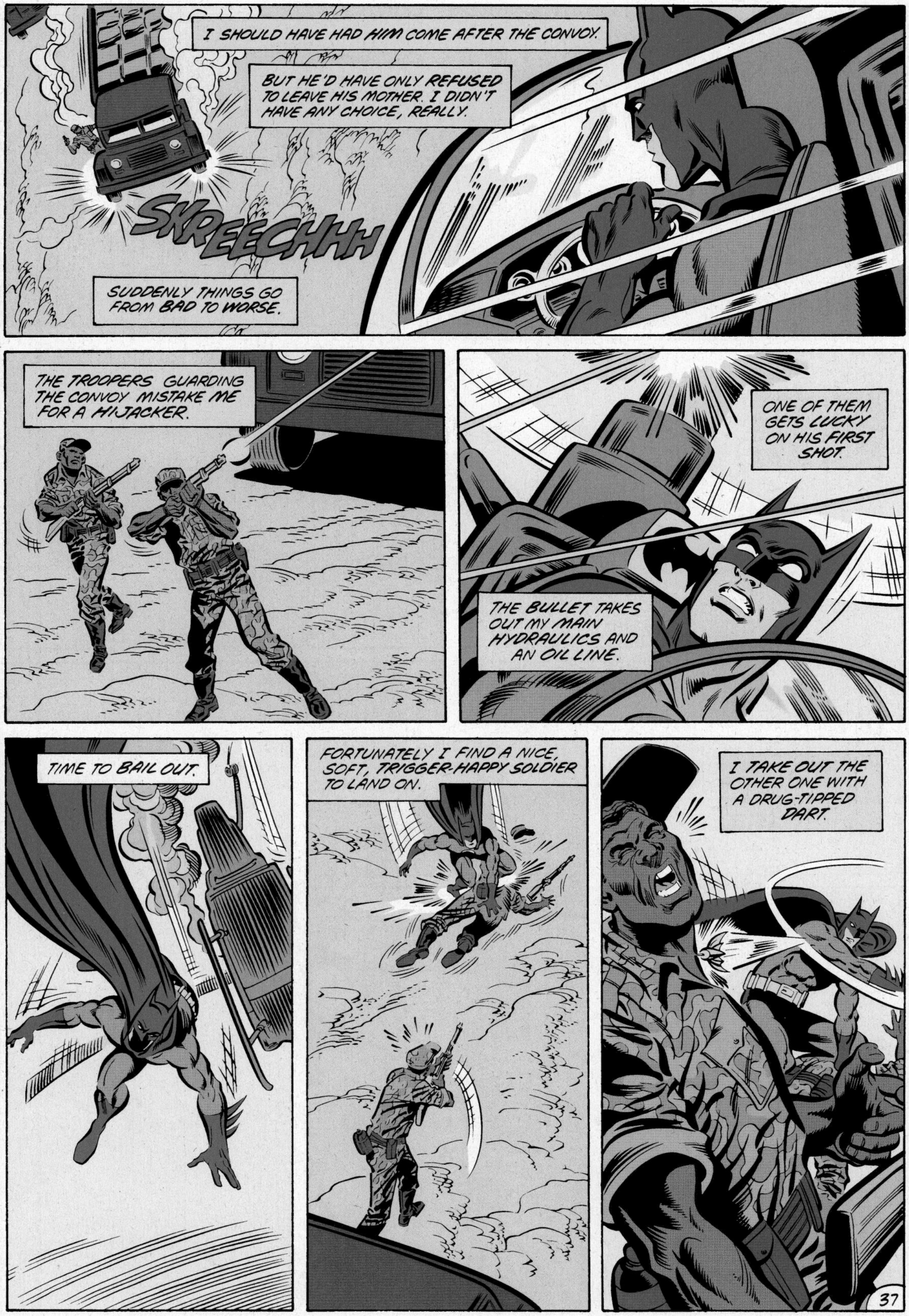
I SHOULD HAVE HAD HIM COME AFTER THE CONVOY.
BUT HE'D HAVE ONLY REFUSED TO LEAVE HIS MOTHER. I DIDN'T HAVE ANY CHOICE, REALLY.
SKREECHHH
SUDDENLY THINGS GO FROM BAD TO WORSE.
THE TROOPERS GUARDING THE CONVOY MISTAKE ME FOR A HIJACKER.
ONE OF THEM GETS LUCKY ON HIS FIRST SHOT.
THE BULLET TAKES OUT MY MAIN HYDRAULICS AND AN OIL LINE.
TIME TO BAIL OUT.
FORTUNATELY I FIND A NICE, SOFT, TRIGGER-HAPPY SOLDIER TO LAND ON.
I TAKE OUT THE OTHER ONE WITH A DRUG-TIPPED DART.
37

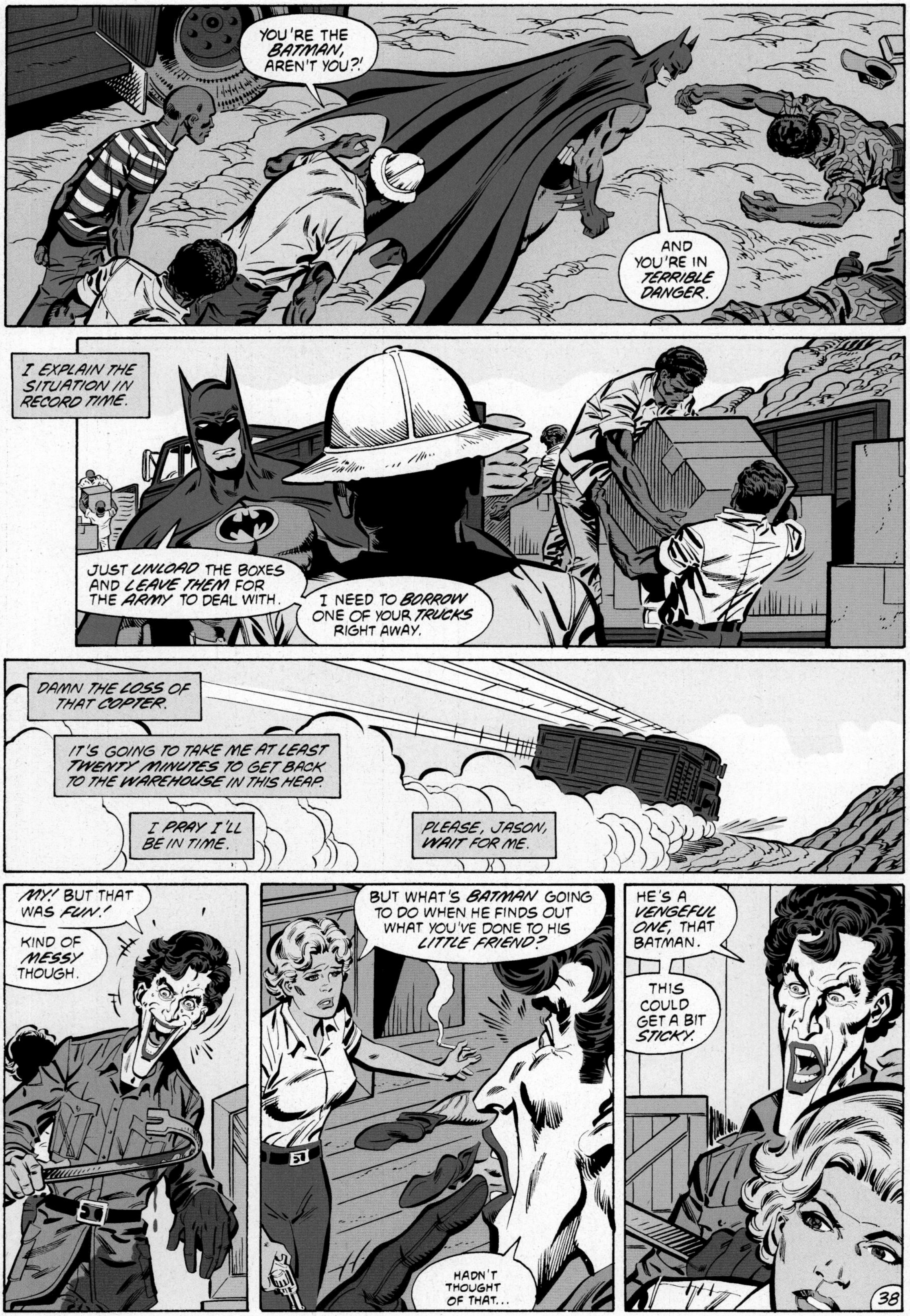
YOU'RE THE BATMAN, AREN'T YOU?!
AND YOU'RE IN TERRIBLE DANGER.
I EXPLAIN THE SITUATION IN RECORD TIME.
JUST UNLOAD THE BOXES AND LEAVE THEM FOR THE ARMY TO DEAL WITH.
I NEED TO BORROW ONE OF YOUR TRUCKS RIGHT AWAY.
DAMN THE LOSS OF THAT COPTER.
IT'S GOING TO TAKE ME AT LEAST TWENTY MINUTES TO GET BACK TO THE WAREHOUSE IN THIS HEAP.
I PRAY I'LL BE IN TIME.
PLEASE, JASON, WAIT FOR ME.
MY! BUT THAT WAS FUN!
KIND OF MESSY THOUGH.
BUT WHAT'S BATMAN GOING TO DO WHEN HE FINDS OUT WHAT YOU'VE DONE TO HIS LITTLE FRIEND?
HADN'T THOUGHT OF THAT...
HE'S A VENGEFUL ONE, THAT BATMAN.
THIS COULD GET A BIT STICKY.
38

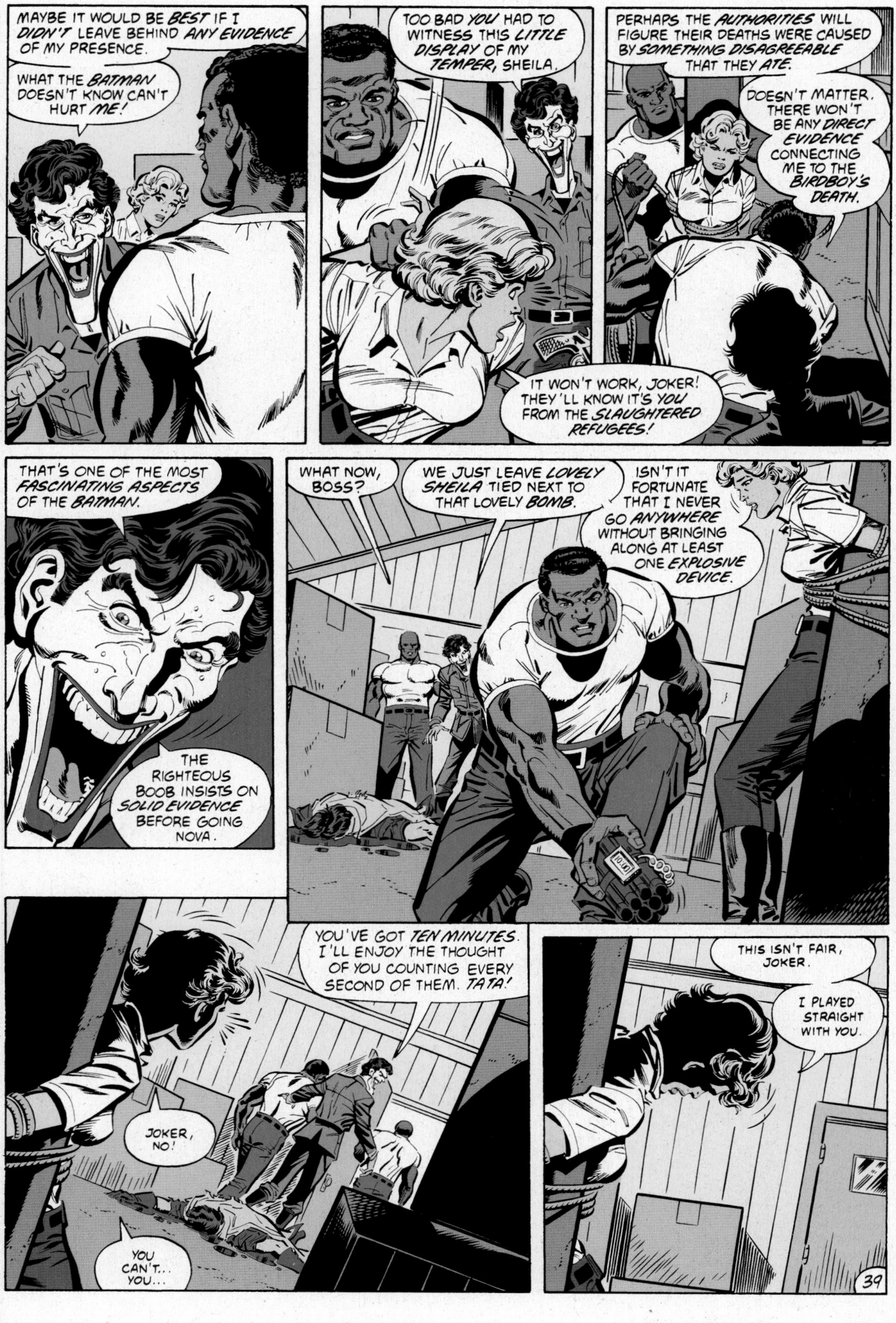
MAYBE IT WOULD BE BEST IF I DIDN'T LEAVE BEHIND ANY EVIDENCE OF MY PRESENCE.
WHAT THE BATMAN DOESN'T KNOW CAN'T HURT ME!
TOO BAD YOU HAD TO WITNESS THIS LITTLE DISPLAY OF MY TEMPER, SHEILA.
PERHAPS THE AUTHORITIES WILL FIGURE THEIR DEATHS WERE CAUSED BY SOMETHING DISAGREEABLE THAT THEY ATE.
DOESN'T MATTER. THERE WON'T BE ANY DIRECT EVIDENCE CONNECTING ME TO THE BIRDBOY'S DEATH.
IT WON'T WORK, JOKER! THEY'LL KNOW IT'S YOU FROM THE SLAUGHTERED REFUGEES!
THAT'S ONE OF THE MOST FASCINATING ASPECTS OF THE BATMAN.
THE RIGHTEOUS BOOB INSISTS ON SOLID EVIDENCE BEFORE GOING NOVA.
WHAT NOW, BOSS?
WE JUST LEAVE LOVELY SHEILA TIED NEXT TO THAT LOVELY BOMB.
ISN'T IT FORTUNATE THAT I NEVER GO ANYWHERE WITHOUT BRINGING ALONG AT LEAST ONE EXPLOSIVE DEVICE.
YOU'VE GOT TEN MINUTES. I'LL ENJOY THE THOUGHT OF YOU COUNTING EVERY SECOND OF THEM. TATA!
JOKER, NO!
YOU CAN'T... YOU...
THIS ISN'T FAIR, JOKER.
I PLAYED STRAIGHT WITH YOU.
39

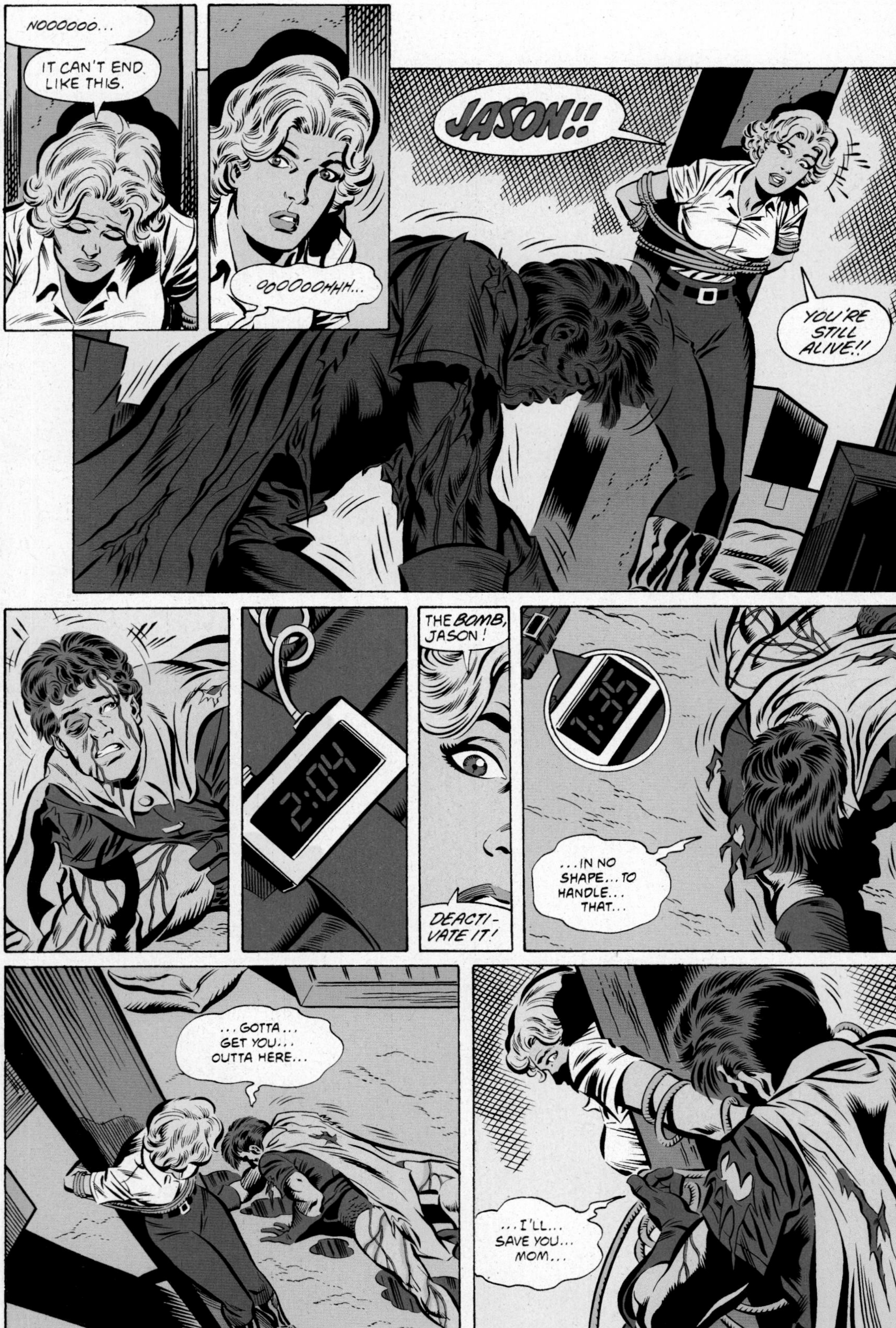
NOOOOOO...
IT CAN'T END LIKE THIS.
OOOOOOHHH...
JASON!!
YOU'RE STILL ALIVE!!
THE BOMB, JASON!
DEACTI-VATE IT!
...IN NO SHAPE...TO HANDLE... THAT...
...GOTTA... GET YOU... OUTTA HERE...
...I'LL... SAVE YOU... MOM...
40

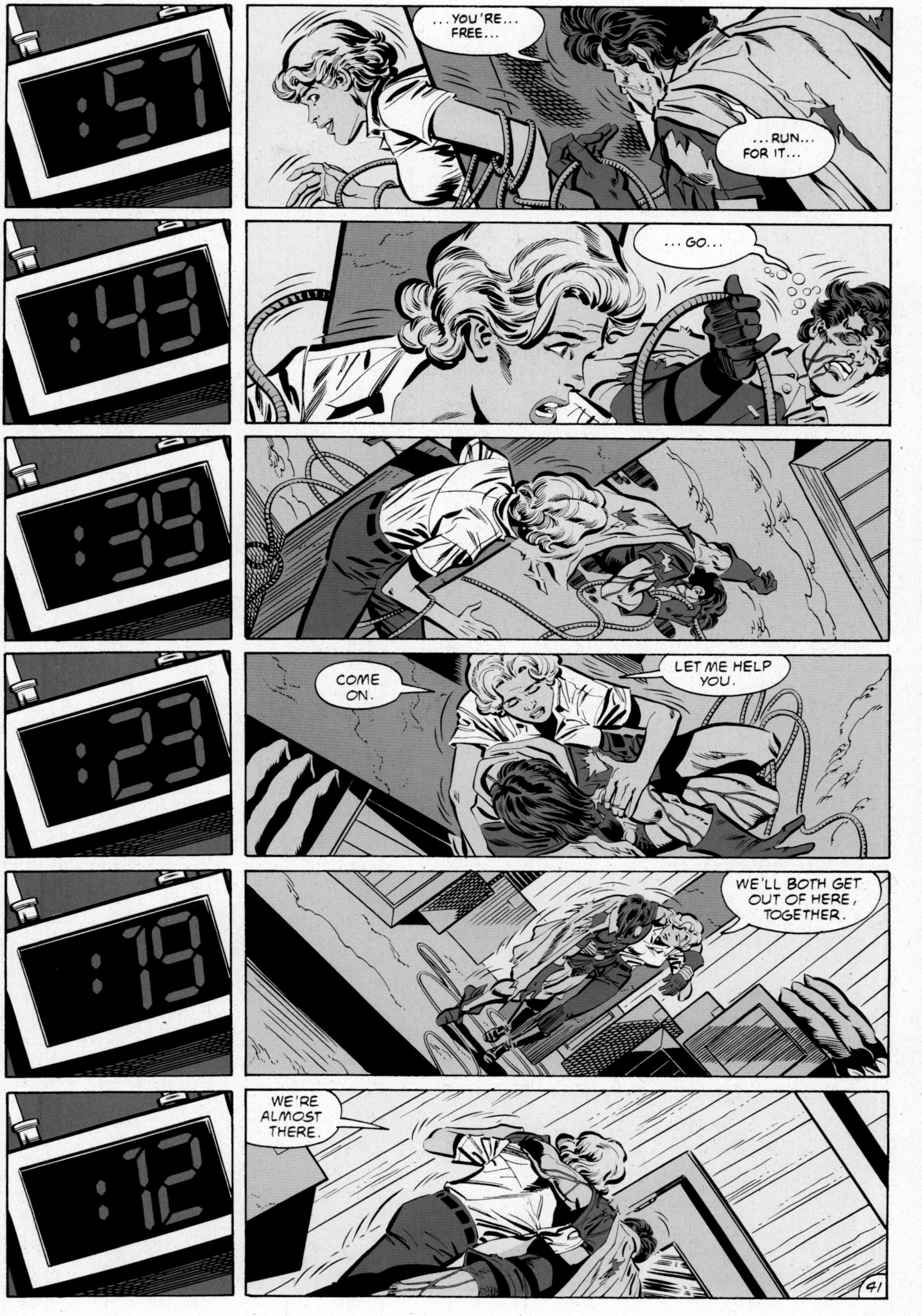
:57
...YOU'RE... FREE...
...RUN... FOR IT...
:43
...GO...
:39
:23
COME ON.
LET ME HELP YOU.
:19
WE'LL BOTH GET OUT OF HERE, TOGETHER.
:12
WE'RE ALMOST THERE.
41

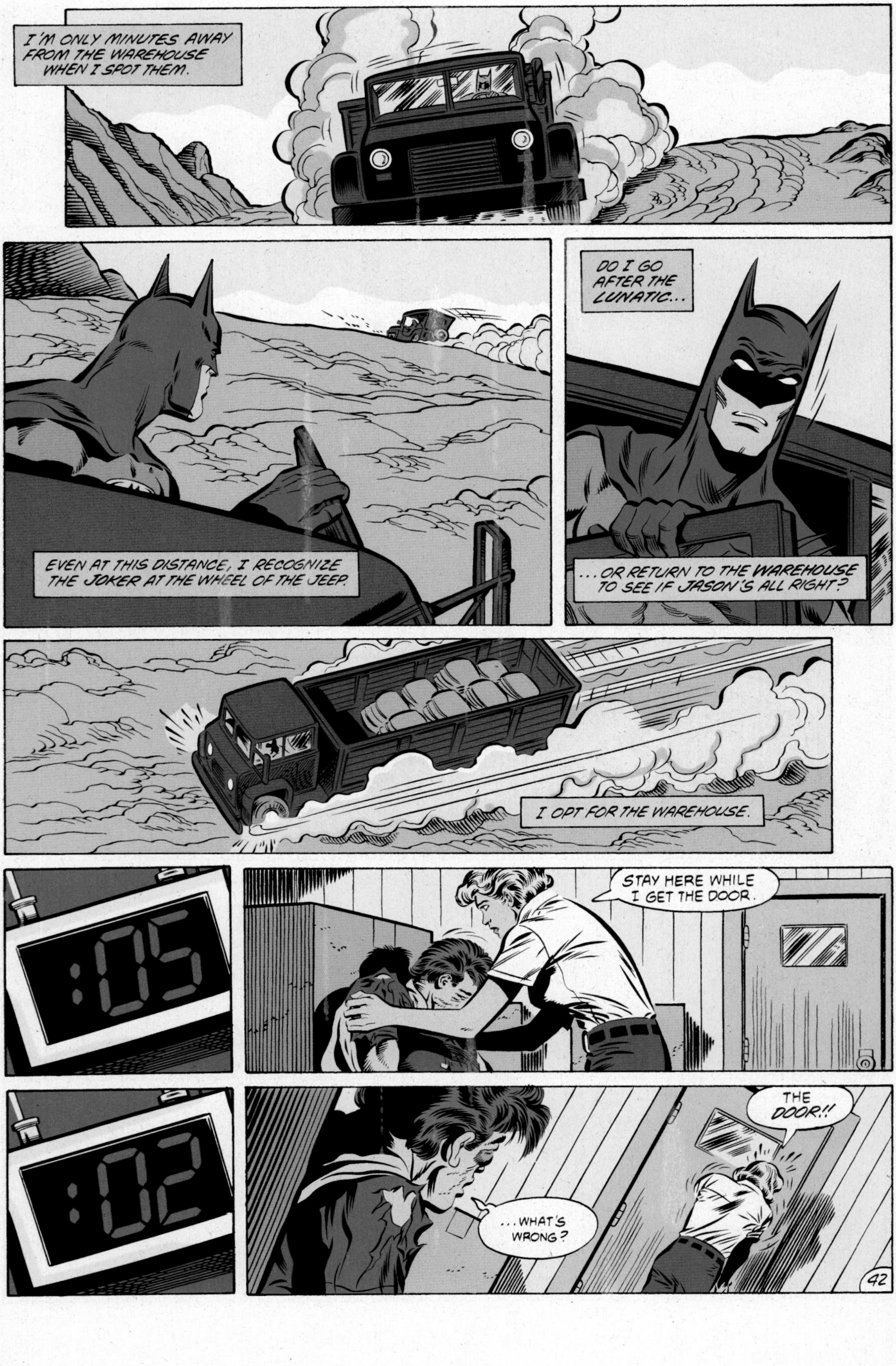

I'M ONLY MINUTES AWAY FROM THE WAREHOUSE WHEN I SPOT THEM.
EVEN AT THIS DISTANCE, I RECOGNIZE THE JOKER AT THE WHEEL OF THE JEEP.
DO I GO AFTER THE LUNATIC...
...OR RETURN TO THE WAREHOUSE TO SEE IF JASON'S ALL RIGHT?
I OPT FOR THE WAREHOUSE.
:05
STAY HERE WHILE I GET THE DOOR.
:02
THE DOOR!!
...WHAT'S WRONG?
42

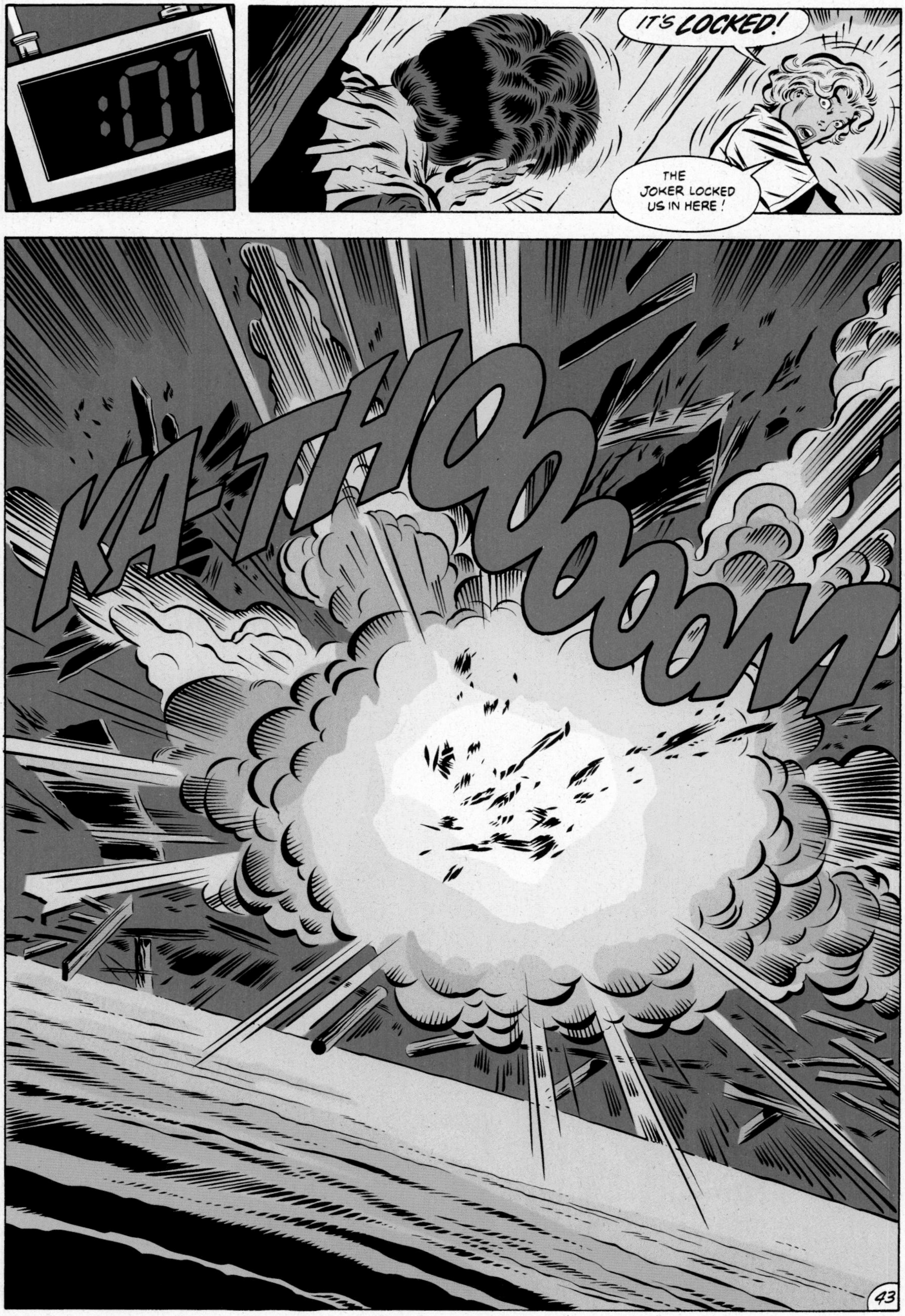

:01
IT'S LOCKED!
THE JOKER LOCKED US IN HERE!
KA-THOOOOOOM
43

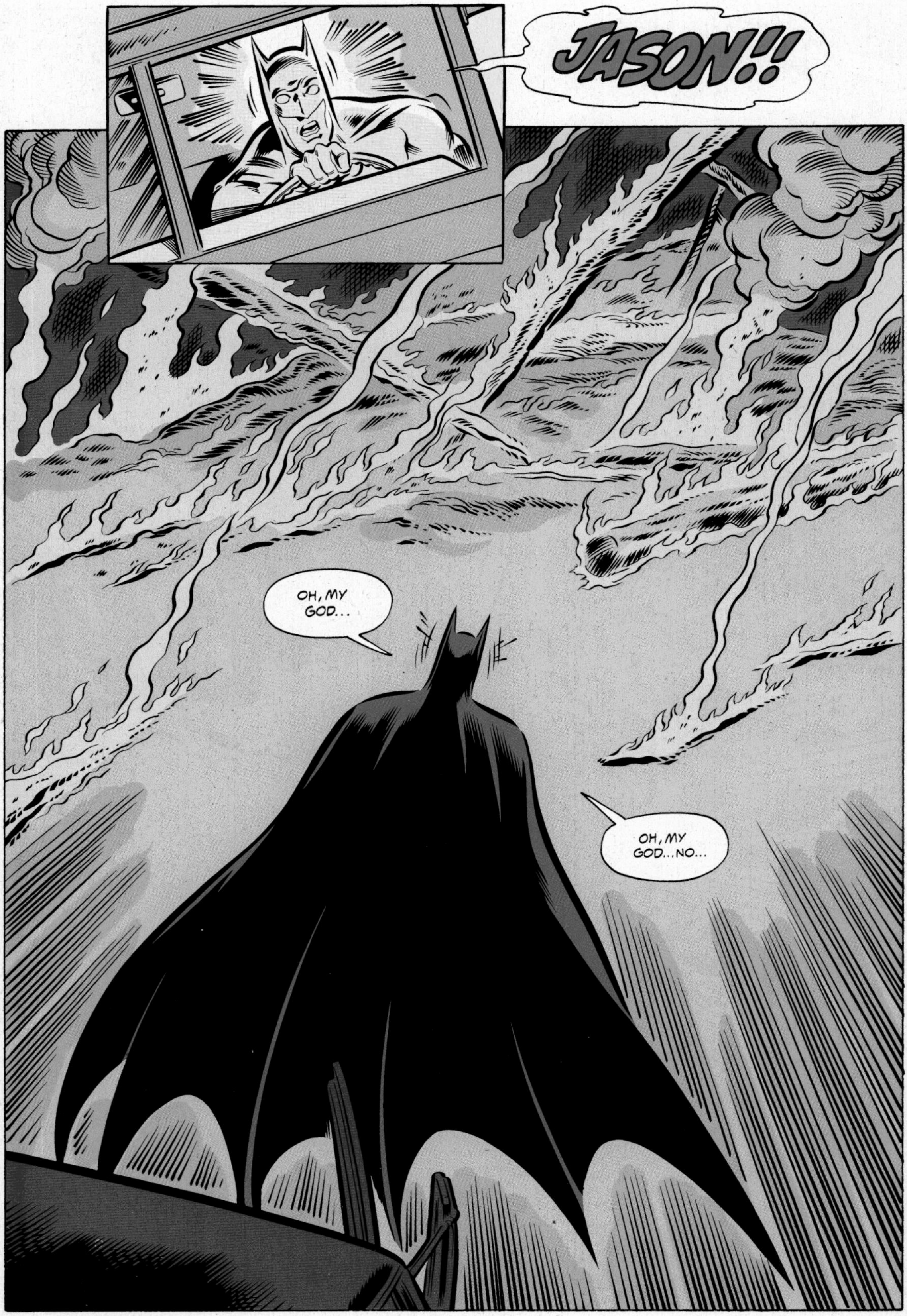
JASON!!
OH, MY GOD...
OH, MY GOD...NO...

Original advertisement — phone numbers are no longer valid.

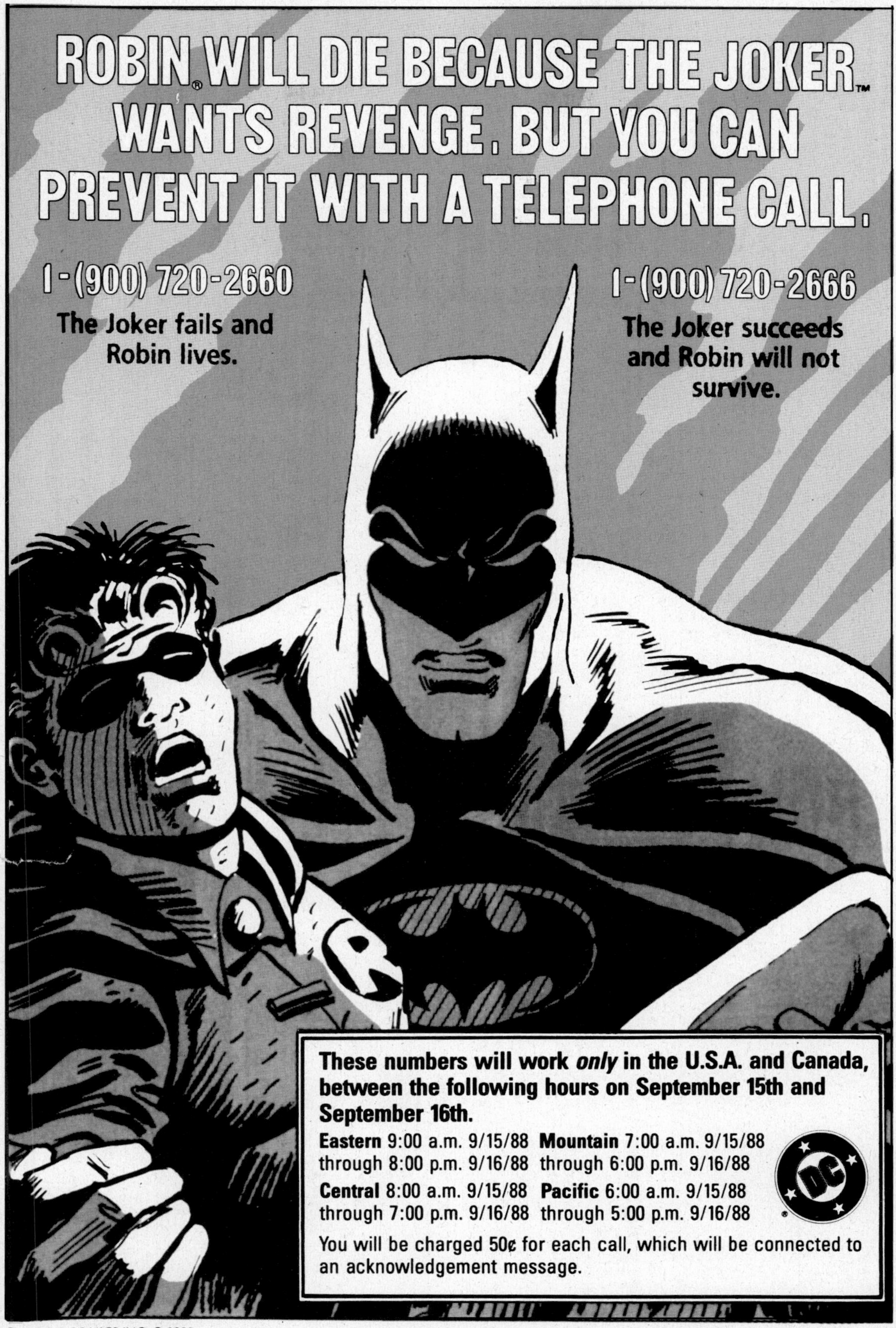

ROBIN® WILL DIE BECAUSE THE JOKER™ WANTS REVENGE. BUT YOU CAN PREVENT IT WITH A TELEPHONE CALL.
1-(900) 720-2660
The Joker fails and Robin lives.
1-(900) 720-2666
The Joker succeeds and Robin will not survive.
These numbers will work only in the U.S.A. and Canada, between the following hours on September 15th and September 16th.
Eastern 9:00 a.m. 9/15/88 through 8:00 p.m. 9/16/88
Mountain 7:00 a.m. 9/15/88 through 6:00 p.m. 9/16/88
Central 8:00 a.m. 9/15/88 through 7:00 p.m. 9/16/88
Pacific 6:00 a.m. 9/15/88 through 5:00 p.m. 9/16/88
You will be charged 50¢ for each call, which will be connected to an acknowledgement message.
DC

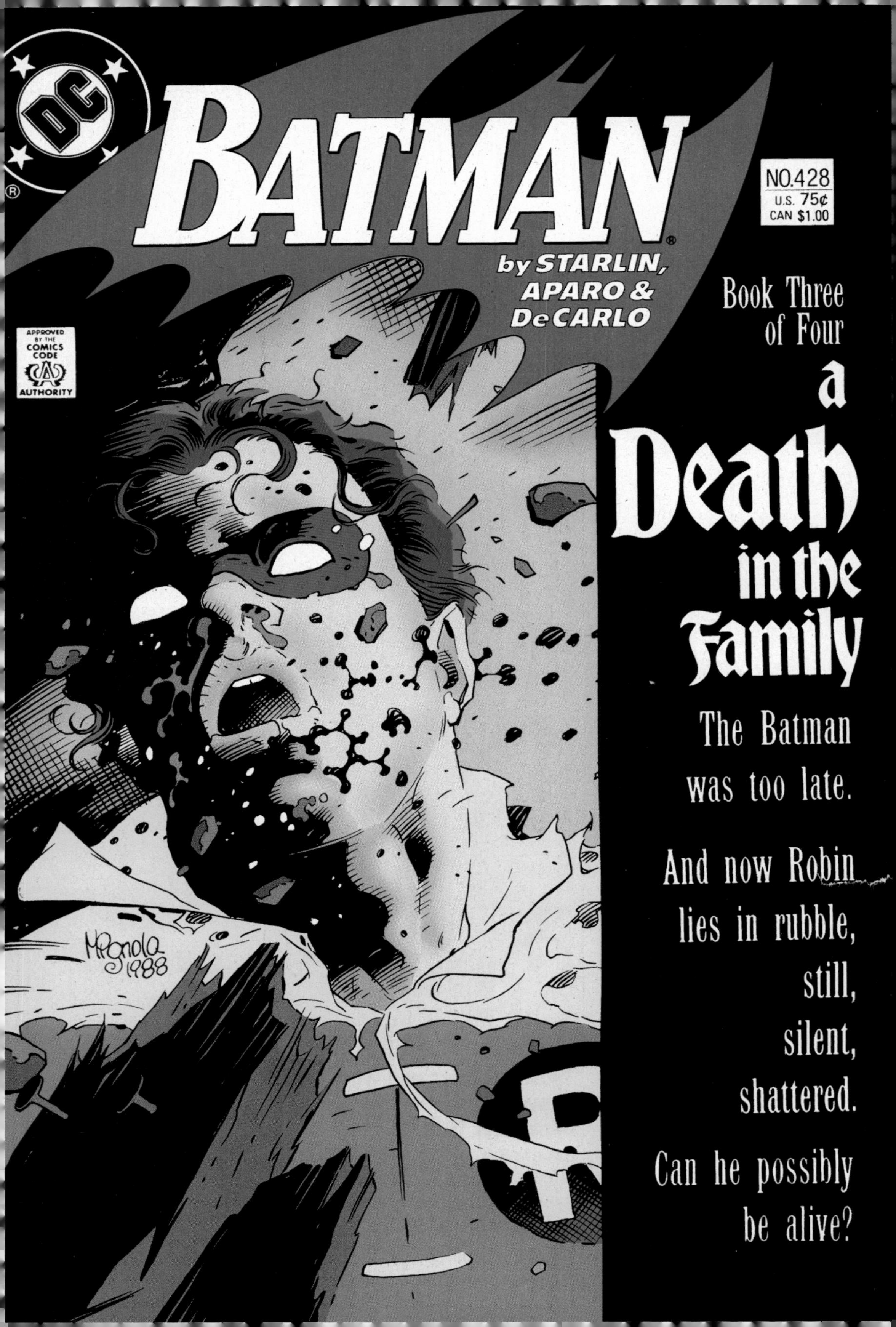
DC
BATMAN
NO.428
U.S. 75¢
CAN $1.00
by STARLIN,
APARO &
DeCARLO
APPROVED BY THE COMICS CODE AUTHORITY
Book Three of Four
a Death in the Family
The Batman was too late.
And now Robin lies in rubble, still, silent, shattered.
Can he possibly be alive?
MIGNOLA 1988

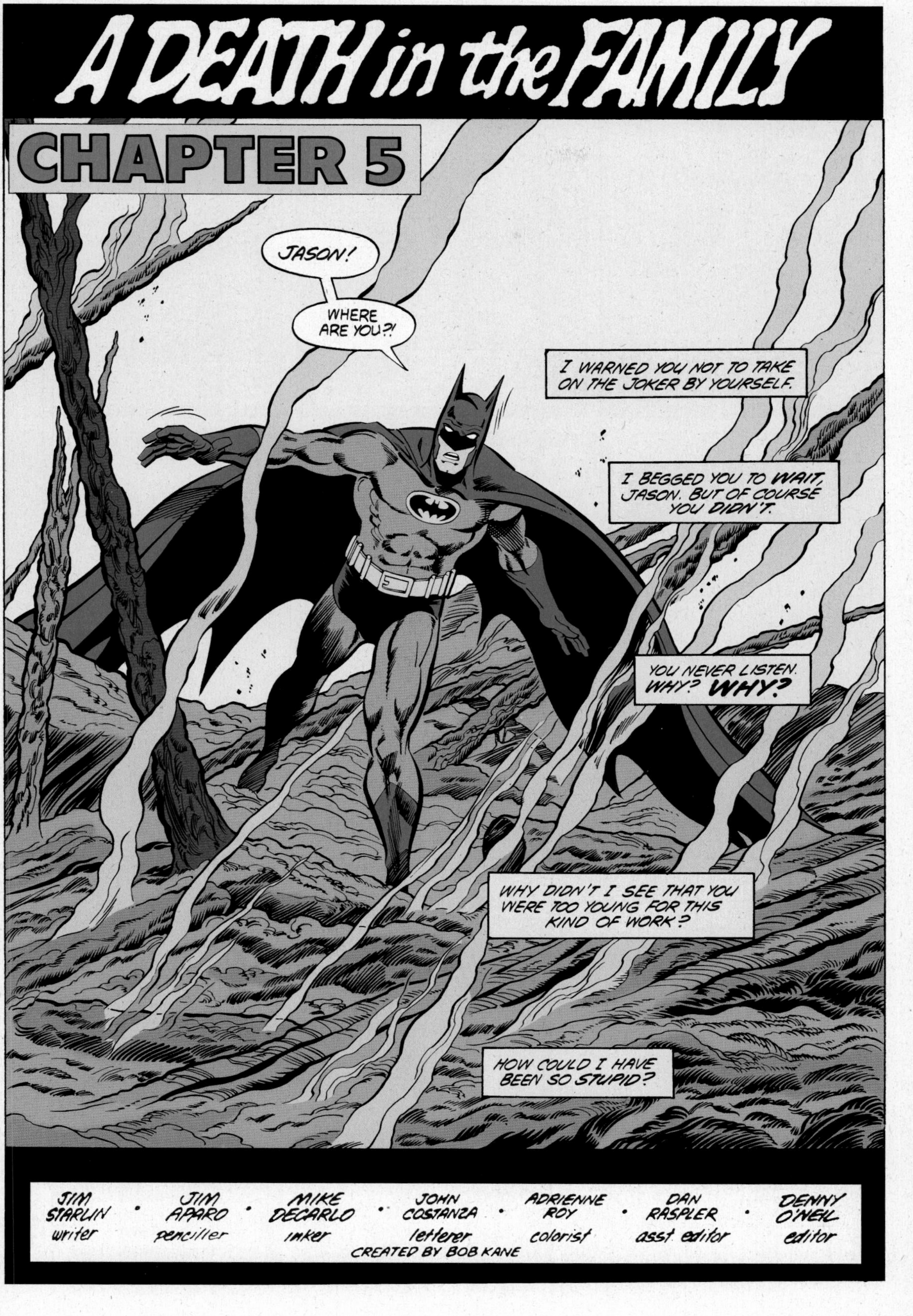
A DEATH in the FAMILY
CHAPTER 5
JASON!
WHERE ARE YOU?!
I WARNED YOU NOT TO TAKE ON THE JOKER BY YOURSELF.
I BEGGED YOU TO WAIT, JASON. BUT OF COURSE YOU DIDN'T.
YOU NEVER LISTEN. WHY? WHY?
WHY DIDN'T I SEE THAT YOU WERE TOO YOUNG FOR THIS KIND OF WORK?
HOW COULD I HAVE BEEN SO STUPID?
JIM STARLIN writer · JIM APARO penciller · MIKE DECARLO inker · JOHN COSTANZA letterer · ADRIENNE ROY colorist · DAN RASPLER asst. editor · DENNY O'NEIL editor
CREATED BY BOB KANE

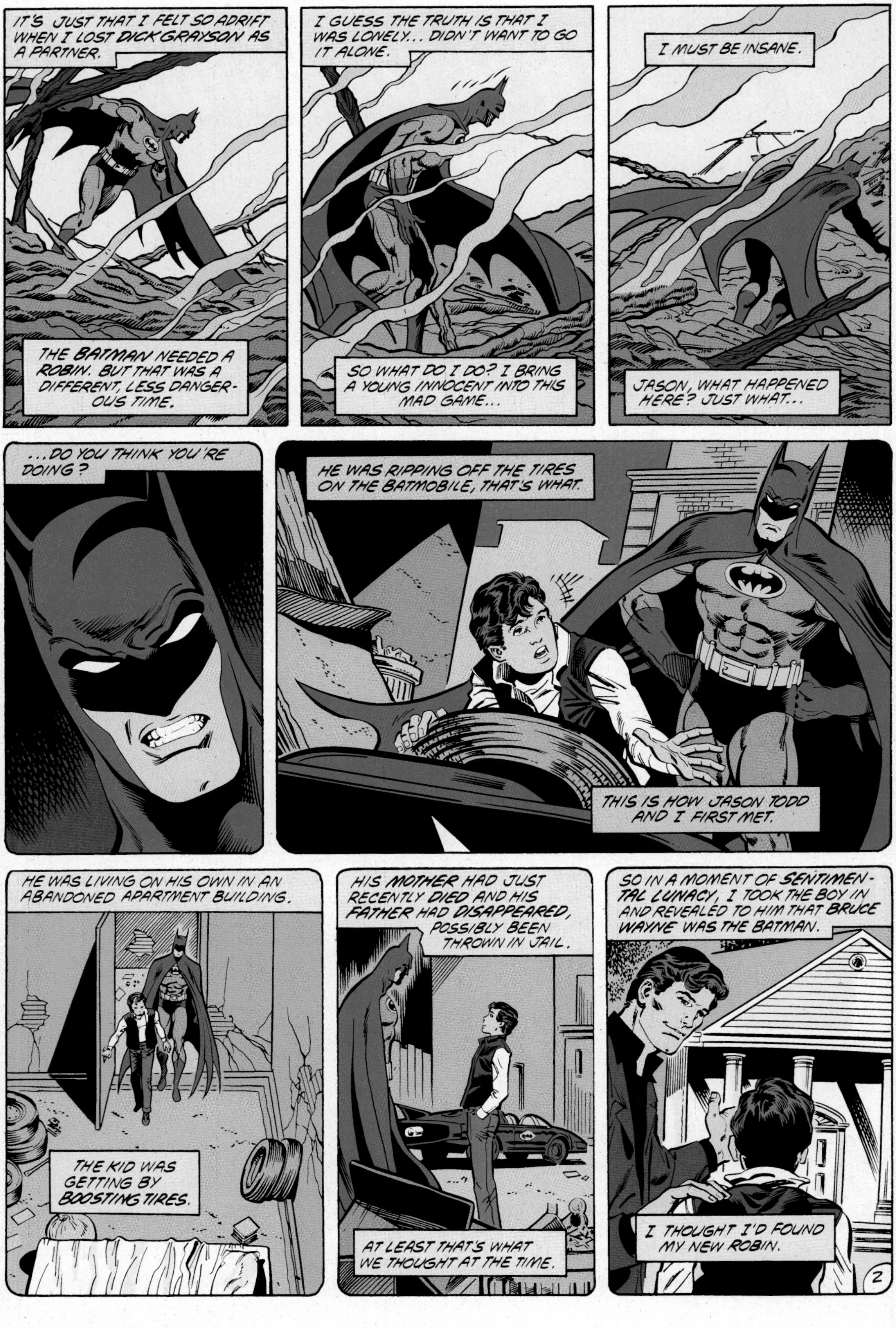
IT'S JUST THAT I FELT SO ADRIFT WHEN I LOST DICK GRAYSON AS A PARTNER.
THE BATMAN NEEDED A ROBIN. BUT THAT WAS A DIFFERENT, LESS DANGER-OUS TIME.
I GUESS THE TRUTH IS THAT I WAS LONELY... DIDN'T WANT TO GO IT ALONE.
SO WHAT DO I DO? I BRING A YOUNG INNOCENT INTO THIS MAD GAME...
I MUST BE INSANE.
JASON, WHAT HAPPENED HERE? JUST WHAT...
...DO YOU THINK YOU'RE DOING?
HE WAS RIPPING OFF THE TIRES ON THE BATMOBILE, THAT'S WHAT.
THIS IS HOW JASON TODD AND I FIRST MET.
HE WAS LIVING ON HIS OWN IN AN ABANDONED APARTMENT BUILDING.
THE KID WAS GETTING BY BOOSTING TIRES.
HIS MOTHER HAD JUST RECENTLY DIED AND HIS FATHER HAD DISAPPEARED, POSSIBLY BEEN THROWN IN JAIL.
AT LEAST THAT'S WHAT WE THOUGHT AT THE TIME.
SO IN A MOMENT OF SENTIMEN-TAL LUNACY, I TOOK THE BOY IN AND REVEALED TO HIM THAT BRUCE WAYNE WAS THE BATMAN.
I THOUGHT I'D FOUND MY NEW ROBIN.
2

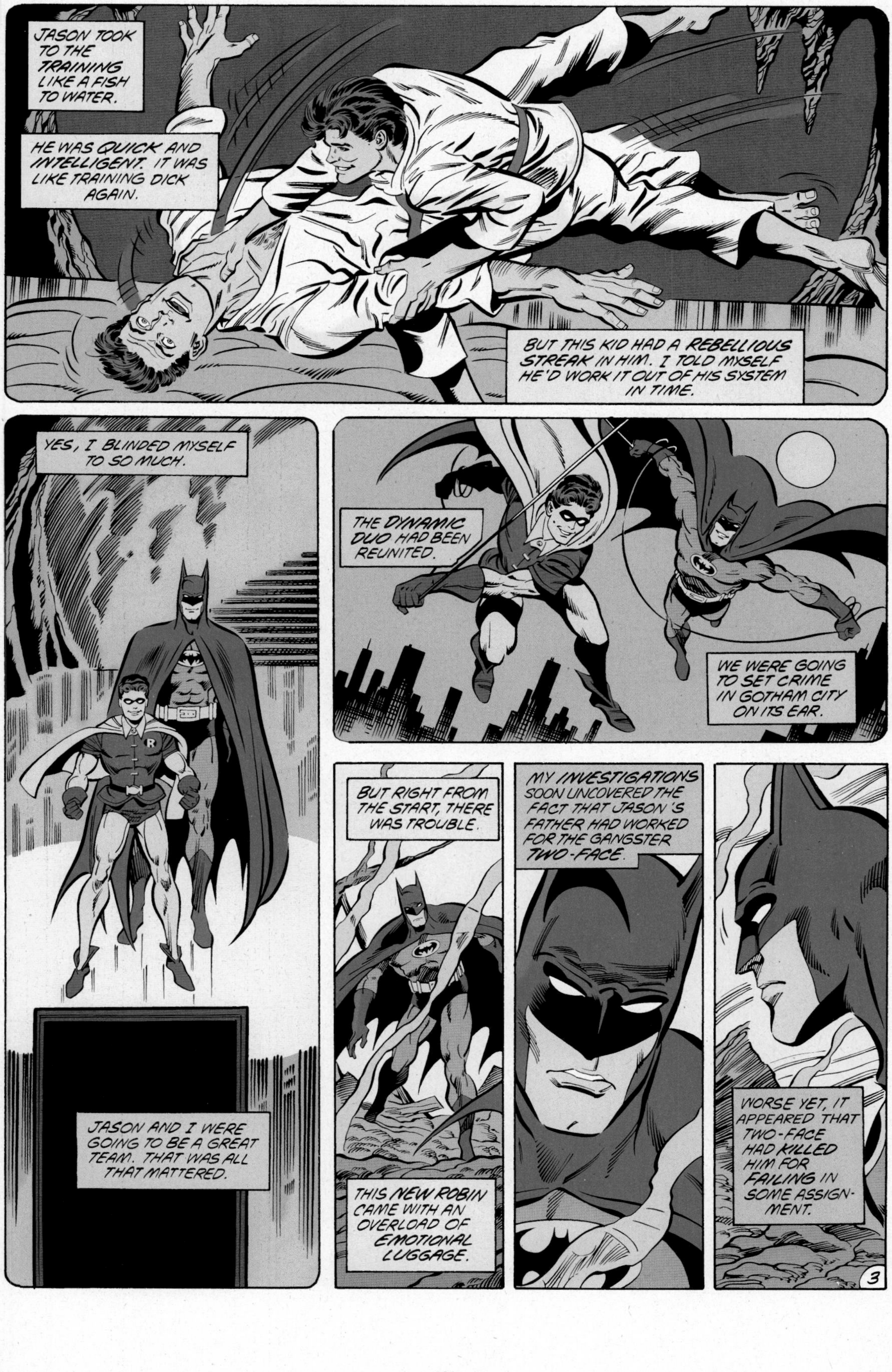
JASON TOOK TO THE TRAINING LIKE A FISH TO WATER.
HE WAS QUICK AND INTELLIGENT. IT WAS LIKE TRAINING DICK AGAIN.
BUT THIS KID HAD A REBELLIOUS STREAK IN HIM. I TOLD MYSELF HE'D WORK IT OUT OF HIS SYSTEM IN TIME.
YES, I BLINDED MYSELF TO SO MUCH.
JASON AND I WERE GOING TO BE A GREAT TEAM. THAT WAS ALL THAT MATTERED.
THE DYNAMIC DUO HAD BEEN REUNITED.
WE WERE GOING TO SET CRIME IN GOTHAM CITY ON ITS EAR.
BUT RIGHT FROM THE START, THERE WAS TROUBLE.
THIS NEW ROBIN CAME WITH AN OVERLOAD OF EMOTIONAL LUGGAGE.
MY INVESTIGATIONS SOON UNCOVERED THE FACT THAT JASON'S FATHER HAD WORKED FOR THE GANGSTER TWO-FACE.
WORSE YET, IT APPEARED THAT TWO-FACE HAD KILLED HIM FOR FAILING IN SOME ASSIGN-MENT.
3

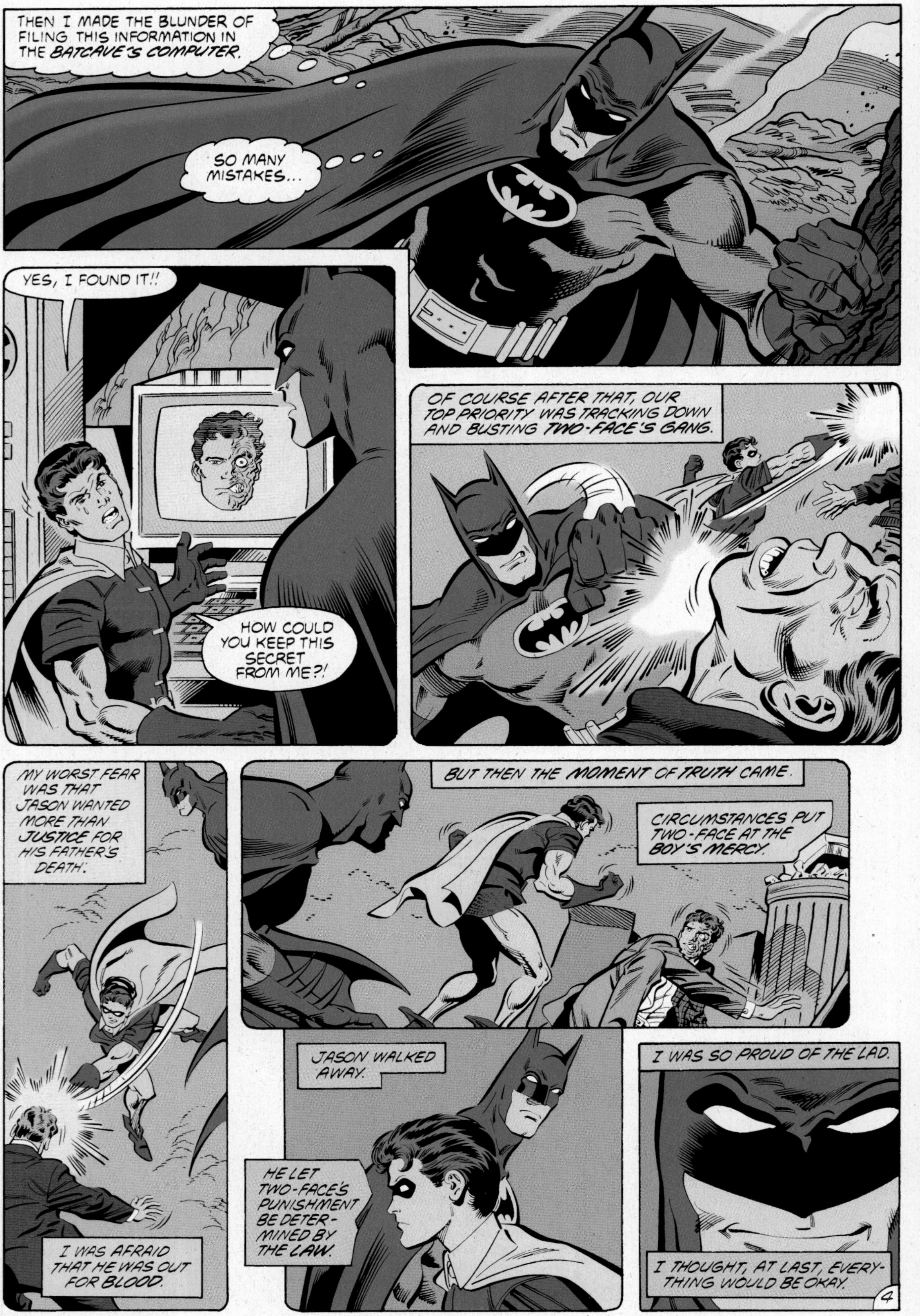
THEN I MADE THE BLUNDER OF FILING THIS INFORMATION IN THE BATCAVE'S COMPUTER.
SO MANY MISTAKES...
YES, I FOUND IT!!
HOW COULD YOU KEEP THIS SECRET FROM ME?!
OF COURSE AFTER THAT, OUR TOP PRIORITY WAS TRACKING DOWN AND BUSTING TWO-FACE'S GANG.
MY WORST FEAR WAS THAT JASON WANTED MORE THAN JUSTICE FOR HIS FATHER'S DEATH.
I WAS AFRAID THAT HE WAS OUT FOR BLOOD.
BUT THEN THE MOMENT OF TRUTH CAME.
CIRCUMSTANCES PUT TWO-FACE AT THE BOY'S MERCY.
JASON WALKED AWAY.
HE LET TWO-FACE'S PUNISHMENT BE DETERMINED BY THE LAW.
I WAS SO PROUD OF THE LAD.
I THOUGHT, AT LAST, EVERYTHING WOULD BE OKAY.
4

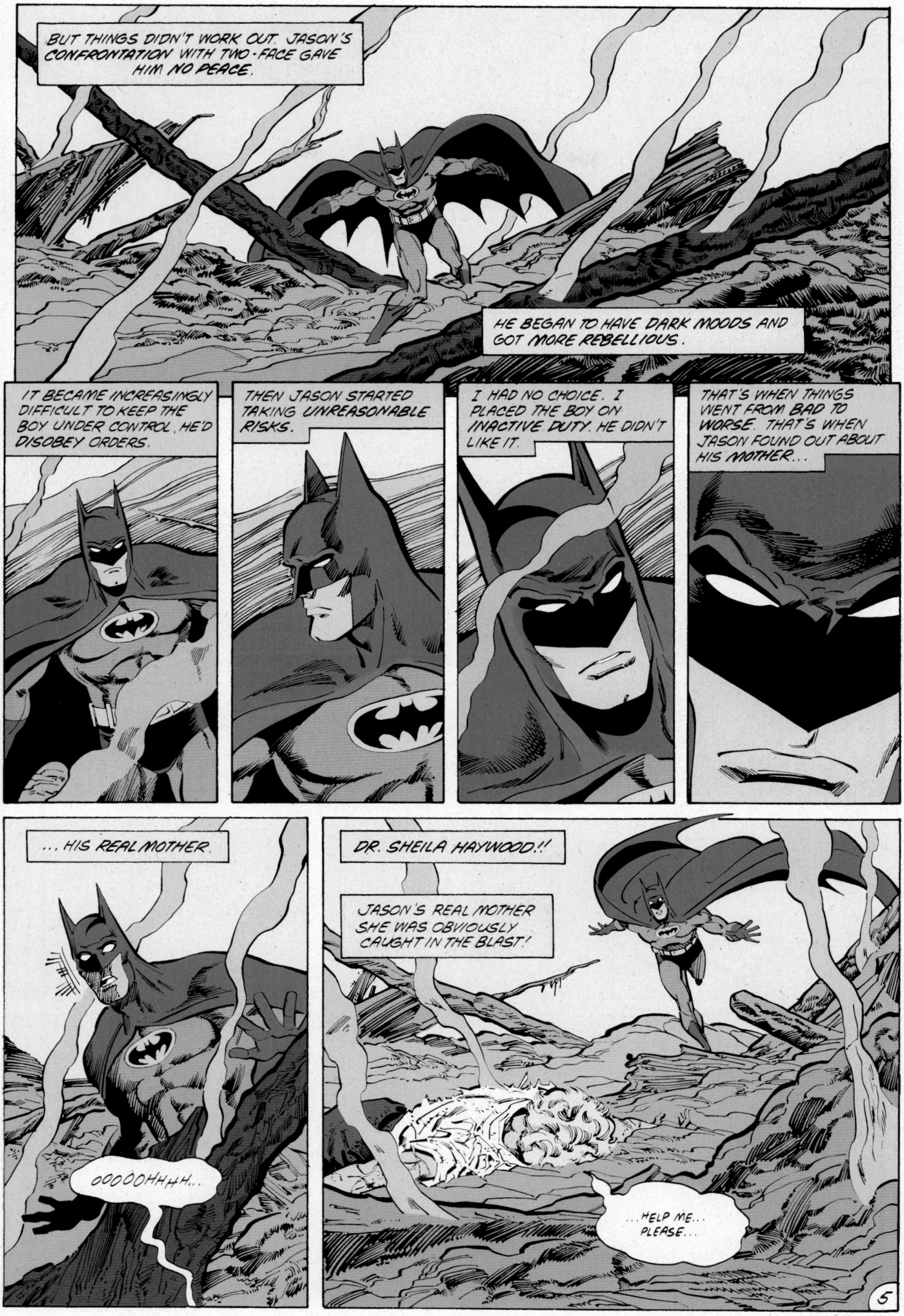
BUT THINGS DIDN'T WORK OUT. JASON'S CONFRONTATION WITH TWO-FACE GAVE HIM NO PEACE.
HE BEGAN TO HAVE DARK MOODS AND GOT MORE REBELLIOUS.
IT BECAME INCREASINGLY DIFFICULT TO KEEP THE BOY UNDER CONTROL. HE'D DISOBEY ORDERS.
THEN JASON STARTED TAKING UNREASONABLE RISKS.
I HAD NO CHOICE. I PLACED THE BOY ON INACTIVE DUTY. HE DIDN'T LIKE IT.
THAT'S WHEN THINGS WENT FROM BAD TO WORSE. THAT'S WHEN JASON FOUND OUT ABOUT HIS MOTHER...
... HIS REAL MOTHER.
OOOOOHHHH...
DR. SHEILA HAYWOOD!!
JASON'S REAL MOTHER SHE WAS OBVIOUSLY CAUGHT IN THE BLAST!
...HELP ME... PLEASE...
5

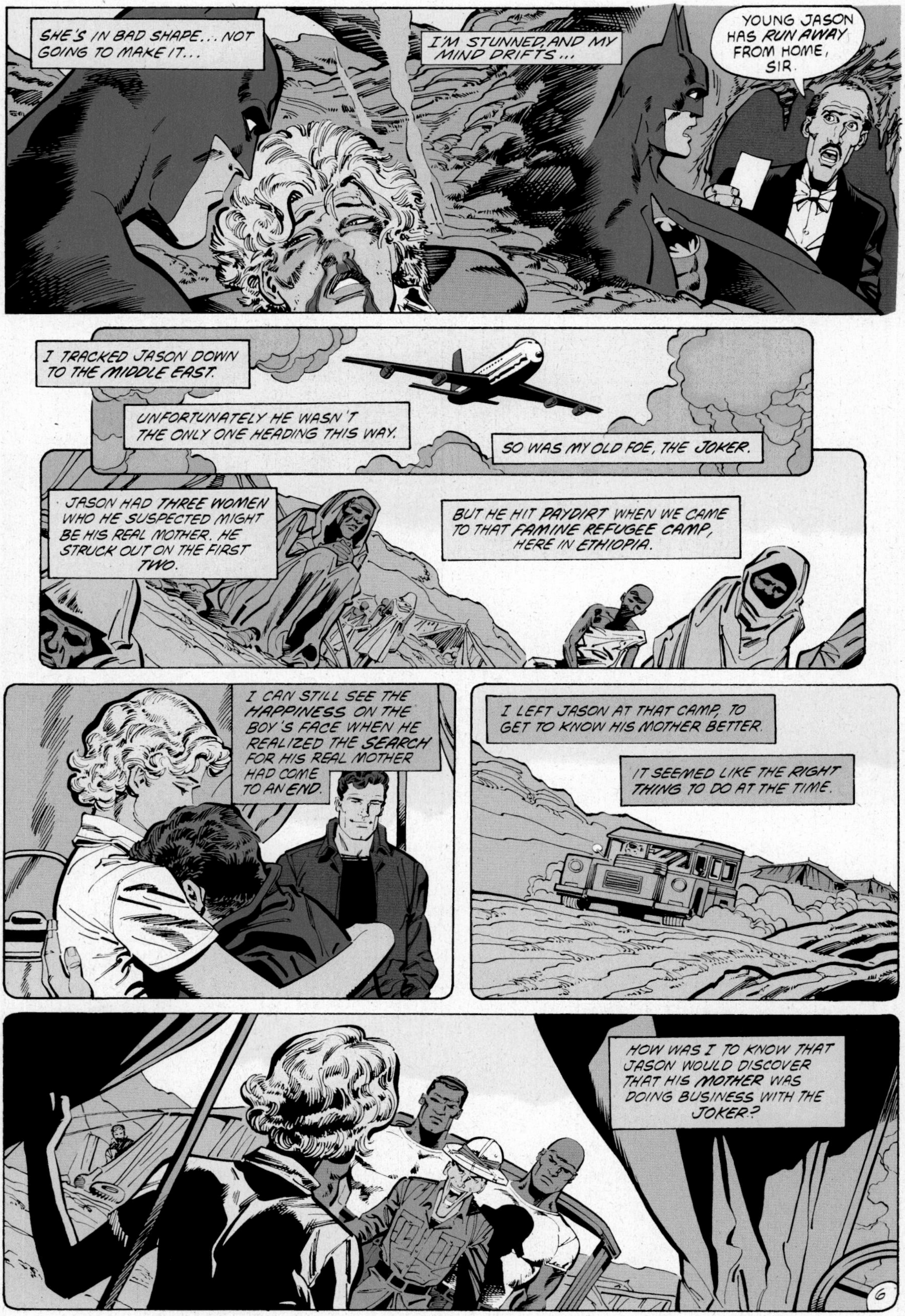
SHE'S IN BAD SHAPE... NOT GOING TO MAKE IT...
I'M STUNNED, AND MY MIND DRIFTS...
YOUNG JASON HAS RUN AWAY FROM HOME, SIR.
I TRACKED JASON DOWN TO THE MIDDLE EAST.
UNFORTUNATELY HE WASN'T THE ONLY ONE HEADING THIS WAY.
SO WAS MY OLD FOE, THE JOKER.
JASON HAD THREE WOMEN WHO HE SUSPECTED MIGHT BE HIS REAL MOTHER. HE STRUCK OUT ON THE FIRST TWO.
BUT HE HIT PAYDIRT WHEN WE CAME TO THAT FAMINE REFUGEE CAMP, HERE IN ETHIOPIA.
I CAN STILL SEE THE HAPPINESS ON THE BOY'S FACE WHEN HE REALIZED THE SEARCH FOR HIS REAL MOTHER HAD COME TO AN END.
I LEFT JASON AT THAT CAMP, TO GET TO KNOW HIS MOTHER BETTER.
IT SEEMED LIKE THE RIGHT THING TO DO AT THE TIME.
HOW WAS I TO KNOW THAT JASON WOULD DISCOVER THAT HIS MOTHER WAS DOING BUSINESS WITH THE JOKER?
6

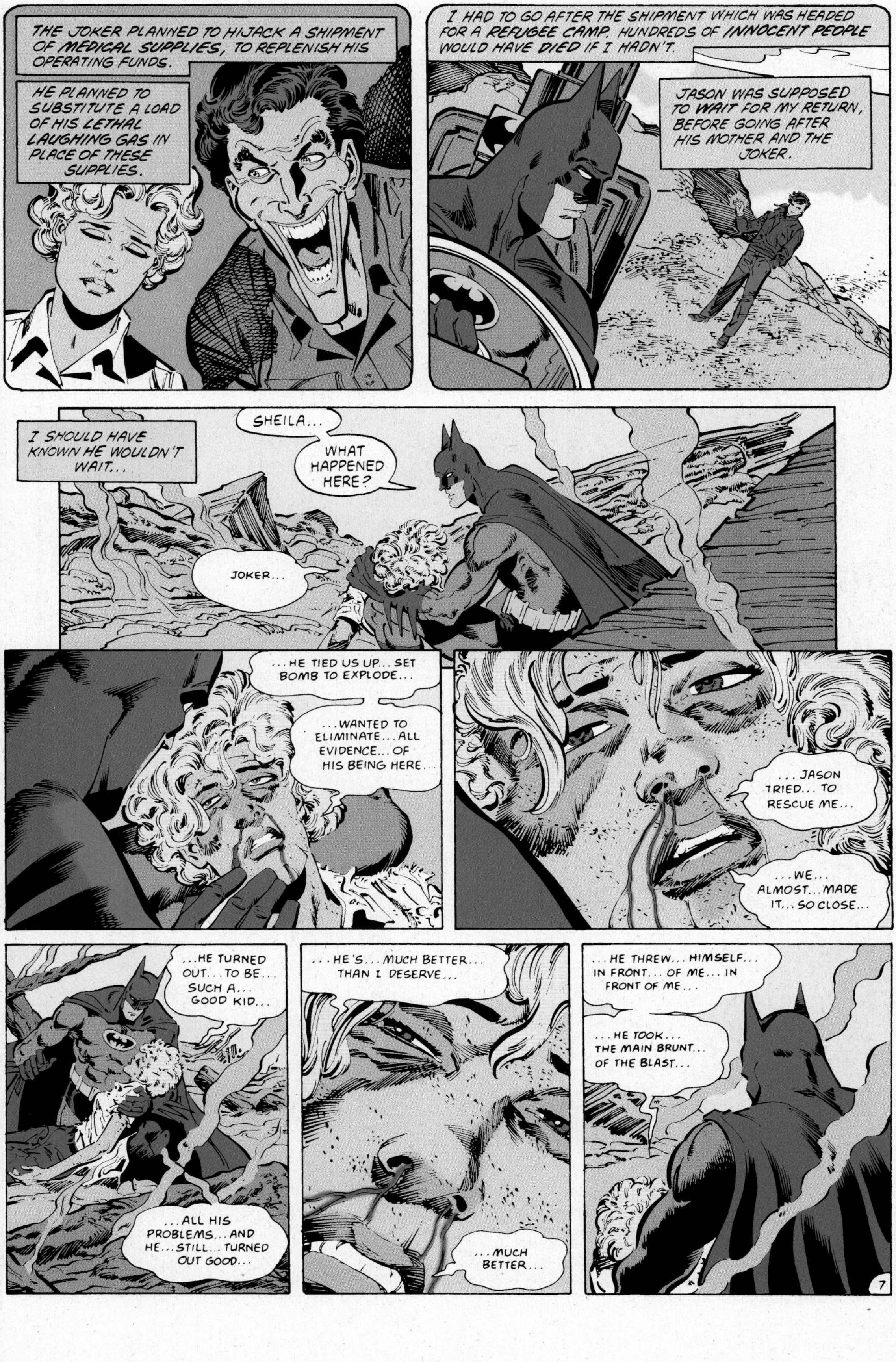
THE JOKER PLANNED TO HIJACK A SHIPMENT OF MEDICAL SUPPLIES, TO REPLENISH HIS OPERATING FUNDS.
HE PLANNED TO SUBSTITUTE A LOAD OF HIS LETHAL LAUGHING GAS IN PLACE OF THESE SUPPLIES.
I HAD TO GO AFTER THE SHIPMENT WHICH WAS HEADED FOR A REFUGEE CAMP. HUNDREDS OF INNOCENT PEOPLE WOULD HAVE DIED IF I HADN'T.
JASON WAS SUPPOSED TO WAIT FOR MY RETURN, BEFORE GOING AFTER HIS MOTHER AND THE JOKER.
I SHOULD HAVE KNOWN HE WOULDN'T WAIT...
SHEILA...
WHAT HAPPENED HERE?
JOKER...
...HE TIED US UP... SET BOMB TO EXPLODE...
...WANTED TO ELIMINATE... ALL EVIDENCE... OF HIS BEING HERE...
...JASON TRIED... TO RESCUE ME...
...WE... ALMOST... MADE IT... SO CLOSE...
...HE TURNED OUT... TO BE... SUCH A... GOOD KID...
...ALL HIS PROBLEMS... AND HE... STILL... TURNED OUT GOOD...
...HE'S... MUCH BETTER... THAN I DESERVE...
...MUCH BETTER...
...HE THREW... HIMSELF... IN FRONT... OF ME... IN FRONT OF ME...
...HE TOOK... THE MAIN BRUNT... OF THE BLAST...
7

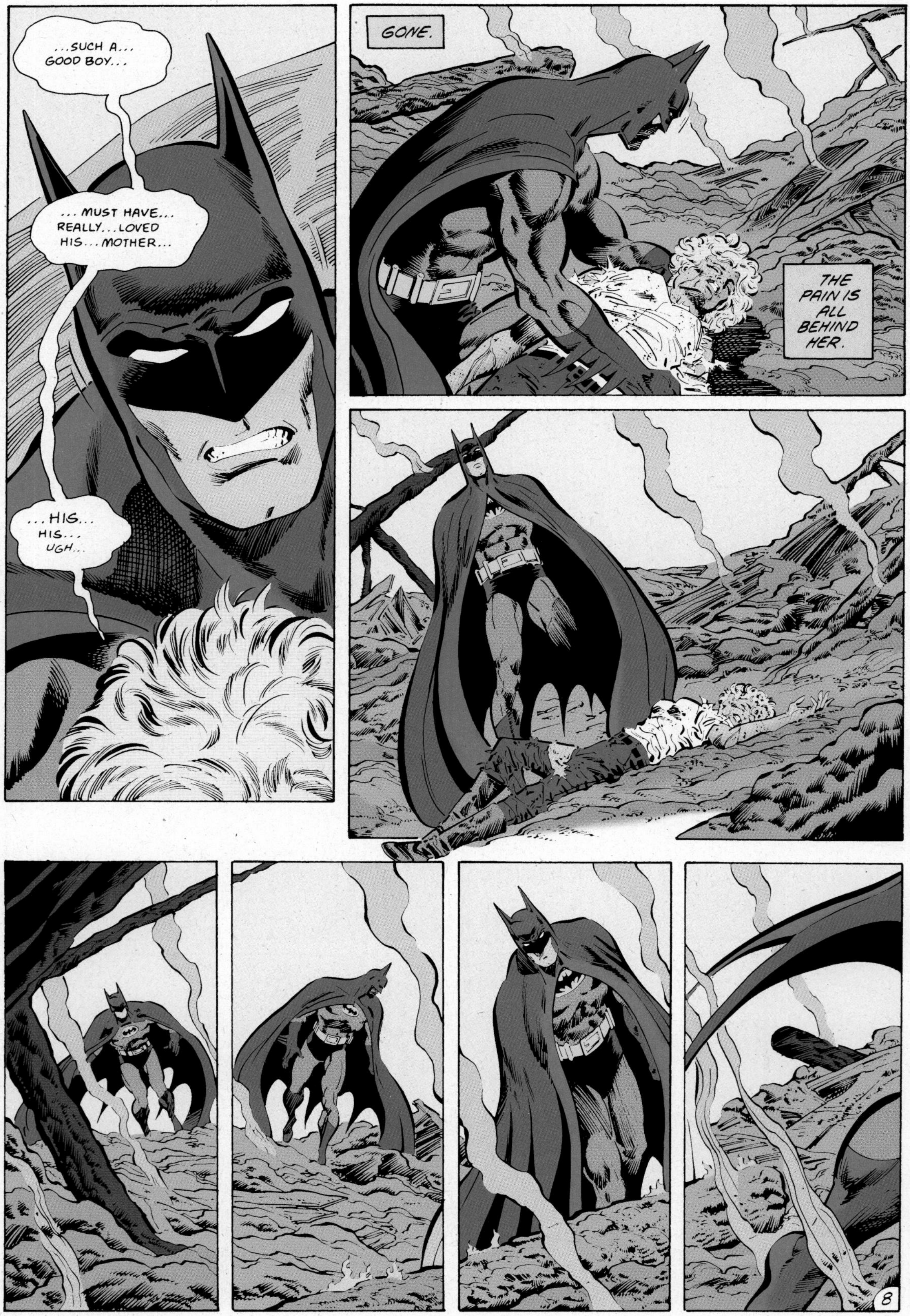
...SUCH A... GOOD BOY...
...MUST HAVE... REALLY...LOVED HIS...MOTHER...
...HIS... HIS... UGH...
GONE.
THE PAIN IS ALL BEHIND HER.
8

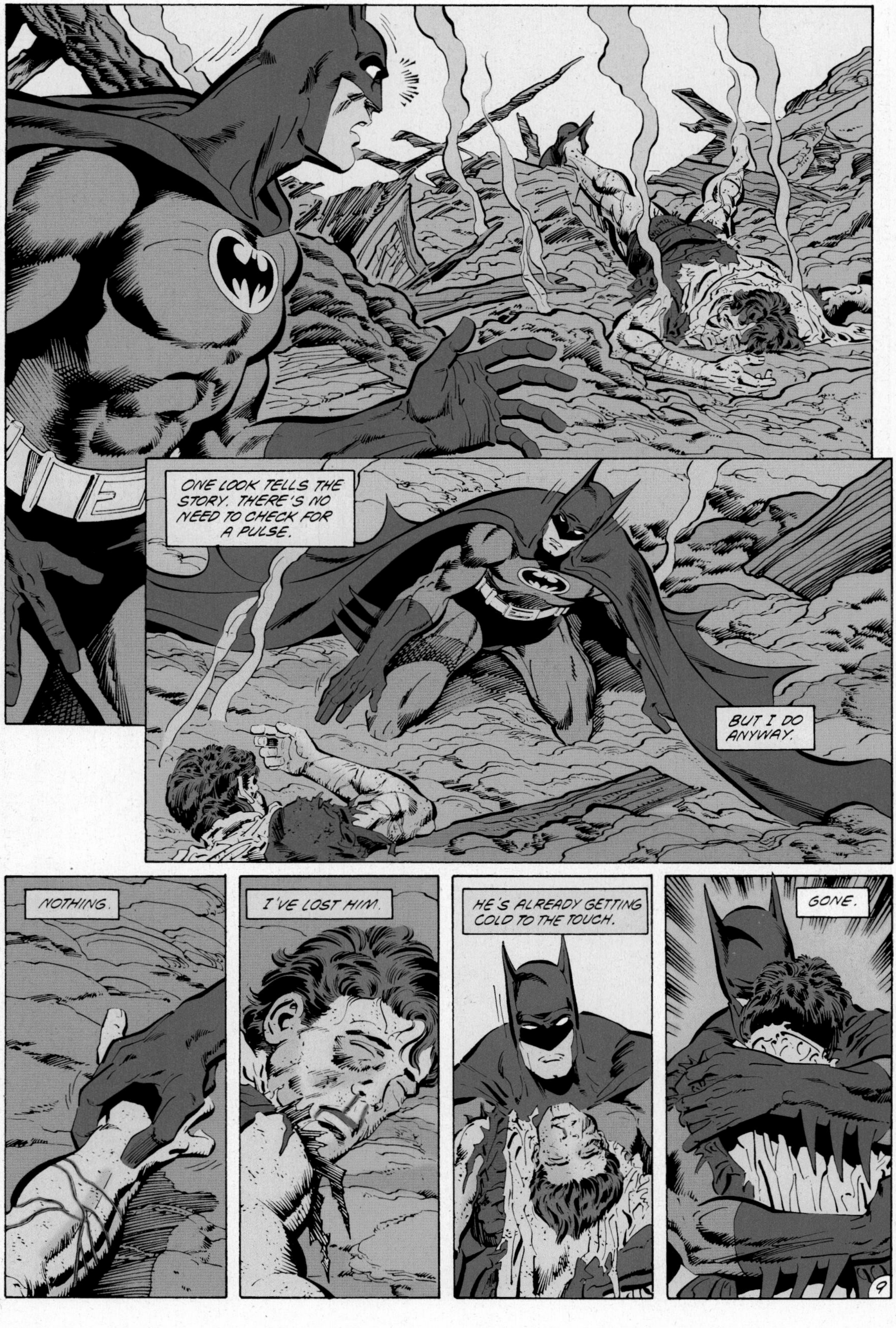
ONE LOOK TELLS THE STORY. THERE'S NO NEED TO CHECK FOR A PULSE.
BUT I DO ANYWAY.
NOTHING.
I'VE LOST HIM.
HE'S ALREADY GETTING COLD TO THE TOUCH.
GONE.
9

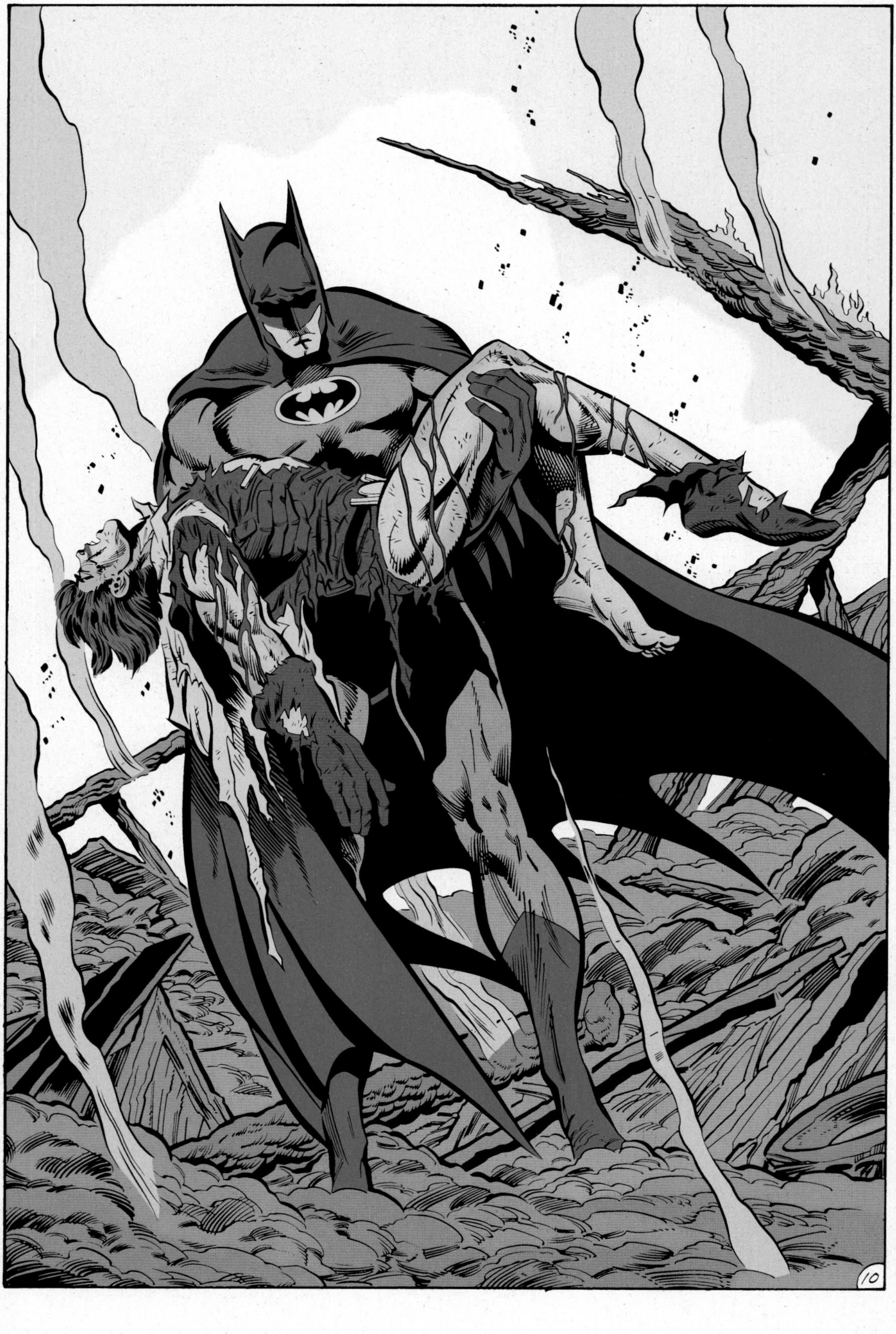
10

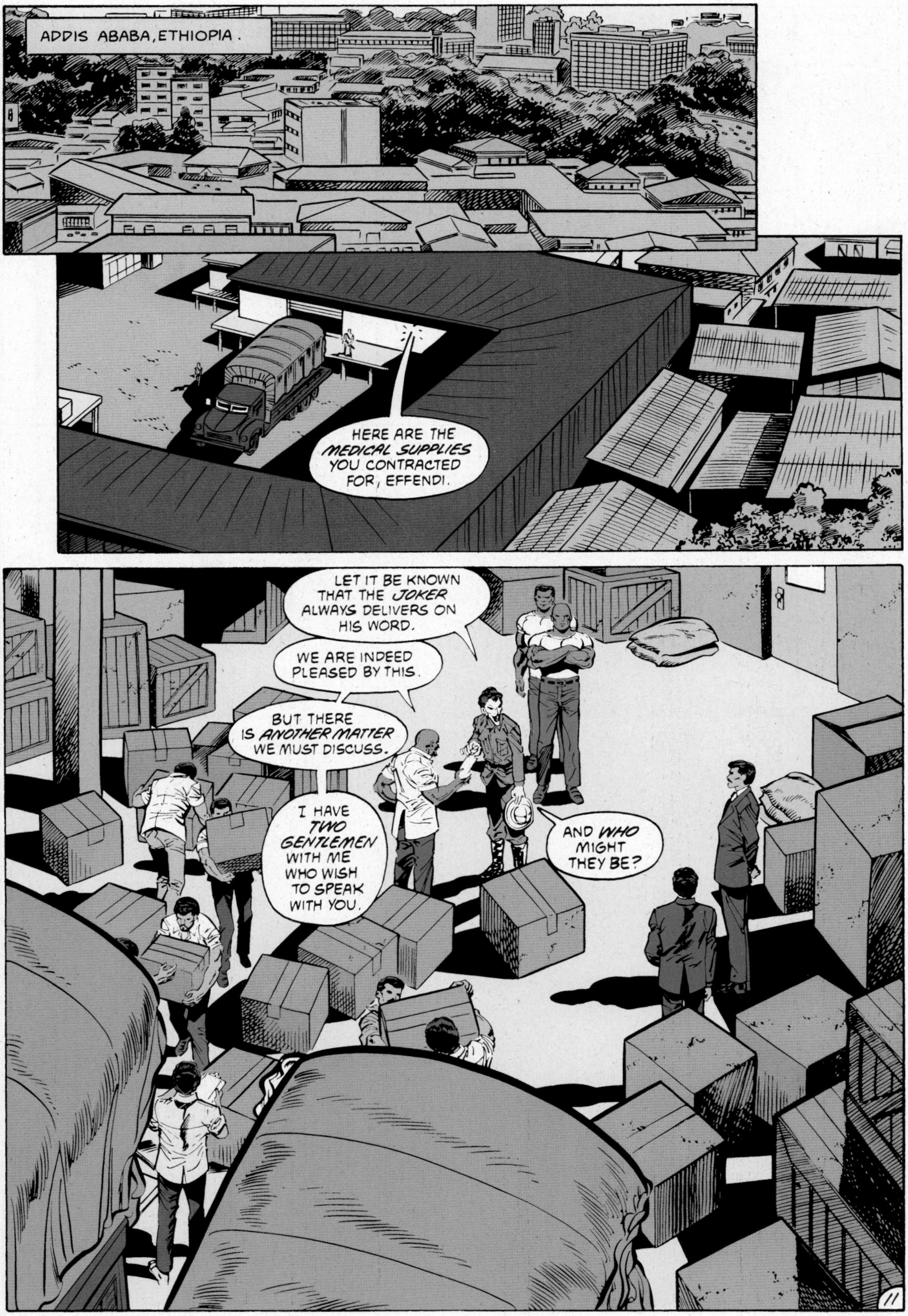
ADDIS ABABA, ETHIOPIA.
HERE ARE THE MEDICAL SUPPLIES YOU CONTRACTED FOR, EFFENDI.
LET IT BE KNOWN THAT THE JOKER ALWAYS DELIVERS ON HIS WORD.
WE ARE INDEED PLEASED BY THIS.
BUT THERE IS ANOTHER MATTER WE MUST DISCUSS.
I HAVE TWO GENTLEMEN WITH ME WHO WISH TO SPEAK WITH YOU.
AND WHO MIGHT THEY BE?
11

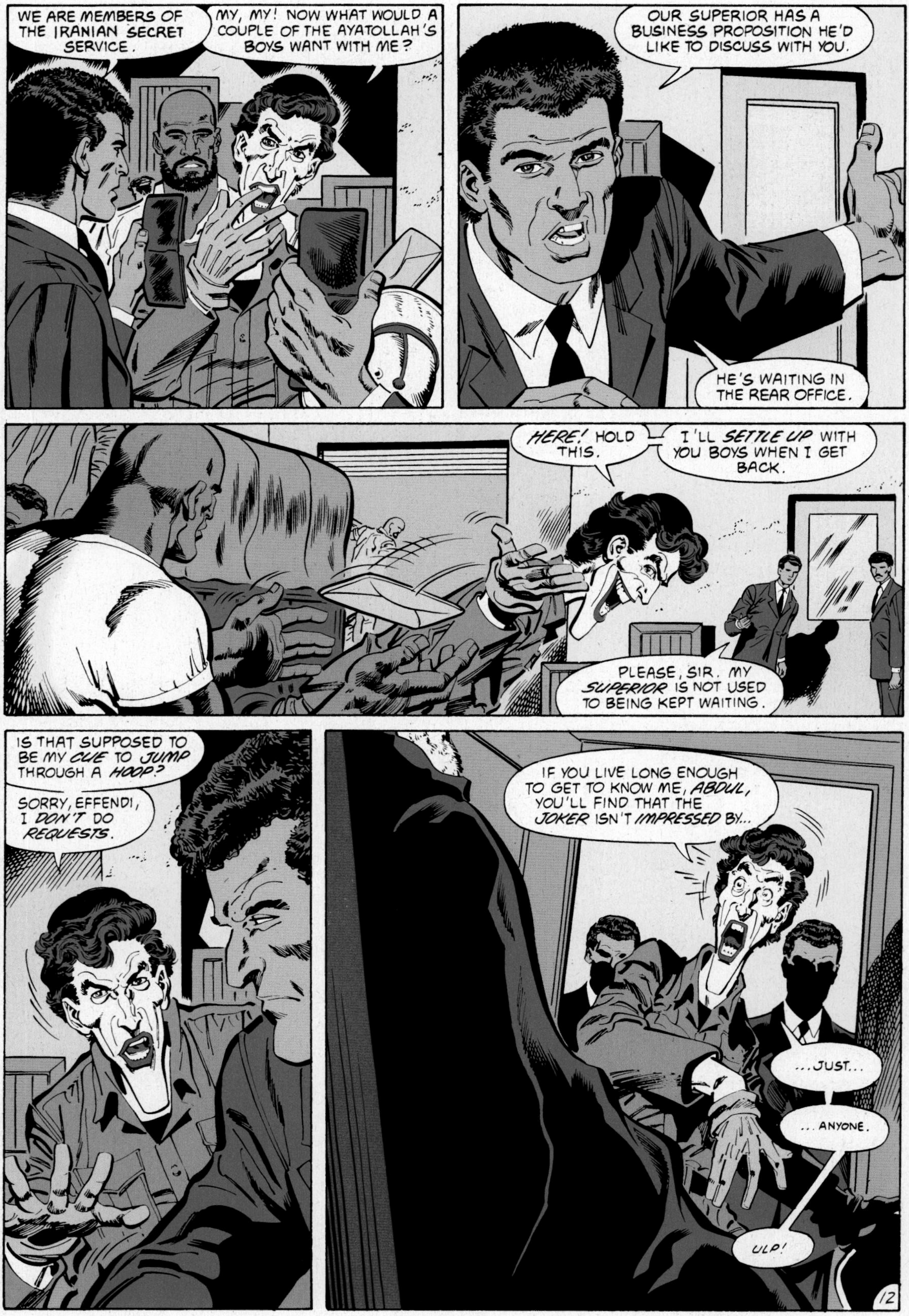
WE ARE MEMBERS OF THE IRANIAN SECRET SERVICE.
MY, MY! NOW WHAT WOULD A COUPLE OF THE AYATOLLAH'S BOYS WANT WITH ME?
OUR SUPERIOR HAS A BUSINESS PROPOSITION HE'D LIKE TO DISCUSS WITH YOU.
HE'S WAITING IN THE REAR OFFICE.
HERE! HOLD THIS.
I'LL *SETTLE UP* WITH YOU BOYS WHEN I GET BACK.
PLEASE, SIR. MY *SUPERIOR* IS NOT USED TO BEING KEPT WAITING.
IS THAT SUPPOSED TO BE MY *CUE* TO *JUMP* THROUGH A *HOOP*?
SORRY, EFFENDI, I *DON'T* DO *REQUESTS*.
IF YOU LIVE LONG ENOUGH TO GET TO KNOW ME, *ABDUL*, YOU'LL FIND THAT THE *JOKER* ISN'T *IMPRESSED* BY...
...JUST...
...ANYONE.
ULP!
12

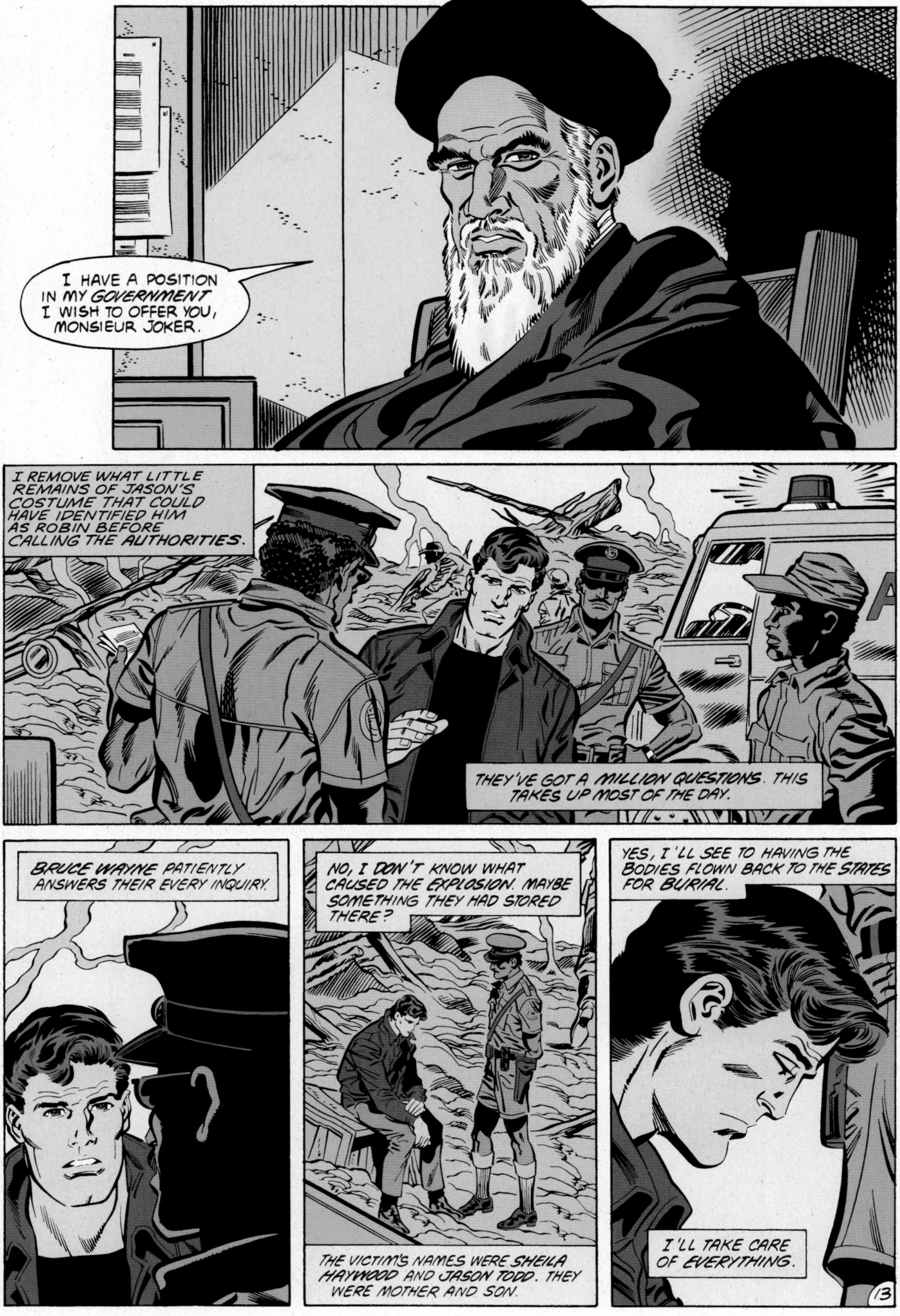

I HAVE A POSITION IN MY GOVERNMENT I WISH TO OFFER YOU, MONSIEUR JOKER.
I REMOVE WHAT LITTLE REMAINS OF JASON'S COSTUME THAT COULD HAVE IDENTIFIED HIM AS ROBIN BEFORE CALLING THE AUTHORITIES.
THEY'VE GOT A MILLION QUESTIONS. THIS TAKES UP MOST OF THE DAY.
BRUCE WAYNE PATIENTLY ANSWERS THEIR EVERY INQUIRY.
NO, I DON'T KNOW WHAT CAUSED THE EXPLOSION. MAYBE SOMETHING THEY HAD STORED THERE?
THE VICTIM'S NAMES WERE SHEILA HAYWOOD AND JASON TODD. THEY WERE MOTHER AND SON.
YES, I'LL SEE TO HAVING THE BODIES FLOWN BACK TO THE STATES FOR BURIAL.
I'LL TAKE CARE OF EVERYTHING.
13

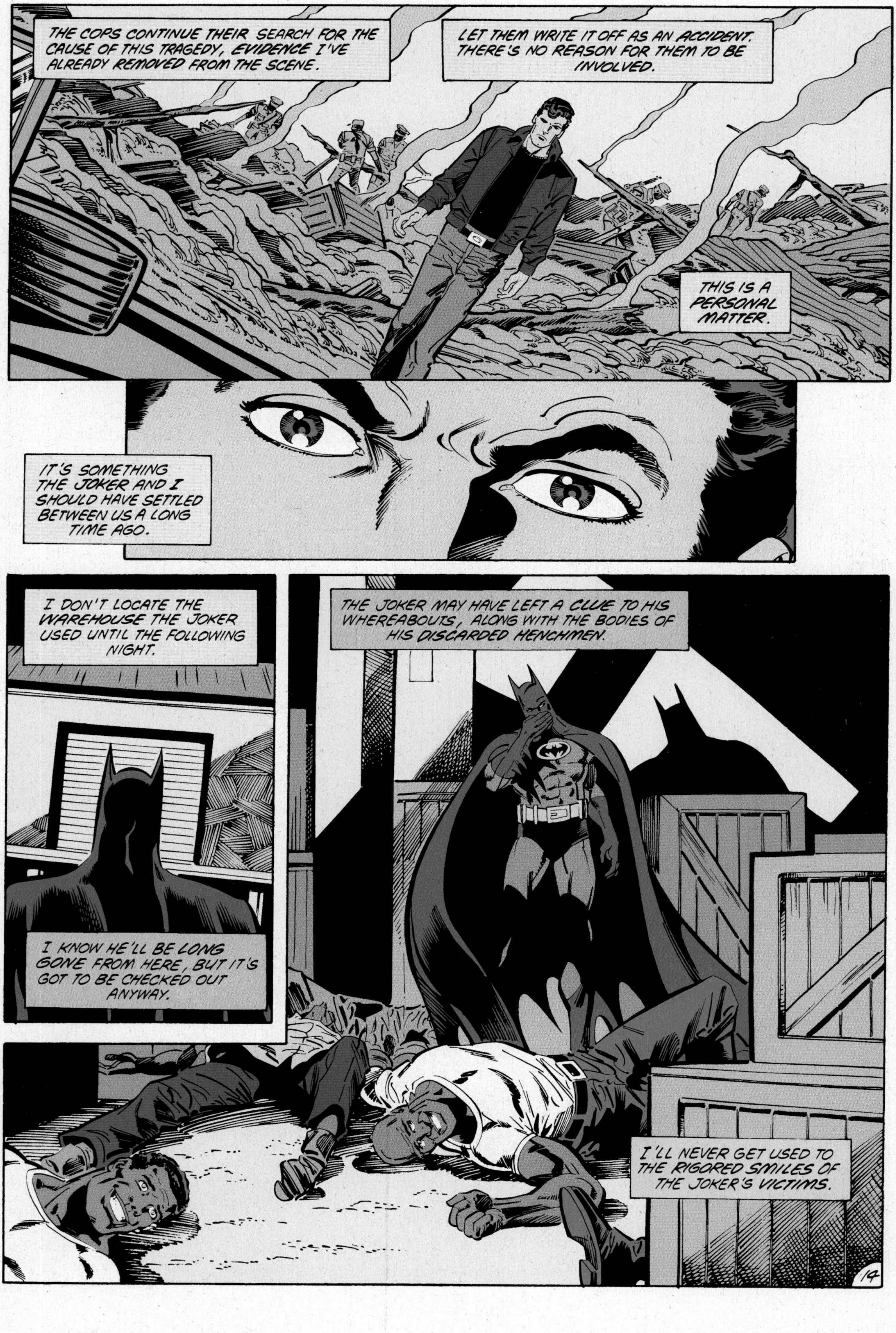
THE COPS CONTINUE THEIR SEARCH FOR THE CAUSE OF THIS TRAGEDY, EVIDENCE I'VE ALREADY REMOVED FROM THE SCENE.
LET THEM WRITE IT OFF AS AN ACCIDENT. THERE'S NO REASON FOR THEM TO BE INVOLVED.
THIS IS A PERSONAL MATTER.
IT'S SOMETHING THE JOKER AND I SHOULD HAVE SETTLED BETWEEN US A LONG TIME AGO.
I DON'T LOCATE THE WAREHOUSE THE JOKER USED UNTIL THE FOLLOWING NIGHT.
I KNOW HE'LL BE LONG GONE FROM HERE, BUT IT'S GOT TO BE CHECKED OUT ANYWAY.
THE JOKER MAY HAVE LEFT A CLUE TO HIS WHEREABOUTS, ALONG WITH THE BODIES OF HIS DISCARDED HENCHMEN.
I'LL NEVER GET USED TO THE RIGORED SMILES OF THE JOKER'S VICTIMS.
14

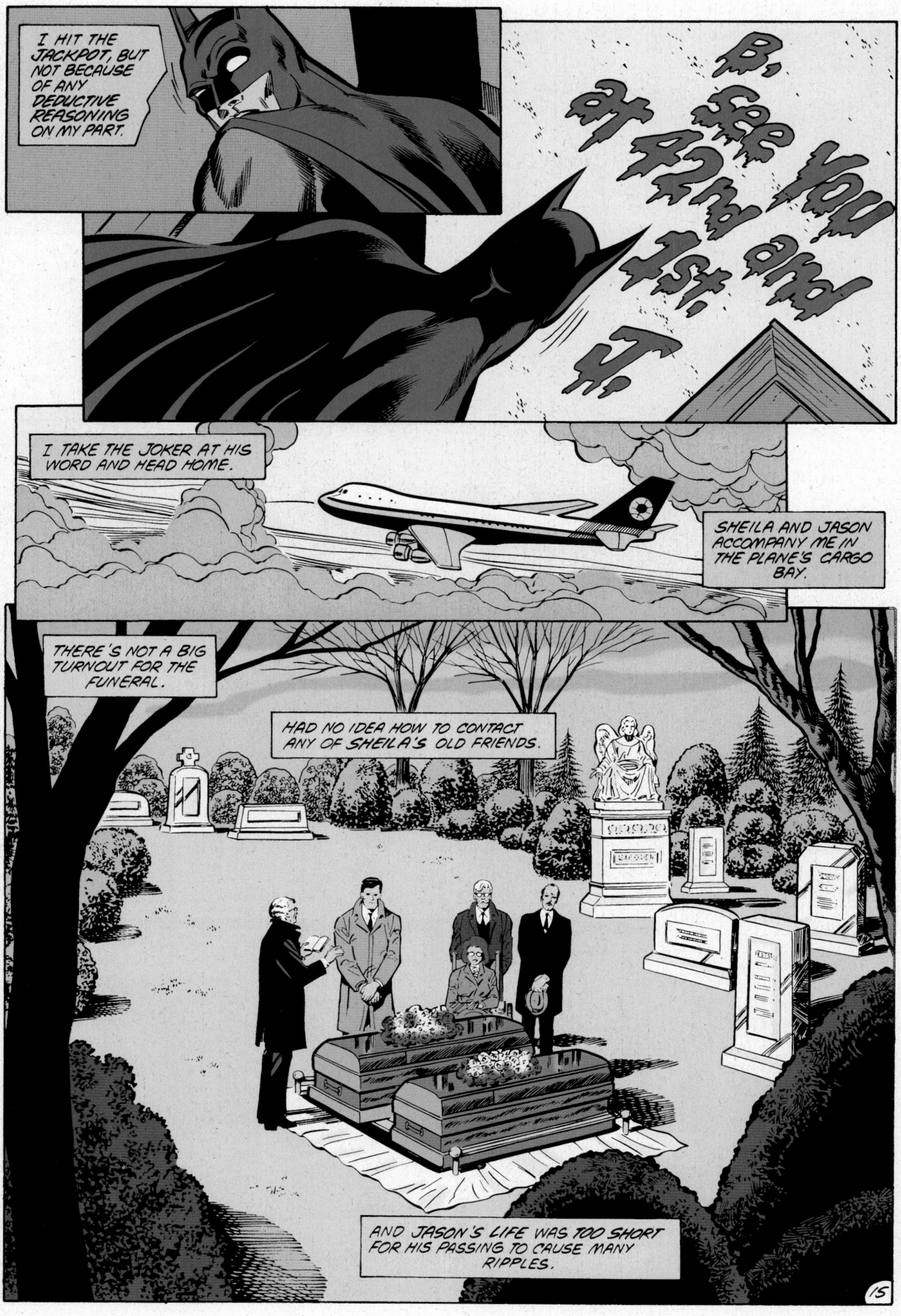
I HIT THE JACKPOT, BUT NOT BECAUSE OF ANY DEDUCTIVE REASONING ON MY PART.
B, See You at 42nd and 1st. J.
I TAKE THE JOKER AT HIS WORD AND HEAD HOME.
SHEILA AND JASON ACCOMPANY ME IN THE PLANE'S CARGO BAY.
THERE'S NOT A BIG TURNOUT FOR THE FUNERAL.
HAD NO IDEA HOW TO CONTACT ANY OF SHEILA'S OLD FRIENDS.
AND JASON'S LIFE WAS TOO SHORT FOR HIS PASSING TO CAUSE MANY RIPPLES.
15

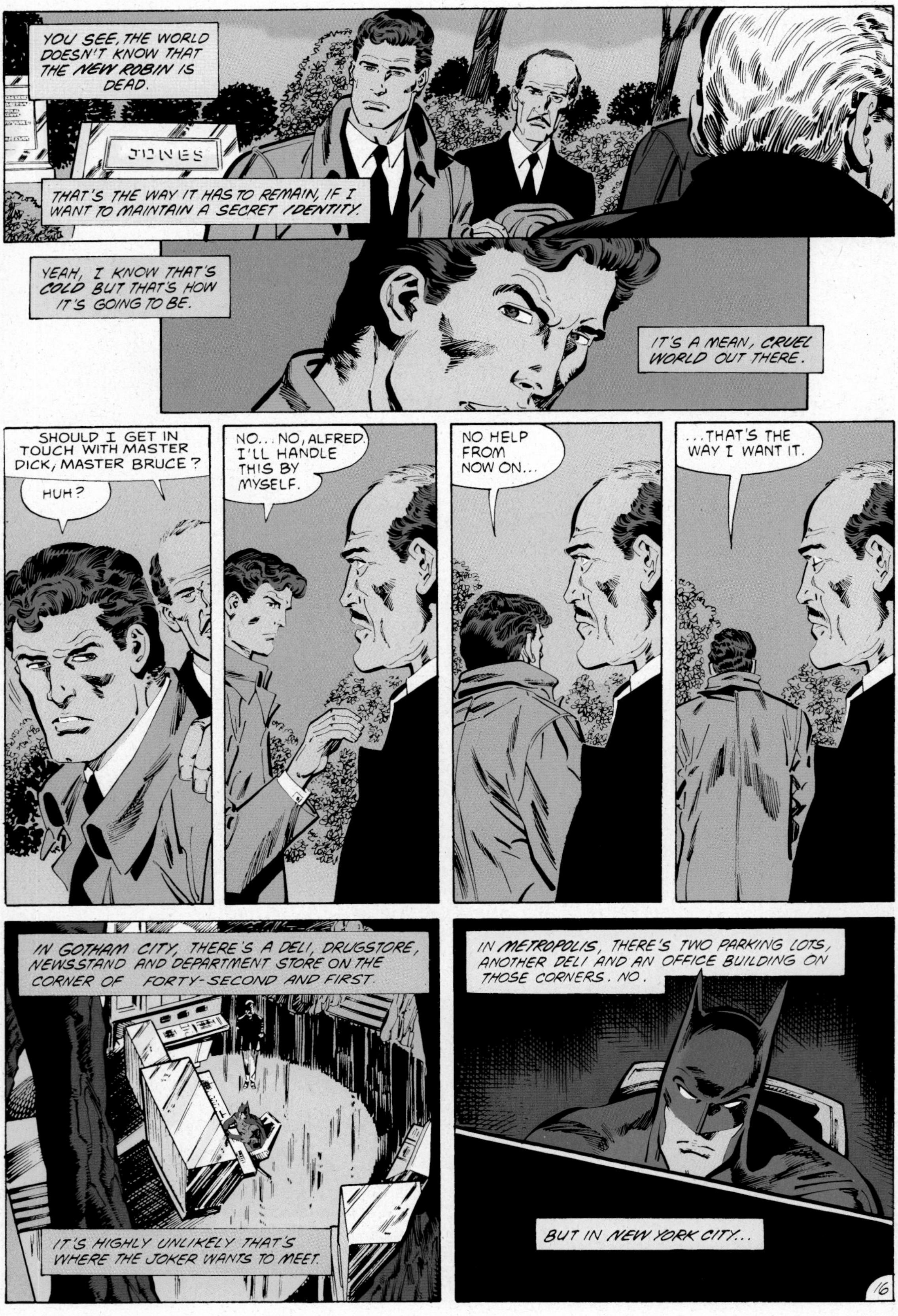
YOU SEE, THE WORLD DOESN'T KNOW THAT THE NEW ROBIN IS DEAD.
JONES
THAT'S THE WAY IT HAS TO REMAIN, IF I WANT TO MAINTAIN A SECRET IDENTITY.
YEAH, I KNOW THAT'S COLD BUT THAT'S HOW IT'S GOING TO BE.
IT'S A MEAN, CRUEL WORLD OUT THERE.
SHOULD I GET IN TOUCH WITH MASTER DICK, MASTER BRUCE?
HUH?
NO... NO, ALFRED. I'LL HANDLE THIS BY MYSELF.
NO HELP FROM NOW ON...
...THAT'S THE WAY I WANT IT.
IN GOTHAM CITY, THERE'S A DELI, DRUGSTORE, NEWSSTAND AND DEPARTMENT STORE ON THE CORNER OF FORTY-SECOND AND FIRST.
IT'S HIGHLY UNLIKELY THAT'S WHERE THE JOKER WANTS TO MEET.
IN METROPOLIS, THERE'S TWO PARKING LOTS, ANOTHER DELI AND AN OFFICE BUILDING ON THOSE CORNERS. NO.
BUT IN NEW YORK CITY...
16

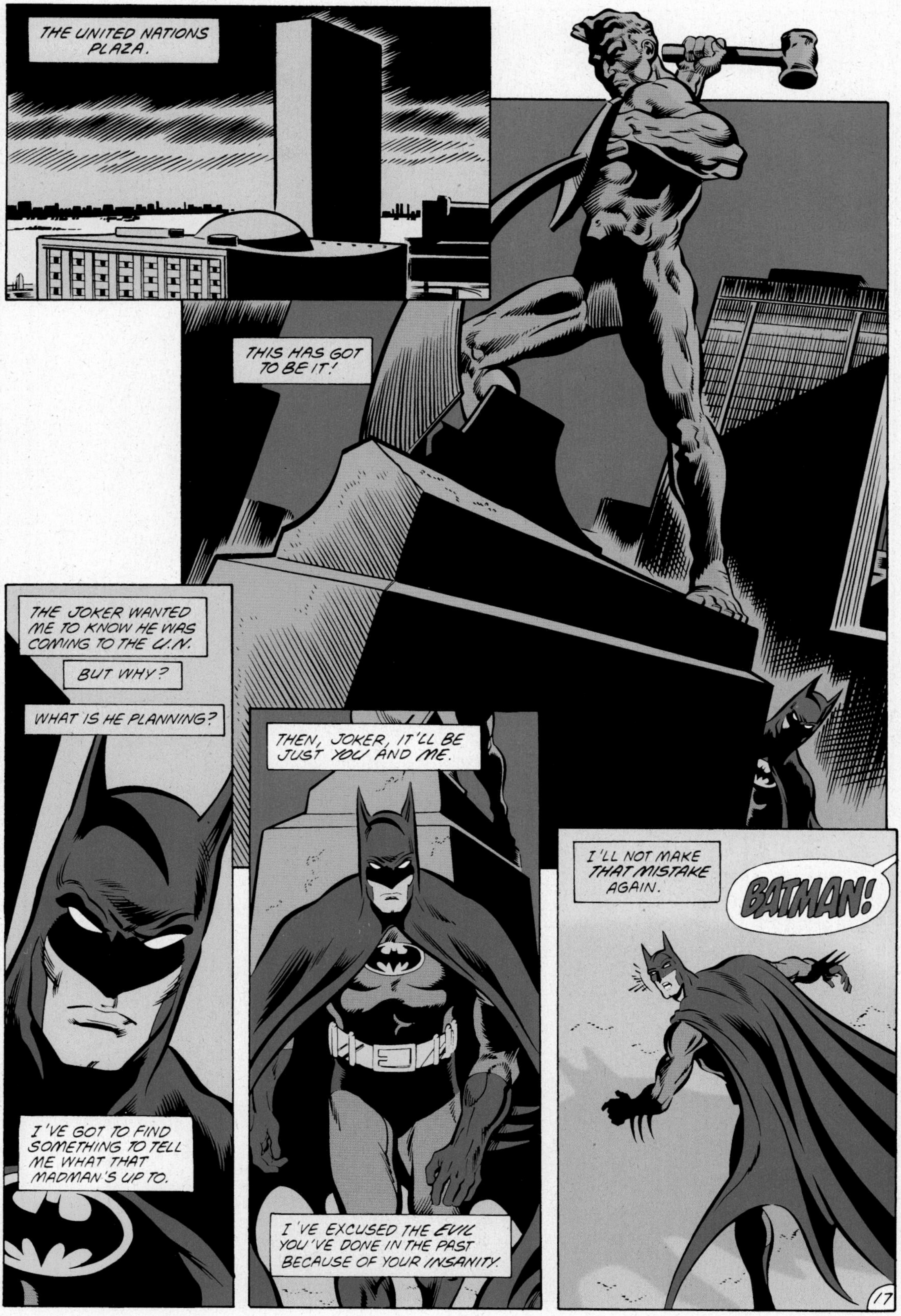

THE UNITED NATIONS PLAZA.
THIS HAS GOT TO BE IT!
THE JOKER WANTED ME TO KNOW HE WAS COMING TO THE U.N.
BUT WHY?
WHAT IS HE PLANNING?
I'VE GOT TO FIND SOMETHING TO TELL ME WHAT THAT MADMAN'S UP TO.
THEN, JOKER, IT'LL BE JUST YOU AND ME.
I'VE EXCUSED THE EVIL YOU'VE DONE IN THE PAST BECAUSE OF YOUR INSANITY.
I'LL NOT MAKE THAT MISTAKE AGAIN.
BATMAN!
17

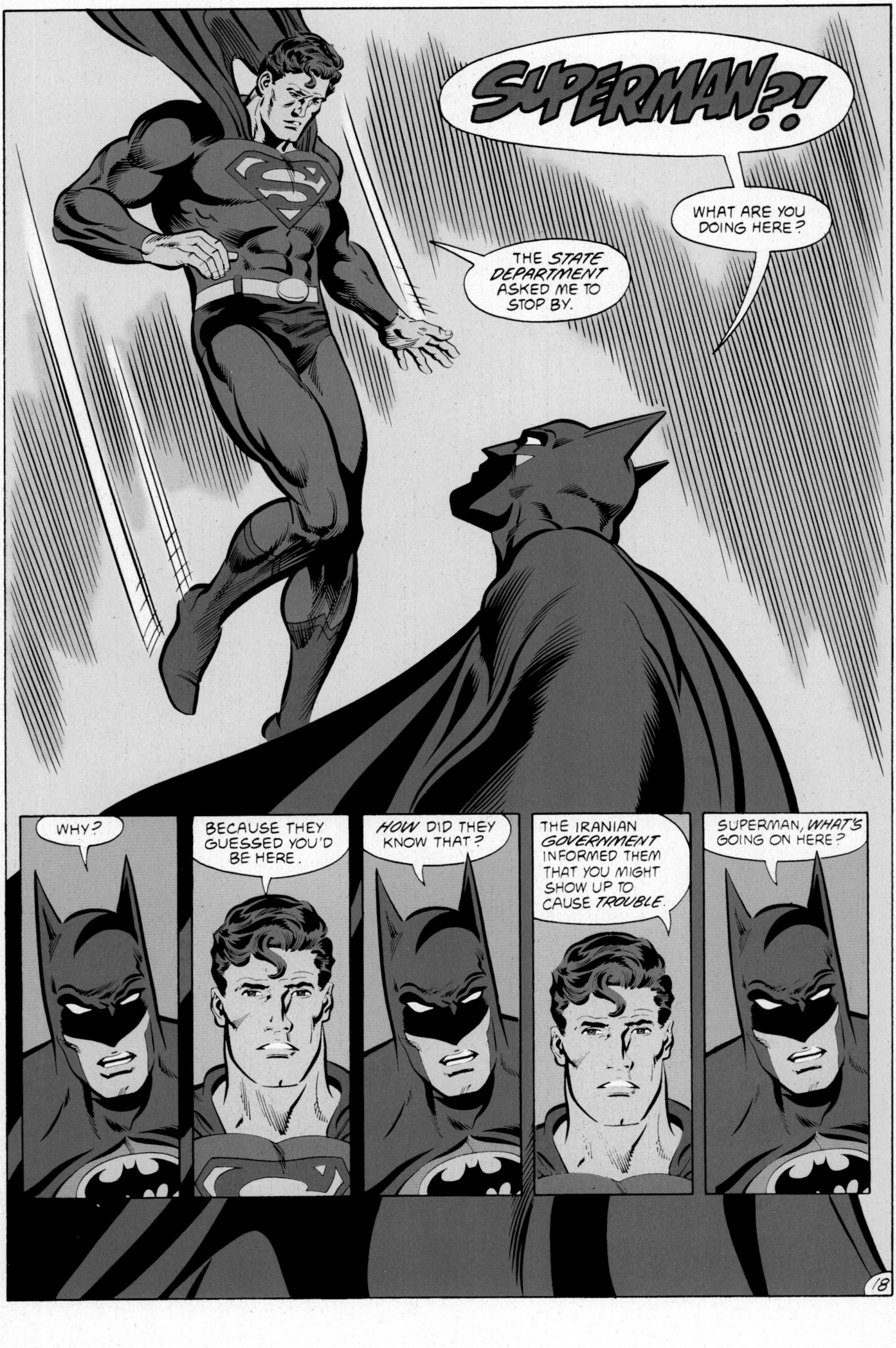
SUPERMAN?!
WHAT ARE YOU DOING HERE?
THE STATE DEPARTMENT ASKED ME TO STOP BY.
WHY?
BECAUSE THEY GUESSED YOU'D BE HERE.
HOW DID THEY KNOW THAT?
THE IRANIAN GOVERNMENT INFORMED THEM THAT YOU MIGHT SHOW UP TO CAUSE TROUBLE.
SUPERMAN, WHAT'S GOING ON HERE?
18

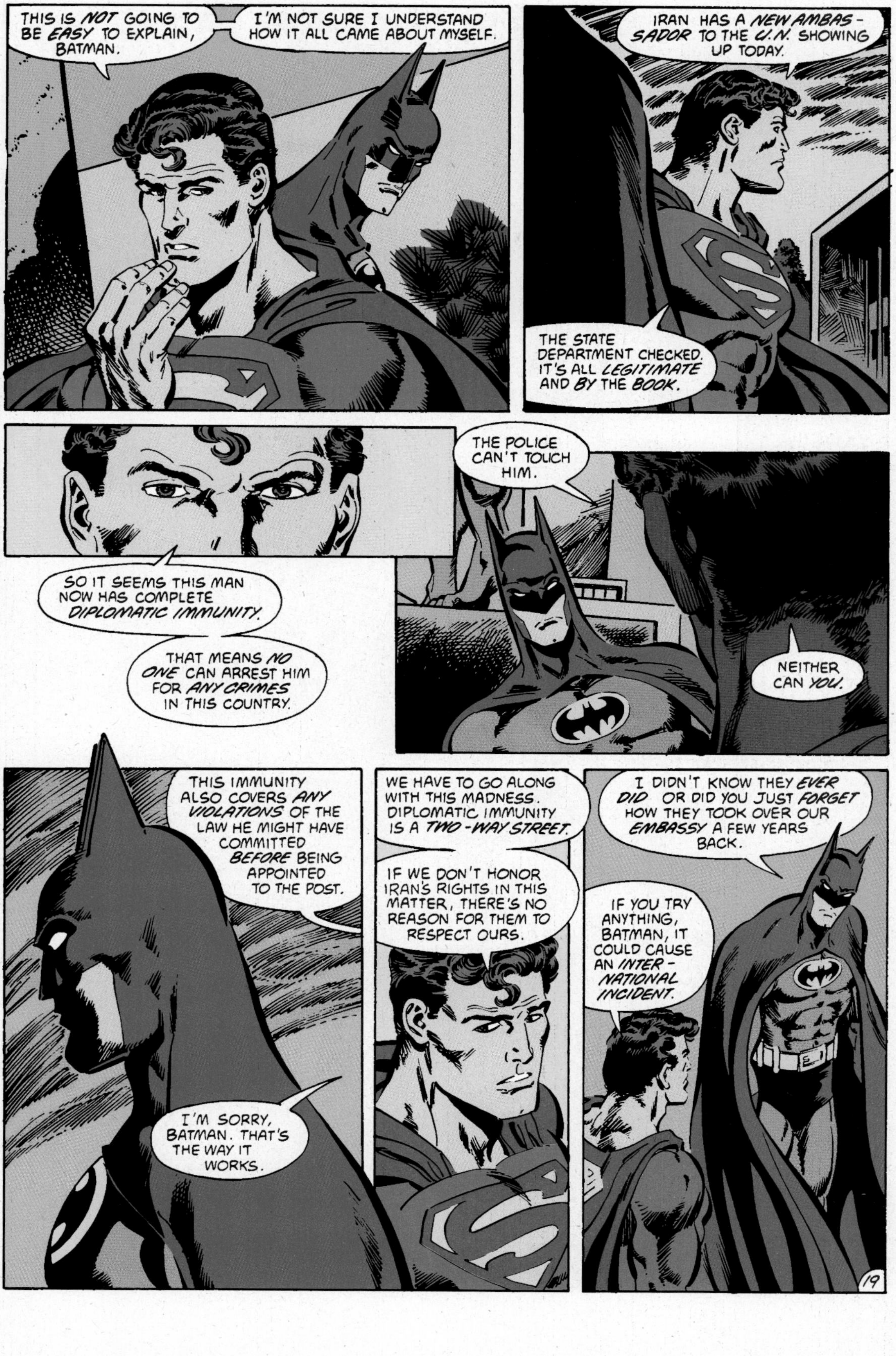

THIS IS *NOT* GOING TO BE *EASY* TO EXPLAIN, BATMAN.
I'M NOT SURE I UNDERSTAND HOW IT ALL CAME ABOUT MYSELF.
IRAN HAS A *NEW AMBASSADOR* TO THE *U.N.* SHOWING UP TODAY.
THE STATE DEPARTMENT CHECKED. IT'S ALL *LEGITIMATE* AND *BY* THE *BOOK*.
SO IT SEEMS THIS MAN NOW HAS COMPLETE *DIPLOMATIC IMMUNITY*.
THAT MEANS *NO ONE* CAN ARREST HIM FOR *ANY CRIMES* IN THIS COUNTRY.
THE POLICE CAN'T TOUCH HIM.
NEITHER CAN *YOU*.
THIS IMMUNITY ALSO COVERS *ANY VIOLATIONS* OF THE LAW HE MIGHT HAVE COMMITTED *BEFORE* BEING APPOINTED TO THE POST.
I'M SORRY, BATMAN. THAT'S THE WAY IT WORKS.
WE HAVE TO GO ALONG WITH THIS MADNESS. DIPLOMATIC IMMUNITY IS A *TWO-WAY STREET*.
IF WE DON'T HONOR IRAN'S RIGHTS IN THIS MATTER, THERE'S NO REASON FOR THEM TO RESPECT OURS.
I DIDN'T KNOW THEY *EVER DID* OR DID YOU JUST *FORGET* HOW THEY TOOK OVER OUR *EMBASSY* A FEW YEARS BACK.
IF YOU TRY ANYTHING, BATMAN, IT COULD CAUSE AN *INTERNATIONAL INCIDENT*.
19

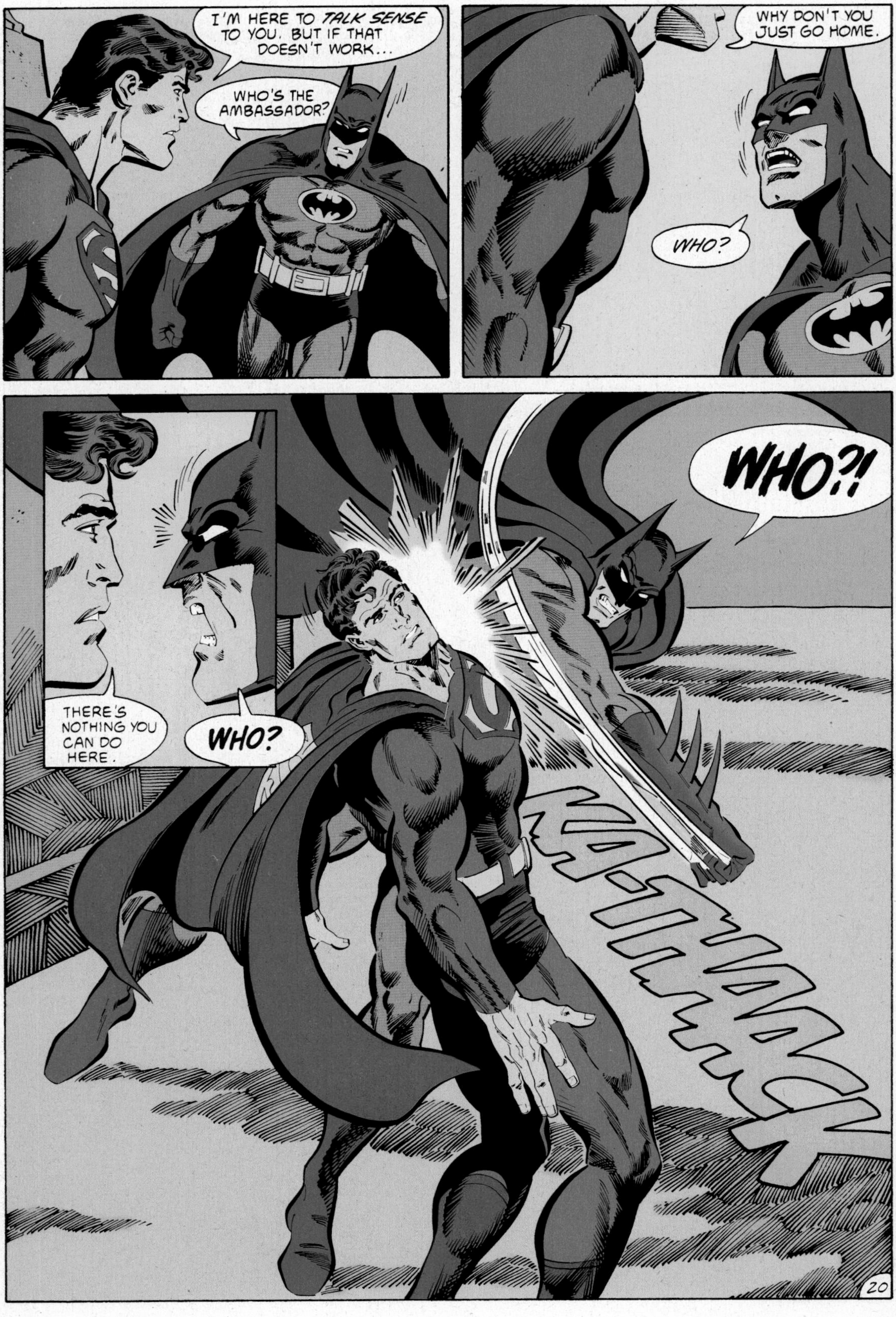
I'M HERE TO TALK SENSE TO YOU. BUT IF THAT DOESN'T WORK...
WHO'S THE AMBASSADOR?
WHY DON'T YOU JUST GO HOME.
WHO?
THERE'S NOTHING YOU CAN DO HERE.
WHO?
WHO?!
KA-THWACK
20

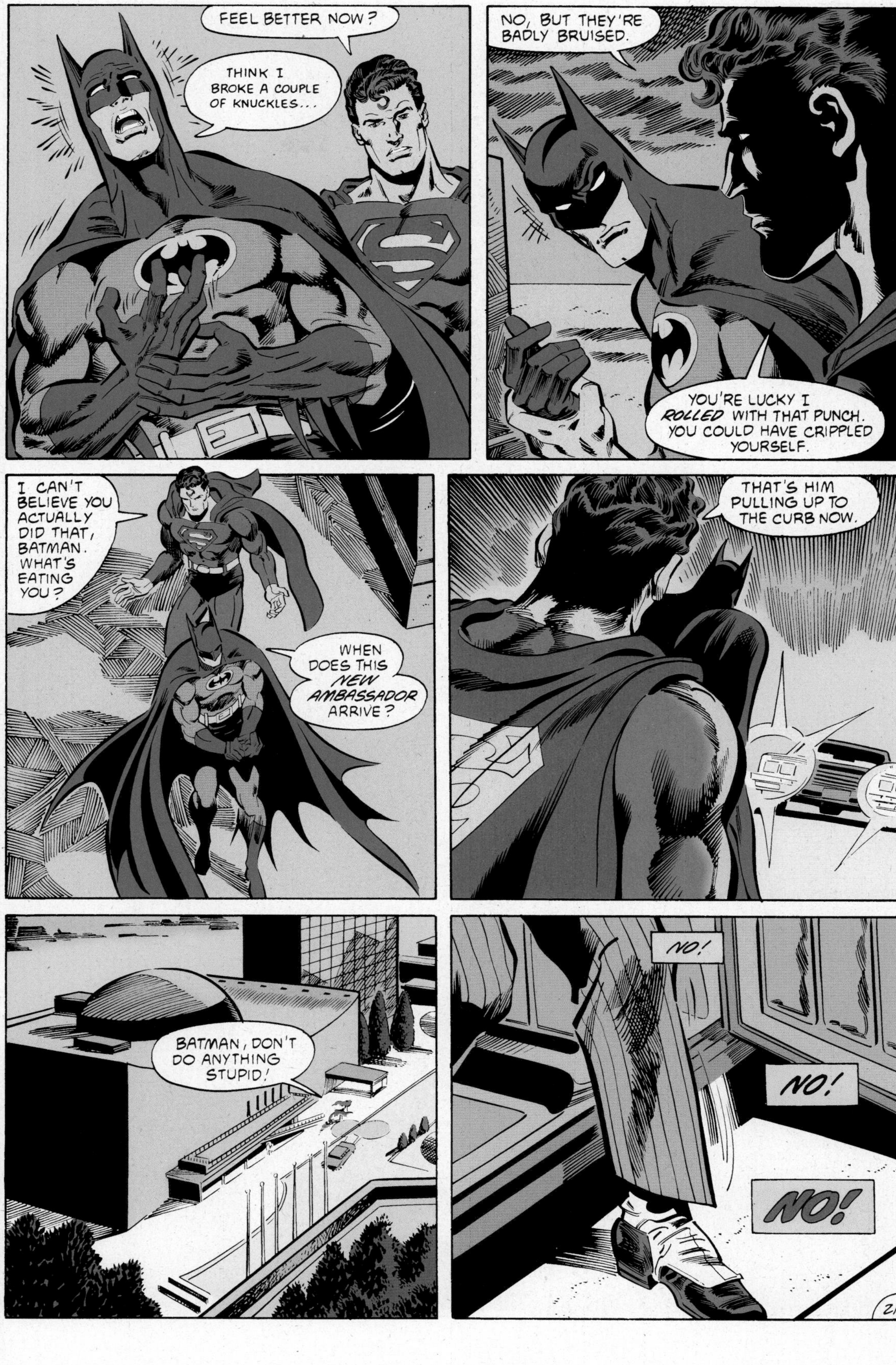

FEEL BETTER NOW?
THINK I BROKE A COUPLE OF KNUCKLES...
NO, BUT THEY'RE BADLY BRUISED.
YOU'RE LUCKY I ROLLED WITH THAT PUNCH. YOU COULD HAVE CRIPPLED YOURSELF.
I CAN'T BELIEVE YOU ACTUALLY DID THAT, BATMAN. WHAT'S EATING YOU?
WHEN DOES THIS NEW AMBASSADOR ARRIVE?
THAT'S HIM PULLING UP TO THE CURB NOW.
BATMAN, DON'T DO ANYTHING STUPID!
NO!
NO!
NO!
21

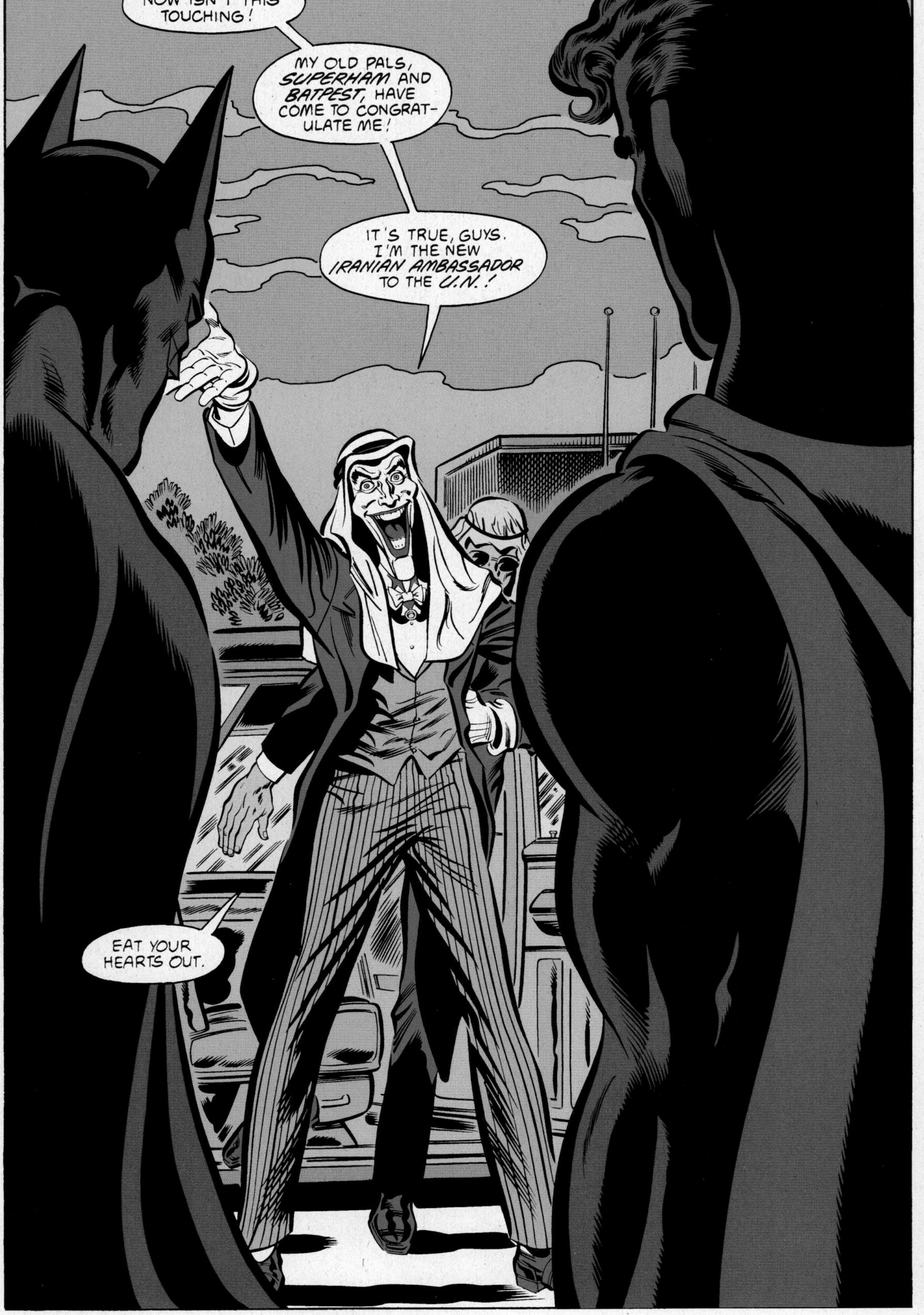
NOW ISN'T THIS TOUCHING!
MY OLD PALS, SUPERHAM AND BATPEST, HAVE COME TO CONGRAT-ULATE ME!
IT'S TRUE, GUYS. I'M THE NEW IRANIAN AMBASSADOR TO THE U.N.!
EAT YOUR HEARTS OUT.

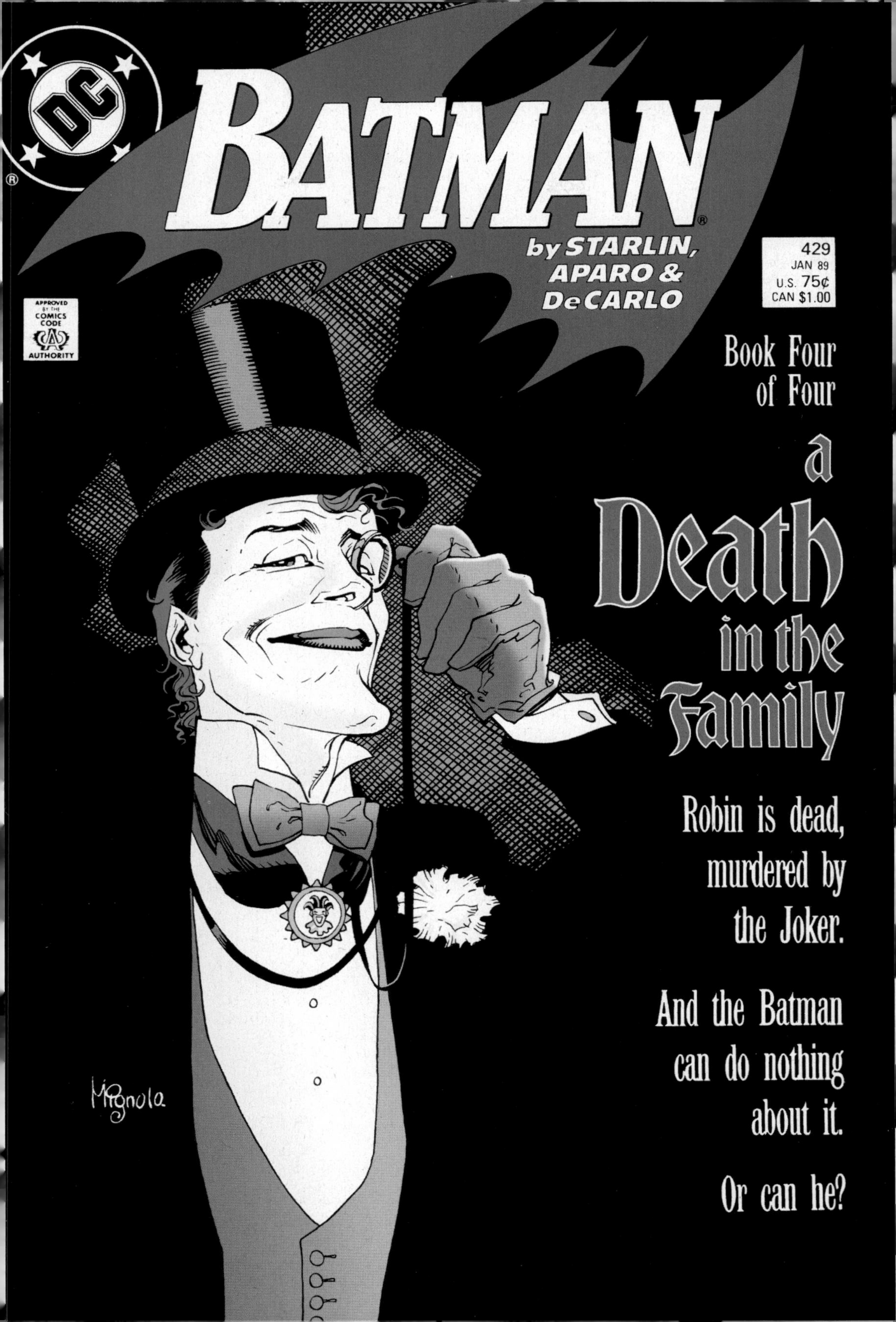

DC
BATMAN
by STARLIN, APARO & DeCARLO
429
JAN 89
U.S. 75¢
CAN $1.00
APPROVED BY THE COMICS CODE AUTHORITY
Book Four of Four
a Death in the Family
Robin is dead, murdered by the Joker.
And the Batman can do nothing about it.
Or can he?
Mignola

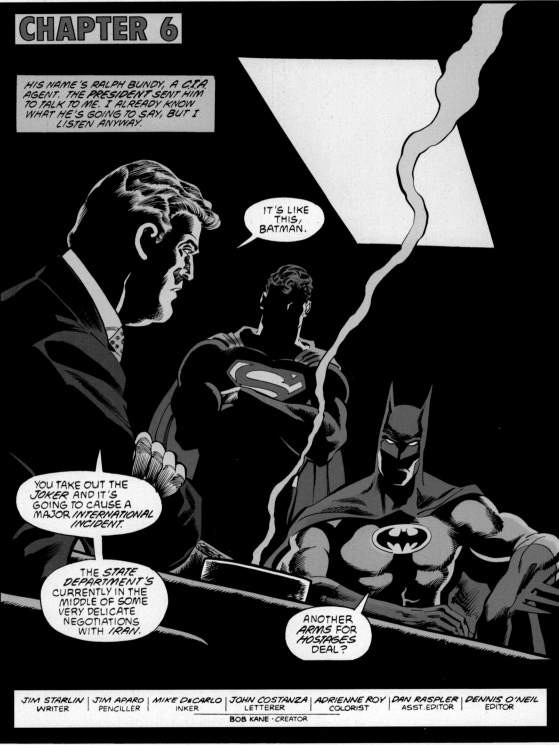

CHAPTER 6

HIS NAME'S RALPH BUNDY, A C.I.A. AGENT. THE *PRESIDENT* SENT HIM TO TALK TO ME. I ALREADY KNOW WHAT HE'S GOING TO SAY, BUT I LISTEN ANYWAY.

IT'S LIKE THIS, BATMAN.

YOU TAKE OUT THE *JOKER* AND IT'S GOING TO CAUSE A MAJOR *INTERNATIONAL INCIDENT.*

THE *STATE DEPARTMENT'S* CURRENTLY IN THE MIDDLE OF SOME VERY DELICATE NEGOTIATIONS WITH *IRAN.*

ANOTHER ARMS FOR HOSTAGES DEAL?

| JIM STARLIN | JIM APARO | MIKE DeCARLO | JOHN COSTANZA | ADRIENNE ROY | DAN RASPLER | DENNIS O'NEIL |
| WRITER | PENCILLER | INKER | LETTERER | COLORIST | ASST. EDITOR | EDITOR |

BOB KANE · CREATOR

THAT'S NONE OF YOUR BUSINESS.

GUYS LIKE US SHOULD JUST DO OUR JOBS AND LET THE *"BIGSHOTS"* DO THEIRS.

THEY KNOW WHAT'S DOING AND THEY SAY *HANDS OFF* IRAN'S NEW *U.N.* AMBASSADOR!

UNDERSTAND?

THE JOKER'S GOT *DIPLOMATIC IMMUNITY.* STATE DOESN'T WANT ANYONE MESSING WITH HIM.

ESPECIALLY *YOU!*

YOU CAN'T BE SERIOUS. THE JOKER'S A *HOMICIDAL MANIAC.*

THEY ONLY MADE HIM AMBASSADOR SO HE CAN *KILL* SOMEONE, PROBABLY THE ENTIRE *U.N.* GENERAL ASSEMBLY.

WE'VE GOT NO *HARD EVIDENCE* TO PROVE THAT.

UNTIL WE DO, THE JOKER HAS TO BE TREATED LIKE ANY OTHER DELEGATE.

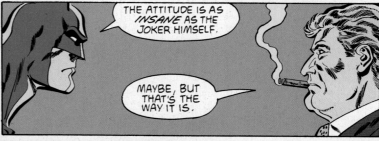

THE ATTITUDE IS AS *INSANE* AS THE JOKER HIMSELF.

MAYBE, BUT THAT'S THE WAY IT IS.

NOT FOR *ME,* IT ISN'T.

AFRAID SO, PAL.

2

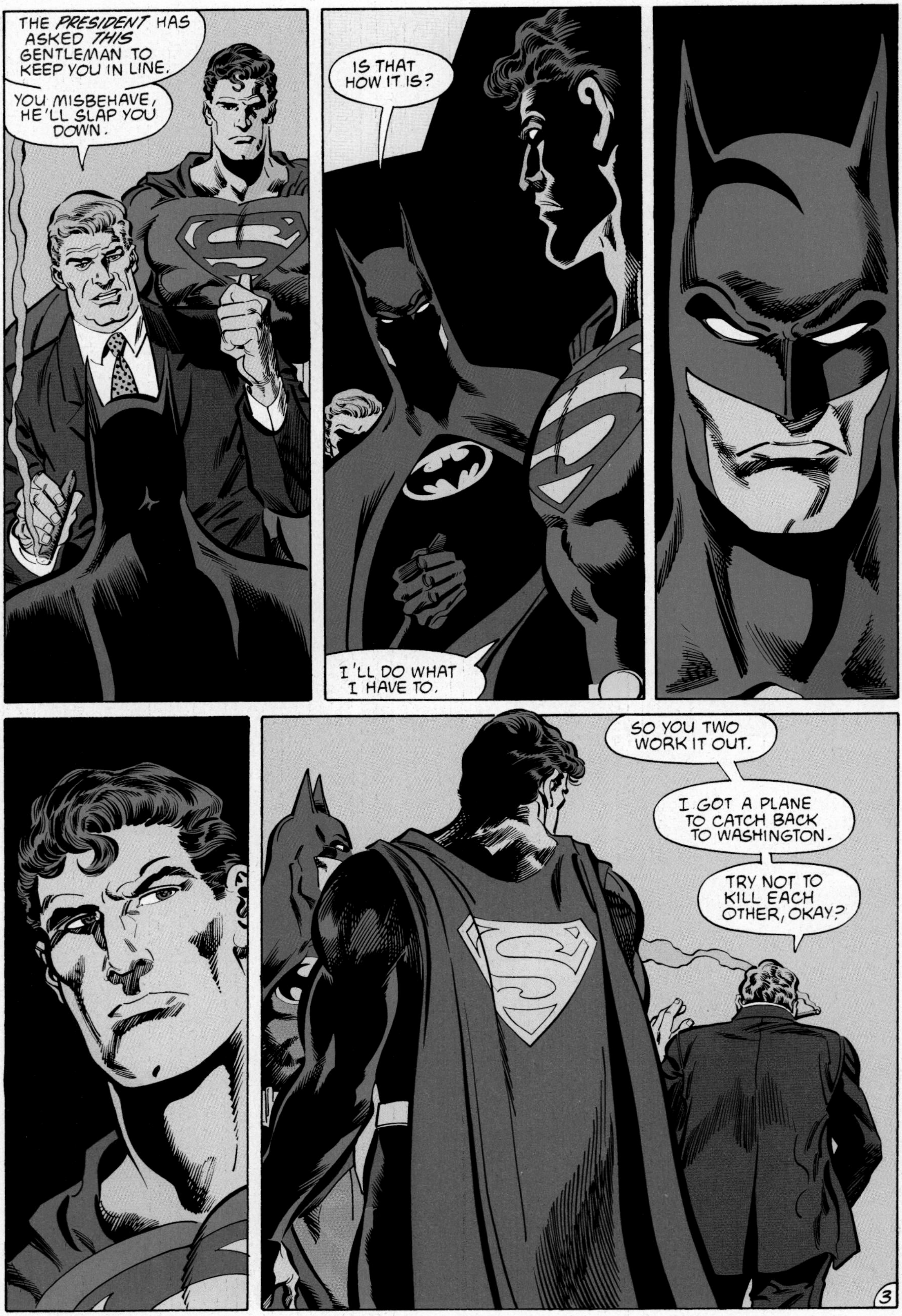
THE *PRESIDENT* HAS ASKED *THIS* GENTLEMAN TO KEEP YOU IN LINE.
YOU MISBEHAVE, HE'LL SLAP YOU DOWN.
IS THAT HOW IT IS?
I'LL DO WHAT I HAVE TO.
SO YOU TWO WORK IT OUT.
I GOT A PLANE TO CATCH BACK TO WASHINGTON.
TRY NOT TO KILL EACH OTHER, OKAY?
3

BATMAN... BRUCE...

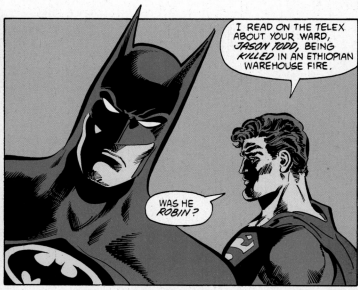

I READ ON THE TELEX ABOUT YOUR WARD, JASON TODD, BEING KILLED IN AN ETHIOPIAN WAREHOUSE FIRE.

WAS HE ROBIN?

YES.

I'M SORRY TO HEAR THAT.

HE SEEMED LIKE A REALLY NICE KID.

HE WAS.

JASON WAS THE BEST.

THE JOKER MURDERED HIM.

YOU HAVE PROOF?

A DEATH BED STATEMENT BY HIS MOTHER. GOOD ENOUGH FOR ME IF NOT A COURT OF LAW.

BUT THE JOKER'S IMMUNIZED FROM RETRIBUTION FOR THAT AND ANY OTHER CRIME THAT HE'S EVER COMMITTED.

THAT'S THE LAW, NOT JUSTICE.

DON'T DO ANYTHING STUPID, BRUCE.

4

YOU CAN'T PUT YOUR *THIRST* FOR *VENGE-ANCE* ABOVE YOUR COUNTRY'S *BEST INTERESTS.*

SPARE ME YOUR *BOY SCOUT SENTIMENTALITIES,* KENT.

TO USE YOUR OWN WORDS... I'LL DO WHAT I HAVE TO.

MAYBE, WITH A LITTLE *LUCK,* WE'LL *NOT* FIND OURSELVES AT *CROSS PURPOSES.*

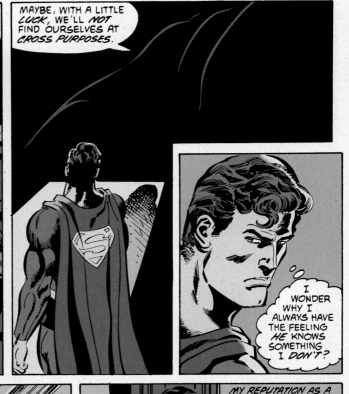

I WONDER WHY I ALWAYS HAVE THE FEELING *HE* KNOWS SOMETHING I *DON'T?*

BACK IN MY *HOTEL ROOM,* I SEE WHAT MY *FEDERAL CONTACTS* CAN DO ABOUT GETTING ME INTO THE *GENERAL ASSEMBLY* AS *BRUCE WAYNE.*

MY REPUTATION AS A *PLAYBOY DILETTANTE* KEEPS ME FROM OBTAINING A POSITION AS A *DELEGATE.*

BUT THEY MANAGE TO SQUEEZE ME IN AS AN *UNOFFICIAL OBSERVER.*

NOW I CAN KEEP AN EYE ON THE *JOKER* WITHOUT MAKING THE *STATE DEPARTMENT* NERVOUS.

THE *FOOLS.*

LOOKS LIKE THIS IS IT.

THE FINAL SHOWDOWN BETWEEN THE JOKER AND MYSELF.

GUESS I ALWAYS KNEW IT WOULD SOMEDAY COME TO THIS.

ONE OF US IS GOING TO DIE. BUT IS THAT REALLY WHAT I WANT TO SEE HAPPEN?

THE MAN'S HOPE-LESSLY INSANE. HOW CAN I HOLD HIM RESPONSIBLE EVEN FOR WHAT HAPPENED TO JASON?

OR AM I JUST LOOKING FOR A COP-OUT?

ADMIT IT, WAYNE. THE JOKER'S COME CLOSE TO FINISHING YOU OFF DOZENS OF TIMES. TOO CLOSE.

YOU'RE STILL NOT BACK TO TOTAL EFFI-CIENCY AFTER THAT ENCOUNTER YOU HAD WITH DEACON BLACK-FIRE.

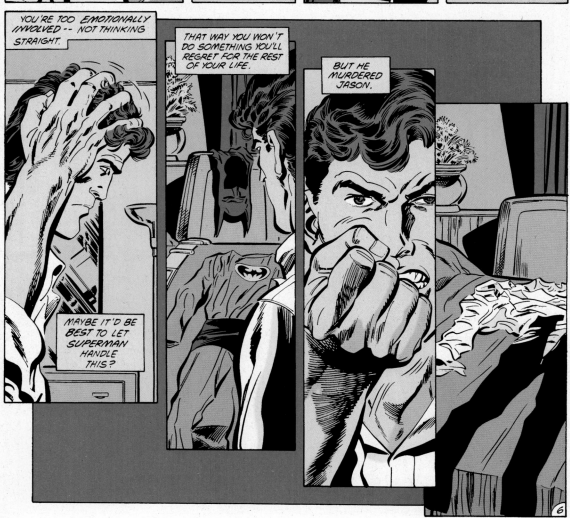

YOU'RE TOO EMOTIONALLY INVOLVED -- NOT THINKING STRAIGHT.

MAYBE IT'D BE BEST TO LET SUPERMAN HANDLE THIS?

THAT WAY YOU WON'T DO SOMETHING YOU'LL REGRET FOR THE REST OF YOUR LIFE.

BUT HE MURDERED JASON.

6

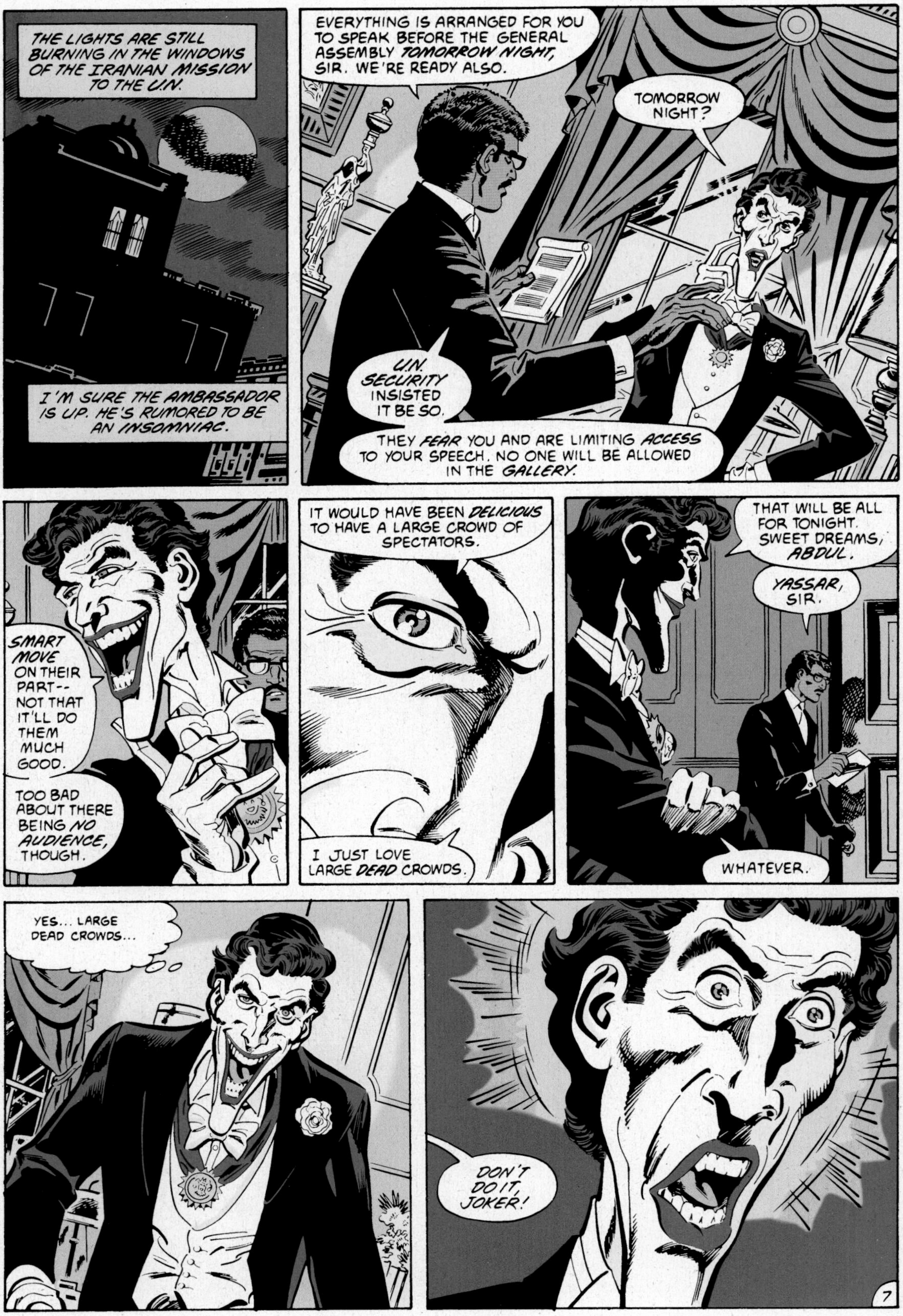
THE LIGHTS ARE STILL BURNING IN THE WINDOWS OF THE IRANIAN MISSION TO THE U.N.
I'M SURE THE AMBASSADOR IS UP. HE'S RUMORED TO BE AN INSOMNIAC.
EVERYTHING IS ARRANGED FOR YOU TO SPEAK BEFORE THE GENERAL ASSEMBLY TOMORROW NIGHT, SIR. WE'RE READY ALSO.
TOMORROW NIGHT?
U.N. SECURITY INSISTED IT BE SO.
THEY FEAR YOU AND ARE LIMITING ACCESS TO YOUR SPEECH. NO ONE WILL BE ALLOWED IN THE GALLERY.
SMART MOVE ON THEIR PART-- NOT THAT IT'LL DO THEM MUCH GOOD.
TOO BAD ABOUT THERE BEING NO AUDIENCE, THOUGH.
IT WOULD HAVE BEEN DELICIOUS TO HAVE A LARGE CROWD OF SPECTATORS.
I JUST LOVE LARGE DEAD CROWDS.
THAT WILL BE ALL FOR TONIGHT. SWEET DREAMS, ABDUL.
YASSAR, SIR.
WHATEVER.
YES... LARGE DEAD CROWDS...
DON'T DO IT, JOKER!
7

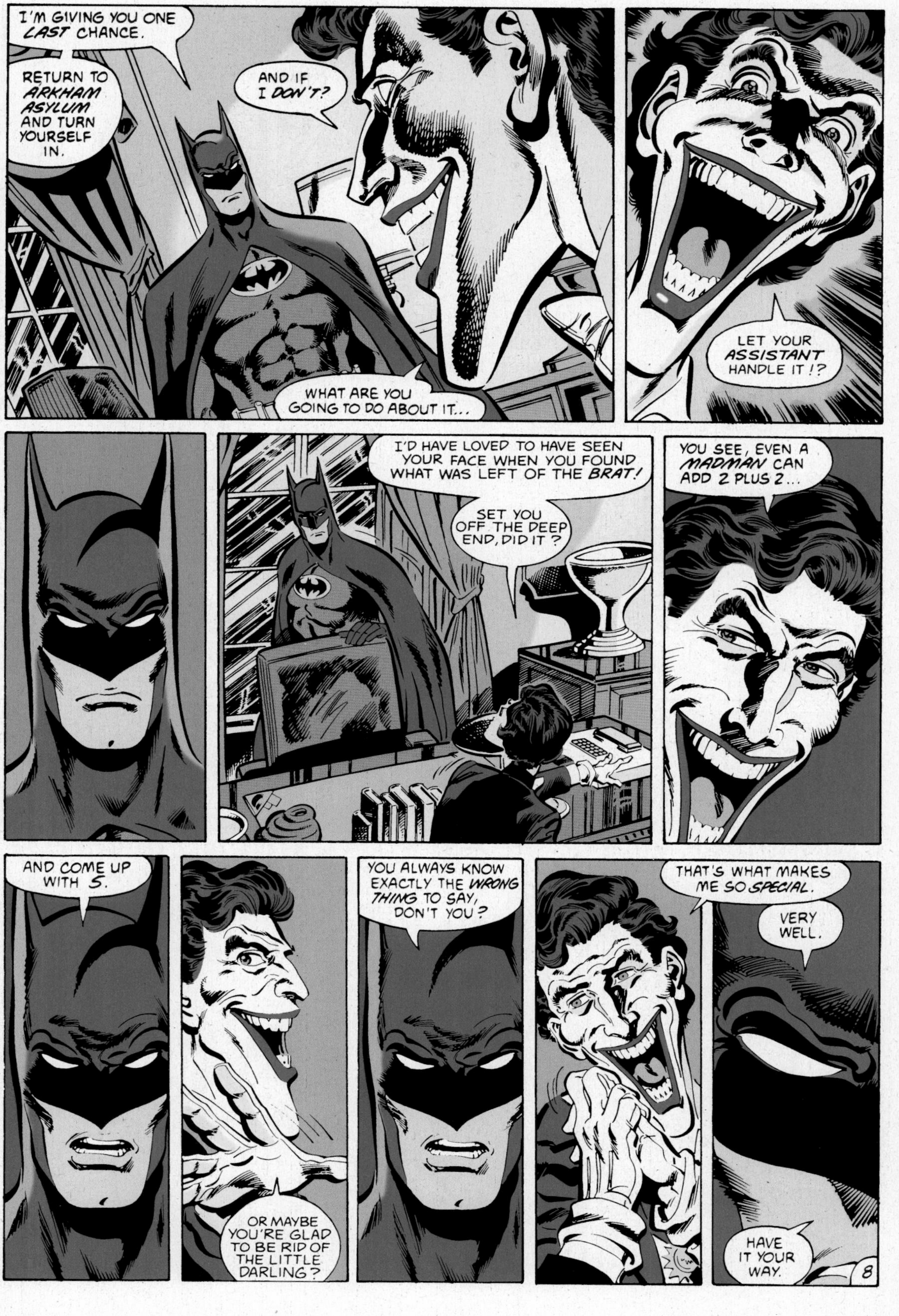
I'M GIVING YOU ONE LAST CHANCE.
RETURN TO ARKHAM ASYLUM AND TURN YOURSELF IN.
AND IF I DON'T?
WHAT ARE YOU GOING TO DO ABOUT IT...
LET YOUR ASSISTANT HANDLE IT!?
I'D HAVE LOVED TO HAVE SEEN YOUR FACE WHEN YOU FOUND WHAT WAS LEFT OF THE BRAT!
SET YOU OFF THE DEEP END, DID IT?
YOU SEE, EVEN A MADMAN CAN ADD 2 PLUS 2...
AND COME UP WITH 5.
OR MAYBE YOU'RE GLAD TO BE RID OF THE LITTLE DARLING?
YOU ALWAYS KNOW EXACTLY THE WRONG THING TO SAY, DON'T YOU?
THAT'S WHAT MAKES ME SO SPECIAL.
VERY WELL.
HAVE IT YOUR WAY.
8

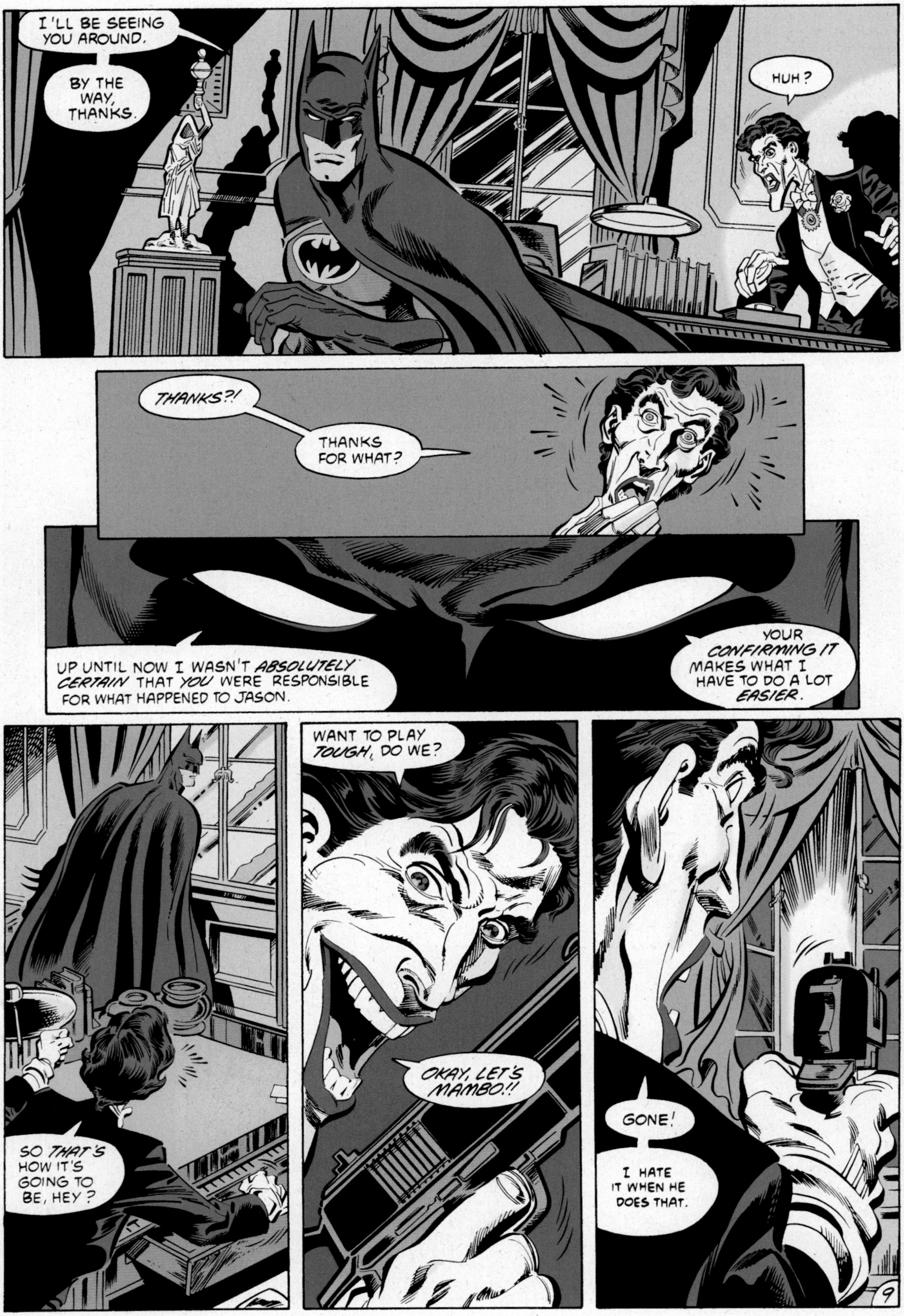
I'LL BE SEEING YOU AROUND.
BY THE WAY, THANKS.
HUH?
THANKS?!
THANKS FOR WHAT?
UP UNTIL NOW I WASN'T ABSOLUTELY CERTAIN THAT YOU WERE RESPONSIBLE FOR WHAT HAPPENED TO JASON.
YOUR CONFIRMING IT MAKES WHAT I HAVE TO DO A LOT EASIER.
SO THAT'S HOW IT'S GOING TO BE, HEY?
WANT TO PLAY TOUGH, DO WE?
OKAY, LET'S MAMBO!!
GONE!
I HATE IT WHEN HE DOES THAT.
9

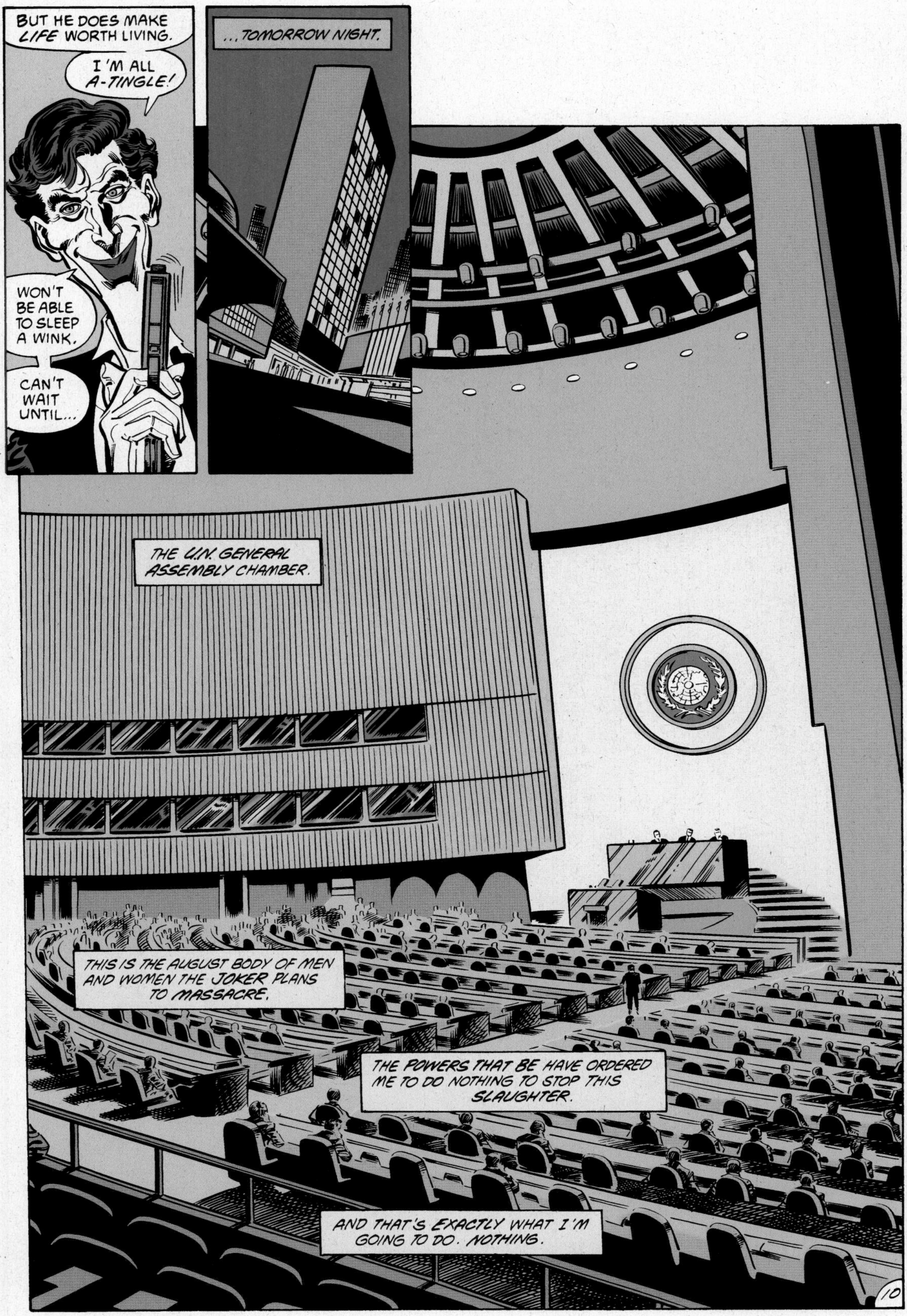

BUT HE DOES MAKE LIFE WORTH LIVING.
I'M ALL A-TINGLE!
WON'T BE ABLE TO SLEEP A WINK.
CAN'T WAIT UNTIL...
...TOMORROW NIGHT.
THE U.N. GENERAL ASSEMBLY CHAMBER.
THIS IS THE AUGUST BODY OF MEN AND WOMEN THE JOKER PLANS TO MASSACRE.
THE POWERS THAT BE HAVE ORDERED ME TO DO NOTHING TO STOP THIS SLAUGHTER.
AND THAT'S EXACTLY WHAT I'M GOING TO DO. NOTHING.
10

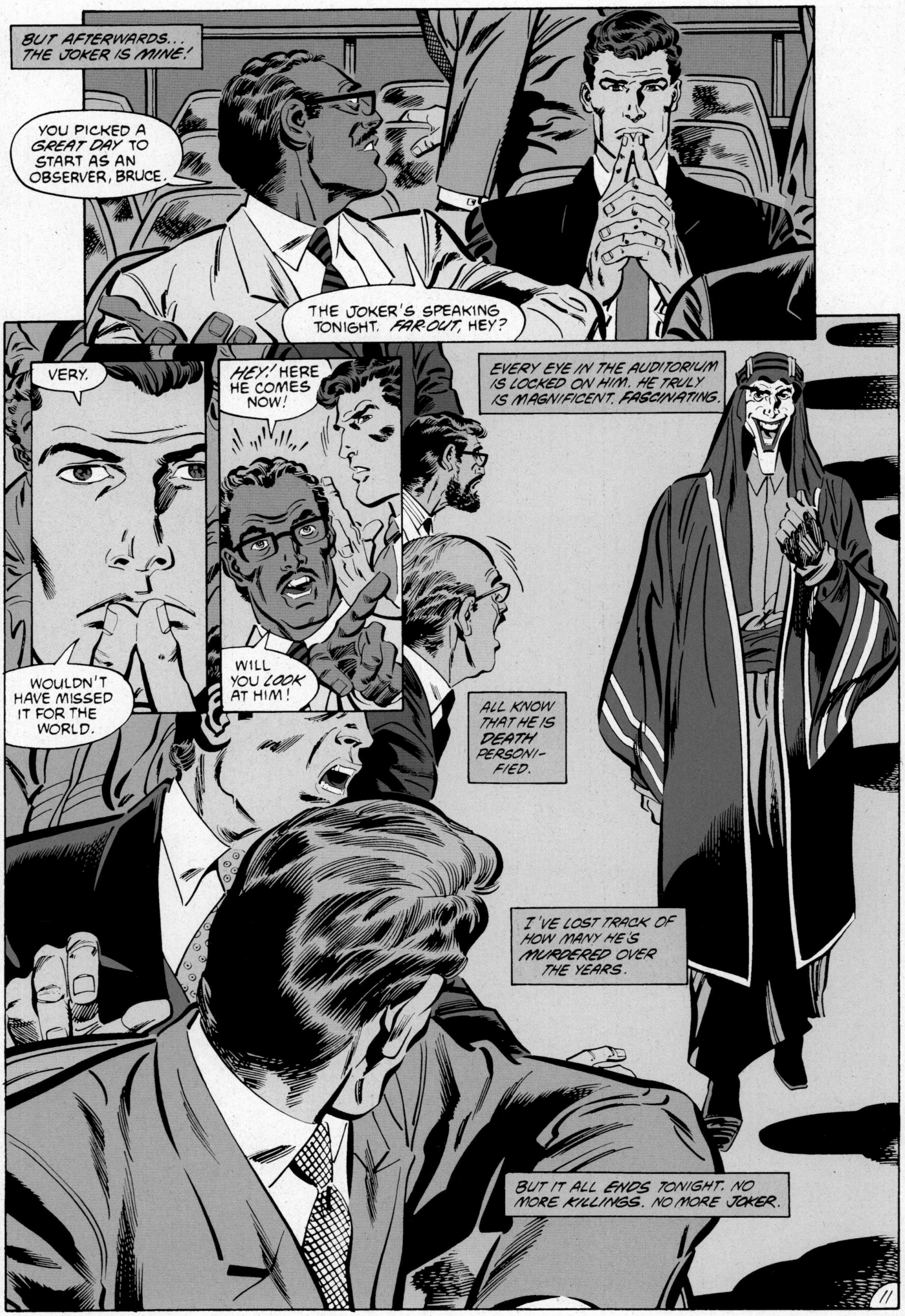
BUT AFTERWARDS... THE JOKER IS MINE!
YOU PICKED A GREAT DAY TO START AS AN OBSERVER, BRUCE.
THE JOKER'S SPEAKING TONIGHT. FAR-OUT, HEY?
VERY.
WOULDN'T HAVE MISSED IT FOR THE WORLD.
HEY! HERE HE COMES NOW!
WILL YOU LOOK AT HIM!
EVERY EYE IN THE AUDITORIUM IS LOCKED ON HIM. HE TRULY IS MAGNIFICENT. FASCINATING.
ALL KNOW THAT HE IS DEATH PERSONIFIED.
I'VE LOST TRACK OF HOW MANY HE'S MURDERED OVER THE YEARS.
BUT IT ALL ENDS TONIGHT. NO MORE KILLINGS. NO MORE JOKER.
11

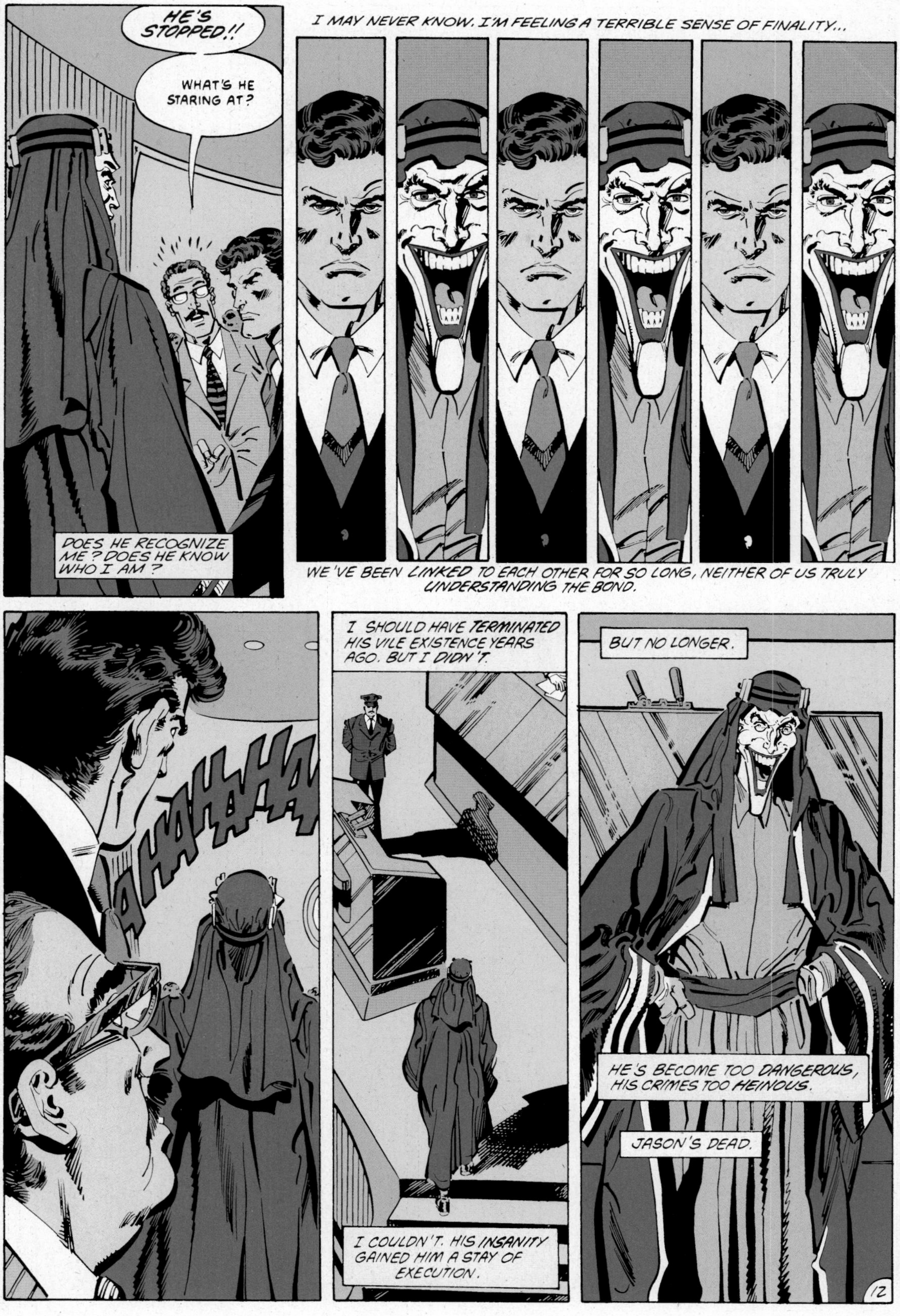
HE'S STOPPED!!
WHAT'S HE STARING AT?
DOES HE RECOGNIZE ME? DOES HE KNOW WHO I AM?
I MAY NEVER KNOW. I'M FEELING A TERRIBLE SENSE OF FINALITY...
WE'VE BEEN LINKED TO EACH OTHER FOR SO LONG, NEITHER OF US TRULY UNDERSTANDING THE BOND.
HAHAHAHAHA
I SHOULD HAVE TERMINATED HIS VILE EXISTENCE YEARS AGO. BUT I DIDN'T.
I COULDN'T. HIS INSANITY GAINED HIM A STAY OF EXECUTION.
BUT NO LONGER.
HE'S BECOME TOO DANGEROUS, HIS CRIMES TOO HEINOUS.
JASON'S DEAD.
12

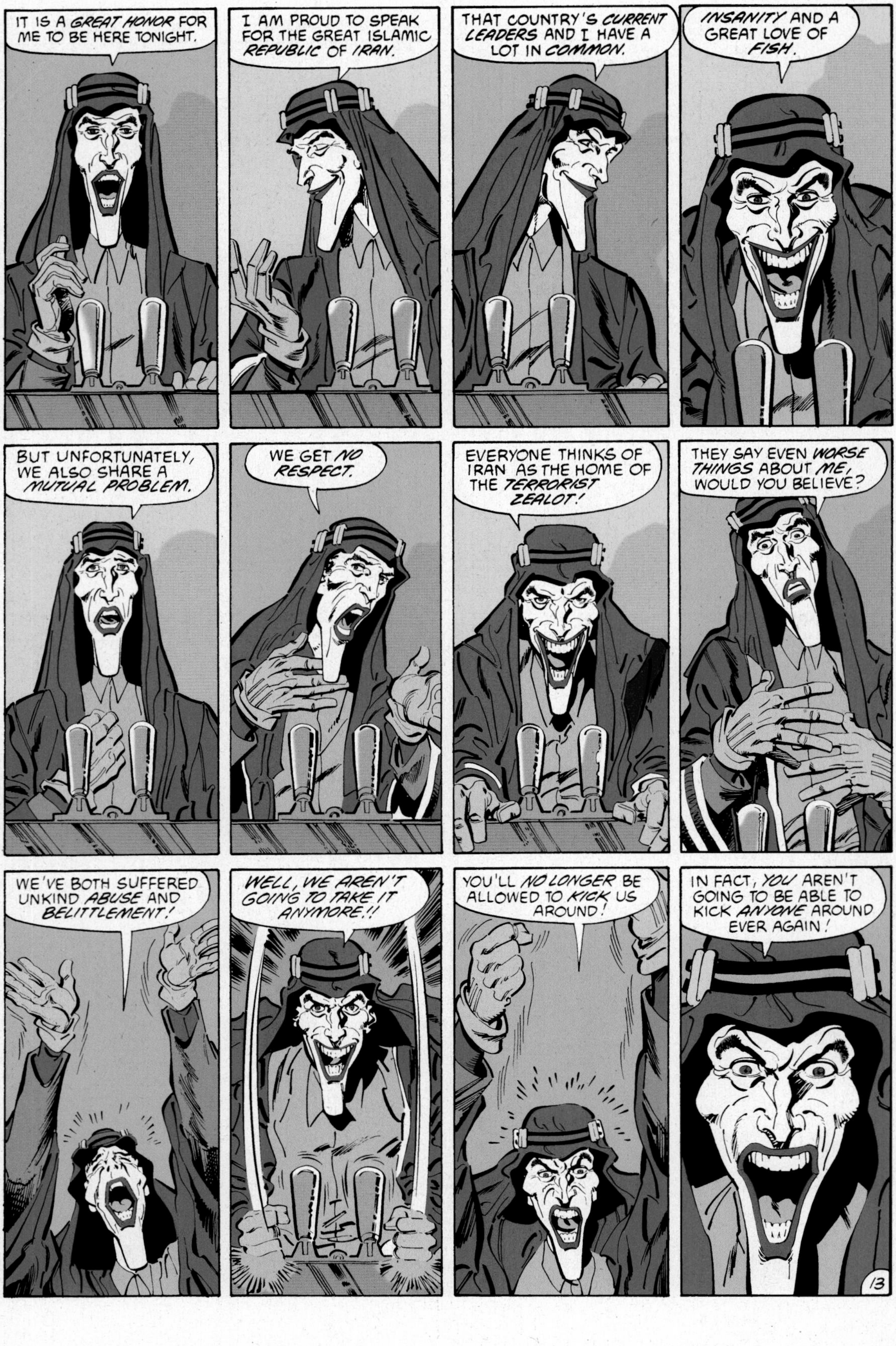
IT IS A GREAT HONOR FOR ME TO BE HERE TONIGHT.
I AM PROUD TO SPEAK FOR THE GREAT ISLAMIC REPUBLIC OF IRAN.
THAT COUNTRY'S CURRENT LEADERS AND I HAVE A LOT IN COMMON.
INSANITY AND A GREAT LOVE OF FISH.
BUT UNFORTUNATELY, WE ALSO SHARE A MUTUAL PROBLEM.
WE GET NO RESPECT.
EVERYONE THINKS OF IRAN AS THE HOME OF THE TERRORIST ZEALOT!
THEY SAY EVEN WORSE THINGS ABOUT ME, WOULD YOU BELIEVE?
WE'VE BOTH SUFFERED UNKIND ABUSE AND BELITTLEMENT!
WELL, WE AREN'T GOING TO TAKE IT ANYMORE!!
YOU'LL NO LONGER BE ALLOWED TO KICK US AROUND!
IN FACT, YOU AREN'T GOING TO BE ABLE TO KICK ANYONE AROUND EVER AGAIN!
13

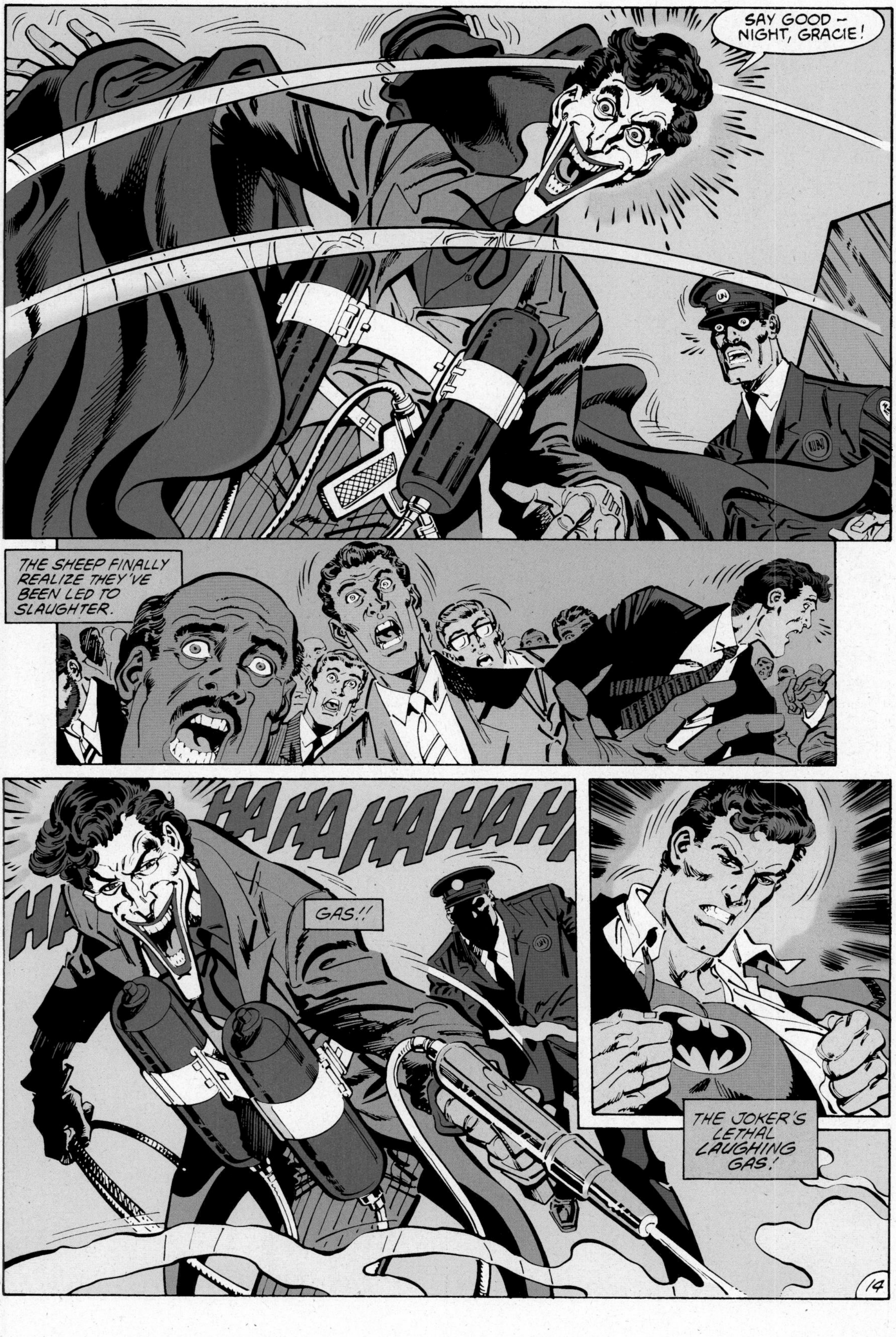
SAY GOOD-NIGHT, GRACIE!
THE SHEEP FINALLY REALIZE THEY'VE BEEN LED TO SLAUGHTER.
HA HA HA HA HA HA H
GAS!!
THE JOKER'S LETHAL LAUGHING GAS!
14

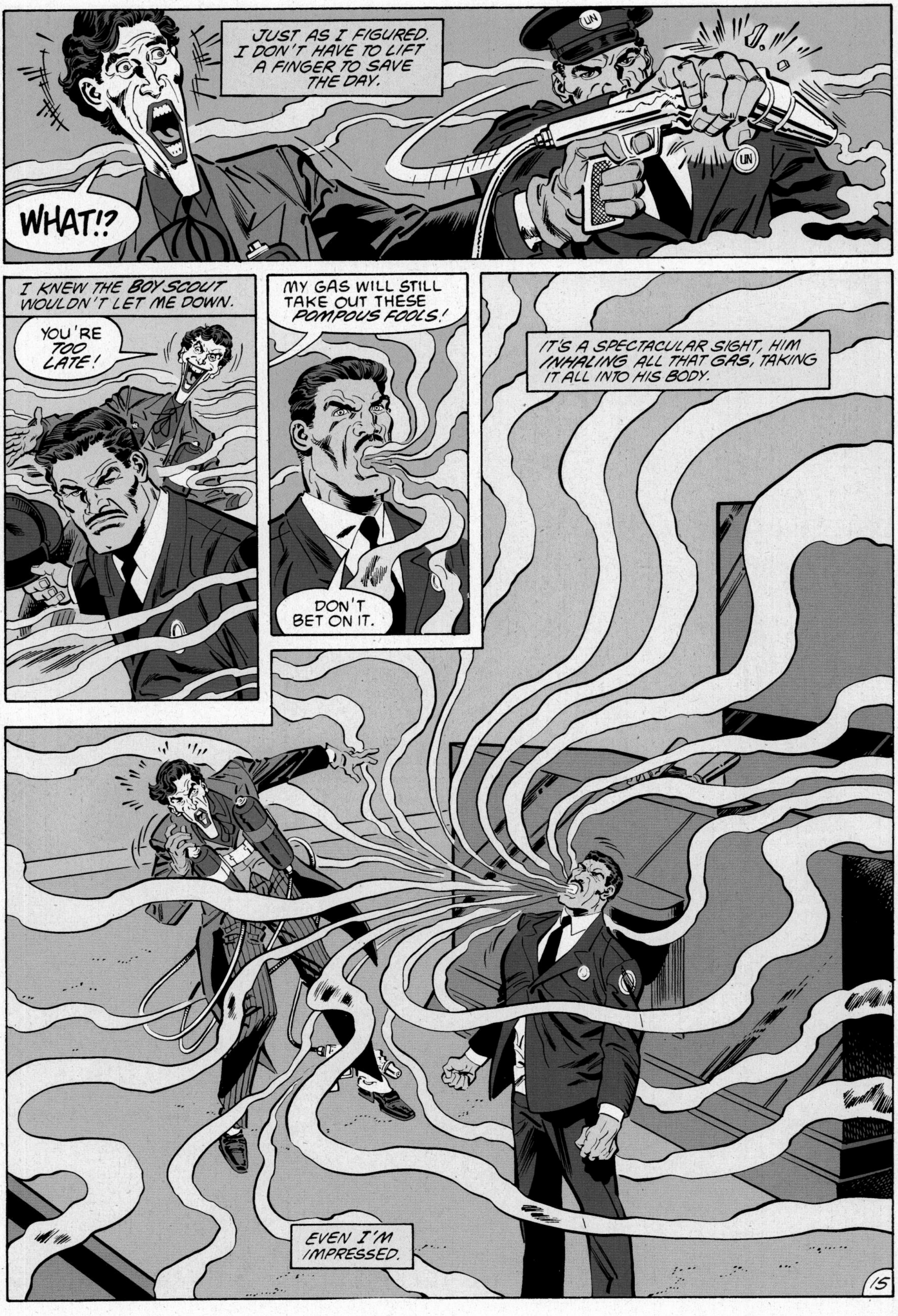
JUST AS I FIGURED. I DON'T HAVE TO LIFT A FINGER TO SAVE THE DAY.
WHAT!?
I KNEW THE BOY SCOUT WOULDN'T LET ME DOWN.
YOU'RE TOO LATE!
MY GAS WILL STILL TAKE OUT THESE POMPOUS FOOLS!
DON'T BET ON IT.
IT'S A SPECTACULAR SIGHT, HIM INHALING ALL THAT GAS, TAKING IT ALL INTO HIS BODY.
EVEN I'M IMPRESSED.
15

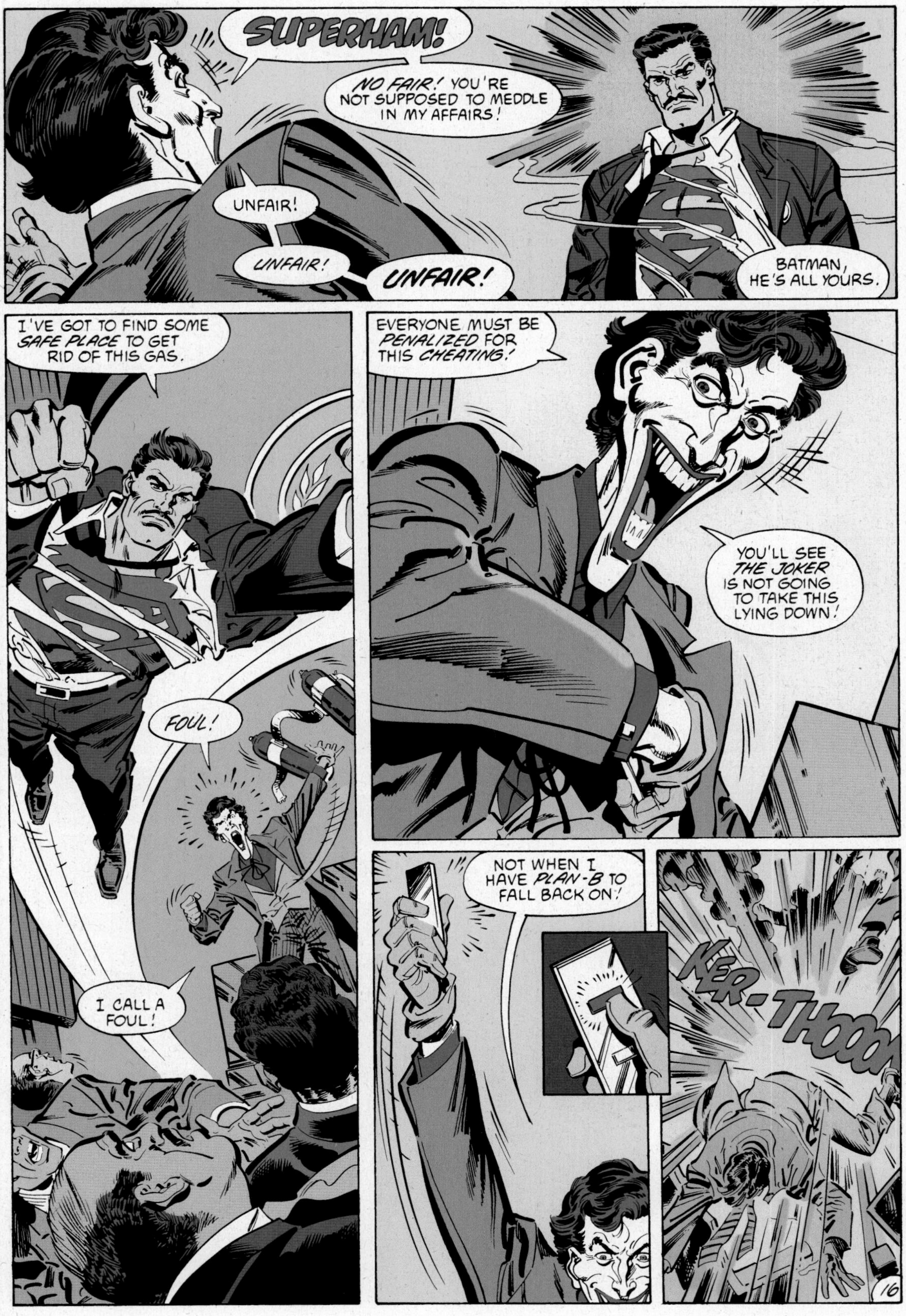
SUPERHAM!
NO FAIR! YOU'RE NOT SUPPOSED TO MEDDLE IN MY AFFAIRS!
UNFAIR!
UNFAIR!
UNFAIR!
BATMAN, HE'S ALL YOURS.
I'VE GOT TO FIND SOME SAFE PLACE TO GET RID OF THIS GAS.
FOUL!
I CALL A FOUL!
EVERYONE MUST BE PENALIZED FOR THIS CHEATING!
YOU'LL SEE THE JOKER IS NOT GOING TO TAKE THIS LYING DOWN!
NOT WHEN I HAVE PLAN-B TO FALL BACK ON!
KER-THOOOM
16

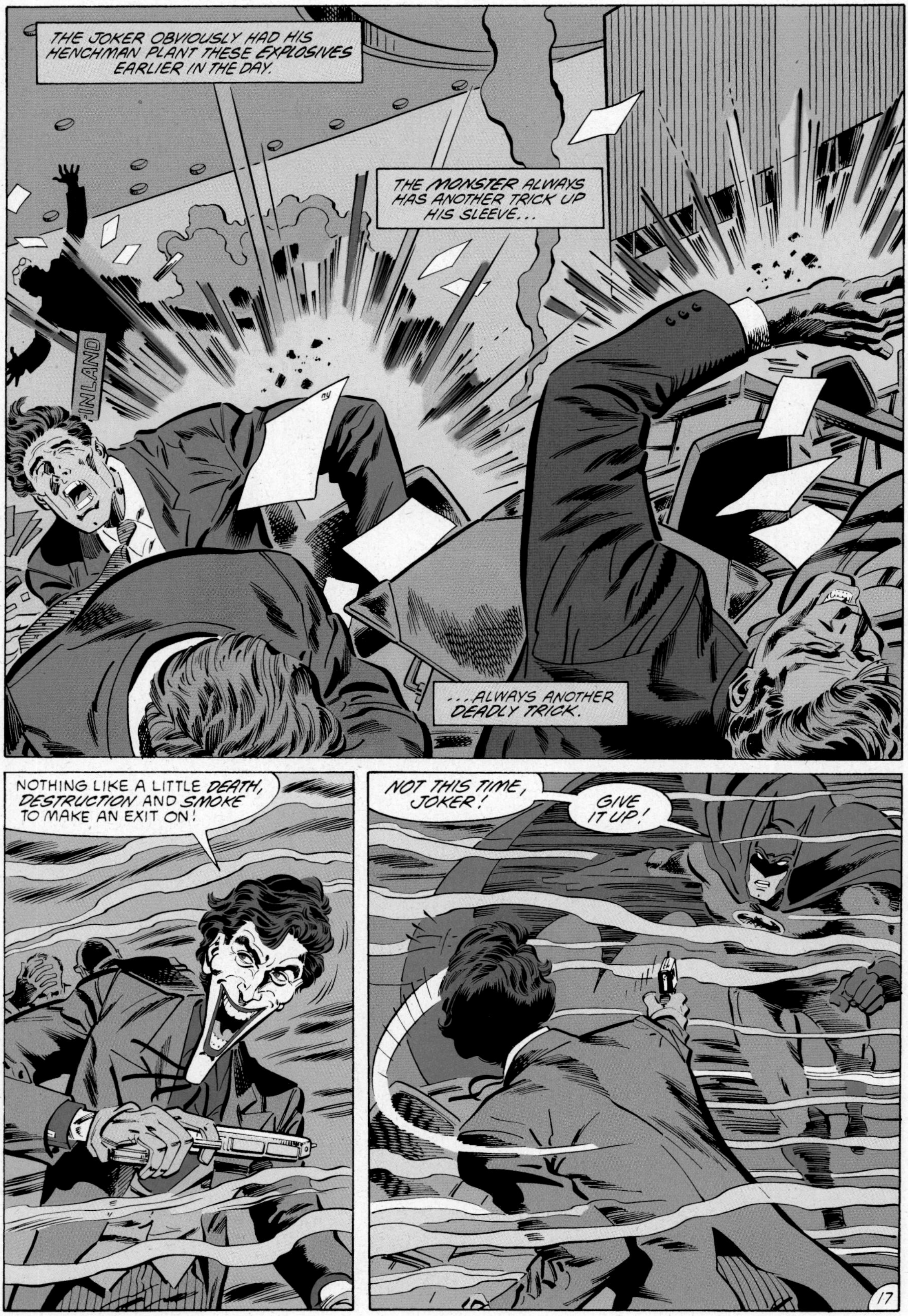
THE JOKER OBVIOUSLY HAD HIS HENCHMAN PLANT THESE EXPLOSIVES EARLIER IN THE DAY.
THE MONSTER ALWAYS HAS ANOTHER TRICK UP HIS SLEEVE...
INLAND
...ALWAYS ANOTHER DEADLY TRICK.
NOTHING LIKE A LITTLE DEATH, DESTRUCTION AND SMOKE TO MAKE AN EXIT ON!
NOT THIS TIME, JOKER!
GIVE IT UP!
17

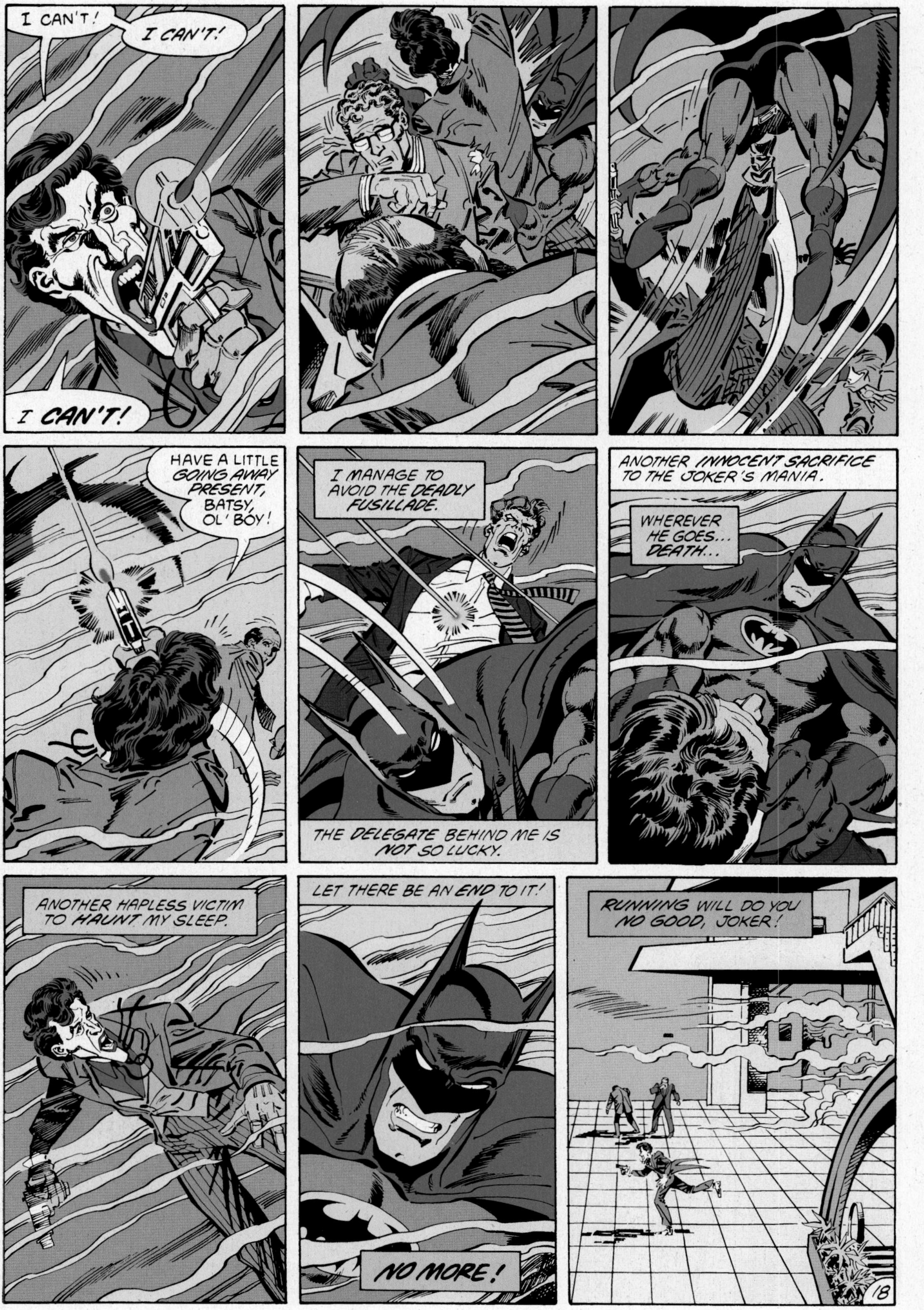
I CAN'T!
I CAN'T!
I CAN'T!
HAVE A LITTLE GOING AWAY PRESENT, BATSY, OL' BOY!
I MANAGE TO AVOID THE DEADLY FUSILLADE.
THE DELEGATE BEHIND ME IS NOT SO LUCKY.
ANOTHER INNOCENT SACRIFICE TO THE JOKER'S MANIA.
WHEREVER HE GOES... DEATH...
ANOTHER HAPLESS VICTIM TO HAUNT MY SLEEP.
LET THERE BE AN END TO IT!
NO MORE!
RUNNING WILL DO YOU NO GOOD, JOKER!
18

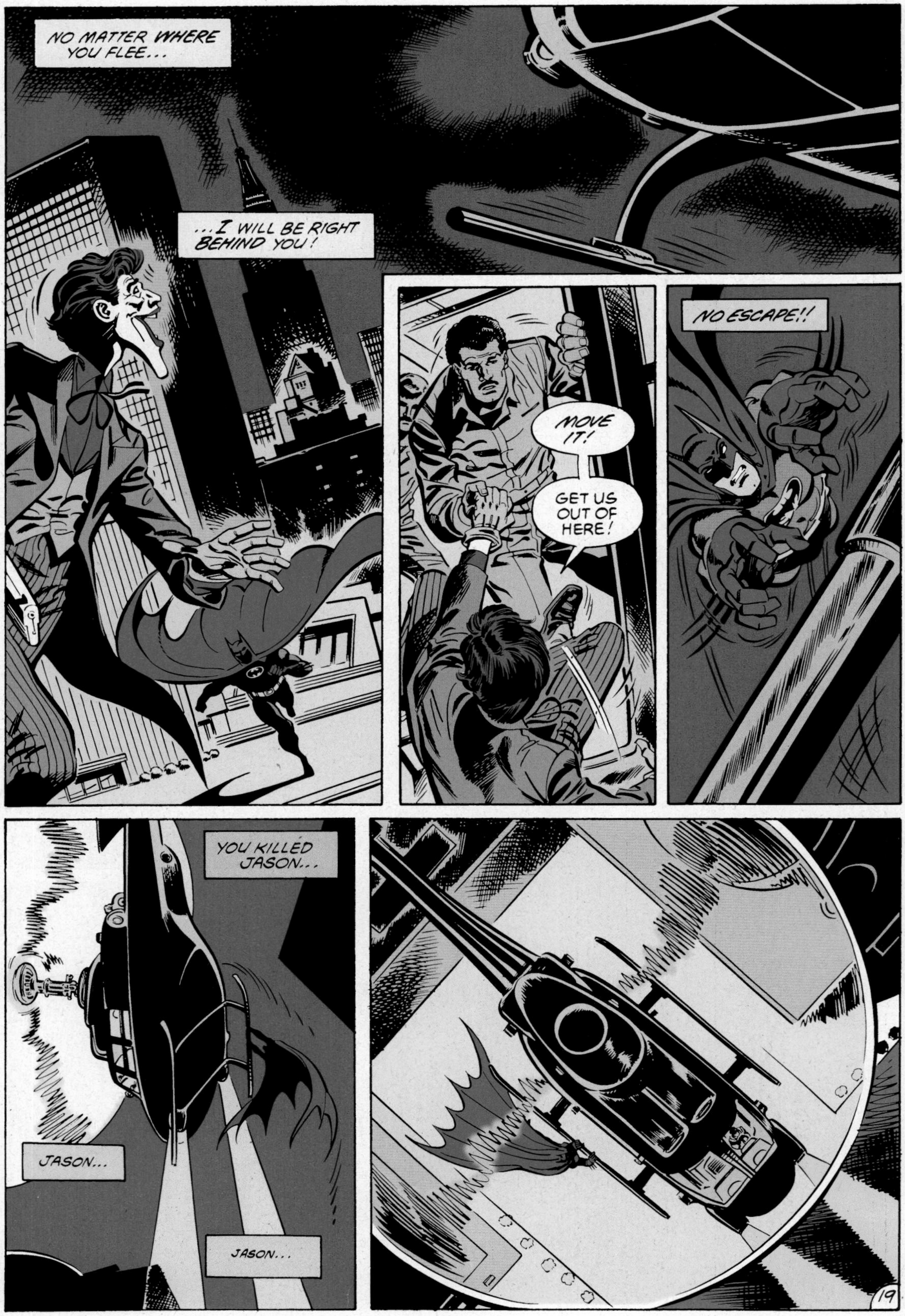
NO MATTER WHERE YOU FLEE...
...I WILL BE RIGHT BEHIND YOU!
MOVE IT!
GET US OUT OF HERE!
NO ESCAPE!!
YOU KILLED JASON...
JASON...
JASON...
19

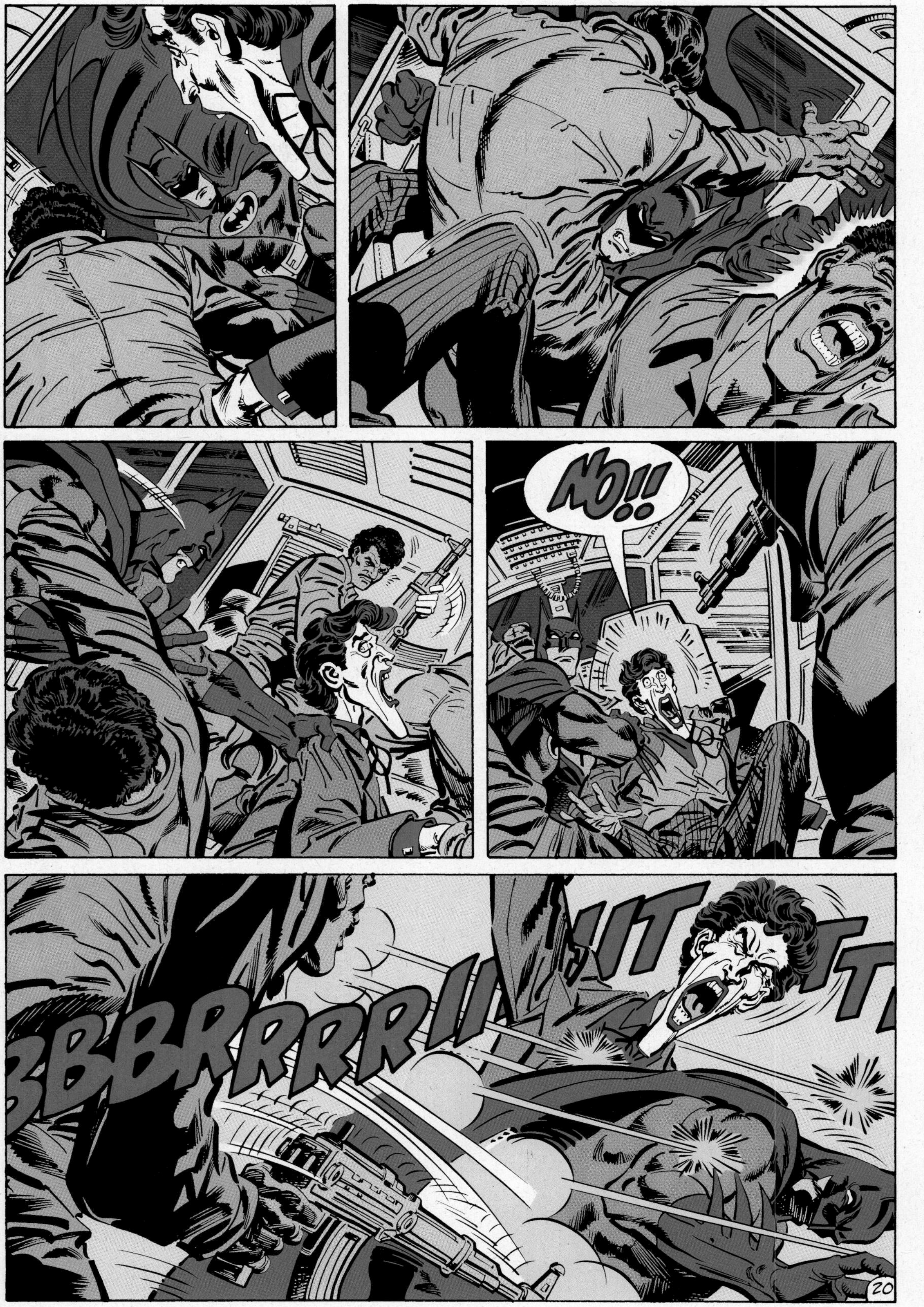
NO!!
BBBRRRRRIIIIIT
20

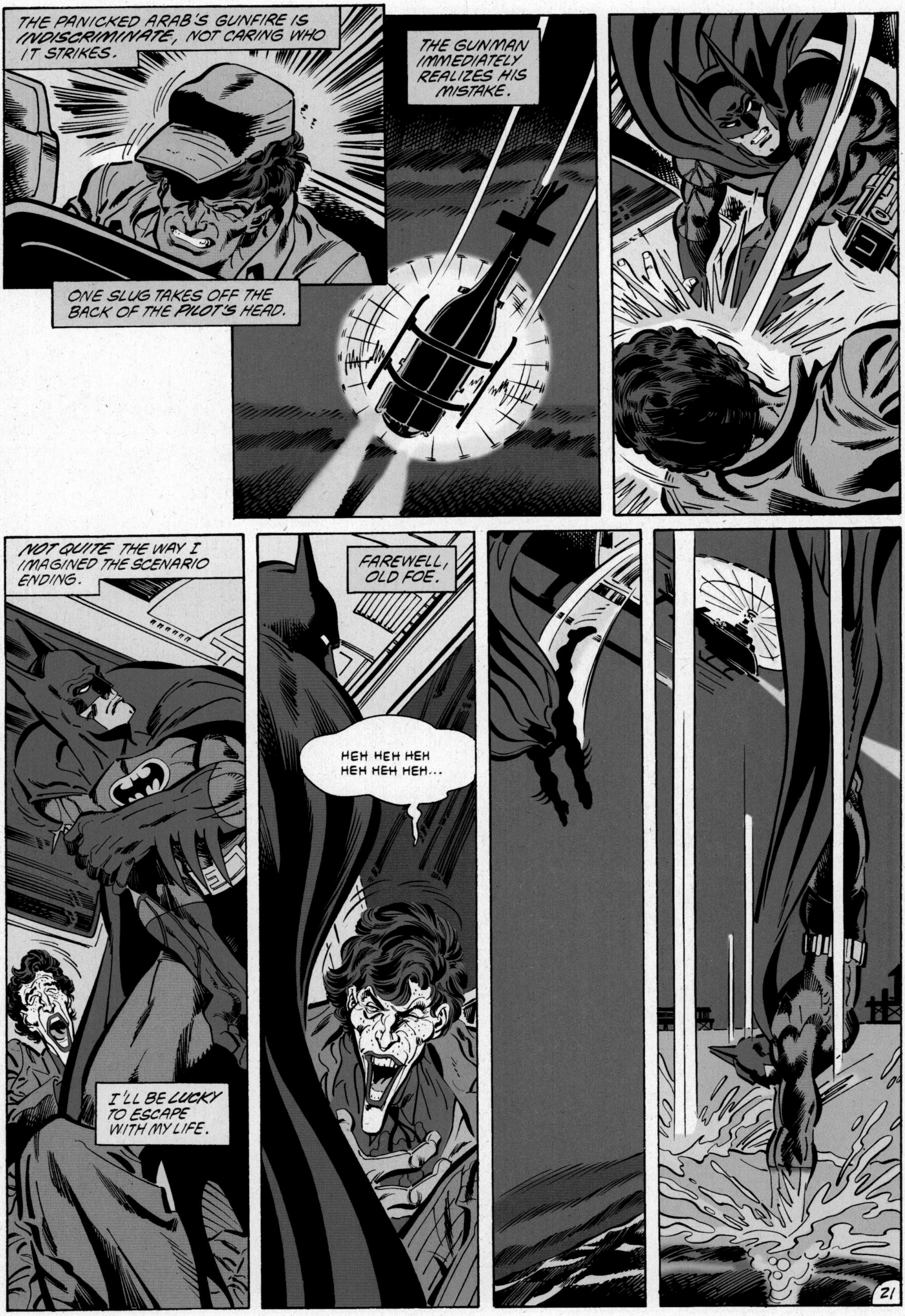
THE PANICKED ARAB'S GUNFIRE IS INDISCRIMINATE, NOT CARING WHO IT STRIKES.
ONE SLUG TAKES OFF THE BACK OF THE PILOT'S HEAD.
THE GUNMAN IMMEDIATELY REALIZES HIS MISTAKE.
NOT QUITE THE WAY I IMAGINED THE SCENARIO ENDING.
I'LL BE LUCKY TO ESCAPE WITH MY LIFE.
FAREWELL, OLD FOE.
HEH HEH HEH HEH HEH HEH...
21

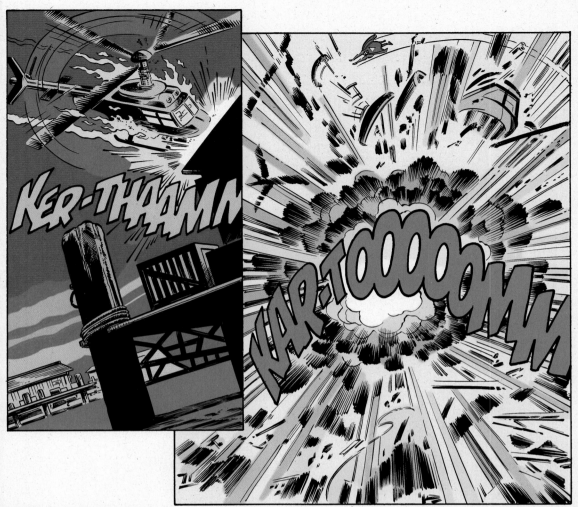

KER-THAAMN

KAR-TOOOOOMM

FIND HIS BODY!

FIND HIS BODY!!

BUT I KNOW THEY WON'T.

THAT'S THE WAY THINGS ALWAYS END WITH THE JOKER AND ME.

UNRESOLVED.

END

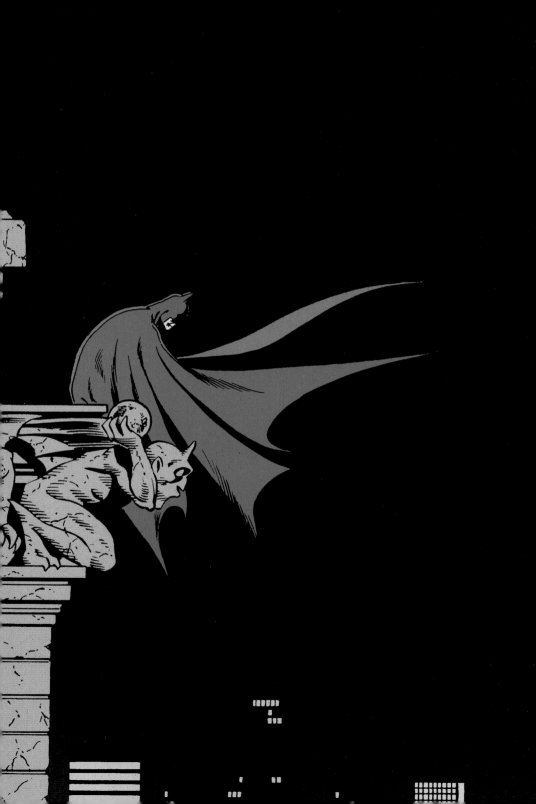

A LONELY PLACE OF DYING
REMEMBRANCES

It's been slightly over twenty years since I got the phone call. I remember it coming from Barbara Randall, who had been my Associate Editor on THE NEW TITANS, but as her name is not on the original stories, I may be wrong. Anyway, I remember Barbara telling me that BATMAN editor Denny O'Neil wondered if I had any ideas for a new version of Robin that they wanted to introduce after the recent murder of Jason Todd (he's recovered since then).

Let me back up a bit. When artist George Pérez and I started the New Teen Titans back in 1980, we began the gradual process of aging then-Robin Dick Grayson. Until then Robin was approximately 15 to 16 years old and while in the middle of fighting villains and such, he tended to spout bad puns. That didn't work for the book I wanted to write, so we bumped his age up to 18 or so, got rid of the puns and gave him a brain instead. I'm not putting down the old Robin; as a kid I loved him, but times had changed and the character that was created in April of 1940 needed to be updated. Besides, in the Titans, he was no longer a sidekick; he was the team leader and he needed to know what he was doing. So little Robin grew up and left the Batman book to take full-time residence in Titans Tower.

Flash forward to 1983. The Batman books wanted Robin back. And they wanted to de-age him to the younger teen he was before we changed him. Their thought was simply that Robin was a necessary component of the Bat titles. The expression is Batman *and* Robin after all, not Batman and some kid named Joey.

But I loved writing the Dick Grayson character, so, in a move motivated totally by greed, I suggested that it would be wrong to de-age Dick Grayson since the readers now liked his older and more serious version, and, though it had never been done before, why couldn't the Bat titles simply create a new Robin? I'd change Dick's hero name in the Titans to something else (Nightwing); he'd grown up and would now want his own name, after all, while DC could call attention to the Bat titles by introducing a brand-new, younger Robin. This could be a win-win scenario. So, in a few short months, the character of Jason Todd was introduced, and a new Robin was born.

Not long afterward I moved to Los Angeles. Time moved on. Continents rose and sank, and the next thing I knew it was 1988 and Jason Todd had been murdered — by both the Joker and the readers. Batman was Robin-less again.

I never did find out why I got the call asking what I'd do to create yet another Robin, but I do remember thinking that in the past Robin was always being groomed to become Batman, should the original die (Batman die? Yeah, like that'll happen!). But why not have a Robin who wanted to be not Batman, but, shock of shocks, Robin? Why not create a character who was so smart that he could deduce that Dick Grayson was Robin and that meant that Bruce Wayne was Batman? Tim Drake (named for upcoming *Batman* director Tim Burton) was brilliant, trained himself to become Robin, and, making him completely different from all previous kid sidekicks, he would have his own family outside of the lead character. Tim's mother and father had no connection to Bruce Wayne and company.

DC liked my take and had me put together a story to introduce him to the world. In order to call further attention to him, the story would move from the Bat-titles to the Titans — DC's most popular title at the time — and back and forth again. I got to work with regular Bat-artist Jim Aparo as well as my Titans partner, George Pérez. It doesn't get better than that.

As for the story, I wanted to use my favorite Batman villain, Two-Face. If ever there was a villain who needed to be psychoanalyzed, it's Harvey Dent's alter ego. I tried to explore his dual psyche as well

as coming up with some different kinds of Two-Face capers. While writing the five-parter I could be found at the research stacks of the library as often as you'd see me behind the computer. Today, the Internet would have made all those "2"-inspired clues easier to research, but I had a ball finding more and more obscure bits I could use to challenge Batman.

I tried to put together a story that would make the readers like Tim almost from day one. That would also make them realize that Batman needed a partner not only to help him fight the bad guys, but to force him to stay human, to remember why he was doing what he was doing, and to prevent him from getting too much into his own head, as they say. Batman without Robin can too easily forget the victims of crime and instead only concentrate on the perpetrators. As Batman himself was a victim of crime, he needs Robin to remind him that the fist alone can't solve the true cost of crime; it also needs to be solved with the heart.

I always liked Tim. I thought that giving him his own family made him stand apart from all the kid heroes we'd seen before. I thought that making him want to be the sidekick and not the main hero meant that he'd not be riddled with angst — already steadily creeping into comics — but that he'd enjoy what he was doing. Fans had not always appreciated Jason Todd, and it was risky to introduce yet another Robin and hope the readers would take to him, but 20 years later Tim is still fighting the good fight. And that pleases me no end.

Marv Wolfman

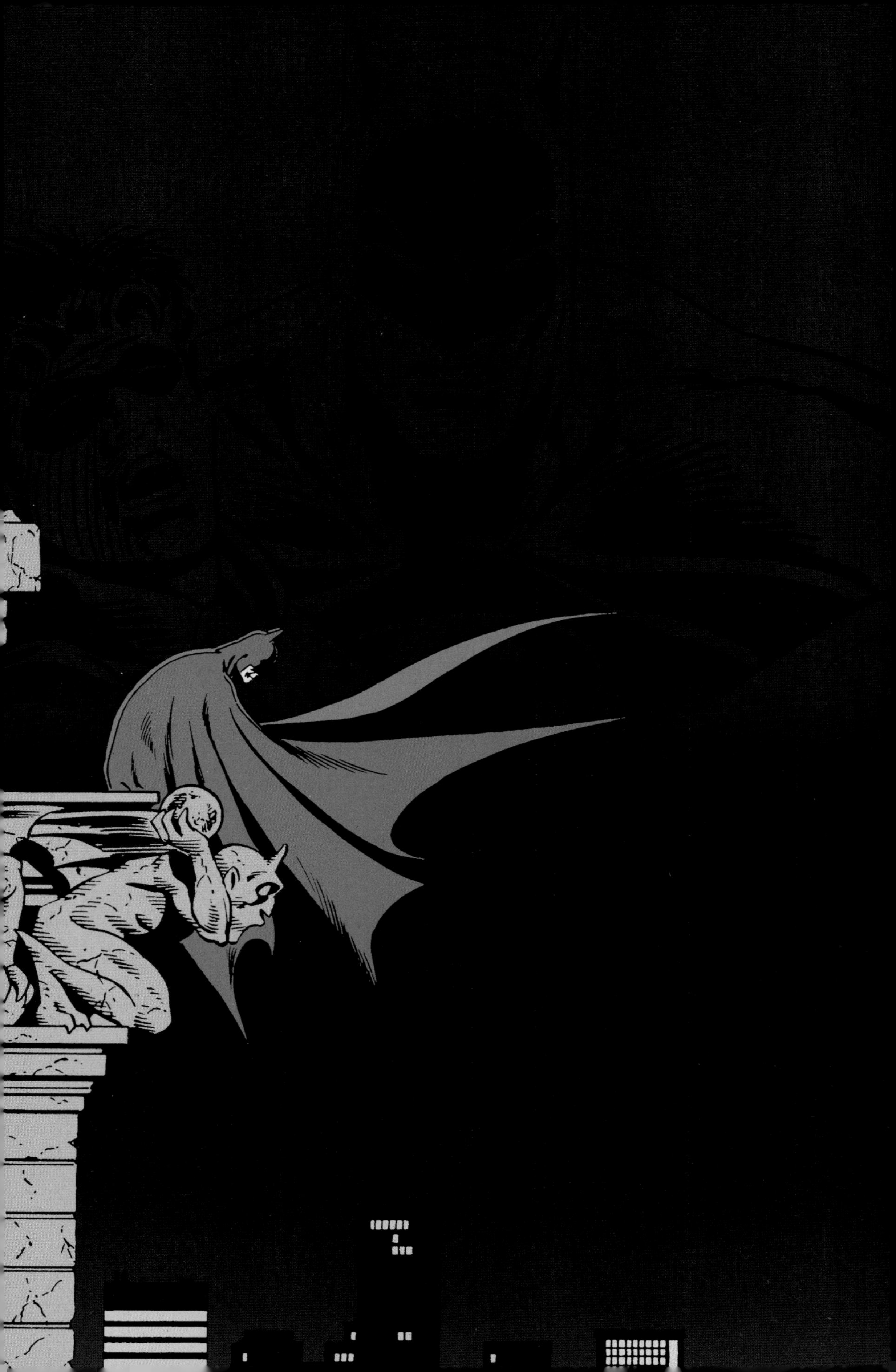

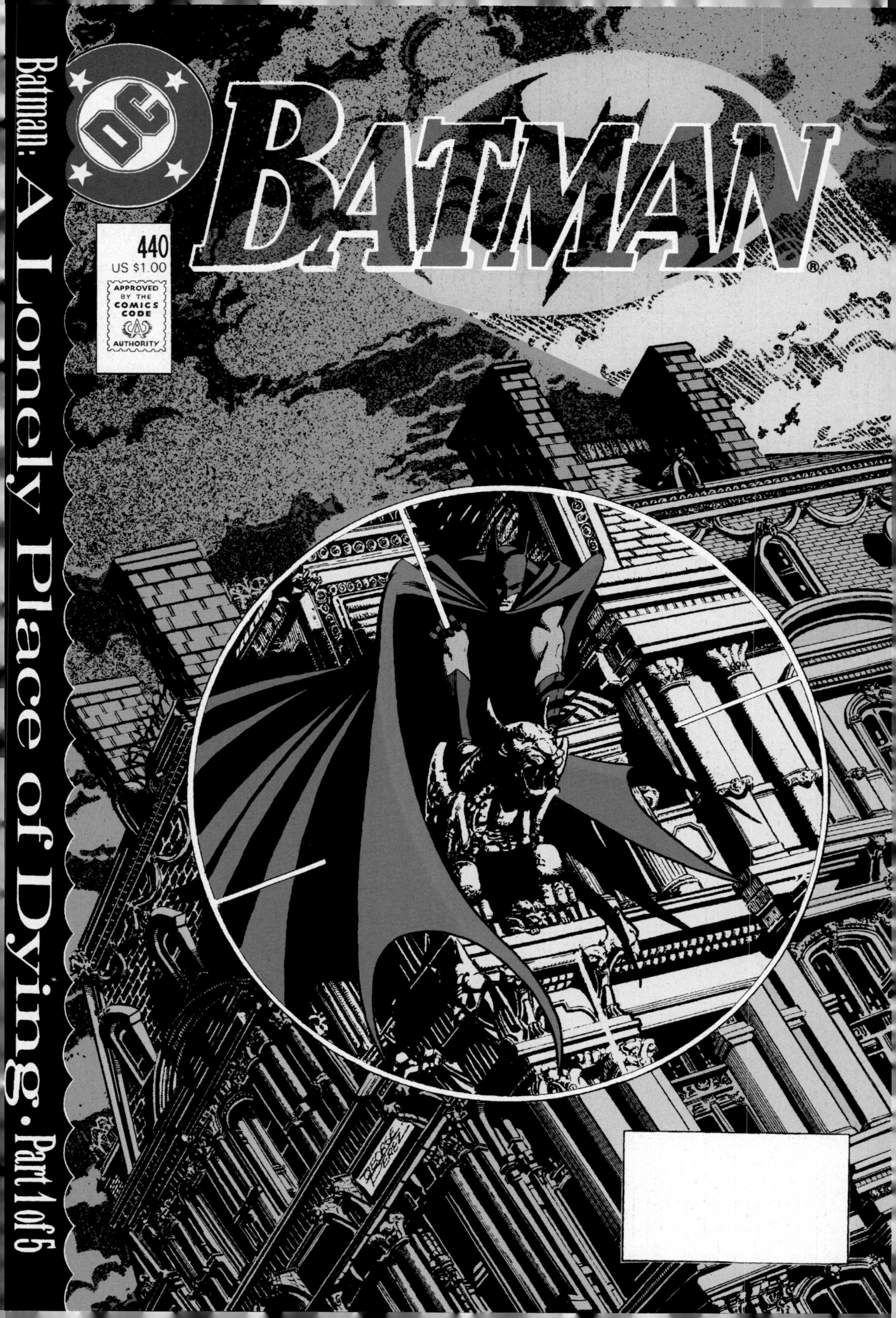
DC
BATMAN
440
US $1.00
APPROVED BY THE COMICS CODE AUTHORITY
Batman: A Lonely Place of Dying • Part 1 of 5

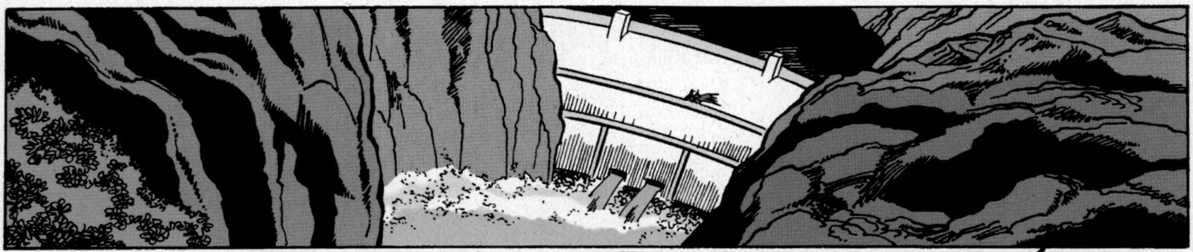

A LONELY PLACE of DYING

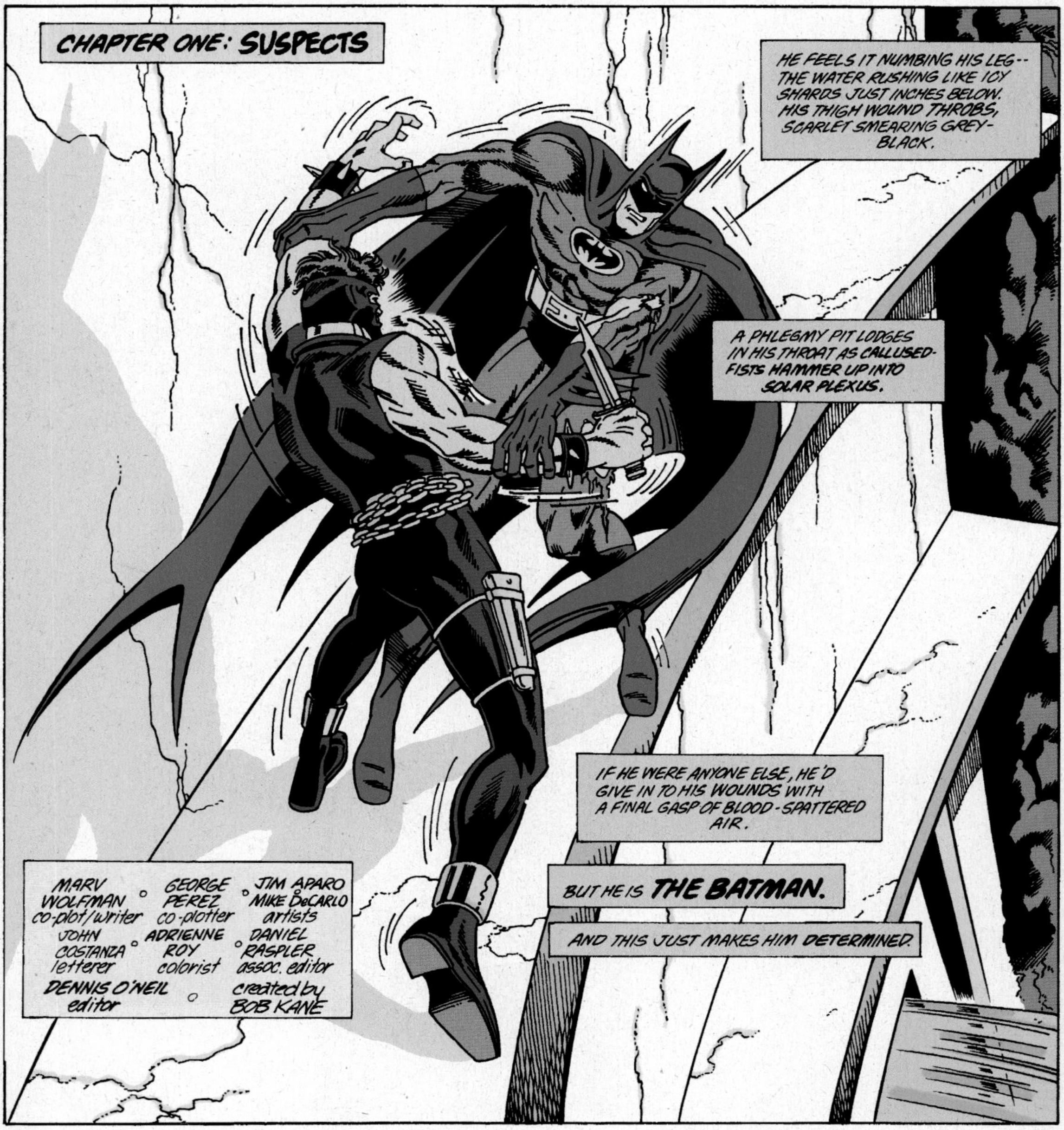
CHAPTER ONE: SUSPECTS
HE FEELS IT NUMBING HIS LEG-- THE WATER RUSHING LIKE ICY SHARDS JUST INCHES BELOW. HIS THIGH WOUND THROBS, SCARLET SMEARING GREY-BLACK.
A PHLEGMY PIT LODGES IN HIS THROAT AS CALLUSED-FISTS HAMMER UP INTO SOLAR PLEXUS.
IF HE WERE ANYONE ELSE, HE'D GIVE IN TO HIS WOUNDS WITH A FINAL GASP OF BLOOD-SPATTERED AIR.
BUT HE IS THE BATMAN.
AND THIS JUST MAKES HIM DETERMINED.
MARV WOLFMAN co-plot/writer
GEORGE PEREZ co-plotter
JIM APARO MIKE DeCARLO artists
JOHN COSTANZA letterer
ADRIENNE ROY colorist
DANIEL RASPLER assoc. editor
DENNIS O'NEIL editor
created by BOB KANE

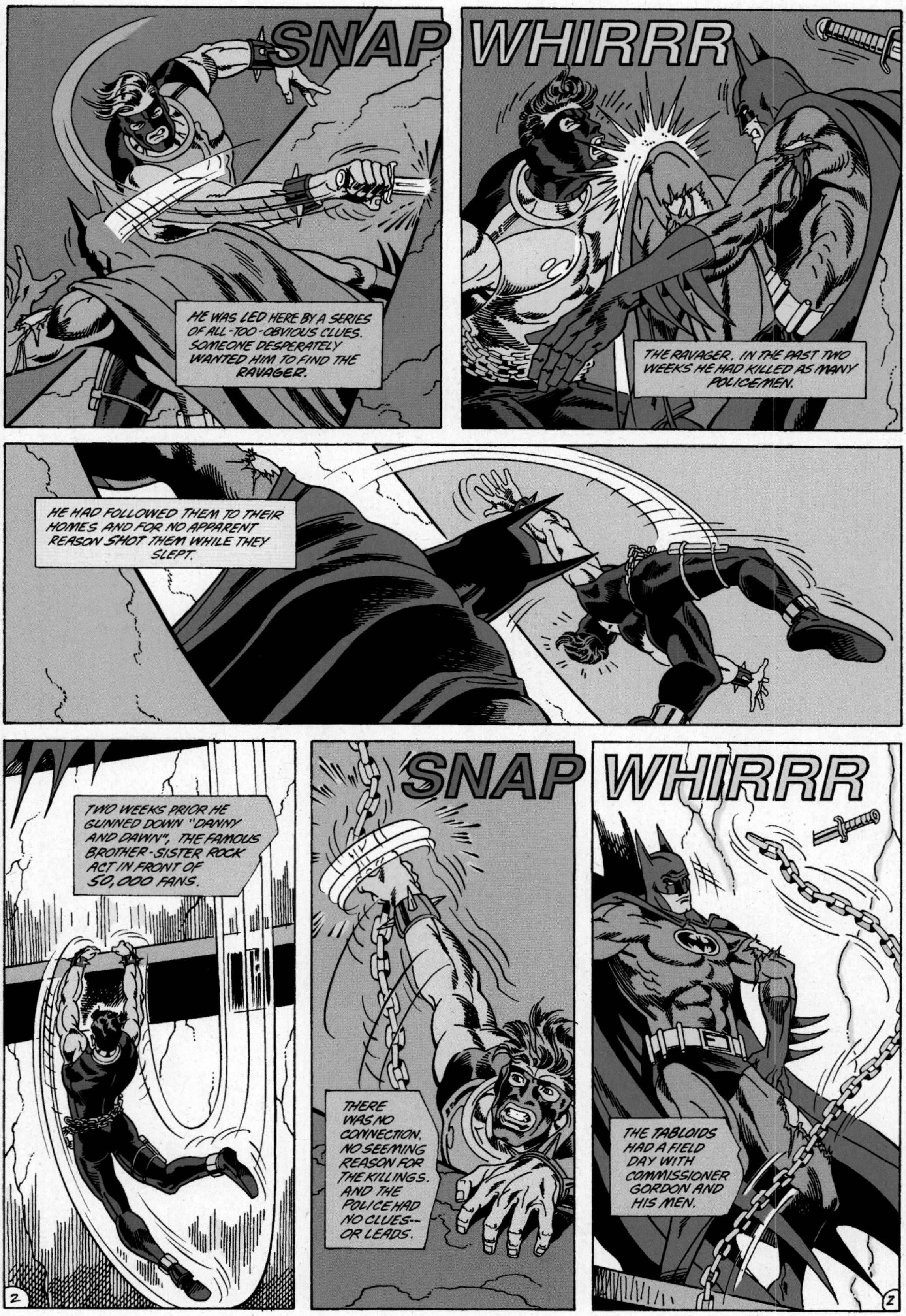
SNAP
WHIRRR
HE WAS LED HERE BY A SERIES OF ALL-TOO-OBVIOUS CLUES. SOMEONE DESPERATELY WANTED HIM TO FIND THE RAVAGER.
THE RAVAGER. IN THE PAST TWO WEEKS HE HAD KILLED AS MANY POLICEMEN.
HE HAD FOLLOWED THEM TO THEIR HOMES AND FOR NO APPARENT REASON SHOT THEM WHILE THEY SLEPT.
TWO WEEKS PRIOR HE GUNNED DOWN "DANNY AND DAWN", THE FAMOUS BROTHER-SISTER ROCK ACT IN FRONT OF 50,000 FANS.
SNAP
WHIRRR
THERE WAS NO CONNECTION, NO SEEMING REASON FOR THE KILLINGS. AND THE POLICE HAD NO CLUES-- OR LEADS.
THE TABLOIDS HAD A FIELD DAY WITH COMMISSIONER GORDON AND HIS MEN.
2
2

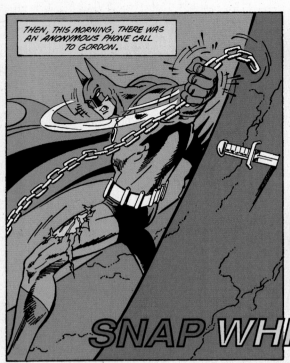

THEN, THIS MORNING, THERE WAS AN *ANONYMOUS* PHONE CALL TO GORDON.

SNAP WHIRRR

FROM THAT, LEADS UNFOLDED LIKE A BLOSSOMING FLOWER. LEADS WHICH BROUGHT HIM HERE.

HIS BREATH COMES IN SHORT SPUTTERING GASPS AS HIS MOUTH FILLS WITH WARM BLOOD...

THE BATMAN FALLS BACK TO THE WALL, TAKING STOCK OF HIS WOUNDS. HIS BREATHING *EASES*... HIS TAUT SKIN LOOSENS, THE NARROW WHITE SLIT OF HIS EYES WIDENS, IF ONLY A FRACTION.

HE WATCHES HIS FOE STRUGGLING IN THE WHITE FOAM.

FOR THE MOMENT, IT IS OVER.

THEY WILL MEET AGAIN.

SNAP WHIRR

3

SNAP WHIRRR

SNAP WHIRRR

SNAP WHIRRR

SNAP WHIRRR

SNAP WHIRRR

HE WAS *HURT,* BUT THAT DIDN'T STOP HIM.

WHIRRR

NOTHING STOPS HIM.

SO MUCH FOR BRUCE WAYNE.

NOW I CAN START ON *DICK GRAYSON.*

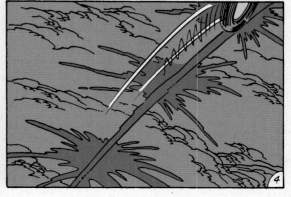

4

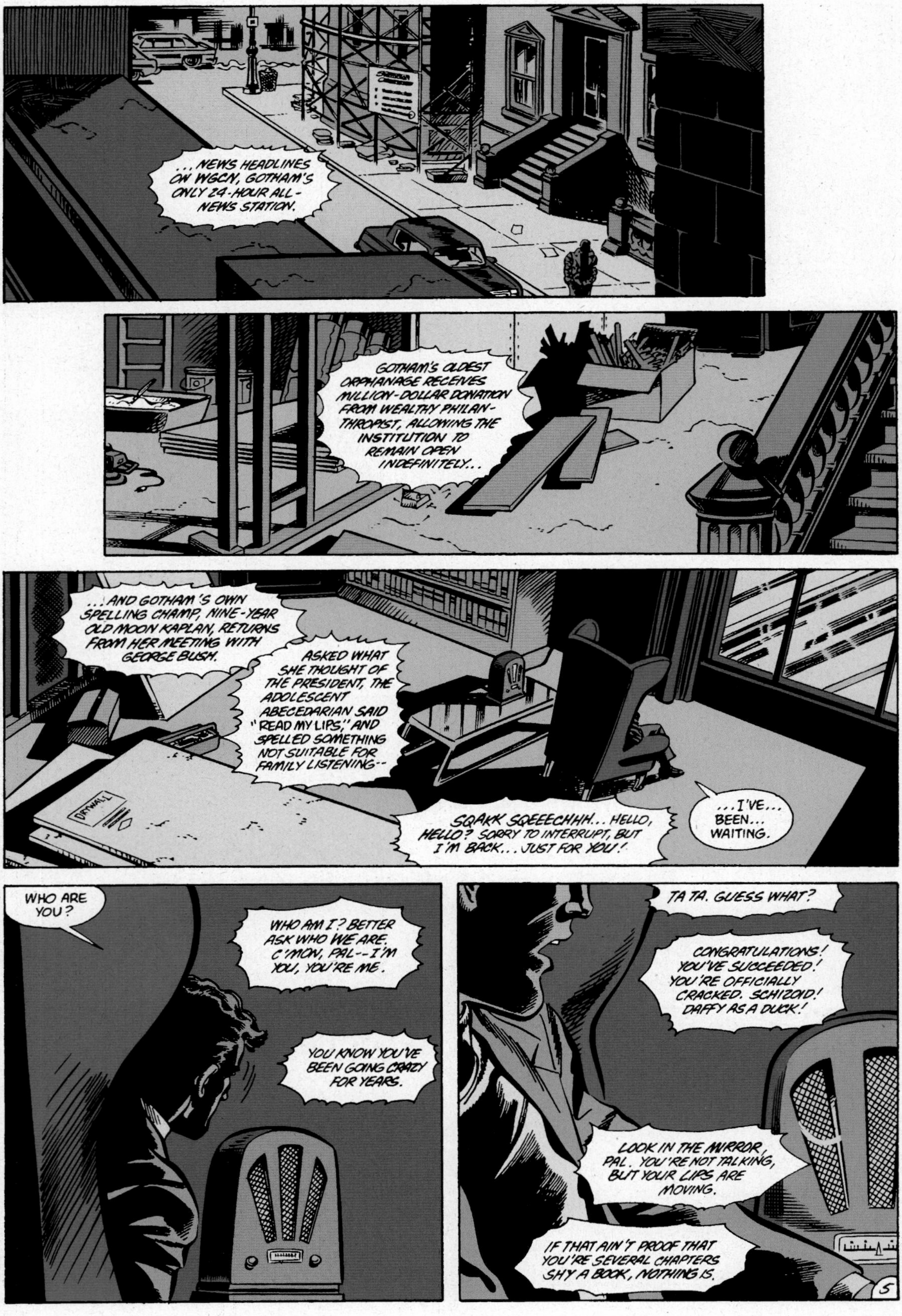
...NEWS HEADLINES ON WGCN, GOTHAM'S ONLY 24-HOUR ALL-NEWS STATION.
GOTHAM'S OLDEST ORPHANAGE RECEIVES MILLION-DOLLAR DONATION FROM WEALTHY PHILANTHROPIST, ALLOWING THE INSTITUTION TO REMAIN OPEN INDEFINITELY...
...AND GOTHAM'S OWN SPELLING CHAMP, NINE-YEAR OLD MOON KAPLAN, RETURNS FROM HER MEETING WITH GEORGE BUSH.
ASKED WHAT SHE THOUGHT OF THE PRESIDENT, THE ADOLESCENT ABECEDARIAN SAID "READ MY LIPS," AND SPELLED SOMETHING NOT SUITABLE FOR FAMILY LISTENING--
SQAKK SQEEECHHH... HELLO, HELLO? SORRY TO INTERRUPT, BUT I'M BACK... JUST FOR YOU!
...I'VE... BEEN... WAITING.
WHO ARE YOU?
WHO AM I? BETTER ASK WHO WE ARE. C'MON, PAL--I'M YOU, YOU'RE ME.
YOU KNOW YOU'VE BEEN GOING CRAZY FOR YEARS.
TA TA. GUESS WHAT?
CONGRATULATIONS! YOU'VE SUCCEEDED! YOU'RE OFFICIALLY CRACKED. SCHIZOID! DAFFY AS A DUCK!
LOOK IN THE MIRROR, PAL. YOU'RE NOT TALKING, BUT YOUR LIPS ARE MOVING.
IF THAT AIN'T PROOF THAT YOU'RE SEVERAL CHAPTERS SHY A BOOK, NOTHING IS.
5

SO WHAT ARE WE GOING TO DO TODAY, PAL? CLIMB A WATER TOWER AND TAKE POT-SHOTS AT PEDESTRIANS?

NAH, DID THAT ALREADY.

WE'RE WAITING. WHAT DO WE WANT TO DO?

C'MON, YOU KNOW WHAT TO DO.

I DON'T *WANT* TO ANY MORE.

SURE YOU DO. YOU JUST DON'T KNOW IT.

FOR US-- JUST SAY IT. C'MON. PWETTY PLEASE.

BUT I SENT RAVAGER TO DO IT AND HE FAILED.

SAY IT, PAL. SAY IT.

OKAY, OKAY. WE KILL BATMAN.

CONGRATULATIONS! YOU GOT THE *RIGHT* ANSWER. DON PARDO, TELL THE MAN WHAT HE'S WON!

WON? WHY FRIEND, YOU'VE WON BATMAN'S ITINERARY FOR ONE FULL WEEK.

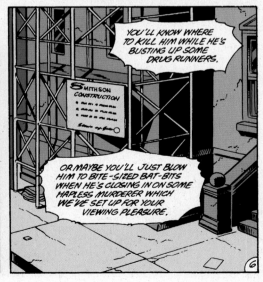

YOU'LL KNOW WHERE TO KILL HIM WHILE HE'S BUSTING UP SOME DRUG RUNNERS.

SMITHSON CONSTRUCTION

OR MAYBE YOU'LL JUST BLOW HIM TO BITE-SIZED BAT-BITS WHEN HE'S CLOSING IN ON SOME HAPLESS MURDERER WHICH WE'VE SET UP FOR YOUR VIEWING PLEASURE.

6

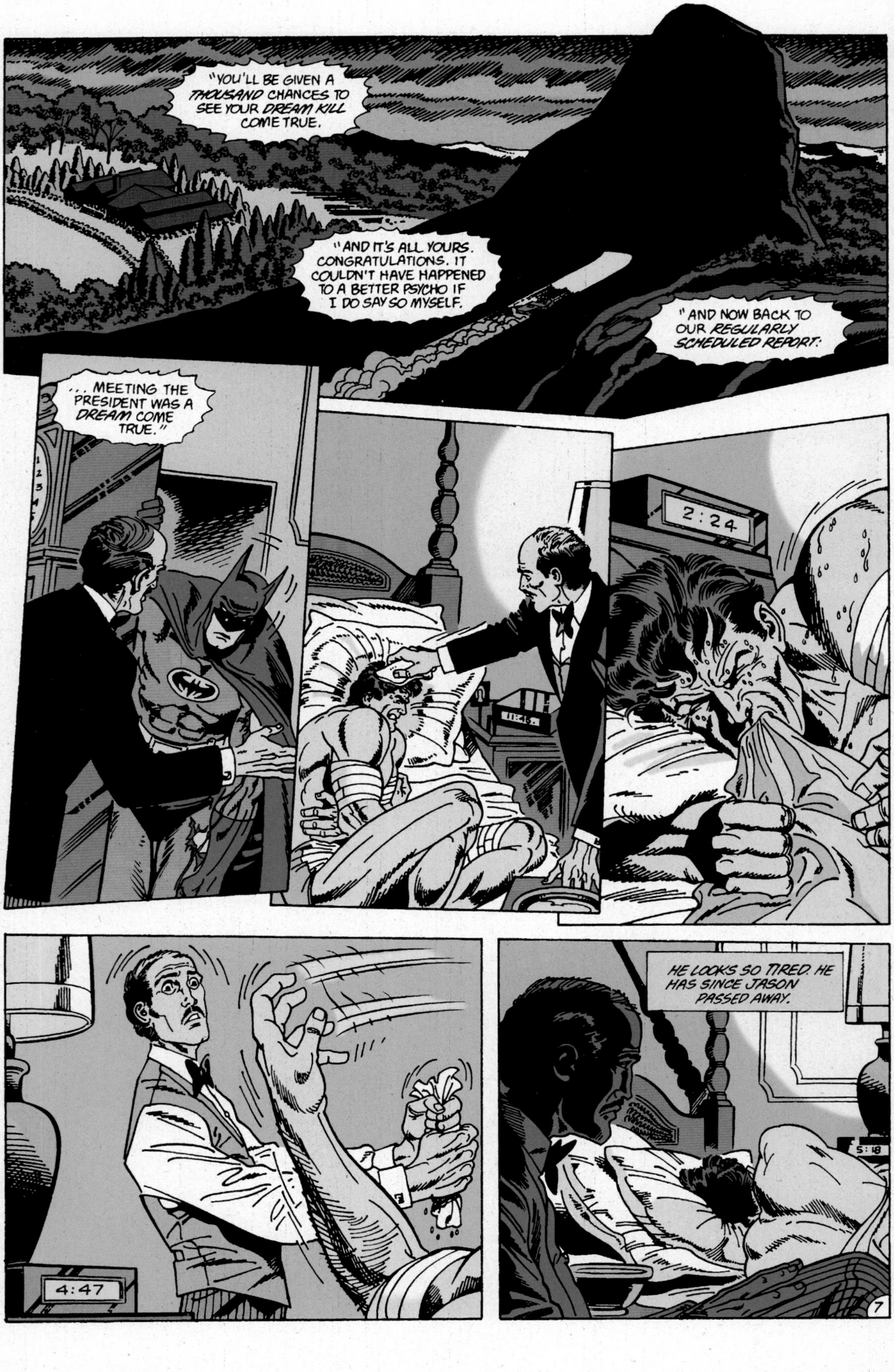
"YOU'LL BE GIVEN A THOUSAND CHANCES TO SEE YOUR DREAM KILL COME TRUE.
"AND IT'S ALL YOURS. CONGRATULATIONS. IT COULDN'T HAVE HAPPENED TO A BETTER PSYCHO IF I DO SAY SO MYSELF.
"AND NOW BACK TO OUR REGULARLY SCHEDULED REPORT:
... MEETING THE PRESIDENT WAS A DREAM COME TRUE."
2:24
4:47
HE LOOKS SO TIRED. HE HAS SINCE JASON PASSED AWAY.
5:18
7

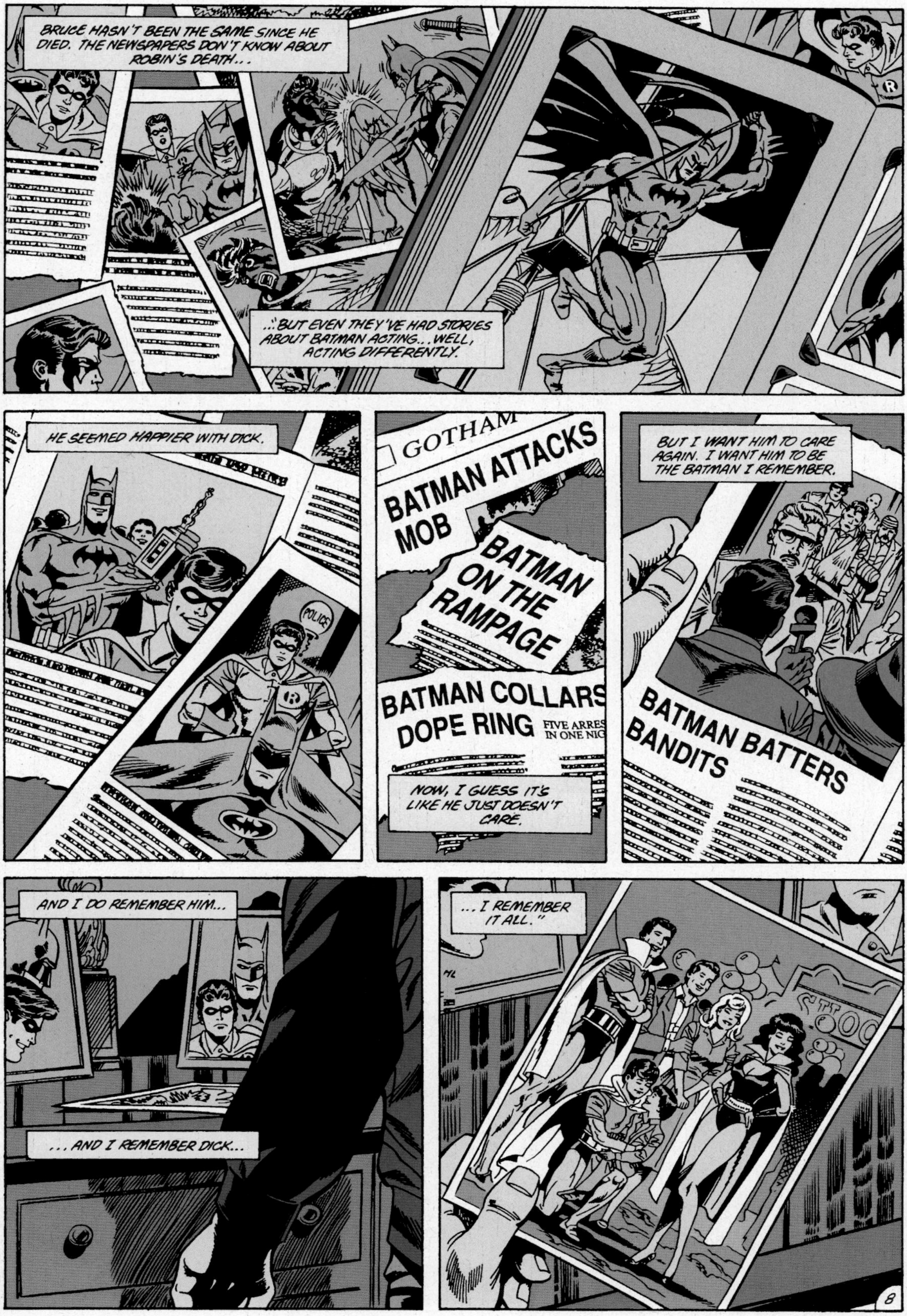
BRUCE HASN'T BEEN THE SAME SINCE HE DIED. THE NEWSPAPERS DON'T KNOW ABOUT ROBIN'S DEATH...
...BUT EVEN THEY'VE HAD STORIES ABOUT BATMAN ACTING... WELL, ACTING DIFFERENTLY.
HE SEEMED HAPPIER WITH DICK.
POLICE
GOTHAM
BATMAN ATTACKS MOB
BATMAN ON THE RAMPAGE
BATMAN COLLARS DOPE RING
FIVE ARRES IN ONE NIG
NOW, I GUESS IT'S LIKE HE JUST DOESN'T CARE.
BUT I WANT HIM TO CARE AGAIN. I WANT HIM TO BE THE BATMAN I REMEMBER.
BATMAN BATTERS BANDITS
AND I DO REMEMBER HIM...
...AND I REMEMBER DICK...
...I REMEMBER IT ALL."
8

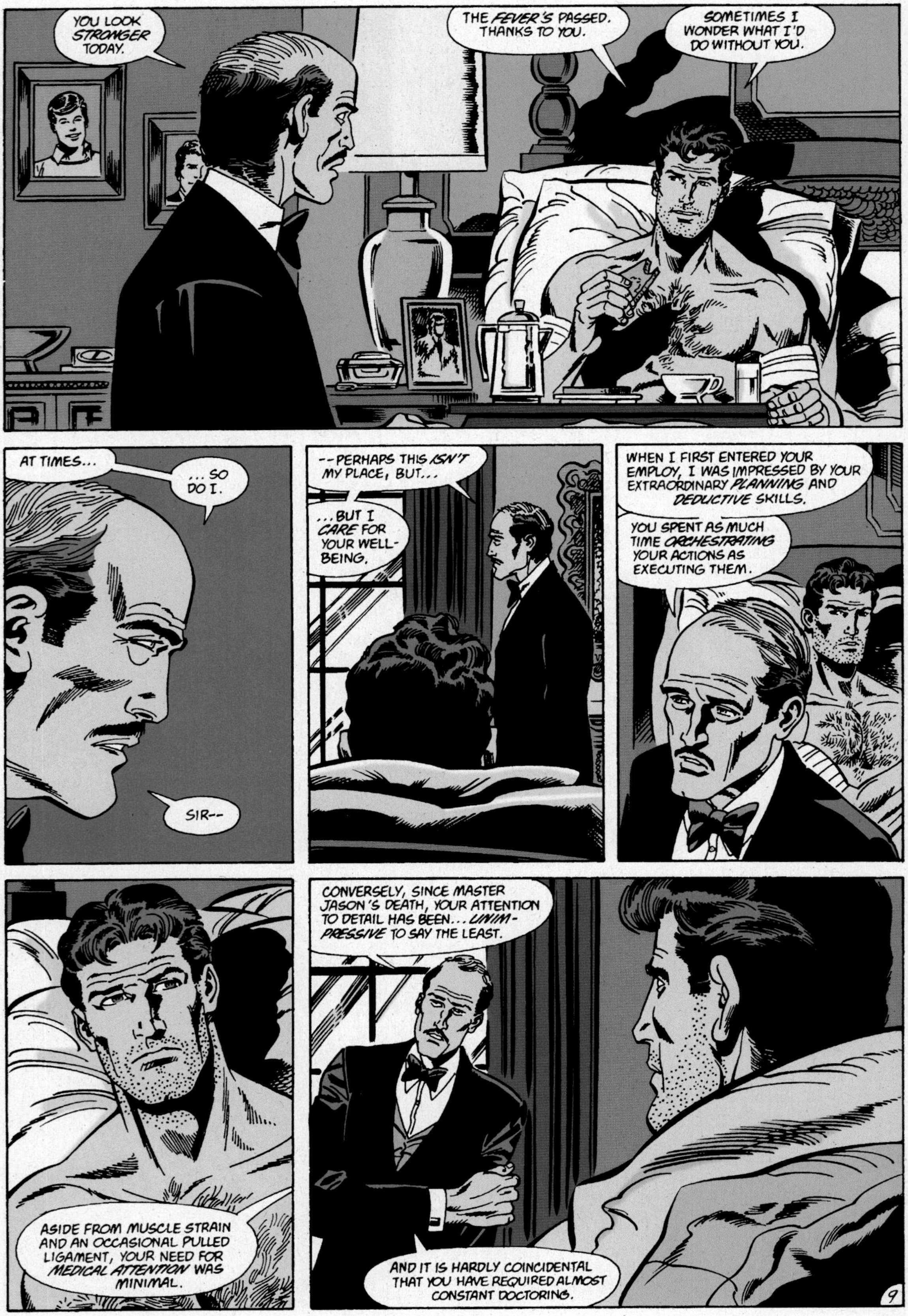
YOU LOOK STRONGER TODAY.
THE FEVER'S PASSED. THANKS TO YOU.
SOMETIMES I WONDER WHAT I'D DO WITHOUT YOU.
AT TIMES...
...SO DO I.
SIR--
--PERHAPS THIS ISN'T MY PLACE, BUT...
...BUT I CARE FOR YOUR WELL-BEING.
WHEN I FIRST ENTERED YOUR EMPLOY, I WAS IMPRESSED BY YOUR EXTRAORDINARY PLANNING AND DEDUCTIVE SKILLS.
YOU SPENT AS MUCH TIME ORCHESTRATING YOUR ACTIONS AS EXECUTING THEM.
ASIDE FROM MUSCLE STRAIN AND AN OCCASIONAL PULLED LIGAMENT, YOUR NEED FOR MEDICAL ATTENTION WAS MINIMAL.
CONVERSELY, SINCE MASTER JASON'S DEATH, YOUR ATTENTION TO DETAIL HAS BEEN... UNIM-PRESSIVE TO SAY THE LEAST.
AND IT IS HARDLY COINCIDENTAL THAT YOU HAVE REQUIRED ALMOST CONSTANT DOCTORING.
9

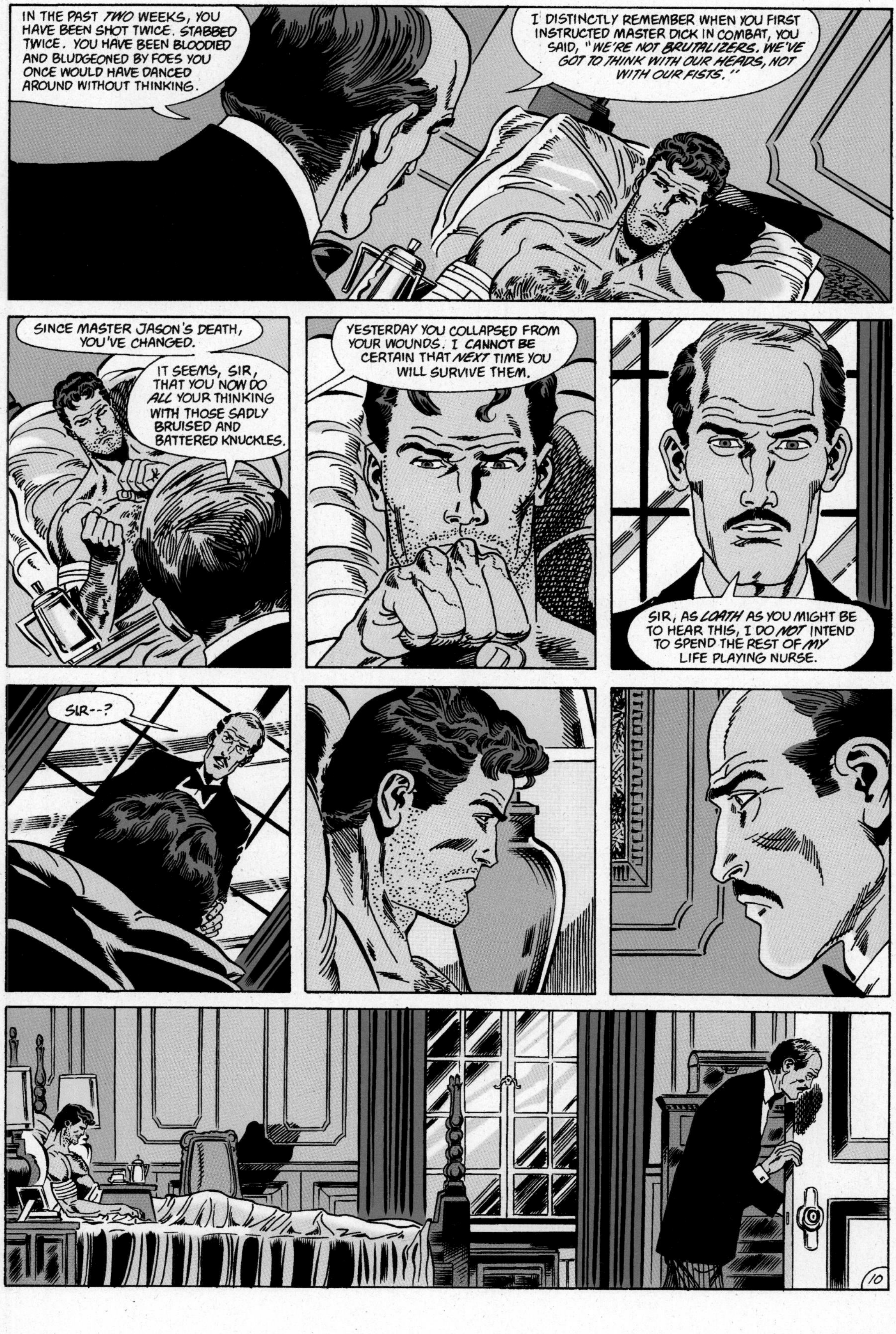
IN THE PAST TWO WEEKS, YOU HAVE BEEN SHOT TWICE. STABBED TWICE. YOU HAVE BEEN BLOODIED AND BLUDGEONED BY FOES YOU ONCE WOULD HAVE DANCED AROUND WITHOUT THINKING.
I DISTINCTLY REMEMBER WHEN YOU FIRST INSTRUCTED MASTER DICK IN COMBAT, YOU SAID, "WE'RE NOT BRUTALIZERS. WE'VE GOT TO THINK WITH OUR HEADS, NOT WITH OUR FISTS."
SINCE MASTER JASON'S DEATH, YOU'VE CHANGED.
IT SEEMS, SIR, THAT YOU NOW DO ALL YOUR THINKING WITH THOSE SADLY BRUISED AND BATTERED KNUCKLES.
YESTERDAY YOU COLLAPSED FROM YOUR WOUNDS. I CANNOT BE CERTAIN THAT NEXT TIME YOU WILL SURVIVE THEM.
SIR, AS LOATH AS YOU MIGHT BE TO HEAR THIS, I DO NOT INTEND TO SPEND THE REST OF MY LIFE PLAYING NURSE.
SIR--?
10

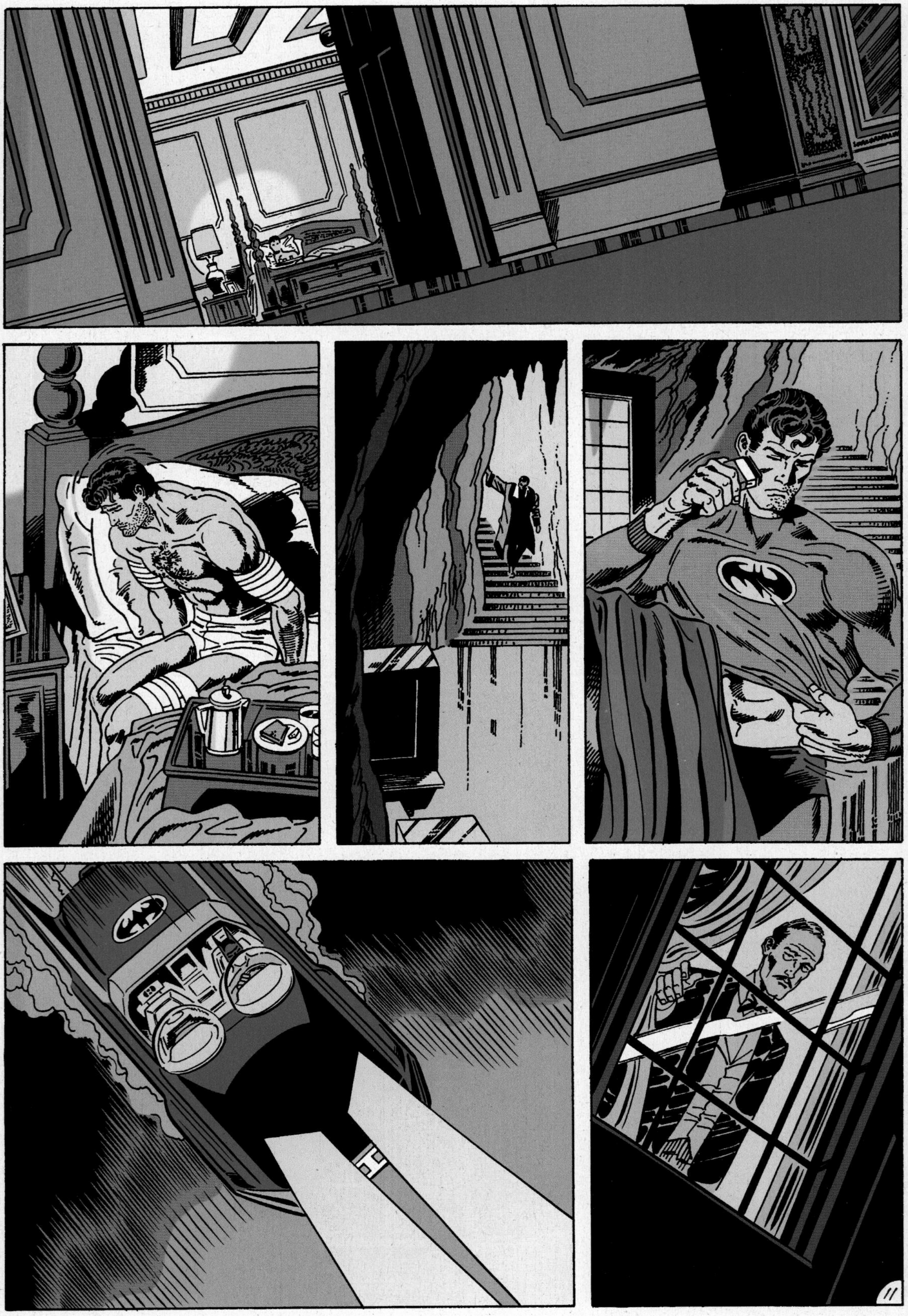
11

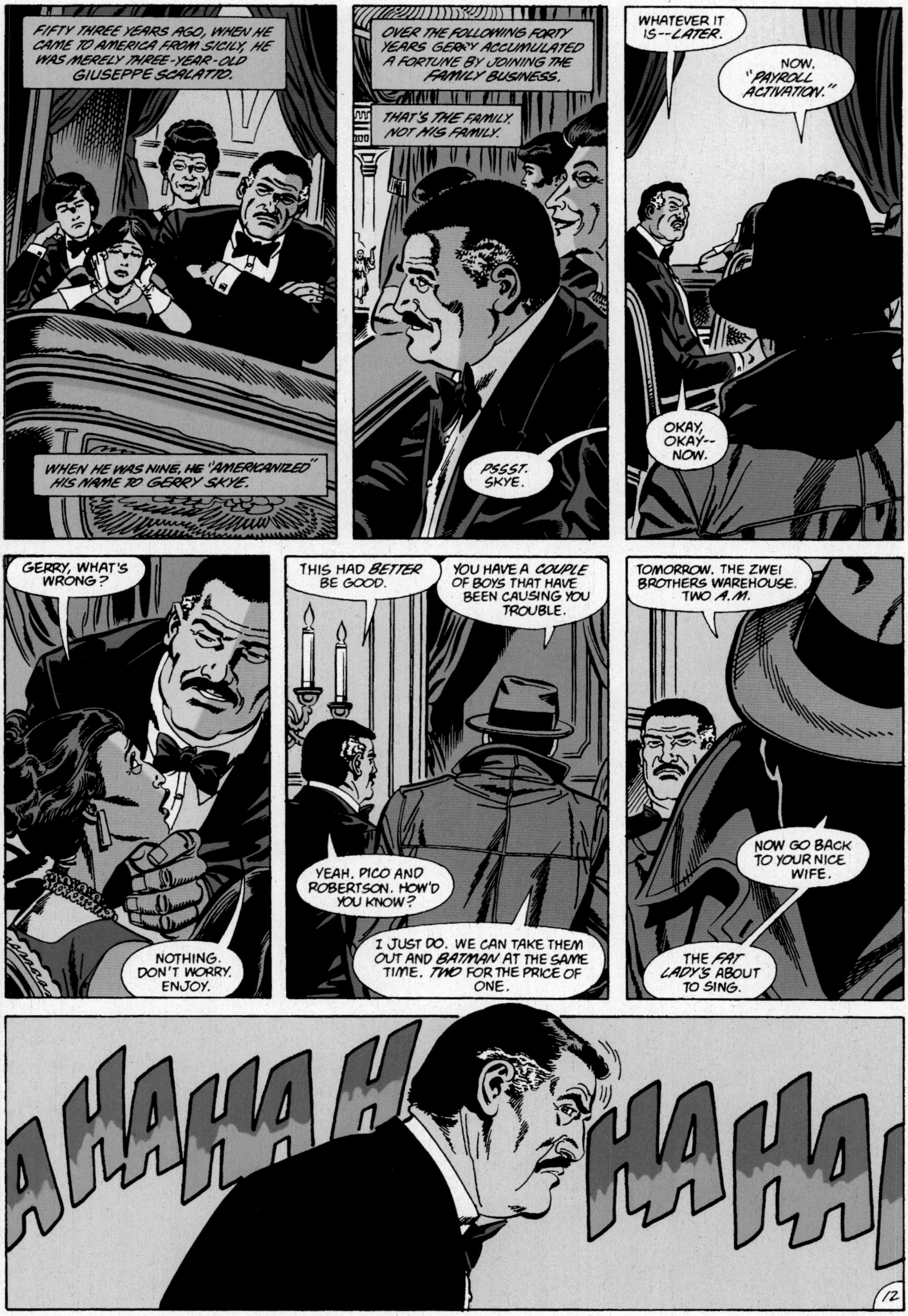
FIFTY THREE YEARS AGO, WHEN HE CAME TO AMERICA FROM SICILY, HE WAS MERELY THREE-YEAR-OLD GIUSEPPE SCALATTO.
WHEN HE WAS NINE, HE "AMERICANIZED" HIS NAME TO GERRY SKYE.
OVER THE FOLLOWING FORTY YEARS GERRY ACCUMULATED A FORTUNE BY JOINING THE FAMILY BUSINESS.
THAT'S THE FAMILY. NOT HIS FAMILY.
PSSST. SKYE.
WHATEVER IT IS--LATER.
NOW. "PAYROLL ACTIVATION."
OKAY, OKAY-- NOW.
GERRY, WHAT'S WRONG?
NOTHING. DON'T WORRY. ENJOY.
THIS HAD BETTER BE GOOD.
YOU HAVE A COUPLE OF BOYS THAT HAVE BEEN CAUSING YOU TROUBLE.
YEAH. PICO AND ROBERTSON. HOW'D YOU KNOW?
I JUST DO. WE CAN TAKE THEM OUT AND BATMAN AT THE SAME TIME. TWO FOR THE PRICE OF ONE.
TOMORROW. THE ZWEI BROTHERS WAREHOUSE. TWO A.M.
NOW GO BACK TO YOUR NICE WIFE.
THE FAT LADY'S ABOUT TO SING.
AHAHAH
HAHAH
12

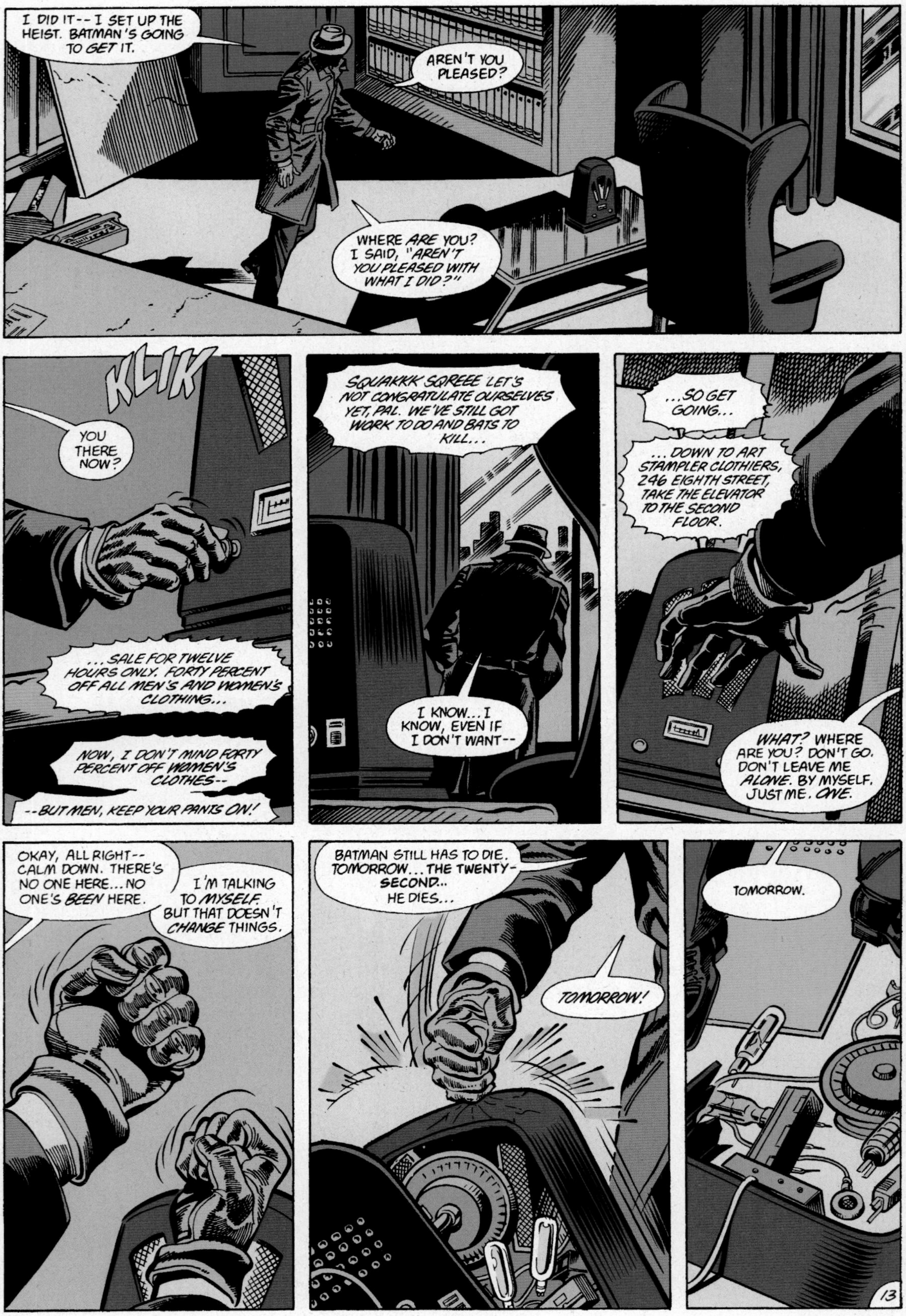
I DID IT-- I SET UP THE HEIST. BATMAN'S GOING TO GET IT.
AREN'T YOU PLEASED?
WHERE ARE YOU? I SAID, "AREN'T YOU PLEASED WITH WHAT I DID?"
KLIK
YOU THERE NOW?
...SALE FOR TWELVE HOURS ONLY. FORTY PERCENT OFF ALL MEN'S AND WOMEN'S CLOTHING...
NOW, I DON'T MIND FORTY PERCENT OFF WOMEN'S CLOTHES--
--BUT MEN, KEEP YOUR PANTS ON!
SQUAKKK SQREEE LET'S NOT CONGRATULATE OURSELVES YET, PAL. WE'VE STILL GOT WORK TO DO AND BATS TO KILL...
I KNOW... I KNOW, EVEN IF I DON'T WANT--
...SO GET GOING...
...DOWN TO ART STAMPLER CLOTHIERS, 246 EIGHTH STREET, TAKE THE ELEVATOR TO THE SECOND FLOOR.
WHAT? WHERE ARE YOU? DON'T GO. DON'T LEAVE ME ALONE. BY MYSELF. JUST ME. ONE.
OKAY, ALL RIGHT-- CALM DOWN. THERE'S NO ONE HERE... NO ONE'S BEEN HERE.
I'M TALKING TO MYSELF. BUT THAT DOESN'T CHANGE THINGS.
BATMAN STILL HAS TO DIE. TOMORROW... THE TWENTY-SECOND... HE DIES...
TOMORROW!
TOMORROW.
13

THERE. *TITANS TOWER.* IT'S JUST A MATTER OF *TIME* NOW. THEY'RE INSIDE. HE'LL HAVE TO LEAVE SOMETIME.

AHH, *TROIA* AND *CHANGELING.* GOOD-- THEIR MEETING'S OVER.

STRANGE--STARFIRE'S LEAVING ALONE. BUT DICK GRAYSON *LIVES* WITH HER.

AND HE USUALLY *LEAVES* WITH HER.

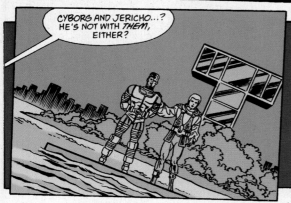

CYBORG AND JERICHO...? HE'S NOT WITH *THEM,* EITHER?

SOMETHING'S DEFINITELY WRONG.

TWENTY MINUTES. HE *CAN'T* STILL BE INSIDE.

BUT IF HE'S NOT, WHERE *IS* HE?

I'VE *GOT* TO FIND HIM.

HE LIVES HERE, BUT I CAN'T *WAIT* FOR HIM FOREVER.

GOT TO GET BACK TO MY *HOTEL* BY SIX.

I KNOW WHAT TO DO.

SHE'S ONLY CARRYING ONE DINNER.

HE'S *NOT* THERE.

BUT I'VE *GOT* TO FIND OUT WHERE HE'S GONE!

I'VE GOT TO TAKE THE *RISK.*

I'VE *GOT* TO SPEAK TO HER.

NOW!

14

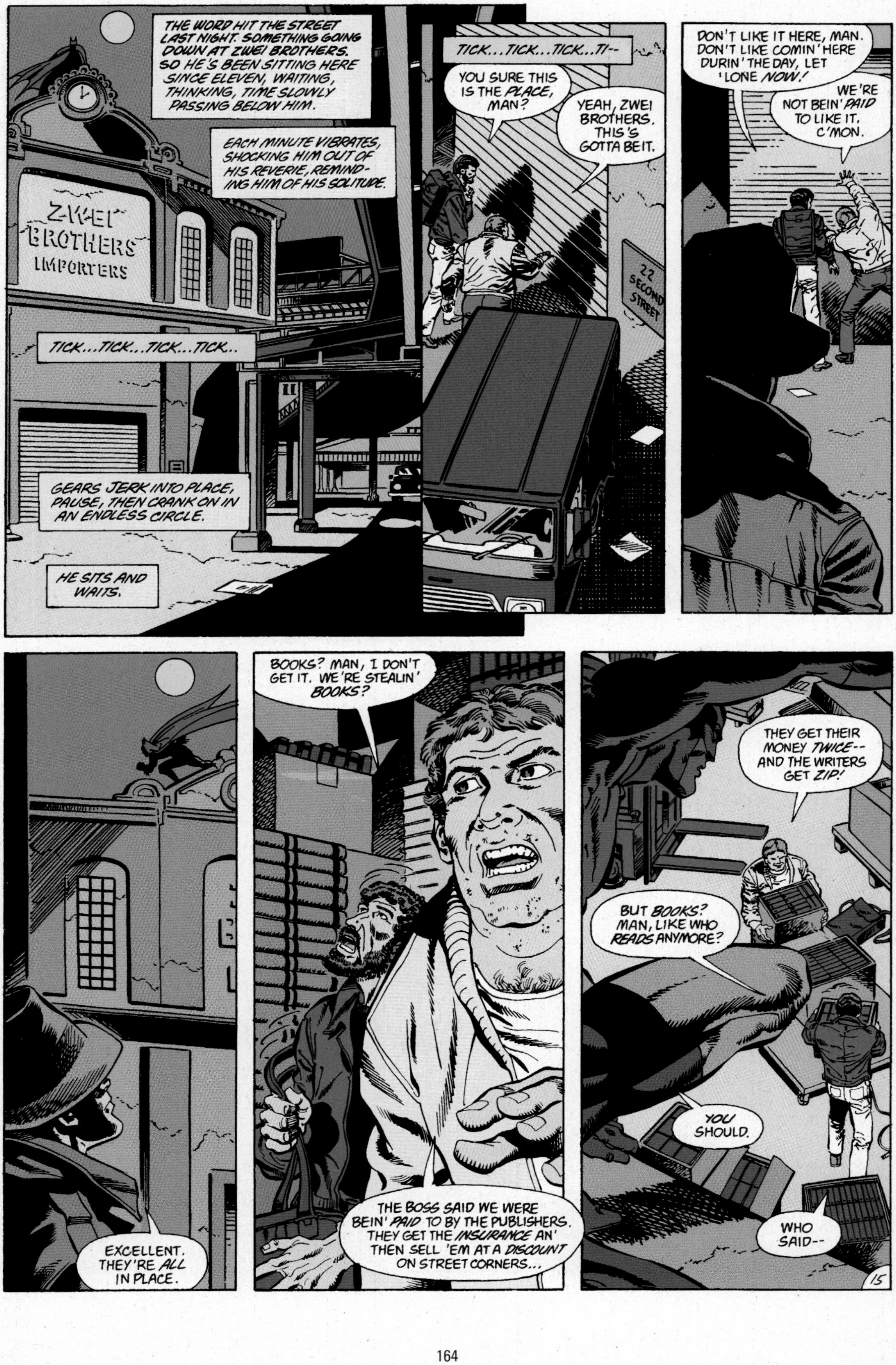
THE WORD HIT THE STREET LAST NIGHT. SOMETHING GOING DOWN AT ZWEI BROTHERS. SO HE'S BEEN SITTING HERE SINCE ELEVEN, WAITING, THINKING, TIME SLOWLY PASSING BELOW HIM.
EACH MINUTE VIBRATES, SHOCKING HIM OUT OF HIS REVERIE, REMINDING HIM OF HIS SOLITUDE.
ZWEI BROTHERS IMPORTERS
TICK...TICK...TICK...TICK...
GEARS JERK INTO PLACE, PAUSE, THEN CRANK ON IN AN ENDLESS CIRCLE.
HE SITS AND WAITS.
TICK...TICK...TICK...TI--
YOU SURE THIS IS THE PLACE, MAN?
YEAH, ZWEI BROTHERS. THIS'S GOTTA BE IT.
22 SECOND STREET
DON'T LIKE IT HERE, MAN. DON'T LIKE COMIN' HERE DURIN' THE DAY, LET 'LONE NOW!
WE'RE NOT BEIN' PAID TO LIKE IT. C'MON.
EXCELLENT. THEY'RE ALL IN PLACE.
BOOKS? MAN, I DON'T GET IT. WE'RE STEALIN' BOOKS?
THE BOSS SAID WE WERE BEIN' PAID TO BY THE PUBLISHERS. THEY GET THE INSURANCE AN' THEN SELL 'EM AT A DISCOUNT ON STREET CORNERS...
THEY GET THEIR MONEY TWICE-- AND THE WRITERS GET ZIP!
BUT BOOKS? MAN, LIKE WHO READS ANYMORE?
YOU SHOULD.
WHO SAID--
15

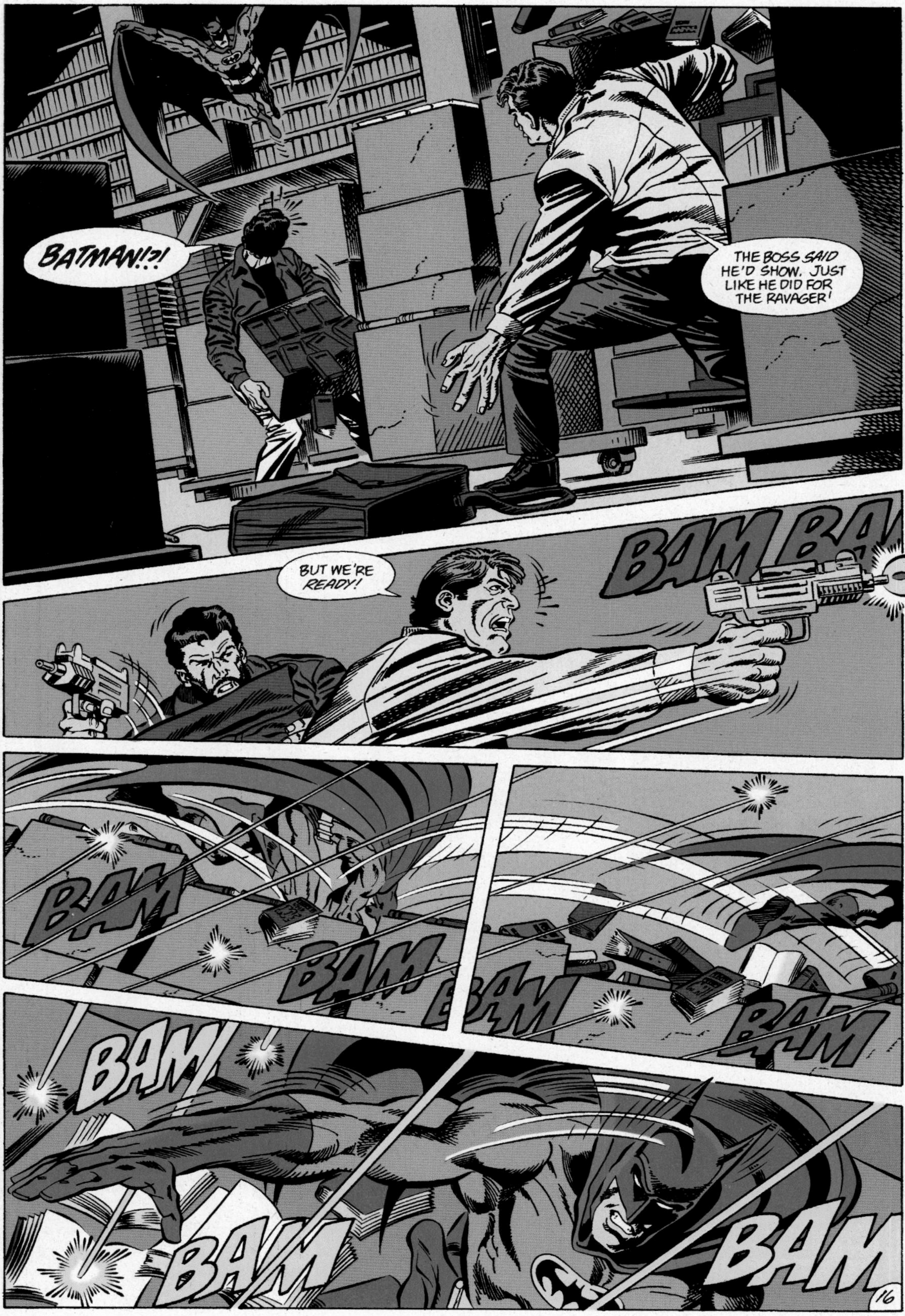
BATMAN!?!
THE BOSS SAID HE'D SHOW. JUST LIKE HE DID FOR THE RAVAGER!
BUT WE'RE READY!
BAM BA
BAM
BAM
BAM
BAM
BAM
BAM
BAM
16

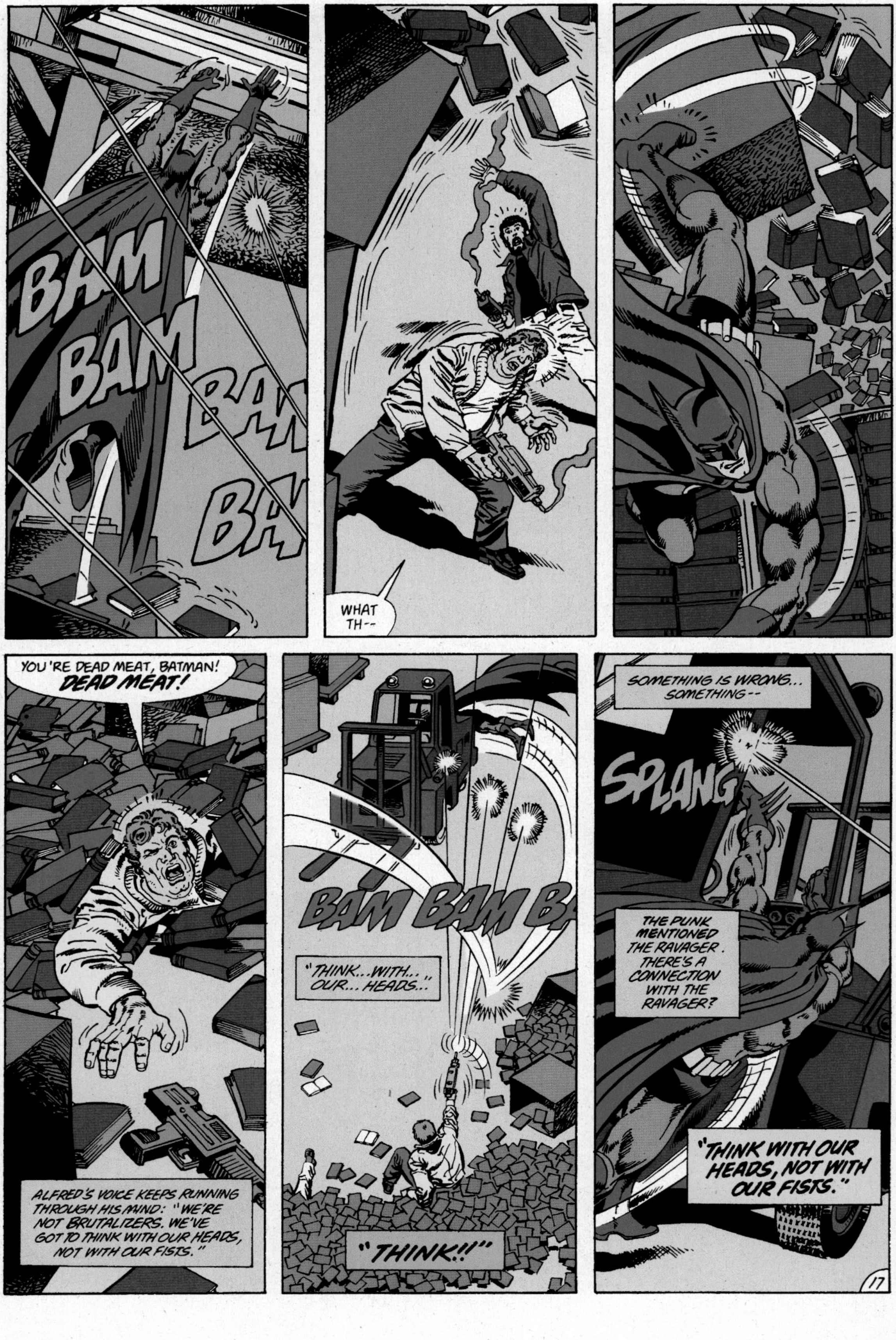

BAM
BAM
BAM
BA
WHAT TH--
YOU'RE DEAD MEAT, BATMAN! DEAD MEAT!
ALFRED'S VOICE KEEPS RUNNING THROUGH HIS MIND: "WE'RE NOT BRUTALIZERS. WE'VE GOT TO THINK WITH OUR HEADS, NOT WITH OUR FISTS."
BAM BAM BAM BA
"THINK...WITH... OUR... HEADS..."
"THINK!!"
SOMETHING IS WRONG... SOMETHING--
SPLANG
THE PUNK MENTIONED THE RAVAGER. THERE'S A CONNECTION WITH THE RAVAGER?
"THINK WITH OUR HEADS, NOT WITH OUR FISTS."
17

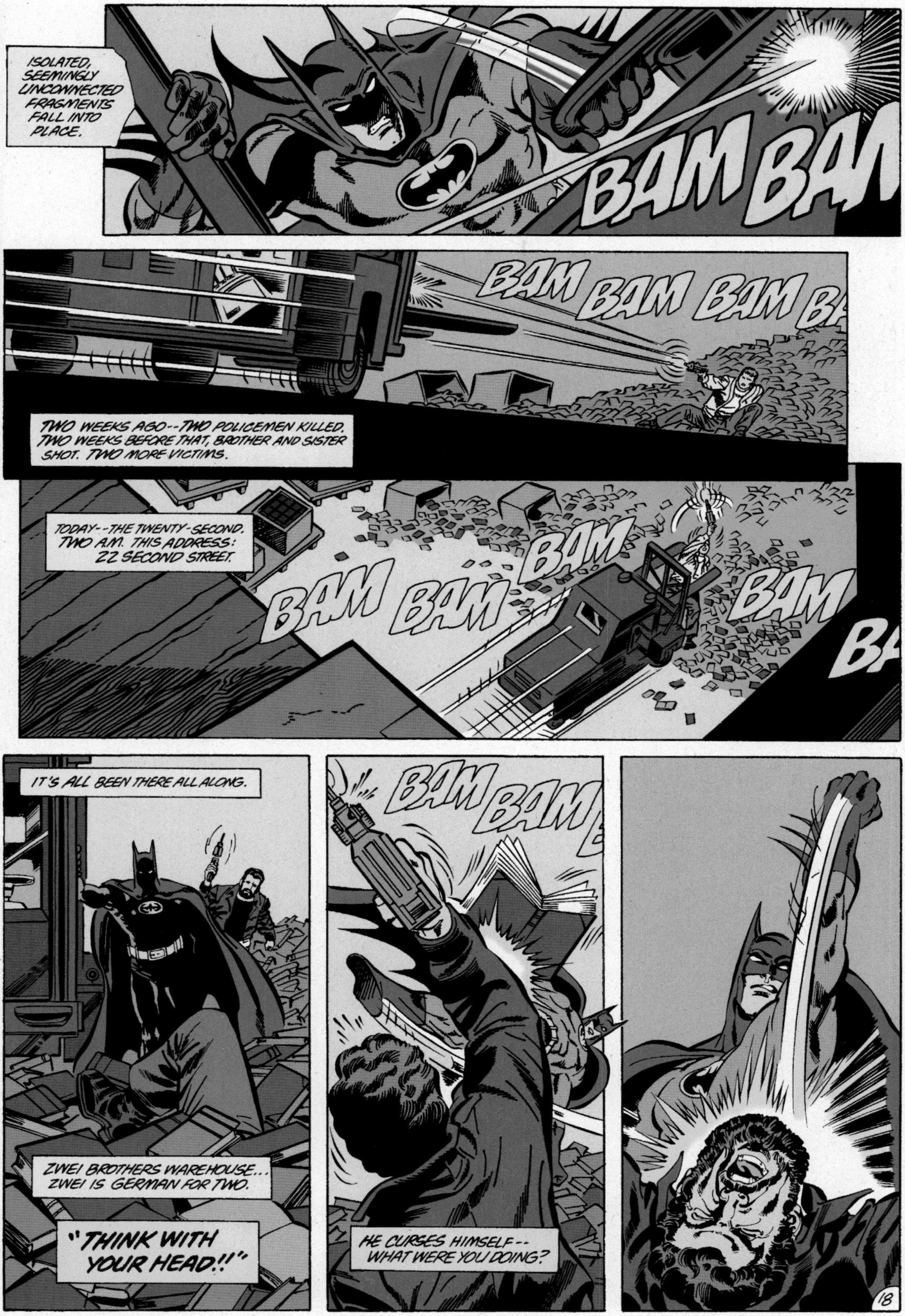
ISOLATED, SEEMINGLY UNCONNECTED FRAGMENTS FALL INTO PLACE.
BAM BAM
BAM BAM BAM BA
TWO WEEKS AGO--TWO POLICEMEN KILLED. TWO WEEKS BEFORE THAT, BROTHER AND SISTER SHOT. TWO MORE VICTIMS.
TODAY--THE TWENTY-SECOND. TWO A.M. THIS ADDRESS: 22 SECOND STREET.
BAM BAM BAM BAM
BA
IT'S ALL BEEN THERE ALL ALONG.
ZWEI BROTHERS WAREHOUSE... ZWEI IS GERMAN FOR TWO.
"THINK WITH YOUR HEAD!!"
BAM BAM
HE CURSES HIMSELF-- WHAT WERE YOU DOING?
18

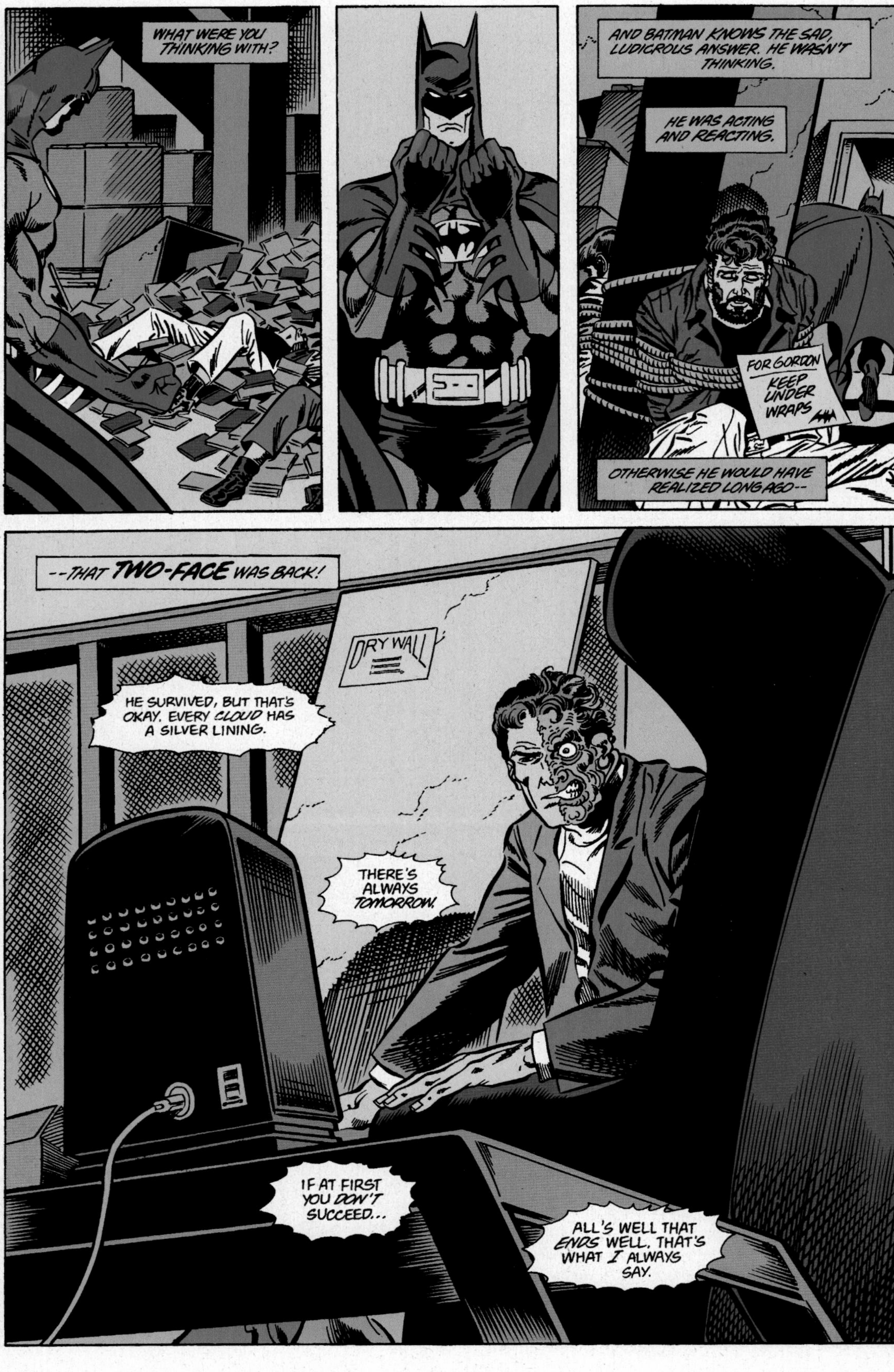
WHAT WERE YOU THINKING WITH?
AND BATMAN KNOWS THE SAD, LUDICROUS ANSWER. HE WASN'T THINKING.
HE WAS ACTING AND REACTING.
FOR GORDON
KEEP UNDER WRAPS
OTHERWISE HE WOULD HAVE REALIZED LONG AGO--
--THAT TWO-FACE WAS BACK!
DRY WALL
HE SURVIVED, BUT THAT'S OKAY. EVERY CLOUD HAS A SILVER LINING.
THERE'S ALWAYS TOMORROW!
IF AT FIRST YOU DON'T SUCCEED...
ALL'S WELL THAT ENDS WELL. THAT'S WHAT I ALWAYS SAY.
19

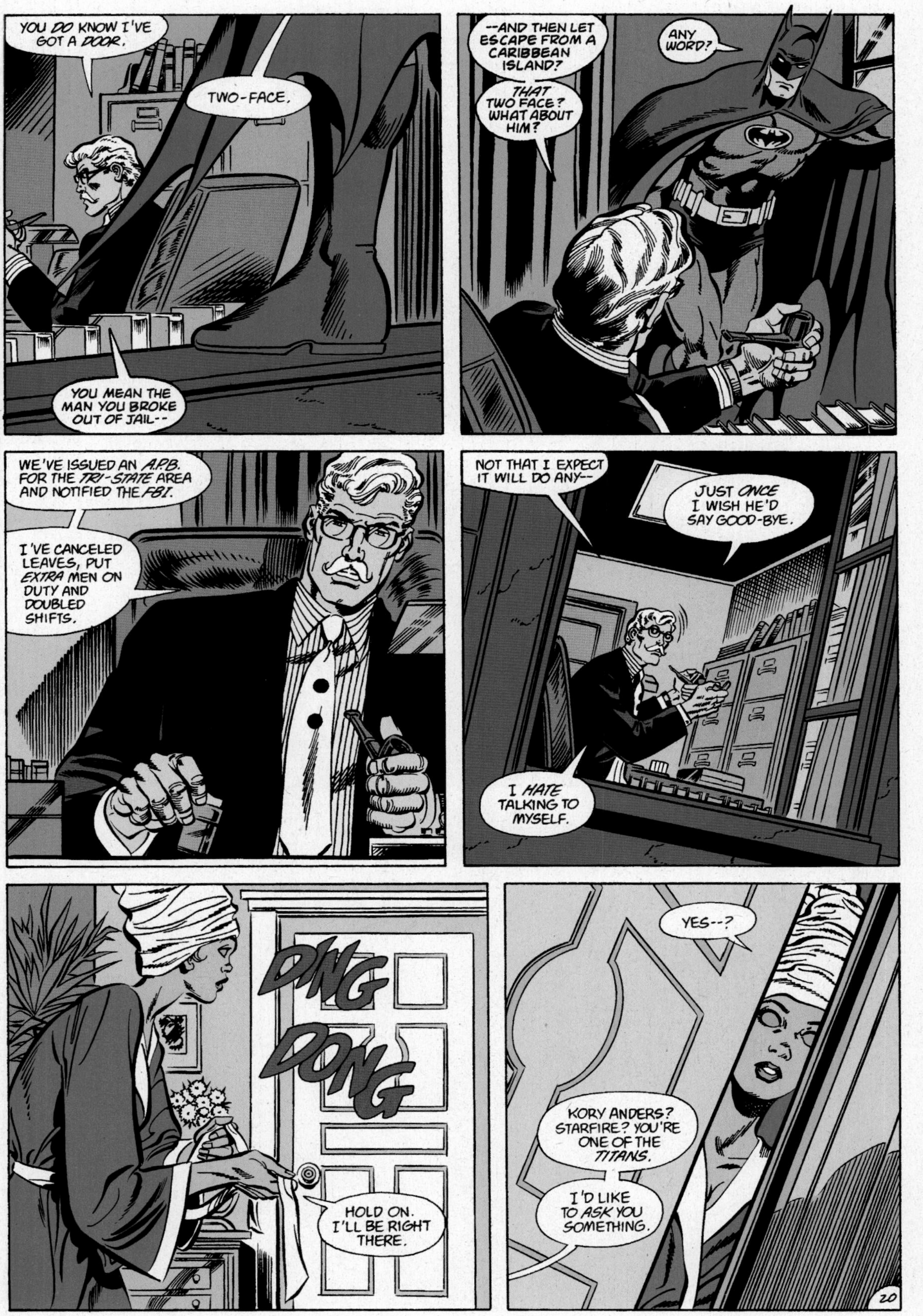
YOU DO KNOW I'VE GOT A DOOR.
TWO-FACE.
YOU MEAN THE MAN YOU BROKE OUT OF JAIL--
--AND THEN LET ESCAPE FROM A CARIBBEAN ISLAND?
THAT TWO FACE? WHAT ABOUT HIM?
ANY WORD?
WE'VE ISSUED AN A.P.B. FOR THE TRI-STATE AREA AND NOTIFIED THE FBI.
I'VE CANCELED LEAVES, PUT EXTRA MEN ON DUTY AND DOUBLED SHIFTS.
NOT THAT I EXPECT IT WILL DO ANY--
JUST ONCE I WISH HE'D SAY GOOD-BYE.
I HATE TALKING TO MYSELF.
DING
DONG
HOLD ON. I'LL BE RIGHT THERE.
YES--?
KORY ANDERS? STARFIRE? YOU'RE ONE OF THE TITANS.
I'D LIKE TO ASK YOU SOMETHING.
20

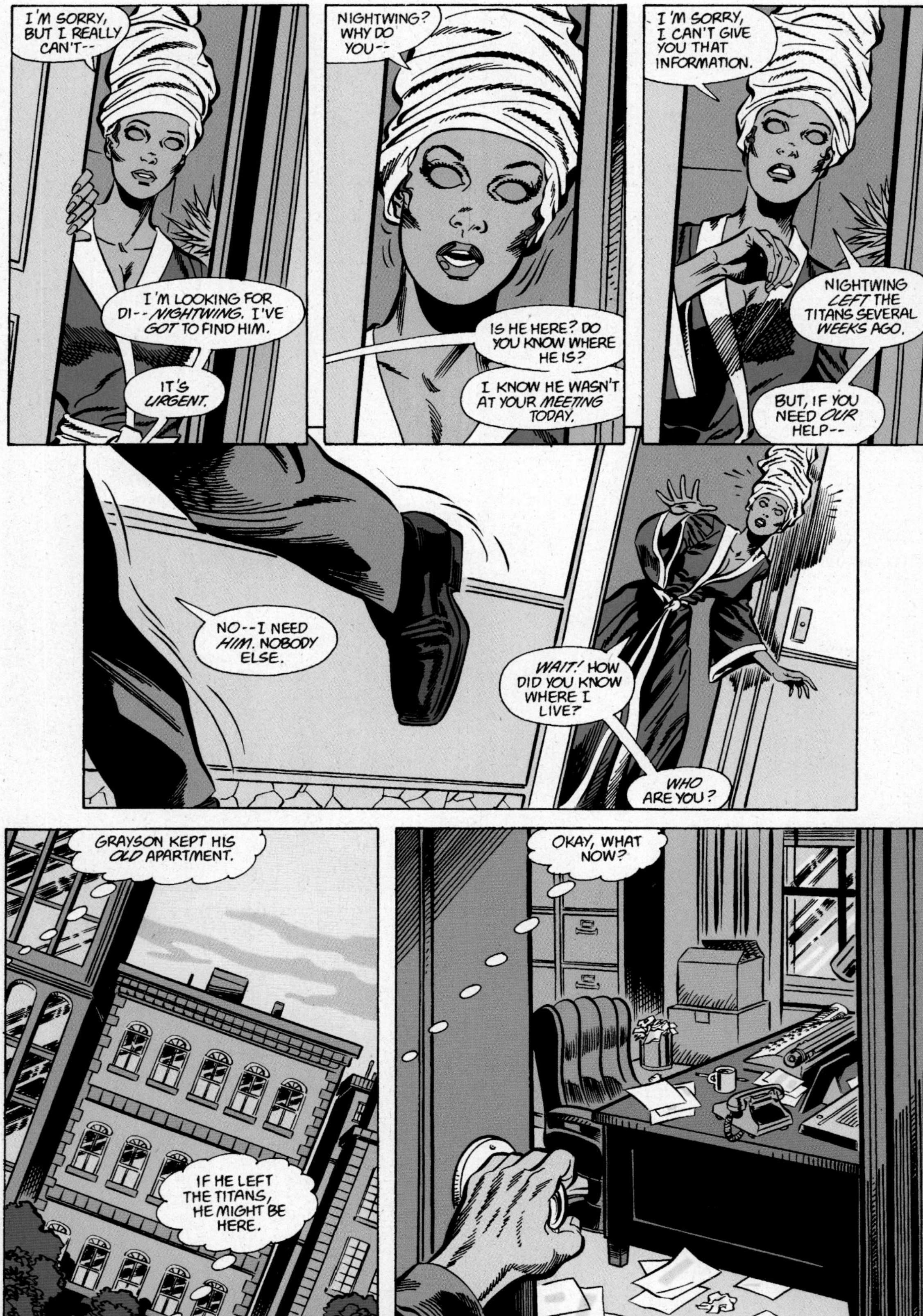
I'M SORRY, BUT I REALLY CAN'T--
I'M LOOKING FOR DI--NIGHTWING. I'VE GOT TO FIND HIM.
IT'S URGENT.
NIGHTWING? WHY DO YOU--
IS HE HERE? DO YOU KNOW WHERE HE IS?
I KNOW HE WASN'T AT YOUR MEETING TODAY.
I'M SORRY, I CAN'T GIVE YOU THAT INFORMATION.
NIGHTWING LEFT THE TITANS SEVERAL WEEKS AGO.
BUT, IF YOU NEED OUR HELP--
NO--I NEED HIM. NOBODY ELSE.
WAIT! HOW DID YOU KNOW WHERE I LIVE?
WHO ARE YOU?
GRAYSON KEPT HIS OLD APARTMENT.
IF HE LEFT THE TITANS, HE MIGHT BE HERE.
OKAY, WHAT NOW?
21

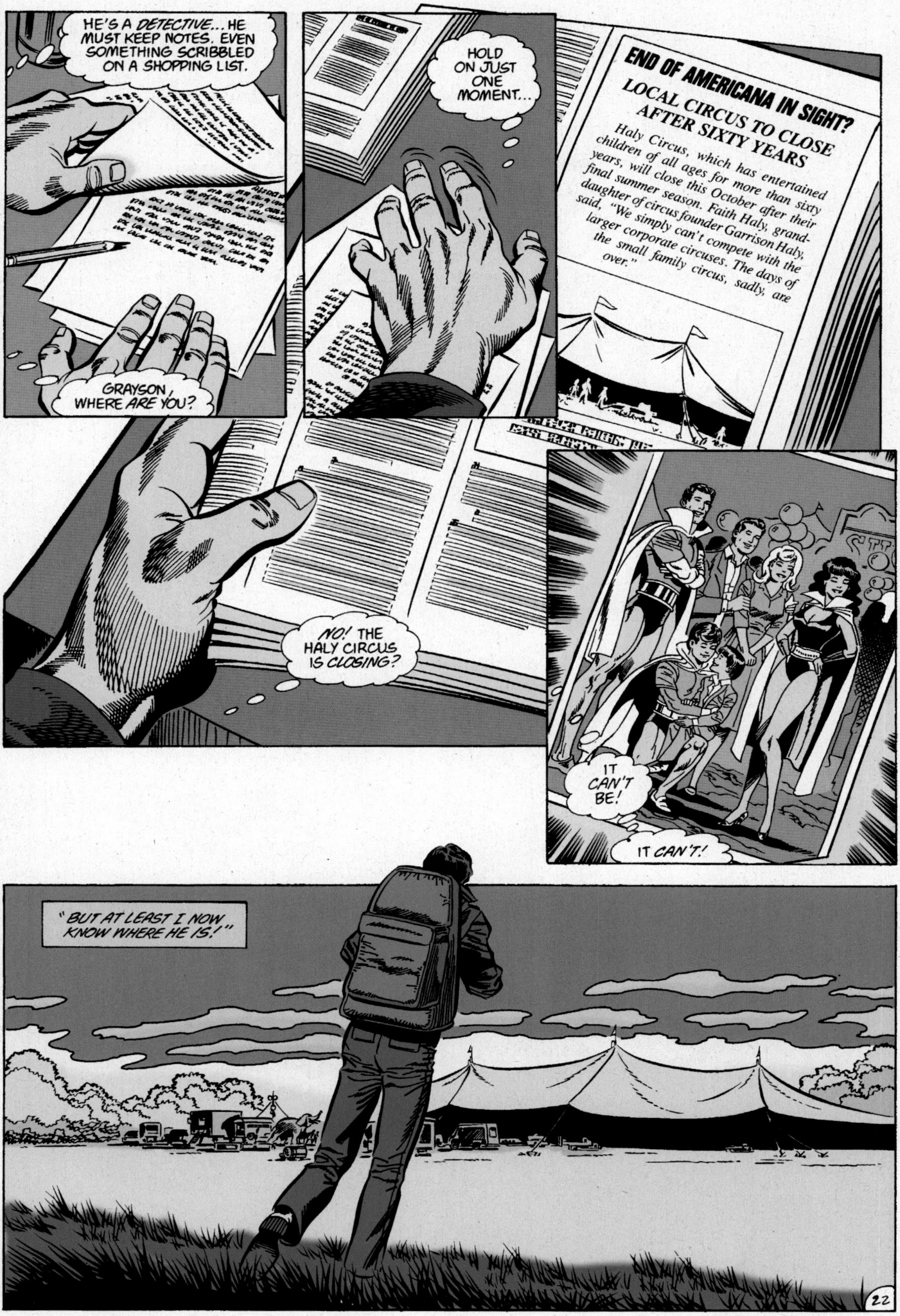
HE'S A DETECTIVE... HE MUST KEEP NOTES. EVEN SOMETHING SCRIBBLED ON A SHOPPING LIST.
GRAYSON, WHERE ARE YOU?
HOLD ON JUST ONE MOMENT...
END OF AMERICANA IN SIGHT?
LOCAL CIRCUS TO CLOSE AFTER SIXTY YEARS
Haly Circus, which has entertained children of all ages for more than sixty years, will close this October after their final summer season. Faith Haly, granddaughter of circus founder Garrison Haly, said, "We simply can't compete with the larger corporate circuses. The days of the small family circus, sadly, are over."
NO! THE HALY CIRCUS IS CLOSING?
IT CAN'T BE!
IT CAN'T!
"BUT AT LEAST I NOW KNOW WHERE HE IS!"
22

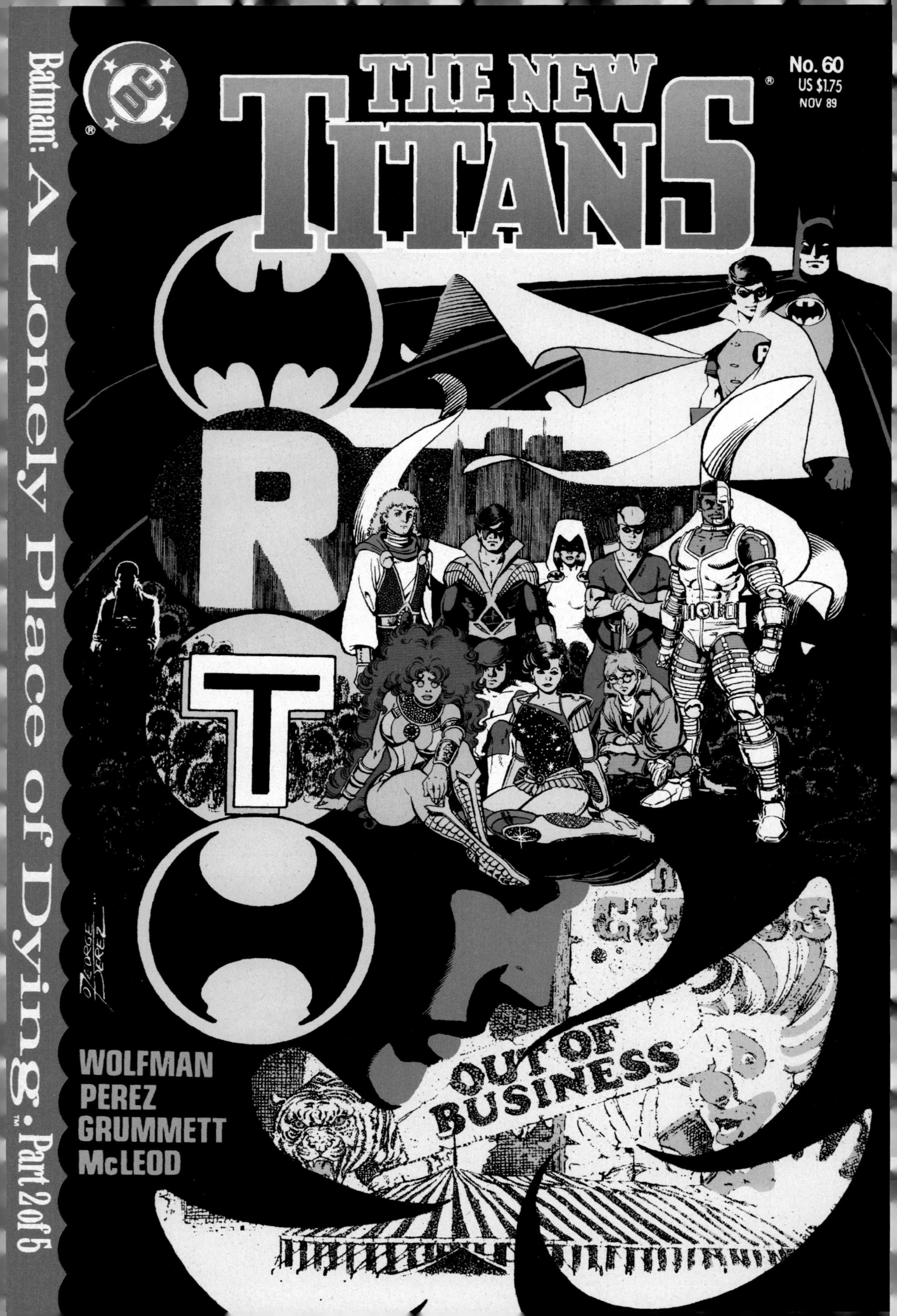

THE NEW TITANS
No. 60
US $1.75
NOV 89
Batman: A Lonely Place of Dying. Part 2 of 5
WOLFMAN
PEREZ
GRUMMETT
McLEOD
OUT OF BUSINESS
GEORGE PEREZ

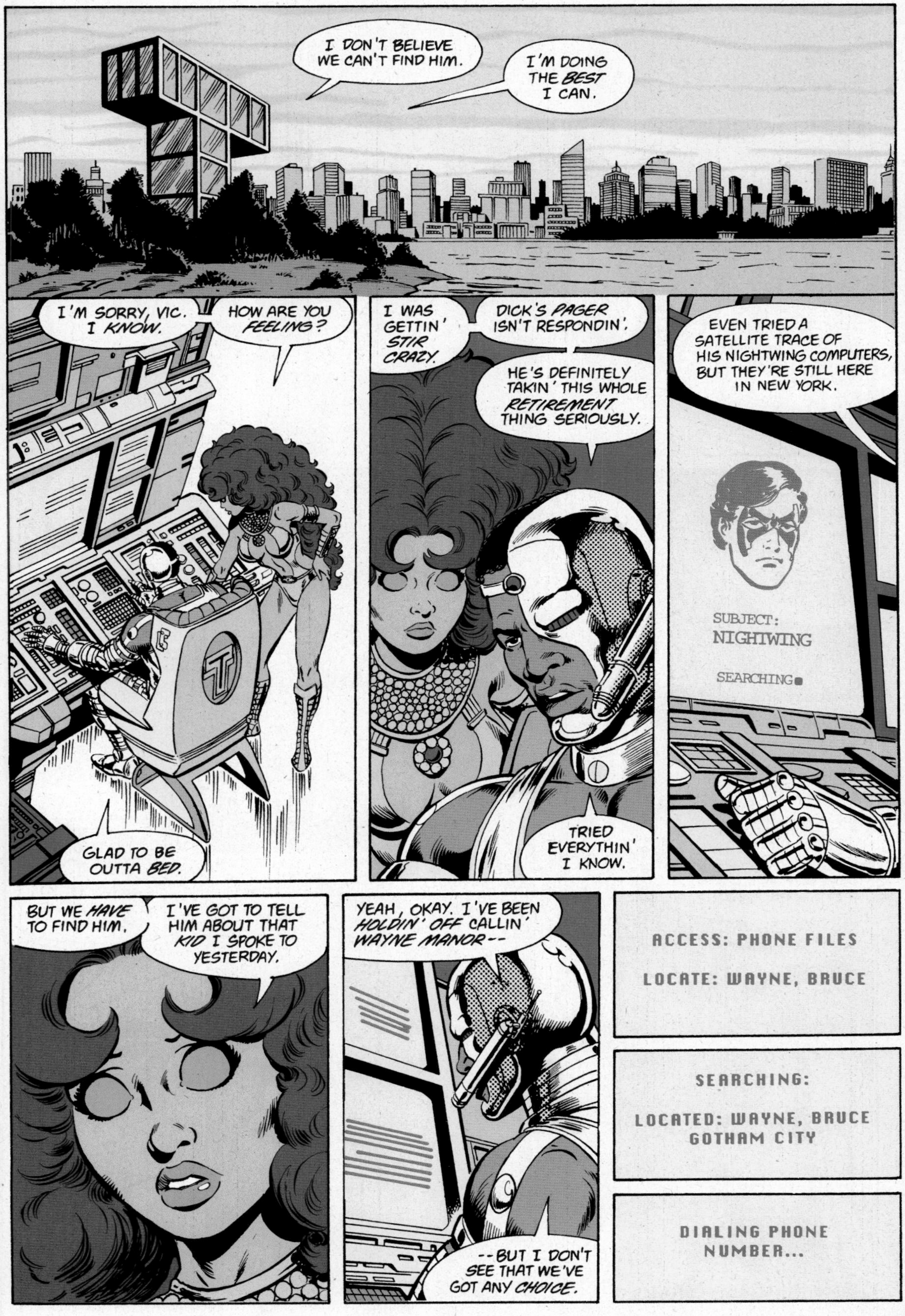
I DON'T BELIEVE WE CAN'T FIND HIM.
I'M DOING THE BEST I CAN.
I'M SORRY, VIC. I KNOW.
HOW ARE YOU FEELING?
GLAD TO BE OUTTA BED.
I WAS GETTIN' STIR CRAZY.
DICK'S PAGER ISN'T RESPONDIN'.
HE'S DEFINITELY TAKIN' THIS WHOLE RETIREMENT THING SERIOUSLY.
TRIED EVERYTHIN' I KNOW.
EVEN TRIED A SATELLITE TRACE OF HIS NIGHTWING COMPUTERS, BUT THEY'RE STILL HERE IN NEW YORK.
SUBJECT: NIGHTWING
SEARCHING
BUT WE HAVE TO FIND HIM.
I'VE GOT TO TELL HIM ABOUT THAT KID I SPOKE TO YESTERDAY.
YEAH, OKAY. I'VE BEEN HOLDIN' OFF CALLIN' WAYNE MANOR--
--BUT I DON'T SEE THAT WE'VE GOT ANY CHOICE.
ACCESS: PHONE FILES
LOCATE: WAYNE, BRUCE
SEARCHING:
LOCATED: WAYNE, BRUCE
GOTHAM CITY
DIALING PHONE NUMBER...

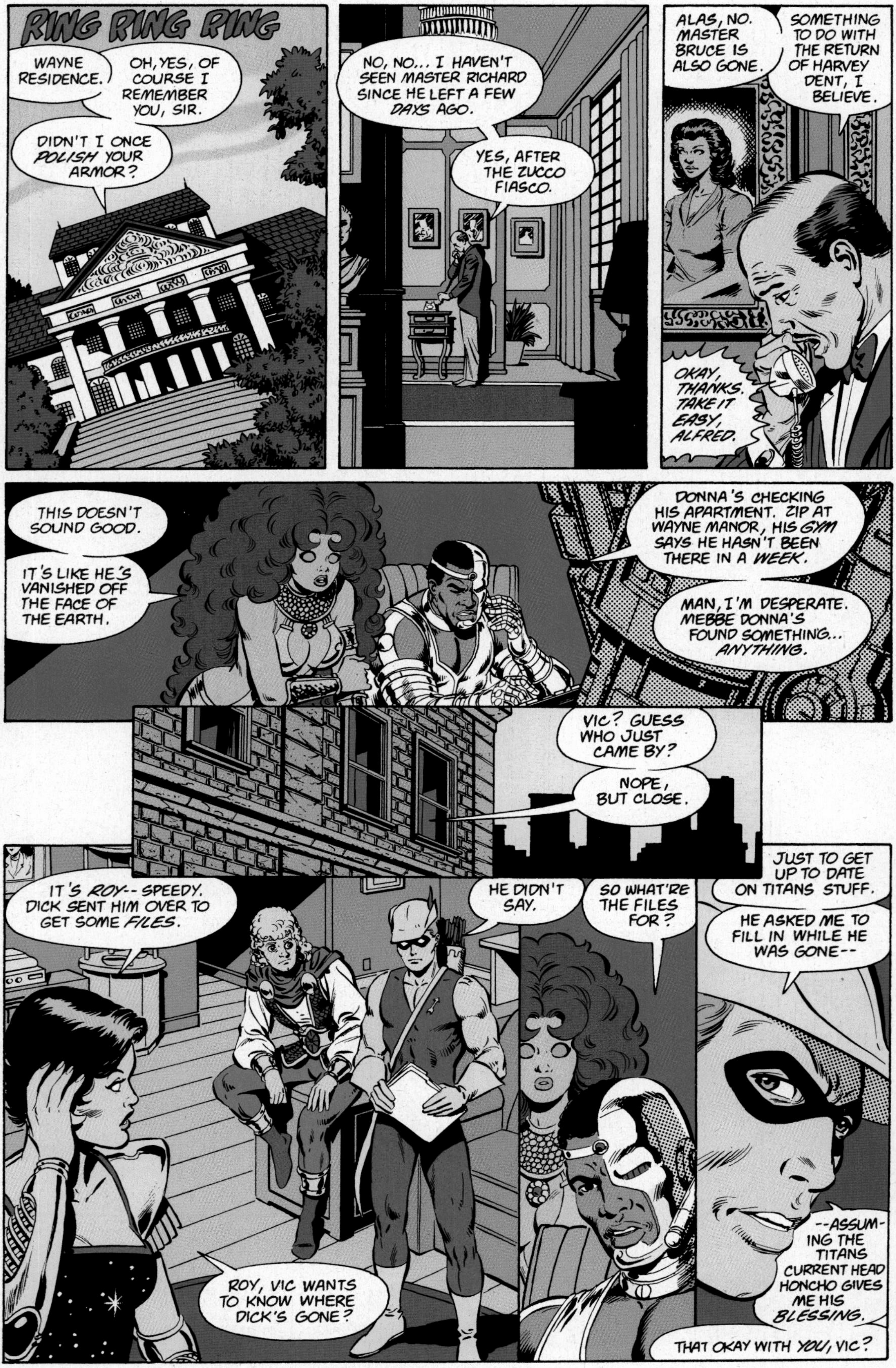
RING RING RING
WAYNE RESIDENCE.
OH, YES, OF COURSE I REMEMBER YOU, SIR.
DIDN'T I ONCE POLISH YOUR ARMOR?
NO, NO... I HAVEN'T SEEN MASTER RICHARD SINCE HE LEFT A FEW DAYS AGO.
YES, AFTER THE ZUCCO FIASCO.
ALAS, NO. MASTER BRUCE IS ALSO GONE.
SOMETHING TO DO WITH THE RETURN OF HARVEY DENT, I BELIEVE.
OKAY, THANKS. TAKE IT EASY, ALFRED.
THIS DOESN'T SOUND GOOD.
IT'S LIKE HE'S VANISHED OFF THE FACE OF THE EARTH.
DONNA'S CHECKING HIS APARTMENT. ZIP AT WAYNE MANOR, HIS GYM SAYS HE HASN'T BEEN THERE IN A WEEK.
MAN, I'M DESPERATE. MEBBE DONNA'S FOUND SOMETHING... ANYTHING.
VIC? GUESS WHO JUST CAME BY?
NOPE, BUT CLOSE.
IT'S ROY-- SPEEDY. DICK SENT HIM OVER TO GET SOME FILES.
HE DIDN'T SAY.
SO WHAT'RE THE FILES FOR?
JUST TO GET UP TO DATE ON TITANS STUFF.
HE ASKED ME TO FILL IN WHILE HE WAS GONE--
ROY, VIC WANTS TO KNOW WHERE DICK'S GONE?
--ASSUMING THE TITANS CURRENT HEAD HONCHO GIVES ME HIS BLESSING.
THAT OKAY WITH YOU, VIC?

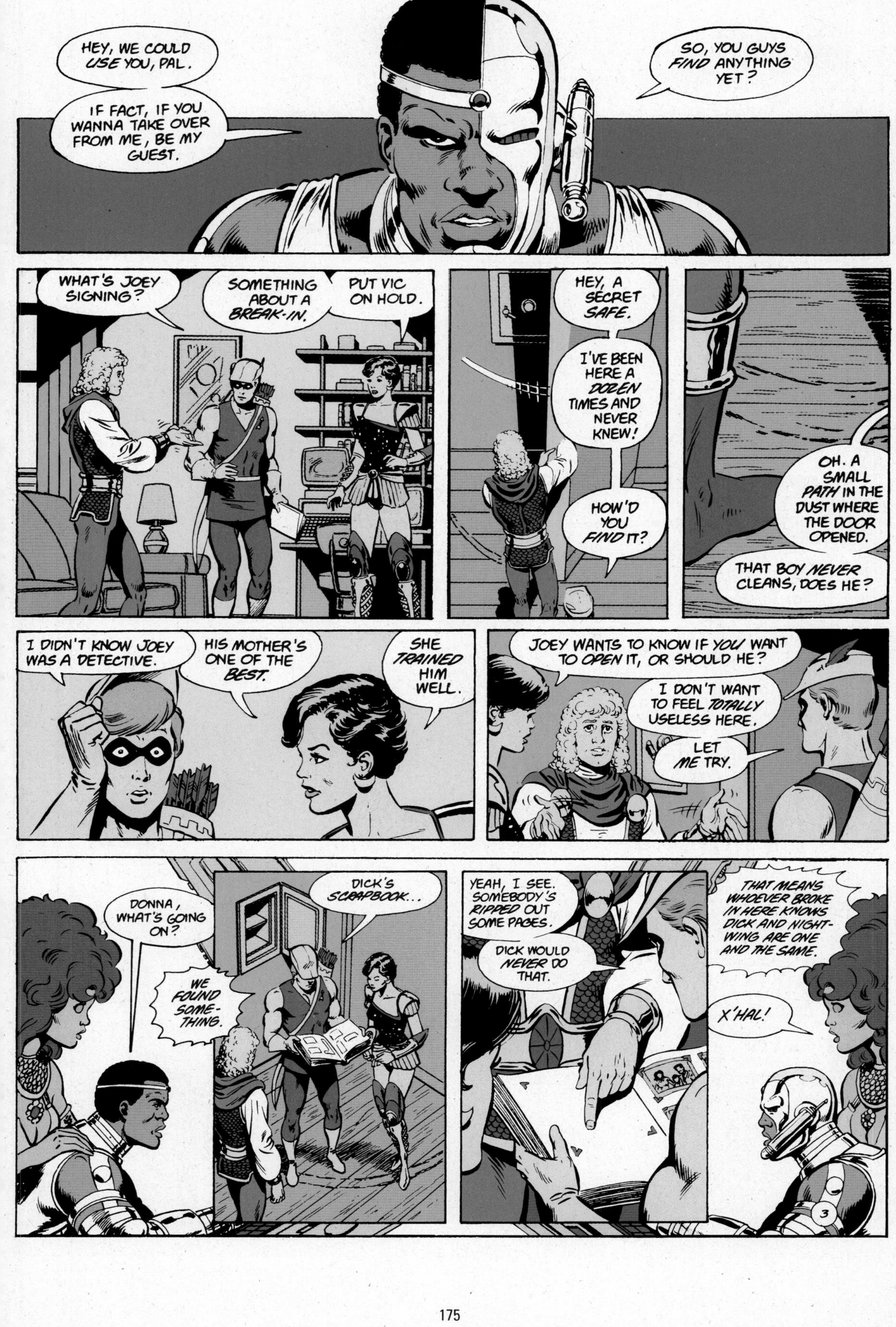
HEY, WE COULD USE YOU, PAL.
IF FACT, IF YOU WANNA TAKE OVER FROM ME, BE MY GUEST.
SO, YOU GUYS FIND ANYTHING YET?
WHAT'S JOEY SIGNING?
SOMETHING ABOUT A BREAK-IN.
PUT VIC ON HOLD.
HEY, A SECRET SAFE.
I'VE BEEN HERE A DOZEN TIMES AND NEVER KNEW!
HOW'D YOU FIND IT?
OH. A SMALL PATH IN THE DUST WHERE THE DOOR OPENED.
THAT BOY NEVER CLEANS, DOES HE?
I DIDN'T KNOW JOEY WAS A DETECTIVE.
HIS MOTHER'S ONE OF THE BEST.
SHE TRAINED HIM WELL.
JOEY WANTS TO KNOW IF YOU WANT TO OPEN IT, OR SHOULD HE?
I DON'T WANT TO FEEL TOTALLY USELESS HERE.
LET ME TRY.
DONNA, WHAT'S GOING ON?
WE FOUND SOME-THING.
DICK'S SCRAPBOOK...
YEAH, I SEE. SOMEBODY'S RIPPED OUT SOME PAGES.
DICK WOULD NEVER DO THAT.
THAT MEANS WHOEVER BROKE IN HERE KNOWS DICK AND NIGHT-WING ARE ONE AND THE SAME.
X'HAL!
3

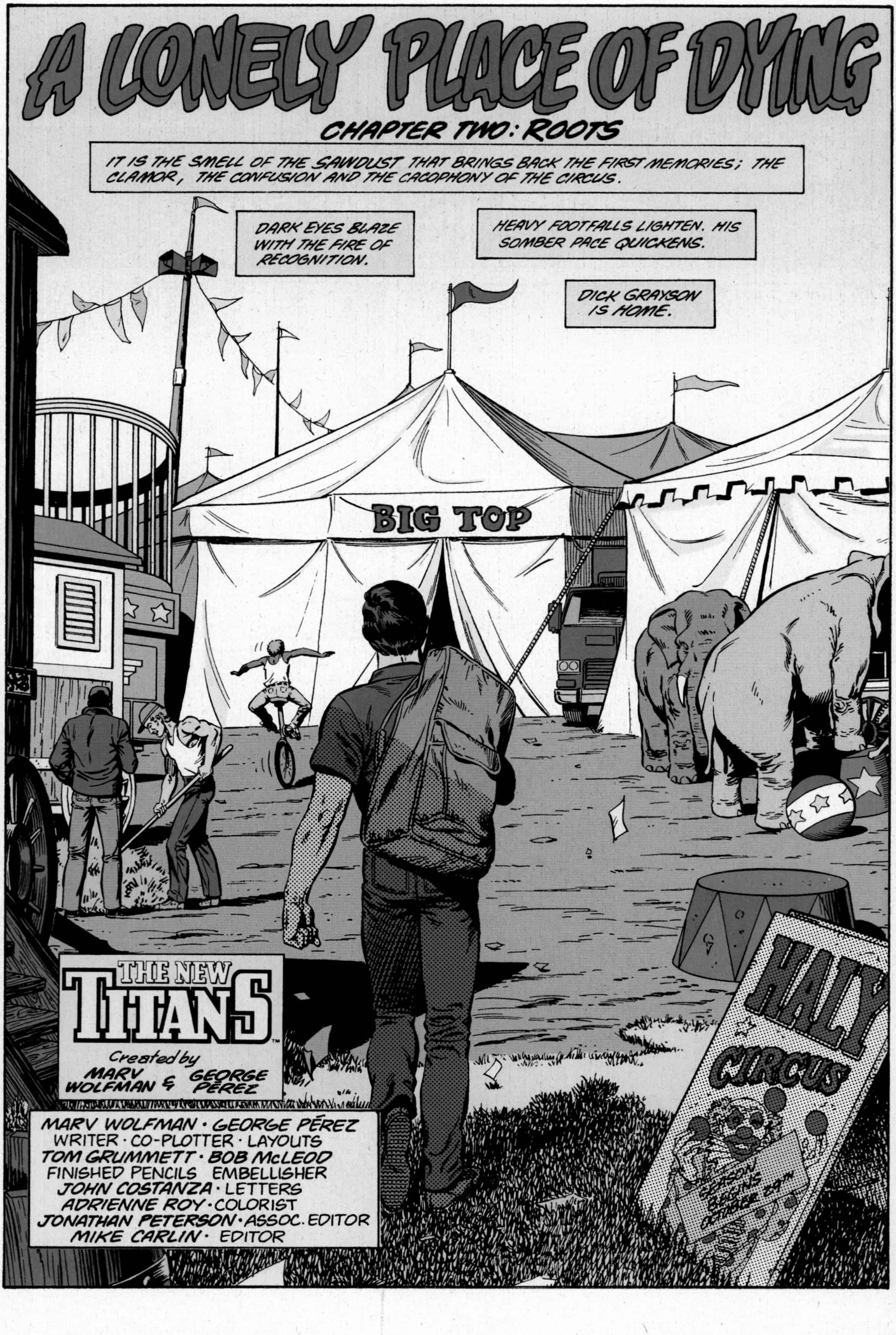
A LONELY PLACE OF DYING
CHAPTER TWO: ROOTS
IT IS THE SMELL OF THE SAWDUST THAT BRINGS BACK THE FIRST MEMORIES; THE CLAMOR, THE CONFUSION AND THE CACOPHONY OF THE CIRCUS.
DARK EYES BLAZE WITH THE FIRE OF RECOGNITION.
HEAVY FOOTFALLS LIGHTEN. HIS SOMBER PACE QUICKENS.
DICK GRAYSON IS HOME.
BIG TOP
THE NEW TITANS
Created by MARV WOLFMAN & GEORGE PÉREZ
MARV WOLFMAN · GEORGE PÉREZ
WRITER · CO-PLOTTER · LAYOUTS
TOM GRUMMETT · BOB McLEOD
FINISHED PENCILS EMBELLISHER
JOHN COSTANZA · LETTERS
ADRIENNE ROY · COLORIST
JONATHAN PETERSON · ASSOC. EDITOR
MIKE CARLIN · EDITOR
HALY CIRCUS

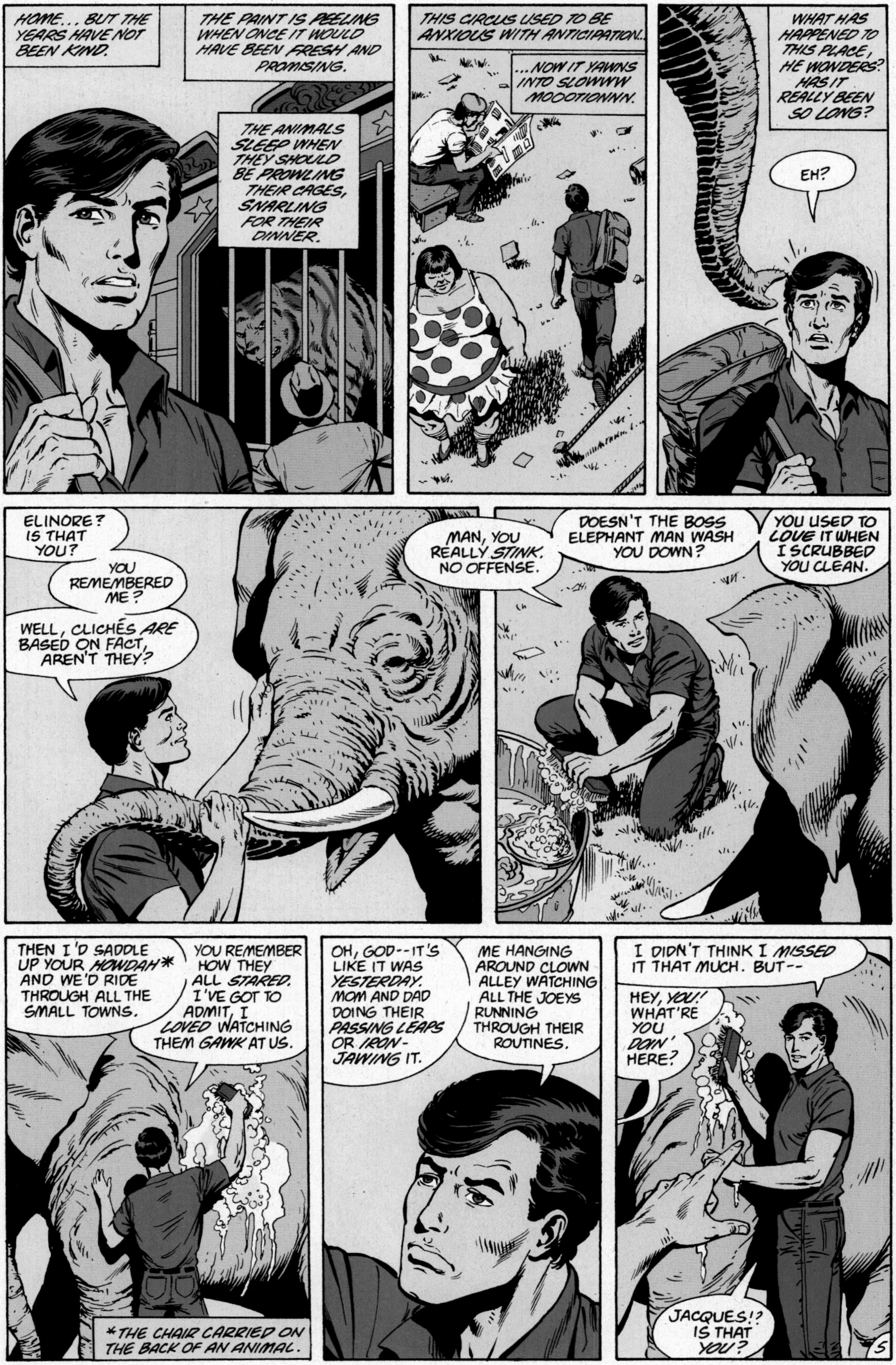
HOME... BUT THE YEARS HAVE NOT BEEN KIND.
THE PAINT IS PEELING WHEN ONCE IT WOULD HAVE BEEN FRESH AND PROMISING.
THE ANIMALS SLEEP WHEN THEY SHOULD BE PROWLING THEIR CAGES, SNARLING FOR THEIR DINNER.
THIS CIRCUS USED TO BE ANXIOUS WITH ANTICIPATION...
...NOW IT YAWNS INTO SLOWWW MOOOTIONNN.
WHAT HAS HAPPENED TO THIS PLACE, HE WONDERS? HAS IT REALLY BEEN SO LONG?
EH?
ELINORE? IS THAT YOU?
YOU REMEMBERED ME?
WELL, CLICHÉS ARE BASED ON FACT, AREN'T THEY?
MAN, YOU REALLY STINK. NO OFFENSE.
DOESN'T THE BOSS ELEPHANT MAN WASH YOU DOWN?
YOU USED TO LOVE IT WHEN I SCRUBBED YOU CLEAN.
THEN I'D SADDLE UP YOUR HOWDAH* AND WE'D RIDE THROUGH ALL THE SMALL TOWNS.
YOU REMEMBER HOW THEY ALL STARED. I'VE GOT TO ADMIT, I LOVED WATCHING THEM GAWK AT US.
*THE CHAIR CARRIED ON THE BACK OF AN ANIMAL.
OH, GOD--IT'S LIKE IT WAS YESTERDAY. MOM AND DAD DOING THEIR PASSING LEAPS OR IRON-JAWING IT.
ME HANGING AROUND CLOWN ALLEY WATCHING ALL THE JOEYS RUNNING THROUGH THEIR ROUTINES.
I DIDN'T THINK I MISSED IT THAT MUCH. BUT--
HEY, YOU! WHAT'RE YOU DOIN' HERE?
JACQUES!? IS THAT YOU?
5

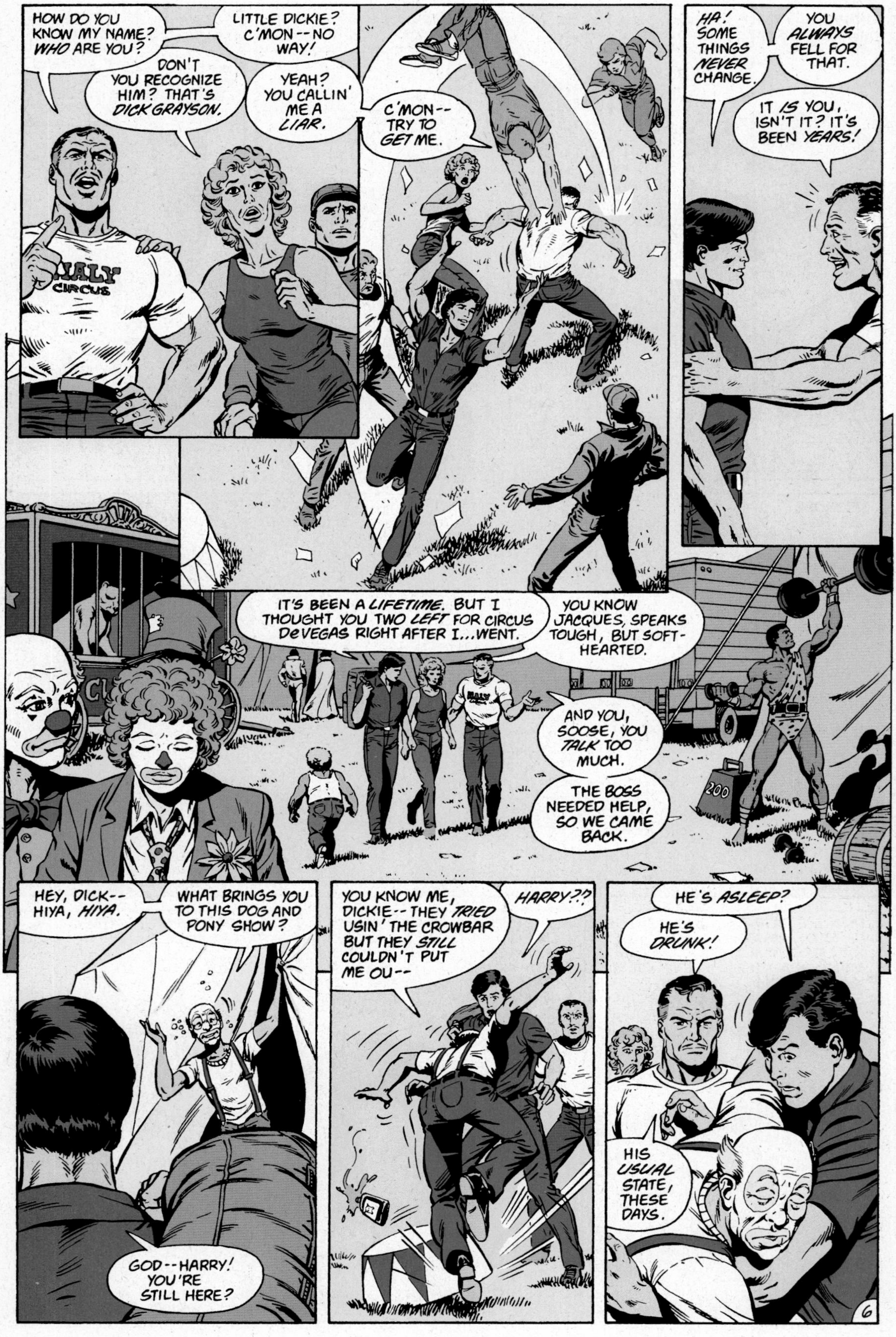
HOW DO YOU KNOW MY NAME? WHO ARE YOU?
LITTLE DICKIE? C'MON--NO WAY!
DON'T YOU RECOGNIZE HIM? THAT'S DICK GRAYSON.
YEAH? YOU CALLIN' ME A LIAR.
HALY CIRCUS
C'MON--TRY TO GET ME.
HA! SOME THINGS NEVER CHANGE.
YOU ALWAYS FELL FOR THAT.
IT IS YOU, ISN'T IT? IT'S BEEN YEARS!
IT'S BEEN A LIFETIME. BUT I THOUGHT YOU TWO LEFT FOR CIRCUS DeVEGAS RIGHT AFTER I...WENT.
YOU KNOW JACQUES, SPEAKS TOUGH, BUT SOFT-HEARTED.
AND YOU, SOOSE, YOU TALK TOO MUCH.
THE BOSS NEEDED HELP, SO WE CAME BACK.
200
HEY, DICK--HIYA, HIYA.
WHAT BRINGS YOU TO THIS DOG AND PONY SHOW?
GOD--HARRY! YOU'RE STILL HERE?
YOU KNOW ME, DICKIE--THEY TRIED USIN' THE CROWBAR BUT THEY STILL COULDN'T PUT ME OU--
HARRY??
HE'S ASLEEP?
HE'S DRUNK!
HIS USUAL STATE, THESE DAYS.
6

I READ ABOUT YOUR CLOSING DOWN, BUT I COULDN'T FIGURE OUT WHY.

NOW THAT I'M HERE, I'M BEGINNING TO UNDERSTAND.

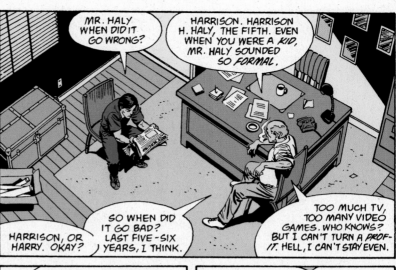

MR. HALY, WHEN DID IT GO WRONG?

HARRISON. HARRISON H. HALY, THE FIFTH. EVEN WHEN YOU WERE A *KID*, MR. HALY SOUNDED SO *FORMAL*.

SO WHEN DID IT GO BAD? LAST FIVE-SIX YEARS, I THINK.

HARRISON, OR HARRY. OKAY?

TOO MUCH TV, TOO MANY VIDEO GAMES. WHO KNOWS? BUT I CAN'T TURN A *PROFIT*. HELL, I CAN'T STAY EVEN.

SO I DECIDED TO SELL, BUT THE ONLY BIDDER WAS SOME *CORPORATION* WHO WANTED THEIR LOGO TATTOOED ON THE ELEPHANTS.

HALY CLOSING

NOT QUITE THE GREATEST SHOW ON EARTH, IS IT, DICK?

LOOK, I DIDN'T WANT TO SELL, SO I CUT DOWN EXPENSES. WOULD'VE WORKED...

...EXCEPT FOR ALL THE *ACCIDENTS* WE'VE HAD.

ACCIDENTS?

YEAH. COST US A FORTUNE AND BROUGHT DOWN OUR SELLING PRICE.

YOU KNOW, SOMETIMES I SIT HERE AND JUST REMEMBER THE GOOD OLD DAYS.

WE WERE BARELY BREAKING EVEN BACK THEN, TOO -- BUT MAN, WERE WE HAVING *FUN*.

AND WE CAN STILL HAVE FUN, KID.

WANT TO SEE THE *BEST* SHOW IN TOWN?

YOU HAVE TO ASK?

7

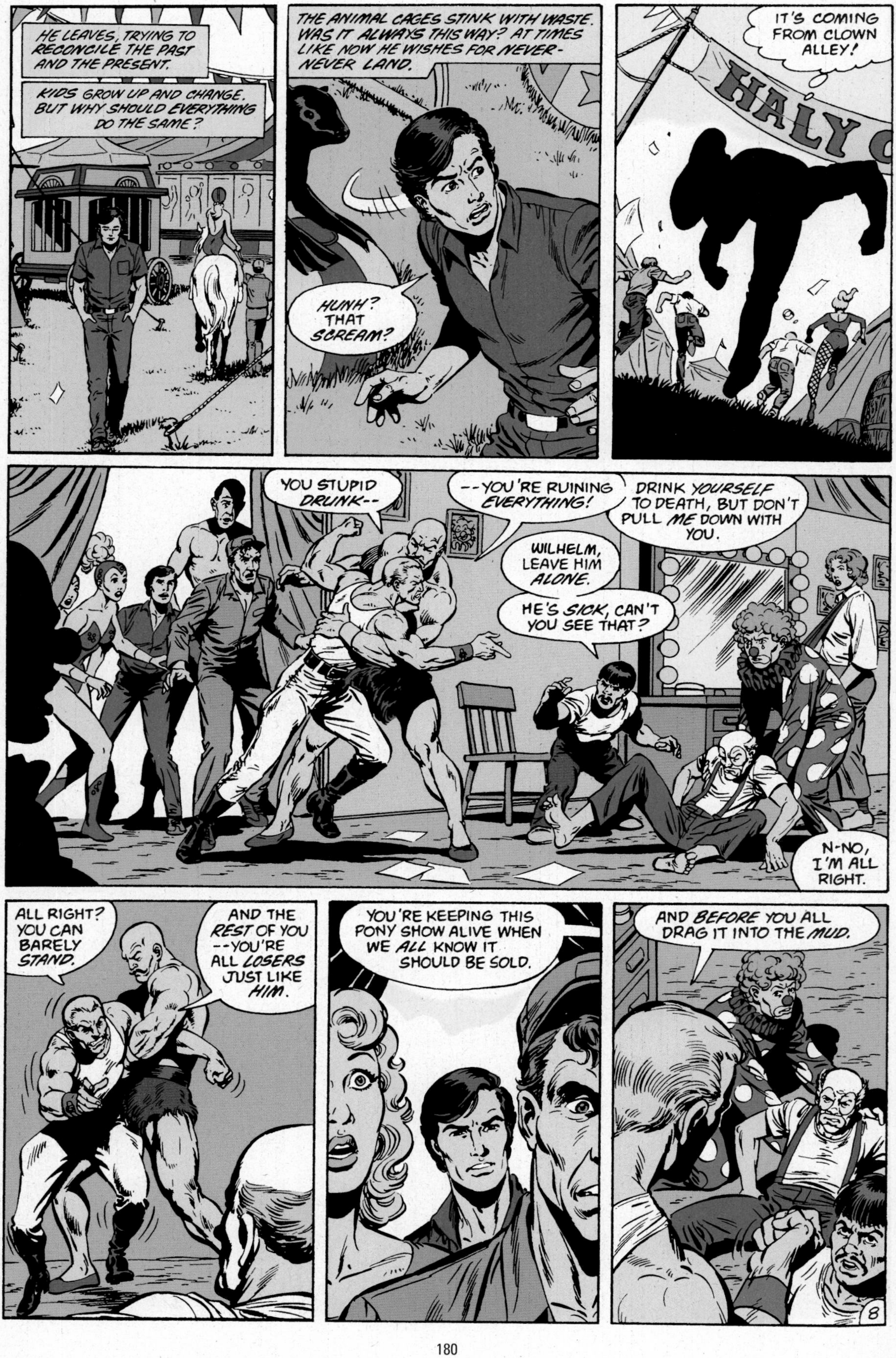
HE LEAVES, TRYING TO RECONCILE THE PAST AND THE PRESENT.
KIDS GROW UP AND CHANGE. BUT WHY SHOULD EVERYTHING DO THE SAME?
THE ANIMAL CAGES STINK WITH WASTE. WAS IT ALWAYS THIS WAY? AT TIMES LIKE NOW HE WISHES FOR NEVER-NEVER LAND.
HUNH? THAT SCREAM?
IT'S COMING FROM CLOWN ALLEY!
HALY
YOU STUPID DRUNK--
--YOU'RE RUINING EVERYTHING!
DRINK YOURSELF TO DEATH, BUT DON'T PULL ME DOWN WITH YOU.
WILHELM, LEAVE HIM ALONE.
HE'S SICK, CAN'T YOU SEE THAT?
N-NO, I'M ALL RIGHT.
ALL RIGHT? YOU CAN BARELY STAND.
AND THE REST OF YOU --YOU'RE ALL LOSERS JUST LIKE HIM.
YOU'RE KEEPING THIS PONY SHOW ALIVE WHEN WE ALL KNOW IT SHOULD BE SOLD.
AND BEFORE YOU ALL DRAG IT INTO THE MUD.
8

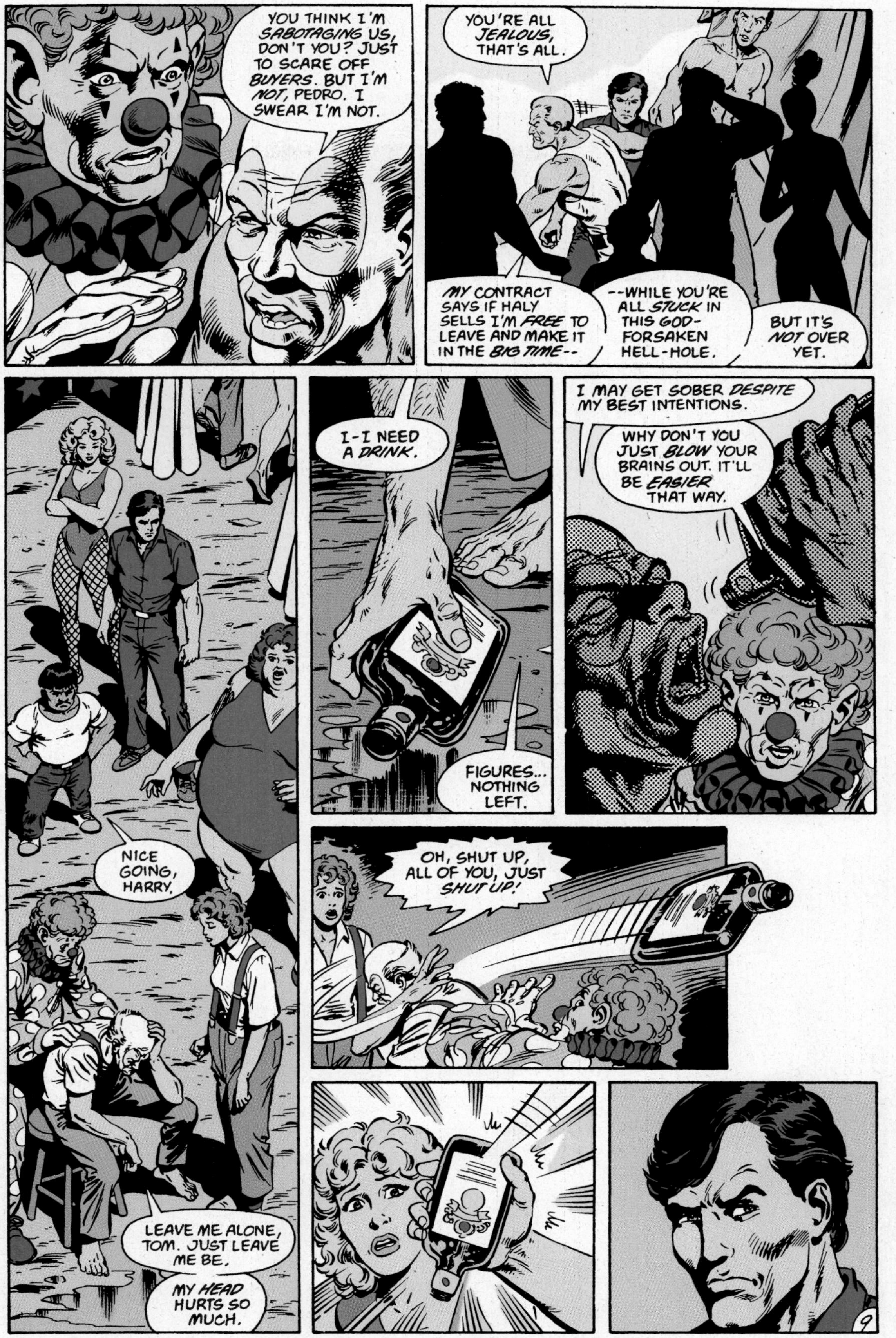
YOU THINK I'M SABOTAGING US, DON'T YOU? JUST TO SCARE OFF BUYERS. BUT I'M NOT, PEDRO. I SWEAR I'M NOT.
YOU'RE ALL JEALOUS, THAT'S ALL.
MY CONTRACT SAYS IF HALY SELLS I'M FREE TO LEAVE AND MAKE IT IN THE BIG TIME--
--WHILE YOU'RE ALL STUCK IN THIS GOD-FORSAKEN HELL-HOLE.
BUT IT'S NOT OVER YET.
I-I NEED A DRINK.
FIGURES... NOTHING LEFT.
I MAY GET SOBER DESPITE MY BEST INTENTIONS.
WHY DON'T YOU JUST BLOW YOUR BRAINS OUT. IT'LL BE EASIER THAT WAY.
NICE GOING, HARRY.
LEAVE ME ALONE, TOM. JUST LEAVE ME BE.
MY HEAD HURTS SO MUCH.
OH, SHUT UP, ALL OF YOU, JUST SHUT UP!
9

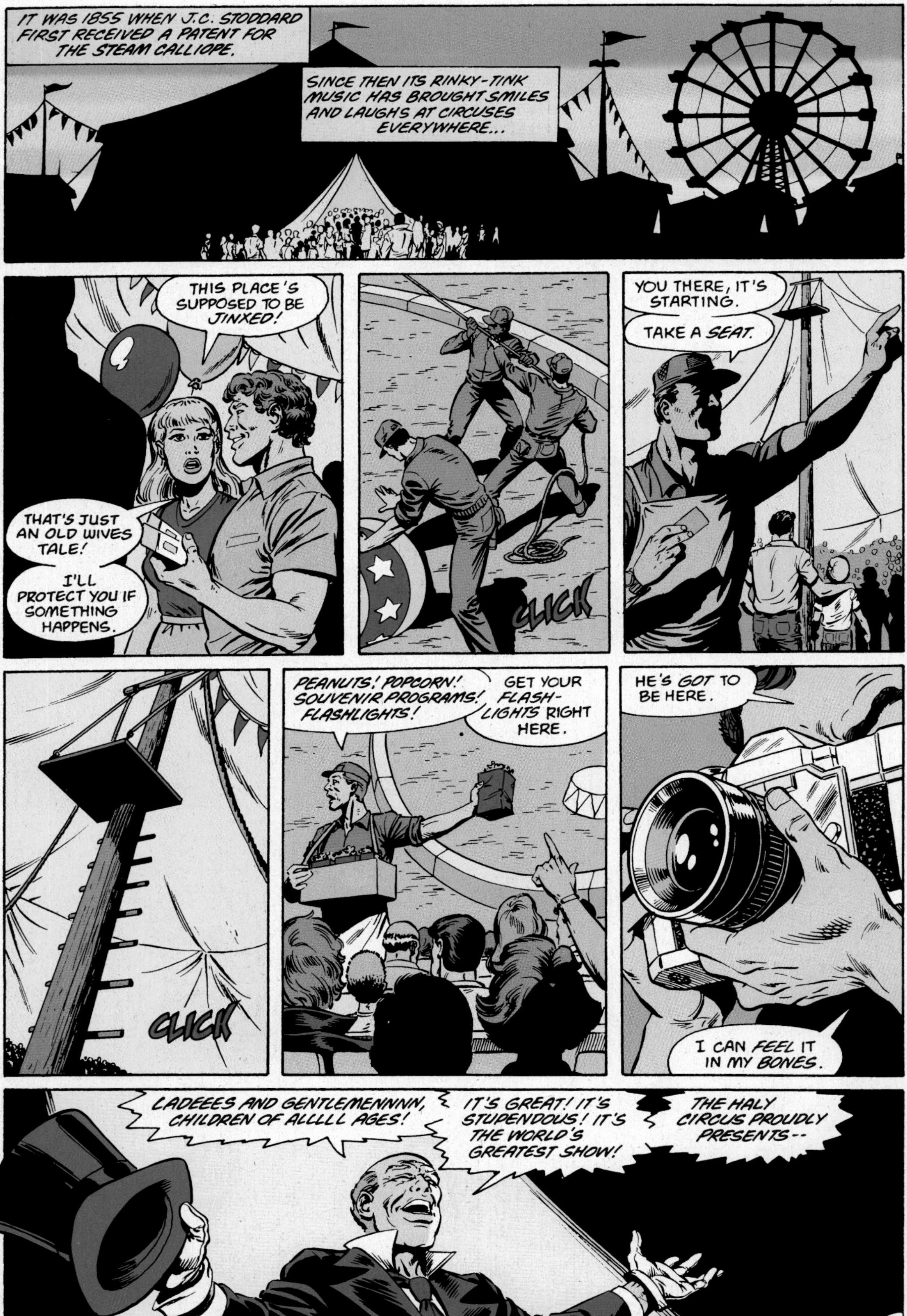
IT WAS 1855 WHEN J.C. STODDARD FIRST RECEIVED A PATENT FOR THE STEAM CALLIOPE.
SINCE THEN ITS RINKY-TINK MUSIC HAS BROUGHT SMILES AND LAUGHS AT CIRCUSES EVERYWHERE...
THIS PLACE'S SUPPOSED TO BE JINXED!
THAT'S JUST AN OLD WIVES TALE!
I'LL PROTECT YOU IF SOMETHING HAPPENS.
CLICK
YOU THERE, IT'S STARTING.
TAKE A SEAT.
CLICK
PEANUTS! POPCORN! SOUVENIR PROGRAMS! FLASHLIGHTS!
GET YOUR FLASH-LIGHTS RIGHT HERE.
HE'S GOT TO BE HERE.
I CAN FEEL IT IN MY BONES.
LADEEES AND GENTLEMENNNN, CHILDREN OF ALLLLL AGES!
IT'S GREAT! IT'S STUPENDOUS! IT'S THE WORLD'S GREATEST SHOW!
THE HALY CIRCUS PROUDLY PRESENTS--
10

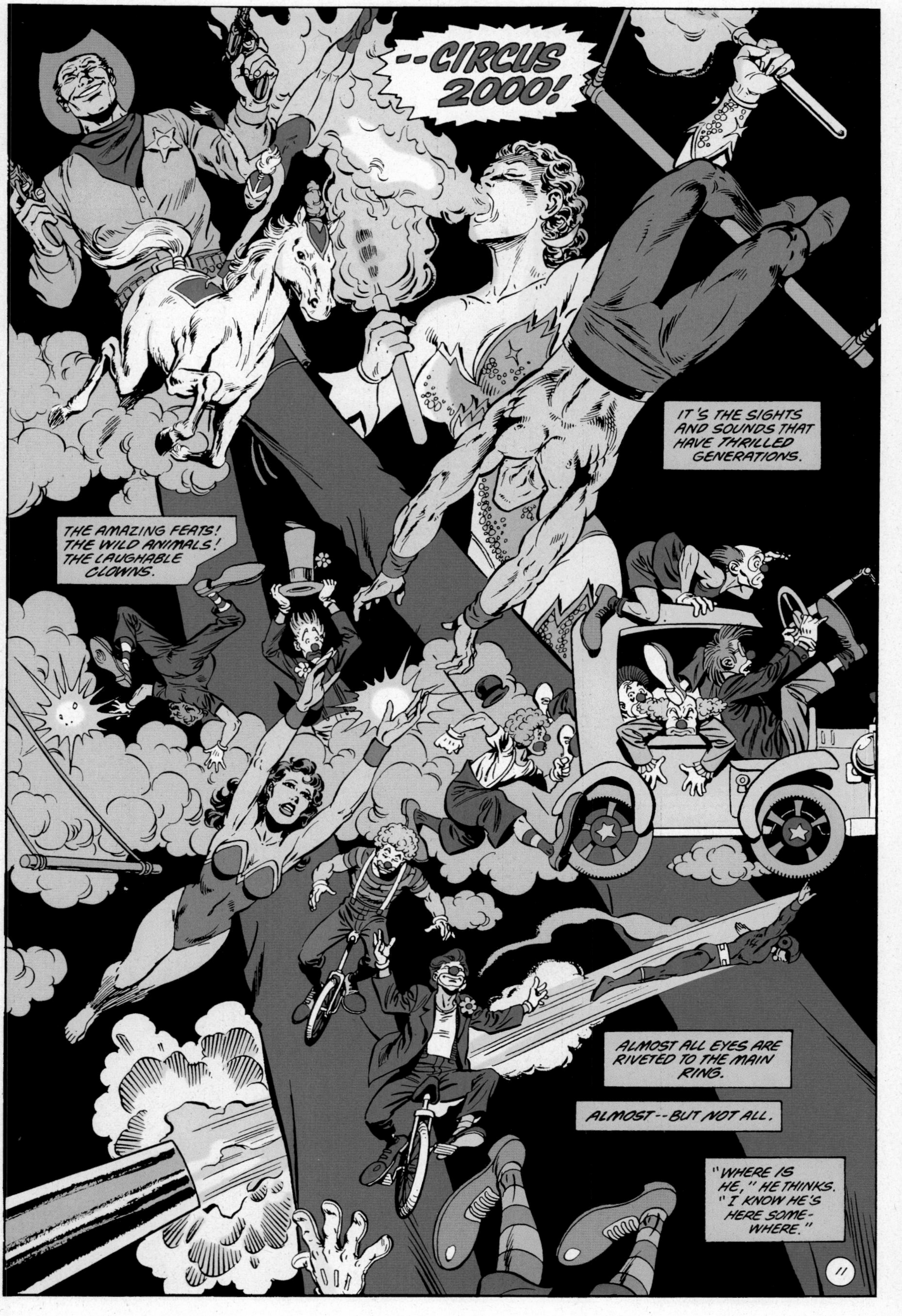
--CIRCUS 2000!
IT'S THE SIGHTS AND SOUNDS THAT HAVE THRILLED GENERATIONS.
THE AMAZING FEATS! THE WILD ANIMALS! THE LAUGHABLE CLOWNS.
ALMOST ALL EYES ARE RIVETED TO THE MAIN RING.
ALMOST--BUT NOT ALL.
"WHERE IS HE," HE THINKS. "I KNOW HE'S HERE SOME-WHERE."
11

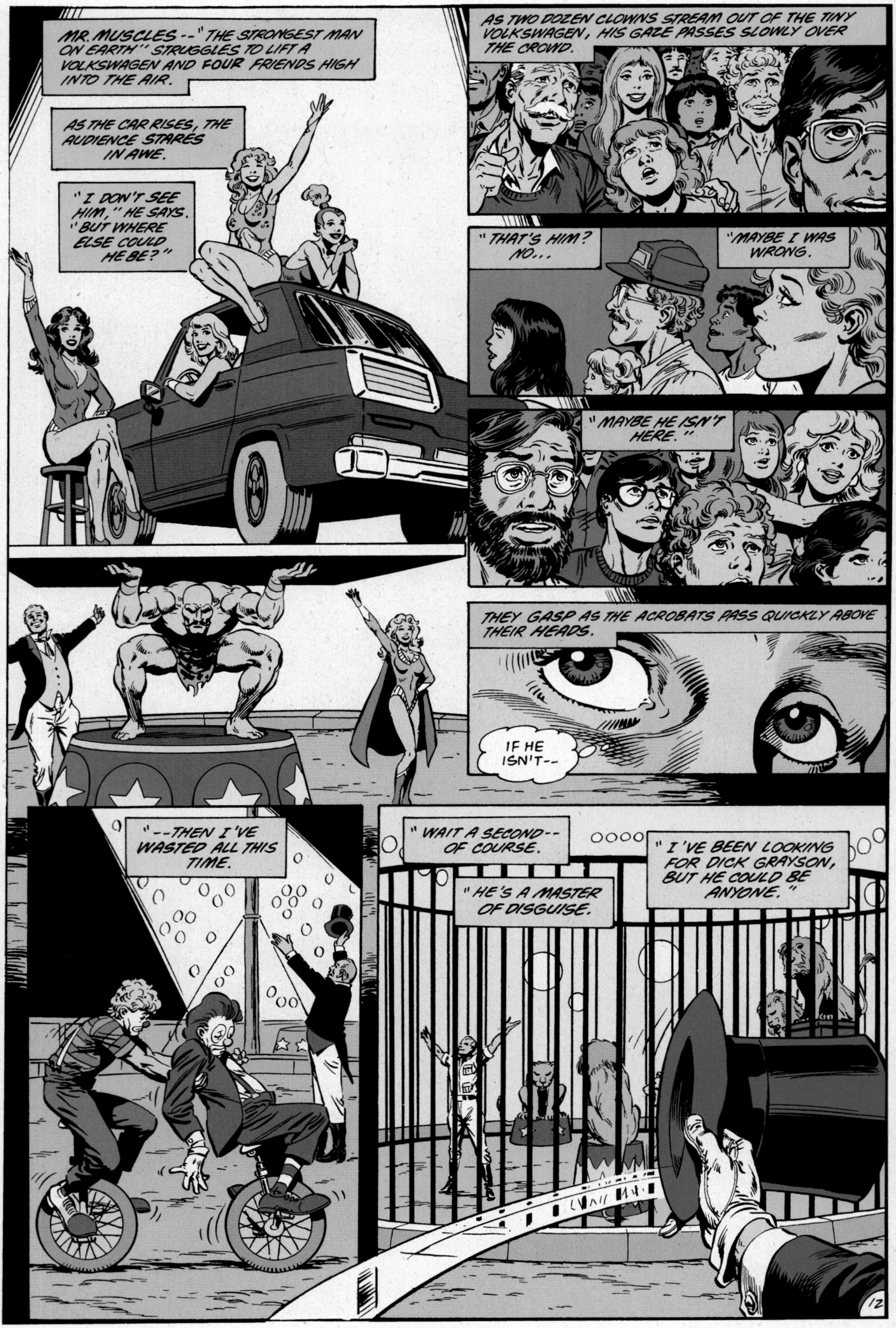

MR. MUSCLES -- "THE STRONGEST MAN ON EARTH" STRUGGLES TO LIFT A VOLKSWAGEN AND FOUR FRIENDS HIGH INTO THE AIR.
AS THE CAR RISES, THE AUDIENCE STARES IN AWE.
"I DON'T SEE HIM," HE SAYS. "BUT WHERE ELSE COULD HE BE?"
AS TWO DOZEN CLOWNS STREAM OUT OF THE TINY VOLKSWAGEN, HIS GAZE PASSES SLOWLY OVER THE CROWD.
"THAT'S HIM? NO...
"MAYBE I WAS WRONG.
"MAYBE HE ISN'T HERE."
THEY GASP AS THE ACROBATS PASS QUICKLY ABOVE THEIR HEADS.
IF HE ISN'T--
"--THEN I'VE WASTED ALL THIS TIME.
"WAIT A SECOND-- OF COURSE.
"HE'S A MASTER OF DISGUISE.
"I'VE BEEN LOOKING FOR DICK GRAYSON, BUT HE COULD BE ANYONE."
12

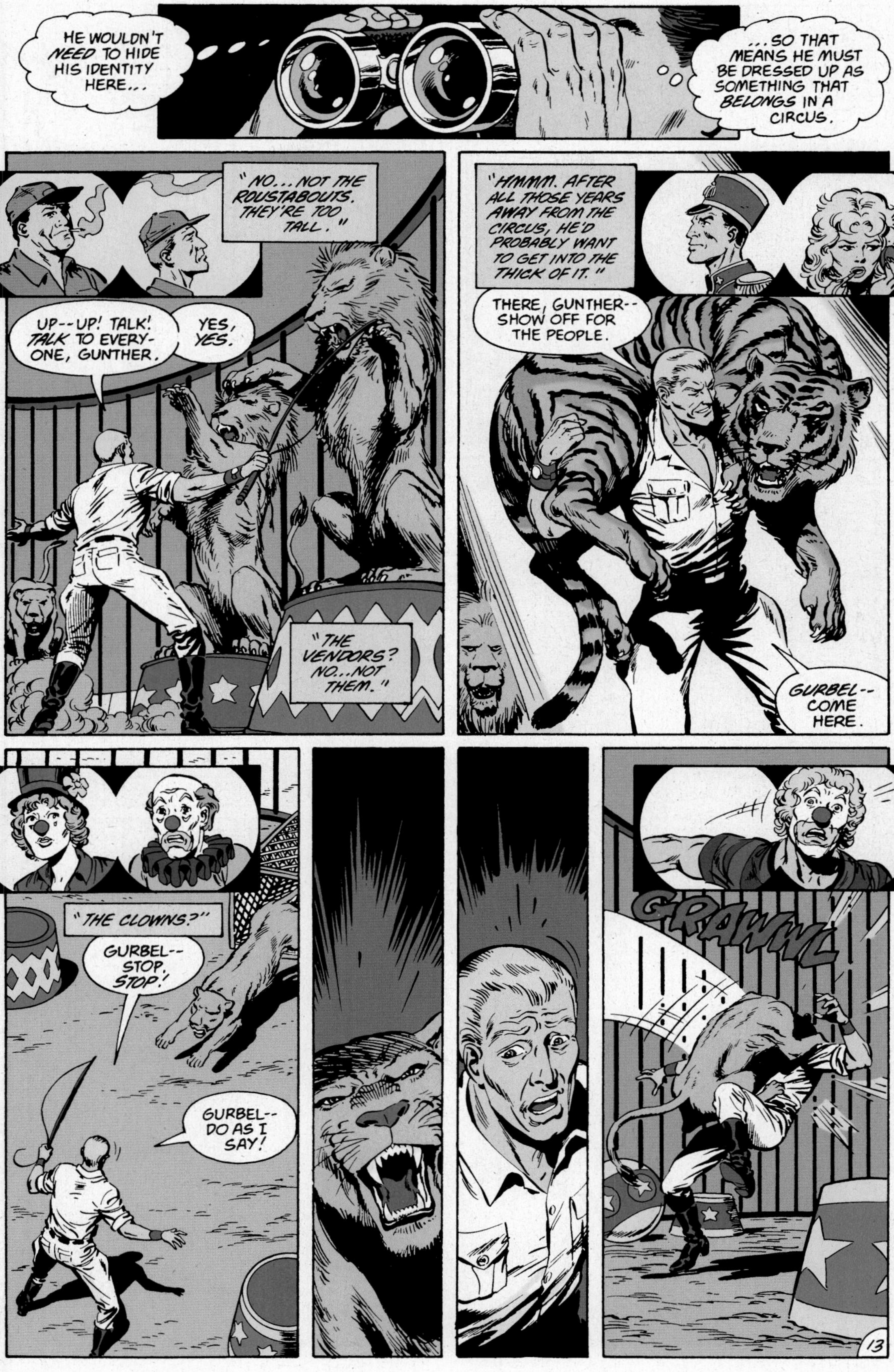
HE WOULDN'T NEED TO HIDE HIS IDENTITY HERE...
...SO THAT MEANS HE MUST BE DRESSED UP AS SOMETHING THAT BELONGS IN A CIRCUS.
"NO... NOT THE ROUSTABOUTS. THEY'RE TOO TALL."
UP--UP! TALK! TALK TO EVERY-ONE, GUNTHER.
YES, YES.
"THE VENDORS? NO...NOT THEM."
"HMMM. AFTER ALL THOSE YEARS AWAY FROM THE CIRCUS, HE'D PROBABLY WANT TO GET INTO THE THICK OF IT."
THERE, GUNTHER--SHOW OFF FOR THE PEOPLE.
GURBEL--COME HERE.
"THE CLOWNS?"
GURBEL--STOP. STOP!
GURBEL--DO AS I SAY!
GRAWWL
13

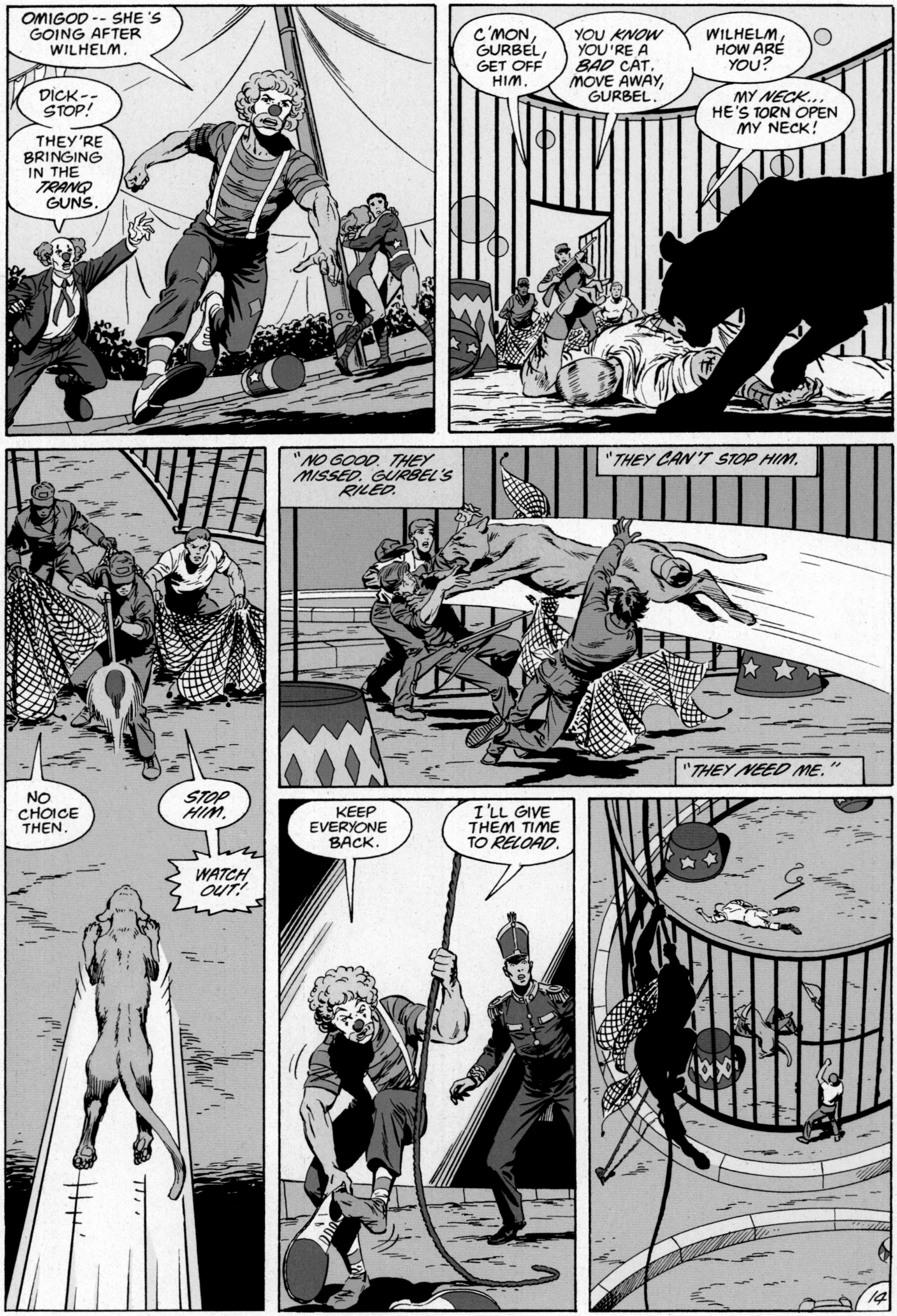
OMIGOD -- SHE'S GOING AFTER WILHELM.
DICK-- STOP!
THEY'RE BRINGING IN THE TRANQ GUNS.
C'MON, GURBEL, GET OFF HIM.
YOU KNOW YOU'RE A BAD CAT. MOVE AWAY, GURBEL.
WILHELM, HOW ARE YOU?
MY NECK... HE'S TORN OPEN MY NECK!
"NO GOOD. THEY MISSED. GURBEL'S RILED.
"THEY CAN'T STOP HIM.
"THEY NEED ME."
NO CHOICE THEN.
STOP HIM.
WATCH OUT!
KEEP EVERYONE BACK.
I'LL GIVE THEM TIME TO RELOAD.
14

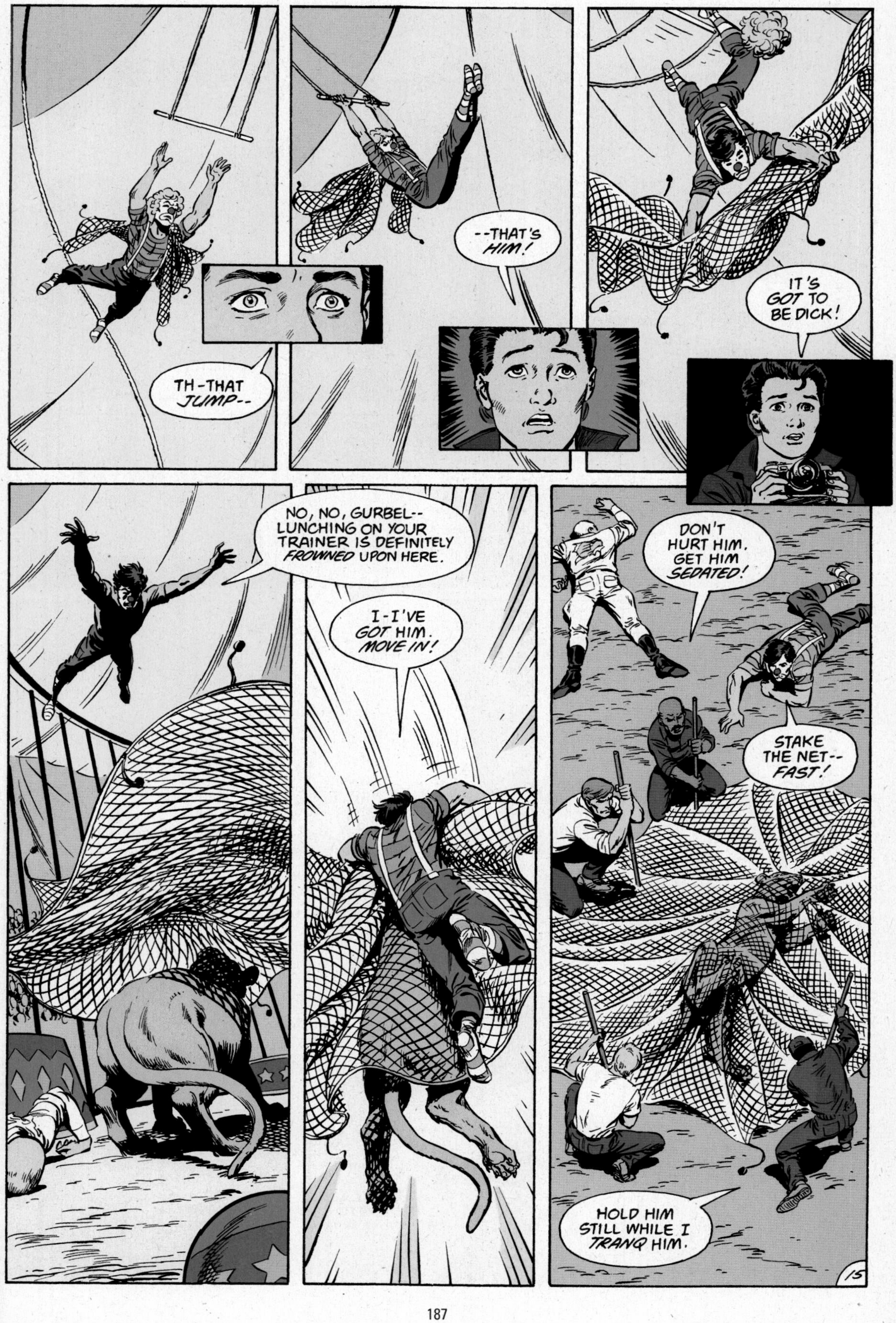
TH-THAT JUMP--
--THAT'S HIM!
IT'S GOT TO BE DICK!
NO, NO, GURBEL-- LUNCHING ON YOUR TRAINER IS DEFINITELY FROWNED UPON HERE.
I-I'VE GOT HIM. MOVE IN!
DON'T HURT HIM. GET HIM SEDATED!
STAKE THE NET-- FAST!
HOLD HIM STILL WHILE I TRANQ HIM.
15

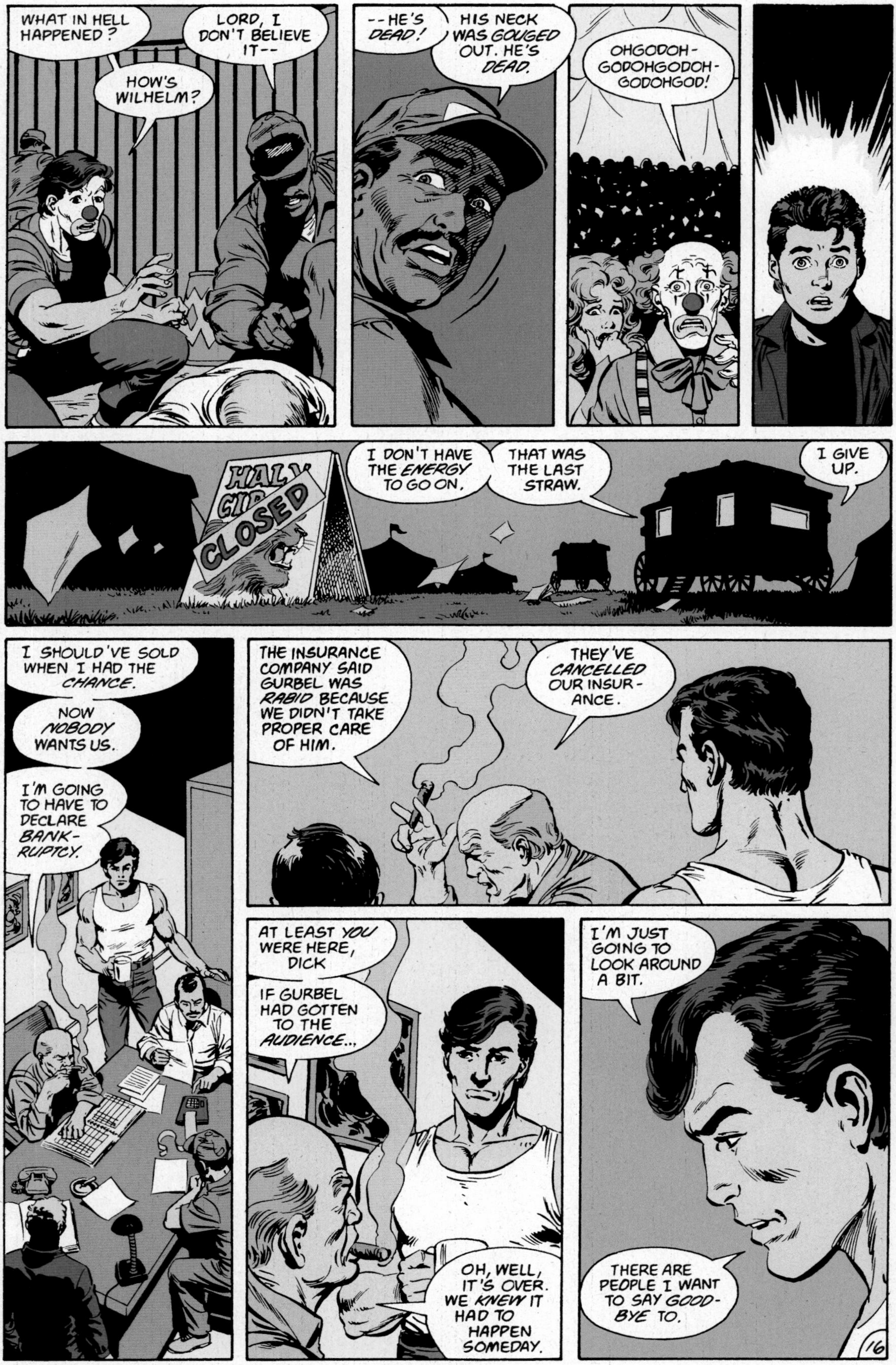
WHAT IN HELL HAPPENED?
LORD, I DON'T BELIEVE IT--
HOW'S WILHELM?
--HE'S *DEAD!*
HIS NECK WAS *GOUGED* OUT. HE'S *DEAD.*
OHGODOH-GODOHGODOH-GODOHGOD!
HALY CIR
CLOSED
I DON'T HAVE THE *ENERGY* TO GO ON.
THAT WAS THE LAST STRAW.
I GIVE UP.
I SHOULD'VE SOLD WHEN I HAD THE *CHANCE.*
NOW *NOBODY* WANTS US.
I'M GOING TO HAVE TO DECLARE *BANK-RUPTCY.*
THE INSURANCE COMPANY SAID GURBEL WAS *RABID* BECAUSE WE DIDN'T TAKE PROPER CARE OF HIM.
THEY'VE *CANCELLED* OUR INSUR-ANCE.
AT LEAST *YOU* WERE HERE, DICK
IF GURBEL HAD GOTTEN TO THE *AUDIENCE...*
OH, WELL, IT'S OVER. WE *KNEW* IT HAD TO HAPPEN SOMEDAY.
I'M JUST GOING TO LOOK AROUND A BIT.
THERE ARE PEOPLE I WANT TO SAY *GOOD-BYE* TO.
16

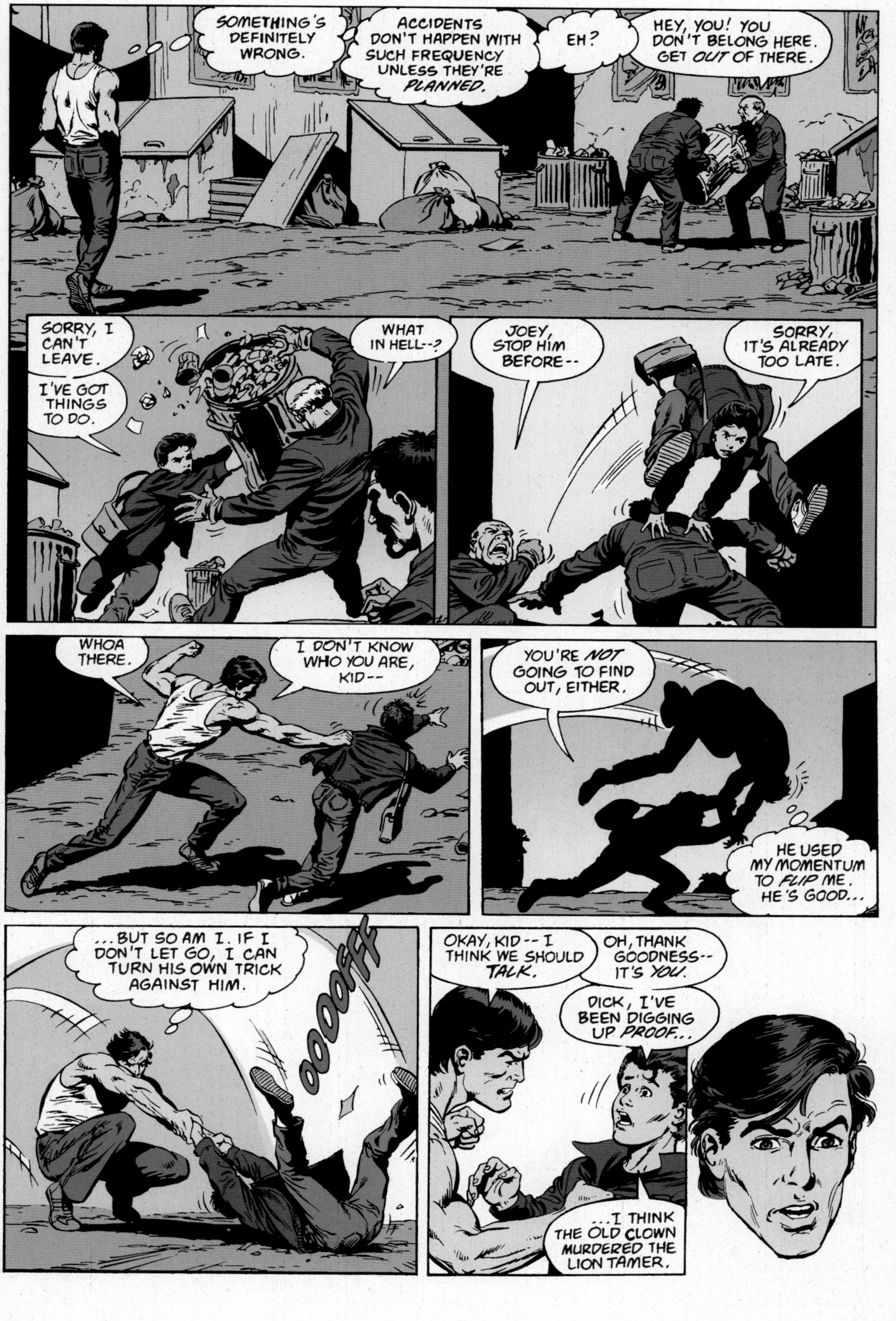
SOMETHING'S DEFINITELY WRONG.
ACCIDENTS DON'T HAPPEN WITH SUCH FREQUENCY UNLESS THEY'RE PLANNED.
EH?
HEY, YOU! YOU DON'T BELONG HERE. GET OUT OF THERE.
SORRY, I CAN'T LEAVE.
I'VE GOT THINGS TO DO.
WHAT IN HELL--?
JOEY, STOP HIM BEFORE--
SORRY, IT'S ALREADY TOO LATE.
WHOA THERE.
I DON'T KNOW WHO YOU ARE, KID--
YOU'RE NOT GOING TO FIND OUT, EITHER.
HE USED MY MOMENTUM TO FLIP ME. HE'S GOOD...
...BUT SO AM I. IF I DON'T LET GO, I CAN TURN HIS OWN TRICK AGAINST HIM.
OOOOFFF
OKAY, KID-- I THINK WE SHOULD TALK.
OH, THANK GOODNESS-- IT'S YOU.
DICK, I'VE BEEN DIGGING UP PROOF...
...I THINK THE OLD CLOWN MURDERED THE LION TAMER.

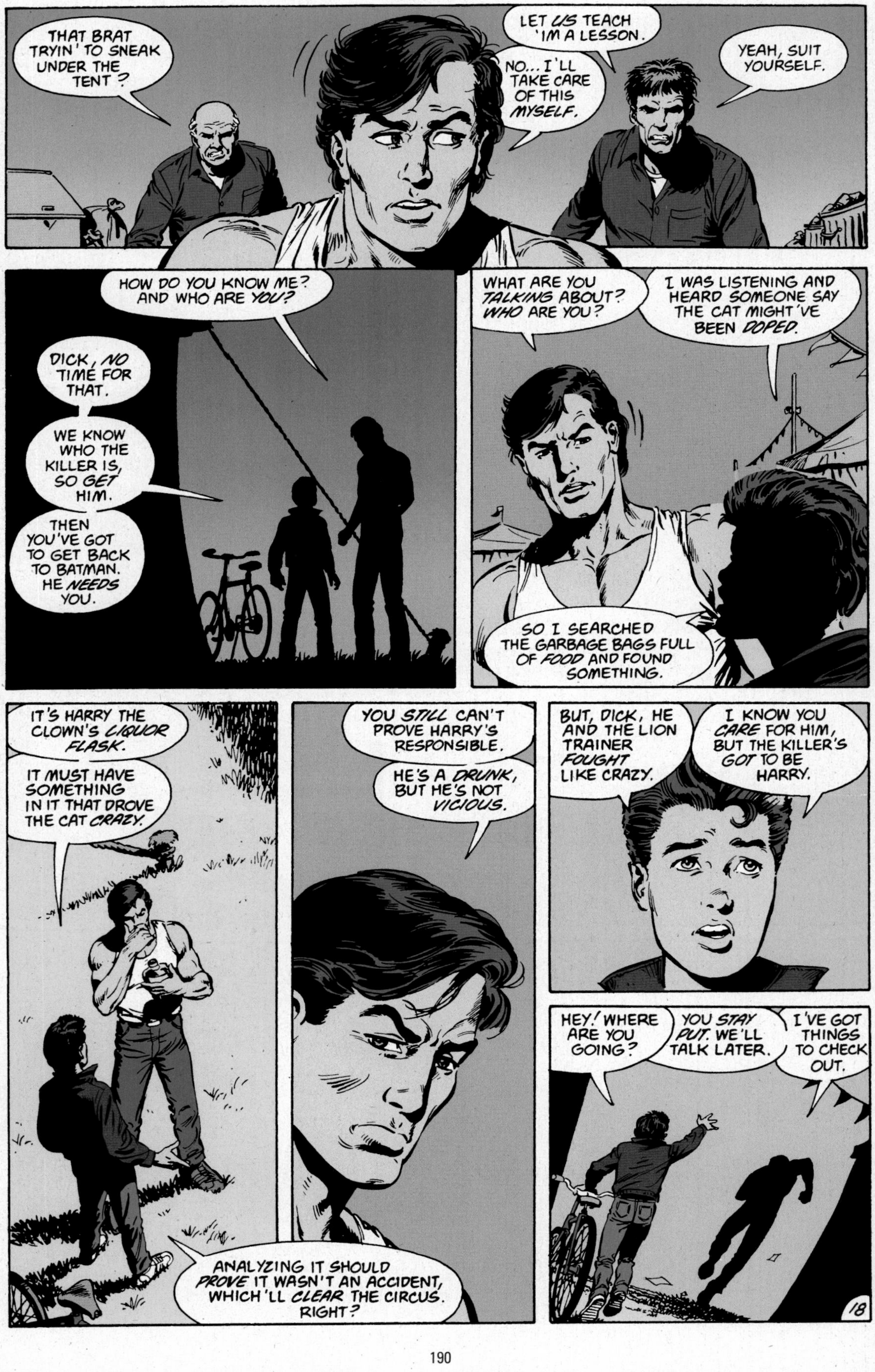
THAT BRAT TRYIN' TO SNEAK UNDER THE TENT?
LET US TEACH 'IM A LESSON.
NO... I'LL TAKE CARE OF THIS MYSELF.
YEAH, SUIT YOURSELF.
HOW DO YOU KNOW ME? AND WHO ARE YOU?
DICK, NO TIME FOR THAT.
WE KNOW WHO THE KILLER IS, SO GET HIM.
THEN YOU'VE GOT TO GET BACK TO BATMAN. HE NEEDS YOU.
WHAT ARE YOU TALKING ABOUT? WHO ARE YOU?
I WAS LISTENING AND HEARD SOMEONE SAY THE CAT MIGHT'VE BEEN DOPED.
SO I SEARCHED THE GARBAGE BAGS FULL OF FOOD AND FOUND SOMETHING.
IT'S HARRY THE CLOWN'S LIQUOR FLASK.
IT MUST HAVE SOMETHING IN IT THAT DROVE THE CAT CRAZY.
ANALYZING IT SHOULD PROVE IT WASN'T AN ACCIDENT, WHICH'LL CLEAR THE CIRCUS. RIGHT?
YOU STILL CAN'T PROVE HARRY'S RESPONSIBLE.
HE'S A DRUNK, BUT HE'S NOT VICIOUS.
BUT, DICK, HE AND THE LION TRAINER FOUGHT LIKE CRAZY.
I KNOW YOU CARE FOR HIM, BUT THE KILLER'S GOT TO BE HARRY.
HEY! WHERE ARE YOU GOING?
YOU STAY PUT. WE'LL TALK LATER.
I'VE GOT THINGS TO CHECK OUT.
18

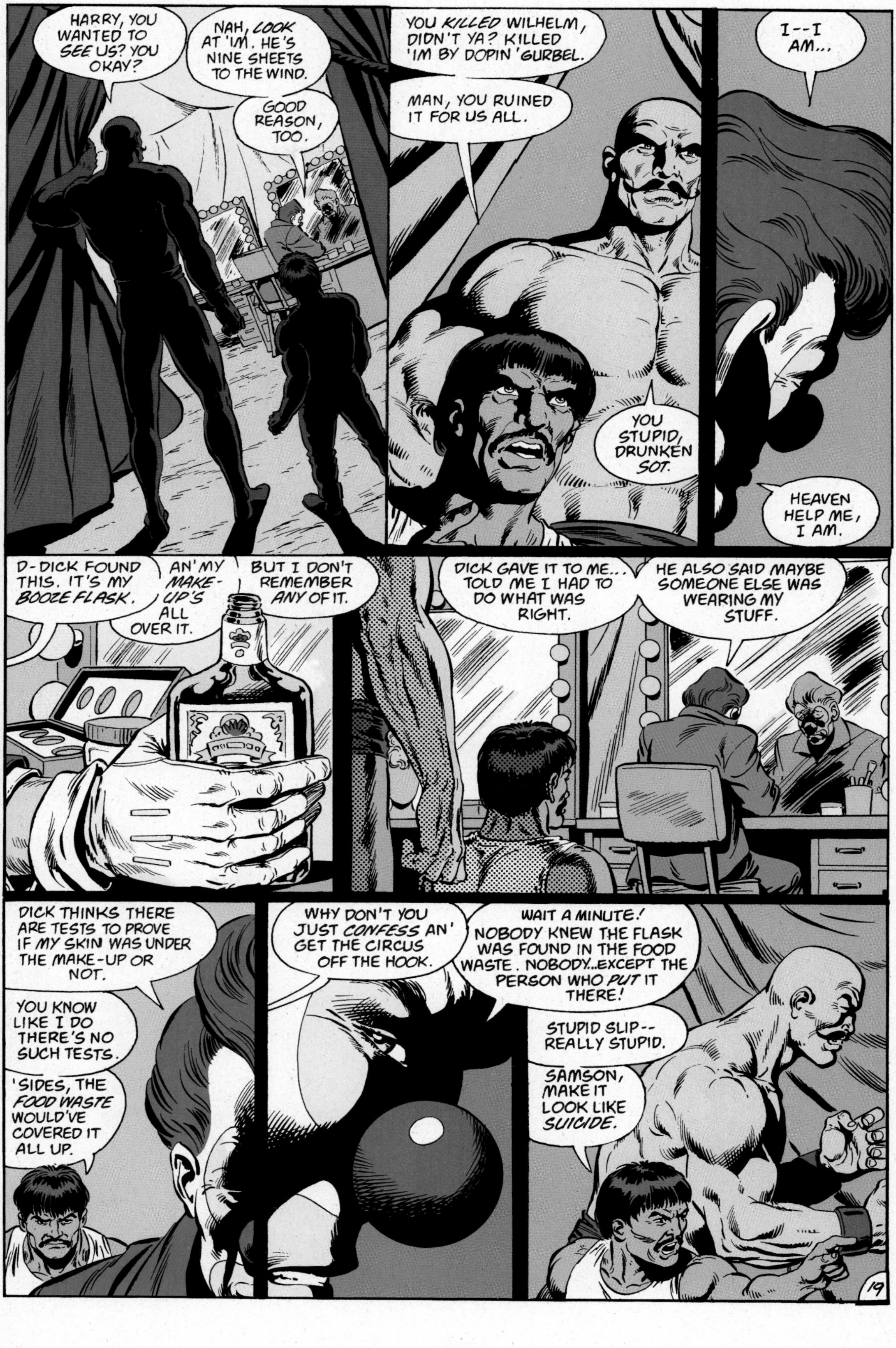
HARRY, YOU WANTED TO SEE US? YOU OKAY?
NAH, LOOK AT 'IM. HE'S NINE SHEETS TO THE WIND.
GOOD REASON, TOO.
YOU KILLED WILHELM, DIDN'T YA? KILLED 'IM BY DOPIN' GURBEL.
MAN, YOU RUINED IT FOR US ALL.
YOU STUPID, DRUNKEN SOT.
I--I AM...
HEAVEN HELP ME, I AM.
D-DICK FOUND THIS. IT'S MY BOOZE FLASK.
AN' MY MAKE-UP'S ALL OVER IT.
BUT I DON'T REMEMBER ANY OF IT.
DICK GAVE IT TO ME... TOLD ME I HAD TO DO WHAT WAS RIGHT.
HE ALSO SAID MAYBE SOMEONE ELSE WAS WEARING MY STUFF.
DICK THINKS THERE ARE TESTS TO PROVE IF MY SKIN WAS UNDER THE MAKE-UP OR NOT.
YOU KNOW LIKE I DO THERE'S NO SUCH TESTS.
'SIDES, THE FOOD WASTE WOULD'VE COVERED IT ALL UP.
WHY DON'T YOU JUST CONFESS AN' GET THE CIRCUS OFF THE HOOK.
WAIT A MINUTE! NOBODY KNEW THE FLASK WAS FOUND IN THE FOOD WASTE. NOBODY...EXCEPT THE PERSON WHO PUT IT THERE!
STUPID SLIP-- REALLY STUPID.
SAMSON, MAKE IT LOOK LIKE SUICIDE.
19

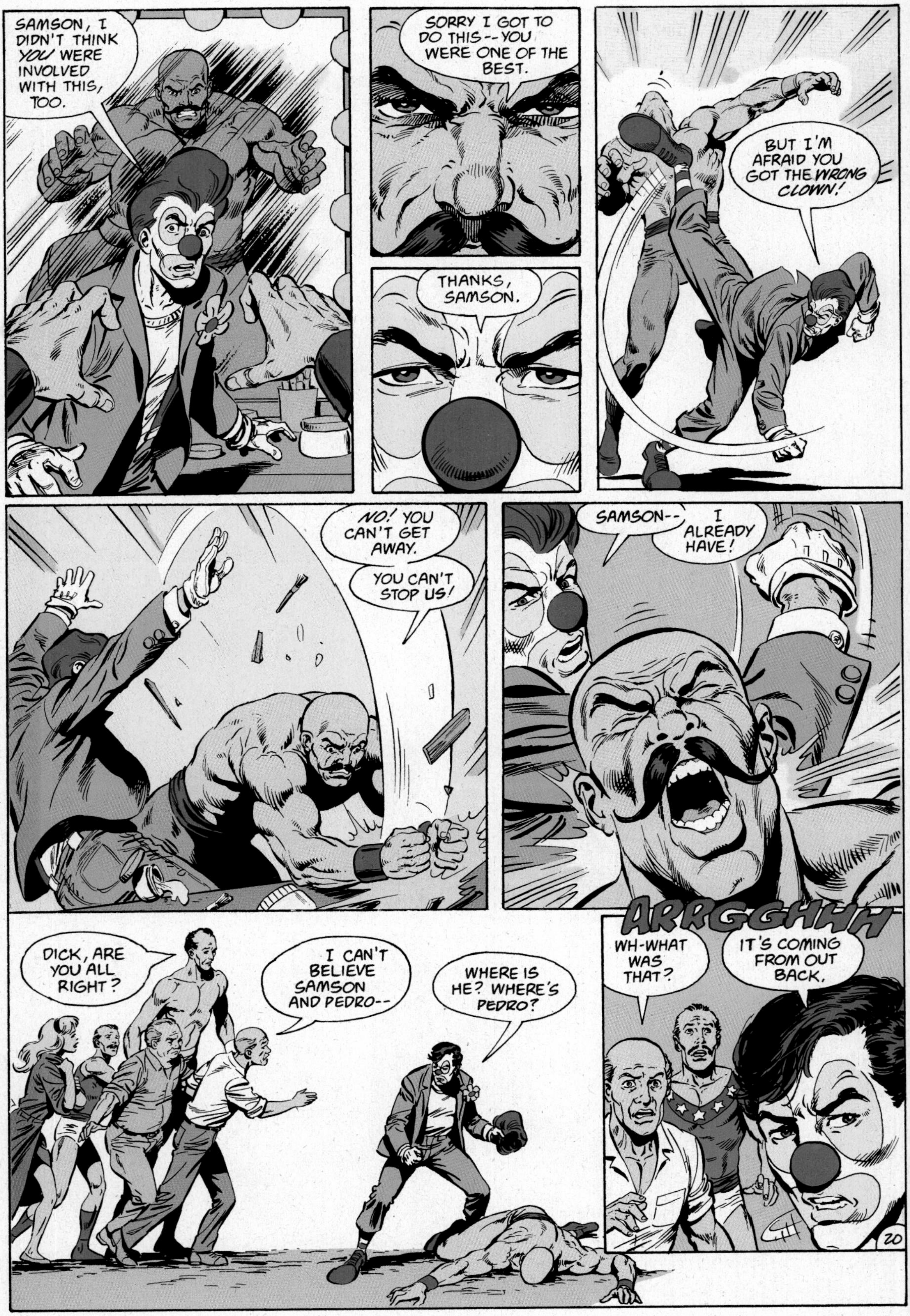

SAMSON, I DIDN'T THINK YOU WERE INVOLVED WITH THIS, TOO.
SORRY I GOT TO DO THIS--YOU WERE ONE OF THE BEST.
THANKS, SAMSON.
BUT I'M AFRAID YOU GOT THE WRONG CLOWN!
NO! YOU CAN'T GET AWAY.
YOU CAN'T STOP US!
SAMSON--
I ALREADY HAVE!
ARRGGHWH
DICK, ARE YOU ALL RIGHT?
I CAN'T BELIEVE SAMSON AND PEDRO--
WHERE IS HE? WHERE'S PEDRO?
WH-WHAT WAS THAT?
IT'S COMING FROM OUT BACK.
20

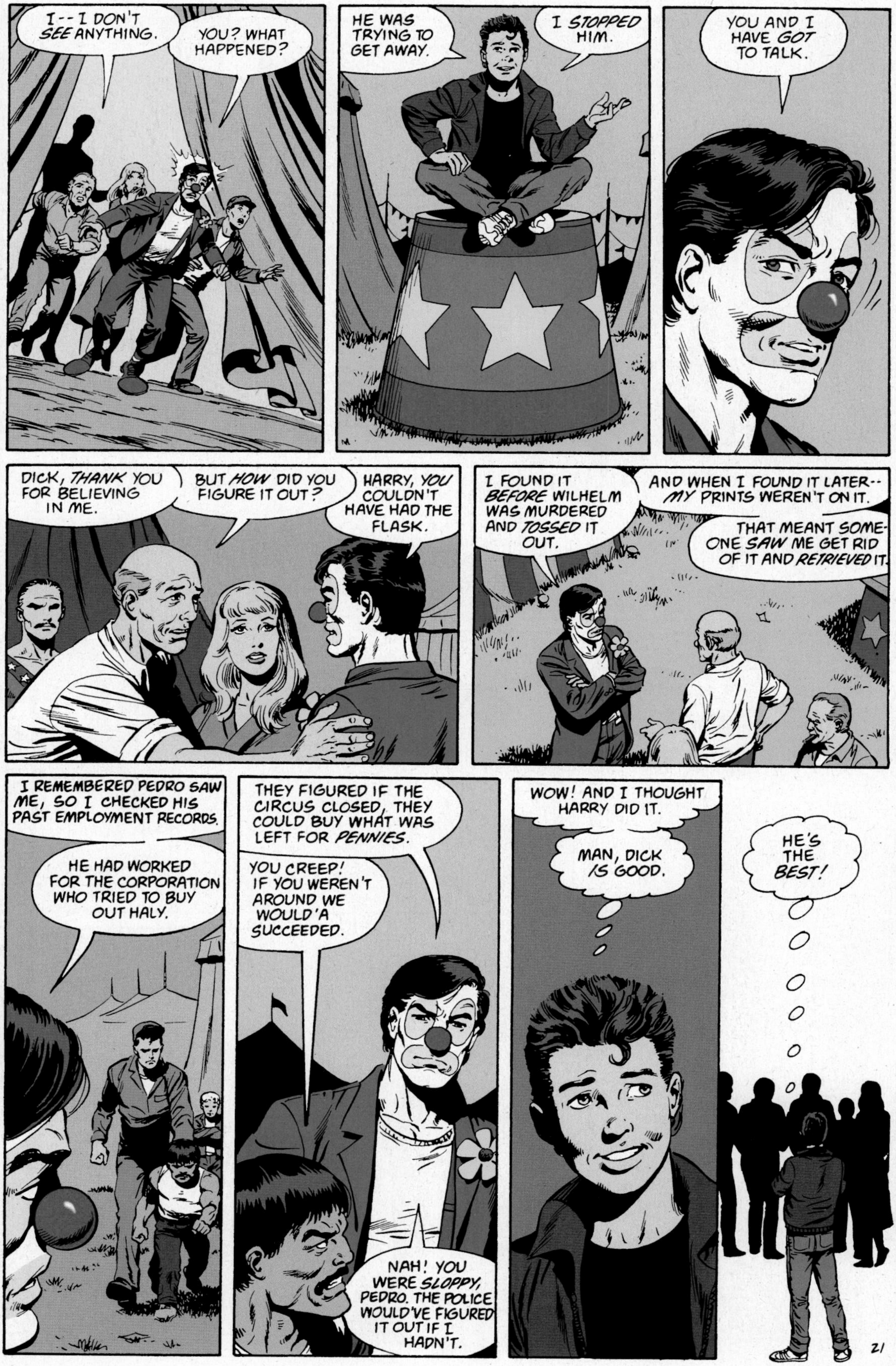
I -- I DON'T SEE ANYTHING.
YOU? WHAT HAPPENED?
HE WAS TRYING TO GET AWAY.
I STOPPED HIM.
YOU AND I HAVE GOT TO TALK.
DICK, THANK YOU FOR BELIEVING IN ME.
BUT HOW DID YOU FIGURE IT OUT?
HARRY, YOU COULDN'T HAVE HAD THE FLASK.
I FOUND IT BEFORE WILHELM WAS MURDERED AND TOSSED IT OUT.
AND WHEN I FOUND IT LATER-- MY PRINTS WEREN'T ON IT.
THAT MEANT SOMEONE SAW ME GET RID OF IT AND RETRIEVED IT.
I REMEMBERED PEDRO SAW ME, SO I CHECKED HIS PAST EMPLOYMENT RECORDS.
HE HAD WORKED FOR THE CORPORATION WHO TRIED TO BUY OUT HALY.
THEY FIGURED IF THE CIRCUS CLOSED, THEY COULD BUY WHAT WAS LEFT FOR PENNIES.
YOU CREEP! IF YOU WEREN'T AROUND WE WOULD'A SUCCEEDED.
NAH! YOU WERE SLOPPY, PEDRO. THE POLICE WOULD'VE FIGURED IT OUT IF I HADN'T.
WOW! AND I THOUGHT HARRY DID IT.
MAN, DICK IS GOOD.
HE'S THE BEST!
21

THANK YOU, DICK.

MY PLEASURE, HARRY. I THINK I'M *HAPPIER* NOW THAN I'VE EVER BEEN.

O F F I C E

OH, NO-- HE'S *JOINING* THE CIRCUS... HE'LL *NEVER* HELP BATMAN NOW.

WE'VE GOT ALL THE *PAPERS* DRAWN UP. WE'LL SEND IT TO YOUR *LAWYER.*

DON'T BE SILLY. YOU'RE *FAMILY.*

I'LL HANDLE IT MYSELF.

YOU TAKE CARE.

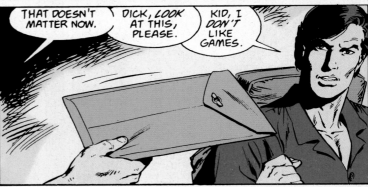

YOU TOO, DICK. I HOPE YOU'LL COME AROUND MORE OFTEN NOW.

HUNH?

DICK, YOU *DIDN'T* REJOIN THE CIRCUS?

BETTER. I'M BECOMING ITS *CO-OWNER.*

NOW, WHO THE HELL ARE YOU?

THAT DOESN'T MATTER NOW.

DICK, *LOOK* AT THIS, PLEASE.

KID, I *DON'T* LIKE GAMES.

NEITHER DO I.

IT'S *IMPORTANT.* I NEED YOU.

BATMAN NEEDS YOU.

22

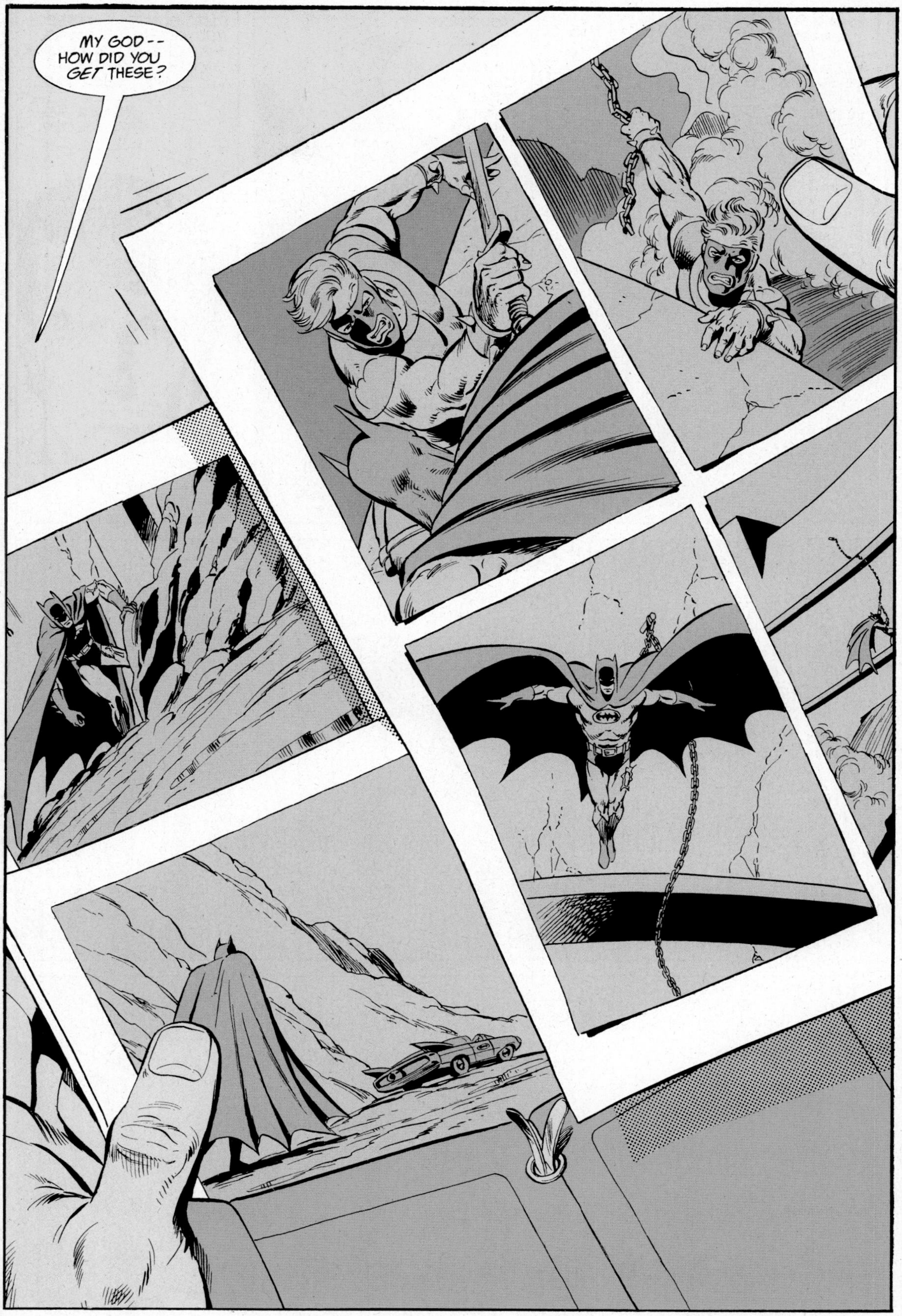
MY GOD-- HOW DID YOU GET THESE?

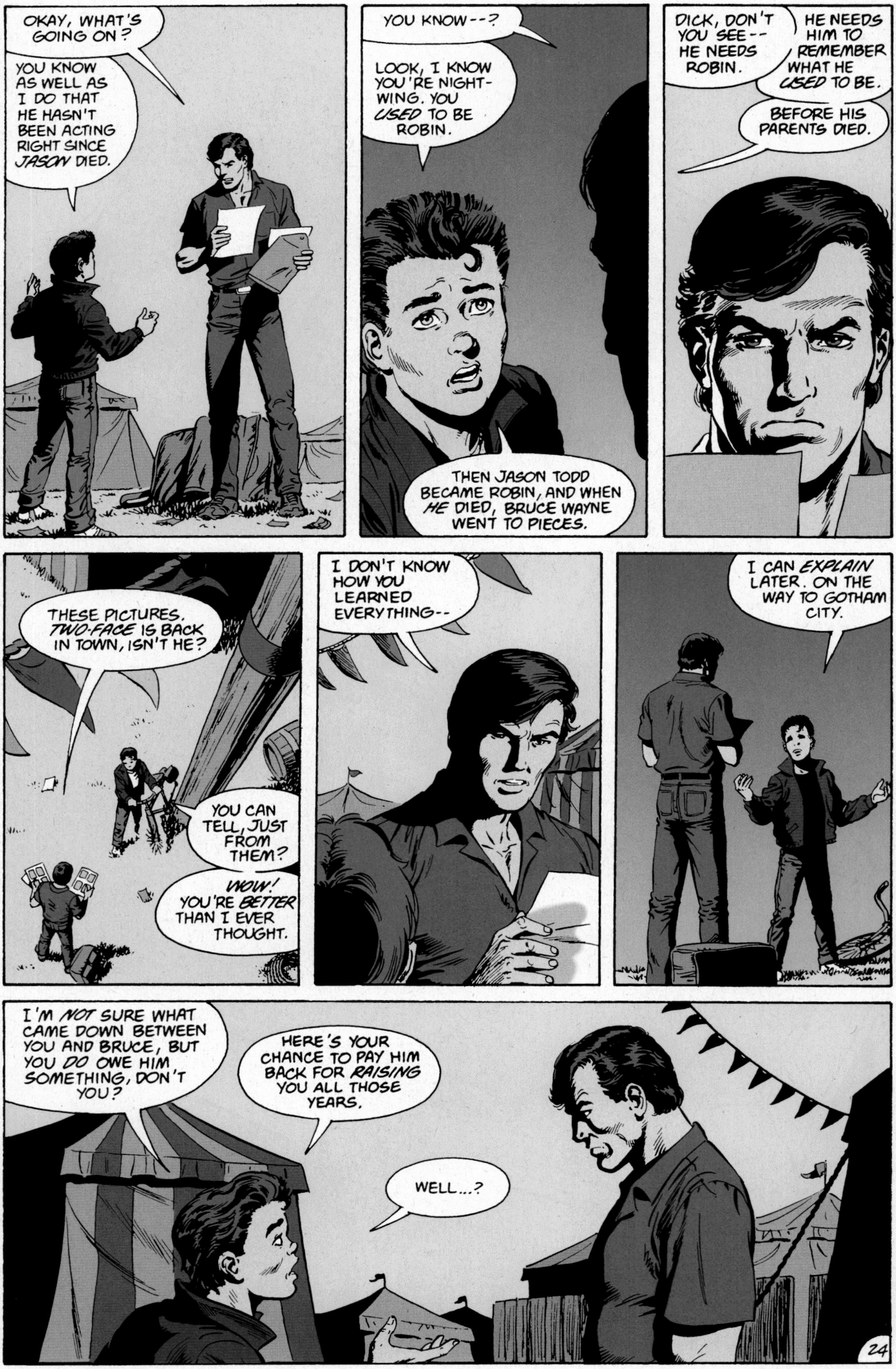
OKAY, WHAT'S GOING ON?
YOU KNOW AS WELL AS I DO THAT HE HASN'T BEEN ACTING RIGHT SINCE JASON DIED.
YOU KNOW--?
LOOK, I KNOW YOU'RE NIGHT-WING. YOU USED TO BE ROBIN.
THEN JASON TODD BECAME ROBIN, AND WHEN HE DIED, BRUCE WAYNE WENT TO PIECES.
DICK, DON'T YOU SEE-- HE NEEDS ROBIN.
HE NEEDS HIM TO REMEMBER WHAT HE USED TO BE.
BEFORE HIS PARENTS DIED.
THESE PICTURES. TWO-FACE IS BACK IN TOWN, ISN'T HE?
YOU CAN TELL, JUST FROM THEM?
WOW! YOU'RE BETTER THAN I EVER THOUGHT.
I DON'T KNOW HOW YOU LEARNED EVERYTHING--
I CAN EXPLAIN LATER. ON THE WAY TO GOTHAM CITY.
I'M NOT SURE WHAT CAME DOWN BETWEEN YOU AND BRUCE, BUT YOU DO OWE HIM SOMETHING, DON'T YOU?
HERE'S YOUR CHANCE TO PAY HIM BACK FOR RAISING YOU ALL THOSE YEARS.
WELL...?
24

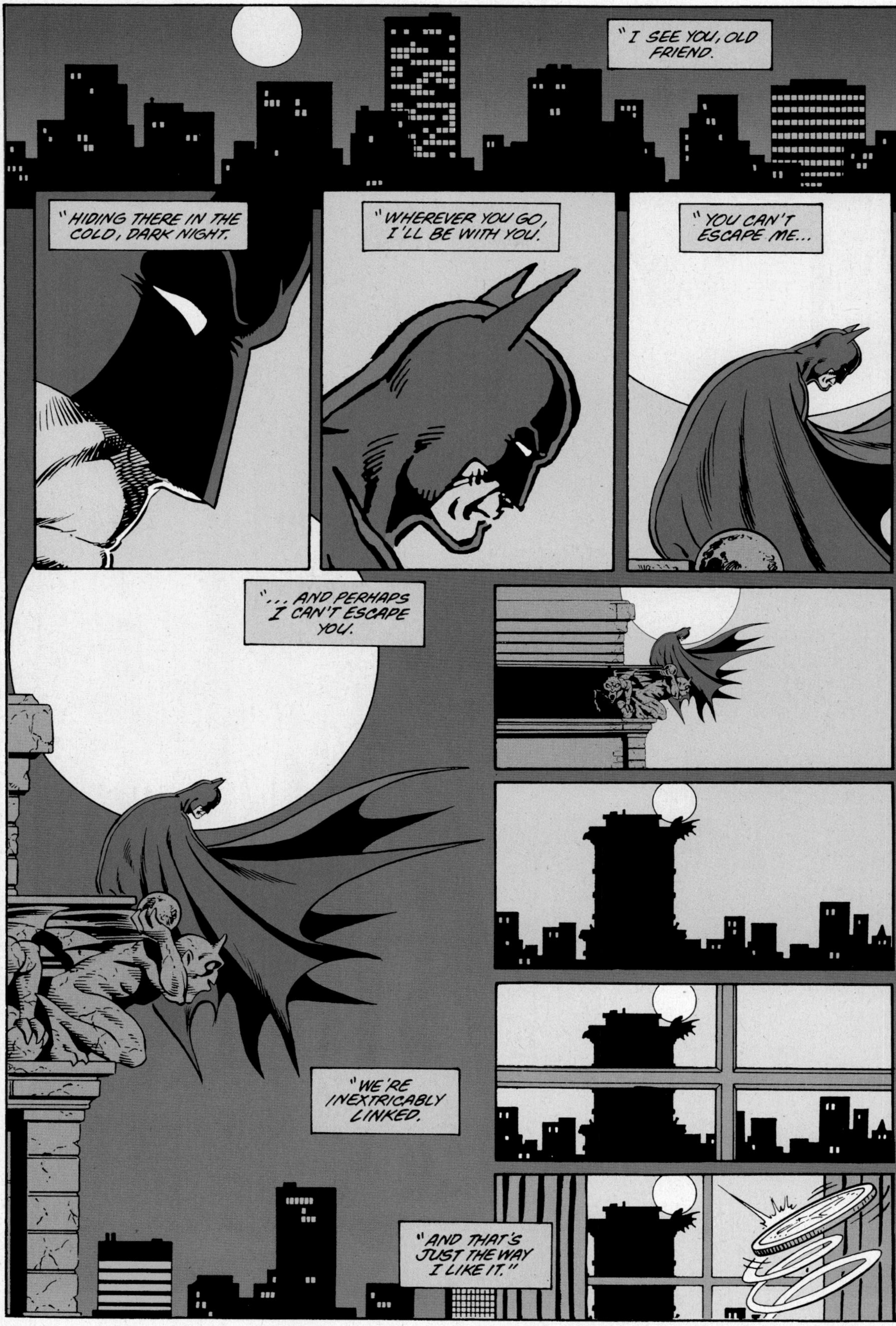
"I SEE YOU, OLD FRIEND.
"HIDING THERE IN THE COLD, DARK NIGHT.
"WHEREVER YOU GO, I'LL BE WITH YOU.
"YOU CAN'T ESCAPE ME...
"...AND PERHAPS I CAN'T ESCAPE YOU.
"WE'RE INEXTRICABLY LINKED.
"AND THAT'S JUST THE WAY I LIKE IT."

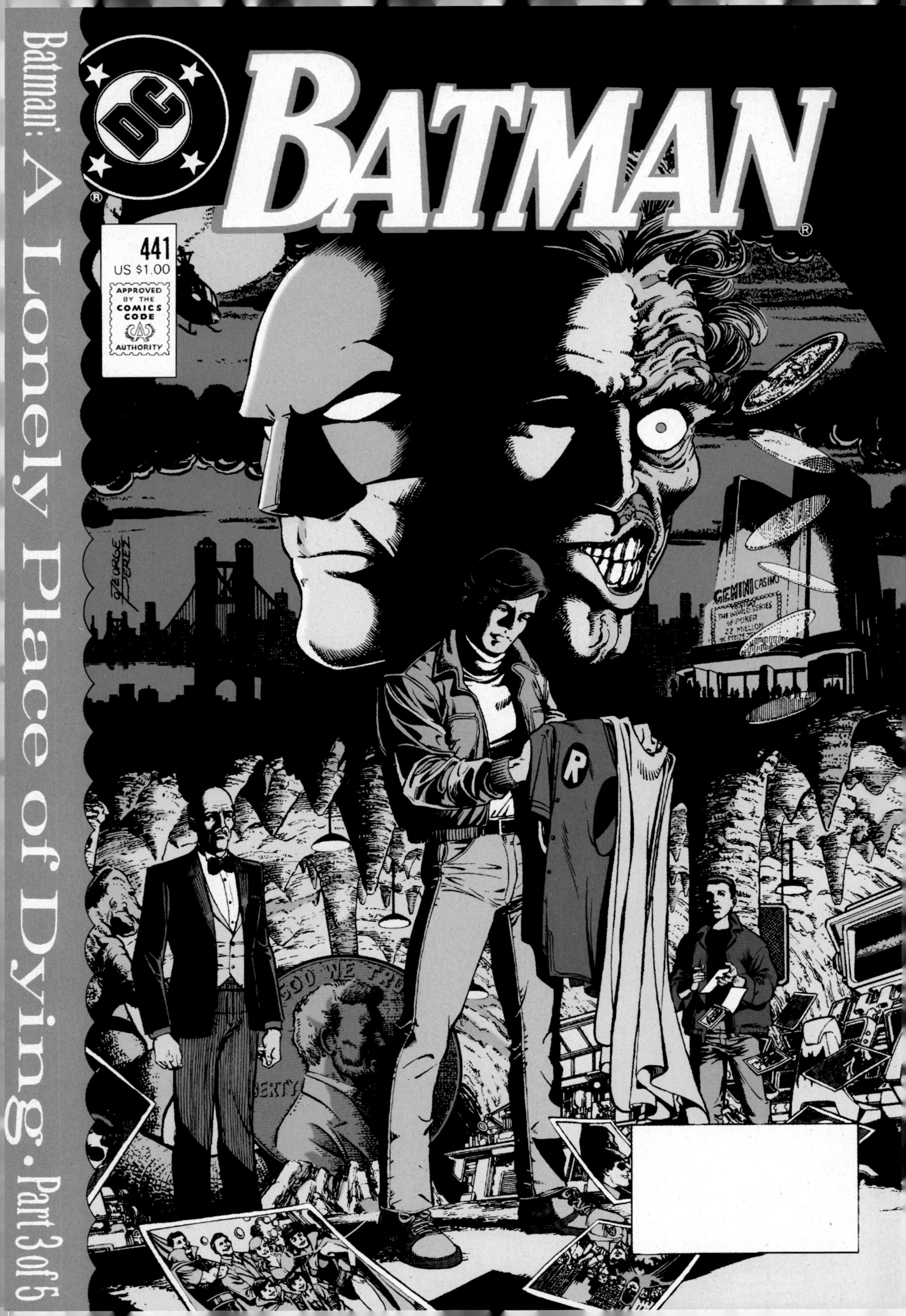
Batman: A Lonely Place of Dying • Part 3 of 5
BATMAN
441
US $1.00
APPROVED BY THE COMICS CODE AUTHORITY
GEORGE PEREZ
GEMINI CASINO
THE WORLD SERIES OF POKER
GOD WE TRUST
LIBERTY

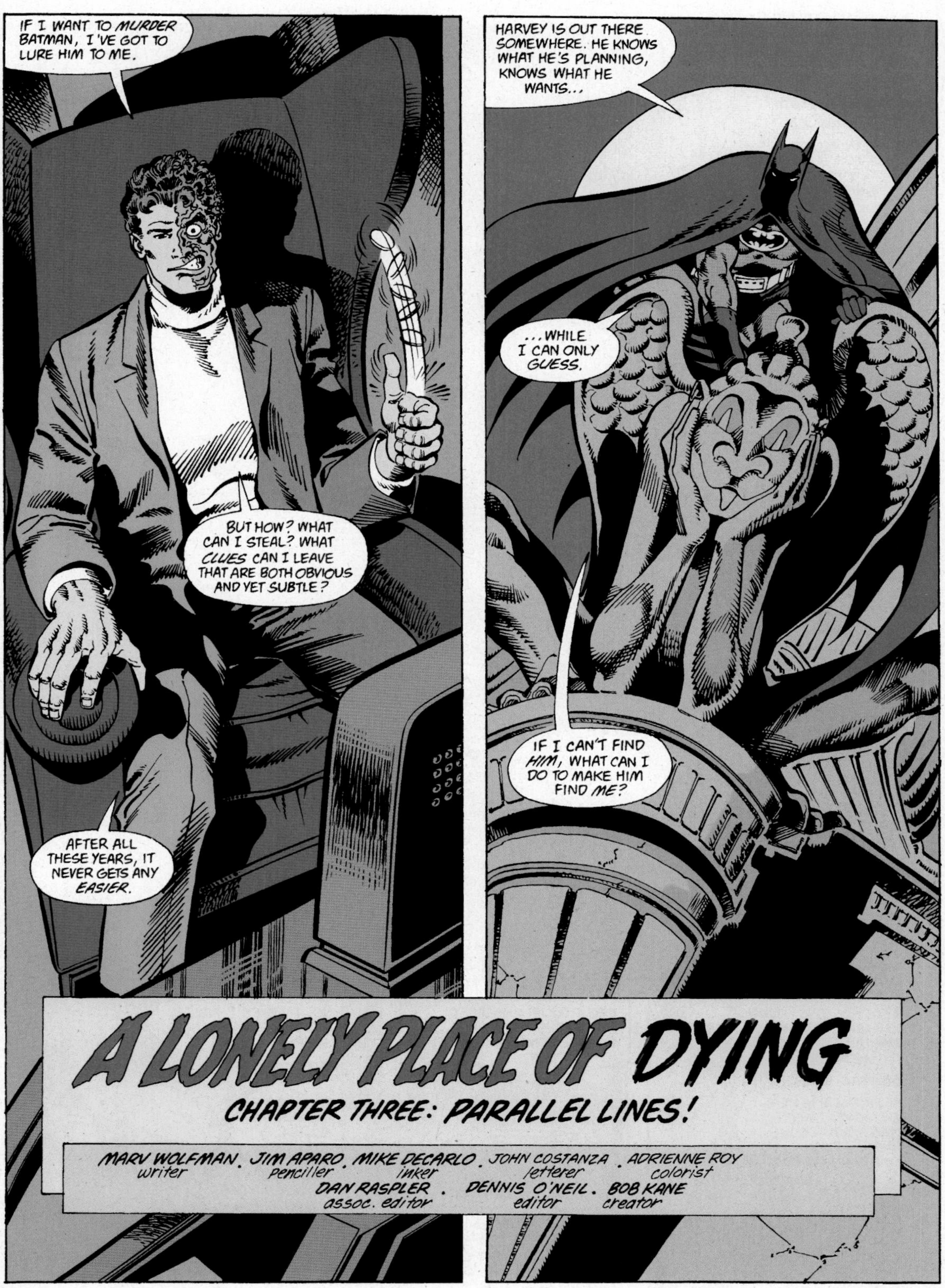

IF I WANT TO MURDER BATMAN, I'VE GOT TO LURE HIM TO ME.
BUT HOW? WHAT CAN I STEAL? WHAT CLUES CAN I LEAVE THAT ARE BOTH OBVIOUS AND YET SUBTLE?
AFTER ALL THESE YEARS, IT NEVER GETS ANY EASIER.
HARVEY IS OUT THERE SOMEWHERE. HE KNOWS WHAT HE'S PLANNING, KNOWS WHAT HE WANTS...
...WHILE I CAN ONLY GUESS.
IF I CAN'T FIND HIM, WHAT CAN I DO TO MAKE HIM FIND ME?
A LONELY PLACE OF DYING
CHAPTER THREE: PARALLEL LINES!
MARV WOLFMAN . writer
JIM APARO . penciller
MIKE DECARLO . inker
JOHN COSTANZA . letterer
ADRIENNE ROY colorist
DAN RASPLER . assoc. editor
DENNIS O'NEIL . editor
BOB KANE creator

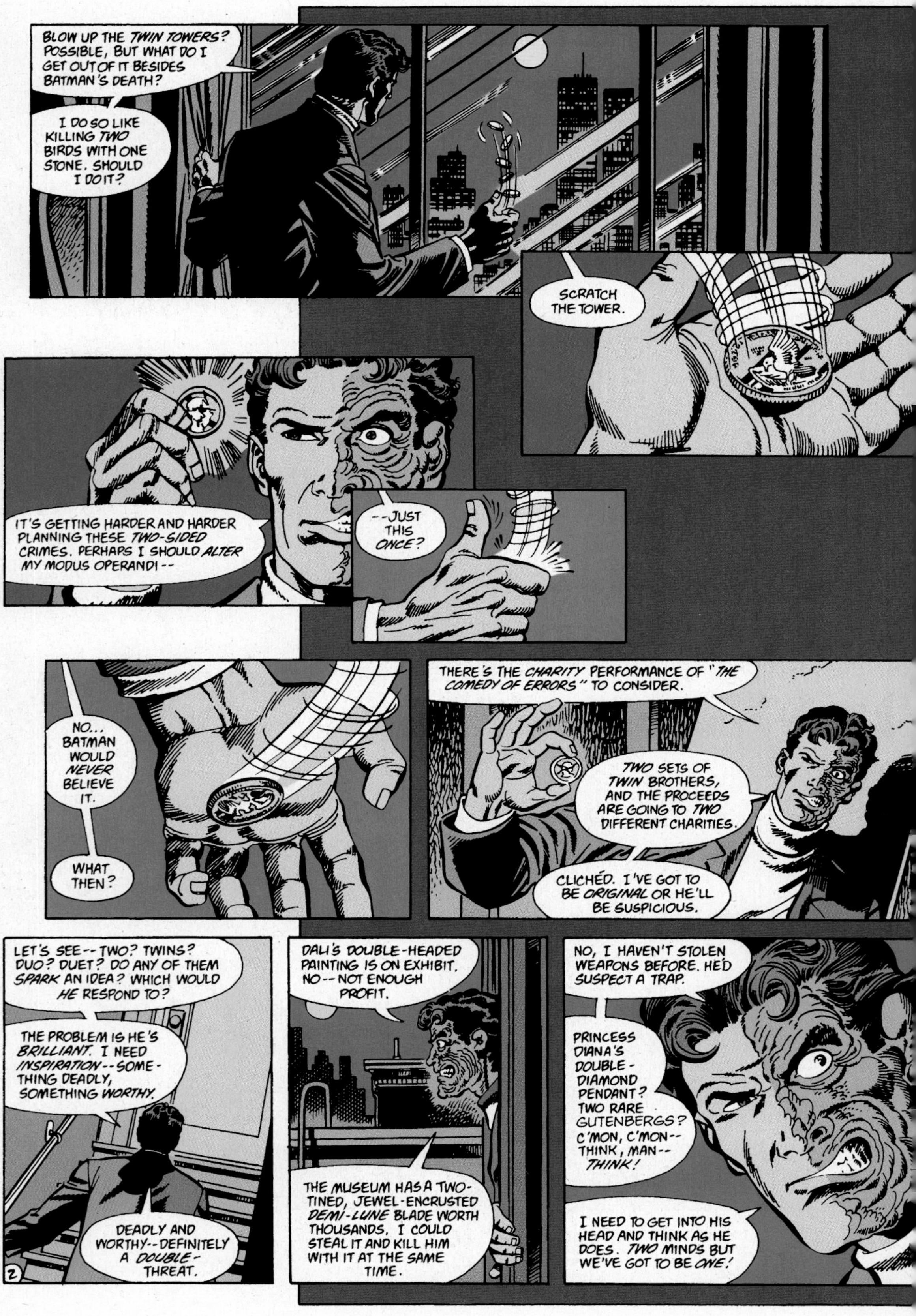
BLOW UP THE TWIN TOWERS? POSSIBLE, BUT WHAT DO I GET OUT OF IT BESIDES BATMAN'S DEATH?
I DO SO LIKE KILLING TWO BIRDS WITH ONE STONE. SHOULD I DO IT?
SCRATCH THE TOWER.
IT'S GETTING HARDER AND HARDER PLANNING THESE TWO-SIDED CRIMES. PERHAPS I SHOULD ALTER MY MODUS OPERANDI--
--JUST THIS ONCE?
NO... BATMAN WOULD NEVER BELIEVE IT.
WHAT THEN?
THERE'S THE CHARITY PERFORMANCE OF "THE COMEDY OF ERRORS" TO CONSIDER.
TWO SETS OF TWIN BROTHERS, AND THE PROCEEDS ARE GOING TO TWO DIFFERENT CHARITIES.
CLICHÉD. I'VE GOT TO BE ORIGINAL OR HE'LL BE SUSPICIOUS.
LET'S SEE--TWO? TWINS? DUO? DUET? DO ANY OF THEM SPARK AN IDEA? WHICH WOULD HE RESPOND TO?
THE PROBLEM IS HE'S BRILLIANT. I NEED INSPIRATION--SOMETHING DEADLY, SOMETHING WORTHY.
DEADLY AND WORTHY--DEFINITELY A DOUBLE-THREAT.
2
DALI'S DOUBLE-HEADED PAINTING IS ON EXHIBIT. NO--NOT ENOUGH PROFIT.
THE MUSEUM HAS A TWO-TINED, JEWEL-ENCRUSTED DEMI-LUNE BLADE WORTH THOUSANDS. I COULD STEAL IT AND KILL HIM WITH IT AT THE SAME TIME.
NO, I HAVEN'T STOLEN WEAPONS BEFORE. HE'D SUSPECT A TRAP.
PRINCESS DIANA'S DOUBLE-DIAMOND PENDANT? TWO RARE GUTENBERGS? C'MON, C'MON--THINK, MAN--THINK!
I NEED TO GET INTO HIS HEAD AND THINK AS HE DOES. TWO MINDS BUT WE'VE GOT TO BE ONE!

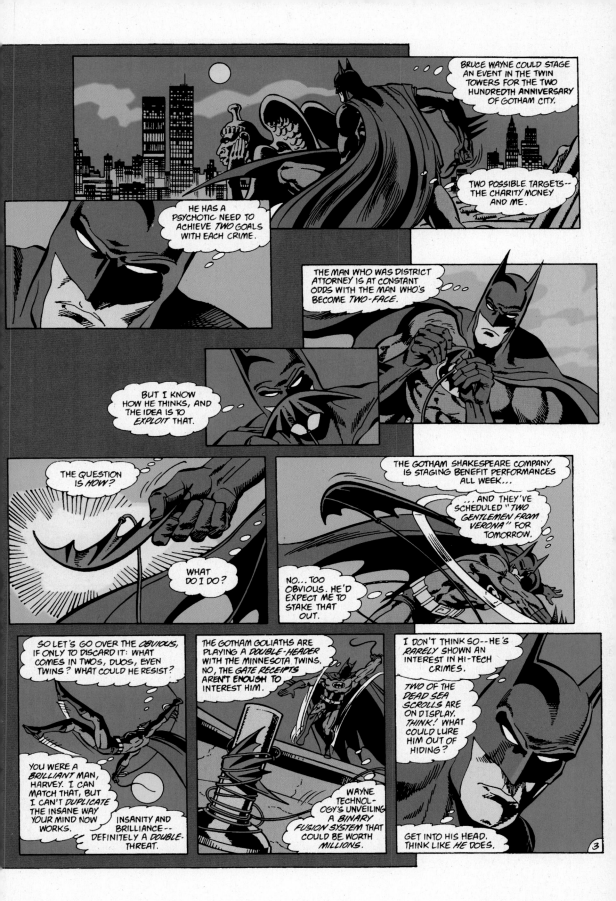

BRUCE WAYNE COULD STAGE AN EVENT IN THE TWIN TOWERS FOR THE TWO HUNDREDTH ANNIVERSARY OF GOTHAM CITY.

TWO POSSIBLE TARGETS-- THE CHARITY MONEY AND ME.

HE HAS A PSYCHOTIC NEED TO ACHIEVE *TWO* GOALS WITH EACH CRIME.

THE MAN WHO WAS DISTRICT ATTORNEY IS AT CONSTANT ODDS WITH THE MAN WHO'S BECOME *TWO-FACE.*

BUT I KNOW HOW HE THINKS, AND THE IDEA IS TO *EXPLOIT* THAT.

THE QUESTION IS *HOW?*

WHAT DO I DO?

THE GOTHAM SHAKESPEARE COMPANY IS STAGING BENEFIT PERFORMANCES ALL WEEK...

...AND THEY'VE SCHEDULED "*TWO GENTLEMEN FROM VERONA*" FOR TOMORROW.

NO... TOO OBVIOUS. HE'D EXPECT ME TO STAKE THAT OUT.

SO LET'S GO OVER THE *OBVIOUS,* IF ONLY TO DISCARD IT: WHAT COMES IN TWOS, DUOS, EVEN TWINS? WHAT COULD HE RESIST?

YOU WERE A *BRILLIANT* MAN, HARVEY. I CAN MATCH THAT, BUT I CAN'T *DUPLICATE* THE INSANE WAY YOUR MIND NOW WORKS.

INSANITY AND BRILLIANCE-- DEFINITELY A *DOUBLE-THREAT.*

THE GOTHAM GOLIATHS ARE PLAYING A *DOUBLE-HEADER* WITH THE MINNESOTA TWINS. NO, THE *GATE RECEIPTS* AREN'T ENOUGH TO INTEREST HIM.

WAYNE TECHNOL-OGY'S UNVEILING A *BINARY FUSION SYSTEM* THAT COULD BE WORTH *MILLIONS.*

I DON'T THINK SO--HE'S *RARELY* SHOWN AN INTEREST IN HI-TECH CRIMES.

TWO OF THE *DEAD SEA SCROLLS* ARE ON DISPLAY. *THINK!* WHAT COULD LURE HIM OUT OF HIDING?

GET INTO HIS HEAD. THINK LIKE *HE* DOES.

3

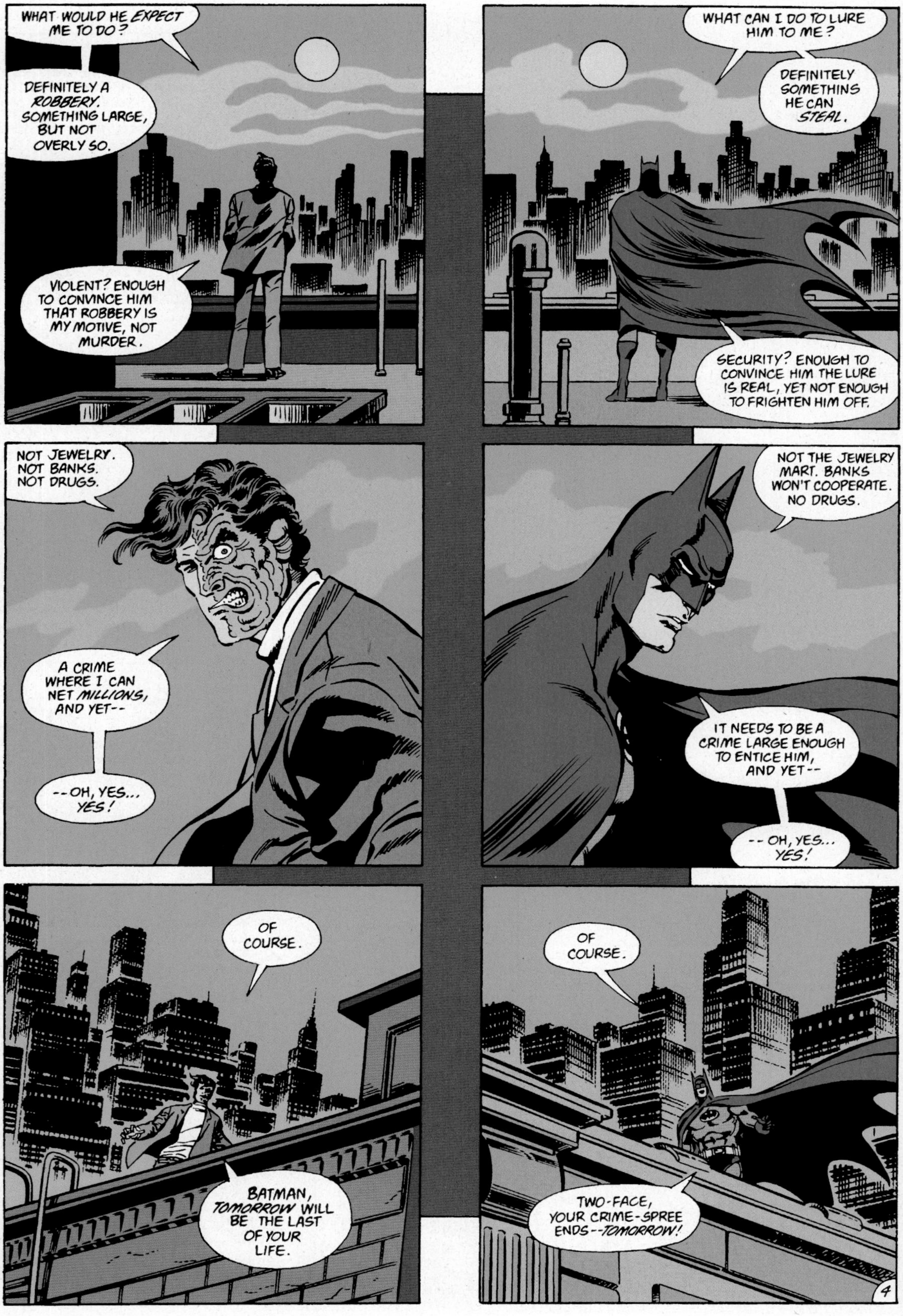
WHAT WOULD HE EXPECT ME TO DO?
DEFINITELY A ROBBERY. SOMETHING LARGE, BUT NOT OVERLY SO.
VIOLENT? ENOUGH TO CONVINCE HIM THAT ROBBERY IS MY MOTIVE, NOT MURDER.
WHAT CAN I DO TO LURE HIM TO ME?
DEFINITELY SOMETHING HE CAN STEAL.
SECURITY? ENOUGH TO CONVINCE HIM THE LURE IS REAL, YET NOT ENOUGH TO FRIGHTEN HIM OFF.
NOT JEWELRY. NOT BANKS. NOT DRUGS.
A CRIME WHERE I CAN NET MILLIONS, AND YET--
--OH, YES... YES!
NOT THE JEWELRY MART. BANKS WON'T COOPERATE. NO DRUGS.
IT NEEDS TO BE A CRIME LARGE ENOUGH TO ENTICE HIM, AND YET--
--OH, YES... YES!
OF COURSE.
BATMAN, TOMORROW WILL BE THE LAST OF YOUR LIFE.
OF COURSE.
TWO-FACE, YOUR CRIME-SPREE ENDS--TOMORROW!
4

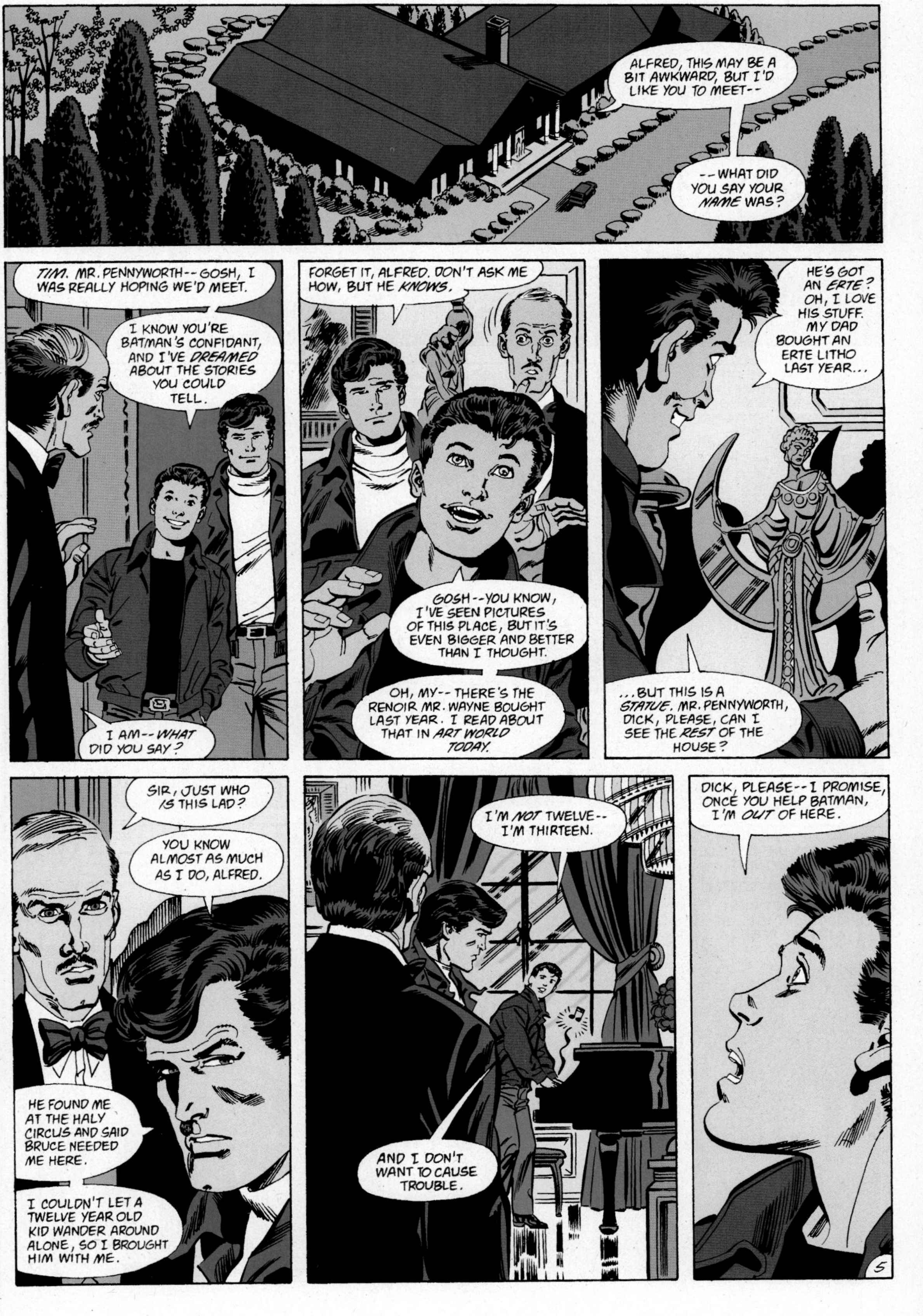
ALFRED, THIS MAY BE A BIT AWKWARD, BUT I'D LIKE YOU TO MEET--
--WHAT DID YOU SAY YOUR NAME WAS?
TIM. MR. PENNYWORTH--GOSH, I WAS REALLY HOPING WE'D MEET.
I KNOW YOU'RE BATMAN'S CONFIDANT, AND I'VE DREAMED ABOUT THE STORIES YOU COULD TELL.
I AM--WHAT DID YOU SAY?
FORGET IT, ALFRED. DON'T ASK ME HOW, BUT HE KNOWS.
GOSH--YOU KNOW, I'VE SEEN PICTURES OF THIS PLACE, BUT IT'S EVEN BIGGER AND BETTER THAN I THOUGHT.
OH, MY--THERE'S THE RENOIR MR. WAYNE BOUGHT LAST YEAR. I READ ABOUT THAT IN ART WORLD TODAY.
HE'S GOT AN ERTE? OH, I LOVE HIS STUFF. MY DAD BOUGHT AN ERTE LITHO LAST YEAR...
...BUT THIS IS A STATUE. MR. PENNYWORTH, DICK, PLEASE, CAN I SEE THE REST OF THE HOUSE?
SIR, JUST WHO IS THIS LAD?
YOU KNOW ALMOST AS MUCH AS I DO, ALFRED.
HE FOUND ME AT THE HALY CIRCUS AND SAID BRUCE NEEDED ME HERE.
I COULDN'T LET A TWELVE YEAR OLD KID WANDER AROUND ALONE, SO I BROUGHT HIM WITH ME.
I'M NOT TWELVE--I'M THIRTEEN.
AND I DON'T WANT TO CAUSE TROUBLE.
DICK, PLEASE--I PROMISE, ONCE YOU HELP BATMAN, I'M OUT OF HERE.
5

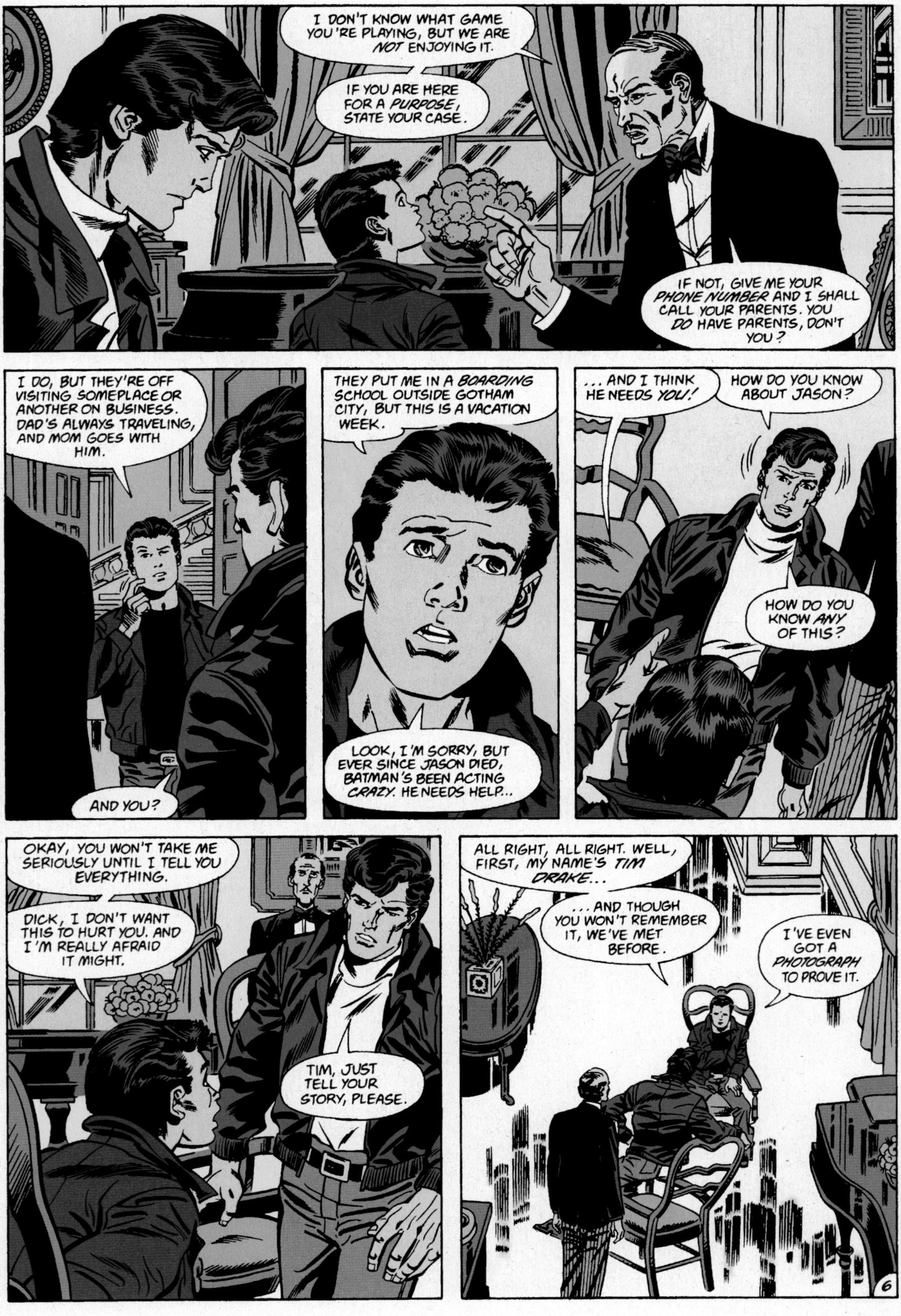
I DON'T KNOW WHAT GAME YOU'RE PLAYING, BUT WE ARE *NOT* ENJOYING IT.
IF YOU ARE HERE FOR A *PURPOSE*, STATE YOUR CASE.
IF NOT, GIVE ME YOUR *PHONE NUMBER* AND I SHALL CALL YOUR PARENTS. YOU *DO* HAVE PARENTS, DON'T YOU?
I DO, BUT THEY'RE OFF VISITING SOMEPLACE OR ANOTHER ON BUSINESS. DAD'S ALWAYS TRAVELING, AND MOM GOES WITH HIM.
AND YOU?
THEY PUT ME IN A *BOARDING* SCHOOL OUTSIDE GOTHAM CITY, BUT THIS IS A VACATION WEEK.
LOOK, I'M SORRY, BUT EVER SINCE JASON DIED, BATMAN'S BEEN ACTING *CRAZY*. HE NEEDS HELP...
... AND I THINK HE NEEDS *YOU!*
HOW DO YOU KNOW ABOUT JASON?
HOW DO YOU KNOW *ANY* OF THIS?
OKAY, YOU WON'T TAKE ME SERIOUSLY UNTIL I TELL YOU EVERYTHING.
DICK, I DON'T WANT THIS TO HURT YOU. AND I'M REALLY AFRAID IT MIGHT.
TIM, JUST TELL YOUR STORY, PLEASE.
ALL RIGHT, ALL RIGHT. WELL, FIRST, MY NAME'S *TIM DRAKE*...
... AND THOUGH YOU WON'T REMEMBER IT, WE'VE MET BEFORE.
I'VE EVEN GOT A *PHOTOGRAPH* TO PROVE IT.
6

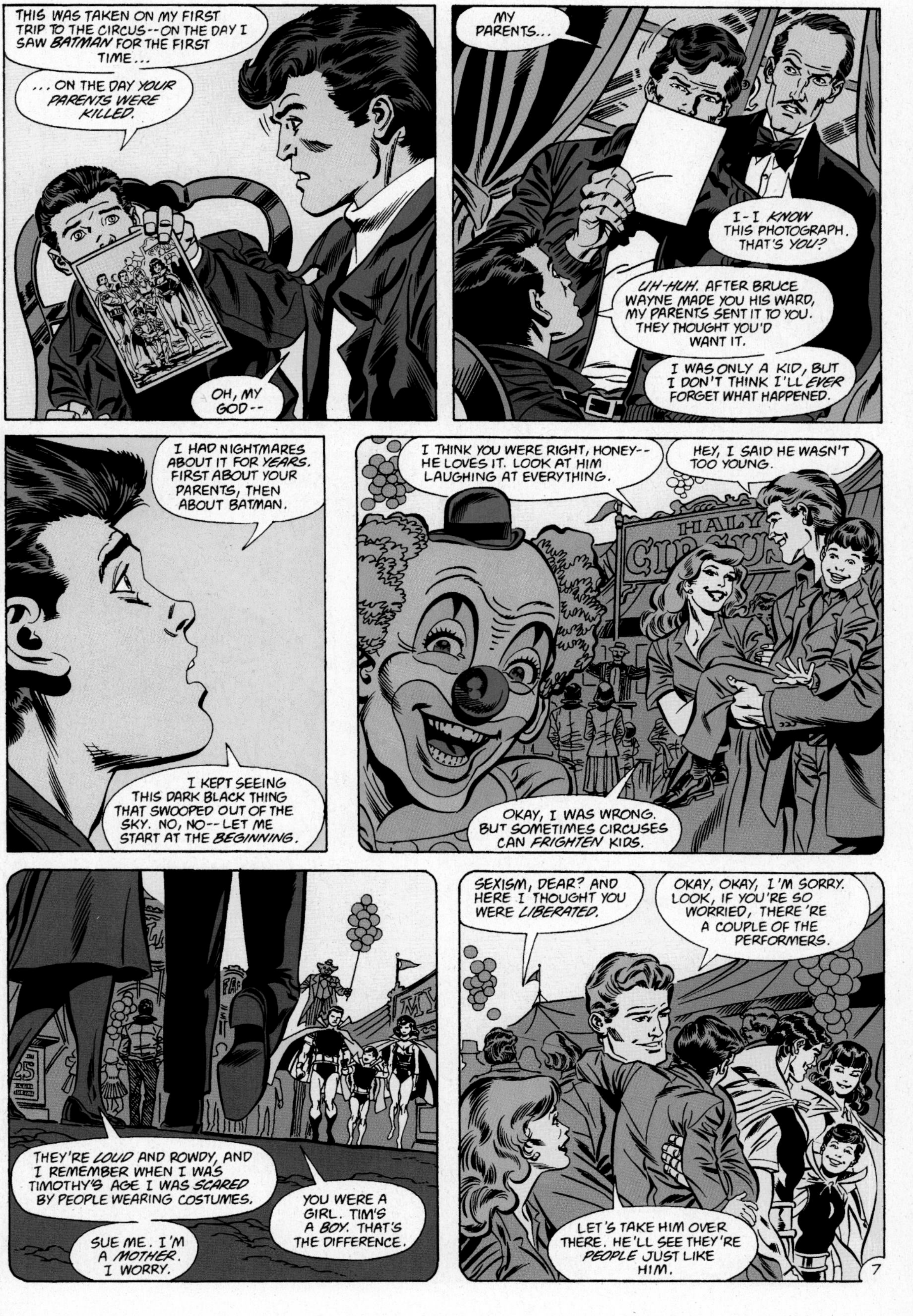
THIS WAS TAKEN ON MY FIRST TRIP TO THE CIRCUS--ON THE DAY I SAW BATMAN FOR THE FIRST TIME...
...ON THE DAY YOUR PARENTS WERE KILLED.
OH, MY GOD--
MY PARENTS...
I-I KNOW THIS PHOTOGRAPH. THAT'S YOU?
UH-HUH. AFTER BRUCE WAYNE MADE YOU HIS WARD, MY PARENTS SENT IT TO YOU. THEY THOUGHT YOU'D WANT IT.
I WAS ONLY A KID, BUT I DON'T THINK I'LL EVER FORGET WHAT HAPPENED.
I HAD NIGHTMARES ABOUT IT FOR YEARS. FIRST ABOUT YOUR PARENTS, THEN ABOUT BATMAN.
I KEPT SEEING THIS DARK BLACK THING THAT SWOOPED OUT OF THE SKY. NO, NO--LET ME START AT THE BEGINNING.
I THINK YOU WERE RIGHT, HONEY--HE LOVES IT. LOOK AT HIM LAUGHING AT EVERYTHING.
HEY, I SAID HE WASN'T TOO YOUNG.
HALY CIRCUS
OKAY, I WAS WRONG. BUT SOMETIMES CIRCUSES CAN FRIGHTEN KIDS.
THEY'RE LOUD AND ROWDY, AND I REMEMBER WHEN I WAS TIMOTHY'S AGE I WAS SCARED BY PEOPLE WEARING COSTUMES.
YOU WERE A GIRL. TIM'S A BOY. THAT'S THE DIFFERENCE.
SUE ME. I'M A MOTHER. I WORRY.
SEXISM, DEAR? AND HERE I THOUGHT YOU WERE LIBERATED.
OKAY, OKAY, I'M SORRY. LOOK, IF YOU'RE SO WORRIED, THERE'RE A COUPLE OF THE PERFORMERS.
LET'S TAKE HIM OVER THERE. HE'LL SEE THEY'RE PEOPLE JUST LIKE HIM.
7

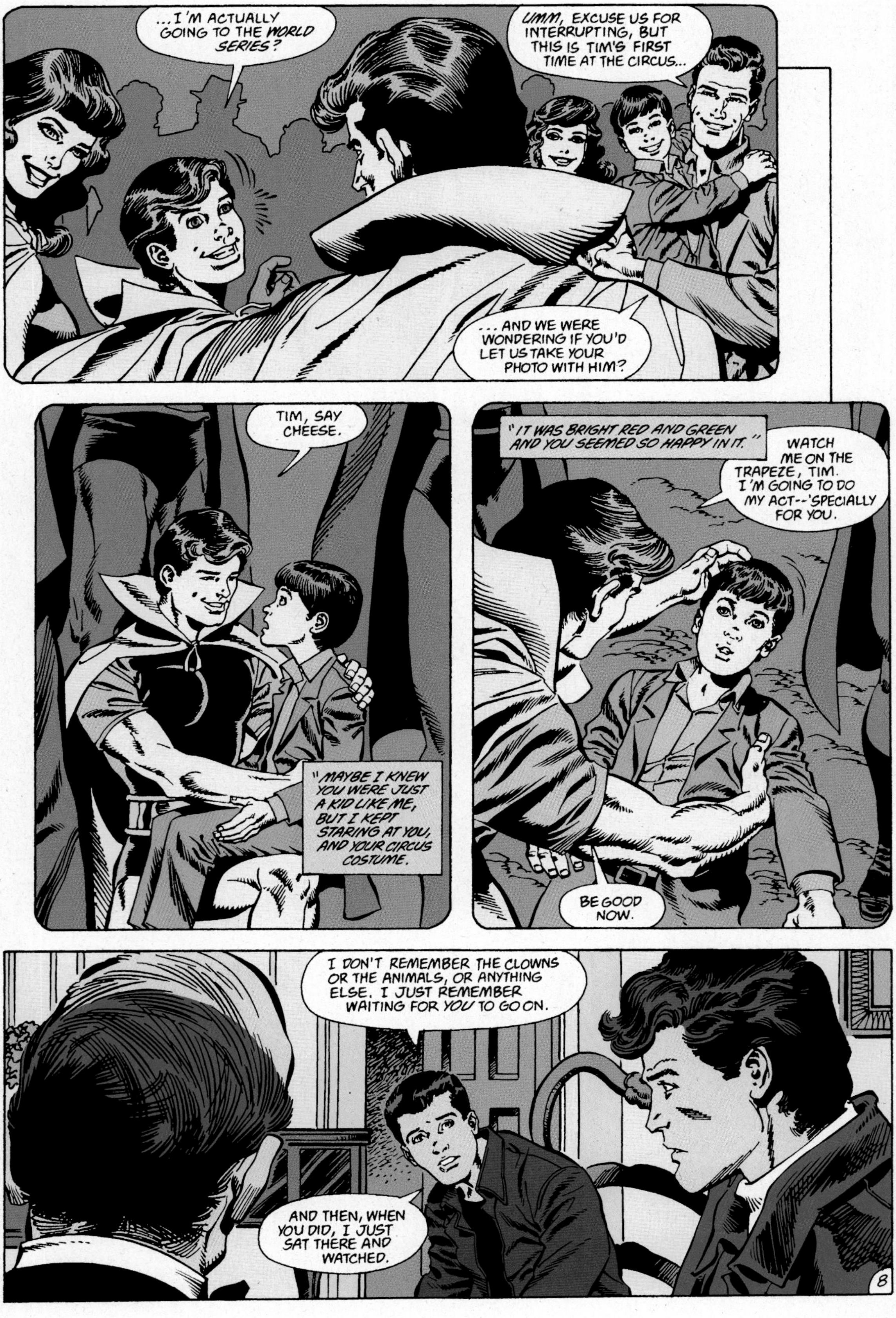
...I'M ACTUALLY GOING TO THE WORLD SERIES?
UMM, EXCUSE US FOR INTERRUPTING, BUT THIS IS TIM'S FIRST TIME AT THE CIRCUS...
...AND WE WERE WONDERING IF YOU'D LET US TAKE YOUR PHOTO WITH HIM?
TIM, SAY CHEESE.
"MAYBE I KNEW YOU WERE JUST A KID LIKE ME, BUT I KEPT STARING AT YOU, AND YOUR CIRCUS COSTUME.
"IT WAS BRIGHT RED AND GREEN AND YOU SEEMED SO HAPPY IN IT."
WATCH ME ON THE TRAPEZE, TIM. I'M GOING TO DO MY ACT--'SPECIALLY FOR YOU.
BE GOOD NOW.
I DON'T REMEMBER THE CLOWNS OR THE ANIMALS, OR ANYTHING ELSE. I JUST REMEMBER WAITING FOR YOU TO GO ON.
AND THEN, WHEN YOU DID, I JUST SAT THERE AND WATCHED.
8

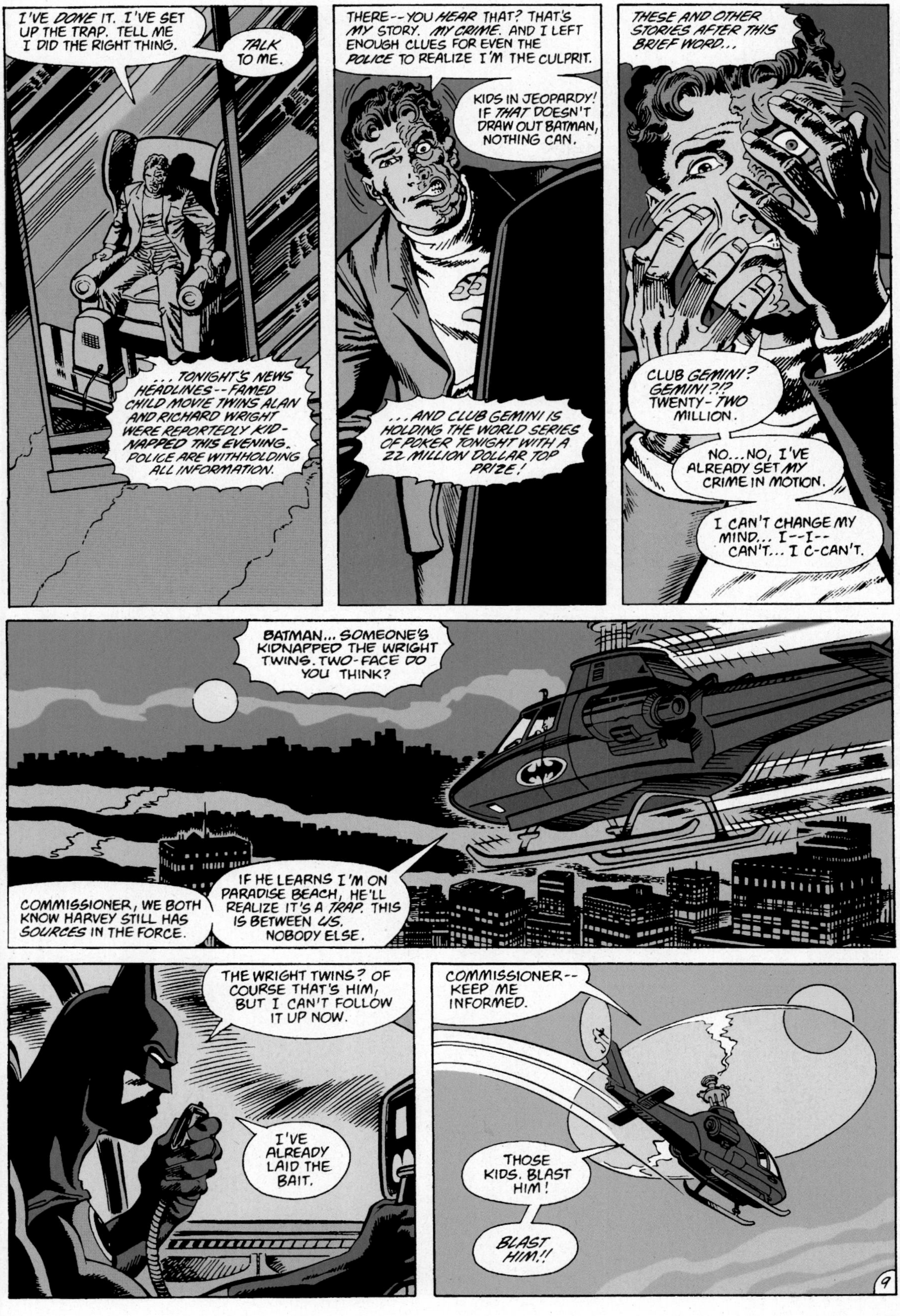
I'VE DONE IT. I'VE SET UP THE TRAP. TELL ME I DID THE RIGHT THING.
TALK TO ME.
...TONIGHT'S NEWS HEADLINES--FAMED CHILD MOVIE TWINS ALAN AND RICHARD WRIGHT WERE REPORTEDLY KIDNAPPED THIS EVENING. POLICE ARE WITHHOLDING ALL INFORMATION.
THERE--YOU HEAR THAT? THAT'S MY STORY. MY CRIME. AND I LEFT ENOUGH CLUES FOR EVEN THE POLICE TO REALIZE I'M THE CULPRIT.
KIDS IN JEOPARDY! IF THAT DOESN'T DRAW OUT BATMAN, NOTHING CAN.
...AND CLUB GEMINI IS HOLDING THE WORLD SERIES OF POKER TONIGHT WITH A 22 MILLION DOLLAR TOP PRIZE!
THESE AND OTHER STORIES AFTER THIS BRIEF WORD...
CLUB GEMINI? GEMINI?!? TWENTY-TWO MILLION.
NO...NO, I'VE ALREADY SET MY CRIME IN MOTION.
I CAN'T CHANGE MY MIND... I--I--CAN'T... I C-CAN'T.
BATMAN... SOMEONE'S KIDNAPPED THE WRIGHT TWINS. TWO-FACE DO YOU THINK?
COMMISSIONER, WE BOTH KNOW HARVEY STILL HAS SOURCES IN THE FORCE.
IF HE LEARNS I'M ON PARADISE BEACH, HE'LL REALIZE IT'S A TRAP. THIS IS BETWEEN US. NOBODY ELSE.
THE WRIGHT TWINS? OF COURSE THAT'S HIM, BUT I CAN'T FOLLOW IT UP NOW.
I'VE ALREADY LAID THE BAIT.
COMMISSIONER--KEEP ME INFORMED.
THOSE KIDS. BLAST HIM!
BLAST HIM!!
9

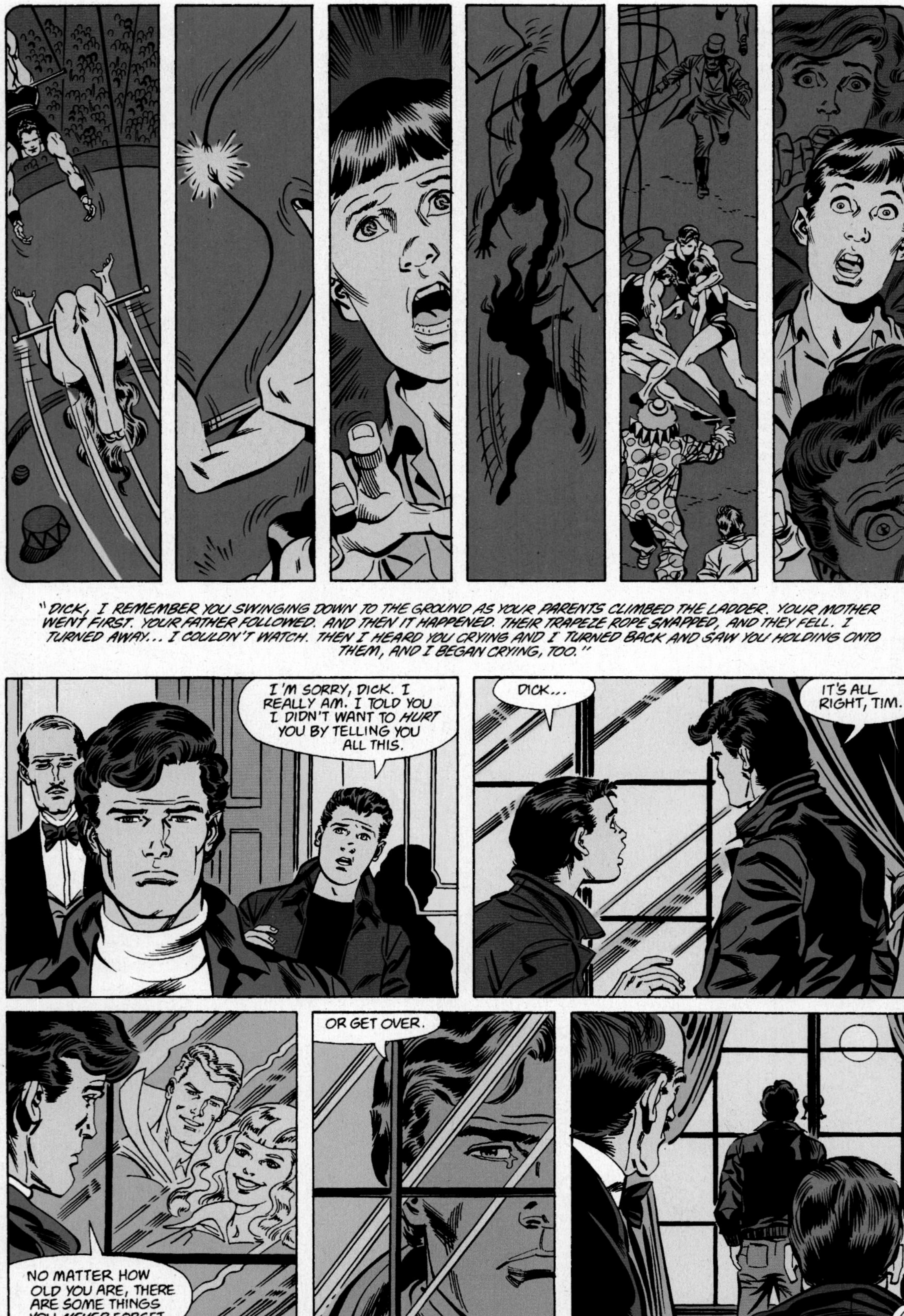
"DICK, I REMEMBER YOU SWINGING DOWN TO THE GROUND AS YOUR PARENTS CLIMBED THE LADDER. YOUR MOTHER WENT FIRST. YOUR FATHER FOLLOWED. AND THEN IT HAPPENED. THEIR TRAPEZE ROPE SNAPPED, AND THEY FELL. I TURNED AWAY... I COULDN'T WATCH. THEN I HEARD YOU CRYING AND I TURNED BACK AND SAW YOU HOLDING ONTO THEM, AND I BEGAN CRYING, TOO."
I'M SORRY, DICK. I REALLY AM. I TOLD YOU I DIDN'T WANT TO *HURT* YOU BY TELLING YOU ALL THIS.
DICK...
IT'S ALL RIGHT, TIM.
NO MATTER HOW OLD YOU ARE, THERE ARE SOME THINGS YOU *NEVER* FORGET.
OR GET OVER.
10

BUT YOU HAVEN'T TOLD ME ANYTHING I DON'T ALREADY KNOW.

I WANT THE REST OF IT. ALL OF IT.

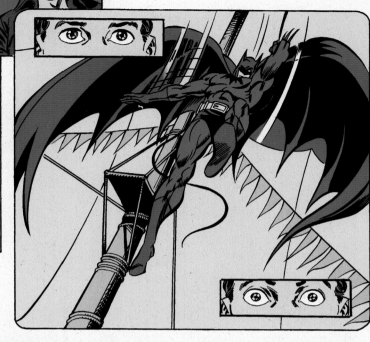

ALL RIGHT. I UNDERSTAND. THE NEXT THING I REMEMBER WAS THIS DARK *SHAPE* FLYING DOWN AT YOU. I DIDN'T KNOW WHAT IT WAS.

BUT I THOUGHT IT HAD HURT YOUR PARENTS AND NOW IT WAS GOING TO HURT YOU.

"I WANTED TO HELP... I DON'T KNOW HOW, BUT I STILL WANTED TO DO SOMETHING.

"MY PARENTS HELD ME BACK AS THE THING MOVED TO YOU. I CRIED OUT TO WARN YOU.

"BUT WHEN HE TOUCHED YOU I REALIZED SOMETHING -- HE WASN'T BAD. HE WASN'T TRYING TO HURT YOU.

"HE WAS THERE TO HELP.

"THAT'S THE FIRST TIME I SAW BATMAN. AND IN THAT MOMENT HE WENT FROM BEING A MONSTER--

"--TO BECOMING SOME GREAT DARK KNIGHT."

11

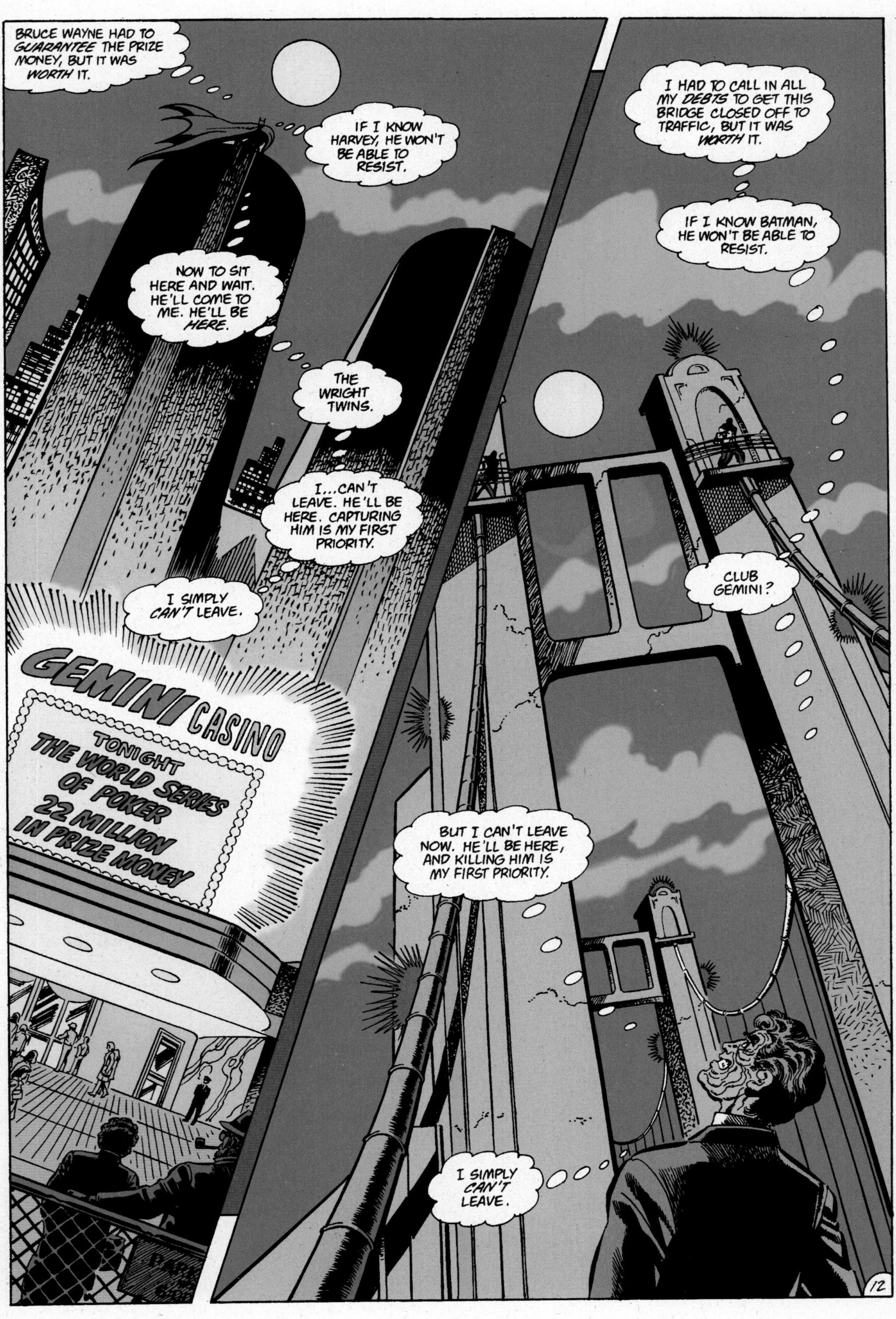
BRUCE WAYNE HAD TO GUARANTEE THE PRIZE MONEY, BUT IT WAS WORTH IT.
IF I KNOW HARVEY, HE WON'T BE ABLE TO RESIST.
NOW TO SIT HERE AND WAIT. HE'LL COME TO ME. HE'LL BE HERE.
THE WRIGHT TWINS.
I...CAN'T LEAVE. HE'LL BE HERE. CAPTURING HIM IS MY FIRST PRIORITY.
I SIMPLY CAN'T LEAVE.
GEMINI CASINO
TONIGHT THE WORLD SERIES OF POKER 22 MILLION IN PRIZE MONEY
I HAD TO CALL IN ALL MY DEBTS TO GET THIS BRIDGE CLOSED OFF TO TRAFFIC, BUT IT WAS WORTH IT.
IF I KNOW BATMAN, HE WON'T BE ABLE TO RESIST.
CLUB GEMINI?
BUT I CAN'T LEAVE NOW. HE'LL BE HERE, AND KILLING HIM IS MY FIRST PRIORITY.
I SIMPLY CAN'T LEAVE.
12

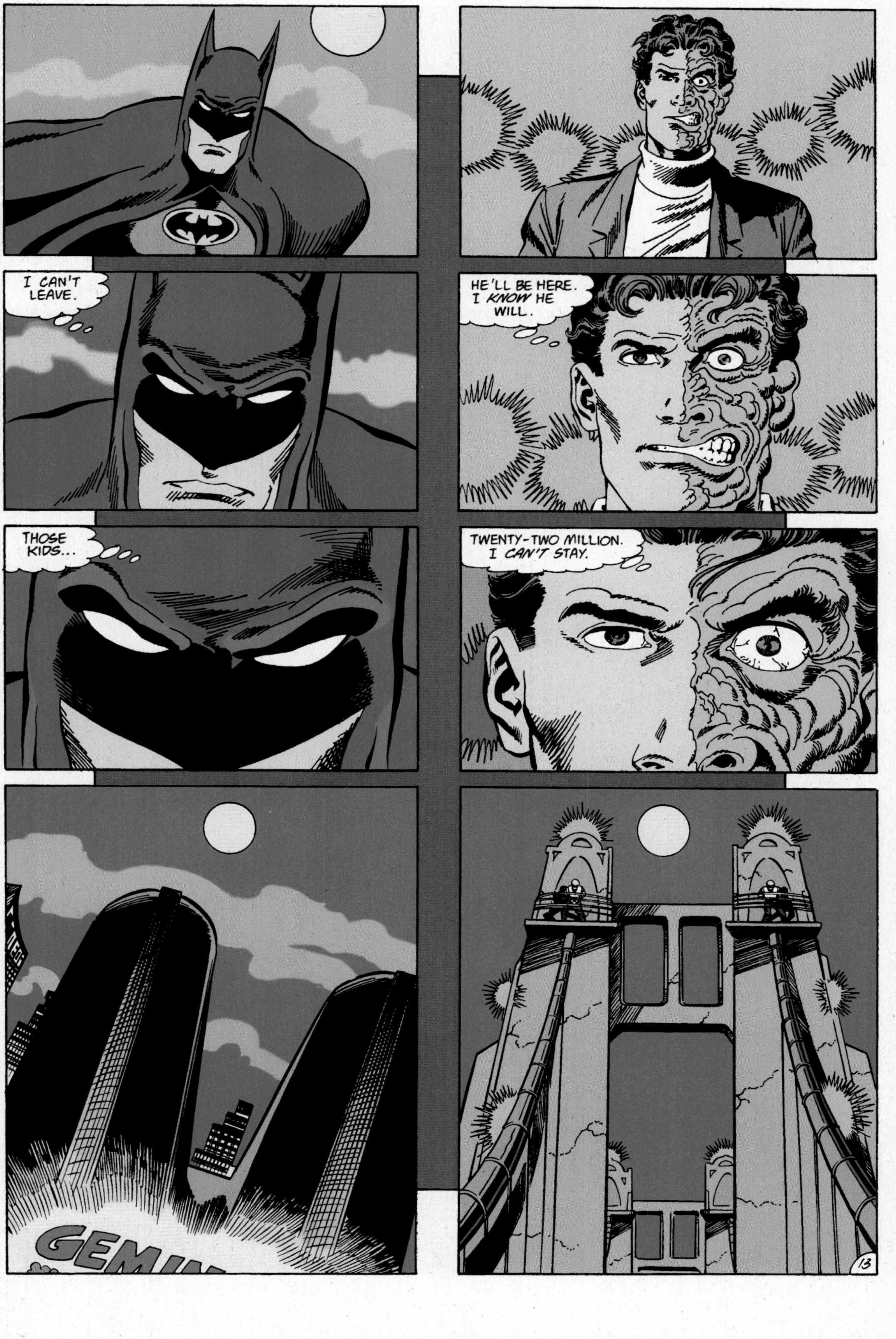
I CAN'T LEAVE.
HE'LL BE HERE. I KNOW HE WILL.
THOSE KIDS...
TWENTY-TWO MILLION. I CAN'T STAY.
GEMIN
13

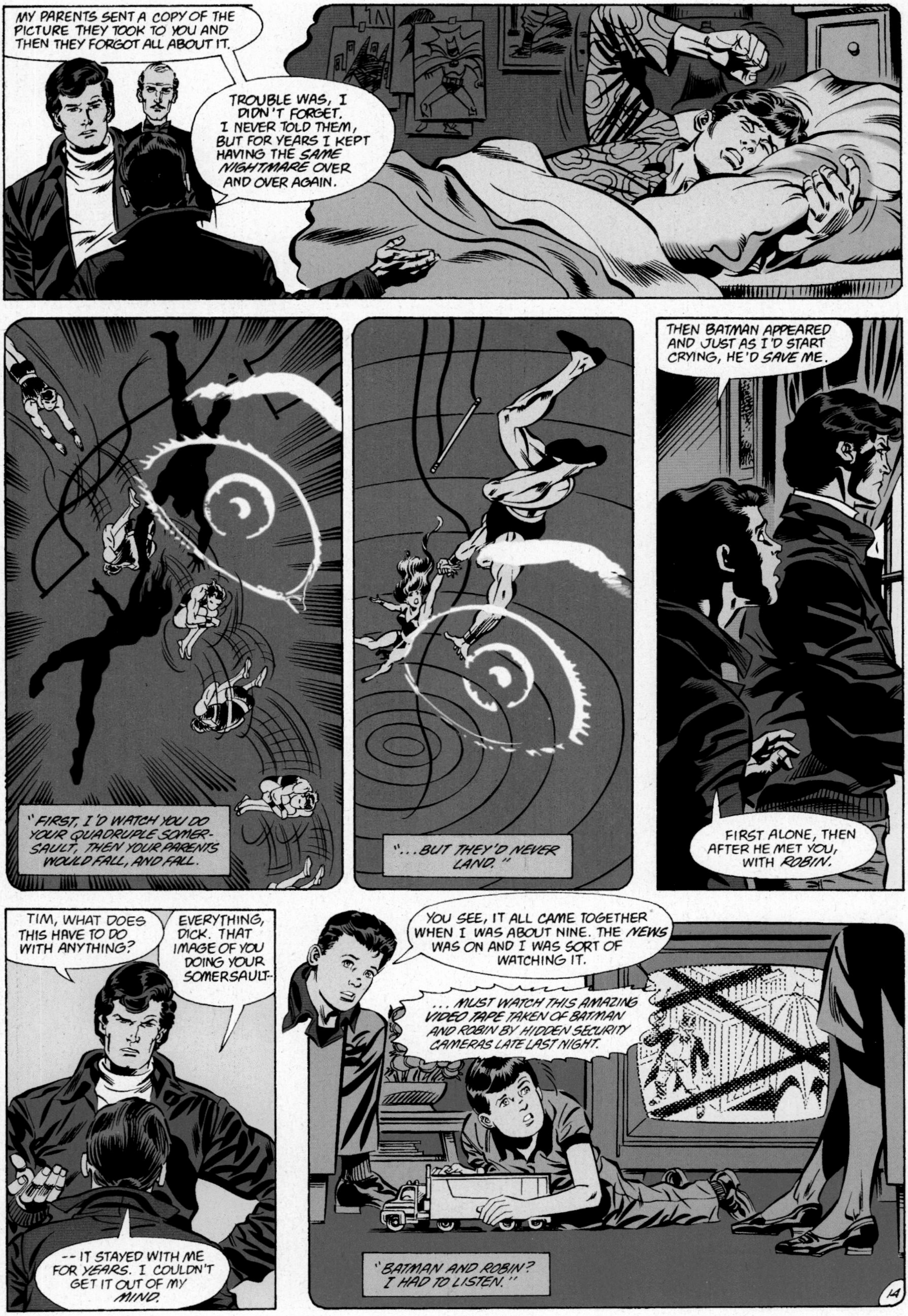

MY PARENTS SENT A COPY OF THE PICTURE THEY TOOK TO YOU AND THEN THEY FORGOT ALL ABOUT IT.
TROUBLE WAS, I DIDN'T FORGET. I NEVER TOLD THEM, BUT FOR YEARS I KEPT HAVING THE SAME NIGHTMARE OVER AND OVER AGAIN.
"FIRST, I'D WATCH YOU DO YOUR QUADRUPLE SOMER-SAULT, THEN YOUR PARENTS WOULD FALL, AND FALL.
"...BUT THEY'D NEVER LAND."
THEN BATMAN APPEARED AND JUST AS I'D START CRYING, HE'D SAVE ME.
FIRST ALONE, THEN AFTER HE MET YOU, WITH ROBIN.
TIM, WHAT DOES THIS HAVE TO DO WITH ANYTHING?
EVERYTHING, DICK. THAT IMAGE OF YOU DOING YOUR SOMERSAULT--
--IT STAYED WITH ME FOR YEARS. I COULDN'T GET IT OUT OF MY MIND.
YOU SEE, IT ALL CAME TOGETHER WHEN I WAS ABOUT NINE. THE NEWS WAS ON AND I WAS SORT OF WATCHING IT.
...MUST WATCH THIS AMAZING VIDEO TAPE TAKEN OF BATMAN AND ROBIN BY HIDDEN SECURITY CAMERAS LATE LAST NIGHT.
"BATMAN AND ROBIN? I HAD TO LISTEN."
14

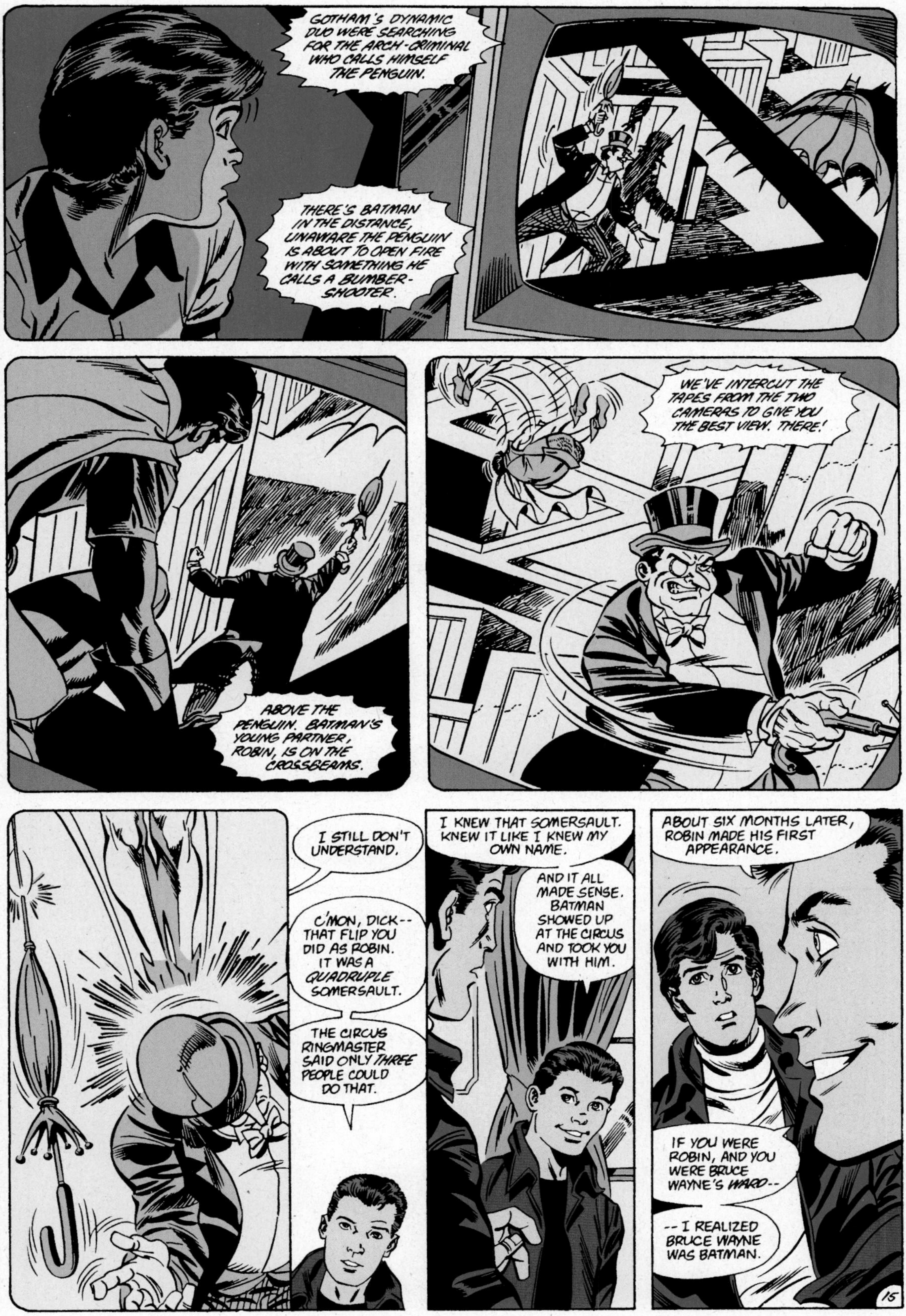
GOTHAM'S DYNAMIC DUO WERE SEARCHING FOR THE ARCH-CRIMINAL WHO CALLS HIMSELF THE PENGUIN.
THERE'S BATMAN IN THE DISTANCE, UNAWARE THE PENGUIN IS ABOUT TO OPEN FIRE WITH SOMETHING HE CALLS A BUMBER-SHOOTER.
ABOVE THE PENGUIN, BATMAN'S YOUNG PARTNER, ROBIN, IS ON THE CROSSBEAMS.
WE'VE INTERCUT THE TAPES FROM THE TWO CAMERAS TO GIVE YOU THE BEST VIEW. THERE!
I STILL DON'T UNDERSTAND.
C'MON, DICK-- THAT FLIP YOU DID AS ROBIN. IT WAS A QUADRUPLE SOMERSAULT.
THE CIRCUS RINGMASTER SAID ONLY THREE PEOPLE COULD DO THAT.
I KNEW THAT SOMERSAULT. KNEW IT LIKE I KNEW MY OWN NAME.
AND IT ALL MADE SENSE. BATMAN SHOWED UP AT THE CIRCUS AND TOOK YOU WITH HIM.
ABOUT SIX MONTHS LATER, ROBIN MADE HIS FIRST APPEARANCE.
IF YOU WERE ROBIN, AND YOU WERE BRUCE WAYNE'S WARD--
--I REALIZED BRUCE WAYNE WAS BATMAN.
15

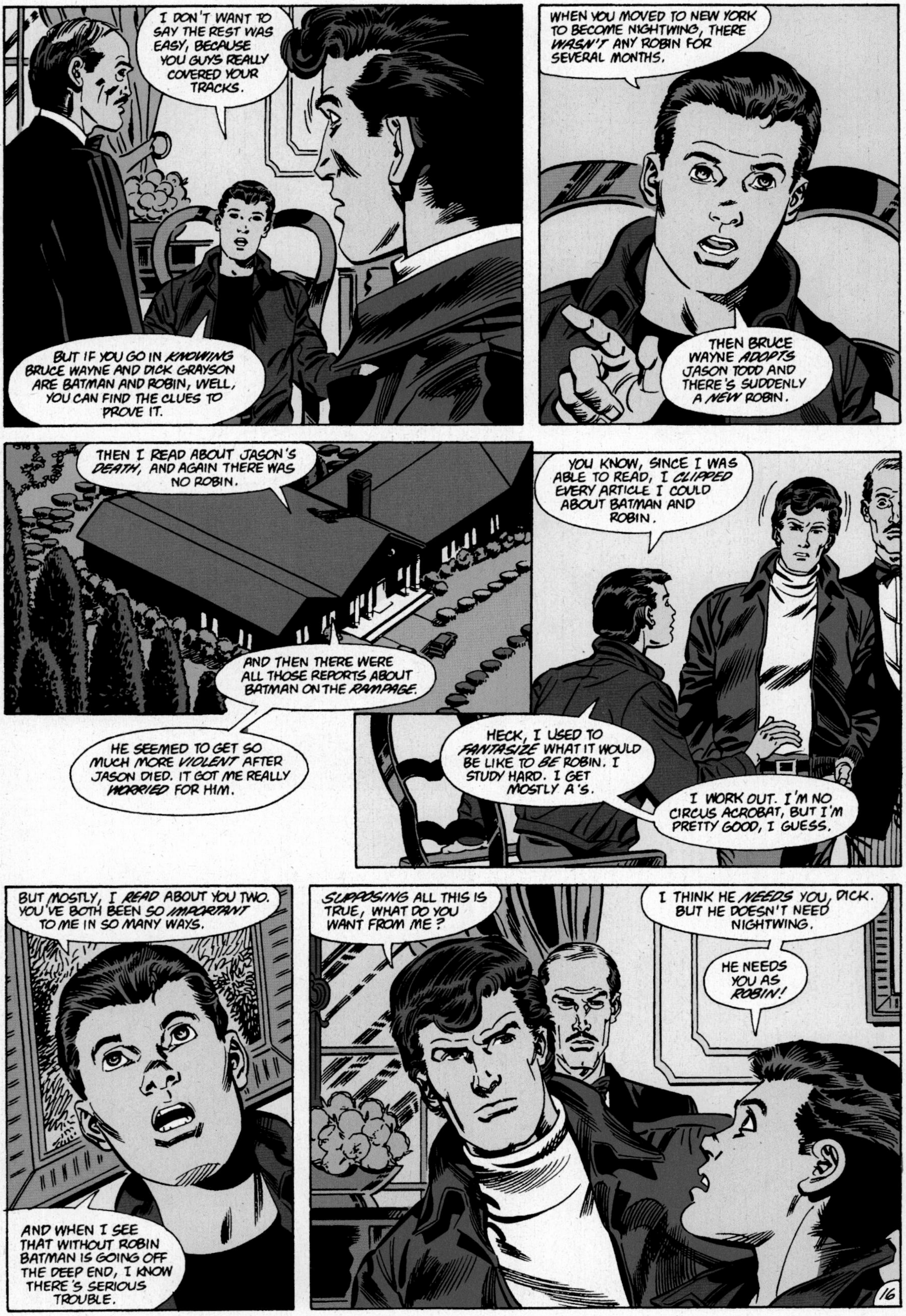
I DON'T WANT TO SAY THE REST WAS EASY, BECAUSE YOU GUYS REALLY COVERED YOUR TRACKS.
BUT IF YOU GO IN KNOWING BRUCE WAYNE AND DICK GRAYSON ARE BATMAN AND ROBIN, WELL, YOU CAN FIND THE CLUES TO PROVE IT.
WHEN YOU MOVED TO NEW YORK TO BECOME NIGHTWING, THERE WASN'T ANY ROBIN FOR SEVERAL MONTHS.
THEN BRUCE WAYNE ADOPTS JASON TODD AND THERE'S SUDDENLY A NEW ROBIN.
THEN I READ ABOUT JASON'S DEATH, AND AGAIN THERE WAS NO ROBIN.
AND THEN THERE WERE ALL THOSE REPORTS ABOUT BATMAN ON THE RAMPAGE.
HE SEEMED TO GET SO MUCH MORE VIOLENT AFTER JASON DIED. IT GOT ME REALLY WORRIED FOR HIM.
YOU KNOW, SINCE I WAS ABLE TO READ, I CLIPPED EVERY ARTICLE I COULD ABOUT BATMAN AND ROBIN.
HECK, I USED TO FANTASIZE WHAT IT WOULD BE LIKE TO BE ROBIN. I STUDY HARD. I GET MOSTLY A'S.
I WORK OUT. I'M NO CIRCUS ACROBAT, BUT I'M PRETTY GOOD, I GUESS.
BUT MOSTLY, I READ ABOUT YOU TWO. YOU'VE BOTH BEEN SO IMPORTANT TO ME IN SO MANY WAYS.
AND WHEN I SEE THAT WITHOUT ROBIN BATMAN IS GOING OFF THE DEEP END, I KNOW THERE'S SERIOUS TROUBLE.
SUPPOSING ALL THIS IS TRUE, WHAT DO YOU WANT FROM ME?
I THINK HE NEEDS YOU, DICK. BUT HE DOESN'T NEED NIGHTWING.
HE NEEDS YOU AS ROBIN!
16

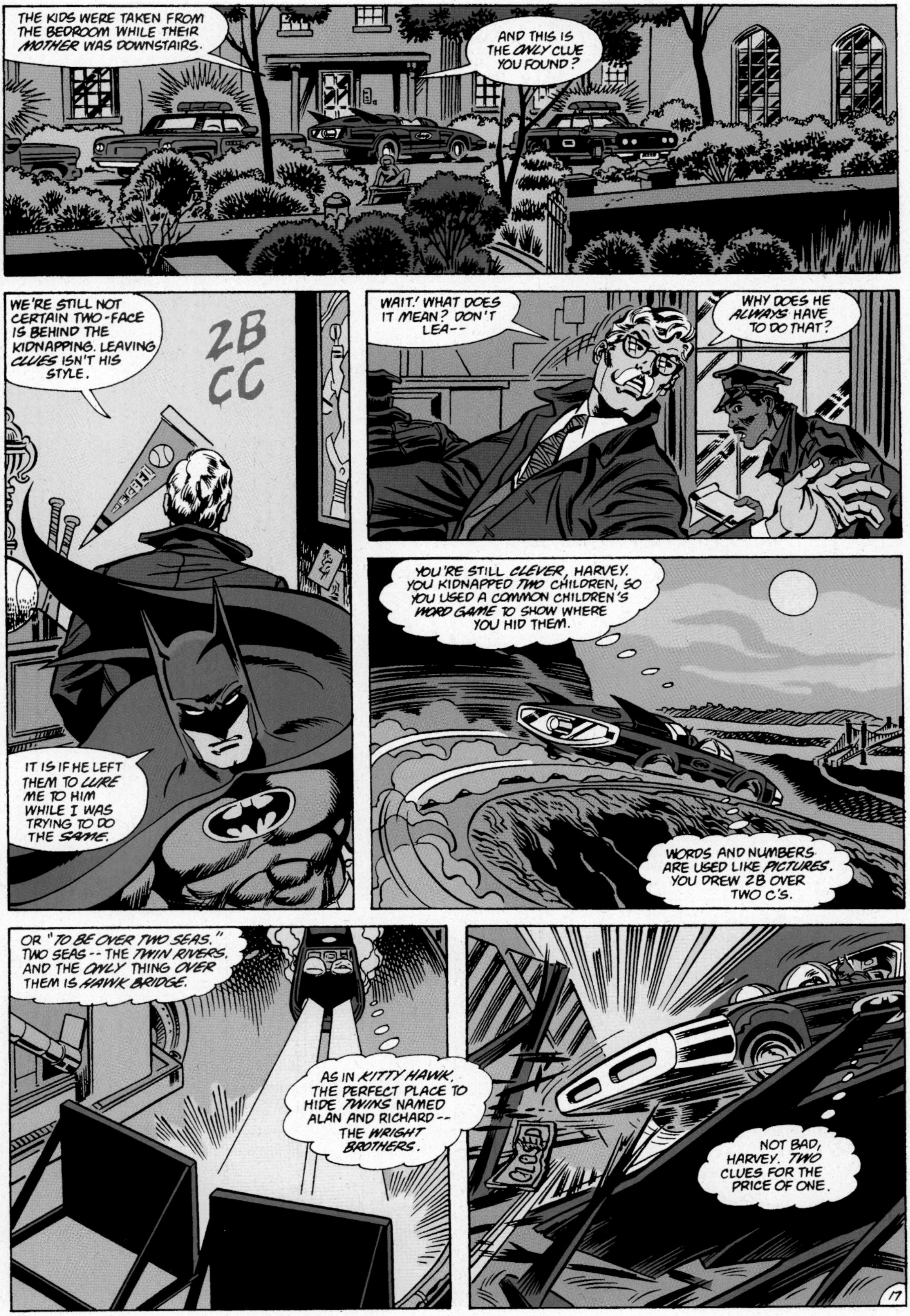
THE KIDS WERE TAKEN FROM THE BEDROOM WHILE THEIR *MOTHER* WAS DOWNSTAIRS.
AND THIS IS THE *ONLY* CLUE YOU FOUND?
WE'RE STILL NOT CERTAIN TWO-FACE IS BEHIND THE KIDNAPPING. LEAVING *CLUES* ISN'T HIS STYLE.
2B
CC
IT IS IF HE LEFT THEM TO *LURE* ME TO HIM WHILE I WAS TRYING TO DO THE *SAME*.
WAIT! WHAT DOES IT *MEAN*? DON'T LEA--
WHY DOES HE *ALWAYS* HAVE TO DO THAT?
YOU'RE STILL *CLEVER*, HARVEY. YOU KIDNAPPED *TWO* CHILDREN, SO YOU USED A COMMON CHILDREN'S *WORD GAME* TO SHOW WHERE YOU HID THEM.
WORDS AND NUMBERS ARE USED LIKE *PICTURES*. YOU DREW 2B OVER TWO C'S.
OR "*TO BE OVER TWO SEAS.*" TWO SEAS -- THE *TWIN RIVERS*, AND THE *ONLY* THING *OVER* THEM IS *HAWK BRIDGE*.
AS IN *KITTY HAWK*, THE PERFECT PLACE TO HIDE *TWINS* NAMED ALAN AND RICHARD -- THE *WRIGHT BROTHERS*.
NOT BAD, HARVEY. *TWO* CLUES FOR THE PRICE OF ONE.
17

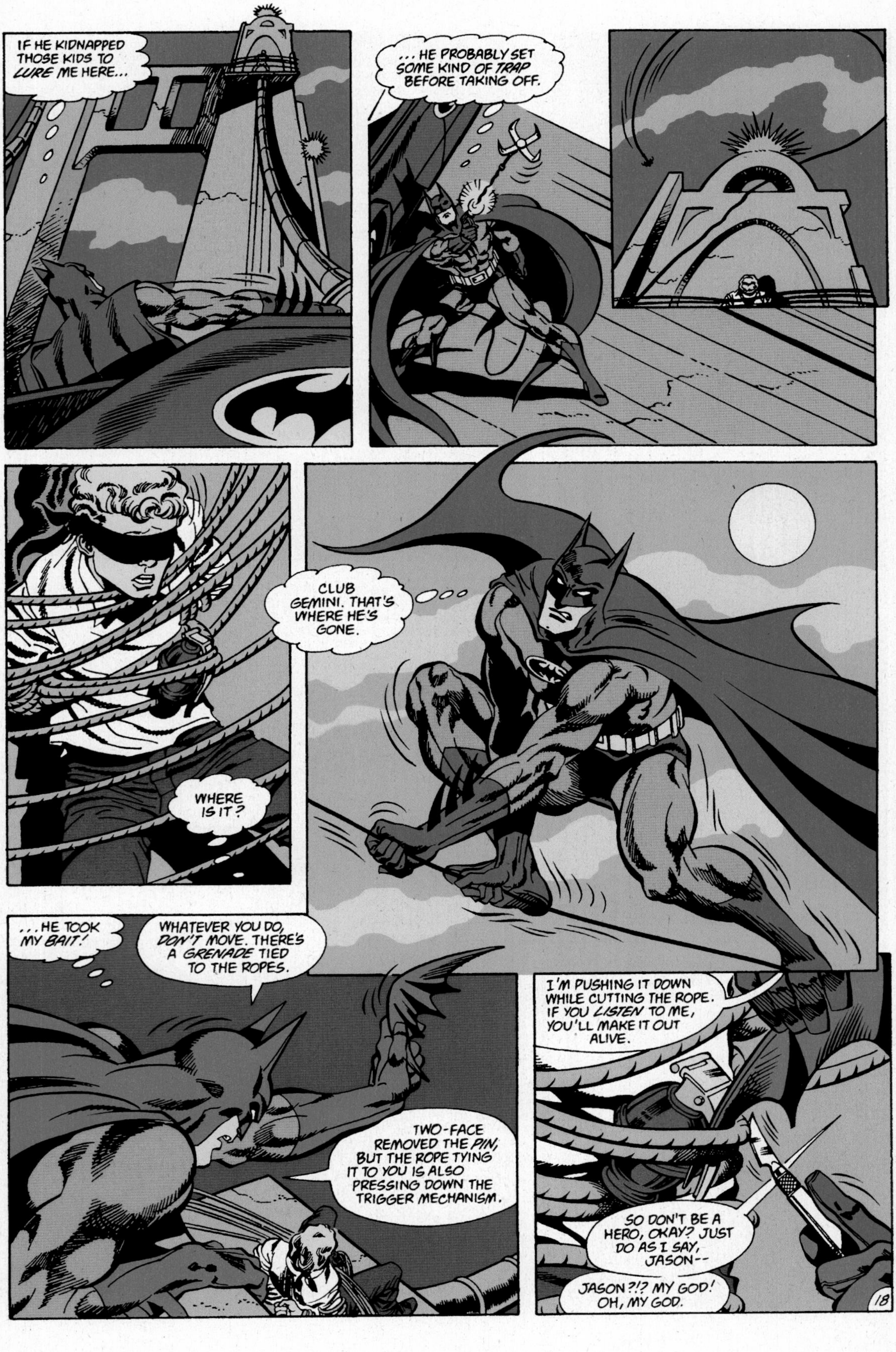
IF HE KIDNAPPED THOSE KIDS TO LURE ME HERE...
...HE PROBABLY SET SOME KIND OF TRAP BEFORE TAKING OFF.
CLUB GEMINI. THAT'S WHERE HE'S GONE.
WHERE IS IT?
...HE TOOK MY BAIT!
WHATEVER YOU DO, DON'T MOVE. THERE'S A GRENADE TIED TO THE ROPES.
TWO-FACE REMOVED THE PIN, BUT THE ROPE TYING IT TO YOU IS ALSO PRESSING DOWN THE TRIGGER MECHANISM.
I'M PUSHING IT DOWN WHILE CUTTING THE ROPE. IF YOU LISTEN TO ME, YOU'LL MAKE IT OUT ALIVE.
SO DON'T BE A HERO, OKAY? JUST DO AS I SAY, JASON--
JASON?!? MY GOD! OH, MY GOD.
18

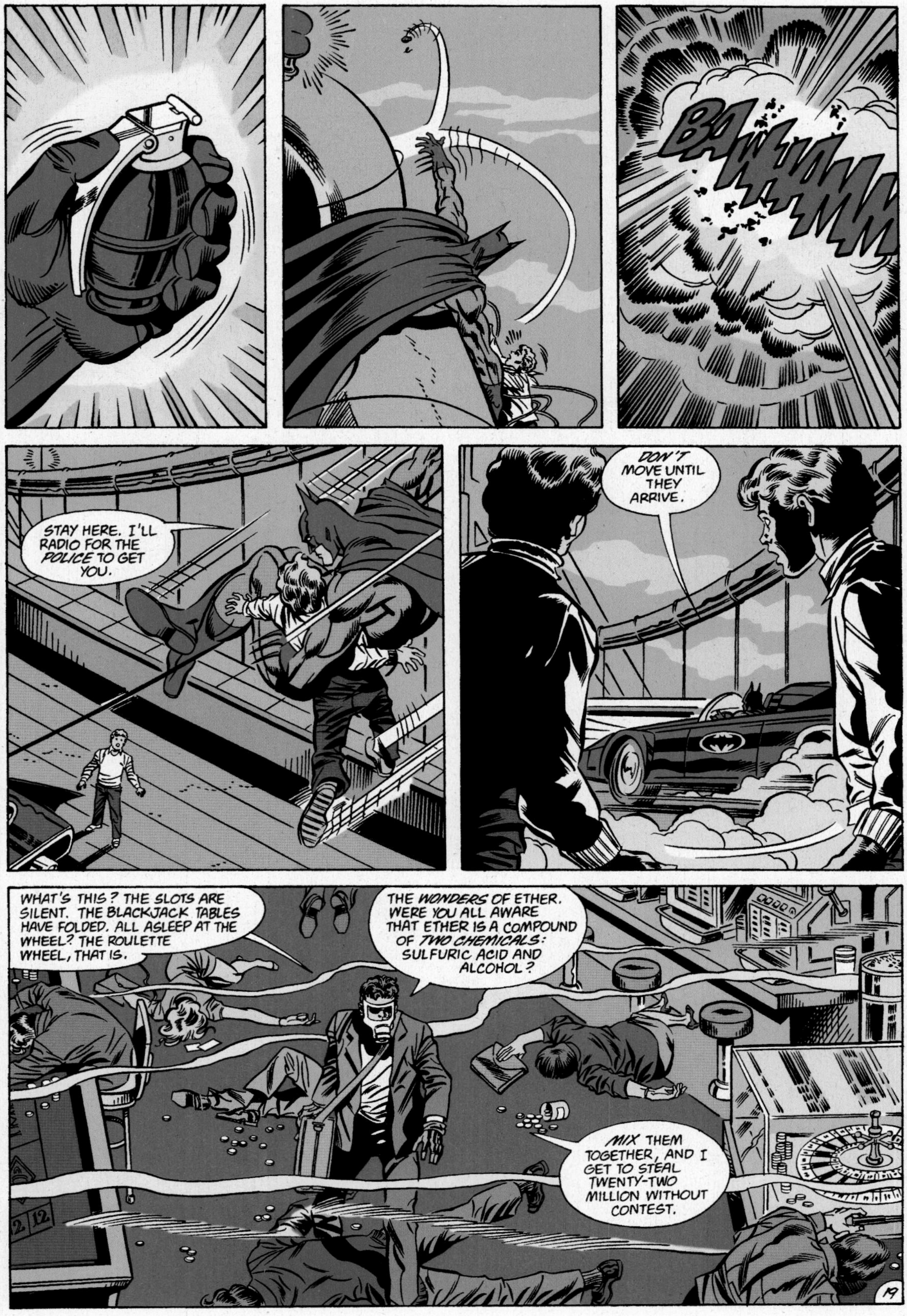
BAWHAMM
STAY HERE. I'LL RADIO FOR THE POLICE TO GET YOU.
DON'T MOVE UNTIL THEY ARRIVE.
WHAT'S THIS? THE SLOTS ARE SILENT. THE BLACKJACK TABLES HAVE FOLDED. ALL ASLEEP AT THE WHEEL? THE ROULETTE WHEEL, THAT IS.
THE WONDERS OF ETHER. WERE YOU ALL AWARE THAT ETHER IS A COMPOUND OF TWO CHEMICALS: SULFURIC ACID AND ALCOHOL?
MIX THEM TOGETHER, AND I GET TO STEAL TWENTY-TWO MILLION WITHOUT CONTEST.
19

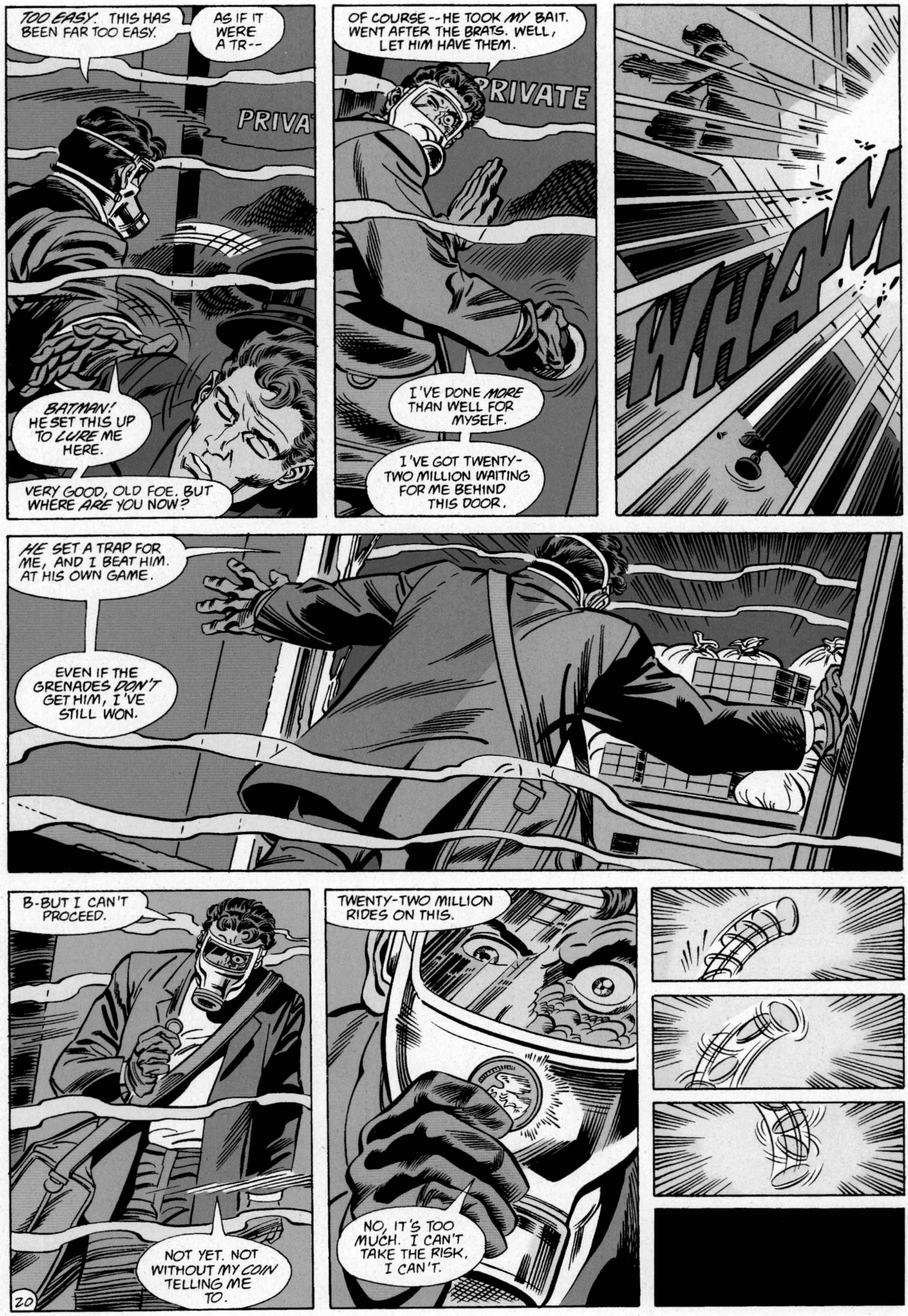
TOO EASY. THIS HAS BEEN FAR TOO EASY.
AS IF IT WERE A TR--
PRIVAT
BATMAN! HE SET THIS UP TO LURE ME HERE.
VERY GOOD, OLD FOE. BUT WHERE ARE YOU NOW?
OF COURSE--HE TOOK MY BAIT. WENT AFTER THE BRATS. WELL, LET HIM HAVE THEM.
PRIVATE
I'VE DONE MORE THAN WELL FOR MYSELF.
I'VE GOT TWENTY-TWO MILLION WAITING FOR ME BEHIND THIS DOOR.
WHAM
HE SET A TRAP FOR ME, AND I BEAT HIM. AT HIS OWN GAME.
EVEN IF THE GRENADES DON'T GET HIM, I'VE STILL WON.
B-BUT I CAN'T PROCEED.
NOT YET. NOT WITHOUT MY COIN TELLING ME TO.
20
TWENTY-TWO MILLION RIDES ON THIS.
NO, IT'S TOO MUCH. I CAN'T TAKE THE RISK. I CAN'T.

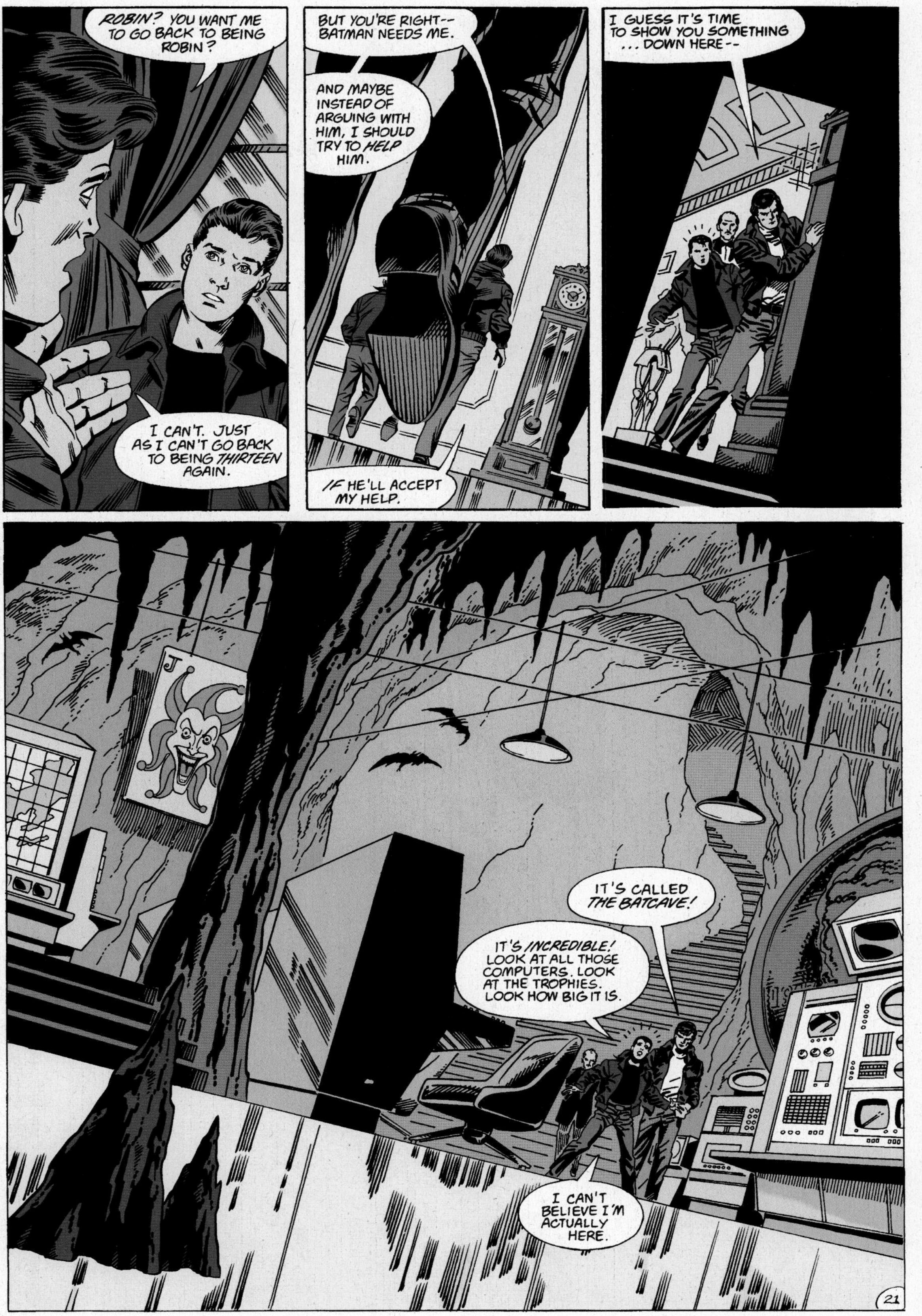
ROBIN? YOU WANT ME TO GO BACK TO BEING ROBIN?
I CAN'T. JUST AS I CAN'T GO BACK TO BEING THIRTEEN AGAIN.
BUT YOU'RE RIGHT-- BATMAN NEEDS ME.
AND MAYBE INSTEAD OF ARGUING WITH HIM, I SHOULD TRY TO HELP HIM.
IF HE'LL ACCEPT MY HELP.
I GUESS IT'S TIME TO SHOW YOU SOMETHING ... DOWN HERE--
IT'S CALLED THE BATCAVE!
IT'S INCREDIBLE! LOOK AT ALL THOSE COMPUTERS. LOOK AT THE TROPHIES. LOOK HOW BIG IT IS.
I CAN'T BELIEVE I'M ACTUALLY HERE.
21

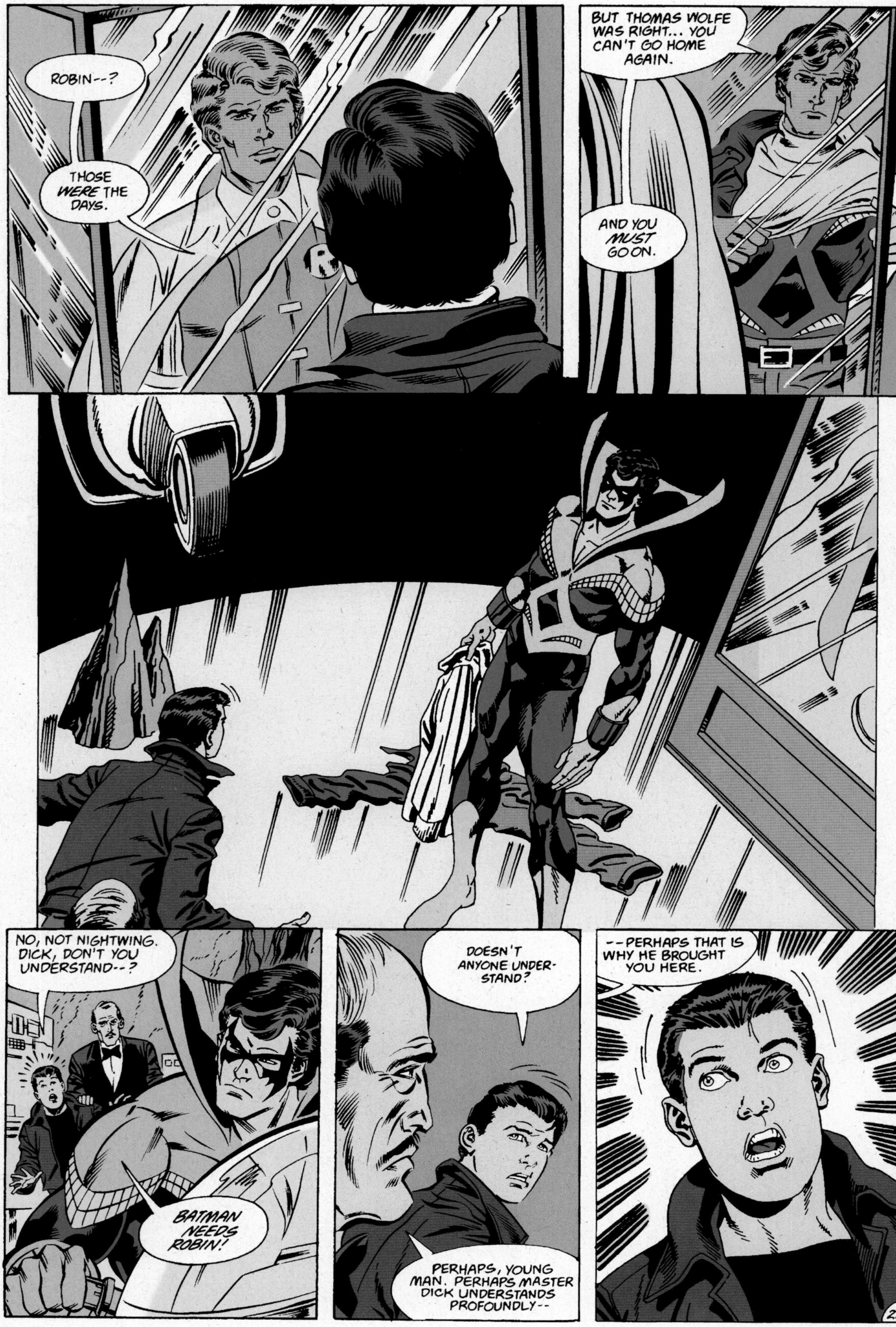
ROBIN--?
THOSE WERE THE DAYS.
BUT THOMAS WOLFE WAS RIGHT... YOU CAN'T GO HOME AGAIN.
AND YOU MUST GO ON.
NO, NOT NIGHTWING. DICK, DON'T YOU UNDERSTAND--?
BATMAN NEEDS ROBIN!
DOESN'T ANYONE UNDERSTAND?
PERHAPS, YOUNG MAN. PERHAPS MASTER DICK UNDERSTANDS PROFOUNDLY--
--PERHAPS THAT IS WHY HE BROUGHT YOU HERE.
22

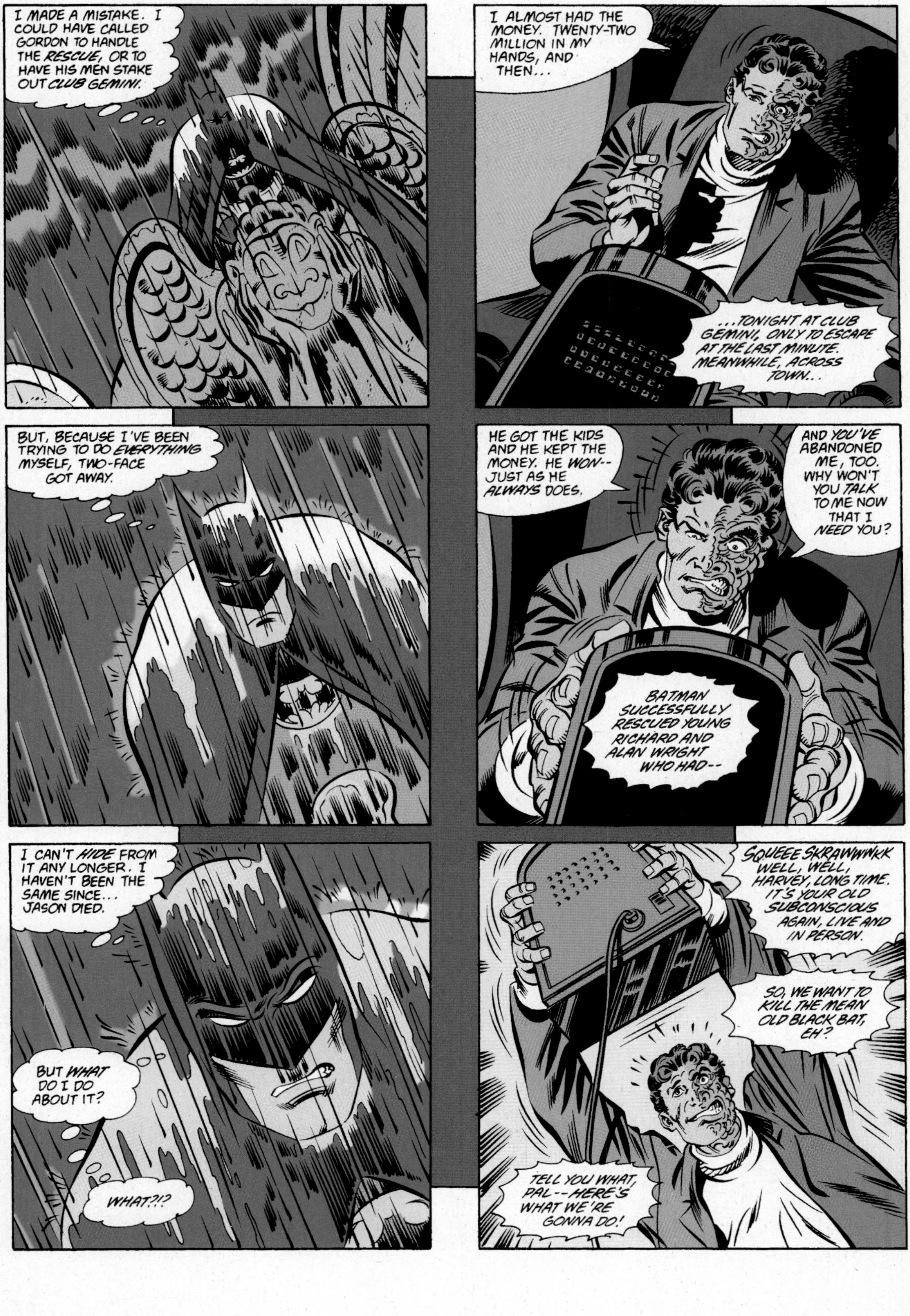
I MADE A MISTAKE. I COULD HAVE CALLED GORDON TO HANDLE THE RESCUE, OR TO HAVE HIS MEN STAKE OUT CLUB GEMINI.
I ALMOST HAD THE MONEY. TWENTY-TWO MILLION IN MY HANDS, AND THEN...
...TONIGHT AT CLUB GEMINI, ONLY TO ESCAPE AT THE LAST MINUTE. MEANWHILE, ACROSS TOWN...
BUT, BECAUSE I'VE BEEN TRYING TO DO EVERYTHING MYSELF, TWO-FACE GOT AWAY.
HE GOT THE KIDS AND HE KEPT THE MONEY. HE WON-- JUST AS HE ALWAYS DOES.
AND YOU'VE ABANDONED ME, TOO. WHY WON'T YOU TALK TO ME NOW THAT I NEED YOU?
BATMAN SUCCESSFULLY RESCUED YOUNG RICHARD AND ALAN WRIGHT WHO HAD--
I CAN'T HIDE FROM IT ANY LONGER. I HAVEN'T BEEN THE SAME SINCE... JASON DIED.
BUT WHAT DO I DO ABOUT IT?
WHAT?!?
SQUEEE SKRAWWWKK WELL, WELL, HARVEY, LONG TIME. IT'S YOUR OLD SUBCONSCIOUS AGAIN, LIVE AND IN PERSON.
SO, WE WANT TO KILL THE MEAN OLD BLACK BAT, EH?
TELL YOU WHAT, PAL--HERE'S WHAT WE'RE GONNA DO!

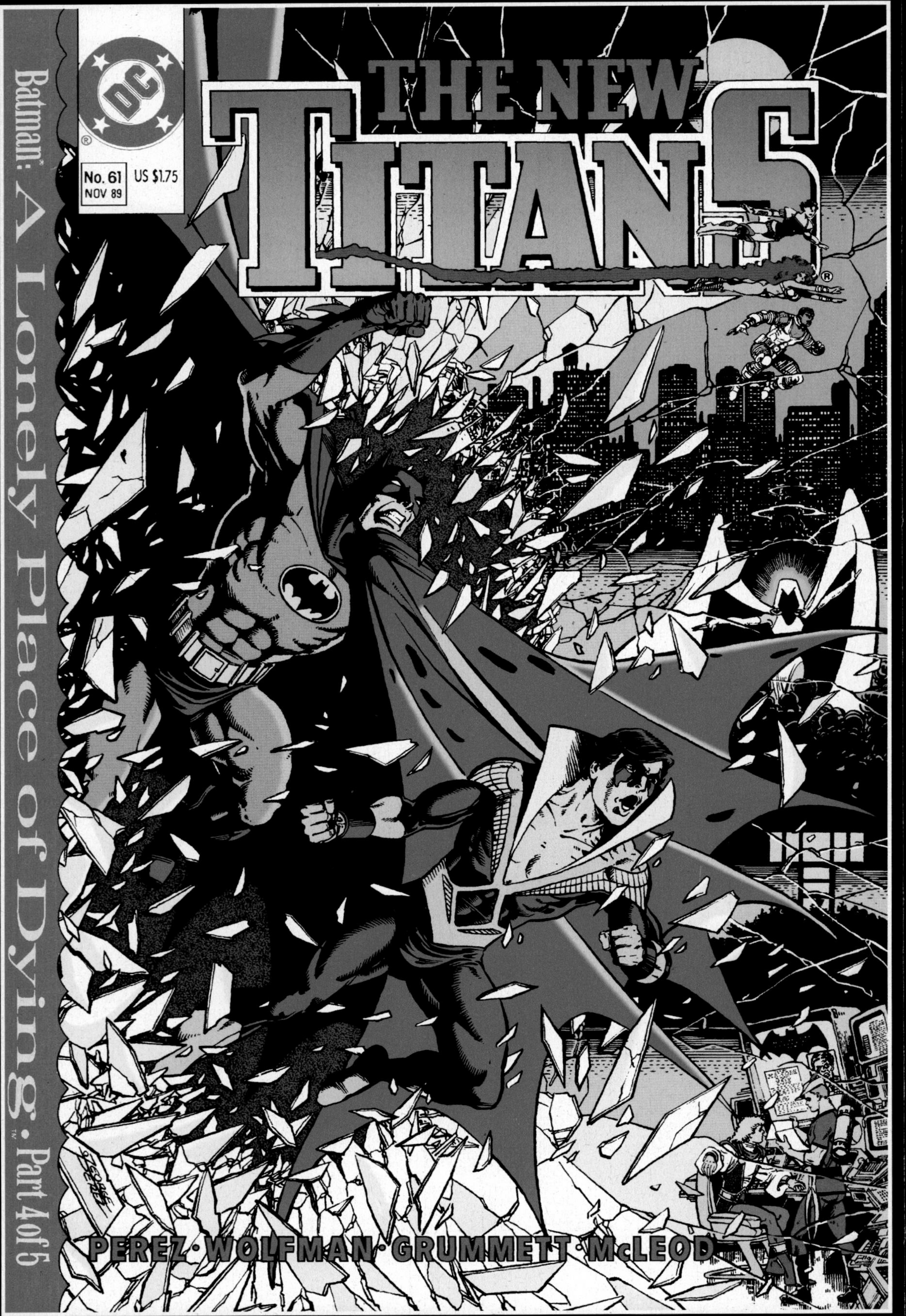
THE NEW
TITANS
No. 61
NOV 89
US $1.75
Batman: A Lonely Place of Dying • Part 4 of 5
PEREZ·WOLFMAN·GRUMMETT·McLEOD

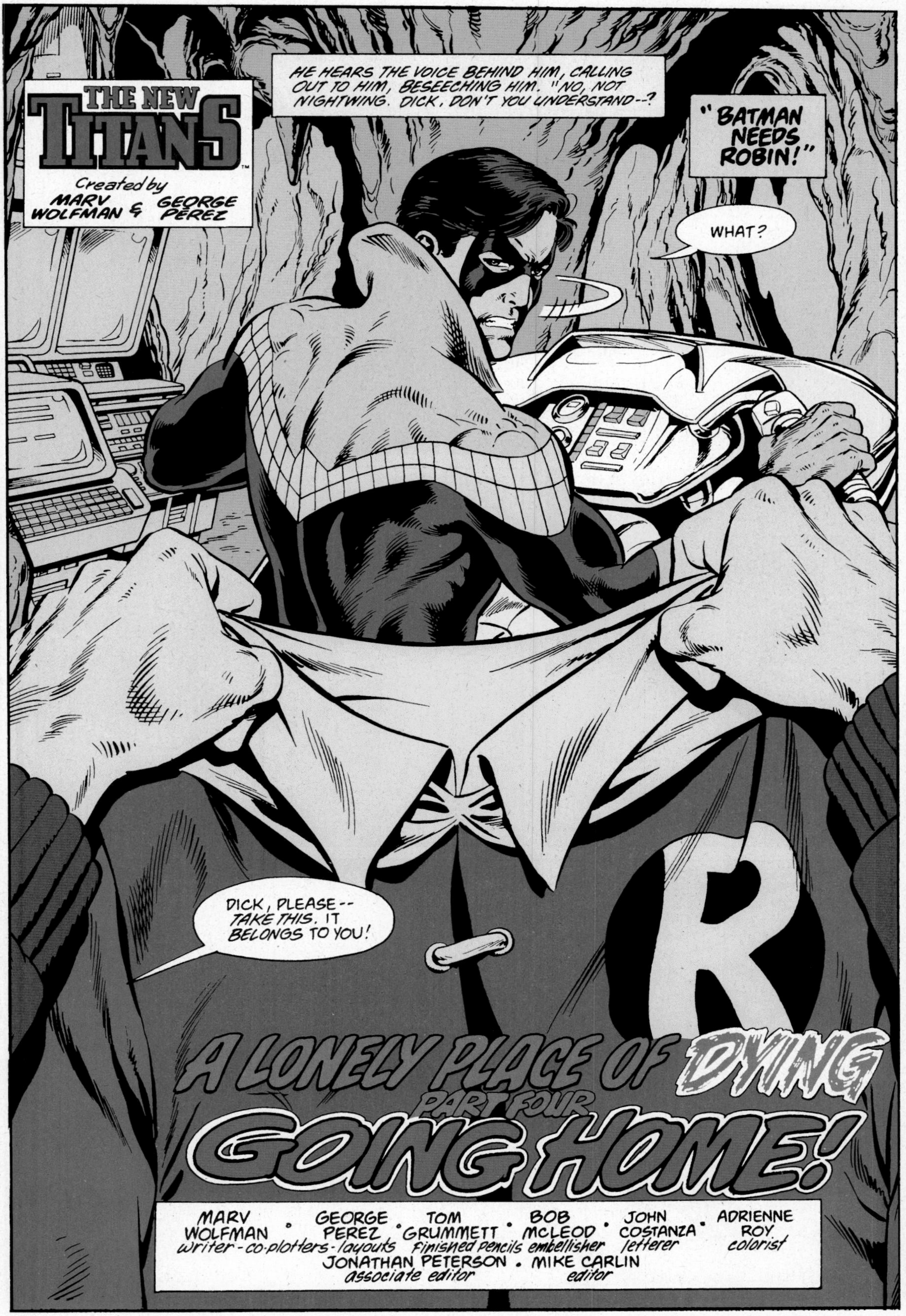
THE NEW TITANS
Created by MARV WOLFMAN & GEORGE PEREZ
HE HEARS THE VOICE BEHIND HIM, CALLING OUT TO HIM, BESEECHING HIM. "NO, NOT NIGHTWING. DICK, DON'T YOU UNDERSTAND--?
"BATMAN NEEDS ROBIN!"
WHAT?
DICK, PLEASE-- TAKE THIS. IT BELONGS TO YOU!
A LONELY PLACE OF DYING
PART FOUR
GOING HOME!
MARV WOLFMAN • GEORGE PEREZ writer-co-plotters-layouts • TOM GRUMMETT finished pencils • BOB McLEOD embellisher • JOHN COSTANZA letterer • ADRIENNE ROY colorist
JONATHAN PETERSON associate editor • MIKE CARLIN editor

WHERE DID YOU *GET* THIS?

FROM THE CASE IN THE TROPHY ROOM. I-IT'S *YOURS!*

I *THOUGHT*--

NO! YOU *DIDN'T* THINK. THAT'S THE PROBLEM...

SIR. THE LAD MAY HAVE A *POINT.*

MASTER BRUCE HAS NOT BEEN THE SAME--

--SINCE HE LOST ROBIN...

...A *SECOND* TIME.

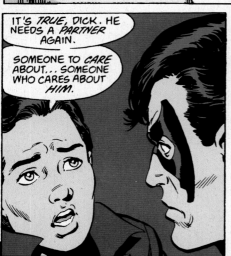

IT'S *TRUE*, DICK. HE NEEDS A *PARTNER* AGAIN.

SOMEONE TO *CARE* ABOUT... SOMEONE WHO CARES ABOUT *HIM.*

I DON'T *BELIEVE* THIS. THAT MAN *RAISED* ME.

I'VE GONE THROUGH HELL *WITH* HIM AND *BECAUSE* OF HIM.

DON'T *LECTURE* ME ABOUT HIM UNTIL YOU'VE *CARED* FOR HIM AND *LOVED* HIM AS LONG AS I HAVE.

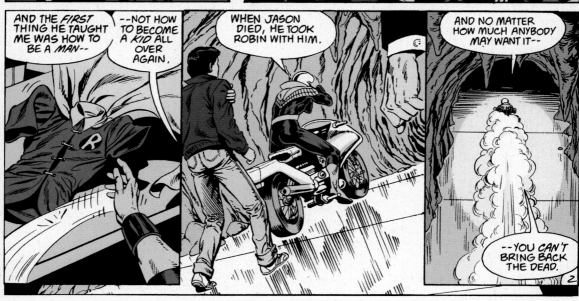

AND THE *FIRST* THING HE TAUGHT ME WAS HOW TO BE A *MAN*--

--NOT HOW TO BECOME A *KID* ALL OVER AGAIN.

WHEN JASON DIED, HE TOOK ROBIN WITH HIM.

AND NO MATTER HOW MUCH ANYBODY MAY WANT IT--

--YOU *CAN'T* BRING BACK THE DEAD.

2

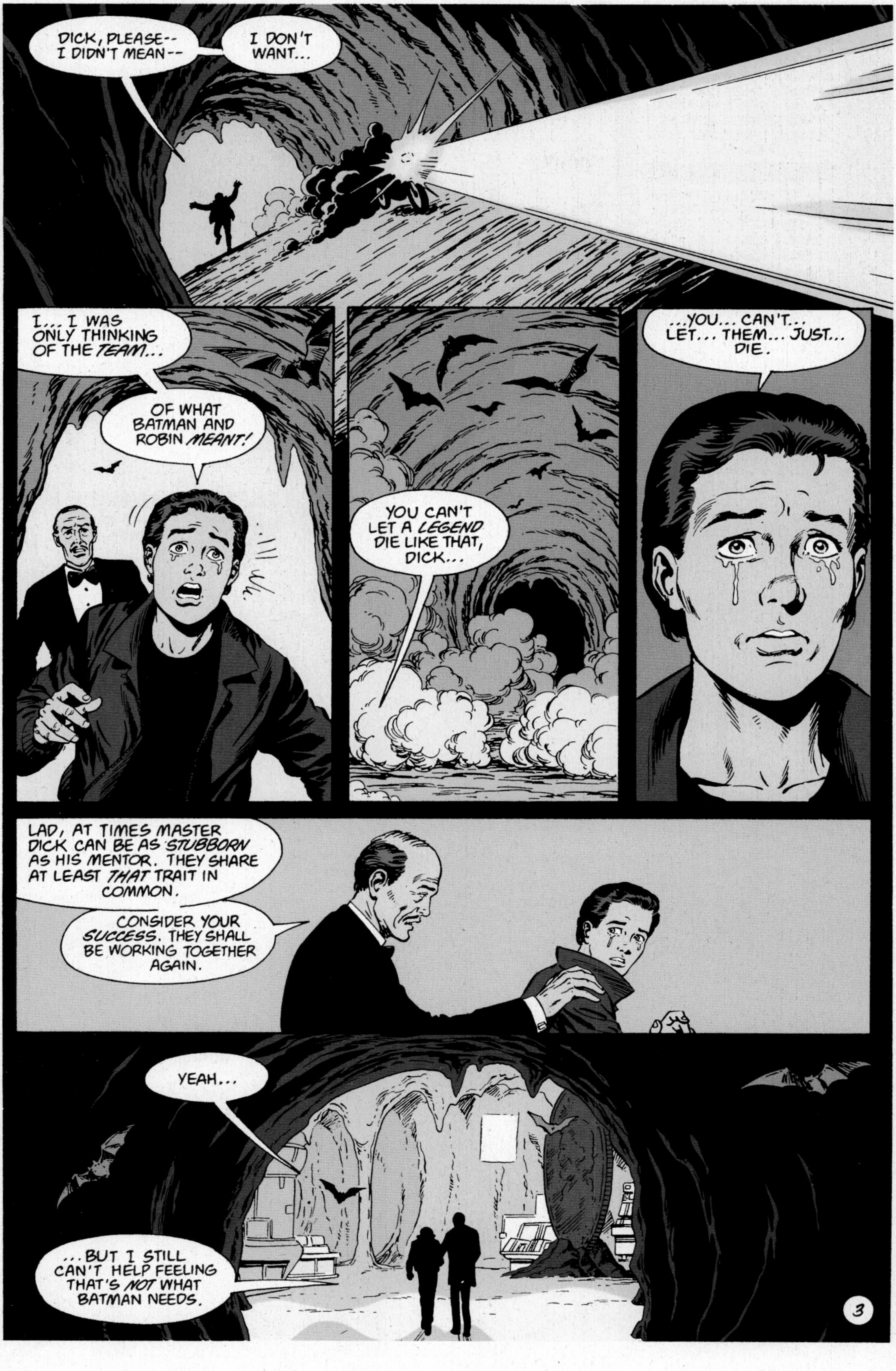
DICK, PLEASE-- I DIDN'T MEAN--
I DON'T WANT...
I... I WAS ONLY THINKING OF THE TEAM...
OF WHAT BATMAN AND ROBIN MEANT!
YOU CAN'T LET A LEGEND DIE LIKE THAT, DICK...
...YOU... CAN'T... LET... THEM... JUST... DIE.
LAD, AT TIMES MASTER DICK CAN BE AS STUBBORN AS HIS MENTOR. THEY SHARE AT LEAST THAT TRAIT IN COMMON.
CONSIDER YOUR SUCCESS. THEY SHALL BE WORKING TOGETHER AGAIN.
YEAH...
...BUT I STILL CAN'T HELP FEELING THAT'S NOT WHAT BATMAN NEEDS.
3

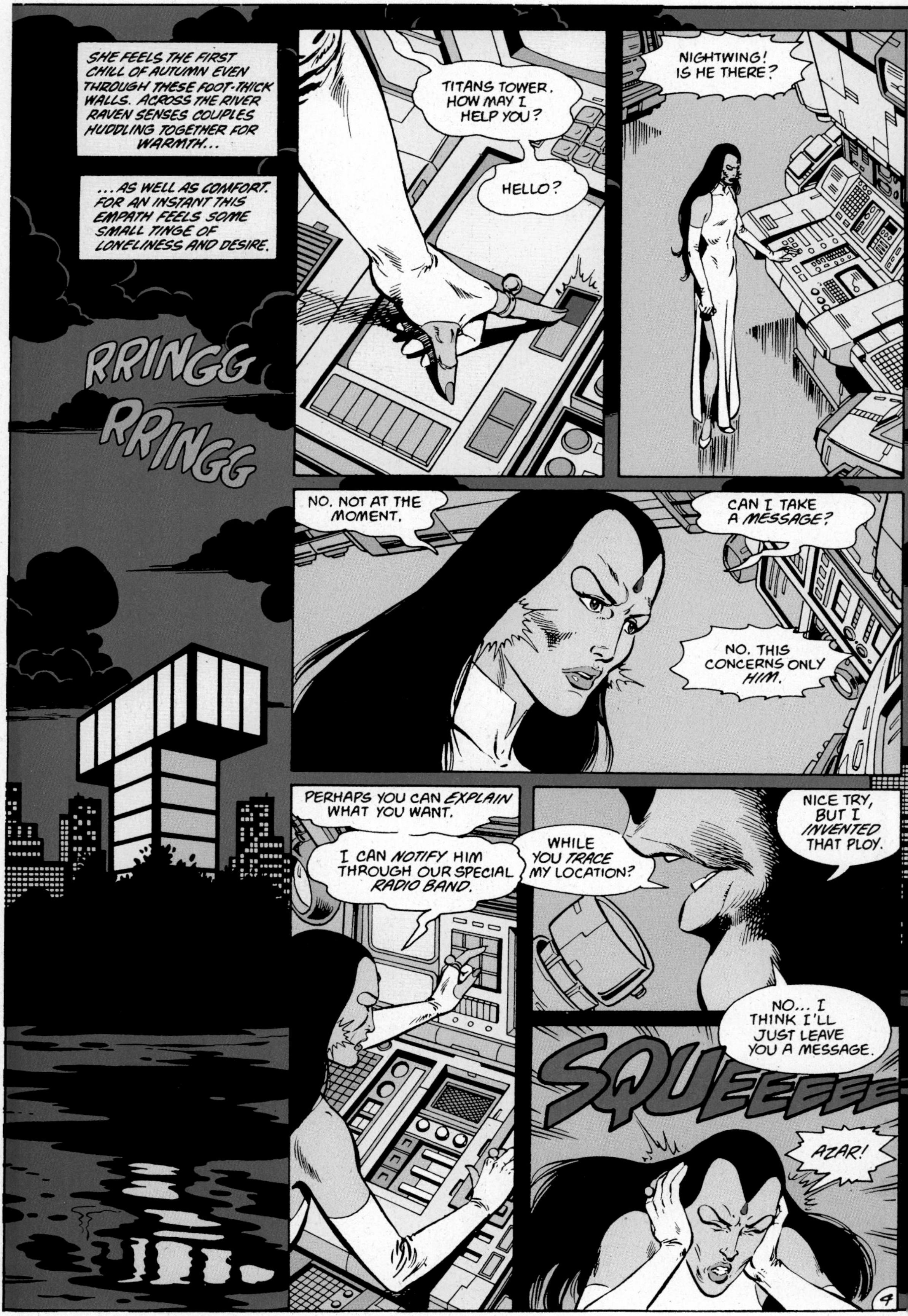

SHE FEELS THE FIRST CHILL OF AUTUMN EVEN THROUGH THESE FOOT-THICK WALLS. ACROSS THE RIVER RAVEN SENSES COUPLES HUDDLING TOGETHER FOR WARMTH...
...AS WELL AS COMFORT. FOR AN INSTANT THIS EMPATH FEELS SOME SMALL TINGE OF LONELINESS AND DESIRE.
RRINGG
RRINGG
TITANS TOWER. HOW MAY I HELP YOU?
HELLO?
NIGHTWING! IS HE THERE?
NO. NOT AT THE MOMENT.
CAN I TAKE A MESSAGE?
NO. THIS CONCERNS ONLY HIM.
PERHAPS YOU CAN EXPLAIN WHAT YOU WANT.
I CAN NOTIFY HIM THROUGH OUR SPECIAL RADIO BAND.
WHILE YOU TRACE MY LOCATION?
NICE TRY, BUT I INVENTED THAT PLOY.
NO... I THINK I'LL JUST LEAVE YOU A MESSAGE.
SQUEEEEE
AZAR!
4

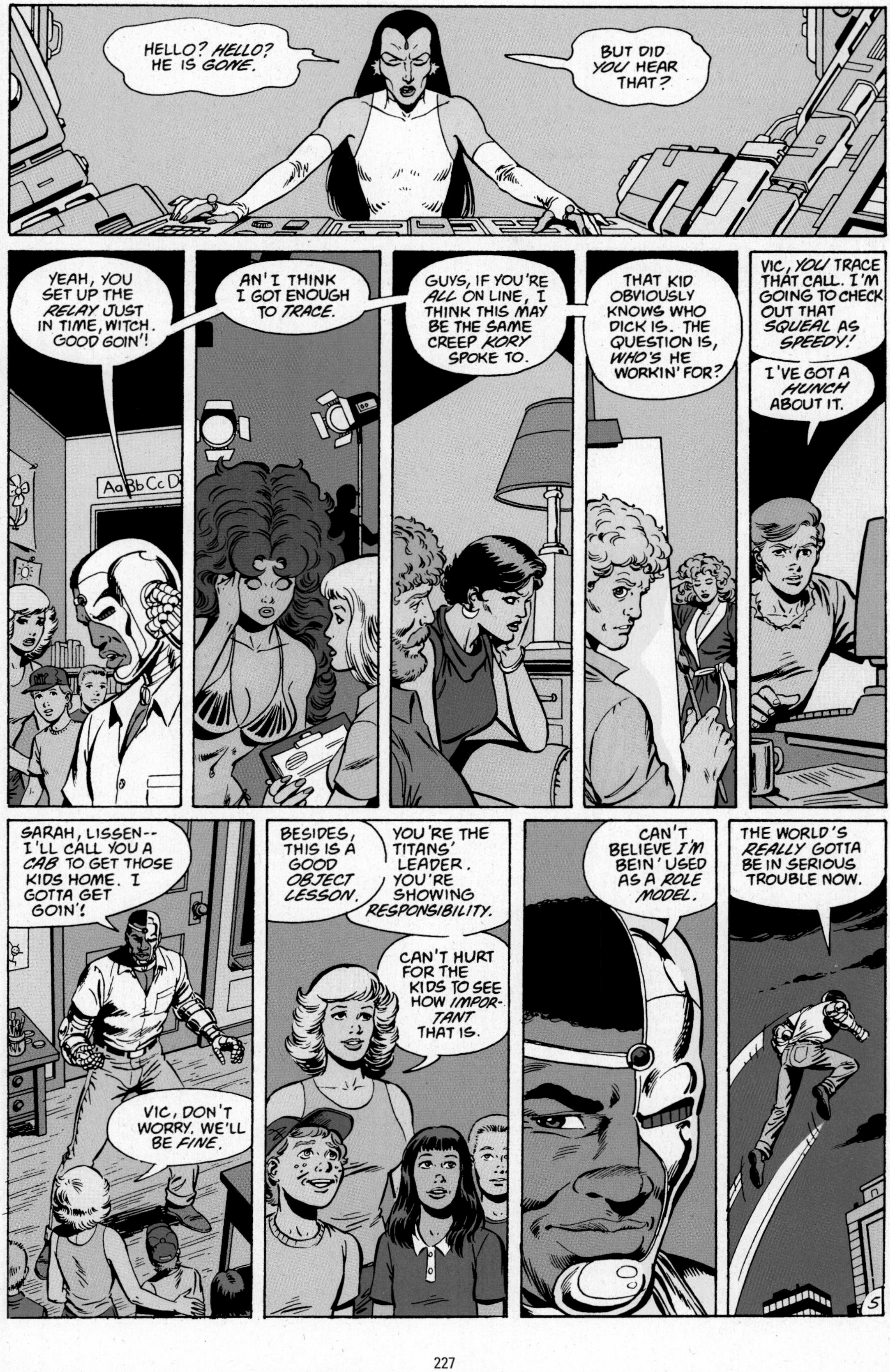
HELLO? HELLO? HE IS GONE.
BUT DID YOU HEAR THAT?
YEAH, YOU SET UP THE RELAY JUST IN TIME, WITCH. GOOD GOIN'!
AN' I THINK I GOT ENOUGH TO TRACE.
GUYS, IF YOU'RE ALL ON LINE, I THINK THIS MAY BE THE SAME CREEP KORY SPOKE TO.
THAT KID OBVIOUSLY KNOWS WHO DICK IS. THE QUESTION IS, WHO'S HE WORKIN' FOR?
VIC, YOU TRACE THAT CALL. I'M GOING TO CHECK OUT THAT SQUEAL AS SPEEDY!
I'VE GOT A HUNCH ABOUT IT.
Aa Bb Cc D
SARAH, LISSEN-- I'LL CALL YOU A CAB TO GET THOSE KIDS HOME. I GOTTA GET GOIN'!
VIC, DON'T WORRY. WE'LL BE FINE.
BESIDES, THIS IS A GOOD OBJECT LESSON.
YOU'RE THE TITANS' LEADER. YOU'RE SHOWING RESPONSIBILITY.
CAN'T HURT FOR THE KIDS TO SEE HOW IMPOR-TANT THAT IS.
CAN'T BELIEVE I'M BEIN' USED AS A ROLE MODEL.
THE WORLD'S REALLY GOTTA BE IN SERIOUS TROUBLE NOW.
5

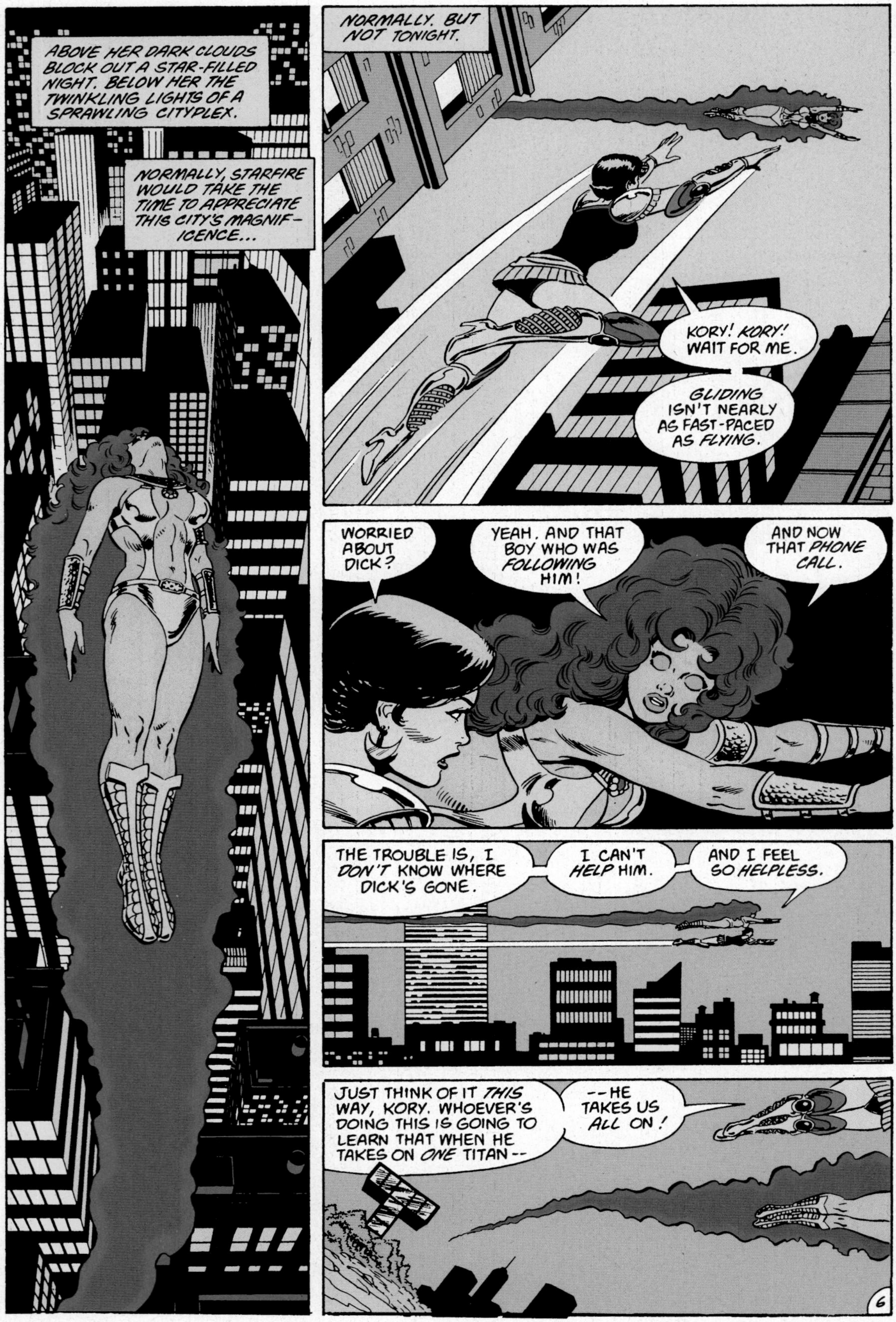
ABOVE HER DARK CLOUDS BLOCK OUT A STAR-FILLED NIGHT. BELOW HER THE TWINKLING LIGHTS OF A SPRAWLING CITYPLEX.
NORMALLY, STARFIRE WOULD TAKE THE TIME TO APPRECIATE THIS CITY'S MAGNIF-ICENCE...
NORMALLY. BUT NOT TONIGHT.
KORY! KORY! WAIT FOR ME.
GLIDING ISN'T NEARLY AS FAST-PACED AS FLYING.
WORRIED ABOUT DICK?
YEAH. AND THAT BOY WHO WAS FOLLOWING HIM!
AND NOW THAT PHONE CALL.
THE TROUBLE IS, I DON'T KNOW WHERE DICK'S GONE.
I CAN'T HELP HIM.
AND I FEEL SO HELPLESS.
JUST THINK OF IT THIS WAY, KORY. WHOEVER'S DOING THIS IS GOING TO LEARN THAT WHEN HE TAKES ON ONE TITAN --
-- HE TAKES US ALL ON!
6

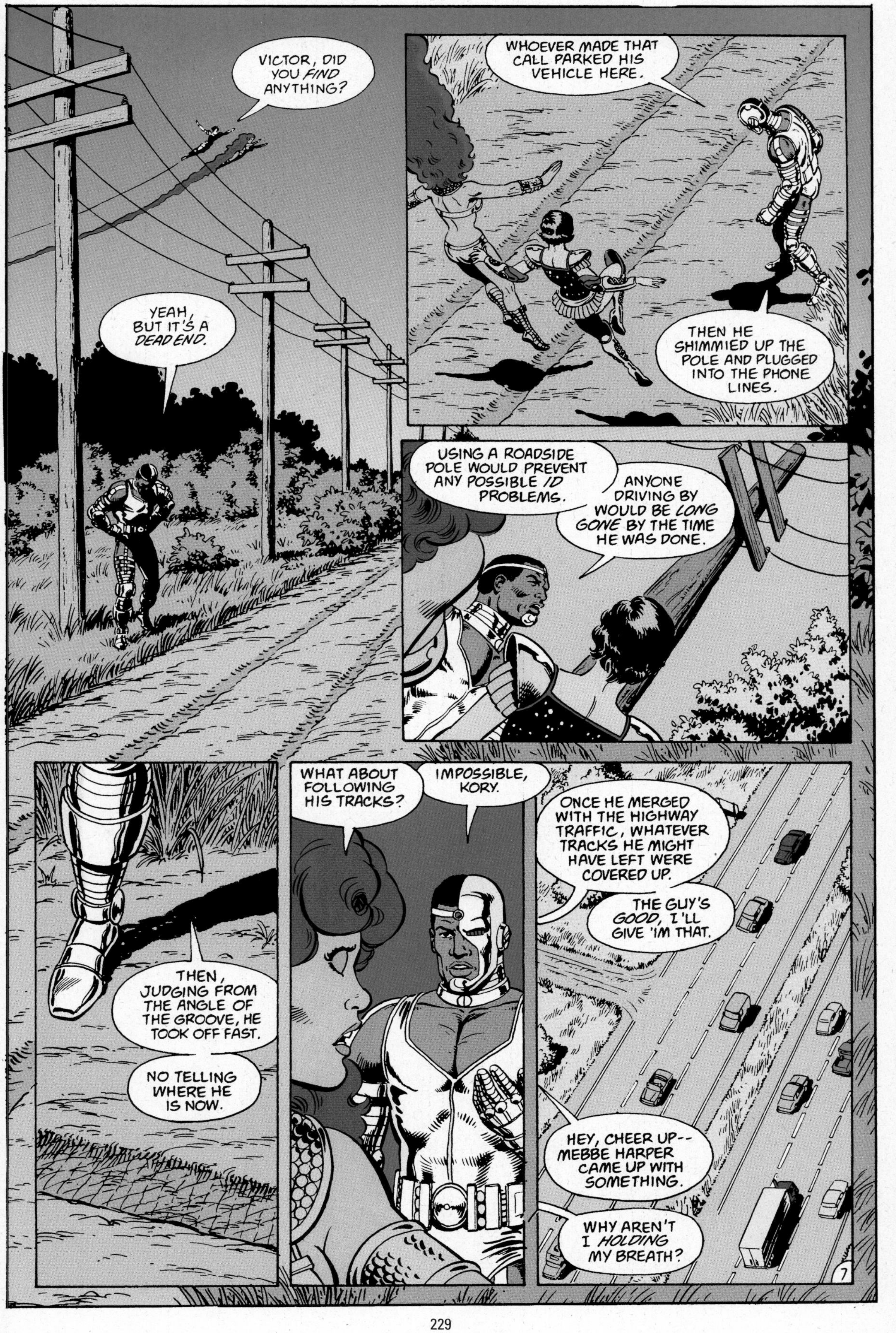
VICTOR, DID YOU FIND ANYTHING?
YEAH, BUT IT'S A DEAD END.
WHOEVER MADE THAT CALL PARKED HIS VEHICLE HERE.
THEN HE SHIMMIED UP THE POLE AND PLUGGED INTO THE PHONE LINES.
USING A ROADSIDE POLE WOULD PREVENT ANY POSSIBLE ID PROBLEMS.
ANYONE DRIVING BY WOULD BE LONG GONE BY THE TIME HE WAS DONE.
THEN, JUDGING FROM THE ANGLE OF THE GROOVE, HE TOOK OFF FAST.
NO TELLING WHERE HE IS NOW.
WHAT ABOUT FOLLOWING HIS TRACKS?
IMPOSSIBLE, KORY.
ONCE HE MERGED WITH THE HIGHWAY TRAFFIC, WHATEVER TRACKS HE MIGHT HAVE LEFT WERE COVERED UP.
THE GUY'S GOOD, I'LL GIVE 'IM THAT.
HEY, CHEER UP-- MEBBE HARPER CAME UP WITH SOMETHING.
WHY AREN'T I HOLDING MY BREATH?
7

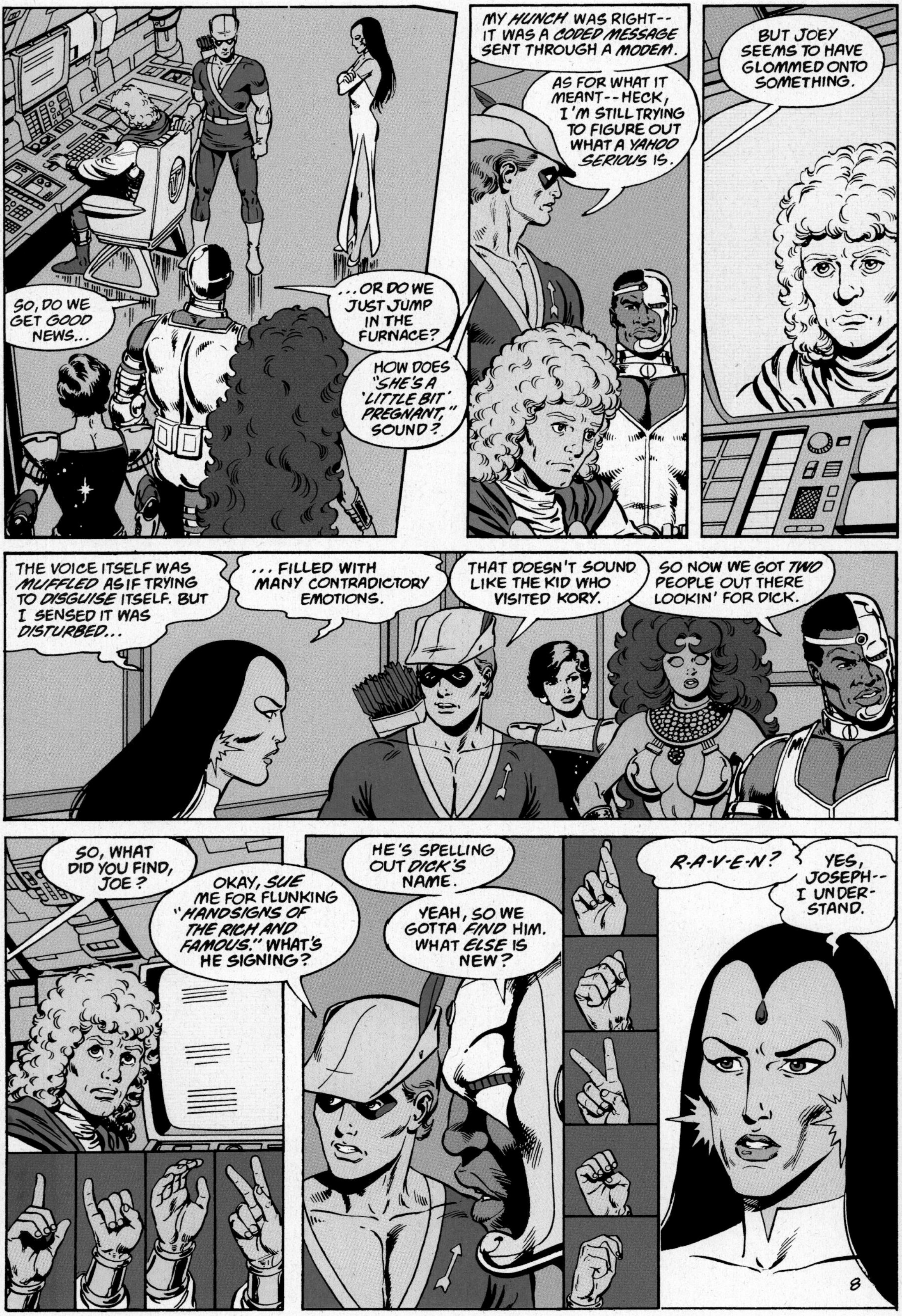
SO, DO WE GET GOOD NEWS...
...OR DO WE JUST JUMP IN THE FURNACE?
HOW DOES "SHE'S A 'LITTLE BIT' PREGNANT," SOUND?
MY HUNCH WAS RIGHT-- IT WAS A CODED MESSAGE SENT THROUGH A MODEM.
AS FOR WHAT IT MEANT--HECK, I'M STILL TRYING TO FIGURE OUT WHAT A YAHOO SERIOUS IS.
BUT JOEY SEEMS TO HAVE GLOMMED ONTO SOMETHING.
THE VOICE ITSELF WAS MUFFLED AS IF TRYING TO DISGUISE ITSELF. BUT I SENSED IT WAS DISTURBED...
... FILLED WITH MANY CONTRADICTORY EMOTIONS.
THAT DOESN'T SOUND LIKE THE KID WHO VISITED KORY.
SO NOW WE GOT TWO PEOPLE OUT THERE LOOKIN' FOR DICK.
SO, WHAT DID YOU FIND, JOE?
OKAY, SUE ME FOR FLUNKING "HANDSIGNS OF THE RICH AND FAMOUS." WHAT'S HE SIGNING?
HE'S SPELLING OUT DICK'S NAME.
YEAH, SO WE GOTTA FIND HIM. WHAT ELSE IS NEW?
R-A-V-E-N?
YES, JOSEPH-- I UNDERSTAND.
8

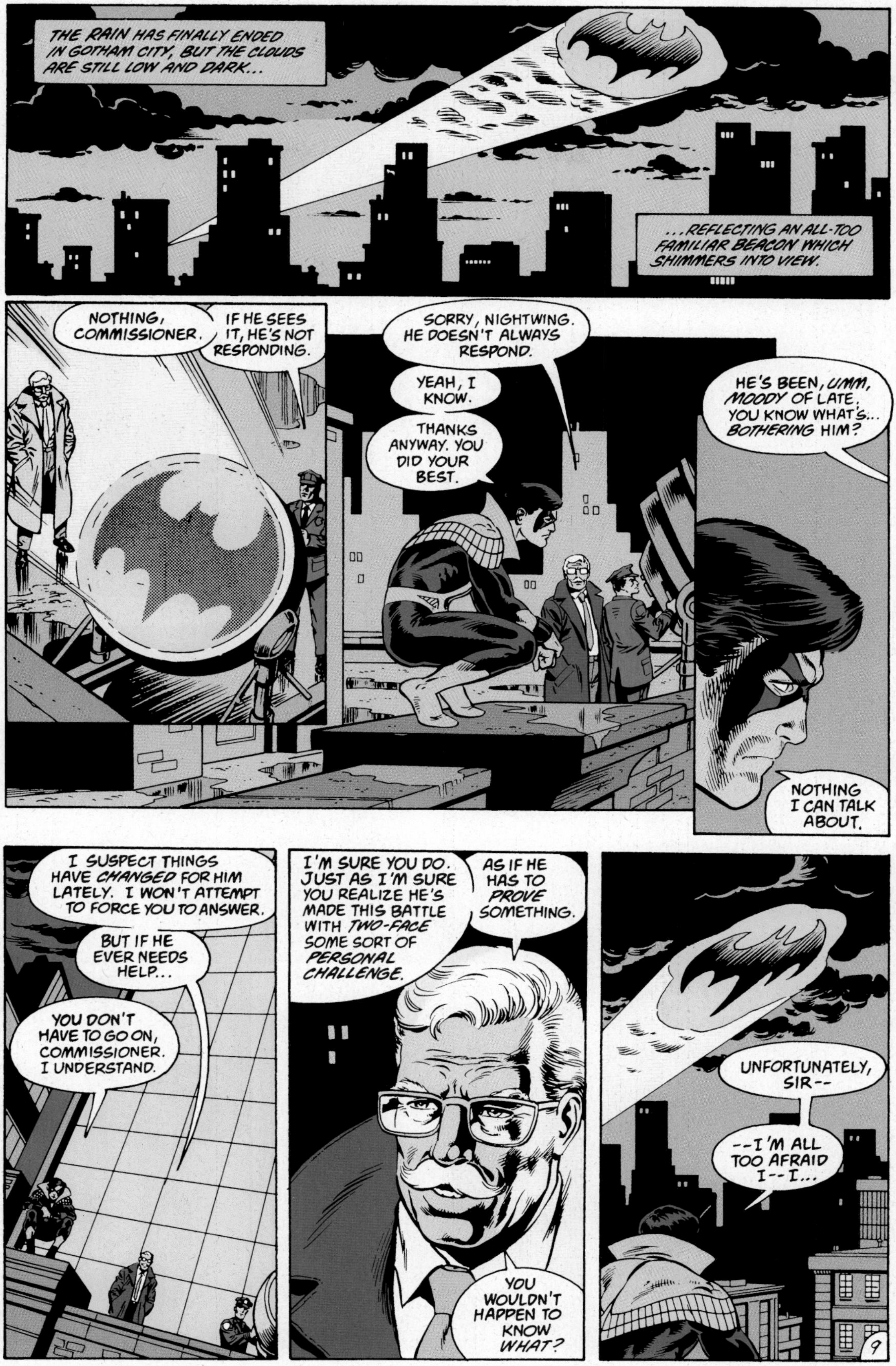
THE RAIN HAS FINALLY ENDED IN GOTHAM CITY, BUT THE CLOUDS ARE STILL LOW AND DARK...
...REFLECTING AN ALL-TOO FAMILIAR BEACON WHICH SHIMMERS INTO VIEW.
NOTHING, COMMISSIONER.
IF HE SEES IT, HE'S NOT RESPONDING.
SORRY, NIGHTWING. HE DOESN'T ALWAYS RESPOND.
YEAH, I KNOW.
THANKS ANYWAY. YOU DID YOUR BEST.
HE'S BEEN, UMM, MOODY OF LATE. YOU KNOW WHAT'S... BOTHERING HIM?
NOTHING I CAN TALK ABOUT.
I SUSPECT THINGS HAVE CHANGED FOR HIM LATELY. I WON'T ATTEMPT TO FORCE YOU TO ANSWER.
BUT IF HE EVER NEEDS HELP...
YOU DON'T HAVE TO GO ON, COMMISSIONER. I UNDERSTAND.
I'M SURE YOU DO. JUST AS I'M SURE YOU REALIZE HE'S MADE THIS BATTLE WITH TWO-FACE SOME SORT OF PERSONAL CHALLENGE.
AS IF HE HAS TO PROVE SOMETHING.
YOU WOULDN'T HAPPEN TO KNOW WHAT?
UNFORTUNATELY, SIR--
--I'M ALL TOO AFRAID I--I...
9

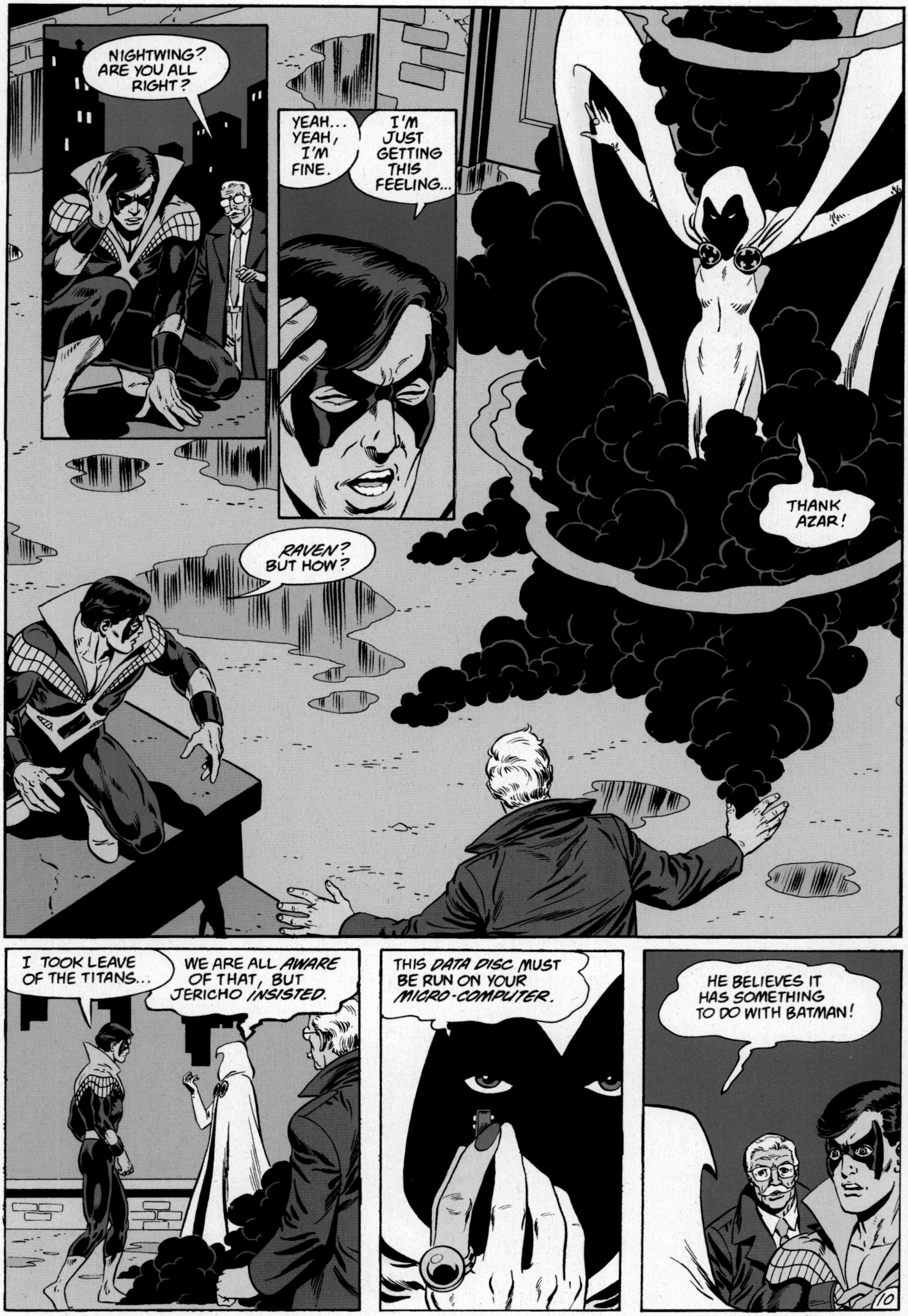

NIGHTWING? ARE YOU ALL RIGHT?
YEAH... YEAH, I'M FINE.
I'M JUST GETTING THIS FEELING...
THANK AZAR!
RAVEN? BUT HOW?
I TOOK LEAVE OF THE TITANS...
WE ARE ALL AWARE OF THAT, BUT JERICHO INSISTED.
THIS DATA DISC MUST BE RUN ON YOUR MICRO-COMPUTER.
HE BELIEVES IT HAS SOMETHING TO DO WITH BATMAN!
10

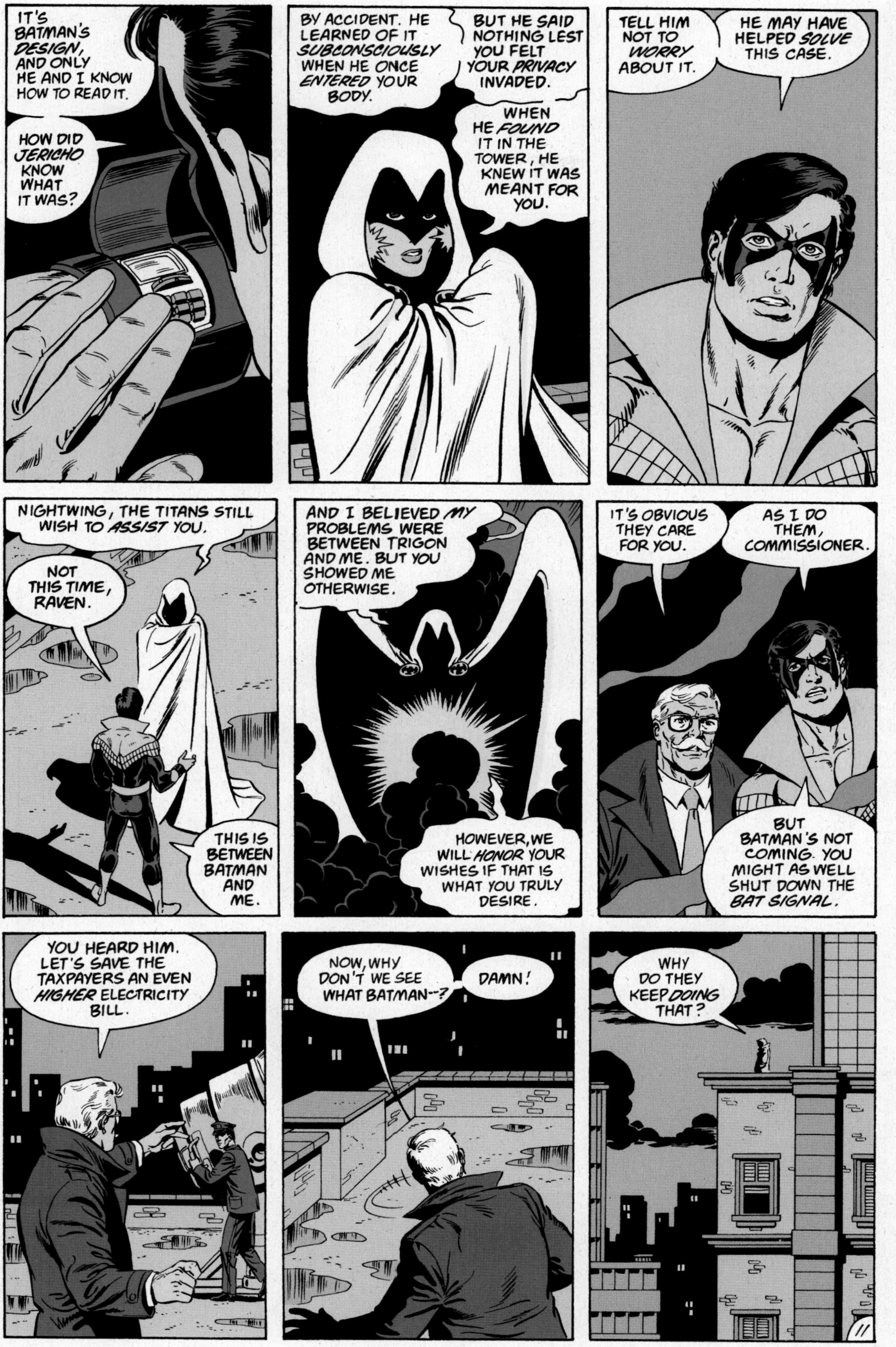
IT'S BATMAN'S DESIGN, AND ONLY HE AND I KNOW HOW TO READ IT.
HOW DID JERICHO KNOW WHAT IT WAS?
BY ACCIDENT. HE LEARNED OF IT SUBCONSCIOUSLY WHEN HE ONCE ENTERED YOUR BODY.
BUT HE SAID NOTHING LEST YOU FELT YOUR PRIVACY INVADED.
WHEN HE FOUND IT IN THE TOWER, HE KNEW IT WAS MEANT FOR YOU.
TELL HIM NOT TO WORRY ABOUT IT.
HE MAY HAVE HELPED SOLVE THIS CASE.
NIGHTWING, THE TITANS STILL WISH TO ASSIST YOU.
NOT THIS TIME, RAVEN.
THIS IS BETWEEN BATMAN AND ME.
AND I BELIEVED MY PROBLEMS WERE BETWEEN TRIGON AND ME. BUT YOU SHOWED ME OTHERWISE.
HOWEVER, WE WILL HONOR YOUR WISHES IF THAT IS WHAT YOU TRULY DESIRE.
IT'S OBVIOUS THEY CARE FOR YOU.
AS I DO THEM, COMMISSIONER.
BUT BATMAN'S NOT COMING. YOU MIGHT AS WELL SHUT DOWN THE BAT SIGNAL.
YOU HEARD HIM. LET'S SAVE THE TAXPAYERS AN EVEN HIGHER ELECTRICITY BILL.
NOW, WHY DON'T WE SEE WHAT BATMAN--?
DAMN!
WHY DO THEY KEEP DOING THAT?
11

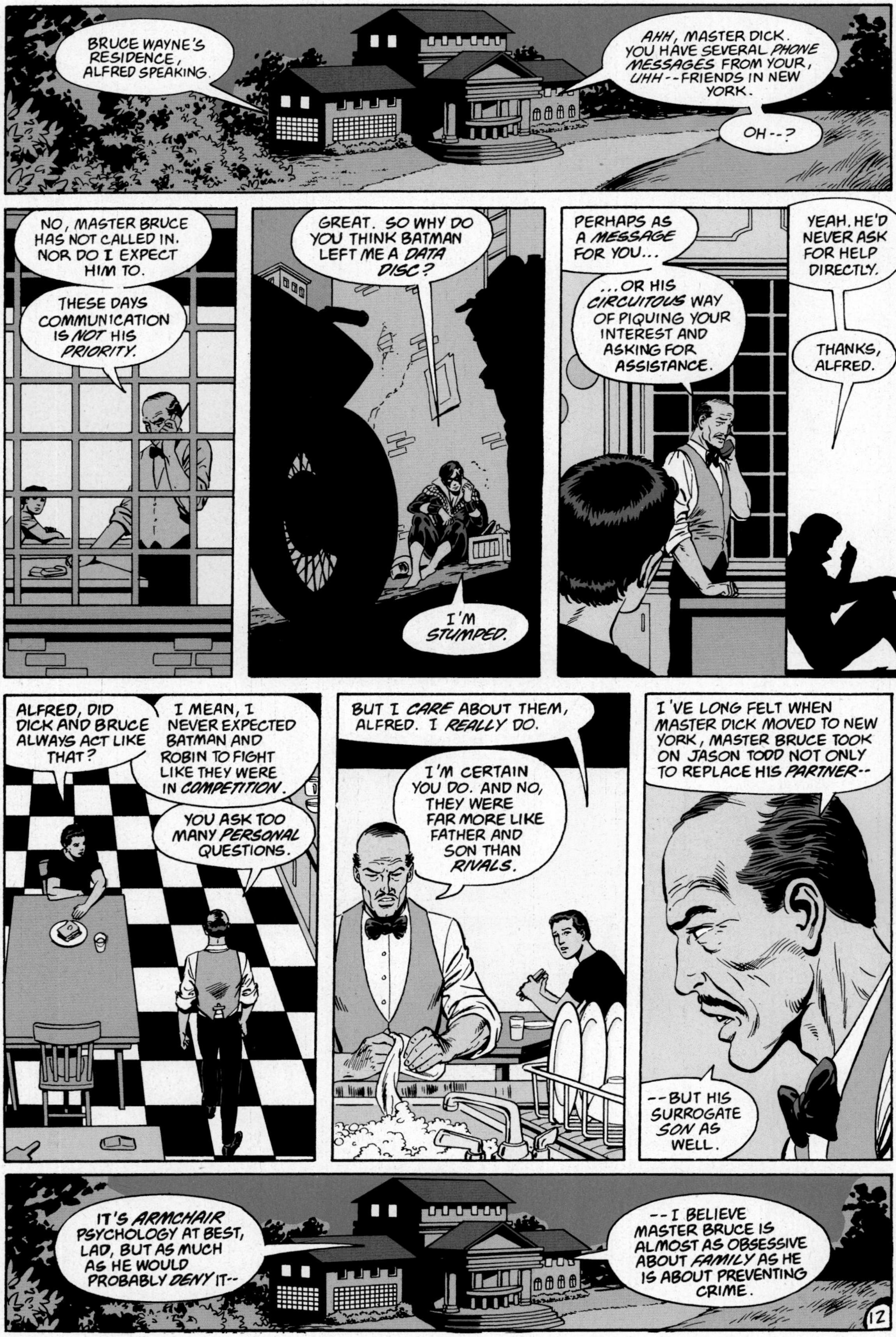
BRUCE WAYNE'S RESIDENCE, ALFRED SPEAKING.
AHH, MASTER DICK. YOU HAVE SEVERAL PHONE MESSAGES FROM YOUR, UHH--FRIENDS IN NEW YORK.
OH--?
NO, MASTER BRUCE HAS NOT CALLED IN. NOR DO I EXPECT HIM TO.
THESE DAYS COMMUNICATION IS NOT HIS PRIORITY.
GREAT. SO WHY DO YOU THINK BATMAN LEFT ME A DATA DISC?
I'M STUMPED.
PERHAPS AS A MESSAGE FOR YOU...
...OR HIS CIRCUITOUS WAY OF PIQUING YOUR INTEREST AND ASKING FOR ASSISTANCE.
YEAH. HE'D NEVER ASK FOR HELP DIRECTLY.
THANKS, ALFRED.
ALFRED, DID DICK AND BRUCE ALWAYS ACT LIKE THAT?
I MEAN, I NEVER EXPECTED BATMAN AND ROBIN TO FIGHT LIKE THEY WERE IN COMPETITION.
YOU ASK TOO MANY PERSONAL QUESTIONS.
BUT I CARE ABOUT THEM, ALFRED. I REALLY DO.
I'M CERTAIN YOU DO. AND NO, THEY WERE FAR MORE LIKE FATHER AND SON THAN RIVALS.
I'VE LONG FELT WHEN MASTER DICK MOVED TO NEW YORK, MASTER BRUCE TOOK ON JASON TODD NOT ONLY TO REPLACE HIS PARTNER--
--BUT HIS SURROGATE SON AS WELL.
IT'S ARMCHAIR PSYCHOLOGY AT BEST, LAD, BUT AS MUCH AS HE WOULD PROBABLY DENY IT--
--I BELIEVE MASTER BRUCE IS ALMOST AS OBSESSIVE ABOUT FAMILY AS HE IS ABOUT PREVENTING CRIME.
12

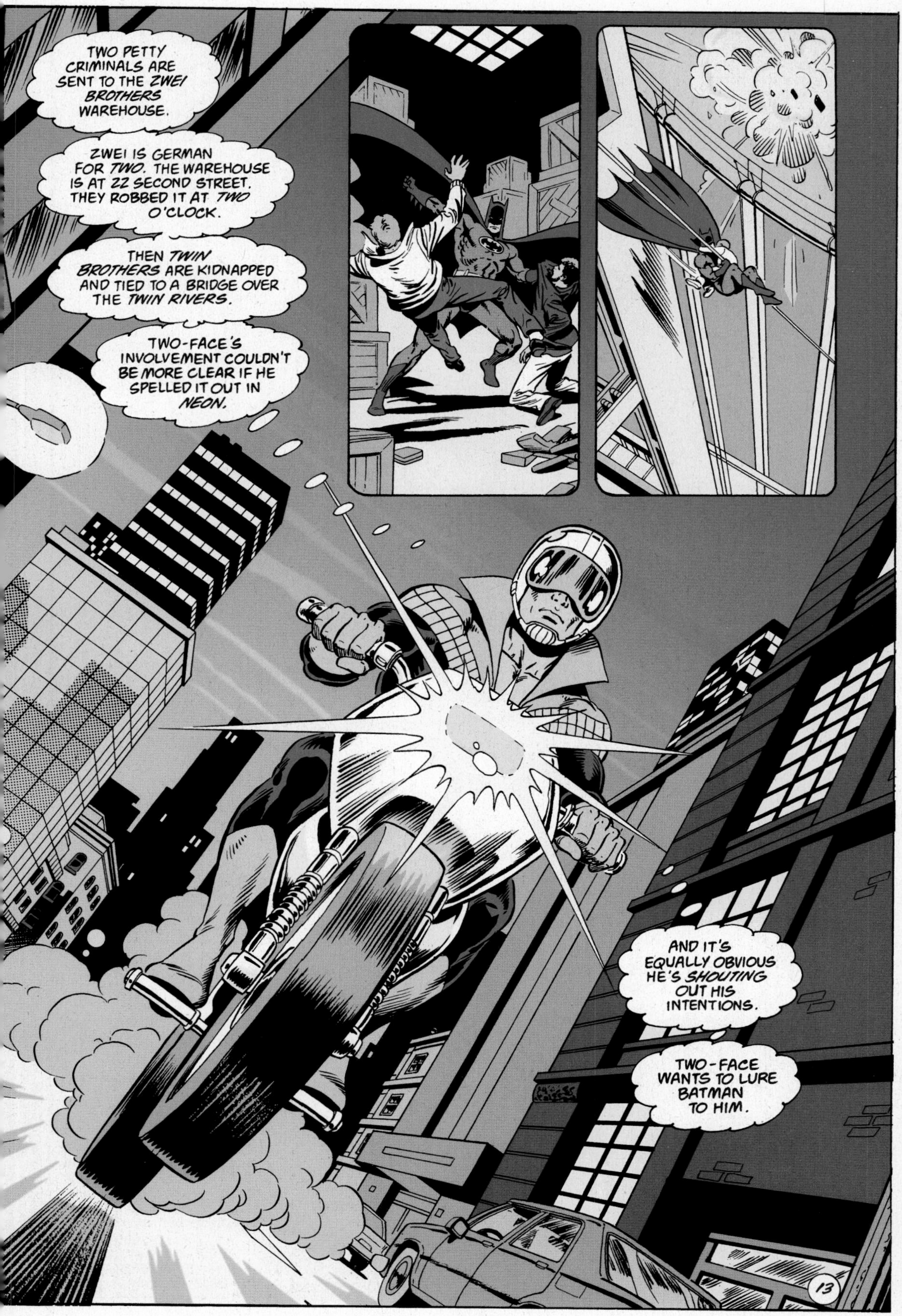
TWO PETTY CRIMINALS ARE SENT TO THE ZWEI BROTHERS WAREHOUSE.
ZWEI IS GERMAN FOR TWO. THE WAREHOUSE IS AT 22 SECOND STREET. THEY ROBBED IT AT TWO O'CLOCK.
THEN TWIN BROTHERS ARE KIDNAPPED AND TIED TO A BRIDGE OVER THE TWIN RIVERS.
TWO-FACE'S INVOLVEMENT COULDN'T BE MORE CLEAR IF HE SPELLED IT OUT IN NEON.
AND IT'S EQUALLY OBVIOUS HE'S SHOUTING OUT HIS INTENTIONS.
TWO-FACE WANTS TO LURE BATMAN TO HIM.
13

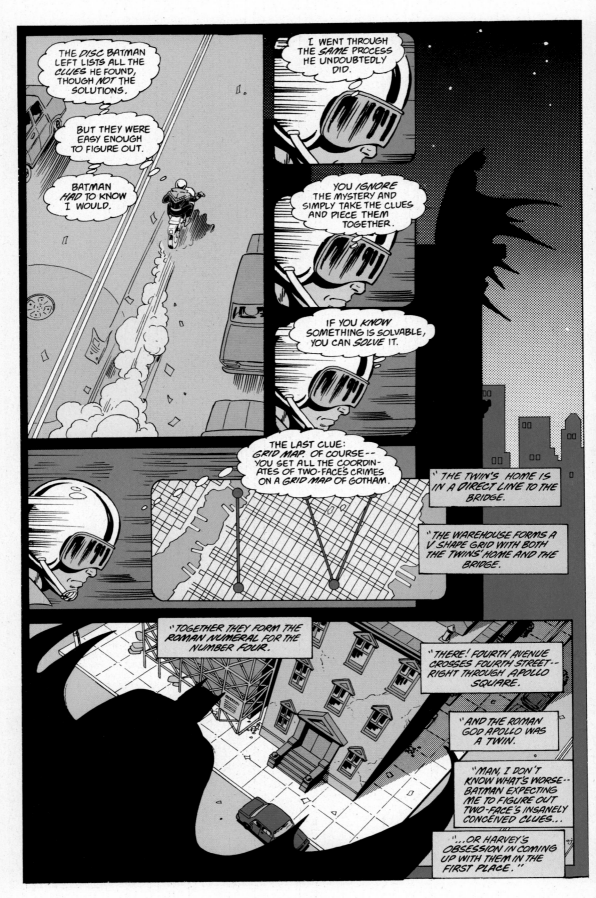

THE *DISC* BATMAN LEFT LISTS ALL THE *CLUES* HE FOUND, THOUGH *NOT* THE SOLUTIONS.

BUT THEY WERE EASY ENOUGH TO FIGURE OUT.

BATMAN *HAD* TO KNOW I WOULD.

I WENT THROUGH THE *SAME* PROCESS HE UNDOUBTEDLY DID.

YOU *IGNORE* THE MYSTERY AND SIMPLY TAKE THE CLUES AND PIECE THEM TOGETHER.

IF YOU *KNOW* SOMETHING IS SOLVABLE, YOU CAN *SOLVE* IT.

THE LAST CLUE: *GRID MAP.* OF COURSE-- YOU SET ALL THE COORDIN- ATES OF TWO-FACE'S CRIMES ON A *GRID MAP* OF GOTHAM.

"THE TWIN'S HOME IS IN A *DIRECT LINE* TO THE BRIDGE.

"THE WAREHOUSE FORMS A *V* SHAPE GRID WITH BOTH THE TWINS' HOME AND THE BRIDGE.

"TOGETHER THEY FORM THE ROMAN NUMERAL FOR THE NUMBER FOUR.

"THERE! *FOURTH* AVENUE CROSSES *FOURTH* STREET-- RIGHT THROUGH *APOLLO SQUARE.*

"AND THE ROMAN GOD *APOLLO* WAS A *TWIN.*

"MAN, I DON'T KNOW WHAT'S WORSE-- BATMAN EXPECTING ME TO FIGURE OUT TWO-FACE'S INSANELY CONCEIVED CLUES...

"...OR HARVEY'S OBSESSION IN COMING UP WITH THEM IN THE FIRST PLACE."

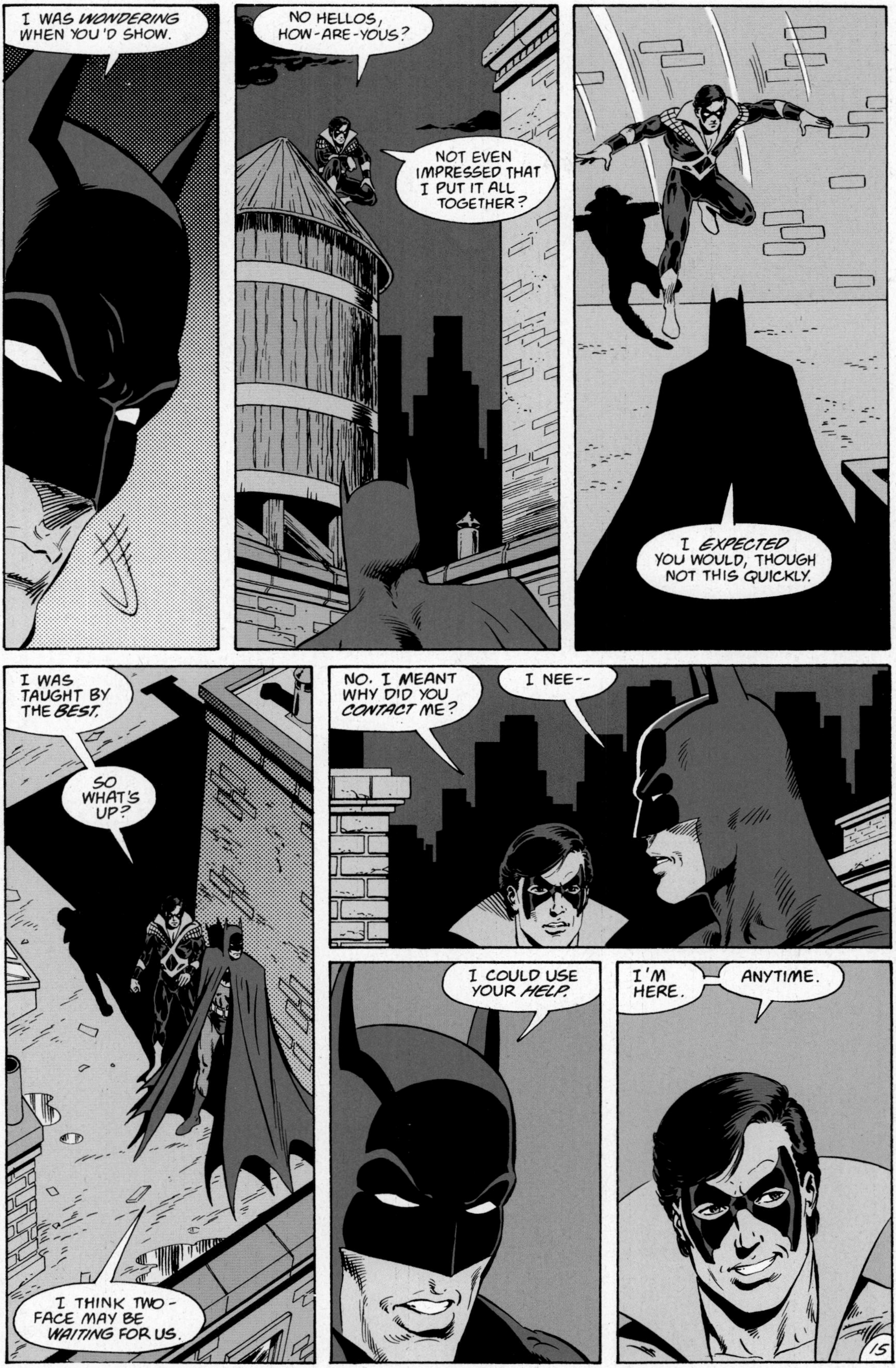
I WAS WONDERING WHEN YOU'D SHOW.
NO HELLOS, HOW-ARE-YOUS?
NOT EVEN IMPRESSED THAT I PUT IT ALL TOGETHER?
I EXPECTED YOU WOULD, THOUGH NOT THIS QUICKLY.
I WAS TAUGHT BY THE BEST.
SO WHAT'S UP?
I THINK TWO-FACE MAY BE WAITING FOR US.
NO. I MEANT WHY DID YOU CONTACT ME?
I NEE--
I COULD USE YOUR HELP.
I'M HERE.
ANYTIME.
15

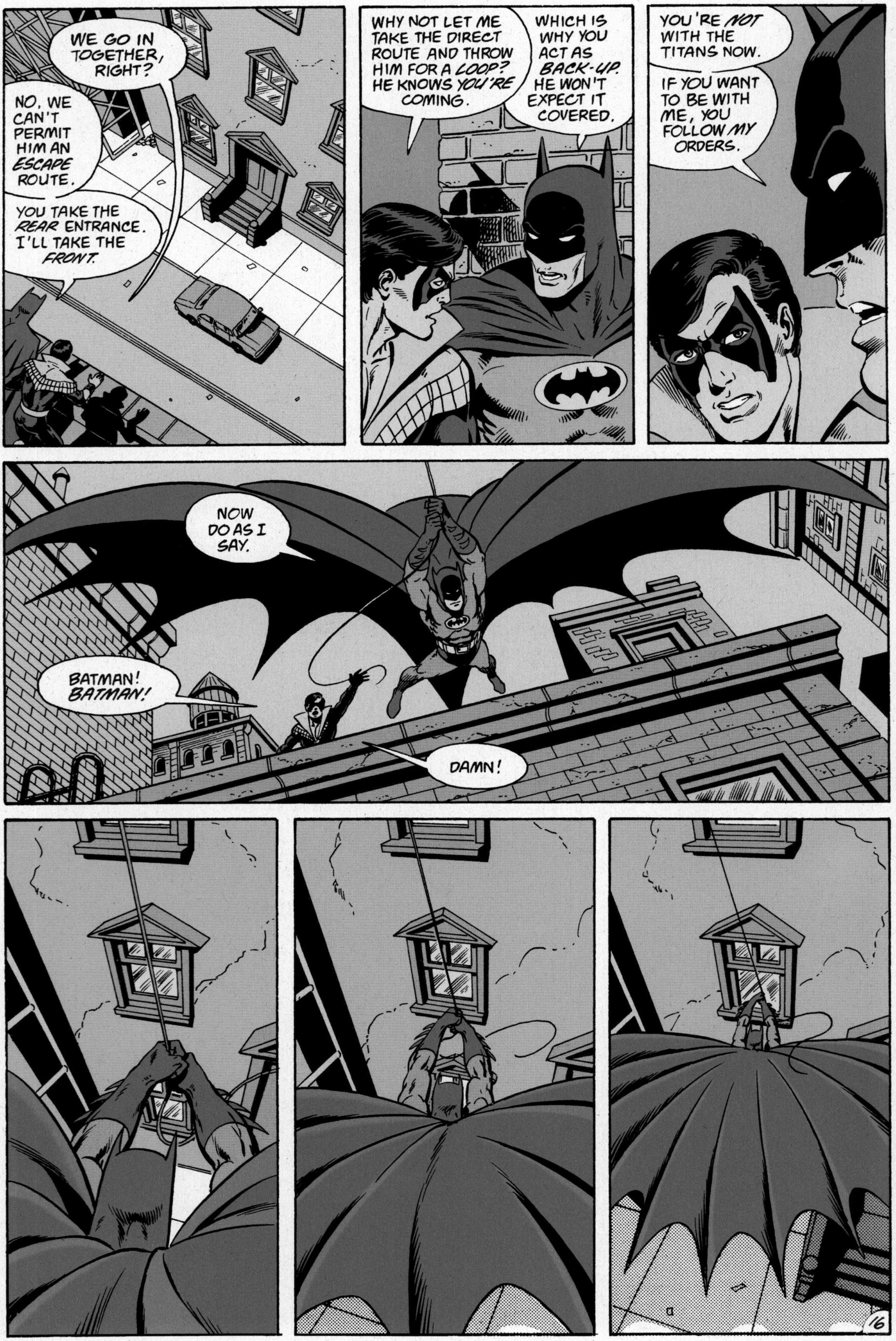

WE GO IN TOGETHER, RIGHT?
NO, WE CAN'T PERMIT HIM AN ESCAPE ROUTE.
YOU TAKE THE REAR ENTRANCE. I'LL TAKE THE FRONT.
WHY NOT LET ME TAKE THE DIRECT ROUTE AND THROW HIM FOR A LOOP? HE KNOWS YOU'RE COMING.
WHICH IS WHY YOU ACT AS BACK-UP. HE WON'T EXPECT IT COVERED.
YOU'RE NOT WITH THE TITANS NOW.
IF YOU WANT TO BE WITH ME, YOU FOLLOW MY ORDERS.
NOW DO AS I SAY.
BATMAN! BATMAN!
DAMN!
16

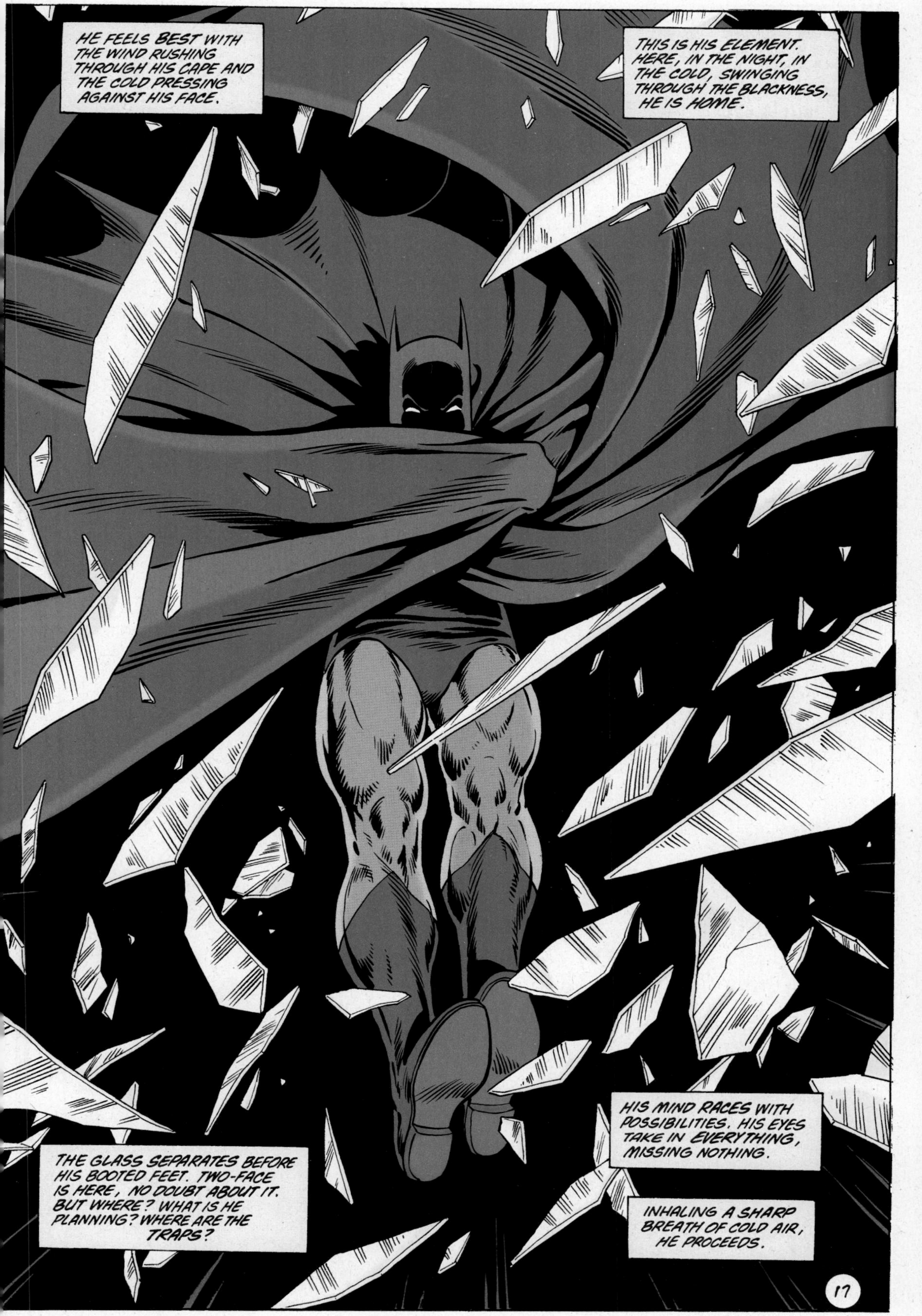
HE FEELS BEST WITH THE WIND RUSHING THROUGH HIS CAPE AND THE COLD PRESSING AGAINST HIS FACE.
THIS IS HIS ELEMENT. HERE, IN THE NIGHT, IN THE COLD, SWINGING THROUGH THE BLACKNESS, HE IS HOME.
THE GLASS SEPARATES BEFORE HIS BOOTED FEET. TWO-FACE IS HERE, NO DOUBT ABOUT IT. BUT WHERE? WHAT IS HE PLANNING? WHERE ARE THE TRAPS?
HIS MIND RACES WITH POSSIBILITIES. HIS EYES TAKE IN EVERYTHING, MISSING NOTHING.
INHALING A SHARP BREATH OF COLD AIR, HE PROCEEDS.
17

TIM IS RIGHT-- BATMAN'S ACTING LIKE A BULL IN A CHINA SHOP.

BUT HE'S NOT *INVULNERABLE.* AND HE'S BARELY PAYING ATTENTION TO THE DANGER.

HE TAUGHT ME TO BE *CAREFUL.* TO USE *STEALTH.*

I HAD TO *LEARN* TO BE CAUTIOUS... TO BE EXTRA CAREFUL.

BUT YOU DON'T *BARGE* IN ANYWHERE, NO MATTER WHAT.

TWO ENTRANCES THROUGH THE BACK. THIS WINDOW OR THE OLD *COAL CHUTE.*

BUT I'VE GOTTEN *TOO BIG* FOR THAT.

AND EVEN THE *WINDOW* IS GOING TO BE A *TIGHT SQUEEZE.*

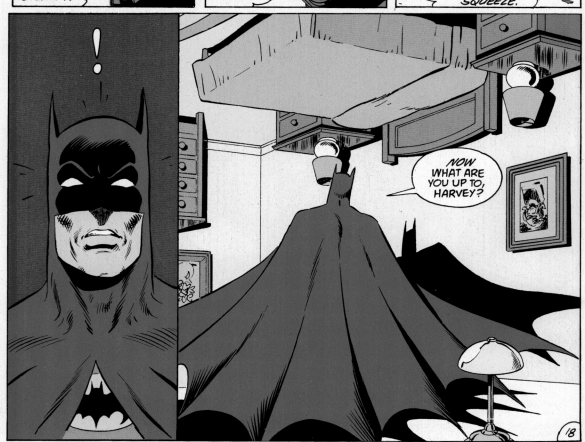

!

NOW WHAT ARE YOU UP TO, HARVEY?

18

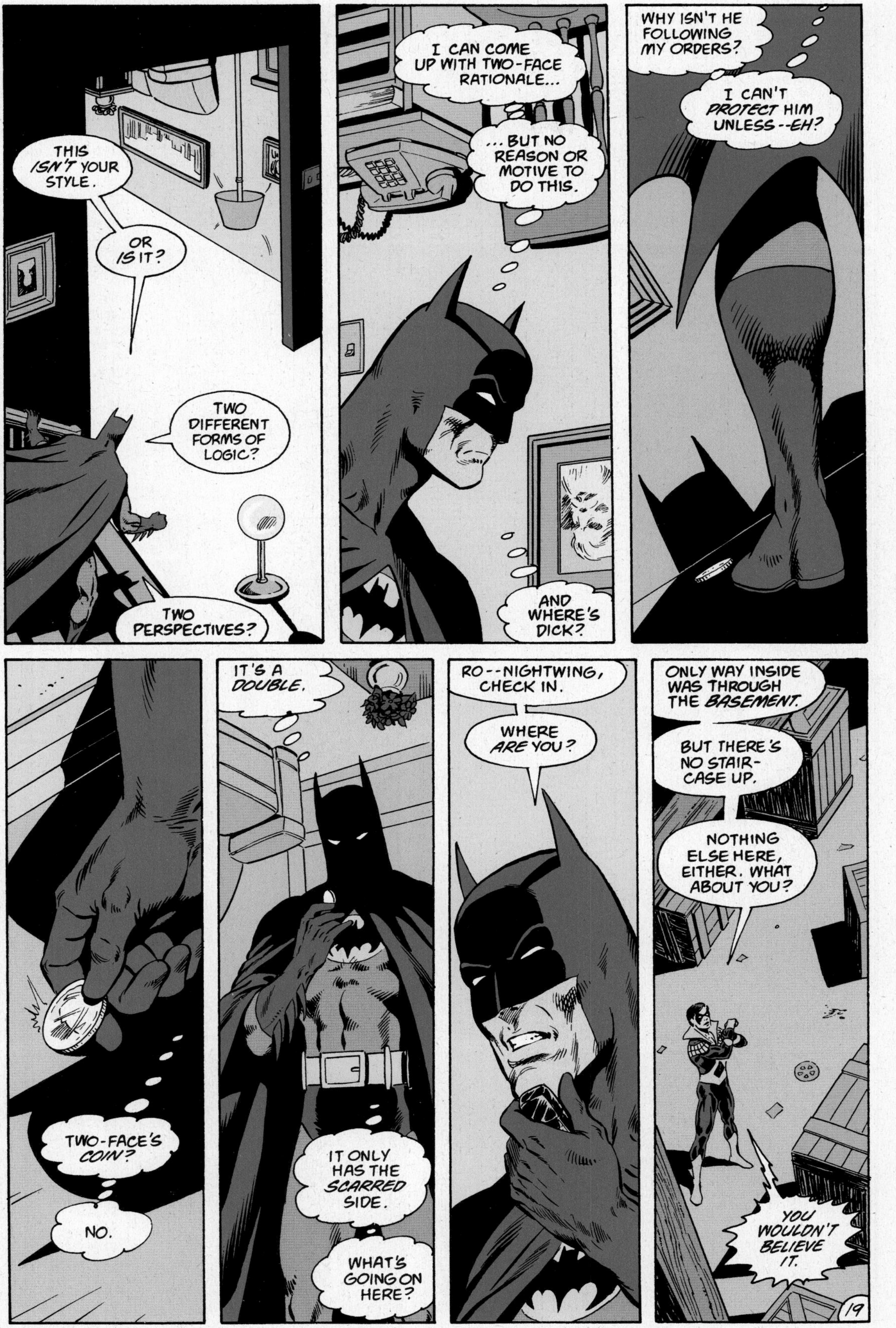
THIS ISN'T YOUR STYLE.
OR IS IT?
TWO DIFFERENT FORMS OF LOGIC?
TWO PERSPECTIVES?
I CAN COME UP WITH TWO-FACE RATIONALE...
...BUT NO REASON OR MOTIVE TO DO THIS.
AND WHERE'S DICK?
WHY ISN'T HE FOLLOWING MY ORDERS?
I CAN'T PROTECT HIM UNLESS--EH?
TWO-FACE'S COIN?
NO.
IT'S A DOUBLE.
IT ONLY HAS THE SCARRED SIDE.
WHAT'S GOING ON HERE?
RO--NIGHTWING, CHECK IN.
WHERE ARE YOU?
ONLY WAY INSIDE WAS THROUGH THE BASEMENT.
BUT THERE'S NO STAIR-CASE UP.
NOTHING ELSE HERE, EITHER. WHAT ABOUT YOU?
YOU WOULDN'T BELIEVE IT.
19

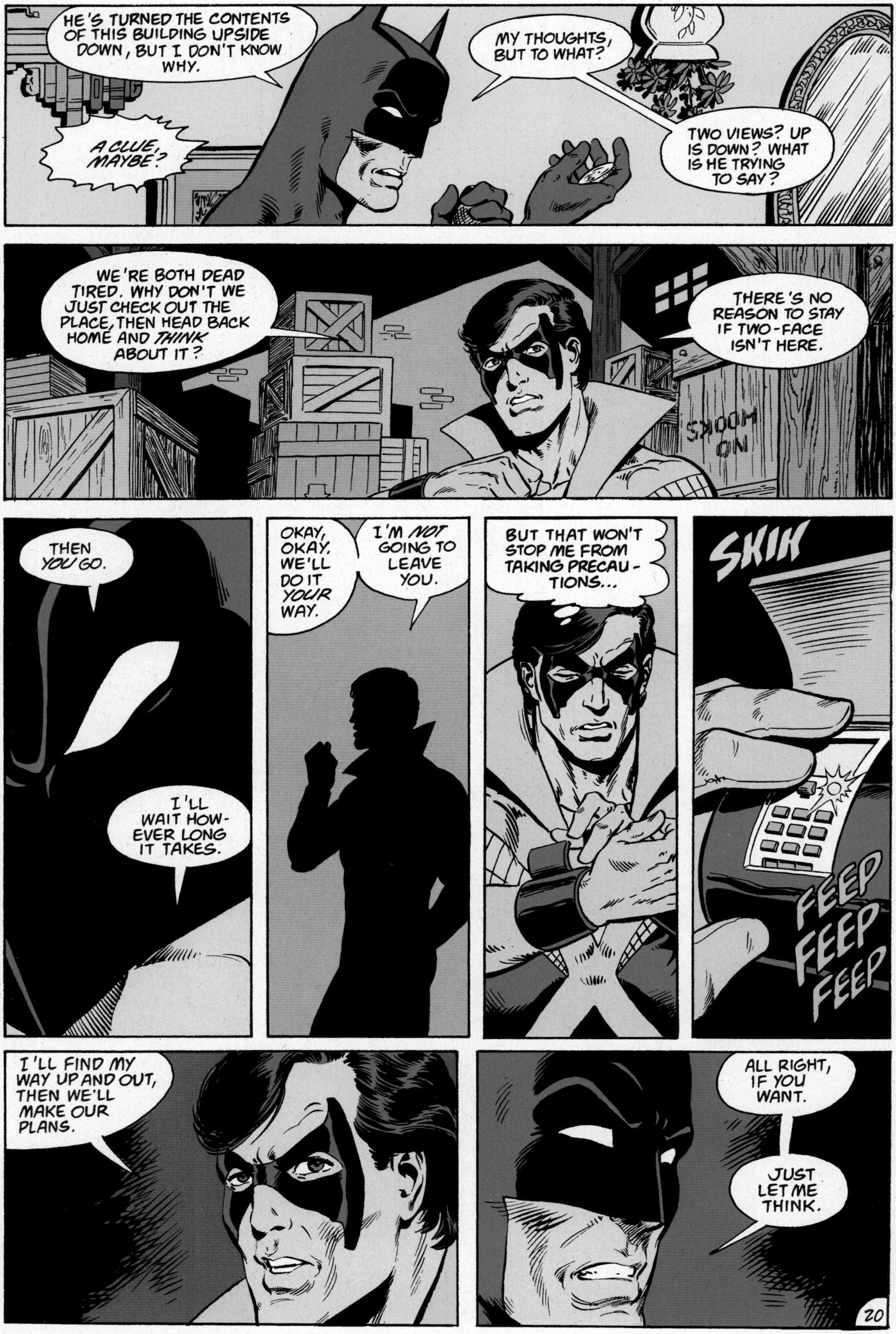

HE'S TURNED THE CONTENTS OF THIS BUILDING UPSIDE DOWN, BUT I DON'T KNOW WHY.
MY THOUGHTS, BUT TO WHAT?
A CLUE, MAYBE?
TWO VIEWS? UP IS DOWN? WHAT IS HE TRYING TO SAY?
WE'RE BOTH DEAD TIRED. WHY DON'T WE JUST CHECK OUT THE PLACE, THEN HEAD BACK HOME AND THINK ABOUT IT?
THERE'S NO REASON TO STAY IF TWO-FACE ISN'T HERE.
THEN YOU GO.
I'LL WAIT HOW-EVER LONG IT TAKES.
OKAY, OKAY, WE'LL DO IT YOUR WAY.
I'M NOT GOING TO LEAVE YOU.
BUT THAT WON'T STOP ME FROM TAKING PRECAU-TIONS...
SKIK
FEEP FEEP FEEP
I'LL FIND MY WAY UP AND OUT, THEN WE'LL MAKE OUR PLANS.
ALL RIGHT, IF YOU WANT.
JUST LET ME THINK.
20

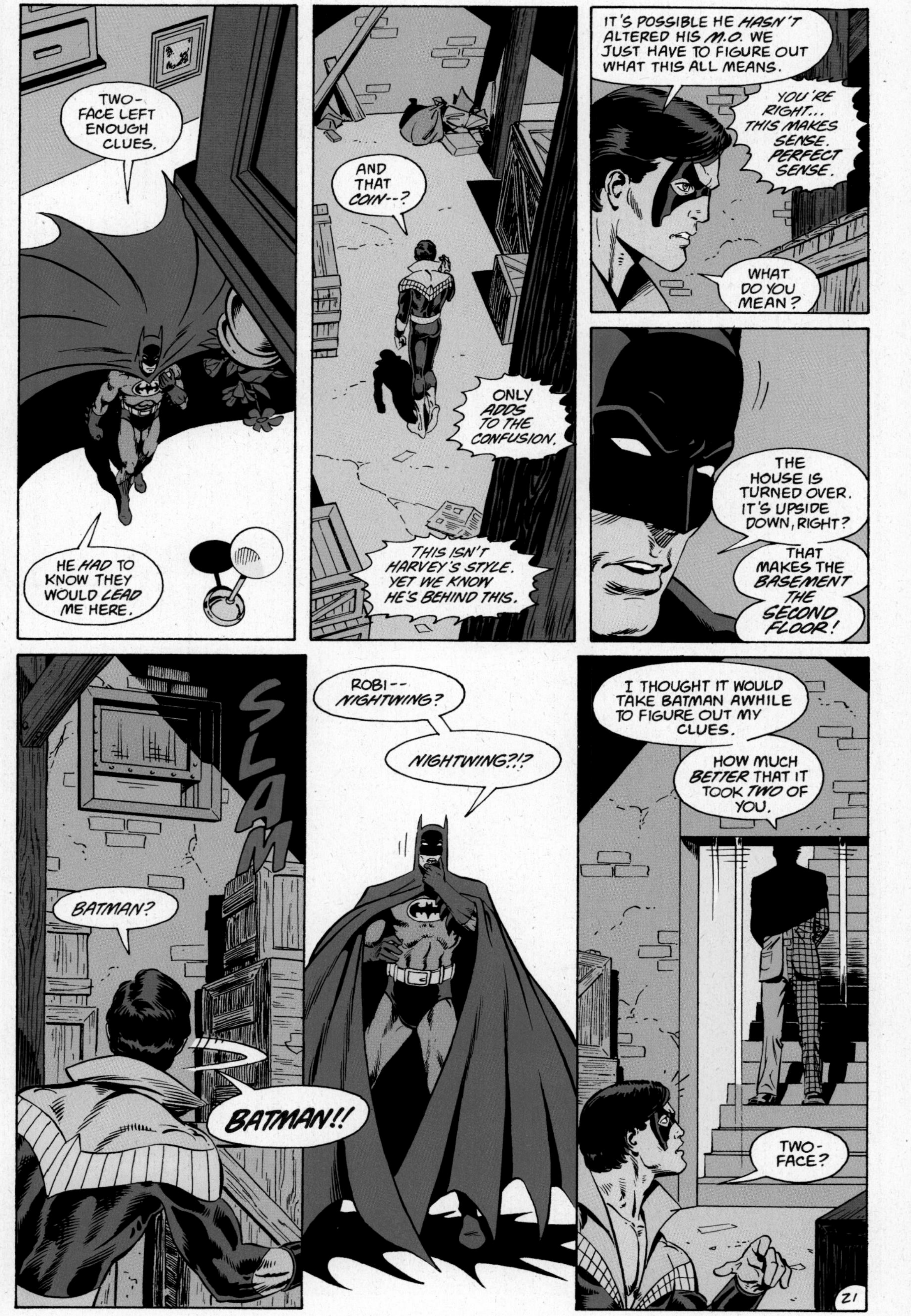
TWO-FACE LEFT ENOUGH CLUES.
HE HAD TO KNOW THEY WOULD LEAD ME HERE.
AND THAT COIN--?
ONLY ADDS TO THE CONFUSION.
THIS ISN'T HARVEY'S STYLE. YET WE KNOW HE'S BEHIND THIS.
IT'S POSSIBLE HE HASN'T ALTERED HIS M.O. WE JUST HAVE TO FIGURE OUT WHAT THIS ALL MEANS.
YOU'RE RIGHT... THIS MAKES SENSE. PERFECT SENSE.
WHAT DO YOU MEAN?
THE HOUSE IS TURNED OVER. IT'S UPSIDE DOWN, RIGHT?
THAT MAKES THE BASEMENT THE SECOND FLOOR!
SLAM
BATMAN?
BATMAN!!
ROBI-- NIGHTWING?
NIGHTWING?!?
I THOUGHT IT WOULD TAKE BATMAN AWHILE TO FIGURE OUT MY CLUES.
HOW MUCH BETTER THAT IT TOOK TWO OF YOU.
TWO-FACE?
21

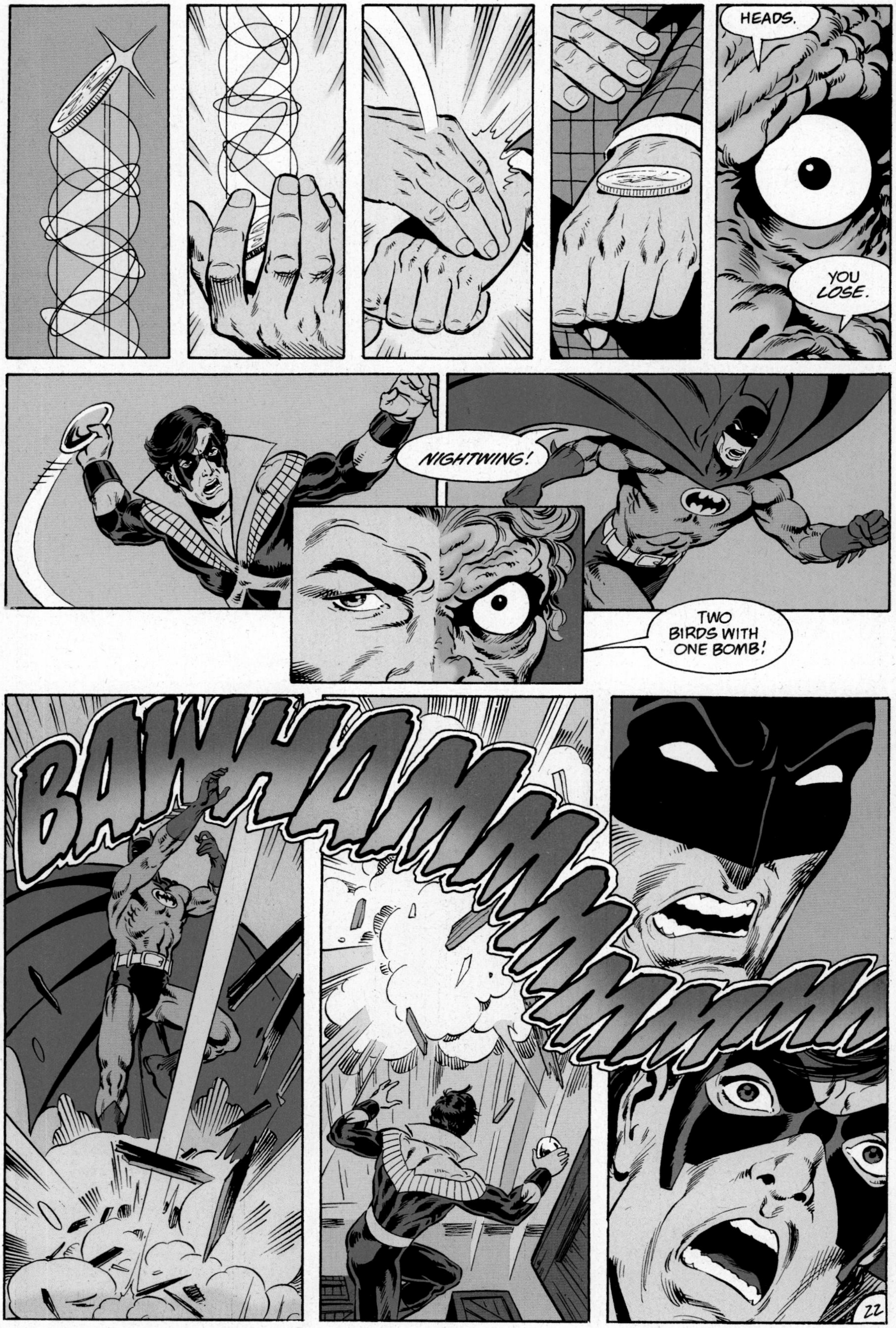

HEADS.
YOU LOSE.
NIGHTWING!
TWO BIRDS WITH ONE BOMB!
BAWHAMMMMMMMMM
22

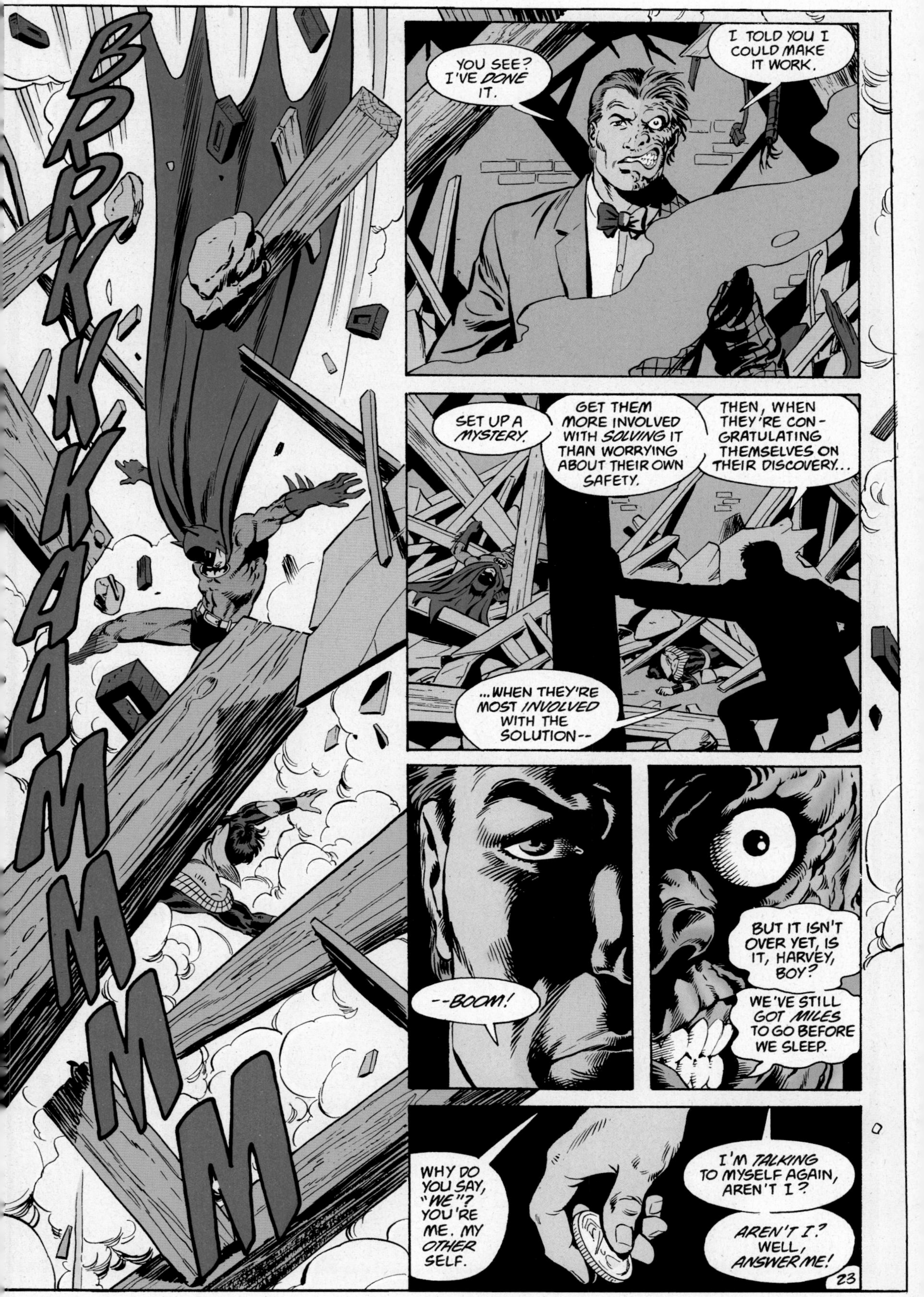
BRRKKKAAAMMMMM
YOU SEE? I'VE *DONE* IT.
I TOLD YOU I COULD MAKE IT WORK.
SET UP A *MYSTERY*.
GET THEM MORE INVOLVED WITH *SOLVING* IT THAN WORRYING ABOUT THEIR OWN SAFETY.
THEN, WHEN THEY'RE CON-GRATULATING THEMSELVES ON THEIR DISCOVERY...
...WHEN THEY'RE MOST *INVOLVED* WITH THE SOLUTION--
--*BOOM!*
BUT IT ISN'T OVER YET, IS IT, HARVEY, BOY?
WE'VE STILL GOT *MILES* TO GO BEFORE WE SLEEP.
WHY DO YOU SAY, "*WE*"? YOU'RE ME. MY *OTHER* SELF.
I'M *TALKING* TO MYSELF AGAIN, AREN'T I?
AREN'T I? WELL, *ANSWER ME!*
23

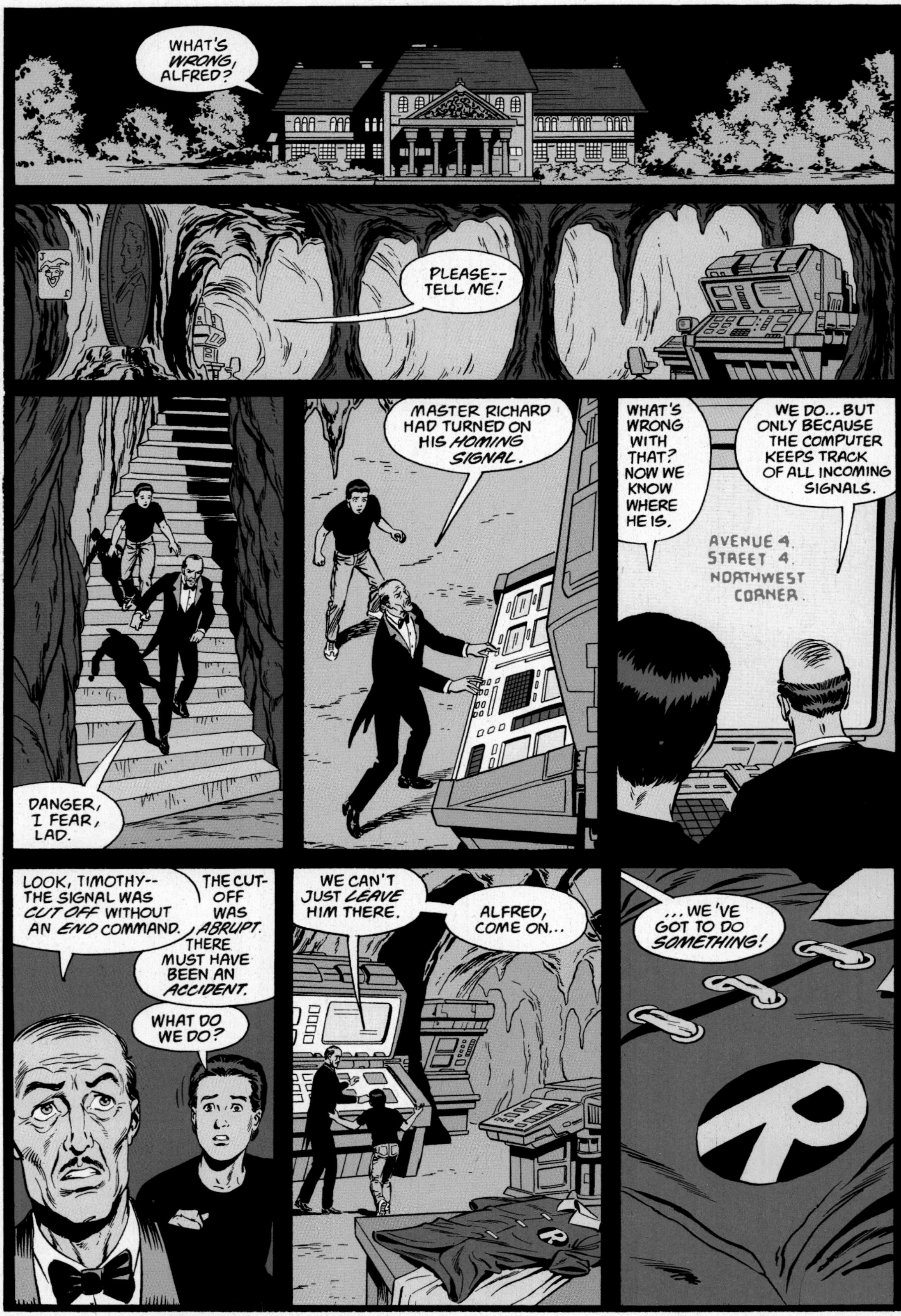
WHAT'S WRONG, ALFRED?
PLEASE-- TELL ME!
DANGER, I FEAR, LAD.
MASTER RICHARD HAD TURNED ON HIS HOMING SIGNAL.
WHAT'S WRONG WITH THAT? NOW WE KNOW WHERE HE IS.
WE DO... BUT ONLY BECAUSE THE COMPUTER KEEPS TRACK OF ALL INCOMING SIGNALS.
AVENUE 4 STREET 4 NORTHWEST CORNER
LOOK, TIMOTHY-- THE SIGNAL WAS CUT OFF WITHOUT AN END COMMAND.
THE CUT-OFF WAS ABRUPT. THERE MUST HAVE BEEN AN ACCIDENT.
WHAT DO WE DO?
WE CAN'T JUST LEAVE HIM THERE.
ALFRED, COME ON...
...WE'VE GOT TO DO SOMETHING!

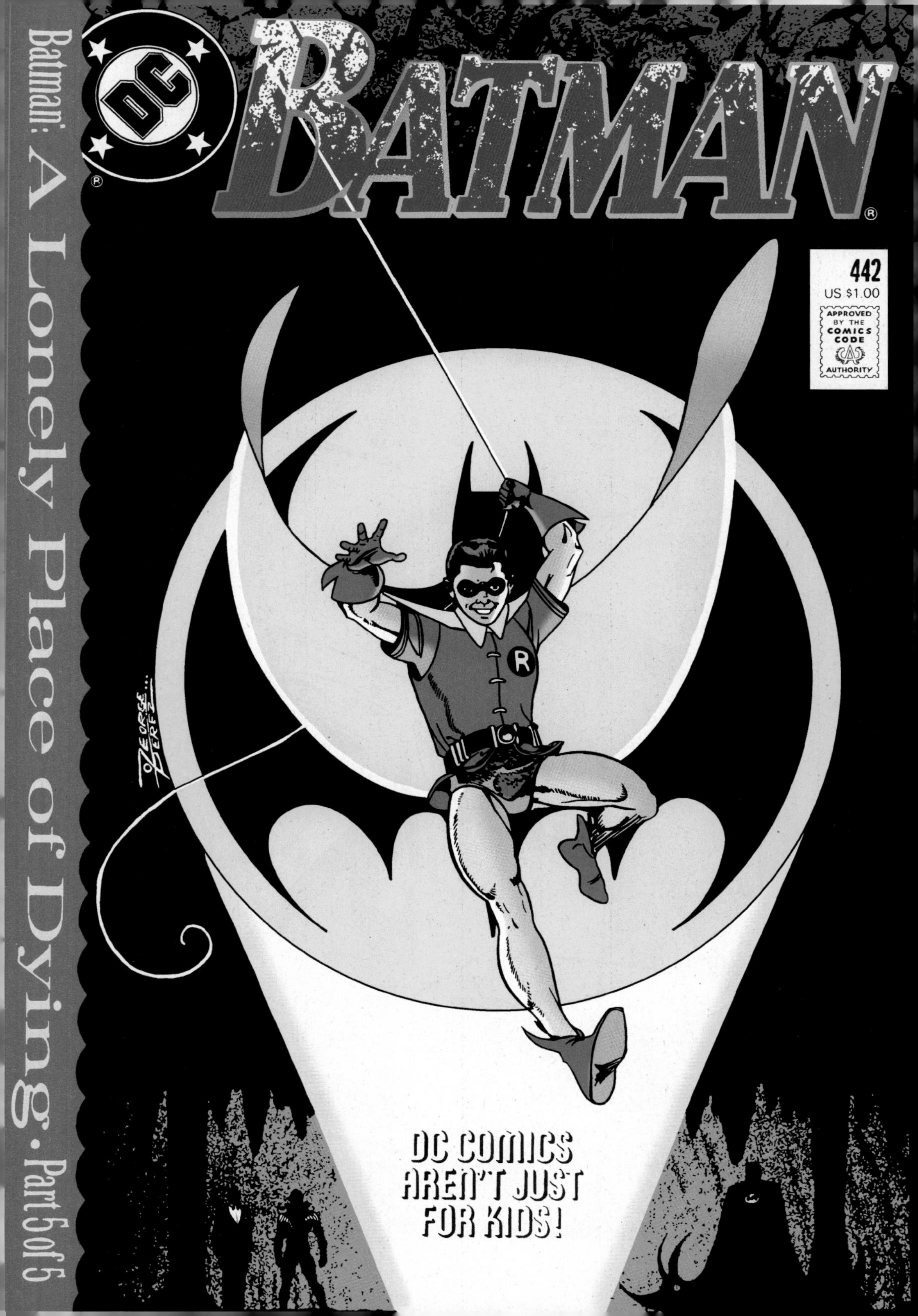
BATMAN
442
US $1.00
APPROVED BY THE COMICS CODE AUTHORITY
Batman: A Lonely Place of Dying • Part 5 of 5
GEORGE PEREZ
DC COMICS AREN'T JUST FOR KIDS!

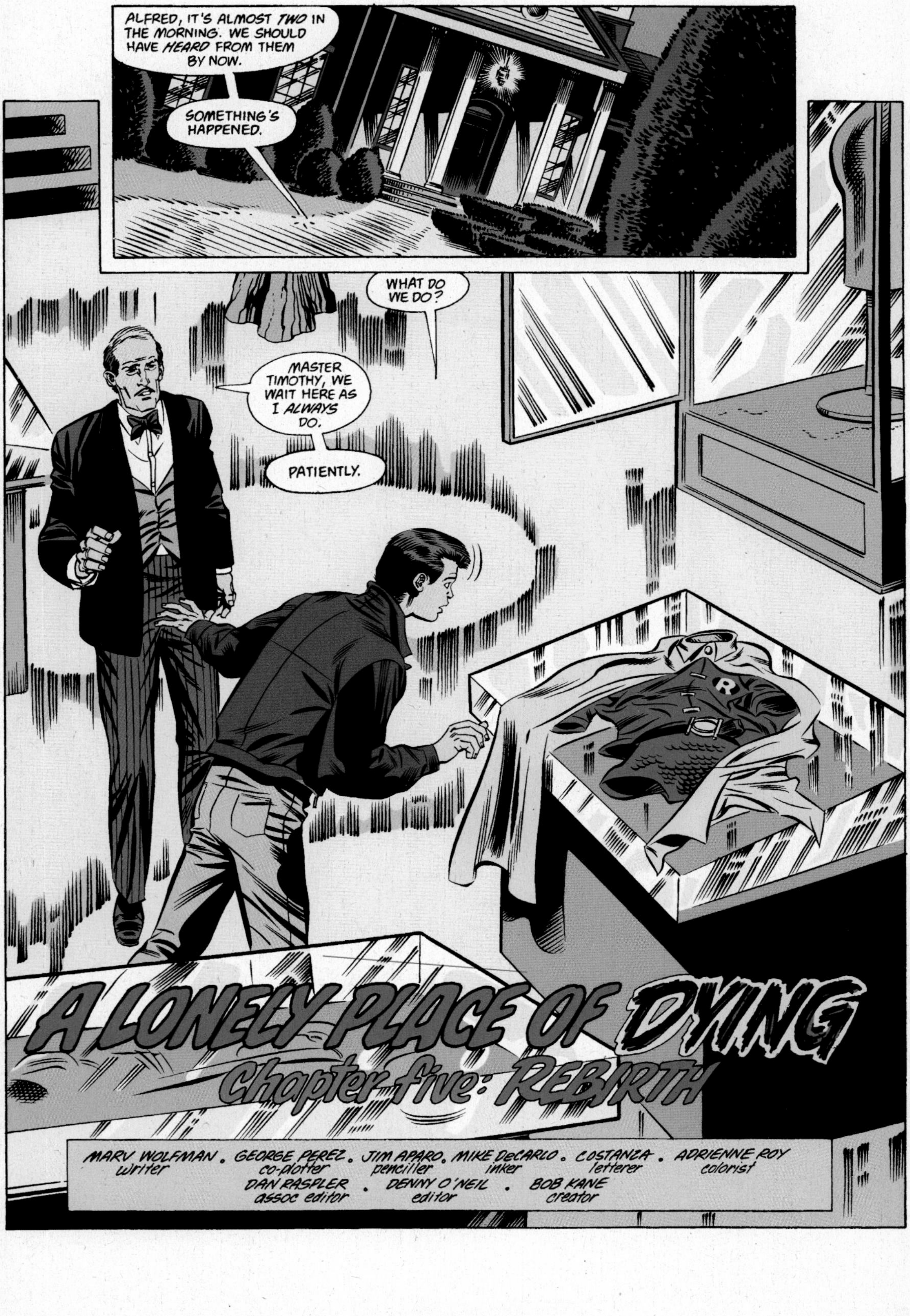

ALFRED, IT'S ALMOST TWO IN THE MORNING. WE SHOULD HAVE HEARD FROM THEM BY NOW.
SOMETHING'S HAPPENED.
WHAT DO WE DO?
MASTER TIMOTHY, WE WAIT HERE AS I ALWAYS DO.
PATIENTLY.
A LONELY PLACE OF DYING
Chapter five: REBIRTH
MARV WOLFMAN writer . GEORGE PEREZ co-plotter . JIM APARO penciller . MIKE DeCARLO inker . COSTANZA letterer . ADRIENNE ROY colorist
DAN RASPLER assoc editor . DENNY O'NEIL editor . BOB KANE creator

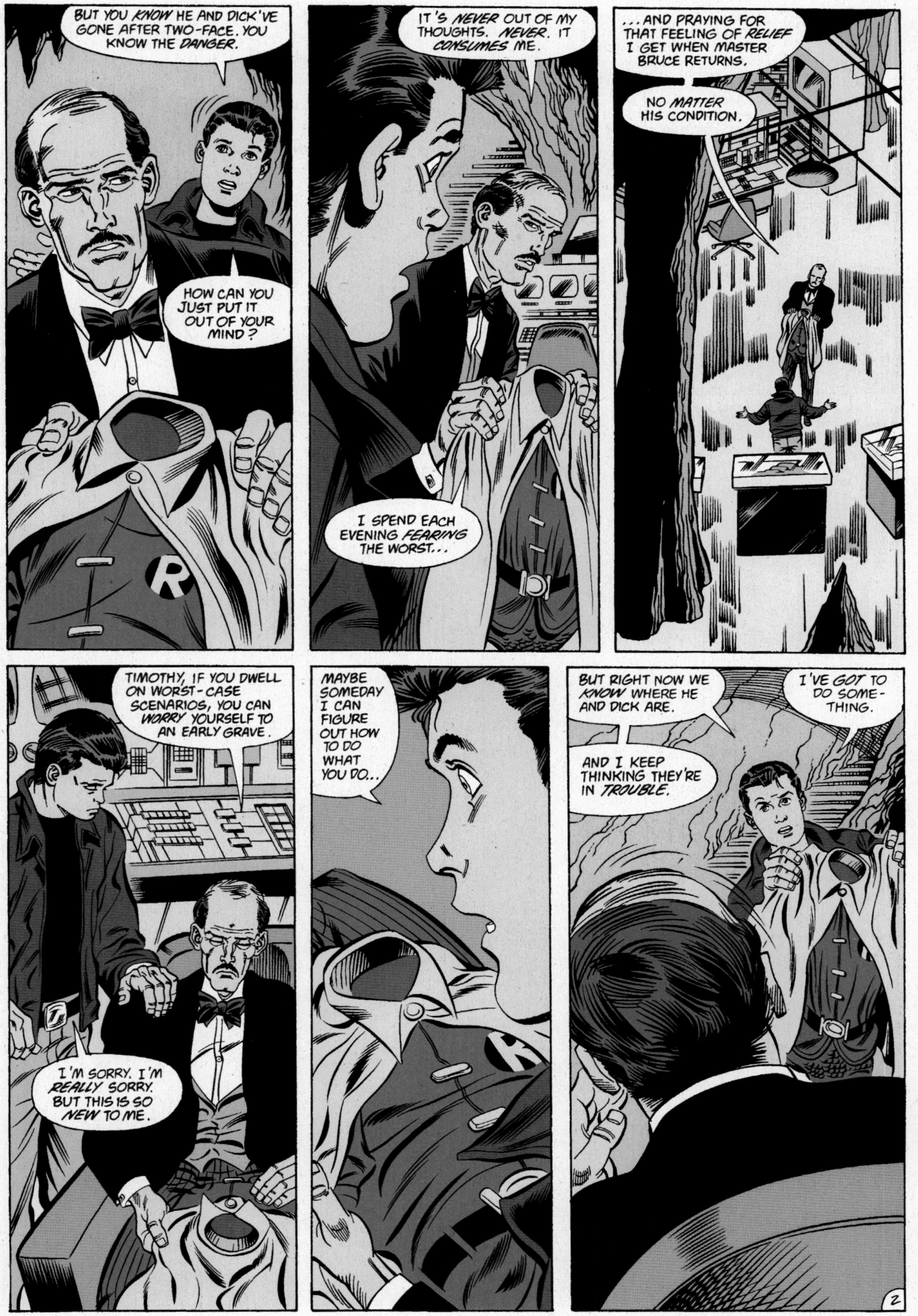
BUT YOU KNOW HE AND DICK'VE GONE AFTER TWO-FACE. YOU KNOW THE DANGER.
HOW CAN YOU JUST PUT IT OUT OF YOUR MIND?
IT'S NEVER OUT OF MY THOUGHTS. NEVER. IT CONSUMES ME.
I SPEND EACH EVENING FEARING THE WORST...
...AND PRAYING FOR THAT FEELING OF RELIEF I GET WHEN MASTER BRUCE RETURNS.
NO MATTER HIS CONDITION.
TIMOTHY, IF YOU DWELL ON WORST-CASE SCENARIOS, YOU CAN WORRY YOURSELF TO AN EARLY GRAVE.
I'M SORRY. I'M REALLY SORRY. BUT THIS IS SO NEW TO ME.
MAYBE SOMEDAY I CAN FIGURE OUT HOW TO DO WHAT YOU DO...
BUT RIGHT NOW WE KNOW WHERE HE AND DICK ARE.
AND I KEEP THINKING THEY'RE IN TROUBLE.
I'VE GOT TO DO SOMETHING.
2

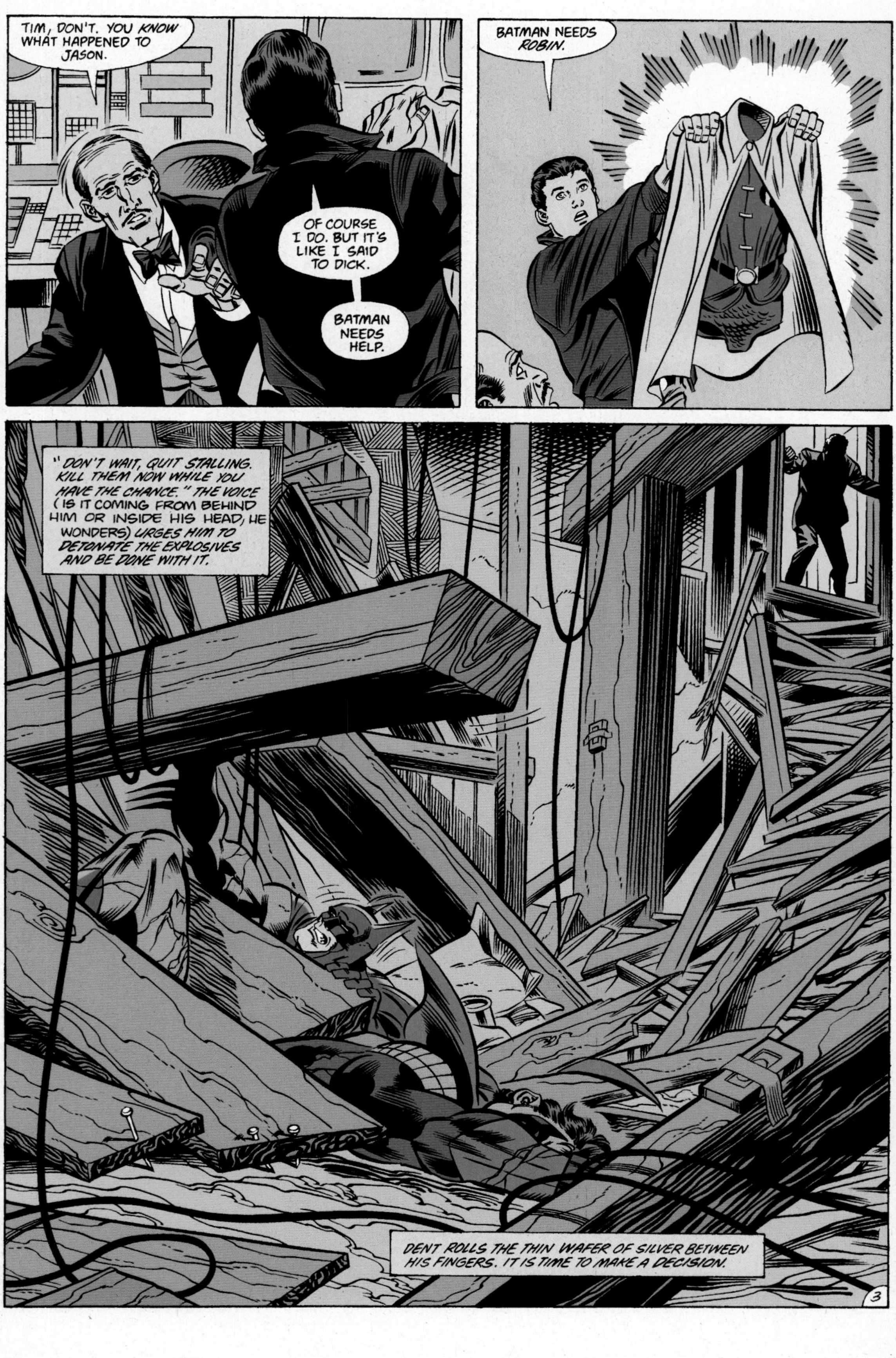
TIM, DON'T. YOU KNOW WHAT HAPPENED TO JASON.
OF COURSE I DO. BUT IT'S LIKE I SAID TO DICK.
BATMAN NEEDS HELP.
BATMAN NEEDS ROBIN.
"DON'T WAIT, QUIT STALLING. KILL THEM NOW WHILE YOU HAVE THE CHANCE." THE VOICE (IS IT COMING FROM BEHIND HIM OR INSIDE HIS HEAD, HE WONDERS) URGES HIM TO DETONATE THE EXPLOSIVES AND BE DONE WITH IT.
DENT ROLLS THE THIN WAFER OF SILVER BETWEEN HIS FINGERS. IT IS TIME TO MAKE A DECISION.
3

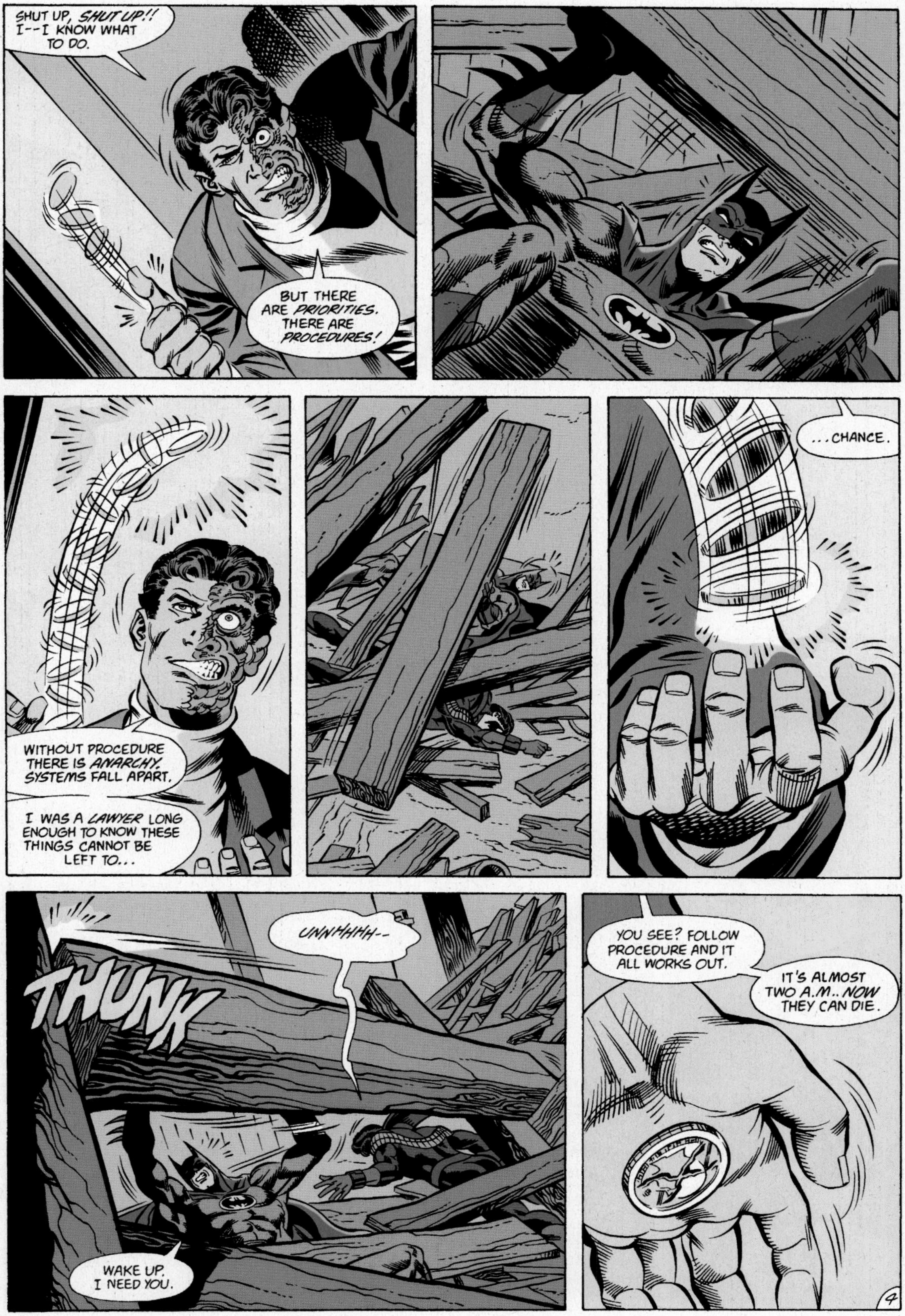
SHUT UP, SHUT UP!! I--I KNOW WHAT TO DO.
BUT THERE ARE PRIORITIES. THERE ARE PROCEDURES!
WITHOUT PROCEDURE THERE IS ANARCHY. SYSTEMS FALL APART.
I WAS A LAWYER LONG ENOUGH TO KNOW THESE THINGS CANNOT BE LEFT TO...
...CHANCE.
THUNK
UNNHHHH--
WAKE UP. I NEED YOU.
YOU SEE? FOLLOW PROCEDURE AND IT ALL WORKS OUT.
IT'S ALMOST TWO A.M.. NOW THEY CAN DIE.
4

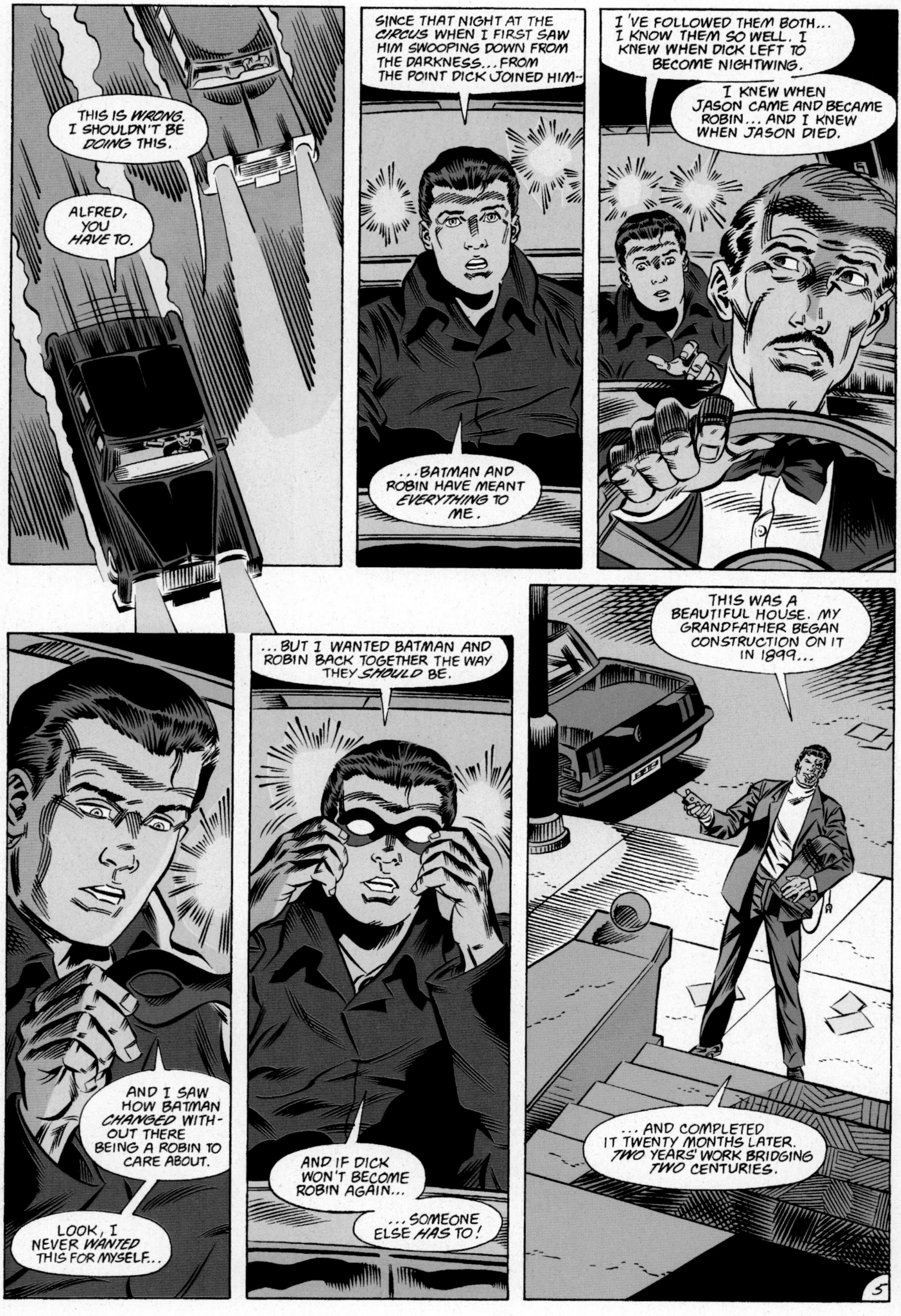

THIS IS WRONG. I SHOULDN'T BE DOING THIS.
ALFRED, YOU HAVE TO.
SINCE THAT NIGHT AT THE CIRCUS WHEN I FIRST SAW HIM SWOOPING DOWN FROM THE DARKNESS...FROM THE POINT DICK JOINED HIM--
...BATMAN AND ROBIN HAVE MEANT EVERYTHING TO ME.
I'VE FOLLOWED THEM BOTH... I KNOW THEM SO WELL. I KNEW WHEN DICK LEFT TO BECOME NIGHTWING.
I KNEW WHEN JASON CAME AND BECAME ROBIN... AND I KNEW WHEN JASON DIED.
AND I SAW HOW BATMAN CHANGED WITH-OUT THERE BEING A ROBIN TO CARE ABOUT.
LOOK, I NEVER WANTED THIS FOR MYSELF...
...BUT I WANTED BATMAN AND ROBIN BACK TOGETHER THE WAY THEY SHOULD BE.
AND IF DICK WON'T BECOME ROBIN AGAIN...
...SOMEONE ELSE HAS TO!
THIS WAS A BEAUTIFUL HOUSE. MY GRANDFATHER BEGAN CONSTRUCTION ON IT IN 1899...
...AND COMPLETED IT TWENTY MONTHS LATER. TWO YEARS' WORK BRIDGING TWO CENTURIES.
5

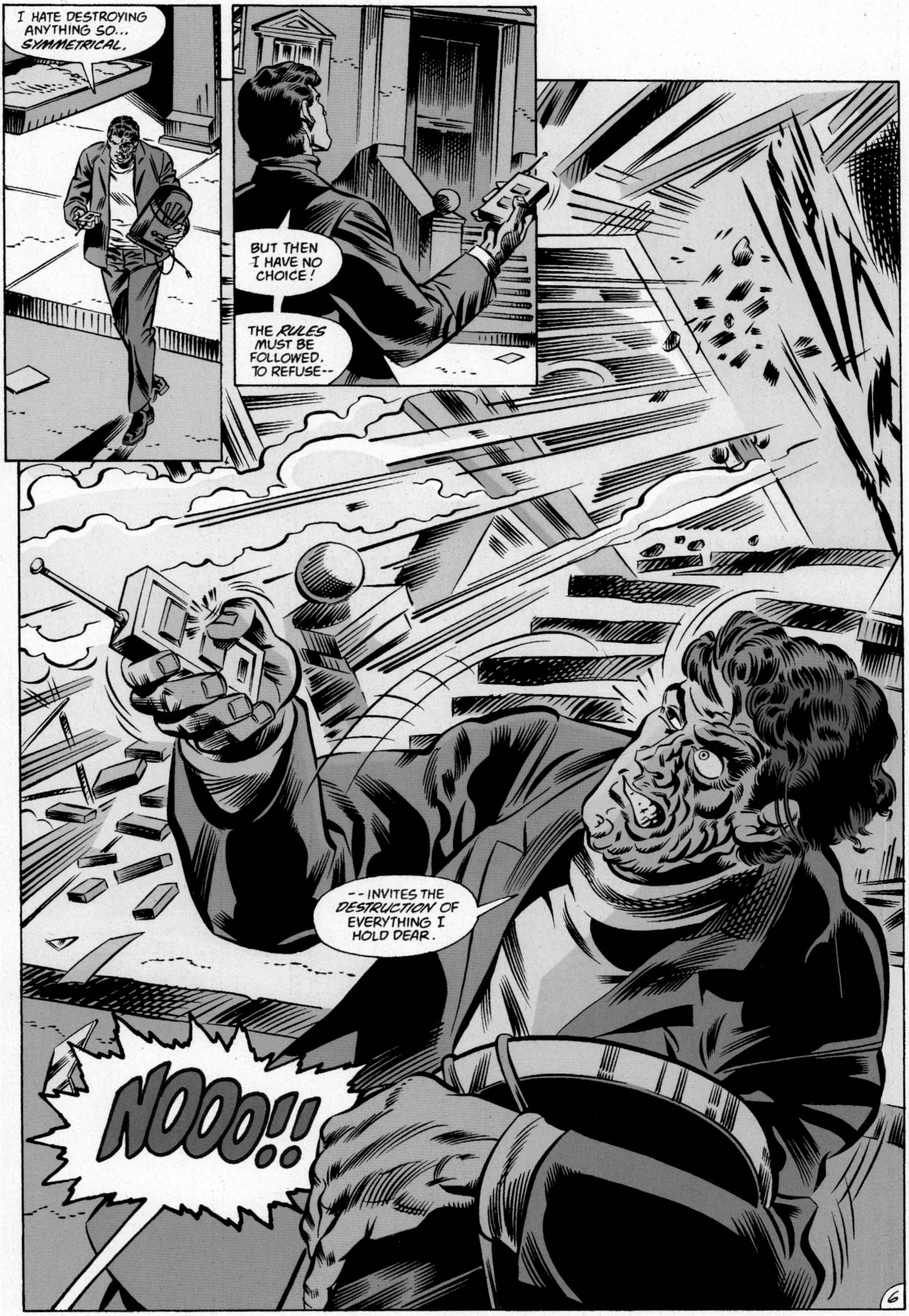
I HATE DESTROYING ANYTHING SO... SYMMETRICAL.
BUT THEN I HAVE NO CHOICE!
THE RULES MUST BE FOLLOWED. TO REFUSE--
--INVITES THE DESTRUCTION OF EVERYTHING I HOLD DEAR.
NOOO!!
6

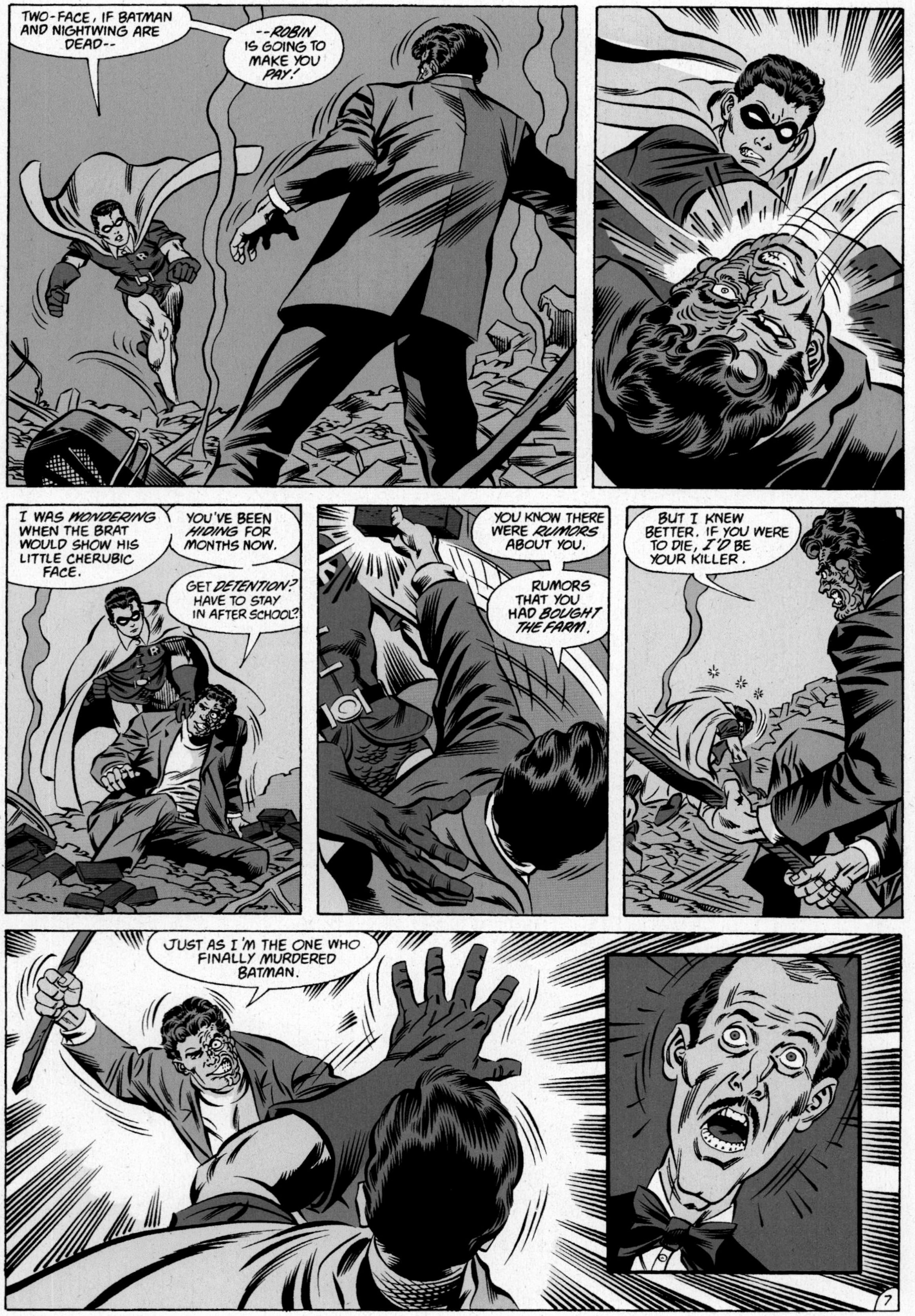

TWO-FACE, IF BATMAN AND NIGHTWING ARE DEAD--
--ROBIN IS GOING TO MAKE YOU PAY!
I WAS WONDERING WHEN THE BRAT WOULD SHOW HIS LITTLE CHERUBIC FACE.
YOU'VE BEEN HIDING FOR MONTHS NOW.
GET DETENTION? HAVE TO STAY IN AFTER SCHOOL?
YOU KNOW THERE WERE RUMORS ABOUT YOU.
RUMORS THAT YOU HAD BOUGHT THE FARM.
BUT I KNEW BETTER. IF YOU WERE TO DIE, I'D BE YOUR KILLER.
JUST AS I'M THE ONE WHO FINALLY MURDERED BATMAN.
7

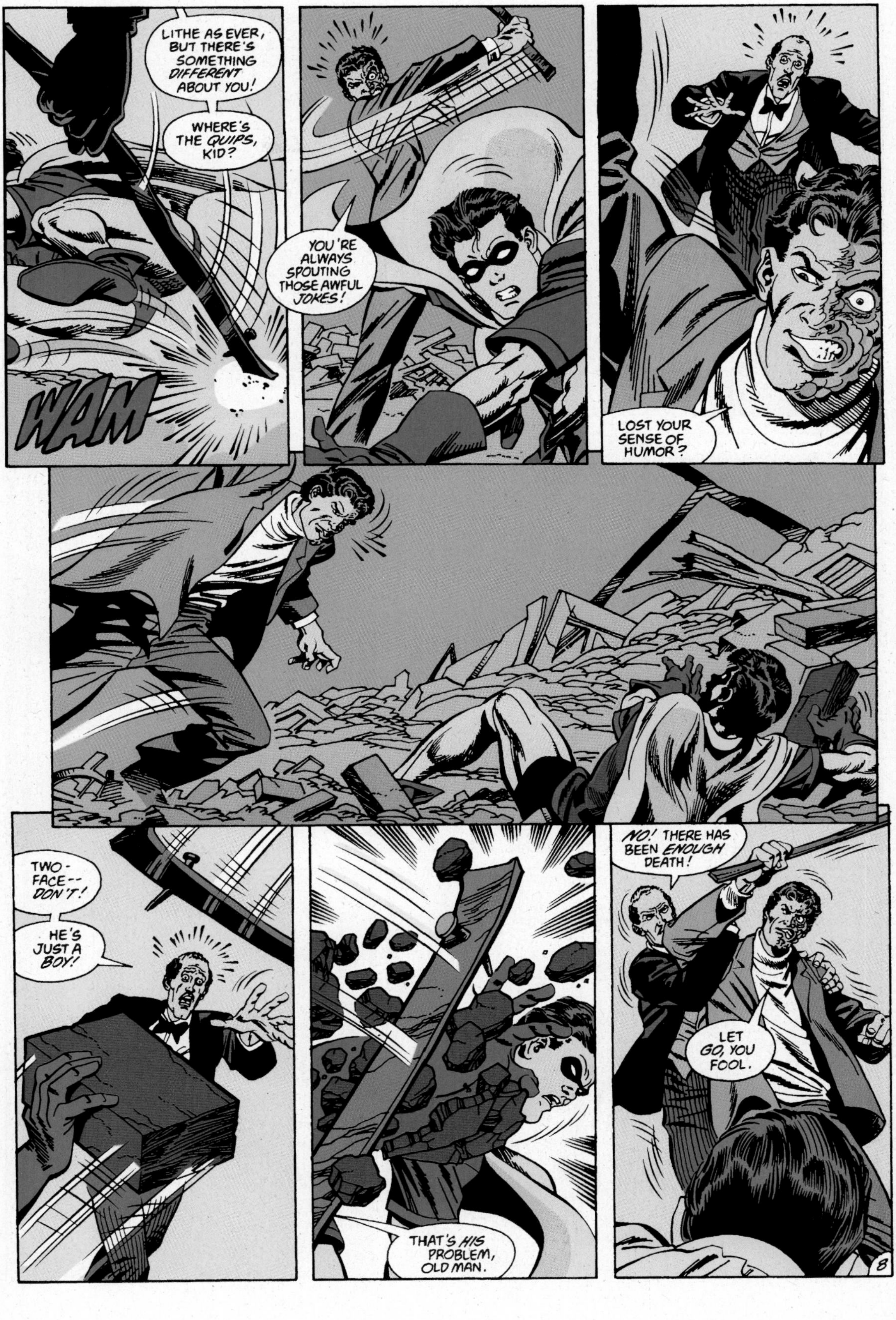

LITHE AS EVER, BUT THERE'S SOMETHING *DIFFERENT* ABOUT YOU!
WHERE'S THE *QUIPS*, KID?
WAM
YOU'RE ALWAYS SPOUTING THOSE AWFUL JOKES!
LOST YOUR SENSE OF HUMOR?
TWO-FACE-- *DON'T*!
HE'S JUST A *BOY*!
THAT'S *HIS* PROBLEM, OLD MAN.
NO! THERE HAS BEEN *ENOUGH* DEATH!
LET *GO*, YOU FOOL.
8

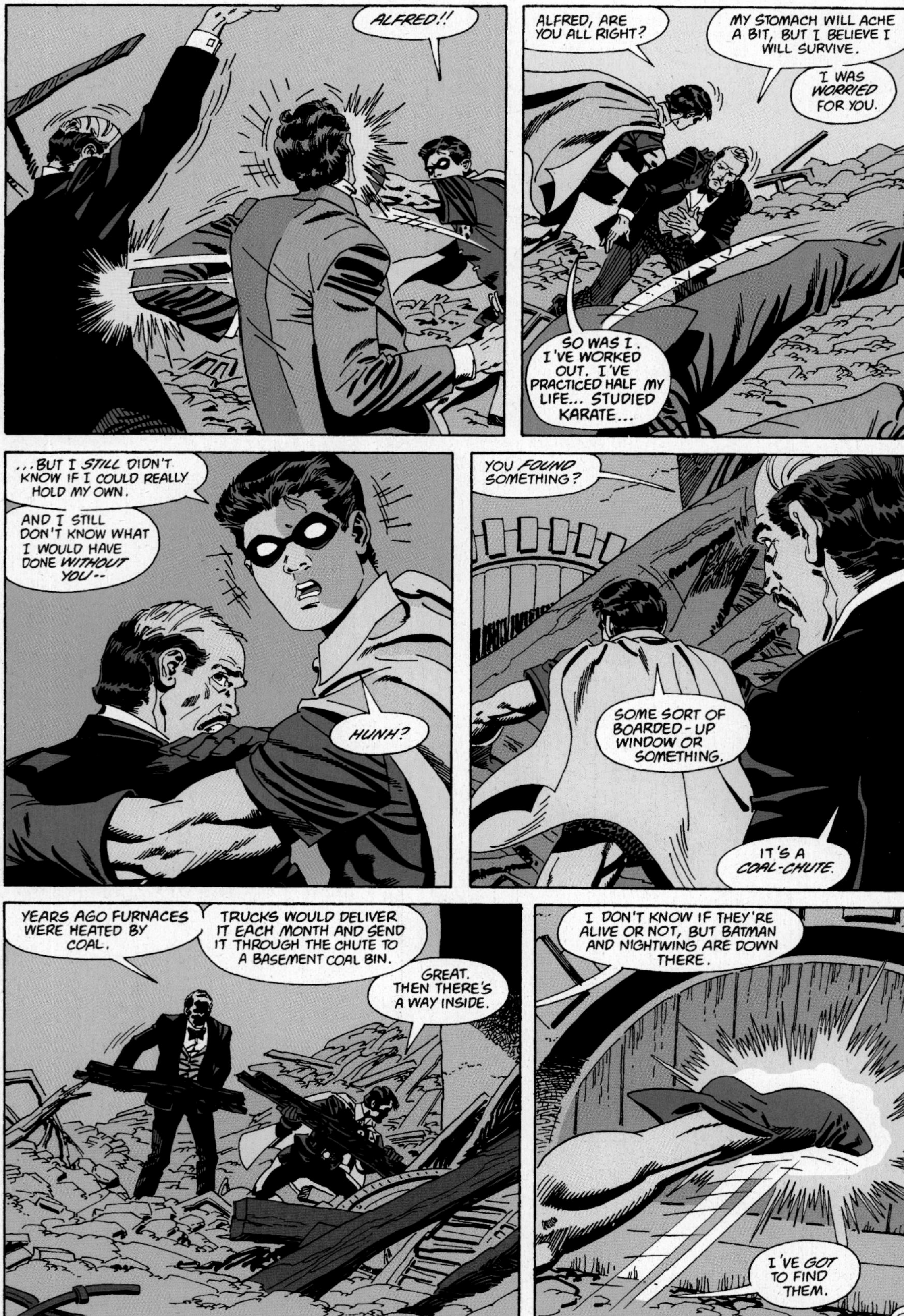
ALFRED!!
ALFRED, ARE YOU ALL RIGHT?
MY STOMACH WILL ACHE A BIT, BUT I BELIEVE I WILL SURVIVE.
I WAS WORRIED FOR YOU.
SO WAS I. I'VE WORKED OUT. I'VE PRACTICED HALF MY LIFE... STUDIED KARATE...
...BUT I STILL DIDN'T KNOW IF I COULD REALLY HOLD MY OWN.
AND I STILL DON'T KNOW WHAT I WOULD HAVE DONE WITHOUT YOU--
HUNH?
YOU FOUND SOMETHING?
SOME SORT OF BOARDED-UP WINDOW OR SOMETHING.
IT'S A COAL-CHUTE.
YEARS AGO FURNACES WERE HEATED BY COAL.
TRUCKS WOULD DELIVER IT EACH MONTH AND SEND IT THROUGH THE CHUTE TO A BASEMENT COAL BIN.
GREAT. THEN THERE'S A WAY INSIDE.
I DON'T KNOW IF THEY'RE ALIVE OR NOT, BUT BATMAN AND NIGHTWING ARE DOWN THERE.
I'VE GOT TO FIND THEM.
9

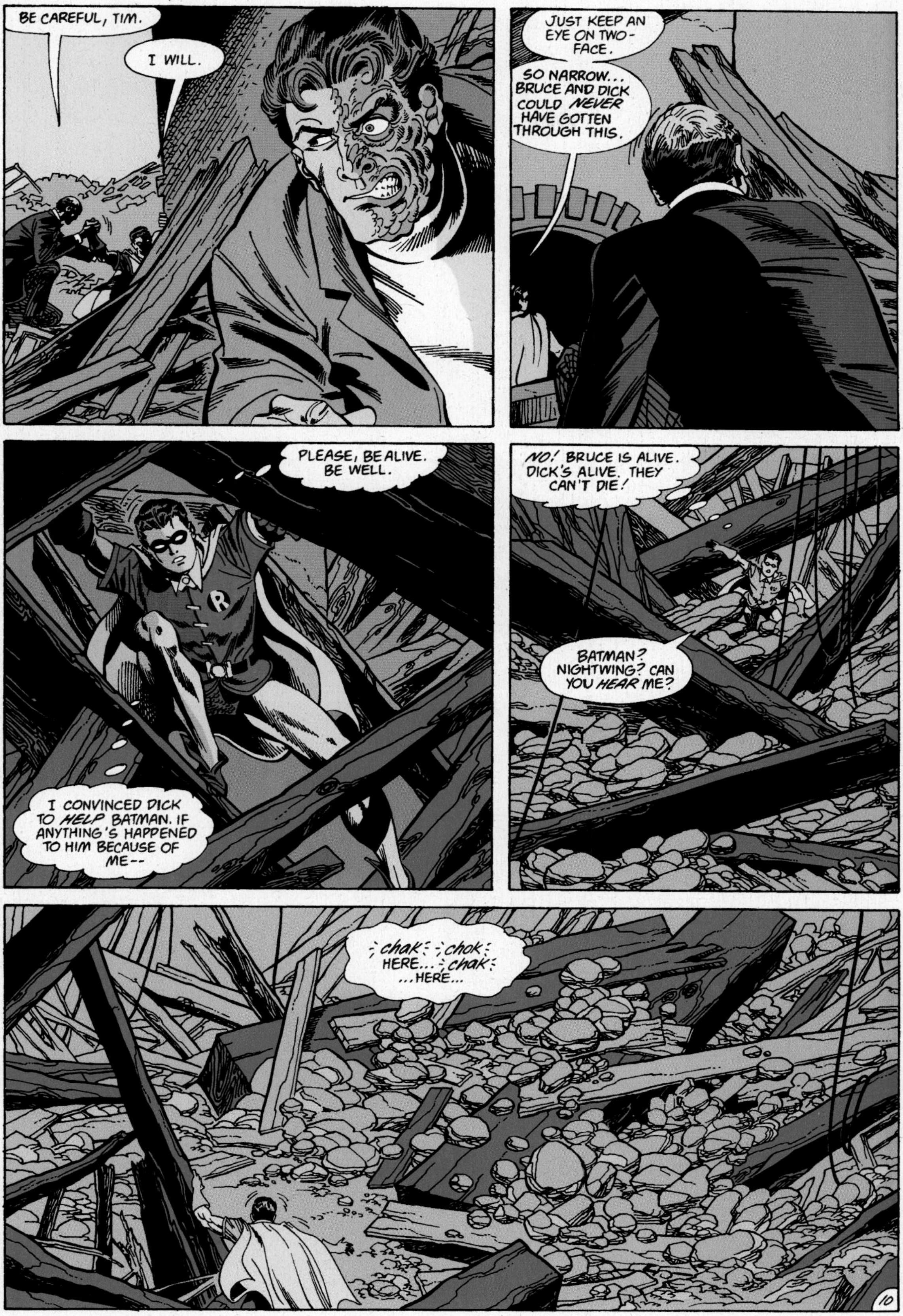
BE CAREFUL, TIM.
I WILL.
JUST KEEP AN EYE ON TWO-FACE.
SO NARROW... BRUCE AND DICK COULD NEVER HAVE GOTTEN THROUGH THIS.
PLEASE, BE ALIVE. BE WELL.
I CONVINCED DICK TO HELP BATMAN. IF ANYTHING'S HAPPENED TO HIM BECAUSE OF ME--
NO! BRUCE IS ALIVE. DICK'S ALIVE. THEY CAN'T DIE!
BATMAN? NIGHTWING? CAN YOU HEAR ME?
chak chok HERE... chak ...HERE...
10

BATMAN? WHERE--?

:CHOKK: UNDER THE CROSSBEAMS...

ARE YOU BOTH ALL RIGHT?

...CAN'T MOVE... PINNED.

AND I CAN'T MOVE THE BEAMS WITHOUT THE ROCKS FALLING ON YOU.

JUST LIE THERE, I'LL HAVE TO CLEAR THE BEAMS BEFORE I CAN GET TO YOU.

TWO-FACE... :CHOK: WHERE IS HE?

I LEFT HIM WITH ALFRED. THE POLICE SHOULD BE COMING.

POLICE? WH-WHO ARE YOU?

...

ROBIN.

FOR NOW, JUST CALL ME ROBIN.

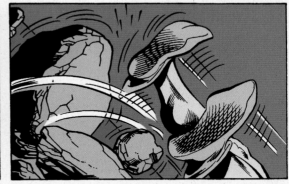

I'VE GOT THE ROCKS OFF THE BEAMS.

BATMAN, HOW ARE YOU TWO DOING?

BATMAN!!

BATMAN!!

11

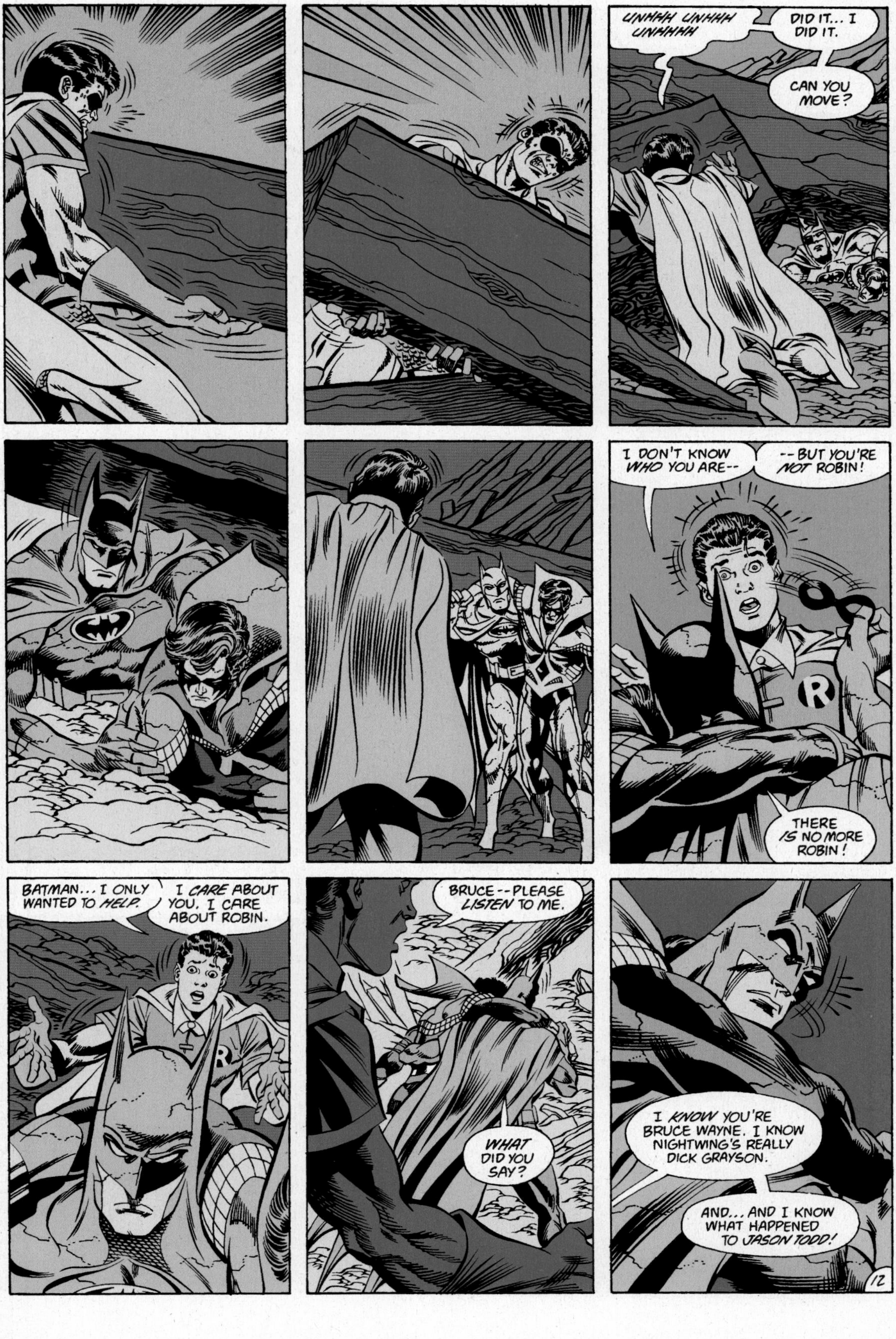
UNHHH UNHHH UNHHHH
DID IT... I DID IT.
CAN YOU MOVE?
I DON'T KNOW WHO YOU ARE--
--BUT YOU'RE NOT ROBIN!
THERE IS NO MORE ROBIN!
BATMAN... I ONLY WANTED TO HELP.
I CARE ABOUT YOU. I CARE ABOUT ROBIN.
BRUCE--PLEASE LISTEN TO ME.
WHAT DID YOU SAY?
I KNOW YOU'RE BRUCE WAYNE. I KNOW NIGHTWING'S REALLY DICK GRAYSON.
AND... AND I KNOW WHAT HAPPENED TO JASON TODD!
12

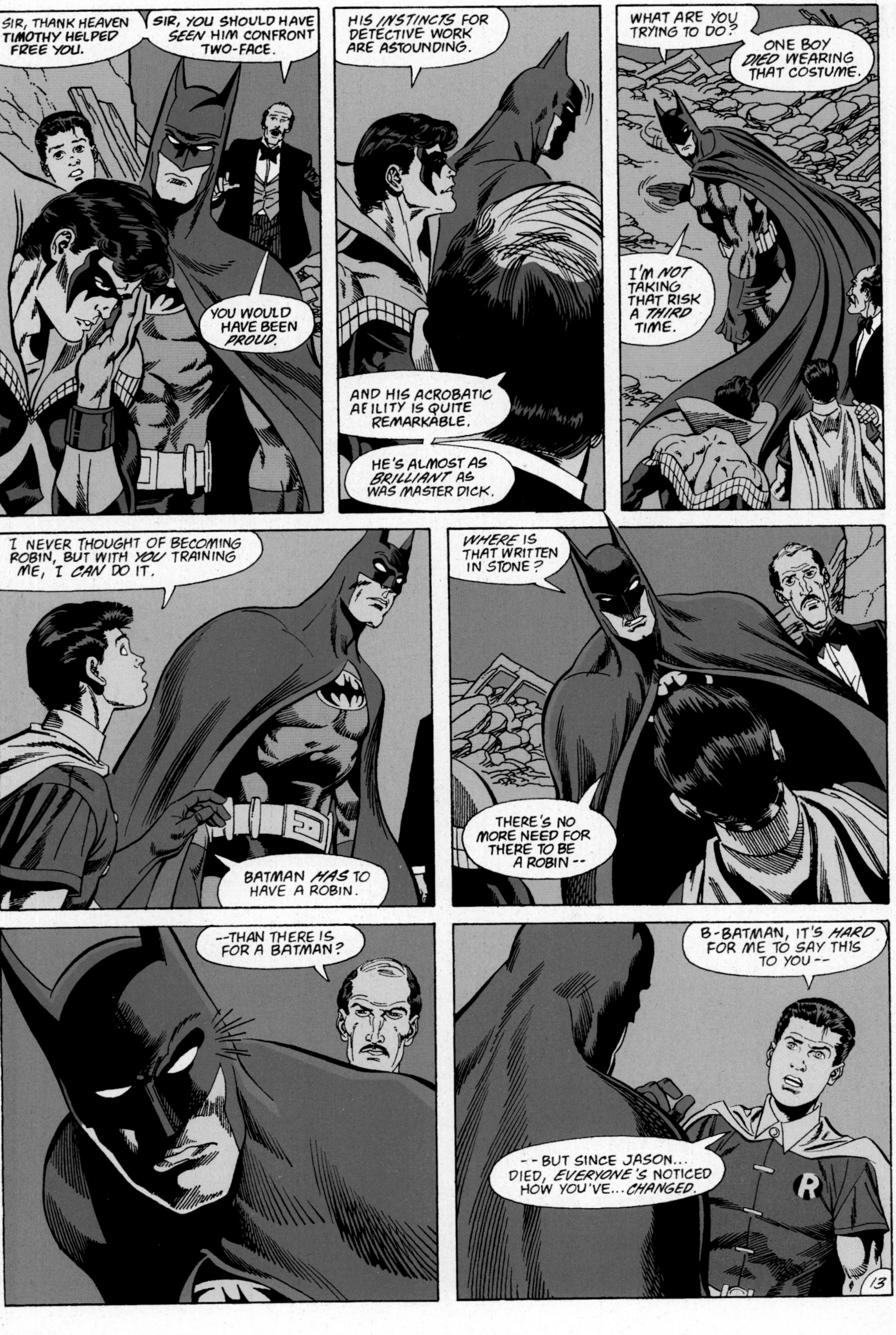
SIR, THANK HEAVEN TIMOTHY HELPED FREE YOU.
SIR, YOU SHOULD HAVE SEEN HIM CONFRONT TWO-FACE.
YOU WOULD HAVE BEEN PROUD.
HIS INSTINCTS FOR DETECTIVE WORK ARE ASTOUNDING.
AND HIS ACROBATIC ABILITY IS QUITE REMARKABLE.
HE'S ALMOST AS BRILLIANT AS WAS MASTER DICK.
WHAT ARE YOU TRYING TO DO?
ONE BOY DIED WEARING THAT COSTUME.
I'M NOT TAKING THAT RISK A THIRD TIME.
I NEVER THOUGHT OF BECOMING ROBIN, BUT WITH YOU TRAINING ME, I CAN DO IT.
BATMAN HAS TO HAVE A ROBIN.
WHERE IS THAT WRITTEN IN STONE?
THERE'S NO MORE NEED FOR THERE TO BE A ROBIN --
--THAN THERE IS FOR A BATMAN?
B-BATMAN, IT'S HARD FOR ME TO SAY THIS TO YOU --
-- BUT SINCE JASON... DIED, EVERYONE'S NOTICED HOW YOU'VE... CHANGED.
13

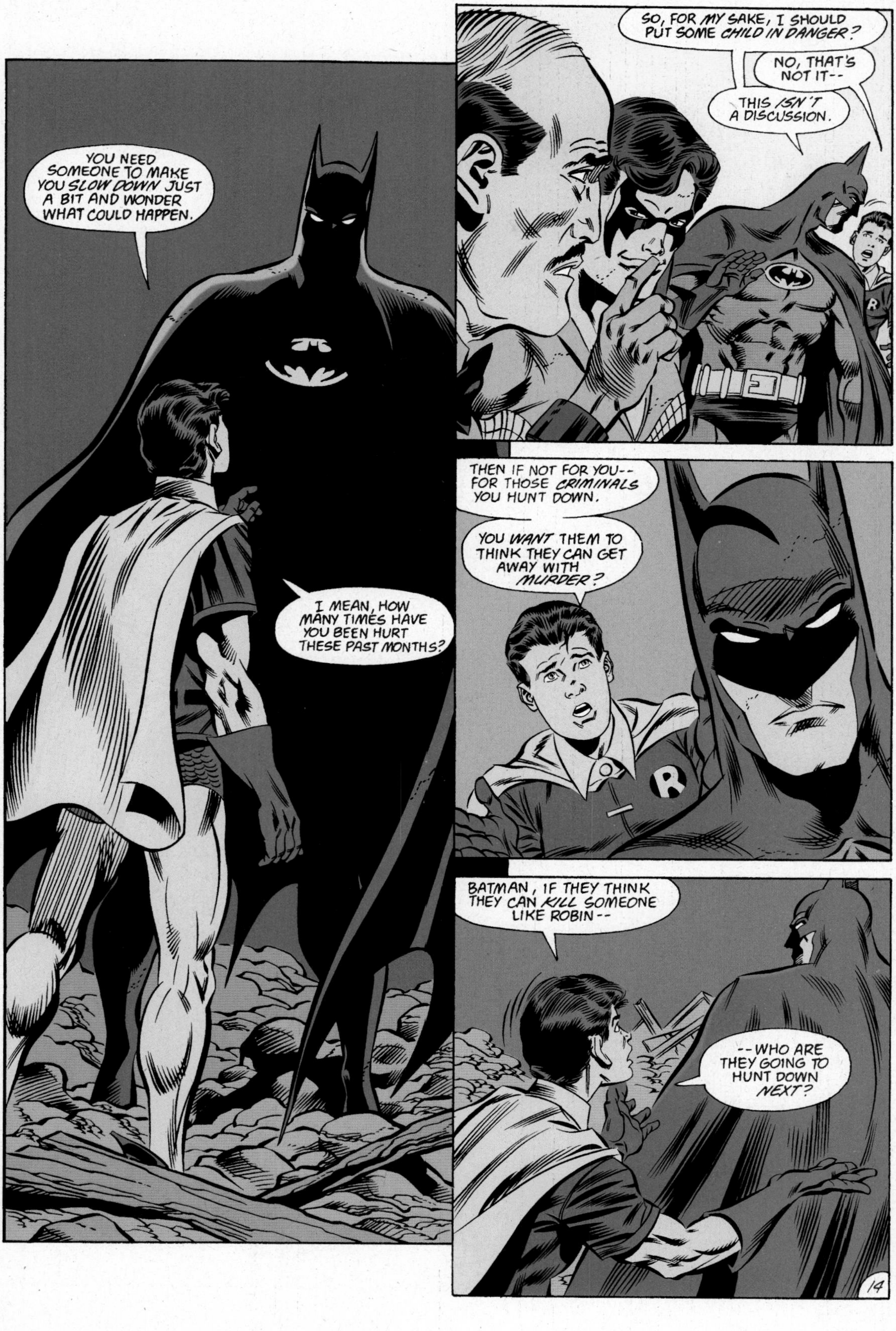
YOU NEED SOMEONE TO MAKE YOU SLOW DOWN JUST A BIT AND WONDER WHAT COULD HAPPEN.
I MEAN, HOW MANY TIMES HAVE YOU BEEN HURT THESE PAST MONTHS?
SO, FOR MY SAKE, I SHOULD PUT SOME CHILD IN DANGER?
NO, THAT'S NOT IT--
THIS ISN'T A DISCUSSION.
THEN IF NOT FOR YOU-- FOR THOSE CRIMINALS YOU HUNT DOWN.
YOU WANT THEM TO THINK THEY CAN GET AWAY WITH MURDER?
BATMAN, IF THEY THINK THEY CAN KILL SOMEONE LIKE ROBIN--
--WHO ARE THEY GOING TO HUNT DOWN NEXT?
14

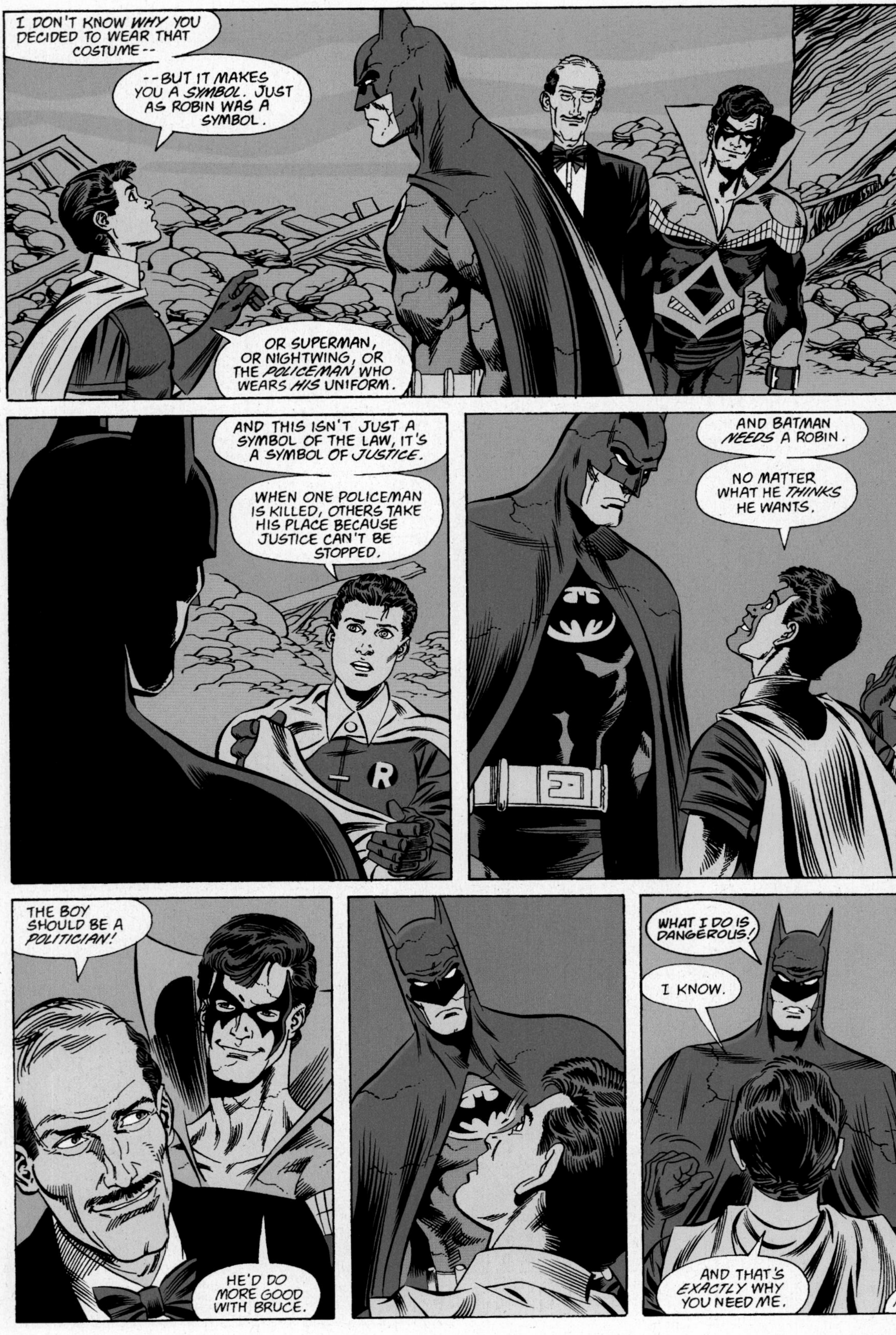
I DON'T KNOW WHY YOU DECIDED TO WEAR THAT COSTUME--
--BUT IT MAKES YOU A SYMBOL. JUST AS ROBIN WAS A SYMBOL.
OR SUPERMAN, OR NIGHTWING, OR THE POLICEMAN WHO WEARS HIS UNIFORM.
AND THIS ISN'T JUST A SYMBOL OF THE LAW, IT'S A SYMBOL OF JUSTICE.
WHEN ONE POLICEMAN IS KILLED, OTHERS TAKE HIS PLACE BECAUSE JUSTICE CAN'T BE STOPPED.
AND BATMAN NEEDS A ROBIN.
NO MATTER WHAT HE THINKS HE WANTS.
THE BOY SHOULD BE A POLITICIAN!
HE'D DO MORE GOOD WITH BRUCE.
WHAT I DO IS DANGEROUS!
I KNOW.
AND THAT'S EXACTLY WHY YOU NEED ME.
15

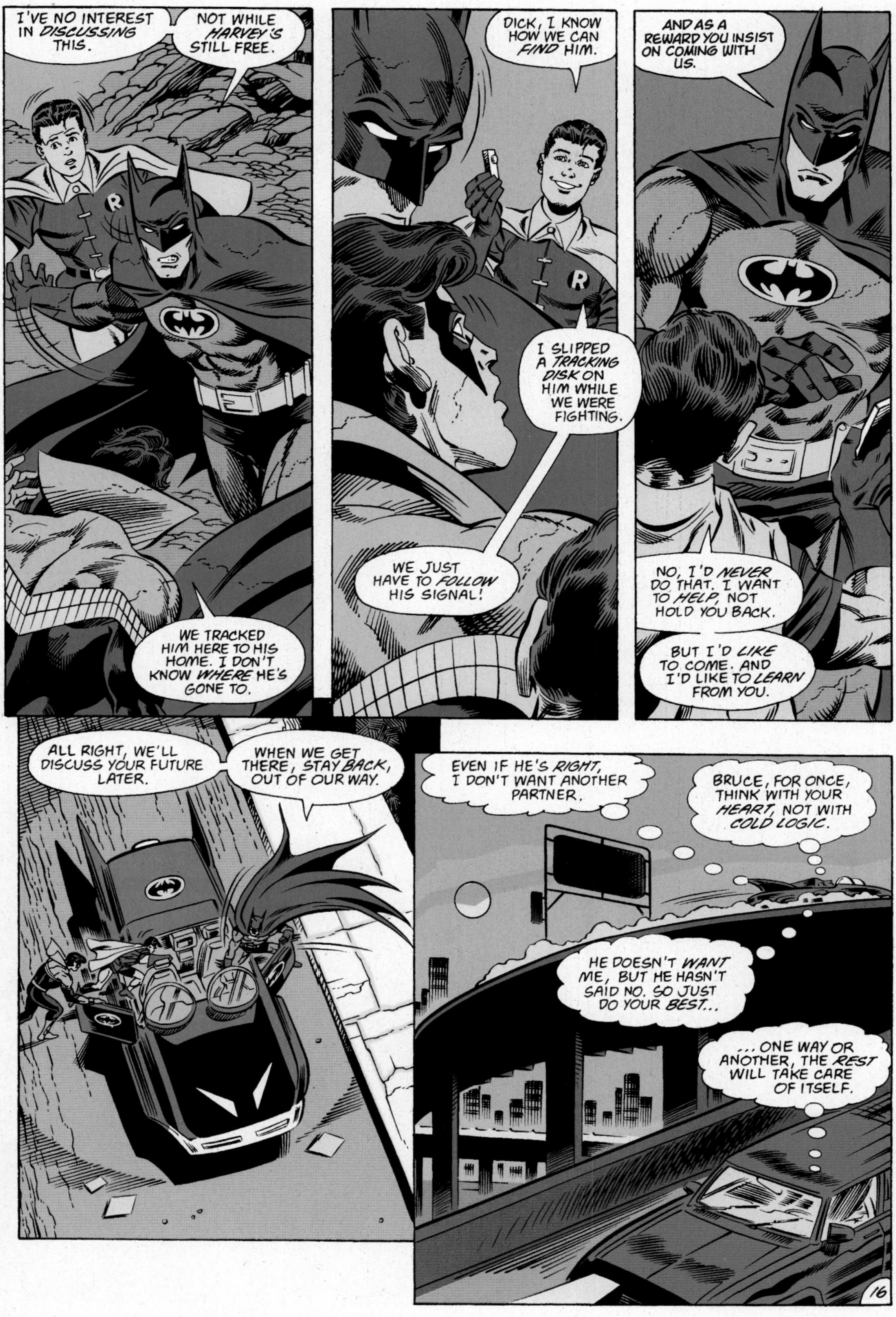
I'VE NO INTEREST IN DISCUSSING THIS.
NOT WHILE HARVEY'S STILL FREE.
WE TRACKED HIM HERE TO HIS HOME. I DON'T KNOW WHERE HE'S GONE TO.
DICK, I KNOW HOW WE CAN FIND HIM.
I SLIPPED A TRACKING DISK ON HIM WHILE WE WERE FIGHTING.
WE JUST HAVE TO FOLLOW HIS SIGNAL!
AND AS A REWARD YOU INSIST ON COMING WITH US.
NO, I'D NEVER DO THAT. I WANT TO HELP, NOT HOLD YOU BACK.
BUT I'D LIKE TO COME. AND I'D LIKE TO LEARN FROM YOU.
ALL RIGHT, WE'LL DISCUSS YOUR FUTURE LATER.
WHEN WE GET THERE, STAY BACK, OUT OF OUR WAY.
EVEN IF HE'S RIGHT, I DON'T WANT ANOTHER PARTNER.
BRUCE, FOR ONCE, THINK WITH YOUR HEART, NOT WITH COLD LOGIC.
HE DOESN'T WANT ME, BUT HE HASN'T SAID NO. SO JUST DO YOUR BEST...
...ONE WAY OR ANOTHER, THE REST WILL TAKE CARE OF ITSELF.
16

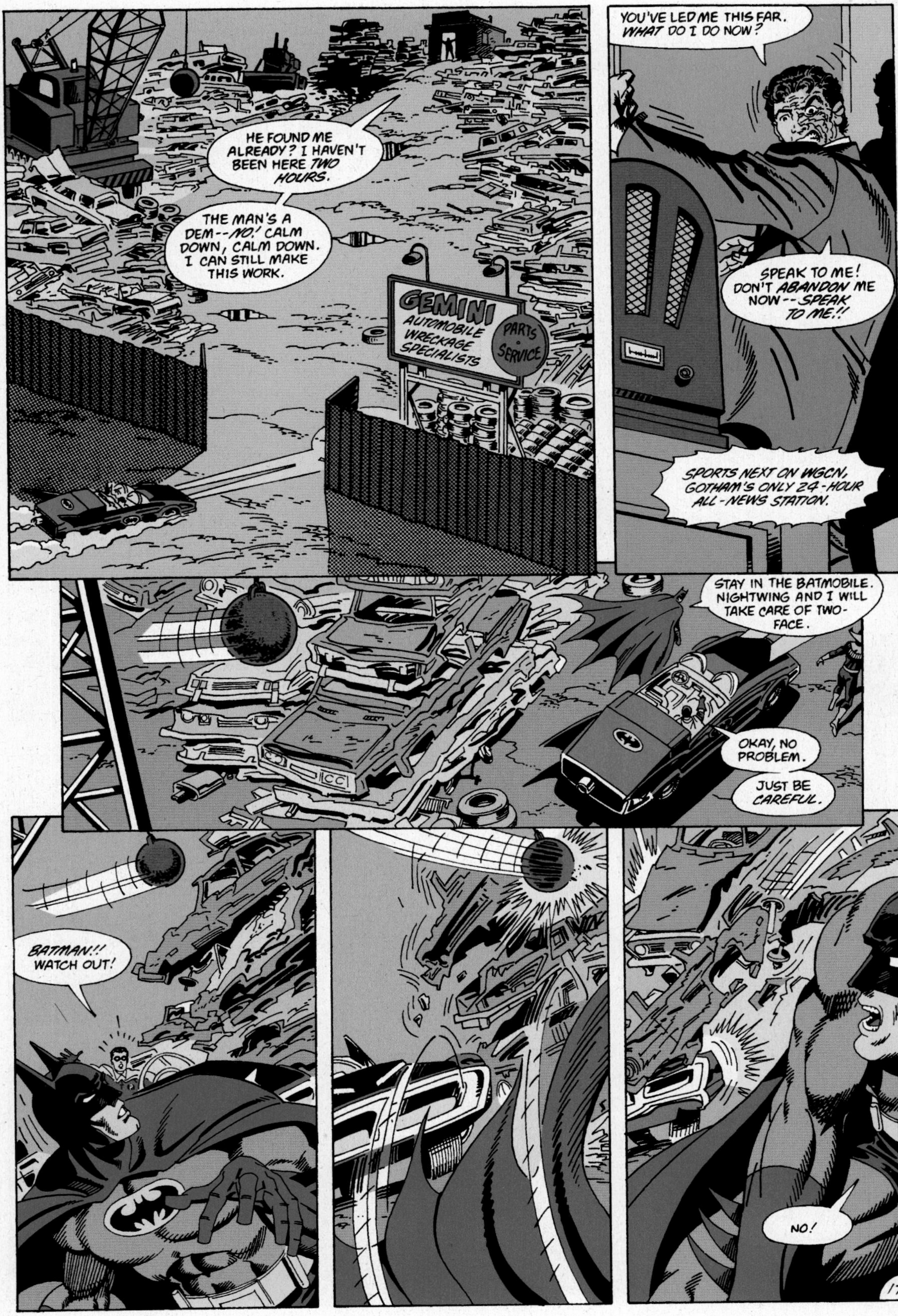
HE FOUND ME ALREADY? I HAVEN'T BEEN HERE TWO HOURS.
THE MAN'S A DEM--NO! CALM DOWN, CALM DOWN. I CAN STILL MAKE THIS WORK.
GEMINI AUTOMOBILE WRECKAGE SPECIALISTS
PARTS • SERVICE
YOU'VE LED ME THIS FAR. WHAT DO I DO NOW?
SPEAK TO ME! DON'T ABANDON ME NOW--SPEAK TO ME!!
SPORTS NEXT ON WGCN, GOTHAM'S ONLY 24-HOUR ALL-NEWS STATION.
STAY IN THE BATMOBILE. NIGHTWING AND I WILL TAKE CARE OF TWO-FACE.
OKAY, NO PROBLEM.
JUST BE CAREFUL.
BATMAN!! WATCH OUT!
NO!
17

TIM!?!

MY GOD! I KNEW I SHOULDN'T HAVE--

...BATMAN...

TIM? HOW--

WHEN I SAW THE BALL, I *JUMPED* OUT THE OTHER DOOR AND *UNDER* THE BATMOBILE.

IT WAS THE *ONLY* THING I COULD *THINK* OF.

I'M SORRY I COULDN'T WARN YOU IN TIME.

DON'T BE. YOU SAVED US *AND* YOURSELF.

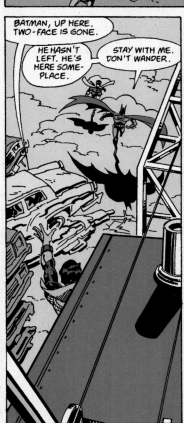

BATMAN, UP HERE. TWO-FACE IS GONE.

HE HASN'T LEFT. HE'S HERE SOME-PLACE.

STAY WITH ME. DON'T WANDER.

NIGHTWING!

THOUGH I PREFERRED IT WHEN I HAD TO DEAL WITH JUST THE *TWO* OF YOU--

-- I'LL GLADLY TAKE ON ONE MORE FOR GOOD LUCK!

KRANNG

18

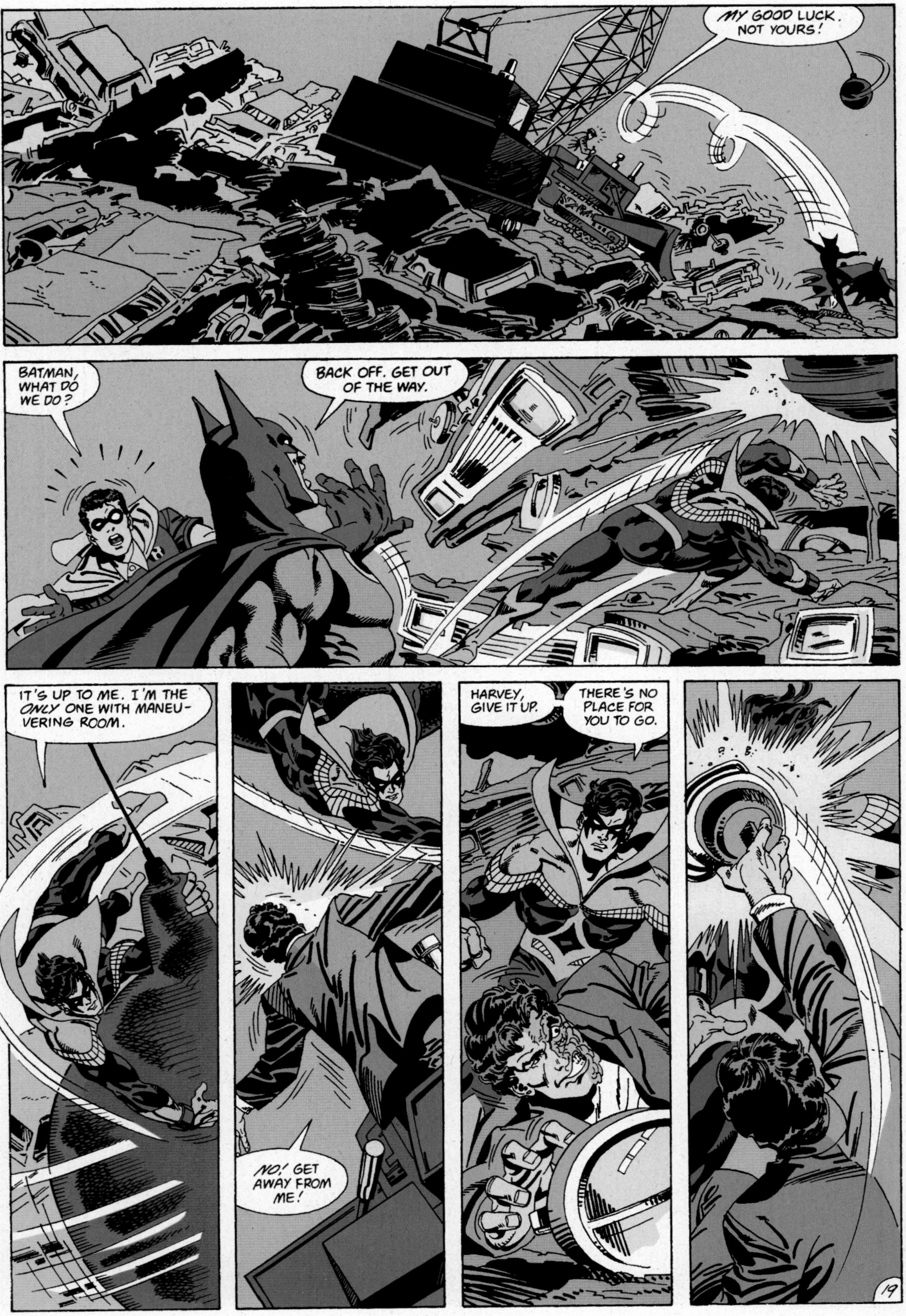
MY GOOD LUCK. NOT YOURS!
BATMAN, WHAT DO WE DO?
BACK OFF. GET OUT OF THE WAY.
IT'S UP TO ME. I'M THE ONLY ONE WITH MANEUVERING ROOM.
NO! GET AWAY FROM ME!
HARVEY, GIVE IT UP.
THERE'S NO PLACE FOR YOU TO GO.
19

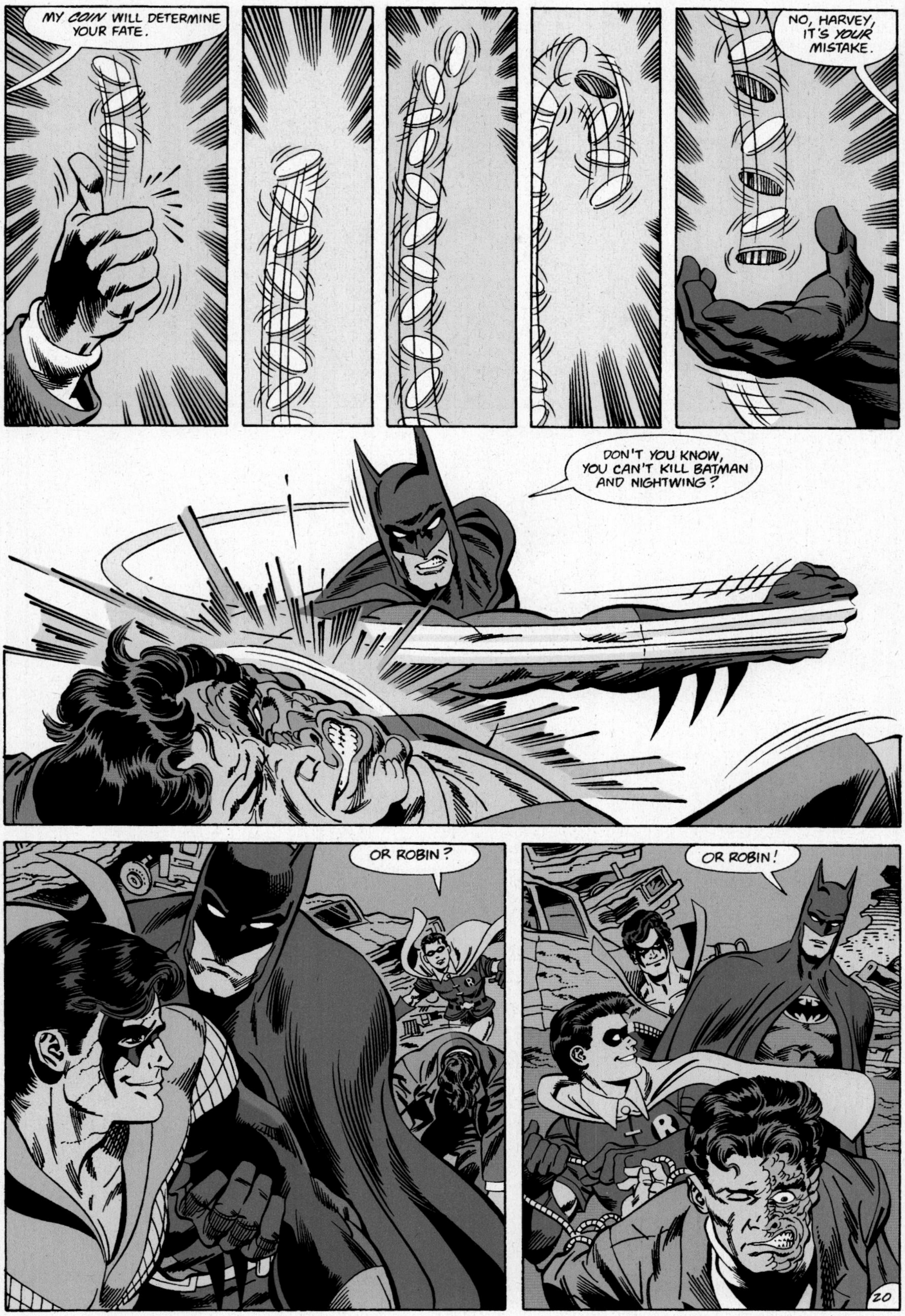
MY COIN WILL DETERMINE YOUR FATE.
NO, HARVEY, IT'S YOUR MISTAKE.
DON'T YOU KNOW, YOU CAN'T KILL BATMAN AND NIGHTWING?
OR ROBIN?
OR ROBIN!
20

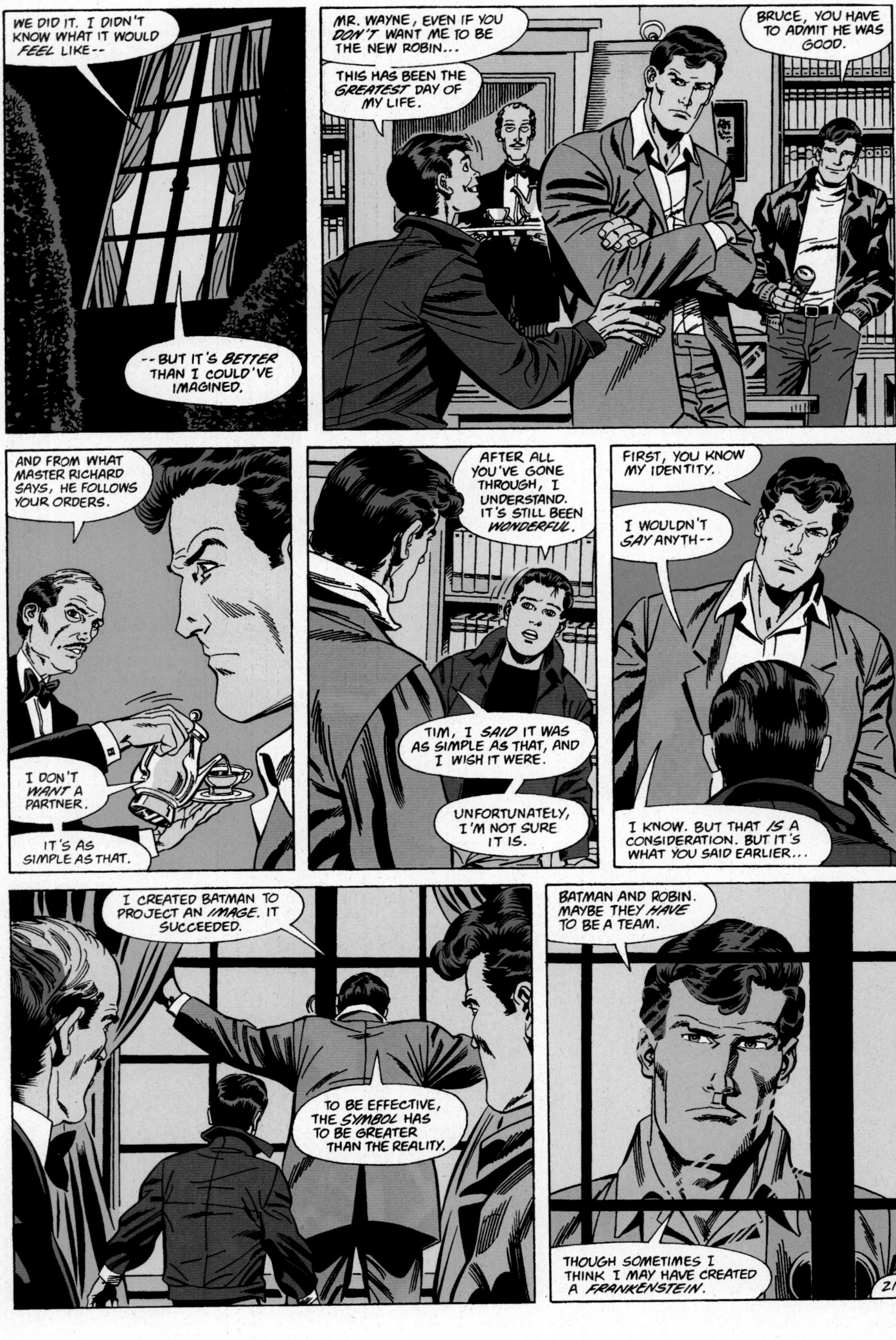
WE DID IT. I DIDN'T KNOW WHAT IT WOULD FEEL LIKE--
--BUT IT'S BETTER THAN I COULD'VE IMAGINED.
MR. WAYNE, EVEN IF YOU DON'T WANT ME TO BE THE NEW ROBIN...
THIS HAS BEEN THE GREATEST DAY OF MY LIFE.
BRUCE, YOU HAVE TO ADMIT HE WAS GOOD.
AND FROM WHAT MASTER RICHARD SAYS, HE FOLLOWS YOUR ORDERS.
I DON'T WANT A PARTNER.
IT'S AS SIMPLE AS THAT.
AFTER ALL YOU'VE GONE THROUGH, I UNDERSTAND. IT'S STILL BEEN WONDERFUL.
TIM, I SAID IT WAS AS SIMPLE AS THAT, AND I WISH IT WERE.
UNFORTUNATELY, I'M NOT SURE IT IS.
FIRST, YOU KNOW MY IDENTITY.
I WOULDN'T SAY ANYTH--
I KNOW. BUT THAT IS A CONSIDERATION. BUT IT'S WHAT YOU SAID EARLIER...
I CREATED BATMAN TO PROJECT AN IMAGE. IT SUCCEEDED.
TO BE EFFECTIVE, THE SYMBOL HAS TO BE GREATER THAN THE REALITY.
BATMAN AND ROBIN. MAYBE THEY HAVE TO BE A TEAM.
THOUGH SOMETIMES I THINK I MAY HAVE CREATED A FRANKENSTEIN.
21

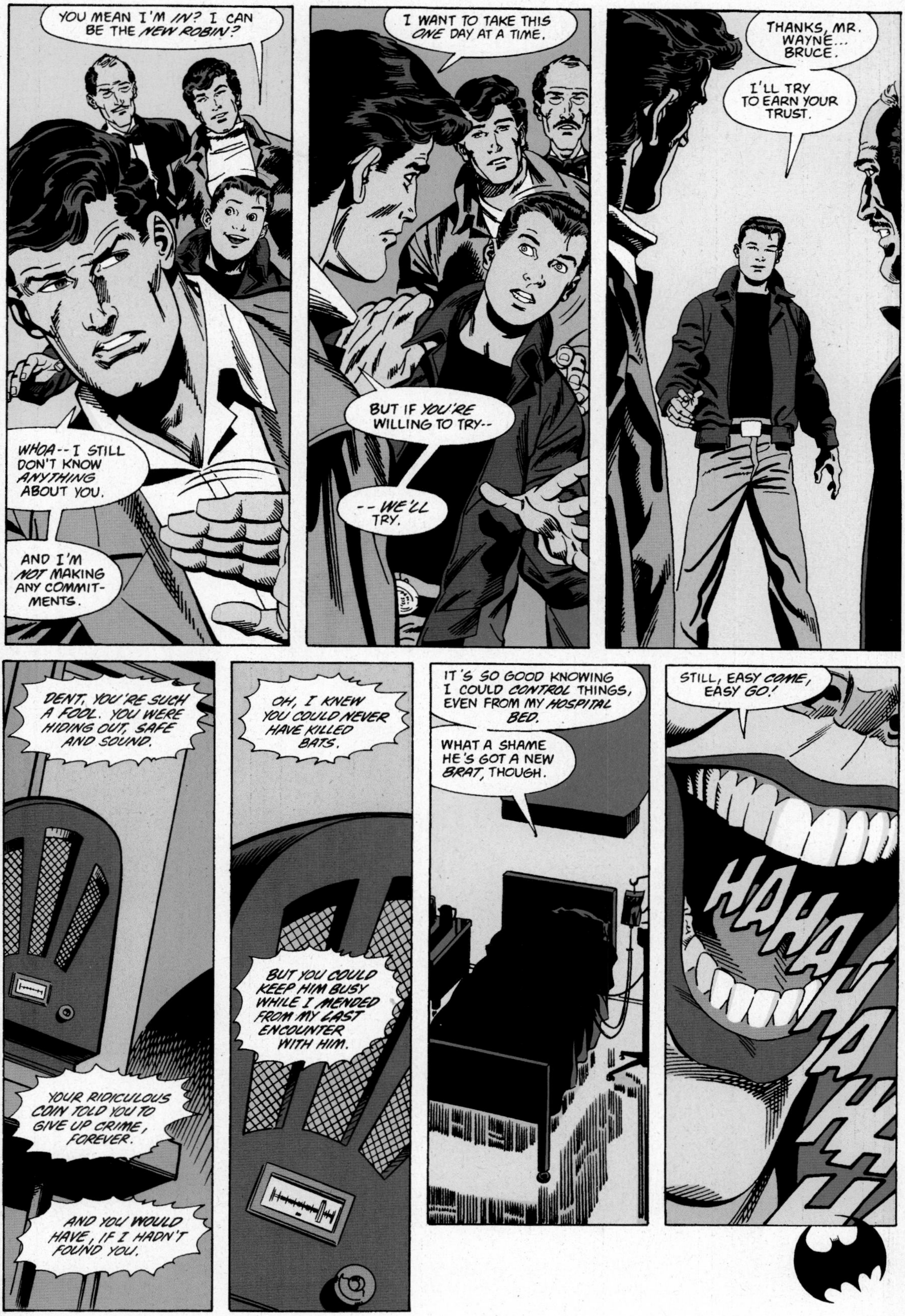

YOU MEAN I'M IN? I CAN BE THE NEW ROBIN?
WHOA-- I STILL DON'T KNOW ANYTHING ABOUT YOU.
AND I'M NOT MAKING ANY COMMITMENTS.
I WANT TO TAKE THIS ONE DAY AT A TIME.
BUT IF YOU'RE WILLING TO TRY--
-- WE'LL TRY.
THANKS, MR. WAYNE... BRUCE.
I'LL TRY TO EARN YOUR TRUST.
DENT, YOU'RE SUCH A FOOL. YOU WERE HIDING OUT, SAFE AND SOUND.
YOUR RIDICULOUS COIN TOLD YOU TO GIVE UP CRIME, FOREVER.
AND YOU WOULD HAVE, IF I HADN'T FOUND YOU.
OH, I KNEW YOU COULD NEVER HAVE KILLED BATS.
BUT YOU COULD KEEP HIM BUSY WHILE I MENDED FROM MY LAST ENCOUNTER WITH HIM.
IT'S SO GOOD KNOWING I COULD CONTROL THINGS, EVEN FROM MY HOSPITAL BED.
WHAT A SHAME HE'S GOT A NEW BRAT, THOUGH.
STILL, EASY COME, EASY GO!
HAHAHAHAHAH

Jim Aparo and Mike DeCarlo drew an alternate final page for the last chapter of A DEATH IN THE FAMILY in case the fans voted to save Robin. It did not see print until the release of BATMAN ANNUAL #25 in 2006, where it was included with the story of Jason Todd's return to the DC Universe.

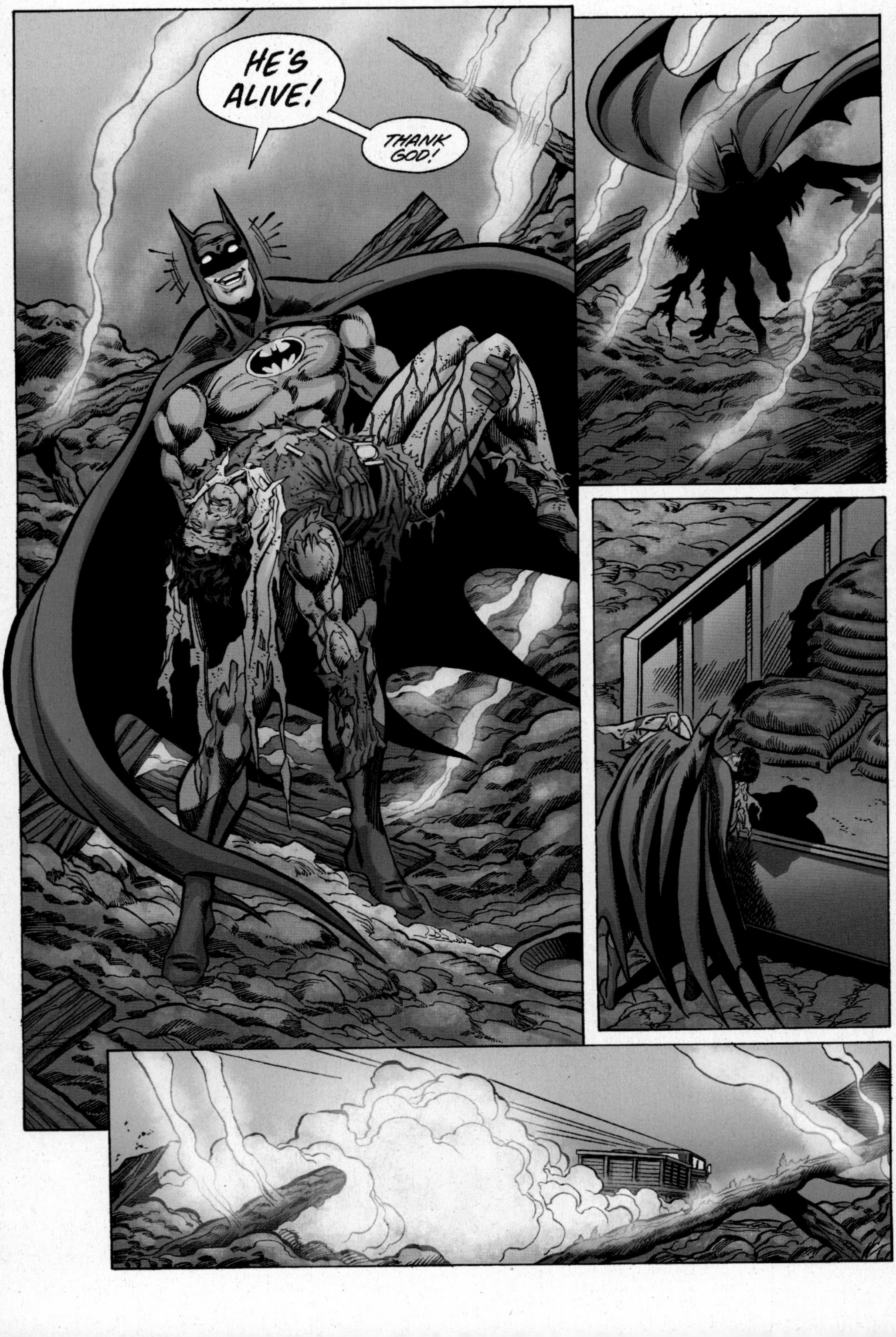
HE'S ALIVE!
THANK GOD!

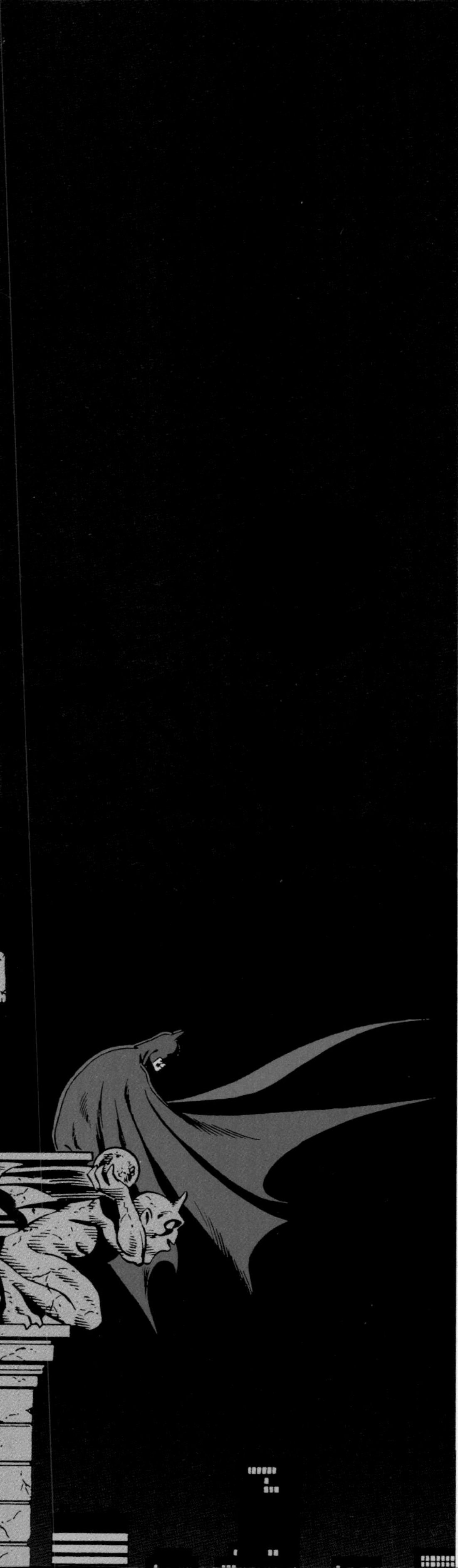

Biographies

JIM STARLIN began his career writing and drawing stories for amateur fanzines, until his first big break in 1972, when he was hired by Marvel Comics to work for Roy Thomas and John Romita as a "finisher" on *Spider-Man*. Early in his career, Starlin co-created Thanos, the most powerful villain in the Marvel Universe, and a character whom he would later use to define their entire cosmic mythology. He is perhaps best known for his work on the critically acclaimed story *The Death of Captain Marvel*, which brought new depth to the super-hero genre with the protagonist being felled by cancer rather than a super-villain. In the late 1980s Starlin began working more for DC Comics, writing a number of Batman stories including BATMAN: THE CULT and A DEATH IN THE FAMILY. Returning to Marvel after these successes, he began creating a vast space opera, starting in *The Silver Surfer* and continuing through the galaxy-spanning miniseries *The Infinity Gauntlet*, *Infinity War* and *Infinity Crusade*. Continuing in his position as one of the preeminent writers of comic-book science fiction, Starlin's recent work for DC includes MYSTERY IN SPACE, DEATH OF THE NEW GODS and RANN-THANAGAR: HOLY WAR,

MARV WOLFMAN, one of the most prolific and influential writers in modern comics, began his career as an artist. Realizing that his talents lay more in writing the stories than in drawing them, Wolfman soon became known for his carefully crafted, character-driven tales. In a career that has spanned nearly three decades, Wolfman has helped shape the heroic careers of DC Comics' Green Lantern, Blackhawk and the original Teen Titans, as well as Marvel Comics' *Fantastic Four*, *Spider-Man* and *Nova*. After co-creating THE NEW TEEN TITANS and the universe-shattering CRISIS ON INFINITE EARTHS with George Pérez, Wolfman was instrumental in the revamp of Superman and the development of THE NEW TEEN TITANS spinoff series VIGILANTE, DEATHSTROKE THE TERMINATOR and TEAM TITANS. He also created such characters as *Blade* for Marvel as well as the series NIGHT FORCE and the retooled DIAL "H" FOR HERO for DC. In addition to his numerous comic-book credits, Wolfman has also written several novels and worked in series television and animation, including the **Superman** cartoon of the late 1980s and the recent hit show **Teen Titans** on Cartoon Network.

JIM APARO was a self-taught artist who first attempted to enter the industry in the early 1950s with the legendary E.C. Comics group. When his work was rejected, Aparo turned to advertising art in his native Connecticut, where he specialized in fashion illustrations for newspaper advertisements while continuing to try to break into comics. His dream was finally realized in 1966 when editor Dick Giordano at Charlton Comics hired him as an artist; his first assignment was a humorous character called Miss Bikini Luv in *Go-Go Comics*. Sharpening his skills on such strips as *The Phantom, Nightshade, Wander* and *Thane of Bagarth*, Aparo followed editor Giordano to DC Comics in 1968. There he quickly gained notice for his smooth, realistic style on such books as AQUAMAN, THE BRAVE AND THE BOLD, THE PHANTOM STRANGER, THE SPECTRE, BATMAN, DETECTIVE COMICS and BATMAN AND THE OUTSIDERS, as well as countless stories for THE HOUSE OF MYSTERY and THE HOUSE OF SECRETS. An artist whose work is still considered a high-water mark for the industry, Aparo died on July 19, 2005.

GEORGE PÉREZ started drawing at the age of five and hasn't stopped since. He began his professional comics career as an assistant to Rich Buckler in 1973, and after establishing himself as a penciller at Marvel Comics he came to DC in 1980, where his highly detailed art style was seen in such titles as JUSTICE LEAGUE OF AMERICA and FIRESTORM THE NUCLEAR MAN. After co-creating THE NEW TEEN TITANS with Marv Wolfman in 1980, Pérez collaborated with Wolfman again on the landmark miniseries CRISIS ON INFINITE EARTHS. In the midst of the post-CRISIS revamps, he also revitalized WONDER WOMAN as the series' writer and artist — reestablishing the Amazon Princess as one of DC's preeminent characters and bringing in some of the best sales the title had ever experienced. Pérez is currently working on Superman. He lives in Central Florida with his beautiful dancer wife, Carol Flynn.

TOM GRUMMETT is based in Saskatoon, Saskatchewan and is best known for his work as a penciller on such DC series as THE NEW TITANS, THE ADVENTURES OF SUPERMAN, SUPERBOY, POWER COMPANY and ROBIN. His runs on these titles gave Grummett the opportunity to draw chapters in some of the biggest publishing events in DC's history, including A LONELY PLACE OF DYING, THE DEATH AND RETURN OF SUPERMAN and the BATMAN story arcs KNIGHTFALL, KNIGHTQUEST and KNIGHTSEND.